The Cassiopaea Experiment Transcripts 1995

The Cassiopaea Experiment is unique in the history of channeling, mediumship, and parapsychology. For years prior to the first Cassiopaean transmission, Laura Knight-Jadczyk went to great lengths to study the channeling phenomenon, including its history, its inherent strengths, weaknesses, dangers, and the various theories and methods developed in the past. After having exhausted the standard literature in search of answers to the fundamental problems of humanity, Laura and her colleagues (including her husband, mathematical physicist Arkadiusz Jadczyk) have held regular sittings for more than twenty years.

With the goal of applying true scientific standards and critical thinking, Laura began her experimentation with the spirit board, chosen for the optimum conditions of conscious feedback it offers. After two years of working through various levels of phenomena, including alleged discarnate entities and denizens of the 'astral realms', a new source came through in 1994. Unlike previous contacts, the Cassiopaeans came through strong and clear, often delivering full paragraphs' worth of complex material at one to two letters per second, with a high density of content and impeccable orthography. After telling Laura, "we are you in the future," the C's have been covering a wide range of topics by transmitting more than one million letters over the last twenty years, answering questions from practically all fields of knowledge, including physics, mathematics, psychology, philosophy, parapsychology, esotericism, history, politics, health, and astronomy. Where the material can be verified, the C's have proven to have an amazing track record, especially when compared to the variable quality of most examples of channeling from the past 150 years.

For the first time in print, this volume includes complete transcripts of 51 experimental sessions conducted in 1995. Questions and answers have been annotated extensively, giving unprecedented insight into the background and interpersonal dynamics of the early Cassiopaea Experiment.

The Cassiopaea Experiment Transcripts 1995

Laura Knight-Jadczyk

Red Pill Press
2015

First Edition, second printing
ISBN 978-0692484517
Red Pill Press (redpillpress.com)

Contents

Editor's Note	i
January 2, 1995	1
January 5, 1995	7
January 7, 1995	23
January 10, 1995	43
January 11, 1995	51
January 14, 1995	57
January 21, 1995	77
February 9, 1995	103
February 11, 1995	109
February 18, 1995	121
February 22, 1995	135
February 25, 1995	141
March 4, 1995	165
March 7, 1995	183
March 11, 1995	189
March 18, 1995	223

April 15, 1995	239
April 18, 1995	257
April 22, 1995	265
April 29, 1995	277
May 7, 1995	287
May 13, 1995	295
May 20, 1995	301
May 26, 1995	311
May 27, 1995	315
May 31, 1995	331
June 3, 1995	339
June 6, 1995	353
June 9, 1995	357
June 10, 1995	361
June 17, 1995	375
July 8, 1995	393
July 19, 1995	409
July 23, 1995	421
August 5, 1995	439
August 12, 1995	455

September 9, 1995	465
September 12, 1995	475
September 16, 1995	481
September 24, 1995	501
October 7, 1995	509
October 14, 1995	513
October 21, 1995	535
November 4, 1995	547
November 11, 1995	565
November 18, 1995	571
November 25, 1995	579
December 2, 1995	585
December 12, 1995	595
December 16, 1995	603
December 30, 1995	607
Chapters of "The Wave"	611
Recommended Reading	615
Index	643

Editor's Note

In the last 20 years, session transcripts of the Cassiopaea Experiment were available only in an electronic format – first shared as text files in a private email group and later, in 2010, republished one by one in the public Cassiopaea Forum[1] for discussion.

Readers have been strongly discouraged from reading the Cassiopaean transcripts on their own, outside of the context provided by Laura's work, since it had been noted that readers often would understand them too literally, misinterpret them and would tend to project their own ideas, beliefs, and biases onto them. Therefore, readers were advised to read them *in context*, that is, by reading about the background of the Cassiopaea Experiment and the unfolding events 'behind the scenes'. For this reason, excerpts of the transcripts have been included, discussed and researched in Laura Knight-Jadczyk's books *Amazing Grace*, *The Wave* series Vols. 1–8, *The Secret History of the World* Vol. 1 and *High Strangeness*. In these and other books (see "Recommended Reading" section), Laura matches a small percentage of 'inspiration' from the Cs with a lot of 'perspiration', i.e. hard work in researching the issues and conveying them to the readers.

This second volume, published one year after the first volume, continues with 51 experimental sessions of the year 1995, for the first time published in paper and electronic books. The advice about getting the necessary context to better understand the material still cannot be emphasized enough. For this reason, the editors have included footnotes pointing to the location where certain excerpts are discussed in detail in the above-mentioned books. The footnotes hopefully will encourage the reader to look up and study the context. A referencing footnote marks the first occurring line of a session excerpt contained in the mentioned books. The footnotes give the book title and the chapter number where the excerpts can be found (e.g. *The Wave* 46).

[1]http://cassiopaea.org/forum

The section "Recommended Reading" and the table "Chapters of 'The Wave'" at the end of this volume give additional details about the inserted references.

For the present volume, Laura has revisited the transcripts from 1995 and extensively annotated questions and answers, again giving unprecedented insight into the background and interpersonal dynamics of the early Cassiopaea Experiment, and comparing certain statements and predictions of the Cs with what she has learned since.

In 1995, the dialog with the Cassiopaeans revolved around topics of 'New Age' and historical disinformation, reincarnation and past lives, karma, soul evolution and the purpose of humanity, the 'Golden Age' and ancient civilizations, weather and Earth changes, 'The Wave' and coming turmoil on our planet, the 'New World Order', hidden government and the all-encompassing control system, higher 'density' experience and the 'fluid' nature of the UFO and alien phenomena, time and the nature of our universe. Also, interspersed with these topics, the sessions of this year document the conflicting interests arising within the group undertaking the Cassiopaea Experiment and the struggle against sometimes obvious skewing of the information and attempted sidetracking of the communications.

An exhaustive index at the end of this volume will hopefully enable the reader to quickly find topics of interest, even though the entire transcripts can and should be read as an amazing, unfolding story, containing numerous gems of wisdom, advice, and information.

January 2, 1995

This is another of the problematic sessions where, in retrospect, it seems that the Cs were managing to convey information to me in spite of the strong emotional component from Frank. As I have detailed in *The Wave*, Franks spent a lot of time complaining about everything and everybody and ranting about the unfairness of life. These rants could go on for hours and the language he used was often quite violent. Over the years, I've learned that venting can be healthy and expressing one's anger can be life-saving, as Gabor Mate points out in his book *When the Body Says 'No'*. The problem here was that Frank used me as the receptacle for his ire and never did anything positive to change his approach to things so as to possibly change the responses he received.

Participants: 'Frank' and Laura

1 **Q**: *(L)* Hello.

2 **A**: Hello.

3 **Q**: *(L)* Who is with us?

4 **A**: Rivia.

5 **Q**: *(L)* And, where are you from?

6 **A**: Cassiopaea.

7 **Q**: *(L)* Have you been listening to Frank talk about his woes and miseries?[1]

A: Yes. 8

Q: *(L)* What do you have in response to 9 his woes and miseries? Since he is the primary channel, it seems to me that it ought to behoove you to give him some kind of a word on this matter.

A: Open.[2] 10

Q: *(L)* What do you mean it is open? 11 Is he going to...

A: Is under attack, as previously de- 12 scribed.[3]

---

[1] *The Wave* 37

[2] This "open" could be in response to my statement that Frank is "the primary channel", which was, of course, his claim. In the years since Frank left, the conversation with the Cs has only gotten richer and more complex, so it could be said that Frank was an inhibiting factor. The Cs actually said this later.

[3] See Sessions 28 October, 2 November, 19 November, 26 November, 1 December 1994, for earlier references to attack. The 2 November 1994 session referred to Frank specifically in a similar context, suggesting that what was going on within him was a battle between dark and light forces. It was advised that one needed

13 **Q**: *(L)* Well, would it not behoove him to not respond negatively in thought, word or deed and to take care of business as best he can and trust that it will all work out? Because, by becoming all discombobulated, he is giving off negative energy...

14 **A**: His methods accomplish the task.

15 **Q**: *(L)* So, in other words, it is alright for him to get all emotionally wrought up and to spout off all these violently...

16 **A**: That repels attacking forces because they thrive upon blase passivity.

17 **Q**: *(L)* Well, we are not talking about passivity here. Are you sure you are a Cassiopaean? It sounds to me like you are saying he ought to be giving off... I think we are pulling in Lizzies because of your negativity...

18 **A**: Incorrect, you have your "way" of repelling attack, and Frank has his.

19 **Q**: *(L)* Well I just don't see how a whole bunch of negative energy in thought and word can repel beings who thrive on negative energy. I mean, they should be just rolling in joy that they are making him so miserable that he has to carry on that way, which then makes me miserable.

20 **A**: Not miserable when repelling.[4]

21 **Q**: *(L)* Well, then, the problem here is that when he does this, everybody else he does it around, it makes them miserable, so, what's the deal here?

22 **A**: Subjective, your methods can cause perception of upset too.

23 **Q**: *(L)* Yes, I know this, but I am working on being totally unmoved by attack. Isn't that the whole point here?

A: If it ain't broke, don't fix it. 24

Q: *(L)* So, I should continue, when I get upset or attacked, to just rave and rant and yell and scream and carry on? 25

A: You don't, you attack back, externally. Frank attacks back internally. The external manifestation is merely overflow and harmless if recognized correctly. 26

Q: *(L)* My understanding is that service to others involves complete lack of concern for self. Therefore, the objective is to have complete lack of concern for self, therefore one would be in such a state of lack of concern for self that when one feels oneself to be under attack, so to speak, or being baited or jabbed, one would simply utterly and entirely disregard this and continue on in a peaceful way. Now, am I misapprehending this in some way? 27

A: Not misapprehending, misinterpreting. 28

Q: *(L)* So, I misinterpret Frank's lack of regard for my feelings because he spouts off and upsets me... that's really a service to others activity and it is only my subjectivity that makes me get upset, therefore, I should eliminate my subjectivity as a service to him so that he can continue to spew off and therefore not upset me, is that what we are getting at here? 29

A: Off base. 30

Q: *(L)* Well, that is what you are saying. 31

to "fight" dark forces but I was having a problem understanding how dumping all his rage on me was fighting as recommended.

[4]Perhaps this was a clue that I should have been repelling Frank's tirades.

32 **A**: That's what you want to believe we are saying, but we are not; we are saying all should strive to be objective.

33 **Q**: *(L)* Well, I don't think it is being objective for every little sling and arrow of misfortune to throw somebody into a tailspin. I think part of the whole process is to learn how to go smoothly through all this stuff. And, what you are saying here is don't worry about going through stuff, just dump...

34 **A**: You are all learning, including Frank.

35 **Q**: *(L)* Well, let's just drop it. It doesn't make any sense.

36 **A**: Your perception, there is much to this whole process that is manifest on other levels, levels other than 3rd...

37 **Q**: *(L)* Well, I just don't think you really understand what is going on. I think that it's...

38 **A**: Yes we do. You do not. Open your mind.

39 **Q**: *(L)* Well the only thing I can change about this whole thing is to just stop listening when Frank moans and groans about things that I know everybody else has gone through without moaning and groaning, because it is entirely, extremely irritating to me to have to listen to it when everybody else has been through it and kept a stiff upper lip.

40 **A**: If Frank tried to keep a "stiff upper lip" it would destroy him because of his make-up, which does not correspond to that of most others; try to recognize differences.[5]

Q: *(L)* Well, I recognize the differences, 41
but I am only human too.

A: If you were asked to be passive to- 42
ward aggressors, how would you feel about that?

Q: *(L)* Well, I thought that was what 43
I was supposed to be practicing and, in fact, have been. I thought that this whole thing was about doing and practicing things to make us different than we had been programmed to be.

A: When it is wholly within your "com- 44
fort zone" not before, remember, in "Bringers of the Dawn" it says to do that which is effortless.

Q: *(L)* OK, it says to do what is effort- 45
less. It takes a lot of effort to put up with Frank when he is like that so he will have to swear and vow that he will never complain to me again. Agreed. It takes too much effort for me to deal with it.

A: Would cause karmic backsliding. 46

Q: *(L)* Now, just a minute here. You 47
just said to do what is effortless. I said it takes a lot of effort for me to put up with that kind of stuff, and now you are saying that this will cause me karmic backsliding?

A: No we said "do" that which is effort- 48
less, "acceptance" is another matter entirely.[6]

Q: *(L)* What does that mean? *(F)* I 49
think that what it means is that if you are doing something that is one thing, accepting is another thing. If I have some sort of foible that you don't like,

[5]This was an important clue, but it went right over my head.

[6]Another clue. Obviously, if I did that which was effortless, I would have stopped having interactions with Frank because it was entirely too upsetting. It was the idea of me continuing the interaction, while asking Frank to forswear his complaining, that suggested "karmic backsliding."

that is not doing. Whether you accept it or not has nothing to do with doing. I accept you, foibles and all, but you are saying that you simply refuse to... *(L)* But I don't attack you, either. *(F)* I don't attack you. *(L)* But, it amounts to the same thing to me. To have to listen to moaning and groaning that repeats over and over is the same thing as being attacked. I listen to everybody's troubles all day long and I get sick of people complaining who never do anything about their problems. *(F)* Well, you don't say that it is my problems that bother you, it's everybody's problems, and it did say that there is karmic significance here, which means that you must have brought yourself into a situation where you are surrounded with other people all moaning and groaning about their problems. And, you chose this. If you didn't want to listen to other people's problems, why did you get married and have kids? *(L)* Well, you would think that my friends would know that I don't need to have problems dumped on me... *(F)* Who is dumping problems on you? You keep saying this as if somehow... *(L)* Well, let's drop it... I want to ask: the other night Frank read my palm and gave me several bits of information. When he reads palms does he direct channel this information?

50 **A**: Some.

51 **Q**: *(L)* Where does the other information come from when he is reading palms?[7]

52 **A**: Varied.

53 **Q**: *(L)* Well, one thing he said to me was about something buried in my cellar. Is there, in fact, something buried in my cellar?

A: Discover. 54

Q: *(L)* How am I to discover it other 55
than digging the whole cellar out?

A: Patience will pave path. 56

Q: *(L)* Does that give me a clue that 57
something is buried under the steps to the cellar rather than under the cellar itself?

A: No. 58

Q: *(L)* Well, I was down there today 59
– I had the kids empty the cellar out – I went around tapping and knocking, and...

A: Yes. 60

Q: *(L)* I used a pendulum and dowsed. 61
I came up with a spot using a pendulum, I found a spot. I used the sledge hammer and broke open a part of the cellar floor, dug down four feet, and there was nothing there. Now, I don't look forward to doing that over a 9 by 7 space, and I certainly don't intend to knock all the walls down...

A: Part of discovery process, test 62
dowsing skill on known entities in order to refine process.

Q: *(L)* Well, either dowsing works or it 63
doesn't, wouldn't you say? Test it on known...

A: Depends upon skill of dowser as in 64
all psychic talents.

Q: *(L)* Well, the clue I am getting from 65
that is that I may not be the one to do the dowsing, is that correct?

A: If you take one piano lesson and fail 66
to produce Chopin, does that mean you should give up the piano?

7 *The Wave* 37

67 **Q**: *(L)* Well, let me ask this, give me a straight answer on this one, is there something down there so that we should continue working on the project?

68 **A**: Yes.

69 **Q**: *(L)* Is it worth tearing up the damn cellar to find it?

70 **A**: Up to you.

71 **Q**: *(L)* Well, let me ask you this, is it worth five thousand dollars?

72 **A**: To some.

Q: *(L)* Is it worth ten thousand dollars? 73

A: Discover. 74

Q: *(L)* What is it? *(F)* Money, it could be gold, it could be jewelry, it could be a valuable stock certificate. *(L)* Speaking of stock certificates, I have an old stock certificate for one share in the Elk's Club. It is very, very old. Is it worth anything and should I pursue having it checked out? 75

A: Yes.[8] 76

End of session

[8] We dug out quite a bit of the cellar and there was possible evidence of something having been there, but that it migrated through the sandy soil over time. In the end, it just became too dangerous to keep digging and we filled the hole back in and poured concrete on the floor to stabilize things.

January 5, 1995

As I recounted in my book *Amazing Grace*, when my son (who is now an adult) was born, he exhibited some peculiarly 'adult' terrors and reactions to a number of things. I will not describe every detail, but, being involved in the work I have been for most of my adult life, I knew that this child had something strange going on from the way he clung to me so desperately as an infant.

Later, when my son was old enough to start talking, he would tell me about his secret friend 'Janie', his black dog 'Sam', and his four brothers. This was really odd because he is the only boy with four sisters.

One day when he was still in diapers, a big military transport plane flew overhead rather low. He began to jump up and down in excitement and point at it and informed me that he could fly such a plane! That this is what he "used to do in the war!"

Being familiar with the work of Ian Stevenson and his *Twenty Cases Suggestive of Reincarnation*, I just asked questions rather than telling him that such things were silly and untrue.

Very early in life, my son developed asthma in a *big* way – hospitalizations almost every week, drugs, oxygen, nebulizers, etc. He also began to have very bad nightmares. Soon, this physically perfect child exhibited some problems running – he was dragging his left leg. The doctor said 'Osgood-Schlatter's disease'. I would see my son sitting on the ground in the shade while other kids were playing, and I would ask him why he wasn't playing. He answered that his "back hurts". Naturally, I took him to numerous specialists, all of whom said that, except for the so-called Osgood-Schlatter's and the asthma, he was perfectly normal.

The nightmares increased and I was at my wits' end. When he turned nine, I decided that it was time to do a session. I had done all I could in the 'accepted' ways; I needed the cavalry to come in. I decided to do a 'past life therapy' session.

As I have already noted in my many remarks on the subject in other articles, even as a hypnotherapist I can't say that I ever actually 'believed' in reincarnation. I used to tell people, "I believe in nothing, I just assign probabilities." I used past life therapy in my work because it *worked*, and not because I believed in it. From my point of view, if a person had to make up an elaborate past life scenario in their subconscious mind to escape from a labyrinth of emotional torment, fine with me!

My son was desperate for relief from the nightly torments, and was ready to try anything. When I was working with hypnosis, I was pretty much a stickler for 'non-leading' questions. If a past life came up, I would work with it (and it often did), but I didn't 'set it up' as the mode beforehand. I would generally use an opening such as "go to the point in space-time when the problem began and describe to me what you are seeing around you." Then that would be the platform from which to discover the experience.

In the case of my son, without any prompting whatsoever, he launched into a terrifying description of being in an airplane – it was unclear if he was the pilot or not, but it seemed so – and his attention being suddenly drawn to the fact that a missile was about to strike the craft. On impact, he began to scream that his leg had been torn off and he was breathing flames. It was so traumatic that I immediately took him away from direct experience and had him view it on a 'screen' at a distance. (This works for getting details where there is a lot of emotion involved.)

The trauma was quite intense and I decided that it would be better to work on this one a little at a time, so we just dealt with part of the experience and I gave some 'feel good' and 'healing' suggestions, and that was that.

This had been about three years before the Cassiopaean transmissions began and he *did* have considerable relief from the asthma and nightmares as a result of the hypnotherapy, so we decided to just leave the issue alone for the time being unless and until more symptoms emerged and became unmanageable.

As a part of the 'testing' phase of the Cassiopaean contact, I decided to ask about any past life information for my son, but I wanted to go about it in a rather 'cagey' way. I was the only one present who knew what he had told me under hypnosis and had never discussed his childhood remarks with anyone in the room, so I thought it would be a good test of the source. If the only information that could be obtained was what was in my mind or my son's mind, that at least would demonstrate a form of telepathy. At the same time, there was the idea that, perhaps my son's description of his 'past life' had been merely a 'drama' in which he could express some other problem that I did not know about. So, I wanted to be very careful in the way I obtained the information.

I was also fully cognizant of the fact that children are very imaginative, and the problem he was having with his leg might simply be that he had injured it at some point or it had some sort of congenital deformity. There were a number of solutions, and I wanted to hear what the Cassiopaeans offered. Thus, the *very* ambiguous form of the questions and my 'indirect' approach in the 7 November 1994 session. In that session part of the exchange was:

> **Q**: *(L)* Why did my son's leg suddenly start giving him problems at about the age of three?
>
> **A**: Reflection of past life. Leg was torn off at death. SAM missile shot by North Vietnamese Army. He was flying a jet. This was 1969. Name was George Raymond. Shot down over Phan bien.

That led off to a series of questions about "scars of the soul" being a source of physical, mental and emotional problems from life to life.

And there the matter lay until a member of the group, Terry Rodemerk, read that session (sometime in December of 1994) and asked me if I had ever checked it out.

I said "no," and he asked if he might do so, so I said "sure." I didn't think he would find anything because my experience had been that finding any confirmation from such things was pretty remote. While many cases *do* produce information that checks out, a lot of them don't, and I wasn't particularly invested in 'proving' anything about reincarnation, especially where my own son was concerned. I just wanted to have tools and ideas to help him. I wasn't sure how Terry planned on going about checking out the details about George Ray or Raymond.

It was a week or two later that Terry produced a little piece of paper that had some notes on it. He thought it might be a 'match'. But, all the info he could get was a person named 'George R. Kidd', who had died in that particular year and was in the AF with the rank of Captain. I think it was from the list of names on the Vienam War Memorial. The records he searched also had the hometown. Surprisingly, it was Punta Gorda, which was only about 150 miles south of our home.

Well, I didn't do anything with it except lay it on the desk and we went on with our session of that evening. I really *didn't* think it was *too* good of a match, because the name on the list was George R. Kidd. We had been given the name George Raymond.

Everybody wanted me to check it out and, with that encouragement, I figured "what the heck!" I might as well *see* if the guy's *middle* name was Ray or Raymond and *how* he died – maybe it *was* a SAM. And, if so, that would be a more definite 'hit'. Since the hometown was given, my idea was to call the newspaper in Punta Gorda to see if there was an obit on file that listed the *full* name and, maybe, that went into more detail about the manner of death. It wasn't going to be a big deal – just a little check with a phone call.

I called information, found the number of the local paper and dialed. I was told that such 'old' records were kept in storage and it would cost to have a search done. Well, I wasn't sufficiently invested in this idea that it might be a 'hit' to spend money on it, so that put me off. *But*, the person on the phone just volunteered that the local library might have such things in their available archives. She gave me the number.

That was easy enough. Why stop with one easy phone call if you can get it with two? I called the library, explained what I was trying to find: an obituary for George R. Kidd that would give me some details about how he died and what his middle name was. The woman said she would look and, after a few minutes, came back and said that yes, they had him in their genealogy section (funny, considering my later plunge into the genealogy project!), but that the records they had did *not* give his middle name, nor the mode of death. It only told where he was buried. Then, just as the lady at the newspaper office had done, she volunteered that 'such and such' funeral home was listed as having handled the arrangements and she knew that they were still in business, so maybe *they* would have a copy of the obituary! She very kindly obtained the number for me.

Well, I was only on my third call in less than a half hour or so, and it seemed like I ought to pursue it until I hit a brick wall, so I decided to call the funeral home. By this time, I began to feel that I really needed to know George R. Kidd's middle name and how he died!

The girl who answered the phone at the funeral home listened to my explanation that I was looking for a copy of the obituary of George R. Kidd, and said that, yes, they might have one in their files. She put me on hold, and a minute later a man came on the phone and said (more or less): "I understand you are looking for information about Captain George Kidd? Can I ask *why*?"

I was *not* prepared to be questioned about this, figuring that it was so old that nobody would really care *why* I wanted to know. I had told the newspaper person that I was doing research on Vietnam, but somehow, the nature of my questions here, so close to the 'jackpot', were not adequately covered by that explanation.

There was a pregnant silence while I calculated how *much* I could say, considering that I might be talking to a person who was not very open to such things, and I decided to leave out the fact that the information had been obtained via channeling, and just stick to the 'information about past lives obtained under hypnosis' story. So, that's what I told him. I said my son had been talking since he was little about having brothers and a dog named Sam and having flown a plane in the war since, and that recently, because of some physical problems, he had undergone hypnosis in an effort to seek relief and had given further information about his name, that he was shot down by a SAM missile, and that all I really wanted to do was confirm his middle name and if, in fact, this was how he died!

The guy was completely amazed. He kept saying over and over: "This is amazing! This is amazing!" Then he said that, yes, he not only had a copy of the obituary and could confirm that George Kidd's middle name was Ray; not only that, but he had also been a personal friend of Captain Kidd, and was still in touch with the family. He said he would fax me the obituary. *Then* he asked me if I would mind if he contacted the family and told them about this.

This was getting out of hand! I did *not* think that was a good idea.

I had enough info to satisfy my curiosity that it had a good probability of being a close-enough 'hit', but I certainly didn't want to interfere in anyone else's life with such a thing. My innocent little venture into finding out two simple facts – middle name and mode of death – was in danger of going way south!

I could imagine the feelings of a person who got a call and was told that there was some strange kid who might be their dead relative reincarnated! But, the funeral-home guy persisted saying that Captain Kidd had two sisters who still lived nearby, and they were very 'open minded', and he just *couldn't* keep such a thing from them, so, reluctantly, I agreed. One was named Ann, and the other was Ruth.

Shortly after I hung up the phone, he faxed me the obituary, which listed the cause of death as "crash on take-off." I was disappointed because it did not confirm the SAM thing, even if we had a partial 'confirmation' about the name. He added a note that he had called Ruth, Captain Kidd's sister, and would be shortly having lunch with her.

I was still cleaning off my desk and feeling nervous that this man was planning on telling some strange woman in Punta Gorda that my son *might* be her dead brother reincarnated. I had such serious misgivings about it that I was actually becoming sick to my stomach. And, I had *no* idea that he was going to do it so quickly!

An hour later, George Ray's sister called me and it was, indeed, the strangest conversation I have ever had. I could tell that she was almost pathetically anxious for this to be true, and my heart broke for her. I tried to play the whole thing down as just a freaky anomaly that had only a small chance of being true, but as she asked me question after question about my son, and I answered them, she became more excited and kept saying that she wanted to meet my son.

For my son's sake, I didn't think that was such a good idea, even though I felt very sorry for this lady who had been grieving for her brother for so many years. I told her that I would think about it, but that it was impossible for us to make the trip anytime soon.

A week or so later, I received a letter from Ruth with directions to her house and a repeated request to let her know as soon as we were able to visit. And, that was where it ultimately lay for *eight months.* As I said, I wasn't anxious to make any moves on this.

I didn't think it was a good idea for pretty obvious reasons. I didn't want to take the risk that my son might identify so much with his past life that he could not focus on this one, and I certainly didn't want him to be further traumatized by waking up memories that might be better left alone. It was only several months later, after the meeting with journalist Tom French, that I did any follow up. I'll cover that in the appropriate context when it comes up.

However, this session was one where I asked some further questions about this matter as a consequence of the above described phone calls and is, in a way, a record of the events.

Participants: 'Frank' and Laura

1 **Q**: *(L)* Hello, who do we have with us tonight?

2 **A**: Turoian.

3 **Q**: *(L)* Where are you from?

4 **A**: Cass.

5 **Q**: *(L)* Cass? Are we abbreviating Cassiopaea now?

6 **A**: Sure, why not.

7 **Q**: *(L)* Well, I am sure that you must be aware of the excitement yesterday with the confirmation of the information received some time ago about [my son's] past incarnation as a pilot in Vietnam...[1]

8 **A**: Yes.

9 **Q**: *(L)* Well, I would like to have a few more details about this George Ray Kidd. Is this, in fact, the individual who is incarnated as my son?

10 **A**: Probably, but up to you to discover so as to learn. Remember, it's all just lessons.

Q: *(L)* Well, what I would like to do is get some information from you and then do a session with [my son] and then compare the information, to have a sort of guideline to go by. Would that be alright? 11

A: Okey dokey. 12

Q: *(L)* The first thing I want to ask is this: George Ray Kidd, the probable individual – could you tell us what kind of plane he was flying? 13

A: EC 121. 14

Q: *(L)* How many other people were on board that plane? 15

A: 15. 16

Q: *(L)* And was that plane shot down? 17

A: Yes. 18

Q: *(L)* It did not just simply crash, is that correct? 19

A: Yes. 20

Q: *(L)* What was it doing when it was shot down? 21

A: Combination reconnaissance and bombing.[2] 22

[1]See session 7 November 1994.

[2]I'll deal with confirmation (or not) of the various questions here in the proper chronological sequence.

23 **Q**: *(L)* Who was the pilot of the plane?

24 **A**: There were two.

25 **Q**: *(L)* What were their names?

26 **A**: George and Glen. The "Two G's."

27 **Q**: *(L)* Now, George Ray's sister called me – what is her reaction to this information?

28 **A**: Anticipation.

29 **Q**: *(L)* What is she anticipating?

30 **A**: Reunion.

31 **Q**: *(L)* Because of this information, [number 2 daughter], of course, has inquired as to who she was in her last lifetime. So, could you tell me this?

32 **A**: Rebecca Rendell.

33 **Q**: *(L)* Where did she live?

34 **A**: Georgia.

35 **Q**: *(L)* What year was she born?

36 **A**: 1900.

37 **Q**: *(L)* When did she die in that lifetime?

38 **A**: 1963.

39 **Q**: *(L)* Is this the lifetime she recalled under hypnosis where she finds herself sitting and waiting and says that everyone is gone, has deserted her, she is alone?

40 **A**: Yes.[3]

41 **Q**: *(L)* What is the situation surrounding that? Why does she feel so abandoned and alone?

A: Alcoholism. 42

Q: *(L)* She was an alcoholic? 43

A: Yes. 44

Q: *(L)* Was she abandoned and left alone because of her alcoholism? 45

A: Husband problems. 46

Q: *(L)* She had problems with her husband because of the alcoholism or did the problems with husband cause the alcoholism? 47

A: Interwoven. 48

Q: *(L)* Did she have children in that lifetime? 49

A: One. 50

Q: *(L)* When was that child born? 51

A: 1919. 52

Q: *(L)* Is that child living today? 53

A: No. 54

Q: *(L)* Did she have any grandchildren? 55

A: Three. 56

Q: *(L)* Was the child a boy or girl? 57

A: Girl. Fonora Jean.[4] 58

Q: *(L)* The next one I want to ask about is my youngest daughter. Who was A___ in her last lifetime? 59

A: Have you finished with [your son]? 60

Q: *(L)* Well, I guess I could ask a few more questions about [my son]. What else could I ask? 61

A: Searing his lungs with flames. 62

---

[3]I actually don't think that this information is correct though I can't formulate why it would have been so skewed. Other information coming via my daughter, and even further on in this session, suggests that her immediate past life may have been in Germany, that she had been one of my children, and that she was tortured and died in a concentration camp.

[4]Or Nora Jean.

63 **Q**: *(L)* Did that happen in the plane crash?

64 **A**: Immediately after missile strike.

65 **Q**: *(L)* Tell us more of what you are seeing at this moment.

66 **A**: Breathing in fire.

67 **Q**: *(L)* Was this the cause of death?

68 **A**: Yes.

69 **Q**: *(L)* Is this the reason [my son] has suffered from asthma?

70 **A**: Yes.

71 **Q**: *(L)* And, you previously said the leg was torn off with the missile strike, is this correct?

72 **A**: Yes.

73 **Q**: *(L)* Are there any other injuries that occurred that he would be experiencing backlash from at this time?

74 **A**: Spine severed 17 locations.

75 **Q**: *(L)* Does this cause him back pain?

76 **A**: Yes.

77 **Q**: *(L)* Any other physical symptoms or experiences?

78 **A**: Psychological.

79 **Q**: *(L)* In this experience, how long after the missile struck did he actually leave the body?

80 **A**: 14 seconds.

81 **Q**: *(L)* It was pretty much instantaneous.

82 **A**: Close.

Q: *(L)* Still, under those circumstances, 14 seconds can be forever. *(F)* No kidding. Time slows down to a standstill. *(L)* What were the last thoughts George Ray had before he left the body? 83

A: He thought of his family and his childhood home.[5] 84

Q: *(L)* If I were to take [my son] to the home GR grew up in, would he remember it? 85

A: That was only one of his homes. 86

Q: *(L)* Did he remember his earliest home? 87

A: Yes![6] 88

Q: *(L)* Was he particularly close to his sister, Ruth? 89

A: More close to brothers. 90

Q: *(L)* Is that... 91

A: Rivalries, other siblings were more assertive. 92

Q: *(L)* Anything else we need to know at this time? 93

A: Body remains were questionable. 94

Q: *(L)* They may have buried the wrong remains in George Ray's grave? 95

A: Open. 96

Q: *(L)* Well, what do you mean the "remains were questionable"? 97

A: All will say. 98

Q: *(L)* That is all you are going to say on that? 99

A: Yes.[7] 100

[5]Which would fit since that's all he talked about when he was little.

[6]An out-of-sequence hint: this turned out to be true.

[7]Obviously, without a lot of hassle, such a thing cannot be falsified. However, as it turned out, the funeral director friend did mention to us that the casket came sealed, with instructions to *not* open it, and he thought that was strange.

101 **Q**: *(L)* Well, that is real curious. Goodness gracious. OK, I would like to know who my youngest daughter was in her last lifetime?

102 **A**: Luther Meinhardt.

103 **Q**: *(L)* Where did Luther Meinhardt live?

104 **A**: Deutschland.

105 **Q**: *(L)* And what year was Luther Meinhardt born in Deutschland?

106 **A**: 1904.

107 **Q**: *(L)* And when did Luther Meinhardt die?

108 **A**: 1947.

109 **Q**: *(L)* What did Luther Meinhardt die from?

110 **A**: Dysentery.

111 **Q**: *(L)* Was there some connection between Luther and me in that lifetime?

112 **A**: Was officer in Gestapo.

113 **Q**: *(L)* Did I know this officer in the Gestapo?

114 **A**: Not directly or by name.

115 **Q**: *(L)* Well, if I didn't know this person directly or by name, did this person have some effect on my life?

116 **A**: Yes.

117 **Q**: *(L)* What effect did this person have on my life. What did they do?

118 **A**: Arrested husband.

119 **Q**: *(L)* And at the time my husband was arrested, what happened then?

120 **A**: Nothing of import.

121 **Q**: *(L)* What happened to the husband after he was arrested? Why was he arrested?

A: Judisch. 122

Q: *(L)* He was arrested because he was 123
Jewish?

A: Yes. 124

Q: *(L)* Was I also Jewish? 125

A: No. 126

Q: *(L)* And how many children did I 127
have?

A: Four. 128

Q: *(L)* What was the result of the ar- 129
rest of my husband? Was he taken to a concentration camp, killed, or what?

A: Killed. 130

Q: *(L)* How was he killed? 131

A: Shot. 132

Q: *(L)* Was this the point at which 133
I committed suicide by diving from a window?

A: Yes.[8] 134

Q: *(L)* OK, there were the four chil- 135
dren; what then happened to the children?

A: Taken to camp "Orphanage." 136

Q: *(L)* What happened to the four of 137
them there?

A: Different fates. 138

Q: *(L)* What was the oldest one's 139
name?

A: Rita. 140

Q: *(L)* What happened to Rita? 141

A: Died in camp. 142

Q: *(L)* How old was Rita when she died 143
in the camp?

A: 17. 144

Q: *(L)* What was the next oldest one's 145
name?

[8] See session 7 November 1994.

146 **A**: Gerta.

147 **Q**: *(L)* What happened to Gerta?

148 **A**: Died in camp.

149 **Q**: *(L)* How old was Gerta when she died?

150 **A**: 15.

151 **Q**: *(L)* What was the next one's name?

152 **A**: Klaus.

153 **Q**: *(L)* What happened to Klaus?

154 **A**: Experimented upon, survived, lives in Austria or Holland.

155 **Q**: *(L)* Why does he live in one or the other?

156 **A**: Hard to decipher because he moves.

157 **Q**: *(L)* Does he move back and forth from one place to the other?

158 **A**: Has or does.

159 **Q**: *(L)* And Klaus is still living. When was Klaus born?

160 **A**: 1929.

161 **Q**: *(L)* What was the last name of the family?

162 **A**: Gerspringer.

163 **Q**: *(L)* What happened to the youngest child?

164 **A**: Ernst. Died 1987.

165 **Q**: *(L)* So, Ernst survived the camp. Are any of the children I have now reincarnations of my children then?

166 **A**: No.[9]

Q: *(L)* Are there any ramifications of this situation that I need to deal with? 167

A: Watch karmic interaction with [youngest daughter]. You may have hidden anger. 168

Q: *(L)* But [youngest daughter] is such a lovable baby! Why did she decide to come into my family if she was part of the Gestapo that destroyed my family? 169

A: Guilt. 170

Q: *(L)* She wanted to come in to assuage her guilt? 171

A: Was Gestapo, but intents were not evil, just "orders." 172

Q: *(L)* And who was my husband in that lifetime? 173

A: Gerhard. 174

Q: *(L)* And who is he in this lifetime? Has he already reincarnated? 175

A: No.[10] 176

Q: *(L)* Didn't you tell me that he had reincarnated and that he was Grant Maciorowski? 177

A: Yes, but has apparently passed and other entity told you, not us. 178

Q: *(L)* So, on the occasion when those questions were being asked, the entity that was telling us that was a corrupted influence? 179

A: Not corrupted, just other. 180

Q: *(L)* Another of the Cassiopaeans told me that? 181

A: Check records.[11] 182

[9] I don't agree since there are numerous signs that at least one of my children was my child in that previous life: my previously mentioned daughter.

[10] Again, I don't agree. I am quite certain that my husband, Ark, was my husband then. There are many signs, synchronicities, memories and feelings on both sides that suggest this to be the case.

[11] There's no way to check the records since that session was not recorded and was lost.

183 **Q**: *(L)* I don't understand. Well, since you brought that subject up, are you intending to say that the entity in this person's body has passed and another entity has taken its place?

184 **A**: No. Grant was husband, but other lifetime.

185 **Q**: *(L)* I see, I guess. OK, well, where is the person who was my husband in that lifetime? Is he still floating around somewhere?

186 **A**: Yes.

187 **Q**: *(L)* OK. What lifetime was it when Grant was my husband?

188 **A**: Before the last one.

189 **Q**: *(L)* What year was that lifetime?

190 **A**: 1800's.

191 **Q**: *(L)* In that particular lifetime, what was the karmic interaction or dynamics?

192 **A**: Husband and wife. Deutschland, Prussia.

193 **Q**: *(L)* What was his name?

194 **A**: Gunther Steinbrandt.

195 **Q**: *(L)* What was my name in that lifetime?

196 **A**: Wilhelmina.

197 **Q**: *(L)* Did we have any children?

198 **A**: No.

199 **Q**: *(L)* What was Gunther Steinbrandt's occupation?

200 **A**: Solderer.

201 **Q**: *(L)* He was a worker with solder?

202 **A**: Yes.

203 **Q**: *(L)* I didn't know they had solder in that time. Sounds like a totally boring life. Did anything dramatic or interesting happen in that life?

A: Subjective. 204

Q: *(L)* My current husband and I seemingly have very strong karma together. What is the source of this karma? 205

A: Were lovers in Persia. 206

Q: *(L)* And that was in the 1600s, as we have been told before, correct? 207

A: Yes. 208

Q: *(L)* Do I have any particular karma toward or with any of my children that is outstanding? Any one or two children with outstanding karma? 209

A: [Youngest daughter]. 210

Q: *(L)* What about [third daughter]? 211

A: No. 212

Q: *(L)* Who was [third daughter] in her last lifetime? 213

A: Brian Jones. 214

Q: *(L)* When did Brian Jones die? 215

A: 1889 216

Q: *(L)* When was Brian Jones born? 217

A: 1803. 218

Q: *(L)* And do all of my children have strong connections to me in terms of affection or karma or whatever? 219

A: As always. 220

Q: *(L)* When was the last lifetime Frank and I were together?[12] 221

A: 1700's. 222

Q: *(L)* Who was Frank in the 1700s? 223

A: Bavarian landowner's son. 224

Q: *(L)* Who was I in this lifetime? 225

A: Daughter. 226

[12] *The Wave* 44

227 **Q**: *(L)* I was Frank's daughter?

228 **A**: No, sister.

229 **Q**: *(L)* Was this the same lifetime when I was married to Grant?

230 **A**: No. Spent 3 lifetimes in what is now Germany.

231 **Q**: *(L)* Was my mother with me in that lifetime?

232 **A**: No.

233 **Q**: *(L)* In that lifetime as Bavarian landowner's children, what was Frank's name?

234 **A**: Heinrig.

235 **Q**: *(L)* What was my name?

236 **A**: Sheila.

237 **Q**: *(L)* What did we do in that lifetime? Argue?

238 **A**: Were sheltered.

239 **Q**: *(L)* Any exceptional talents or abilities?

240 **A**: Piano and harp.

241 **Q**: *(L)* So, all I did was sit around and play the piano and harp all the time?

242 **A**: Close.

243 **Q**: *(L)* And read books? What did Frank do, smoke cigars and gaze out the window?

244 **A**: Read.

245 **Q**: *(L)* Must have been nice, Frank. What area of Bavaria was this?

246 **A**: Muenchen near. South of there. On Braunau.

247 **Q**: *(L)* Was this a very large house?

248 **A**: Castle.

249 **Q**: *(L)* Sounds better all the time. Is the castle still standing?

A: Yes. 250

Q: *(L)* Would we know that castle by name? 251

A: No. 252

Q: *(L)* What was our last name, surname, family name? 253

A: Von Endersohn. 254

Q: *(L)* Did we live long and fulfilling and happy lives? 255

A: Open. 256

Q: *(L)* Did we experience tragedy? 257

A: Was turbulent era. 258

Q: *(L)* Well, how old was I when I died? 259

A: 43. 260

Q: *(L)* How old was Frank when he died? 261

A: 43. 262

Q: *(L)* Were we twins? 263

A: No. 264

Q: *(L)* Who was older, me or him? 265

A: Year apart. 266

Q: *(L)* What did he die from? 267

A: Heart attack. 268

Q: *(L)* What did I die from? 269

A: Pneumonia. 270

Q: *(L)* Did we die still living in our castle? 271

A: Yes. 272

Q: *(L)* Did either of us have any children? 273

A: No. Were sheltered from turbulence directed at wealthy. 274

Q: *(L)* How were we sheltered from this turbulence? 275

A: Kept isolated. Never married. 276

277 **Q**: *(L)* Well, I guess that is one way to shelter yourself from turbulence, just never go out. We just sat around, played the piano and harp and read books. That sounds like a pretty ideal existence to me. Did we ride horses too?

278 **A**: Yes.

279 **Q**: *(L)* I guess we worked hard to entertain ourselves. *(F)* That must be why we both yearn for security, peaceful reading and so on. *(L)* I have always wanted to live in Europe. Would I be happy doing so?

280 **A**: Up to you.

281 **Q**: *(F)* Well, that is probably why you yearn to live in Europe, because you spent 3 lifetimes in that area. *(L)* If I used hypnosis, could I improve my piano playing? Also, would I be able to automatically play the harp?

282 **A**: Open.

283 **Q**: *(L)* Has it ever been done before?

284 **A**: Yes.

285 **Q**: *(L)* The other night, on New Year's Eve, you said there was a whole group of celestial visitors, and among these you included my great-grandmother, Laura, is that correct?

286 **A**: Yes.

287 **Q**: *(L)* Well, does this mean that she has not gone into the light or can people come who have done so?

288 **A**: Latter.

289 **Q**: *(L)* I would like to know what my grandmother thinks of being dead?

290 **A**: Relief.

291 **Q**: *(L)* Well, I think that one of the things that made her hang on so long was that she was worried about me. I think about her a lot. When I do, is she aware of it?

A: Maybe. 292

Q: *(L)* Now, getting back to the idea of walk-ins – this is an idea that Ruth Montgomery promulgated – does this ever happen? 293

A: Rarely. 294

Q: *(L)* What about the case of the individual known as Lobsang Rampa? Was Lobsang Rampa a walk-in? 295

A: No. 296

Q: *(L)* What was the source of the material Lobsang wrote about in his books? 297

A: An active imagination. 298

Q: *(L)* So, Lobsang's books were basically his imagination and were not channeled in any way? 299

A: Open. 300

Q: *(L)* Is there a possibility that he channeled some of that information? 301

A: Yes. 302

Q: *(L)* I sent out a batch of mail today, I sent a copy to MF with a cover letter, etc. I am curious as to whether this will open his eyes in any way to the fact that what is going on with [this experiment] is far more interesting than what is going on with Scarlett? 303

A: Doubtful. 304

Q: *(L)* I also sent a copy of it to Leonard S and a copy to this metaphysical group over here on 54 and a copy to Jean and Gene B... How will Mary N react to our information? 305

A: Open. 306

Q: *(L)* Are you going to give me any indication about how any of these people 307 are going to react to any of this information? Can you look into the future and give me any idea of what I can expect from the different people?[13]

308 **A**: Wait and see.

309 **Q**: *(L)* As far as I can see, having found out about the network [internet], until I can get an access line, it seems that our use of this network is going to be severely limited.

310 **A**: Look into 800 number.

311 **Q**: *(L)* Well, in order to get an 800 number, I would have to get the company to do it. I'll look into it, but I don't think so. Now, this person on the [internet], IrishSir – I have basically decided that I am not going to respond to him because he is very offensive in his responses. It is as though he is attempting to draw me into a situation where he can attack. Is this course of action acceptable?

312 **A**: Open.

313 **Q**: *(L)* Is there anything I could say to this guy that would have an impact on him?

314 **A**: Of course.

315 **Q**: *(L)* Give me a clue as to what approach to take?

316 **A**: Up to you to learn communication with challenging subjects.[14]

317 **Q**: *(L)* The other night when we were talking about Jesus, I asked if there was any historical person we knew who resembled him and you said you were scanning.

A: No. 318

Q: *(L)* What was Jesus' actual name? 319

A: Jesinavarah. 320

Q: *(L)* What is the source of [eldest 321 daughter's] aversion to what I do and think?

A: Different orientation. 322

Q: *(L)* And what is her orientation? 323

A: Material. 324

Q: *(L)* Is [eldest daughter] a 4th den- 325 sity candidate?

A: Open. 326

Q: *(L)* We have been having a lot of 327 very unusual cloud shapes and formations. What is the source of this...

A: Upper level wind convergence. 328

Q: *(L)* When this occurs, does it repre- 329 sent anything from other dimensions? Or is it something to do with EM wave formations from the Earth?

A: Vague. 330

Q: *(L)* In other words, can these upper 331 level winds and strange cloud patterns be 4th, 5th or 6th density interactions?

A: Maybe. 332

Q: *(L)* Could these cloud patterns be 333 a result of strange electromagnetic patterns on the Earth such as those that presage earthquakes and volcanic eruptions?

[13]My main concern here was the information about aliens and abductions. Up to this point in time, the 'ancient astronauts', 'space brothers here to help us' meme was all that was out there and it was clear to me that there was something darkly disturbing about the UFO/alien reality. There were very, very few sources that talked about the negative aspects that were kept hidden, for the most part.

[14]Obviously, I was just getting my toes wet on the internet and my awareness of what we now know as trolls was non-existent.

334 **A**: Can.

335 **Q**: *(L)* Do we have an upcoming volcanic eruption or earthquake in the, say, next ten days?

336 **A**: Yes.

337 **Q**: *(L)* Which?

338 **A**: Earthquake. Andes. 7.6 Peru.[15]

339 **Q**: *(L)* Is there anything we need to know before we shut down for the night?

A: No. 340

Q: *(L)* What time of day was George 341
Ray born?

A: a.m. 6:21. 342

Q: *(L)* I apologize for asking so 343
many personal questions, but this thing about [my son] has definitely given a lot of credibility to the source here.

A: Goodnight. 344

End of session

[15]There was a 7.4 on 21 February 1996 off the coast of northern Peru, near the Peru-Chile Trench. So, no cigar for that one. Not enough details and the earthquake epicenter was not in the Andes.

January 7, 1995

This session was all over the place and, as a result, some very interesting responses came through about sex. I won't spoil it here at the beginning, but I'll just note that it is an idea that is quite startling in its implications and usefulness for solving other sex-related issues, however, I don't think it is the whole banana. We came back to the issue in later sessions and obtained more clarity on the topic and I'll comment on that as it appears in the text.

Participants: 'Frank', Laura, Terry, Jan, Violette, Diana M, Tom M

1 **Q**: *(L)* Hello.

2 **A**: Hello. Victim Violette. [Laughter]

3 **Q**: *(L)* Who do we have with us tonight?

4 **A**: Powder.

5 **Q**: [Powder added to board] *(L)* Now, I guess you'll want aftershave too.

6 **A**: Aftershave, please.

7 **Q**: *(L)* Who do we have with us tonight?

8 **A**: Lomarra.

9 **Q**: *(L)* Are you a discarnate?

10 **A**: No.

11 **Q**: *(L)* What or who are you?

12 **A**: Light being.[1]

13 **Q**: *(L)* And where are you communicating from?

A: Cassiopaea. 14

Q: *(L)* We have a few interesting ques- 15
tions tonight. I think the first thing on everybody's mind is the strange events during the night and early morning hours, reported by Terry and Jan compared with events that happened which John W said that he experienced and also, Terry's dad, and also something woke [#2 daughter] up with a start and I was awakened with a strange feeling. We are a little bit curious about this event, this occurrence, and we would like to have some information on it. What exactly was it?

A: Thunder. 16

Q: *(L)* It seemed to be an extraordi- 17
narily massive strike, and it seemed to have been heard at a great distance in several directions. Where, in fact, did this lightning bolt strike?[2]

A: Cell was uniformly structured 18
throughout region.

[1]It occurs to me as I comb through these texts for insight that a "light being" is something like a consolidated information field.

[2]*The Wave* 2

19 **Q**: *(T)* So we all heard that particular blast because of that?

20 **A**: No. Each zone received similar EM profile, thus one particularly heavily charged event in each zone.

21 **Q**: *(L)* What is an EM profile?

22 **A**: Electromagnetic.

23 **Q**: *(L)* Was there any particular significance to this type of blast since it is not something any of us has experienced in our immediate memory? Is there any implication to this blast in terms of 4th density activity?

24 **A**: You have, and yes, as always.

25 **Q**: *(L)* Since this was such a boomer, what exactly was going on on 4th density that produced a boomer like this?

26 **A**: Overlapping densities, lasting approximately 1.3 seconds, as you measure time i.e.: for 1.3 seconds, you lived completely in 4th density.

27 **Q**: *(T)* So this was a significant event for us to have noticed?

28 **A**: The noticing was more significant than the event.

29 **Q**: *(V)* Can I ask... so every time there is... am I wrong in assuming that every time there is thunder there is a mix of 4th density? *(L)* No, no. *(V)* It's just this one time? (Tom) What about if you didn't notice? I didn't hear it. *(T)* What was the answer? *(L)* The noticing was more important than the event. *(T)* So it was important that we were aware that something had happened...

30 **A**: You did at another level of consciousness.[3]

31 **Q**: *(L)* Did this event have anything to do with [my daughter's] experience this morning of being awakened by a rustling in her room and thinking that she heard a squeaky voice calling her name?

A: Yes. 32

Q: *(L)* OK, what was it that she experienced? 33

A: 4th density "resident." 34

Q: *(L)* And what kind of 4th density resident was this? 35

A: Om. 36

Q: *(L)* Who is Om? *(V)* Is it a name? *(T)* Is Om the name of the being? 37

A: Type. 38

Q: *(L)* What is a type Om? 39

A: You would rather not know! 40

Q: *(L)* No, I would rather know. If something is going to be visiting my daughter in her bedroom, I definitely want to know who or what it is. 41

A: Who says this will be regular event? 42

Q: *(V)* So, in other words, if it is not going to happen all the time, don't worry about it, is that right? 43

A: Yes. 44

Q: *(T)* This was just a one-time event? 45

A: Yes. 46

Q: *(V)* Was the reason [my daughter] was so aware of this is because she is psychically open when she is asleep? 47

A: Yes. 48

Q: *(V)* Is there anything she needs to do to control her psychic openness in order not to be harmed? 49

A: Why control something beneficial? 50

Q: *(V)* Well, it's just that Laura was concerned because you know... (Tom) 51

[3]Obviously addressed to Tom M who had just said he didn't notice/hear the event.

Is this something that we all encounter every now and again?

52 **A**: Three of you have... no, make that five. Terry, Tom, Frank, Diana, Laura.

53 **Q**: *(D)* The thumps that I hear in my house, this is not my grandmother, is this correct?[4]

54 **A**: Yes.

55 **Q**: *(D)* Are these visitors?

56 **A**: Yes.

57 **Q**: *(D)* What can you tell me about that?

58 **A**: What do you want to know?

59 **Q**: *(D)* Are these Cassiopaeans?

60 **A**: We do not "Thump." [Laughter]

61 **Q**: *(L)* What is causing the thumping phenomenon in Diana's house?

62 **A**: 5th and 4th [density] visitors of varying description your many activities have attracted.

63 **Q**: *(T)* Are they harmful? *(D)* My many activities like reading... psychic readings? *(L)* No, no, stop. Are these beings in general STS or STO oriented?

64 **A**: STS.

65 **Q**: *(L)* So, varying activities of Diana's have attracted them. What initial activities did Diana do that opened the doorway for this type of activity?

66 **A**: Networking.

67 **Q**: *(L)* Networking with who or what?

68 **A**: Her recent contacts.

Q: *(L)* With who or what? 69

A: People. 70

Q: *(L)* Who, specifically? *(D)* Are we 71
talking about Eddie Page?[5]

A: That is one. 72

Q: *(D)* Marti T? 73

A: Yes. 74

Q: *(D)* Jiles H? 75

A: Yes. 76

Q: *(V)* Laura and Frank? 77

A: No. 78

Q: *(D)* Patty K? 79

A: No. 80

Q: *(D)* Anyone from the [metaphysical] 81
church?

A: Yes. 82

Q: *(D)* Ben? 83

A: No. 84

Q: *(D)* Don W? 85

A: Yes. 86

Q: *(D)* Did it start with my association 87
with Don W?[6]

A: Yes. 88

Q: *(D)* Was that the first time? 89

A: Yes. 90

Q: *(D)* How can I stop these visits? 91

A: Complicated. 92

Q: *(D)* Where do I start? What is the 93
first step? *(L)* Well, you have an EM

[4]Notice the bizarre way the question is posed. This was typical of Diana M.

[5]Review the sordid Eddie Page saga from the previous sessions, 17 and 31 December 1994.

[6]It's interesting that all of the individuals assessed as being initiators of 4th/5th density STS contact were very active in the local UFO/abductee/contactee community, not so much psychic or metaphysically oriented.

opening. Closing that would be the first step.

94 **A**: You have begun already.

95 **Q**: *(D)* With reading. *(T)* By asking?

96 **A**: Yes. Yes.

97 **Q**: *(D)* What is the next step?

98 **A**: This is not a "step by step process."

99 **Q**: *(L)* Is it that she is going to have to have knowledge and awareness?

100 **A**: The light is knowledge, which is protection.

101 **Q**: *(L)* I guess that means that you need to visualize light around yourself and your house. *(D)* I guess some sage and holy water... *(L)* No, no, no, no, no rituals. Knowledge. The power of the mind only. *(T)* If she stops associating with Page and group, will this be a good step in the right direction?

102 **A**: We do not condone recommendations for friendships and associations; that is free will.

103 **Q**: *(L)* So, they are not going to tell you who to associate with, it is your own choice. *(J)* But, now that you have the knowledge, you can make an informed choice. *(D)* Well, there is no choice... that is it.

104 **A**: Up to you.

105 **Q**: *(L)* I would like to bring up before we get sidetracked, that we have Tom M with us this evening and...

106 **A**: Hi Tom.

Q: *(L)* Tom has a couple of questions 107
he would like to ask about moving and his direction in life – this will be brief. So, I will just let him ask his questions.[7]

A: Now you are beginning to see what 108
happens when you let emotions take over, Tom. We warned you in a subtle way.

Q: *(T)* What do I need to do to get my- 109
self back on track on a spiritual path?

A: We were talking directly to you with 110
the last 2 answers.

Q: *(T)* Did you get some kind of a warn- 111
ing?

A: Do you remember, Tom. 112

Q: (Tom) No, I don't remember the 113
warning.

A: Okay, now think carefully, access 114
memories of first day of "union."

Q: (Tom) Are you talking about my re- 115
lationship with Andrea?

A: We were being discreet. 116

Q: *(L)* You blabbed it out, they were 117
being discreet. Did you get some kind of warning? *(V)* Did you get any 'gut' feelings? *(L)* Have you not learned that your relationship is taking you away from your spiritual path? *(D)* Did she ask you to give up anything? *(V)* Did the relationship make you feel uncomfortable? *(D)* Did it give you negative thoughts about spirituality?

A: Let Tom figure it out. This is rather 118
of a private nature.

Q: (Tom) OK. Well, I'm thinking of... 119

[7]It was typical for Tom M. He would show up to ask a few questions for advice, completely ignore the advice, and then show up later to try to get himself out of a nasty situation.

[8]This was a definite hint. Tom had been involved with some of the people of the metaphysical church that caused me so many problems and I had even been asked

120 **A**: Tom has a tendency to be rebellious and secretive.[8]

121 **Q**: *(J)* Well, that's not such a bad combination. *(T)* Yeah, I'm working on that... *(V)* We all have our crosses to bear... *(L)* Tom now has a plan where he is going to... his relationship has led to other situations that have caused unpleasantness in his life; he is now going to travel half-way across the country to escape this...

122 **A**: Repeating syndrome.

123 **Q**: *(T)* No matter where you go, there *you* are. *(L)* The scenery may change, but you will be the same with the same problems until you change yourself. (Tom) It is really because I know I can support myself better out there and I know that we can support ourselves better out there.

124 **A**: How do you know that?

125 **Q**: (Tom) Because I have checked with the papers, I have looked at what is out there... There's more jobs out there, there's more apartments, more opportunity, better chance to really get ahead... *(L)* Who are you trying to convince?

126 **A**: Really???

127 **Q**: (Tom) I just feel like it's time for a change.

128 **A**: You have felt that way often before.

129 **Q**: (Tom) OK, let me ask this: could I have some kind of place out there, do something that needs to be done out there?

A: Many have lived under the illusion 130
that relocation improves destiny. All have failed.

Q: *(L)* If you can't succeed where you 131
are, you probably won't succeed anywhere else. *(J)* You always carry yourself with you wherever you go. If you are what's wrong, moving doesn't change that. *(L)* And, in fact, it can make things worse. *(T)* Yeah, you lose a lot because you lose your connections and contacts, your support system, your network, everything. (Tom) Well, part of it is that I just want to go. *(L)* Maybe wanting to go is part of your problem. *(J)* Are you running away? (Tom) No. *(L)* Is Tom running away? [Terry gives his seat to Tom at the board.]

A: Yes. 132

Q: *(L)* Is there anything you can tell 133
Tom...

A: The community he is considering is 134
much more 3rd density. It is not metaphysically oriented.

Q: *(L)* In other words, if he moves, he 135
will get more in the soup? [Break for discussion.] Tom thinks he can make it work... comments please.

A: Well, this plan is related to and con- 136
tingent on shaky emotional considerations. His relationship is unstable and that is at the root of the issue.

Q: (Tom) What do I have to do to make 137
the relationship stable? *(V)* Oh, the youngsters! "We are going to make this

to do an emergency Spirit Release session with him as a result of some of their prescribed activities, like mirror gazing and calling up spirits. After that, he had sworn he wasn't going to have anything further to do with that sort of thing, but apparently that wasn't the case and he was not being entirely forthcoming at this session.

square peg fit into this round hole no matter what!"

138 **A**: Open.

139 **Q**: (Tom) Can you give me a hint as to what I need to do... *(L)* What they are saying is that you can't make this relationship stable... *(J)* Either it is or it isn't.

140 **A**: Let Tom decide.

141 **Q**: (Tom) Let me just ask this: can I make this relationship stable?

142 **A**: Discover. But moving won't accomplish this.

143 **Q**: (Tom) I know I can make this work, but should I stay here?

144 **A**: Better chance of survival of the relationship if you remain and work things out.

145 **Q**: (Tom) But her best friend is out there...

146 **A**: Friendships are not stable with this one.

147 **Q**: *(L)* They are saying Andrea is not capable of a stable friendship and that may extend to relationships. (Tom) Can I help her attain spirituality or a level of enlightenment?

148 **A**: What we told you with the first answer applies. Does not have to be painful.

149 **Q**: (Diana) I have been married twice. The day before I was to marry the man who I thought was wonderful, of course, I was told that no one was going to make me marry him, and that if I wanted to I could change my mind. I had reservations but I did not feel that I could back out because the wedding was already set. And it turned out to be a very destructive marriage and divorce. So, what I am saying to you is that if everything is not perfect about your mate, in terms of your expectations and needs, if there is anything that you think you can or have to change about this person, or that involvement with you will change her, you are wrong. You can't change them, they won't change, and the relationship will deteriorate destructively. If you are now asking what you have to do to 'make' it work, it is already on the road to destruction. It is never too late to come to your senses and back out.

A: Yes. 150

Q: *(L)* Is there a past life or karmic tie between Tom and Andrea? 151

A: As always. It is up to him to discover. He is rebellious and is not listening. We have given much, now it is up to him. 152

Q: *(L)* Is anyone in this room not rebellious? *(Chorus)* I am! *(L)* Have we not all learned the hard way? *(Chorus)* I certainly have... yes... *(V)* We have all learned the lesson we see Tom facing. It's easy for us to sit back and know the end result because we have all been through it before. It's easy for us to tell him to back away and rethink because we have all been forced to do it but we need to remember how painful it was to us at the time and how we all thought it was the end of the world. *(L)* Yes. We all thought that ending destructive relationships was the hardest thing in the world to do... other people gave us advice when we were younger like we are advising Tom now, and we didn't take it... But how much easier on us it would have been if we had the wisdom then to do what we see now... *(Chorus)* Amen! 153

154 **A**: Real love is not strictly hormonal.

155 **Q**: (Tom) So, what they are saying is that I can make this work here but I can't make it work there? *(L)* No, Tom, the chances are not good either way, but you have something of a chance here with a good support system and your metaphysical network. There, it is certain to fail and then you will be in emotional turmoil, probably broke, and stuck far away from everybody. *(V)* There is not a pat answer on your relationship, they just said if you stay here, it has a better chance. They didn't say that if you stay, you definitely will succeed... And, if you are seeking spirituality right now, it is definitely a bad move to make...

156 **A**: Yes.

157 **Q**: *(J)* Going back to the event of this morning, when JW related his experience of it to me, he said that when he opened his eyes that the light looked yellow... *(V)* I noticed the discoloration too... *(J)* Was that related to the event?

158 **A**: Yes.

159 **Q**: *(J)* What caused the light to change color?[9]

160 **A**: Leftover 4th density effects.

161 **Q**: *(L)* Is this something that is going to be happening more and more as we move to 4th density?

162 **A**: Yes.

163 **Q**: *(L)* Is this electromagnetic charging of the atmosphere – I am assuming that is what it is, and that it is occurring as part of the shifting of densities...

A: Yes. 164

Q: *(L)* If it is an electromagnetic charging of the atmosphere, is this charging coming about because of this oncoming wave and effects that we are beginning to feel more and more of, are they part of the wave, its presence or approach? 165

A: It is a buildup, similar to the early effects preceding the arrival of a sea wave. 166

Q: *(T)* Are the extremely high winds they have been experiencing in North Carolina and California and the earthquakes in Japan all related to this? 167

A: Yes. 168

Q: *(T)* Yes. The media is playing that down... 140-mile-an-hour winds up in the Carolinas and out in California they were hitting 160-miles-an-hour winds. *(L)* Well, they told us we were going to have really weird weather. *(T)* There was another earthquake in Japan today. This has been ongoing for the last couple of weeks. Japan is supposed to go. *(V)* Sylvia Brown was on a talk show. Sylvia Brown is known as a highly aware psychic. How do you feel about her psychic abilities? 169

A: Okay. 170

Q: *(V)* She had said that there was going to be a big earthquake in Alaska... a huge one... what can you tell us about this? 171

[9] *The Wave* 2

[10] This is something that we often forget. The Cs have said repeatedly that Earth changes and related matters are a long-term process, not just a one-day pole shift and Boom! everything is changed and everyone ascends or something. Considering the fact that this session was in 1995 and I am annotating now in 2015, it is clear now exactly what was meant. Indeed, things have changed dramatically if

172 **A**: One of many events of the buildup lasting years, as you measure time.[10]

173 **Q**: *(V)* That's interesting because I followed Sylvia Brown for a number of years. *(L)* Let me ask this: I got a letter from Piers A and he was giving me the big pooh pooh and....

174 **A**: Piers is misguided.

175 **Q**: *(L)* Well, my question about this is, in addition to that really revolting letter I got from that creep on the network, my feeling about this is: I really want these people to open their eyes, will they?[11]

A: Those who will, will. 176

Q: *(T)* Look at it this way, you have an 177
open enough mind to allow those who have their minds closed to keep them closed. You have tried, you don't have to take it any further. *(L)* You guys said that we were going to have a whole big, bodacious bunch more of UFO activity this year, is that correct?

A: Bingo! 178

Q: *(L)* And I guess it has already 179
started because some guy in Michigan filmed a UFO in broad daylight and they showed it on the news three days

incrementally over these past 20 years; but indeed, there are moments when singular, dramatic events occur, such as 9/11 and the Chelyabinsk Meteor explosion. Things are definitely picking up and it may be, indeed, something like childbirth!

[11]I had been sharing the Cs perspective on the internet and a few other people by snail mail. It seems that what people were looking for was 'love and light' and everything is going to be rainbows and unicorns, not a prediction that we were facing a global lockdown on our freedoms and a possible alien takeover (whether literal or via human agents). I think the Cs' perspective has been proven correct by now.

[12]Reported by Hildebrand Communications, Inc., for *United Press International*, December 22, 1994:

> Kingsley, Michigan, December 21, 1994 *(UPI)* – A Michigan State Trooper responding to a woman's UFO report Wednesday confirmed seeing "a cylindrical mass, with a large amount of individual lights."
>
> A 5-minute videotape shot by the woman and broadcast on local television provided additional evidence that something was indeed out there, police said.
>
> "This one is apparently a valid report," said one of the trooper's superiors, State Police Sgt. Bill Sholten. "He is credible. I saw the tape and there was definitely something out there," Sholten said.
>
> The trooper, who asked not to be identified because he doesn't want publicity, reported seeing three military jets in the area while the UFO was near. His report also noted that after the siting, a request for information was turned down by the U. S. Air Force for unknown reasons.
>
> A Regional Air Traffic Control Center in Minnesota reported spotting something on radar screens to support the report.
>
> A woman who lives on a farm near Kingsley said she saw the object hovering above her barn at 6:30 am EST, December 21st. She called police about an hour later and the trooper arrived at about 7:45 a.m. The trooper watched the UFO through binoculars until it disappeared about 20 minutes later. The woman, who got a closer look at the UFO, described the object as about three times larger than her barn, or some 60 feet in diameter. She also said it had white and blue lights

in a row and I don't think they were being snide in their comments...[12] *(F)* Yes they were. I saw it on channel 13 and they were being definitely snide. *(T)*

---

and what appeared to be a haze surrounding it.

Sholten said the woman told police she saw a similar UFO on Thanksgiving, but didn't tell anyone "because she was afraid everyone would think she was nuts."

This December sighting followed a veritable flap that had occurred the previous March.

March 13, 1995, by Ellen Creager, Knight-Ridder/*Tribune*:

One year ago last Wednesday, something strange happened in western Michigan. A 911 call recorded the scene:

National Weather Service radar operator: "What is really going on down there?"

Holland, Mich., Police Officer Jeff Velthouse: "We don't know. People are calling in and telling us about these strange objects. ..."

Radar operator: "What did it look like?"

Velthouse: "Witnesses are seeing five or six objects, some cylindrically shaped, circles with blue, red, white and green lights. We've had reports from south Holland (Mich.) and over in northern Allegan County. Lots of lights moving all over the place."

Radar operator: "There were three and sometimes four blips, and they weren't planes. Planes show as pinpoints on the scope, these were the size of half a thumbnail. They were from 5 to 12,000 feet at times, moving all over the place. Three were moving toward Chicago. I never saw anything like it before, not even when I'm doing severe weather."

In one of Michigan's greatest unsolved mysteries, nobody has been able to explain the UFOs seen by hundreds of people in western Michigan on March 8, 1994.

What has happened to the people who saw the lights that night? The radar operator who saw the UFOs has transferred out. Velthouse still works as a Holland police officer. Other witnesses are eager to recall their awesome experience – and still wonder, what were those lights in the sky?

"These sightings would have to fall into the category of a true unidentified flying object," says Dr. Michael Swords, professor of natural science at Western Michigan University and former editor of the *Journal for UFO Studies*, a scholarly journal. "The radar returns were definitely anomalous, completely unexplained."

But was it, you know ... aliens?

"It's not unreasonable to think it could be something from another galaxy," says Randee Murphy of Ada, Mich., who saw the lights directly above her house that night.

"I don't believe for a minute that it was any kind of alien structure; I think there is a fairly strong earthly explanation for what occurred," says Leo Grenier, director of the National Weather Service in Muskegon.

The UFO sighting was the largest in the United States in 1994, based on the number of people who reported it. UFO researchers called it a "major, radar-confirmed UFO flap" with more than 300 witnesses, including a police officer. Most important, it showed up on the radar of an operator at the National Weather Service at Muskegon County Airport.

"We can explain away 80 to 90 percent of UFO sightings," says Walter Andrus of the Mutual UFO Network, a Texas-based investigation group. "It's that other 10 percent that we're interested in."

And those guys lost their network affiliation, too! *(L)* That fellow in Michigan, could you identify that craft for us and who it belonged to?

180 **A**: It was the Grays.

181 **Q**: *(L)* Now, are the Grays going to allow themselves to be seen more and more in 3rd density in the upcoming years?

182 **A**: Yes.

183 **Q**: *(L)* Is there a reason behind this exposure?

184 **A**: All of these events are related to that with which you are now familiar.

185 **Q**: *(L)* This is part of their movement to land on the planet, interact with human beings, say, via the media... *(T)* They are already landing on the planet...

186 **A**: No, for all is related to approach of oncoming wave, what the details are will remain to be seen.[13]

187 **Q**: *(L)* By the way, Tom, your information about the bases in Appalachia happens to have been confirmed. *(T)* Are there military bases in the Appalachian mountains?

188 **A**: Yes.

189 **Q**: *(L)* Hidden ones?

190 **A**: Yes.

191 **Q**: *(T)* Are they for the subjugation of the U.S. when they start to implement the final stages of the New World Order in this country?

A: Remains to be seen. 192

Q: *(L)* Do they actually have buildings or places set up in this country to be crematoriums and labor camps as I have read about in several articles? 193

A: Yes. 194

Q: *(T)* When do they intend to initiate this plan? 195

A: Open. 196

Q: *(T)* Last I heard was March of 1995. *(V)* Goodness gracious. *(L)* I have been saying for years now after doing the [astrological] charts that 1995 is going to be one strange year.[14] *(V)* A lot of other people are saying that too. *(D)* There is supposed to be something big, some big organization fall... *(L)* If we sat here and visualized a clockwise vortex of light and energy, would it greatly enhance the energy flow? 197

A: Not necessary any longer. 198

Q: *(V)* Last night I all of a sudden got a flash to do a Tarot reading. Now, I hadn't done this in months because I know it is not a super clear channel, but, I had the overwhelming feeling that it was OK to do this. Was the reading I did for myself last night a valid and factual true reading? 199

A: If you wish it to be. 200

[13]Notice the question that this "no" was in response to. The Cs were pretty clearly saying that just how the 'takeover of Earth by aliens' would transpire was not defined. Nowadays, I say "who needs aliens when we have psychopaths running our planet?" But, for all we know, psychopaths in charge, and the thuggish militarized police all over the planet, are simply agents of 4th density negative beings who are, I keep saying, somewhat 'paranormal'.

[14]As it turned out, we weren't very far away from the Oklahoma City bombing, which was a big part of laying the groundwork for 9/11 and all that has followed.

201 **Q**: *(V)* Well, I was hoping with the reading that I was drawing on your energy – was I?

202 **A**: You do not need cards to "draw on our energy." Your strong feeling was to meditate for information. You misinterpreted it as a need for Tarot. Cards can confuse, meditation never does.

203 **Q**: *(V)* Well, they were nice cards and I threw a spread this morning that was beautiful... the last card was the moon card... and in my perception of that card I haven't been able to signify whether that meant psychic energy or deception... what was the meaning within my perception?

204 **A**: We have given enough personal data for this session.

205 **Q**: *(T)* What is a good way to meditate?

206 **A**: The way that feels "effortless" for you.

207 **Q**: *(V)* OK, if we are getting off of personal stuff here, and moving on to more generalized... I would like to know... there is a common knowledge kind of thing among metaphysical people that when a soul is born onto the planet, that soul, that little baby, has infinite knowledge, and as we grow and learn we were conditioned to lose our knowledge – is this true?

208 **A**: No.

209 **Q**: *(L)* How could a baby have infinite knowledge, it only has imprint of its past life experiences? *(V)* You have heard that also...

210 **A**: That is nonsense.

211 **Q**: *(V)* That's fine... I was just... I'm sure you've heard that...

A: Souls are not "born" into this planet. 212
Souls were never born! And, will never die!

Q: *(V)* I understand, my question was 213
loose; I'm sorry. *(D)* Are there any new souls being created?

A: Just answered if you use your head. 214
Diana does not know the real concept of "time."

Q: *(D)* Well, that is a concept that is 215
very difficult for me. *(L)* Well, for everybody. We can talk about it and play with it... but there really is no time. It's an illusion, it's a lie... *(T)* It's part of the 3rd density world we have created... *(D)* I'm trying real hard...

(F) OK, let me give you an example: Take yourself off the planet, take yourself farther away so you can't see the sun anymore except as a speck.

(D) OK, I'm there...

(F) Now you are floating out there in space... there is no direction, everything is just out from you... there is no up or down or sideways... nothing... You see stars every way you look, but there is no point of orientation... Now, being no longer on the planet, the sun doesn't rise and the sun doesn't set... you have no watch or clock... how do you know what was before and what was after...

(Tom) Have you ever heard of people who go down into caves to do research experiments, and they come out thinking that only 45 days have passed when it has really been 65 or a hundred... because time slows down and virtually stops. Time is a human concept.

(F) I read the book about the Barbara Mackle abduction. She was kidnapped by a guy who put her into an underground coffin with gadgets to help

her survive, and she was buried... she thought, when she was pulled out, 83 hours later, she thought she had only been in there one night.

(L) Let's ask this question: In a state where there are no artificial considerations such as the delineation of night and day, in such a state, what would be the natural cycle of the human physical body in terms of, say, sleeping or eating, and refer this back to our concept of time. In other words, how long would we naturally stay awake, and then how long would we naturally sleep if we were not constrained by artificial time references, in a general sense?

216 **A**: Your entire existence would be radically different and would not cycle in the same ways at all.

217 **Q**: *(L)* Can you tell us how it would?

218 **A**: It depends on the environment.

219 **Q**: *(L)* So, we are so interactive with our environment that we almost can't separate ourselves from it, is that what you are saying?

220 **A**: Close.

221 **Q**: *(L)* If our solar system motion was such that, according to our present time delineations, we had 48 hours of daylight and 48 hours of night, would there be a concomitant extension of lifetime in the same terms?

222 **A**: Maybe.

223 **Q**: *(L)* Sitchin has an interesting idea about his theorized planet Nibiru, that their solar year is 3,600 of our years, and, therefore, for every one year of their life, 3,600 years pass on Earth, and therefore a being who theoretically was on such a planet, one with a 3,600-year orbit, would live many multiple thousands of years. Is this a valid concept insofar as it goes?

A: That is a confused cross conceptualization. 224

Q: *(L)* Now, is that confusion as I presented it, or confusion as Sitchin theorized it? 225

A: It's the whole gang. 226

Q: *(T)* We have to remember that time is only relative to Earth, and it came about the way it is now only because of mathematics based on base 10 counting system. If you go to the moon, time is not reflected in the same way, if you have to measure it, as it is here. We use Earth time on the moon. If we were to go to Mars, Mars time would be different. It is all based on rotation and orbit, which is only one way of doing it. As an example, not exactly having to do with time, but the idea of *pi*, 3.1416. On the SETI program they send out *pi* on a radio program saying: "Intelligent life will understand *pi* because *pi* is a basic idea in circular mathematics." You have to be able to figure *pi* in order to calculate circumference and diameter and so on in circles and arcs. So, I ask, what is the good of sending out *pi* in base ten when, say, the Grays only have 8 digits on their fingers? What is *pi* in base 8? 3.1416 means absolutely nothing to someone who is working in another system base. 227

A: Grays are cybergenetic beings, therefore they use mathematics they are programmed to use. 228

Q: *(T)* You all missed the point. I understand that Grays are... 229

A: No, we did not. Why do you look "up" when talking to us? 230

Q: *(L)* Well, where should we look? 231

232 **A**: Anywhere.

233 **Q**: *(L)* OK now, the Grays are programmed to use mathematics. I am assuming that they are programmed to use the mathematics of the Lizard beings, their creators, is that correct?

234 **A**: Variable.

235 **Q**: *(L)* Well, the question I am trying to get at here is, what base do the Lizards use?

236 **A**: The Lizards have a form of mathematics you would not even begin to understand.

237 **Q**: *(L)* Well, I would imagine so. Now, if a line is defined as the movement of a point in a single direction, and a plane is defined as a line moving at right angles to itself, and the 3rd dimension is defined as a plane moving at right angles to itself, and the 4th dimension is defined as a three dimensional object moving at right angles to itself, then what we are talking about in 4th density, something that we simply cannot grasp. If we look at a three dimensional apple, we are only seeing a slice, so to speak, of a 4th dimensional object. If we could see the apple in its true, 4th dimensional state, we would see something, probably more like a long, red tubular type thing that goes onto infinity. Is this a correct assessment?

238 **A**: Close.

239 **Q**: *(T)* And then there is 5th, 6th and 7th density levels. The whole point is to demonstrate that time doesn't exist and is irrelevant. It could be defined in any countless numbers of ways.

240 **A**: Yes.

241 **Q**: *(L)* Look at the Mayans... they counted in base 20. (Tom) Once you remove all references to time, it slows down and eventually stops. *(J)* Yes, look at what happens to those who are in sensory deprivation chambers. (Tom) Exactly. *(L)* An imploding infinity, so to speak.

A: If you were out in space, you might sleep for thousands of years or remain "awake" for millions of "years." 242

Q: (Tom) This refers back to Frank's explanation of floating in space along with how time might be perceived without reference points. 243

A: It really does not matter, because you would not be under the same illusion that "Time" even exists. 244

Q: *(L)* Let me ask this: I am kind of drifting into another subject, but we are talking about being in space. We talked at one point, I believe, of the matrices of the various planets and our perceptions of the planets in our solar system, and these matrices being almost like a doorway to another density, and that if we were in the proper dimensional mode that we would see the other planets of our own solar system quite differently from how we see them in our 3rd density mode, and that we would, in fact, be able to look upon Venus, which manifests in 3rd density as a pretty hellish place, with temperatures 900 degrees or thereabouts, and we would find it to be something else altogether with beings inhabiting it – is this correct? 245

A: Yes. Beings live absolutely everywhere in one realm or another. 246

Q: *(L)* Are the beings who live on the planet Venus aware of us on the planet Earth? 247

A: Yes. 248

249 **Q**: *(L)* Are there beings also living on Mars?

250 **A**: Yes.

251 **Q**: *(L)* Are they aware of us?

252 **A**: Yes.

253 **Q**: *(L)* Are the beings on all the other planets in our solar system aware of us here, on planet Earth?

254 **A**: Yes, because they are all of higher density.

255 **Q**: *(L)* Why is it that the Earth seems to be the lower density planet and we seem to be kind of left out in the cold, so to speak? They know of us, but we can't perceive them. Why is this? Why are we singled out for this? *(D)* Was Earth created after all the others?

256 **A**: No, no, no.

257 **Q**: *(T)* Are they interacting with us?

258 **A**: Okay, stop, whoa! A review session follows: Who is 1st density?

259 **Q**: *(L)* Rocks and minerals, right?

260 **A**: And?

261 **Q**: *(L)* Plants?

262 **A**: Yes. Now, what awareness do you suppose they have of you?

263 **Q**: *(L)* What awareness do rocks and plants have of *us*?! Oh, dear God! *(V)* That's an interesting way to put it. An excellent example. *(T)* When we ask why higher beings have awareness of us but we are not aware of them, we need to ask what awareness beings lower than us have of us. *(J)* Obviously no more than we have of 4th density. *(T)* But when you play music to a plant, it has some awareness because it makes it grow better. *(L)* But music is not a being. (Tom) It's an energy wave. *(J)* Wait a minute... what they are saying is: they have no more awareness of us than we, as 3rd density beings, have of 4th density beings. (Tom) Does this mean that they interact with us the way we interact with plants?

A: Who is "on" 2nd level. 264

Q: *(L)* Animals. *(T)* Insects, lower life 265
forms.

A: Now, think carefully, what level of 266
awareness, and more importantly, understanding, do they have of you?

Q: *(L)* Well, I guess they are aware 267
of us in some way, but they don't understand us... (Tom) Some do at some point... *(T)* They understand us to a certain extent... *(F)* But their understanding is entirely different from our understanding of them. In other words, they see these big hulking beings, but they don't know what's going on. *(L)* Was Ouspensky's explanation of how animals perceive humans very close to the truth?[15]

A: Close. Now, what about 1st level 268
understanding and perception of 2nd level?

Q: *(L)* OK, 1st density, minerals and 269
plants... now rocks and minerals combine with plants through growing actions, water dissolution, erosion, and so on, they have a real limited existence. And what happens is that mostly animals come along and eat them. *(F)* Bees pollinate flowers. *(L)* Different kinds of animals live in trees. *(T)* Some animals live in the ground and in caves. *(L)* So, rocks and minerals and plants have a really limited understanding of the animals above them which interact

[15] See Ouspensky's *Tertium Organum.*

with them in various ways.

270 **A**: Yes, and you have a limited understanding of the densities above you.

271 **Q**: *(L)* Well, that is still not answering my question, my question was... *(T)* As an example, today we all experienced something we call thunder, but we were all aware that it was something more. Something happened in 4th density that we experienced in a certain way, and it was a limited understanding of that level.

272 **A**: Laura, unblock, do rocks and plants "see" you?

273 **Q**: *(J)* Probably not. *(D)* We don't really know. (Tom) We see the 3rd density manifestations of 1st density objects. We don't see the 1st density perception of itself. So, how do we see the 4th density manifestations, they see us on a 4th density level... not necessarily as we perceive ourselves.

274 **A**: Tom, you are making rapid progress. Laura better watch her Butt! [Laughter]

275 **Q**: *(V)* So, I am curious... what do rocks look like to each other? *(L)* Yes, what do rocks see when they look at each other?

276 **A**: They sense each other.

277 **Q**: *(L)* What example of our sensory apparatus would be close to an example of what a rock senses when it is aware of another rock?

278 **A**: That is a cross conceptualization and will not work.

279 **Q**: *(L)* So there is no way we can interpret what a rock senses. Well, another 1st density example is plants. We know that plants can react positively to certain persons and negatively to others. They have experimented with hooking them up to polygraph machines and measured these responses. *(J)* They also react to music... (Tom) 3rd density reactions...

A: Yes. 280

Q: *(L)* If plants interact with each 281 other, do they feel, say, fondness for one another?

A: Something akin to that. 282

Q: *(L)* Does it hurt a plant when we 283 eat it?[16]

A: Does it hurt you when a "Lizzie" 284 eats you?

Q: (Tom) Yes, you see, on 4th density... 285 we are on 3rd density and we eat 1st and 2nd density, the 4th density eats us. *(D)* If we hurt plants by eating them like the Lizzies hurt us when they eat us, how are we to survive without eating?

A: When you no longer crave physical- 286 ity, you no longer need to "eat."

Q: *(L)* So part of the 'Fall' into 287 the physical existence and part of the Edenic story of the whole business, "you shall eat by the sweat of your brow," has to do with being physical and needing to eat?

A: Lucifer, "The fallen Angel." This is 288 you.

Q: *(L)* So, 'falling' means going into 289 physical existence wherein you must feed on other life, other beings, is that it?

A: Yes. 290

Q: *(T)* When plants feed on 1st level 291 beings such as rocks and water and so

[16] *The Wave* 23

forth, do the 1st density beings feel pain?

292 **A**: That is redundant. We have already covered this.

293 **Q**: *(T)* So when a plant absorbs nutrients.... *(L)* Well, a plant is the same density as minerals, so it is almost like... *(T)* Like two separate entities becoming one? *(V)* Like Jeffrey Dahmer... [Laughter] *(L)* [Sings] "My bologna has a first name..." *(LM)* [Entered the room a few minutes earlier.] Minerals dissolve in water and are then absorbed by the plant, what pain could there be in this?

294 **A**: Subjective, LM.

295 **Q**: *(L)* Maybe the dissolution of, say, phosphate in water, is a "death" to it...

296 **A**: Close. You limit when you perceive on 3rd level only and think that your perception is all there is.

297 **Q**: *(L)* So, in other words, we should be able to perceive on 1st and 2nd as well as 3rd while working on 4th level understanding?

298 **A**: No. Work on 4th, 5th and 6th.

299 **Q**: *(L)* Is it not also beneficial to understand the 1st and 2nd density levels as well, just simply for the exercise in understanding that which is below us?

300 **A**: Strive always to rise.

301 **Q**: *(V)* Haven't we already done our 1st and 2nd level work as evolving souls?

302 **A**: Yes.

303 **Q**: *(V)* So there is no reason to step back. (Tom) Who eats the Lizzies on the 4th level?

304 **A**: No one. 4th is the last density for full manifestation of STS.

Q: (Tom) So, beings on the 5th and 6th 305
level exist in pure energy?

A: Yes. 306

Q: *(T)* The 4th level is the last for full 307
STS. Does that mean that the 5th level, which you have described as the "contemplative" level... what is the state of existence of a STS being on the 5th level?

A: Souls of 1, 2, 3, and 4 go to 5th. 308

Q: *(T)* So 5th level is where they go to 309
while waiting to go back to one of the 4 for their next incarnation?

A: Exactly. 310

Q: *(T)* That is why it's called the con- 311
templation level. You go and think about what you have done. *(T)* What about souls on 6th density? *(L)* Are there 6th density STS beings?

A: No, when you get to 6th you no 312
longer need to recycle.

Q: *(L)* But still, is there an STS experi- 313
ence at 6th density, like the 6th density Orions?

A: These are only reflections of individ- 314
uals, not unified entities. These reflections exist for balance. They are not whole entities, just thought forms.[17]

Q: *(L)* Are these 6th density beings 315
what the Bible describes as a 'gathering' of angels as in the story of Job where 'Lucifer' came in before the Lord...

A: Yes. 316

Q: *(L)* So, there are STS and STO at 317
6th density which balance? And they are just there, they exist?

A: Reflection for balance. 318

---

[17] *Secret History* 12; *The Wave* 26

319 **Q**: *(L)* Is there any kind of hierarchy to this thing? Do these beings come before some kind of 'Grand Council' and make plans and discuss things, and make decisions and implement them?[18]

320 **A**: No.

321 **Q**: *(L)* Well, how do things happen? Do things just sort of happen as a natural interaction of things and energies?

322 **A**: Yes.

323 **Q**: *(V)* If we are on the 3rd density and you are working with us and we are striving to make 4th density, at the same time are you, at 6th density, striving to reach 7th?

324 **A**: Yes.

325 **Q**: *(T)* Is helping us, helping you to reach 7th density? *(V)* Are there others at higher densities working with you as you are working with us?

326 **A**: No, we all reach 7th level together.

327 **Q**: *(L)* So, in other words, you guys are trying to bring us up and everybody else is coming up, and when all the pieces are back together, we then go to 7th, is that it?

328 **A**: Yes.

329 **Q**: *(T)* So that is your purpose in helping us?

330 **A**: It's a natural process.

331 **Q**: (Tom) Will our function be, when we are at 6th density, to help others on 3rd, as you are doing?

332 **A**: Yes. We are you in the future.

333 **Q**: (Tom) When more than 50 per cent of the souls reach 6th density in preparation to go to 7th density, will all the rest of them automatically manifest into that density?

A: Not correct concept. You are using 3rd density "Brotherhood" inspired mathematical calculations and ideas. 334

Q: *(J)* So, there are no percentages involved in it. *(T)* So, we have to get every single soul up there. *(V)* I don't think it is as much that as that you can't apply 3rd density mathematics to that level. (Tom) Let's say a majority. 335

A: No. Still using 3rd density mathematics. 336

Q: *(L)* OK, what criteria constitutes the means of this ultimate translation into 7th density? 337

A: The lessons completed. 338

Q: *(J)* OK. (Tom) When all the souls transition to 7th density, will all the souls be integrated into one soul? 339

A: Close. 340

Q: (Tom) So that is why we have to get everybody, because we all become one on 7th density. *(D)* What will we then do to change the game and make it interesting again? 341

A: Don't have to "do" anything, has, will, is!!! 342

Q: *(L)* The fellow who wrote *The Ultimate Frontier*, was he channeling that information or did those events he described actually take place? 343

A: Yes and yes. 344

Q: *(L)* Was he, in fact, the reincarnation of King David as he claimed? 345

A: If he prefers. 346

Q: *(L)* He lost me when he went off on his thing about women and that souls 347

[18] *The Wave* 71

reincarnated as only one sex. *(J)* No, that's not so and I think switching sex has a lot to do with homosexuality. *(L)* Yes. (Tom) But I do think that a soul has a tendency to be more of one than the other.

348 **A**: No.

349 **Q**: *(L)* I think it ends up being balanced.

350 **A**: It is all just lessons.

351 **Q**: *(J)* Does the human state of sexuality, such as homosexuality, have something to do with changing sexes from one lifetime to another?

352 **A**: Sometimes.

353 **Q**: *(L)* Of all the modes of sexual expression, which one is more likely to advance one to 4th density more rapidly?

354 **A**: Total celibacy.

355 **Q**: *(D)* Well then I'm OK! [Laughter] *(V)* Can you explain why total celibacy?

356 **A**: Because you are then "letting go" of the cravings for physicality.[19]

357 **Q**: (Tom) It is a 3rd density act which entices you to 3rd density. *(L)* OK, now, what is the second most likely for advancement? [Laughter] *(D)* We have me taken care of, now we're going to get you taken care of! *(J)* In order of importance... [Laughter]

358 **A**: Does it matter?

359 **Q**: *(D)* It does to Laura. Would you please answer? *(L)* I suppose that everyone should get to the point that they would simply desire to be totally celibate and totally let go of all physical things and so forth, but, we have left to us, at this point, heterosexuality, homosexuality, bisexuality and multisexuality. [Laughter] *(D)* We also have the ability to take pleasure in our physical bodies in those forms of sexuality. We have the ability to have pleasure in the flesh and they can't. And, what I have read, is that they envy that. *(L)* Is that true, that you envy our physicality?

A: No. Not in the least! 360

Q: *(L)* I have read that when you are 361
at the higher spiritual levels that you can do a spiritual merge which is better than orgasm. Is that true?[20]

A: Why do you need orgasm of any 362
kind?

Q: *(L)* Well, it does seem to be like one 363
of the ultimate experiences of physicality. (Tom) That's exactly it... it's physicality... *(L)* If that is so, isn't everything that exists in the physical, 3rd density world, in some way a reflection of experiences or states of being on higher realms?

A: 3rd density as you experience it is 364
an illusion you have been fed to continue your imprisonment therein.

Q: *(L)* So, in other words, there is no 365
cosmic orgasm that keeps the worlds in existence as exemplified by the eternally copulating Vishnu and Shiva?

A: That is Bull! [Laughter] 366

Q: *(L)* Well, they teach this stuff in the 367
Eastern religions and they even have the idols sculpted in this posture...

[19] That is, celibacy when one has let go of cravings is effortless. Celibacy that is an effort is probably not positive because it is done in an effort to *get* something, i.e., advance to 4th density.

[20] *High Strangeness* 11

368 **A**: That is a rationalization to continue the illusion.

369 **Q**: *(L)* So, in other words, the orgasmic experience is quite literally a lure to keep us... *(D)* Controlled... (Tom) And in the 3rd level... *(L)* Is that true?

370 **A**: Yes.

371 **Q**: *(L)* Let's go back to a question I asked in another session on this same subject: what happens to our energy at the point of orgasm? Where does that energy go?

372 **A**: Drains to 4th level STS.

373 **Q**: *(T)* Is this a manifestation of the Lizards feeding off of us?

374 **A**: STSers there retrieve it.

375 **Q**: *(T)* So, orgasm is a 3rd density manifestation of the 4th density consumption of 3rd density energy?

376 **A**: One of their methods.

377 **Q**: *(D)* In *Bringers of the Dawn* it talks about sex and it says that it is an expression of love and so forth and that you should not have sex with someone who does not really love you.

378 **A**: Love is all that is needed.

379 **Q**: *(L)* If two individuals, as an expression of true love at higher levels, desire to express this love in a physical way, is it possible to channel the energy in a positive way without feeding the 4th level STS guys?

380 **A**: Nope.[21]

381 **Q**: *(L)* In other words, no matter what you do, how you think, or whatever, that's where it goes?

A: Sex is a physical craving. 382

Q: *(V)* So, when the big transition comes, let me assume, anybody who is having sex at the time or has any kind of sexual relationships around that time is not going to transition because of that? *(L)* I don't think so... *(V)* Well, I just want to get this clear. Is that true? 383

A: No. Transition is the "Millennium." A thousand years is the 3rd level interpretation. 384

Q: *(L)* So, for a thousand years we will be living as physical beings in 4th density, so to speak, making this transition during this period... and, by the time it is over we will have done away with our physical appetites? 385

A: Close. Some will be there at the beginning, others will need more "time." 386

Q: *(T)* So, when we are on the 4th density, we are still in the physical, and we will still be consuming, will we then be consuming that energy from 3rd density, the orgasmic energy, or something like that? 387

A: Some. 388

Q: *(D)* Even if we are STO? 389

A: Not if completely STO. 390

Q: *(D)* Then how do we get energy... we get energy from each other. Which is more powerful... the service... well we have to be service to others... *(L)* That is because STO multiplies and grows... STS just fragments, segregates, and gets smaller and smaller... *(J)* The law 391

[21] The topic of sex will come up again and again through the sessions, so just hang on. Hint in advance: it is not *always* true that sexual energy drains to 4D STS; the responses here were most likely very strongly influenced by Frank, who had a powerful, emotional rejection of sex and sexuality.

of diminishing returns. *(D)* We can access or receive others' energies as we give our own?

392 **A**: Yes.

393 **Q**: *(D)* Well, then, that is where service to others is service to self. *(L)* Any last messages? I feel a lot of changing going on here. Is there anything for any of us in the way of guidance?

394 **A**: Only if requested specifically.

395 **Q**: *(D)* Am I contacting you when I channel at home?

A: Yes but be careful of corrupting in- 396
fluences. Soulsearch, Terry.

Q: *(T)* I've been soul searching and 397
soul surfing, too! Is Keen Industries going to do anything with me?

A: Wait and see. 398

Q: *(T)* Will I be able to contact you? 399

A: Here. 400

End of Session

January 10, 1995

The initial questions of this session had to do with the pain I was experiencing as a consequence of the auto accident reported in a December 1994 session. My condition was actually deteriorating and I found it difficult to do ordinary tasks. I had been advised by a surgeon to have my neck vertebrae fused but I was determined *not* to take the surgery route, so I was struggling through with alternative therapies.

The second item was more information about the alleged cache of whatever that may have been buried under our house. I didn't think that whatever it was could be very valuable, but for me, it was a sort of 'test' of the Cs.

Next, there was some concern about Violette, who was a confirmed 'love and light' New Age type.

Finally, once the juices got flowing, I thought I would try to confirm some of the many New Age–type ideas that were flying around the internet.

Participants: 'Frank' and Laura

1 **Q**: *(L)* Hello. I wonder if they will show up?

2 **A**: We always show up.

3 **Q**: *(L)* Thank you very much. I have some pretty serious questions I want to ask tonight, so please be patient with me even if I do ask questions that are not quite in line.

4 **A**: Okay but such sessions drain you physically, thus must be kept short.

5 **Q**: *(L)* OK, it will be short. I just have a few questions. The first question is: my doctor sent me to a chiropractor. This chiropractor does not adjust me like any chiropractor I have ever been to. In fact, I feel that he is making me worse.

A: Go to another. 6

Q: *(L)* Is this, in fact, some sort of a scam? 7

A: Money is only concern there. Not your welfare. 8

Q: *(L)* OK, could you, at this point, access the names of chiropractors in our area and give me a recommendation... should I go to DH? It's an awful long 9

[1] This actually turned out to be a local chiropractor; I went to him and had good results.

drive to make after adjustments.

10 **A**: That must be up to you. McG.[1]

11 **Q**: *(L)* I have here a diagram of my cellar and I am going to put it on the board and I would like you to please locate it on this diagram.[2]

12 **A**: Okay.

13 **Q**: *(L)* [Places diagram on table; planchette indicates location.] Is that the spot right there? [Puts finger on spot.]

14 **A**: Yes.

15 **Q**: *(L)* OK, thank you very much.

16 **A**: More than one place.

17 **Q**: *(L)* Oh, well sorry. [Places diagram back on table; planchette moves and indicates location.] OK, this sector here? Any other places? [Planchette indicates another place.]

18 **A**: Across steps underneath.

19 **Q**: *(L)* Is that all of it, now?

20 **A**: Maybe. Eccentric former owner died before he could retrieve.

21 **Q**: *(L)* What year was this put there?

22 **A**: Between 1933 and 1945.

23 **Q**: *(L)* On this one spot where I have my finger, how deep must we dig?

24 **A**: Near surface.

25 **Q**: *(L)* And this spot that goes under the steps?

26 **A**: Deeper.

27 **Q**: *(L)* So, he dug the hole and buried stuff and then he built the cellar and built the stairs on top of it, is that it? About how deep is this going to be?

A: Discover, but be careful of shifting sands. 28

Q: *(L)* I bet he dug the cellar and put it in to cover up his activities. What was this guy up to other than digging this cellar? 29

A: Seek records at city hall. 30

Q: *(L)* Do we have a well, a usable well, on our property? 31

A: Useable for what? 32

Q: *(L)* For drinking water. 33

A: It is 260 feet to good drinking water. To get crystalline water. 34

Q: *(L)* Is there a well here that would still pump water even if not for drinking? 35

A: Iron high. 36

Q: *(L)* Is there a pipe in the ground on this property that was formerly used as a well that could still be used? 37

A: Yes. Iron is too high for drinking. 38

Q: *(L)* Now, I am sure you are aware of how Violette is feeling. I think she took offense at the fact that you used the word 'bullshit' the other night... 39

A: Violette should talk!! Mirth! Word is used commonly by your people. 40

Q: *(L)* Well, I know that and I wasn't offended. I didn't say anything. Some words are offensive to me and I don't use them. She was also upset because you guys would not tell me about the Om 4th density resident that was in my 41

---

[2]This was to collect more information about the possibility of something interesting being buried in the little cellar under our house which was mentioned in the 2 January 1995 session.

[3]See 7 January 1995 session.

daughter's room. Is Om an abbreviation for a type of being?[3]

42 **A**: No, it is full word.

43 **Q**: *(L)* What is an Om being, for the benefit of the whole world which waits breathlessly to discover the nature of this type of being?

44 **A**: Poltergeist-type being.

45 **Q**: *(L)* Was that Om being brought in because of the dimensional overlap or is it strictly related to my daughter?

46 **A**: Former mostly.

47 **Q**: *(L)* So poltergeist-type beings can enter our density through these dimensional overlaps?

48 **A**: Sure.

49 **Q**: *(L)* Violette is talking about dropping out of the group because she says it is 'no longer personal.' I would like to know what she really means by this?

50 **A**: The answers conflict with her personal desires and expectations.

51 **Q**: *(L)* Well, I had the feeling from the beginning that Violette was not capable of the type of objectivity needed to deal with absolutes. And then, every once in a while I would think that her dedication and determination would carry her far. But, apparently she is only dedicated and determined when it satisfies her own point of view. At times I was very sympathetic toward her struggle and then at other times I would get very agitated toward her because I don't suffer fools gladly. I expect that you guys are a lot more patient than I am. As things are at this moment, what are the chances she will come back to the group?

A: Open. 52

Q: *(L)* I didn't think you would tell 53
me that one. Now, I have some articles in this magazine here: This is Lyssa Royal and she has "channeled for thousands around the globe since 1985. Her books and magazine articles are published in six languages worldwide. Etc., etc." She writes here: "The human consciousness is roughly divided into three different areas for the sake of this illustration: the conscious mind, the subconscious mind and the unconscious mind." Now, are these labels generally correct?

A: Roughly. 54

Q: *(L)* She says: "The unconscious 55
mind is a link to your greater self, it is also used as a wasteland where scary, dark things are stored that you really don't want to bring up." Is this a fairly accurate statement?[4]

A: Semi-accurate.[5] 56

Q: *(L)* Is there anything you can say to 57
make the statement more accurate?

A: The unconscious mind is also a con- 58
duit for connecting with the higher self, other selves, and the universal mind.

Q: *(L)* Lyssa also says: "When you are 59
a child and have a traumatic event, the subconscious not only finds a way to immediately process the information and store it, but also to protect you from further fragmentation. It must seek to create a balance." So, she says, the "very intense raw energy that is generated from trauma gets stuffed into the unconscious mind." Is this true?

A: Close enough. 60

[4] *The Wave* 10
[5] *High Strangeness* 7

61 **Q**: *(L)* She then goes on to say: "When an extraterrestrial looks at us, we seem like multiple personality cases to them because of our mind divisions." Is this true?

62 **A**: Irrelevant.

63 **Q**: *(L)* Why is that irrelevant? Is it because when a higher density being looks at us they know what they are looking at?

64 **A**: Yes. They know and understand the separations of your minds quite precisely. That would be like saying "when a human looks at a rodent, they notice that they are excessively furry."

65 **Q**: *(L)* She goes on to say: "The ET often does not know how to communicate with a fragmented human. Sometimes they fly their ships by and few people may see them, but the greater percentage do not see them as that data gets sucked into the subconscious and the triage occurs." She means triage in the sense of the mind being so flabbergasted that it immediately shunts information into the unconscious. Is this true, that ETs are having problems communicating with us because we are the ones blocking contact?

66 **A**: No.

67 **Q**: *(L)* Is it true that some people may not see ETs or UFOs because they block it from their own minds?

68 **A**: This can happen or the blockage may be inspired by the alien.

69 **Q**: *(L)* Now, she says: "For the most part, the average person in society does not know how to interpret telepathic contact... (Lyssa's alien talking) in the moment you start perceiving us reality starts shifting because, remember, you are one frequency and we are another." Is this true?

A: It is irrelevant. 70

Q: *(L)* Why is that irrelevant? 71

A: This is not an obstacle, as suggested 72
by this statement.

Q: *(L)* Anyway, the article goes on: 73
"So an ET walks up to you in your backyard and for a fragment of a moment you may perceive us. But what commonly happens is that the human will suddenly shut down usually by becoming very sleepy and falling into a sleep or type of trance state such as one that is produced by alpha or theta brain waves." Is this true? When a person sees an ET do they just turn off from the shock? Is this why most ET contact is not remembered?

A: It can happen but does not usually. 74

Q: *(L)* It says that when you start clear- 75
ing out the stuff in your subconscious mind that the first layer that comes out of the subconscious is simply the top layer of priorities that were given to your subconscious mind to store and process. For the most part the first layer is not scary. It represents procrastinated perceptions that are waiting for processing by the conscious mind... then you start peeling off more layers through hypnosis or meditation and then...

A: We do not wish to further critique 76
this as we can give all relevant and related information when needed. You are "comparing notes" which is fine if in moderation, but remember, separated sources are subject to variable corruption.

Q: *(L)* What is a separated source? 77

A: That which is separated from yours. 78

79 **Q**: *(L)* Somebody different from us? OK, let me work on this. Our source is you, correct?

80 **A**: Yes.

81 **Q**: *(L)* So, the source this person is getting her information from is separated from you?

82 **A**: From you, thus unverifiable.[6]

83 **Q**: *(L)* Well, I don't exactly get what you mean. The whole point of this article is to say that ET's who abduct people are here to help us evolve and that it is only us, if we have dark and dirty unconscious minds, who perceive them as negative.

84 **A**: Wrong, you do not need "help" evolving, nor does anything else.[7]

85 **Q**: *(L)* Well, the thing that concerns me about this particular point of view is that a lot of people are using this to rationalize seeing the ETs and the abductions... can I read you just a little more?

86 **A**: Overall gist is enough for us.

87 **Q**: *(L)* This woman here, Dorothy Ann, claims she channels dolphins and whales. Dolphins and whales are telling her that they are here to keep frequencies and to awaken energy centers on the Earth, and that they are very high-level beings, for eons they have kept the electromagnetic grids in the oceans, they follow the old paths, etc. The grids are now in the process of being reset and the whales will be instrumental in this change of the vibrational patterns on the planet.

A: No. 88

Q: *(L)* The dolphin kingdom has been empowered to communicate more easily with humans; the whales are awakening to their mission of greater contact and communication with other beings... 89

A: Nonsense. 90

Q: *(L)* So, I don't really need to go on because all of this is nonsense. Now, this guy here who channels this being called Kryon writes an article about the metaphysical Christ. I read this article and really liked it. It made me feel nice and good and pleasant. Well, I'm not even going to ask you because I like him. It says here on another page that the Milky Way galaxy is part of a system of loosely 20 other galaxies. Is this true? 91

A: Too vague, all systems can be measured thusly if desired. 92

Q: *(L)* So that is too arbitrary. 93

A: Also a system of every conceivable combination. 94

Q: *(L)* In any event, it says that all of these universes expand at the rate of 90% of the speed of light. The ultimate central sun of it all is what we vaguely call God. 95

A: We have already covered these areas and "God" is "Everything," not a central sun. 96

Q: *(L)* Well, he is talking about this 25-thousand-year cycle where the Earth passes into a photon belt that circles 97

[6] I think that the Cs' point was that the internal nature of any given channel must determine the kind of source they connect with and the reality they experience. Just speculating.

[7] *High Strangeness* 7; *The Wave* 21, 23

the Pleiadian system,[8] and when this photon belt hits us it is going to make all kinds of changes and it one of the small cycles, and the harmonic convergence is...

98 **A**: Fragmented channel.

99 **Q**: *(L)* This guy is a fragmented channel? Is there such a thing as the harmonic convergence?

100 **A**: If you wish to converge harmonically, you may.

101 **Q**: *(L)* So there is no photon belt circling around the Pleiades that hits us every 25,000 years?

A: If this was true, don't you think we 102
would have informed you by now?

Q: *(L)* Well, sometimes you don't in- 103
form us of things because we don't ask the specific questions. I just wanted to check this out. OK, he is fragmented and I can forget that! Now, next question: As you know, there is some major flooding going on in California right now.

A: Yes. 104

Q: *(L)* You didn't tell us about this, 105
did you?

A: Yes we did. We specifically men- 106

[8]In astronomy, the Pleiades, or Seven Sisters, is an open star cluster containing middle-aged hot B-type stars located in the constellation of Taurus. It is among the nearest star clusters to Earth and is the cluster most obvious to the naked eye in the night sky. The cluster is dominated by hot blue and extremely luminous stars that have formed within the last 100 million years. The Pleiades are a prominent sight in winter in both the Northern Hemisphere and Southern Hemisphere, and have been known since antiquity to cultures all around the world, including the Celts, Māori, Aboriginal Australians, the Persians, the Arabs (known as Thurayya), the Chinese, the Japanese, the Maya, the Aztec, and the Sioux and Cherokee. In Hinduism, the Pleiades are known as Krittika and are associated with the war-god Kartikeya (Murugan, Skanda), who derives his name from them. The god is raised by the six Krittika sisters, also known as the Matrikas. He is said to have developed a face for each of them. The Babylonian star catalogues name the Pleiades MUL.MUL or "star of stars", and they head the list of stars along the ecliptic, reflecting the fact that they were close to the point of vernal equinox around the 23rd century BC. The earliest known depiction of the Pleiades is likely a bronze age artifact known as the Nebra sky disk, dated to approximately 1600 BC. Some Greek astronomers considered them to be a distinct constellation, and they are mentioned by Hesiod, and in Homer's Iliad and Odyssey. The rising of the Pleiades is mentioned in the Ancient Greek text Geoponica. The Greeks oriented the Hecatompedon temple of 550 BC and the Parthenon of 438 BC to their rising. Galileo Galilei was the first astronomer to view the Pleiades through a telescope. He thereby discovered that the cluster contains many stars too dim to be seen with the naked eye. He published his observations, including a sketch of the Pleiades showing 36 stars, in his treatise Sidereus Nuncius in March 1610. The nine brightest stars of the Pleiades are named for the Seven Sisters of Greek mythology: Sterope, Merope, Electra, Maia, Taygeta, Celaeno, and Alcyone, along with their parents Atlas and Pleione. As daughters of Atlas, the Hyades were sisters of the Pleiades. [http://en.wikipedia.org/wiki/Pleiades]

tioned weird weather all over.

107 **Q**: *(L)* OK, I have communicated with this woman, this Marilynne, from the computer net, and she says she wants to move down here. She seems to be a very nice person. Anybody who does Reiki and cans applesauce is OK in my book. Is there anything you could say to her about her desire to move to this area?

108 **A**: Good idea!

109 **Q**: *(L)* Is one of the things I am supposed to be doing responding to Irish-Sir from the network even though he is so negative?

110 **A**: Of course, if you only network with those of like mind, what have you accomplished???

111 **Q**: *(L)* Now, our other little friend, SF-Pro, who says his mother is experiencing a ghost, whom she thinks is her deceased husband – is this the case?

112 **A**: Maybe. Not crucial information.

113 **Q**: *(L)* Was the advice and information I gave him adequate?

114 **A**: Okay.

115 **Q**: *(L)* Should I see a lawyer about my accident?

A: Up to you. We are not here to lead 116
you by the hand, because then you do not learn.

Q: *(L)* I would say you are right about 117
that. L came over and told me that he thought that the information we were getting was quite accurate, based upon independent verification. Was he being sincere in this?

A: Yes. 118

Q: *(L)* Helen D told me that I was 119
going to meet an older, retired person around the end of the year who was going to be very instrumental in my work. Is this going to happen?

A: Wait and see.[9] 120

Q: *(L)* Are S___ and N___ going to be 121
helpful?[10]

A: Open. 122

Q: *(L)* Any information for either of us 123
here?

A: No. 124

Q: *(L)* Well, thank you. *(F)* They give 125
you information about yourself when it is necessary to prevent you from falling into a black hole.

Q: *(L)* Goodnight. 126

End of Session

[9]This Helen D was actually a fairly good psychic and I think, in retrospect, that what she was seeing was my meeting Ark, my husband, who finally came on the scene in 1996.

[10]New Age/MUFON people who had called and expressed interest in the experiment.

January 11, 1995

Participants: 'Frank', Laura, Barry and Susy Konicov, publishers of a popular New Age magazine, via telephone

1 **Q**: *(L)* Is anyone with us?

2 **A**: Yes.

3 **Q**: *(L)* Frank is talking with Susy Konicov. We'll put her on speakerphone.

4 **A**: Channel disrupted.

5 **Q**: *(S)* Are you from the same group as the Pleiadians?

6 **A**: Same. When at Pleiades, Pleiadians, when at Cassiopaea, Cassiopaeans. Light beings.

7 **Q**: *(S)* What kind of source are you?

8 **A**: 6th density.

Q: *(S)* Why are you choosing Laura 9
and Frank to transmit this information?[1]

A: Because balancing fields are cor- 10
rect.[2]

Q: *(B)* Maitreya... What is the destiny 11
of this person in this lifetime?[3]

A: Plays prominent role in disinforma- 12
tion process.

Q: *(B)* Is Benjamin Creme aware of 13
that?[4]

A: No. 14

Q: *(B)* Are the ETs putting thoughts 15
in Benjamin Creme's head?

A: Yes. 16

---

[1] *The Wave* 26, 37

[2] *The Wave* 2

[3] According to Buddhist tradition, Maitreya is a bodhisattva who will appear on Earth in the future, achieve complete enlightenment, and teach the pure dharma. According to scriptures, Maitreya will be a successor to the present Buddha, Gautama Buddha.

[4] Apparently, some guy named Benjamin Creme was making claims that Maitreya was alive and well in London. Creme says he was first contacted telepathically by his Master in January 1959, who asked him to make tape recordings of his messages to Creme. He first began to speak publicly of his mission on 30 May 1975, in London, England. His central message announced the emergence of a group of enlightened spiritual teachers who could guide humanity forward into the new Aquarian Age of peace and brotherhood based on the principles of love and sharing. At the head of this group would be a great Avatar, Maitreya, the World Teacher, expected by all the major religions as their "Awaited One" – the Christ to the Christians, the Mahdi to the Muslims, the Messiah for Jews, and the 5th Buddha (Maitreya) for Buddhists. Check Wikipedia for more of this nonsense. Obviously, Barry Konicov was quite taken with the idea.

17 **Q**: *(B)* What is their purpose in this?

18 **A**: To cause confusion, diversion, and deception so that reality channels may be cloaked. Self explanatory.

19 **Q**: *(B)* Does this mean so that what we think is real really isn't?

20 **A**: Close.

21 **Q**: *(B)* This must mean that the aliens want to give us one person to focus on which is so spectacular, so that we cannot see the truth.

22 **A**: Remember warnings about false prophets in the "desert."

23 **Q**: *(B)* Does this mean that Benjamin Creme is an STS person?

24 **A**: Yes, indirectly.

25 **Q**: *(B)* Is he the antichrist?

26 **A**: No. The "antichrist" is not an individual, but consortium.

27 **Q**: *(B)* Who is the Consortium?

28 **A**: Term refers to idea of large body of individuals.

29 **Q**: *(L)* Who specifically? *(F)* Human beings?

30 **A**: Yes and others.[5]

31 **Q**: *(B)* Are these beings who have lived longer than most people live in one lifetime?

32 **A**: Confused thought patterns.

33 **Q**: *(B)* Are these people who have reincarnated for lifetime after lifetime and have kept the same memory to continue the same plan?

A: Only a select few. 34

Q: *(B)* Is this channeling going to go 35 beyond the primitive method of one letter at a time, or is it going to go into the method of writing or typing or direct channeling consciously or unconsciously?[6]

A: Can now, less danger of corruption 36 through this method.[7]

Q: *(B)* What is the purpose of this con- 37 tact?[8]

A: To help you to learn, thus gain 38 knowledge, thus gain protection, thus progress.

Q: *(B)* What do the Cassiopaeans gain 39 from this contact?

A: By helping you, we are moving to- 40 ward fulfilling of our destiny of union with you and all else, thus completing the grand cycle.

Q: *(B)* Is this the only probability open 41 to you or is this the best probability open to you?

A: Both. 42

Q: *(B)* Are you a great distance from 43 us in light years?

A: Distance is a 3rd density idea. 44

Q: *(B)* Light years is 3rd density? 45

A: Yes. 46

Q: *(B)* What do you mean by traveling 47 on the wave?

---

[5] *The Wave* 7, 22

[6] *The Wave* 26, 37

[7] This is an important bit of data. Despite the fact that it could be said that I am constantly 'in contact' with the Cs – i.e., myself in the future – at some subliminal level which often rises strongly into full consciousness, I still prefer to use the board with other participants for the sake of limiting corruption.

[8] *Secret History* 12; *The Wave* 71

48 **A**: Traveling on thoughts.

49 **Q**: *(F)* Our thoughts or your thoughts?

50 **A**: Not correct concept.[9]

51 **Q**: *(L)* What is the correct concept?

52 **A**: All is just lessons.

53 **Q**: *(L)* Whose thoughts are they?

54 **A**: Thoughts unify all reality in existence and are all shared.[10]

55 **Q**: *(S)* You travel on a wave of energy created by all thought forms?

56 **A**: Thought forms are all that exists!

57 **Q**: *(B)* Have those that are STS acknowledged that those that are STO are going to win in this race or conflict?

58 **A**: No, absolutely not! In fact, the STS cannot conceive of "losing" but instinctively feel pressure building upon them, that is the reason for the impending turmoil.[11]

59 **Q**: *(B)* What happens to them when they lose – does this mean that they are degaussed, or does that mean that they have to go back and do the whole evolutionary process all over again on the other polarity?

60 **A**: Latter.[12]

61 **Q**: *(B)* So, there is a nexus point coming up?

62 **A**: Close. When we said "close" we meant concept was "close" to reality. Not close in terms of time or distance.

Q: *(B)* At that point do they experi- 63
ence the pain that they have caused? *(L)* Good question!

A: No, that is what happens on 5th 64
level only.

Q: *(B)* What is the proper protocol 65
when meeting a Lizard?[13]

A: Up to you! 66

Q: (F to Barry on phone) I don't think 67
I'll repeat that Barry. *(L)* Did he use the 'F' word? *(F)* No, he referred to a part of the anatomy.[14] *(B)* Are Lizards shape shifters?

A: All on 4th level of density have that 68
ability.

Q: *(B)* Do they have the ability to 69
block their true appearance?

A: Yes. 70

Q: *(B)* Are they walking around 71
amongst us now?

A: Infrequently, they use "agents" to 72
do most of their tasks on 3rd level.

Q: *(B)* Are these agents the 'Men in 73
Black' or are they the 'Grays'?

A: Both and many others. Men in 74
Black are often Lizards cloaked as human types, and can remain on 3rd density level for limited periods called short wave cycle. Men in Black claim to be government in order to have excuse to have direct contact with selected humans.

---

[9] *The Wave* 43, 64

[10] See Pierre Lescaudron's recent book on information as the substrate of the Universe/Cosmos, *Earth Changes and the Human-Cosmic Connection.*

[11] Notice that this was back in 1995, pre-9/11, and well before any of us was aware of how bad it could and would get; witness the state of the planet at present.

[12] This is an interesting point that most people seldom notice.

[13] *The Wave* 52

[14] People who demand answers that conform to their expectations are often unhappy with the Cs.

75 **Q**: *(B)* Have these Men in Black killed humans?

76 **A**: No.

77 **Q**: *(F)* They just threaten?

78 **A**: Yes.

79 **Q**: *(B)* Have the Lizards killed humans?

80 **A**: Oh yes!!!

81 **Q**: *(B)* There is a book out that says that if you meet the Buddha on the road you should kill him – should we do the same with a Lizard?

82 **A**: Strange.

83 **Q**: *(B)* Is there a physical confrontation going on in other than 3rd density that is resulting in bodies being blown apart and death and destruction and so on?

84 **A**: Not exactly, remember, you are applying 3rd level ideas to 4th level reality, which does not fit.

85 **Q**: *(B)* Does that mean that blowing bodies apart does not fit?

86 **A**: Yes.

87 **Q**: *(B)* But they do have physical bodies on the 4th level, don't they?

88 **A**: Transitory.

89 **Q**: *(B)* So are ours.

90 **A**: No, yours aren't.

91 **Q**: *(B)* Because they can shape-shift does that mean that if they were to be shattered they could bring their bodies back together again into the shape they just were?

92 **A**: Close.[15]

Q: *(B)* Are the Lizards behind any of the apparitions of the Virgin Mary around the world? 93

A: Yes. All of them. 94

Q: *(B)* What is the purpose behind this? 95

A: Diversions and disinformation so that knowledge will be dispersed, therefore more will be open to attack. 96

Q: *(L)* If you think about it, propagating belief in the 'old time religions', which include belief in hell or purgatory, tends to put a person in a very vulnerable position because then they are open to thoughts of guilt, sin, and are therefore susceptible to thought control and terror. 97

A: Yes. 98

Q: *(S)* Theo, through the "Ashtar Command" channeled through Yvonne Cole, predicted a landing of aliens in December 1994 – was this a fabrication or was this a miscalculation? 99

A: Fabrication. 100

Q: *(S)* She is such a nice person... 101

A: Channel is deceived. 102

Q: *(S)* Who is really channeling through Yvonne Cole? 103

A: Agents of the Lizards, more disinformation. Who is not receiving disinformation, then, you ask? Well, you will know when you have opened your mind and have received much information; now message to you: Konicovs, we are aware of your work, and you are close to a major "breakthrough," however, beware that STS forces are trying to defeat you, and we would suggest you slow down your battles against 104

[15] This, too, is an extremely interesting answer that might deserve some follow-up one day.

STS forces a little, so as to prevent too much heat from them coming down upon you!!

105 **Q**: *(S)* Are you talking about the de-taxing work Barry is doing?

106 **A**: Precisely.

107 **Q**: *(L)* Are they marking them?

108 **A**: Have already been watched closely.

109 **Q**: *(L)* Barry is not one to step back, so what can they do to protect themselves?

110 **A**: Knowledge is protection. Two calls recently.

111 **Q**: *(L)* Did you have two calls? About what or from who?

112 **A**: Had to do with "business" but was ruse.

113 **Q**: *(L)* OK, I think that is all their questions. We thank you. [Phone conversation is terminated.] Are you still with us?

114 **A**: Yes.

115 **Q**: *(L)* Tell us what Barry and Susy think of the reading you just gave them?

116 **A**: Enthralled.

117 **Q**: *(L)* Well, they may call it a primitive method, but all the people who are doing straight channeling are producing straight crap. [Change of topic.] As you know we have a very large hole in our cellar and we haven't reached anything yet. Are you sure there is something under there?

118 **A**: Search carefully.

119 **Q**: *(L)* Could it be in the dirt that has already been taken out?

A: No. 120

Q: *(L)* Which way to go from where the hole is? How much deeper? I mean, I know you told us to keep on, but if we don't find something pretty soon... I mean, how much can you dig? The whole cellar will disappear into this hole. 121

A: Patience pays. 122

Q: *(L)* Well can you just tell me how much deeper... 123

A: Sift carefully. 124

Q: *(L)* Sift the sand that's already taken out or the sand that's coming out? 125

A: All. 126

Q: *(L)* Do we need to go deeper? 127

A: Maybe. 128

Q: *(L)* Do we need to go wider? 129

A: Patience!!! 130

Q: *(L)* Frank, do you know how big a hole there is in that cellar? *(F)* No, but I'd love to see it. [Laughter] *(L)* You and I could take this table and sit in that hole comfortably. *(F)* How long did it take you to dig that? *(L)* They've just been working on it today. *(F)* There could be tons of stuff inside the dirt. *(L)* Now, I'm in a real tough spot, guys. I've either got to go with P___, and his deal is pretty poor or do something else and I don't know what that would be. At least that is the only option I see.[16] 131

A: Sorry, but you must decide what to do it's part of learning process. 132

Q: *(L)* Are Barry and Susy going to play an important part in the work we are doing in the future? 133

[16] I was referring to a real estate transaction.

134 **A**: Probably, but wait and see.

135 **Q**: *(L)* What is P___ thinking about the deal just now?

136 **A**: Money.

137 **Q**: *(L)* He wants the mortgage?

138 **A**: Why not negotiate and explain your position honestly?

139 **Q**: *(L)* That is what I am going to do.

140 **A**: He will understand delays better, no one can blame you for wanting best "deal."

141 **Q**: *(L)* I want to ask one other thing. Recently the personal effects of JO were found – can you tell us what kind of vehicle was driven out to that area in which those items were...[17]

A: Time for you to move on past this 142
issue.

Q: *(L)* Jeannie[18] was talking to me and 143
she said that she really thought JO was trying to get people to solve this mystery...

A: Aunt Clara strikes again.[19] 144

Q: *(L)* Should I send Frank to 145
Sharky?[20]

A: Up to you. Time to go. 146

Q: *(L)* Thank you and goodnight. 147

End of Session

[17]Referring to an unsolved local murder.
[18]Psychic of my acquaintance who was generally very accurate!
[19]I wrote about "Aunt Clara" in *The Wave*.
[20]My dentist.

January 14, 1995

This session contains a number of very interesting exchanges respecting 4th density realities, STS vs. STO, and a whole range of UFO/alien-related questions. It's almost embarrassing to have our ignorance about such things exposed this way. But everybody has to start learning somewhere and not everybody had *The Wave* to read!!

Participants: 'Frank', Laura, Terry and Jan, Tom M and Andrea

1 **Q**: *(L)* Is anyone with us?

2 **A**: Yes.

3 **Q**: *(L)* Who do we have with us tonight?

4 **A**: Hnorra.

5 **Q**: *(L)* Where are you from?

6 **A**: Cassiopaea.

7 **Q**: *(L)* Why is the movement so slow this evening?[1]

8 **A**: It will speed up dramatically, so be patient. Send the little one away, please.[2]

9 **Q**: *(L)* Why do the children have to be kept at a distance?

10 **A**: As protection against possible psychic damage as soul is not yet fully blossomed!

11 **Q**: *(L)* Does this mean that when a person's soul comes into their body at birth that it is kind of like reduced to a seed form or like the bud of a flower, and that the growing-up years are either the rooting or...

12 **A**: It is a reawakening period.

13 **Q**: *(L)* Does that mean that when the soul comes into the body that it cannot, at that point, remember any of its past experiences...

14 **A**: Cycle.

15 **Q**: *(L)* So it cycles like ebbing and flowing and that is the ebb point where there is very little awareness?

16 **A**: Something like that.

17 **Q**: *(L)* We have some questions and the first one is: You have told us in the past

[1]This is a bothersome effect that I've noticed many times over the years that generally occurs when someone is present who has a fearful or hostile attitude.

[2]As a general rule, we usually began the sessions after the children's bed-time. My youngest daughter was extremely curious about 'what the grownups were doing' and had sneaked into the adjacent room and was peeking around the door. I hadn't noticed her and I don't think anyone else had, so only the Cs knew she was there. I sent her off to bed.

[3]*Secret History* "Afterword"

that you are us in the future and that you are moving this way to merge with us.[3]

18 **A**: Yes.

19 **Q**: *(L)* As we measure time, how far in the future are you us?[4]

20 **A**: Indeterminate as you measure time.

21 **Q**: *(L)* Does this mean that at the point in time when the Wave arrives on the Earth in this upcoming event that you have given us the information to plot the ETA, is that the time at which you will merge with us and become us in the future?

22 **A**: No, that is not the correct concept.

23 **Q**: *(L)* You have said that when the Wave arrives that you will merge with us. Is this the same thing that you are talking about when you say that you are us in the future?[5]

24 **A**: No.

25 **Q**: *(L)* So, we are talking about two separate events or subjects, or two separate points in space-time, is that correct?

26 **A**: No. You are again slipping into trying to apply 3rd density logic to higher levels of density reality.

27 **Q**: *(L)* So, this is pick on Laura night!

28 **A**: No. We are trying to help everyone to advance.

Q: *(L)* So, we are not talking about the same event... 29

A: What is "future," anyway? 30

Q: *(L)* The future is simultaneous events, just different locales in space-time, just a different focus of consciousness, is that correct?[6] 31

A: Yea, so if that is true, why try to apply linear thinking here, you see, we are merging with you right now! 32

Q: *(L)* I see.[7] *(T)* So, what you are trying to say is that when the Wave comes it is going to take us to 4th density, if we are ready, but we are not actually going to merge with you in 6th density at that point, but we may experience a 'merge' at that point because all points of focus merge during transition from one density to another? 33

A: Partly correct, partly way off. 34

Q: *(J)* What part is right and what part is wrong? *(T)* The Wave is going to take those of us who are, at that point, ready, to move us into 4th density – is this part correct? 35

A: Open. 36

Q: *(T)* Which part of it is open? 37

A: You are a 4th density candidate.[8] 38

Q: *(T)* So, we are 4th density candidates but that doesn't necessarily mean 39

---

[4] *The Wave* 2, 71

[5] *The Wave* 3

[6] *Secret History* "Afterword"

[7] Actually, I didn't really see at the time but now, after 20 years, I understand much better exactly what the Cs meant. By gaining and gathering all the knowledge and experiences that they were urging me to pursue, I have become more like them though certainly, only in a limited respect as to what is possible at this level of existence.

[8] Terry was assuming that he was going to move to 4th density and the Cs' answer made it clear that this was not a certainty.

that we will make it into 4th density, true?

40 **A**: Partly.

41 **Q**: *(T)* As 4th density candidates, anyone that is, when the Wave comes, if they have reached the correct frequency vibration, and have raised themselves up to the point that the Wave will take them, they will, at that point, move into 4th density, true?

42 **A**: Close enough.

43 **Q**: *(T)* Now, when those who move into 4th density make the move, will they experience a completeness or merge with all other densities of their being, at that point, even if it is for a short time?

44 **A**: For one immeasurably small instant, this is what is meant by "illumination"![9]

45 **Q**: *(T)* But, for that small instant, because there really is no time, maybe an instant or an aeon, depending on how any individual might measure it, we might experience oneness with ourselves?

46 **A**: It may seem to last "forever."

47 **Q**: *(L)* Is this what is known as the 'rapture'?

48 **A**: Some have attempted to explain instinctive thought patterns this way.[10]

49 **Q**: *(L)* Is the moving into 4th density, and the understanding we have of it, which is the possible transcending or leaving a 3rd density Earth, which is under great assault in terms of cataclysmic activity and so forth, and moving to a place where none of that is apparent, is this what is known as the 'rapture'?

A: Laura, you are reaching. 50

Q: *(L)* Well, Jan and I were talking 51 about it this week, it's her fault. Don't blame it on me. *(J)* It's my fault. *(L)* Jan made me do it. [Laughter]

A: Jan is the "boogie" man! 52

Q: *(L)* That's right, Jan is the boogie 53 man, she did it. *(J)* Wait a minute! *(T)* You took responsibility. *(J)* No, I kinda like that! Thank you. *(L)* We have a couple of questions that can be answered, I think, fairly quickly, so let's get them out of the way. Jan, as you know, her mother passed away yesterday morning, and she is very interested in knowing where her mother is at this point, and what condition she finds herself in. Can you give her this information?

A: She is at 5th level density now. 54

Q: *(L)* Is she finding her introduction 55 to this level to be pleasant?

A: That is subjective. 56

Q: *(L)* I knew that was coming. Any 57 more questions on that, Jan? I don't want to get fussed at. *(J)* No, that's alright. Has my mother been having OBEs in the last month?

A: Yes. 58

Q: *(L)* Now, Terry had a very interest- 59 ing experience when he was standing outside his house.

[9] *The Wave* 6

[10] Which suggests that the Apostle Paul was on to something, he just didn't really know how to interpret, much less describe, what he saw and experienced in his visions.

60 **A**: Terry has many of those.

61 **Q**: *(T)* Yes, thank you, I do. It's amazing how they come to me. I was standing outside. There's a lot of cats in the neighborhood and we, ourselves, have six cats. They look at one a lot and I recognize cats for cats and don't think it is possible that I made a mistake in this. A cat came around one of the trees across the street from me, and it wasn't a regular cat. It was much larger. It looked at me and hunched down into its cat-like stance and locked on me. Was this a real cat, or a bob cat?

62 **A**: Yes, it was a bobcat from Northeastern Pinellas Piney woods preserve.

63 **Q**: *(L)* Is there a preserve in that direction from you? *(T)* Yes, it is up on the Pasco/Pinellas border, down from us here as a matter of fact.

64 **A**: Up from you, Terry. Learn direction better, please. Compass awareness is to be vital in the future.

65 **Q**: *(T)* I know it is up from me, but I am north of the place now and I'm talking as if I am in St. Petersburg, saying up from me, but it is south of me at the moment.

66 **A**: Incorrect, you were speaking from home in your mind.

67 **Q**: *(T)* True. *(L)* Busted! *(T)* You guys are cool! *(L)* What was it you said, "Love a 6th density dude with a sense of humor!"

68 **A**: Yes.

69 **Q**: *(T)* Are there dudes and dudesses up there?

70 **A**: Yes, cool dudes and dudesses! [Laughter]

Q: *(L)* Now, come on, stop it, I am try- 71
ing to get a question in here!

A: Stop what? 72

Q: *(L)* Stop fooling around, I want to 73
get these questions done.

A: But we are having fun, is there any- 74
thing wrong with that?

Q: *(L)* No, but I want to get through 75
my questions. *(T)* Lighten up, a fun session is something we need.

A: Uptight. [Laughter] 76

Q: *(T)* We got a live one tonight. 77

A: Yes. 78

Q: *(L)* It's because of you, Terry. *(T)* 79
Thank you. *(L)* You got all this practical joke business going...

A: No, Andrea. 80

Q: *(T)* Andrea! My goodness. [Laugh- 81
ter] Why Andrea?

A: She is fun loving. 82

Q: *(T)* OK, we're having fun tonight. 83
Go on, ask the next question. *(L)* Can I ask my question now?

A: Oh, what the hell, go for it! 84

Q: *(T)* I didn't know W. C. Fields had 85
made it to 6th level. [Laughter] *(L)* Seriously now...

A: Seriously now, folks! 86

Q: *(L)* The other night as I was read- 87
ing by the window, I saw something white pass by the window. In order for anything to pass that window, it would have to be very tall or floating. Also, my dogs would not have allowed anything to be passing by my window unless they were dead, drugged or paralyzed in some way. After a few minutes I explained it to myself as having just seen my cigarette smoke float by in

my peripheral vision, but, after thinking awhile, I realized that after all these years of smoking, I have an acute sense of what smoke is and where it is around me. Therefore, I think that some sort of awareness cued me that I was seeing something besides a waft of smoke. Can you tell me what it was, outside my window, or was it just my cigarette smoke?

88 **A**: You are gradually experiencing more and more "bleed-throughs" of 4th density.

89 **Q**: *(L)* What did I see go by my window?

90 **A**: Fourth density energy source.

91 **Q**: *(L)* Is an energy source like an entity or being?

92 **A**: Tell us what you imagine 4th density to be like, Laura?

93 **Q**: *(L)* Well, I have no idea. *(T)* Good answer.

94 **A**: Okay, then please try harder to discover.

95 **Q**: *(L)* Do you mean right now?

96 **A**: Yes.

97 **Q**: *(J)* Can we help?

A: Yes. You see without further 98
progress in this area, we cannot adequately explain details of 4th density life.

Q: *(L)* Alright guys, how do we imag- 99
ine 4th density life to be? *(T)* Let me ask a question first.

A: Free association. 100

Q: *(T)* Is this energy source that she 101
saw not necessarily a being or an entity, but loose energy being transmitted from 4th density?

A: Answer to that depends upon 102
greater understanding of 4th level reality.

Q: *(L)* Why do I have this gripping and 103
pinching sensation on the back of my neck right at this moment?

A: We are blasting open your learning 104
chakra.[11]

Q: *(T)* Did it just start? *(L)* Oh, yes. 105
It feels like I am being gripped by a pair of pincers right at the base of my neck. OK, 4th density is like, am I correct, that it is similar to the dream state? The instant you think something or focus on it, it happens or becomes real?

A: Continue. 106

[11]This was definitely an interesting sensation because it was definitely physical but it was more than that in ways I can't even describe. Of course, one has to keep in mind that I had recently suffered a severe neck injury in an auto accident and one cannot exclude some random nerve participation in the effect. Nevertheless, it is interesting that the Cs referred to this area, around the C6 and C7 vertebrae, right at the nape of the neck, as the "learning chakra". According to traditional systems, the throat chakra is the fifth fhakra and is the seat of self-expression, the crossroads between the head and the heart, serving as mediator between thought and emotion. Since, some years earlier, I had experienced an opening of the heart chakra, perhaps, if one assumes this event to be something that really meant what the Cs said it did, then it merely signaled that the energy was continuing to move upward. I should note that if this is the process that was taking place, it took literally years to manifest.

107 **Q**: *(L)* And that, for example, if you wished to be on a boat on the water, that you would find yourself on a boat on what is actually a more real ocean than the ocean we experience here, because, in every way it matches your expectations, down to the glints of sunlight on the water...

108 **A**: Slip 4th.

109 **Q**: *(J)* Like slipping gears? *(L)* Am I slipping?

110 **A**: Yes. Why do you need a boat?

111 **Q**: *(L)* Well, just because in that particular fantasy the idea is to be on a boat. *(T)* But it is not a fantasy. *(L)* It is reality. OK. So, in other words, 4th density is a realm where your thoughts instantly manifest as reality. If, for example, you think of yourself being a princess in a tower, a castle would manifest and you would be in a tower, and if you wanted your hair to hang down to the ground, it would hang down too.

112 **A**: That is 5th level stuff.

113 **Q**: *(L)* OK, so, we have something in between that and 3rd level.

114 **A**: Continue.

115 **Q**: *(T)* Does it closely resemble 3rd density, but different in some manner?

116 **A**: No.

117 **Q**: *(T)* You were saying that when the transition comes about that there would be a 3rd and 4th level Earth, and some people would be 3rd density on the 3rd density Earth, and some would be 4th density on the 4th level Earth.

118 **A**: One possibility for you to ponder.

Q: *(L)* OK, let's take a short break... 119

[Break]

Q: *(L)* Now, guys, I guess you have 120
been listening to our discussion and you listened to Jan read the paragraph from [previous session] about 4th density experience being the highest level of wishful thinking, that wishful thinking becomes reality... *(J)* Or did I take it out of context?

A: Close. STS. 121

Q: *(L)* So, STO wishful thinking... 122

A: STO does not wishfully think. 123

Q: *(L)* Well, how does STO think? *(T)* 124
Responsibly... *(L)* [Experiencing acute pinching feeling at nape of neck.] God! You guys are doing strange things to my body...[12]

A: Helpful and balanced. Wishes are 125
strictly STS.

Q: *(L)* So, acceptance of experience in 126
the sense of just allowing things to happen and responding in a balanced and helpful way is an STO response or experience in 4th density, is that correct?

A: Close. 127

Q: *(L)* And therefore, seeing things 128
moving past such as what I saw by my window, and responding to them basically in an open, curious, and allowing way would have been an STO response, is that correct?

A: Maybe. 129

Q: *(T)* It depends on how you respond 130
curiously. *(T)* The Lizzies are hanging out in 4th density too, and they are not STO, are they?

[12]It really did feel like I was being picked up by the back of the neck! I've experienced lots of weird physical sensations as a consequence of various experiences and injuries, but nothing like that was!

131 **A**: Correct.

132 **Q**: *(T)* So, they are not having STO helpful, responsible...

133 **A**: True.

134 **Q**: *(T)* So, in 4th density, both types can still happen?

135 **A**: Yes.

136 **Q**: *(T)* The desired type is the STO-type thinking...?

137 **A**: Yes.

138 **Q**: *(T)* But STS thinking is also available if that is the way you decide to go when you get there?

139 **A**: Yes.

140 **Q**: *(T)* This of course limits you in your ability to move up to 6th density?

141 **A**: Yes.

142 **Q**: *(T)* Once you are in 4th density, if you choose STS, can you change it to STO?

143 **A**: Yes.

144 **Q**: *(T)* So you can move back and forth as you so desire and it is all still free will?

145 **A**: If you move from STS to STO in 4th level, you don't move back.

146 **Q**: *(T)* Once you are STS in 4th density you have to stay there? *(L)* No. *(J)* If you move from STS to STO in 4th density you don't go back to STS, you stay at STO, is that correct? *(T)* That's what I mean, once you have decided to do STO, that's where you stay because you don't have any desire to go back to STS?

A: Yes. 147

Q: *(T)* So, it is not so much that you don't have a choice, it is just that you don't want to go back to STS? 148

A: Yes. 149

Q: *(T)* So if you move up and do what the Lizards are doing, then you continue to do that until you get tired of it or see different, or become enlightened and then move to STO and then that's where you will want to stay? 150

A: Open.[13] 151

Q: *(T)* Can you move from STO back to STS? I know you said you can't, but that's because you choose not to? 152

A: Natural factors prohibit this. 153

Q: *(L)* So, I guess that once you get to STO natural factors, the nature of that position is that you just simply don't... it just doesn't happen. 154

A: Now, blockbuster for you: 3rd level beings who reach total STO profile automatically and instantaneously go to 4th level at moment achieved! 155

Q: *(T)* They just vanish? Have people done that before here? 156

A: Yes.[14] 157

Q: *(F)* Yeah, I've heard of that. *(T)* Sure, people disappear like that all the time. *(L)* Well, I don't think it happens that often, but I think it happens... *(F)* It has happened. *(J)* People disappear and you never hear what happened to them. *(F)* There have been cases where people have suddenly vanished, where a flash of light has just hit them and *Poof!* *(T)* Like spontaneous combustion... *(F)* No... *(J)* Not spontaneous 158

[13] I think it was "open" because of the assumption that Lizzies might change polarity.

[14] So, if the Apostle Paul was trying to describe moving from 3D to 4D realities, perhaps his insight about being changed in the 'twinkling of an eye' was correct?

combustion because the body is left behind. *(F)* There have been cases where people were actually sitting with other people and suddenly everybody present suddenly sees a blinding flash of light and that person is *Spffft!* Gonzerooni! *(L)* Gonzerooni? *(F)* Once and for all![15] *(T)* I want to ask this question – if it has already been asked, somebody stop me – what is the total STO profile? *(L)* Total lack of concern for self.

159 **A**: Yes.

160 **Q**: *(L)* So, in other words, you don't do anything or think anything in terms of fulfilling or doing for self. You always think in terms of doing or fulfilling for others. *(T)* Damn, I've got a long way to go then... *(Chorus)* Don't we all! *(J)* Was Gandhi?

161 **A**: No.

162 **Q**: *(T)* Mother Theresa?

163 **A**: No. Political deceptions.[16]

164 **Q**: *(J)* Mother Theresa is a political deception? [Laughter] *(L)* Let me ask this question... it is on a little bit different subject right now, but I am kind of stretching my brain right now and I need a little bit of a relief there and then we will come back...

165 **A**: You are off balance this session due to a "bug" in your body. You have a bacterial overgrowth in your intestines.

166 **Q**: *(L)* OK, I was talking to Jan earlier about real estate in Pasco and Pinellas counties and the differences and so forth, and I made the suggestion or statement that they might want to sell their house in St. Petersburg and move to Pasco County. What do you think of that?

A: Okay. 167

Q: *(L)* Is that all you think of it? 168

A: What else? 169

Q: *(L)* I just wanted to know if you 170
thought it would be advisable?

A: Open. 171

Q: *(L)* Now, I want to ask about these 172
KRLL documents that Sally has told me about and is sending. Tell us what is the background and validity of the KRLL papers. Terry knows more about them than I do. Supposedly it is some kind of exposition written by an alien being revealing the government conspiracy. Were the KRLL papers valid? *(T)* KRLL was supposedly a prisoner of the United States. *(L)* Was there really such a being as KRLL?

A: Semi. 173

Q: *(T)* Is there any validity to the 174
KRLL papers?[17]

A: Semi. 175

Q: *(T)* Was it dictated by this alien be- 176
ing?

A: Maybe. 177

Q: *(T)* Was it put together by a hu- 178
man?

A: Semi. 179

Q: *(T)* Is this in the same area of UFO 180
lore as the Cooper and Lear and Lazar and Bennewitz stuff?

A: We have told you many times... 181
Laura, pay attention... Listen!

[15] I actually haven't looked for any such cases that can be verified.

[16] This certainly turned out to be true as books published in recent years have demonstrated!

[17] *The Wave* 64

182 **Q**: *(L)* Well, you say semi. Semi means half-way. Is it half true or half-way true?

183 **A**: Whoa! Calm down! Patience, my love!

184 **Q**: *(T)* Should we put about the same amount of validity we have in the other UFO documents?

185 **A**: Stop now!!!!

186 **Q**: *(L)* Is this an area we can't talk about now because it is too delicate?

187 **A**: No!!!!!

188 **Q**: *(F)* What the H is going on?

189 **A**: We are trying to tell you something important, and you keep asking questions. Now, please, silence for a moment!!!! We have told you many times to communicate with each other and network and share ideas, because that is how you LEARN and PROGRESS! But, you are beginning to rely on us for all your answers, and you do not LEARN that way!!!!!!! Now, try this, you will be thunderstruck with the results: Each of you has stored within you unlimited amounts of factual and "Earthshaking" information. This information was put into your consciousness in order for you to retrieve it in order for you to learn. Now just start by holding a discussion about the last series of questions you were trying to ask us, and "let it flow."

190 **Q**: *(T)* I have a question for you Laura, does that feel weaker? [Tom is giving Reiki to Laura's neck.] *(L)* Well, it's not hot like it used to be, and I am just wondering, since you took the second attunements from Jim G... let's just ask: Is Tom's Reiki canceled by Jim G's initiation?

A: Faltering. 191

Q: *(L)* But he had good Reiki to begin with and it will be OK for me right now? 192

A: Open.[18] 193

Q: *(L)* Who is Don Ware? I asked about him because JW gave me a list of names... 194

(T) OK, Don Ware used to be the regional MUFON director over on the East Coast, and he got run out because he was moving into the metaphysical side of the phenomenon and MUFON is a nuts-and-bolts operation. They don't want to hear this kind of stuff at all. *(F)* I know they don't because they are looking strictly at it as... *(T)* They are trying to get scientific credibility...

(F) Well, yes, and they want a UFO to land that you can go up to and take a hammer and go "Plink, plink, plink! It's Here!"

(T) They want to know where the aliens are from, what they are up to, what kind of propulsion systems they use, how they build them, which... I have reached the opinion that MUFON is the continuation of Project Bluebook. When they closed Project Bluebook, they went out and subverted the

[18] At this point the group reviewed the comments that had been made regarding several persons prominently involved in UFO research who had also been involved or quoted in the KRLL document. This gave us a starting point in evaluating the material. The reader may wish to recall said comments from earlier sections. Don Ware was brought up because he was also mentioned, though he had not been involved in the KRLL papers.

UFO groups starting with NICAP and APRO, and MUFON is one of the latest of the groups that changes from one type of group to another and all the information that is gathered in the field goes to Texas and there it disappears and no one ever hears about it again. The Black Hole of Texas.

(L) So, in other words, if John Lear and William Cooper are getting the Cassiopaean Seal of Approval, and they are saying basically the same thing the KRLL document is saying, where did they get their information?

(T) One of the thoughts on that was Moore or Lear or Bennewitz, one of these, was the one that had written the KRLL papers. There was some talk that KRLL may have been an acronym used by the government to identify this being who gave the information which is the basis of this document.

(L) To your knowledge, would Lear or Cooper ever have been in a position, or did they ever at any time claim to have been in a position, to observe any of this activity written up in this document themselves?

(T) I don't believe that either of them have ever claimed to have been in a position to have physically observed any of this or to have been in the underground bases. They were working with information they claimed to have gotten from other sources.

(L) And what do they claim their other sources are, unnamed?

(T) A lot of them are unnamed. Moore and Cooper claim they have inside government sources. I believe Cooper is the one who claims that he at one time worked for the military. In fact he was Air Force, I believe.

(L) Is he the one who claims that he was the intelligence analyst for the Admiral of the Pacific Fleet?

(T) Yes. There are several versions of the Cooper papers as he modifies and updates them. He didn't change anything really, he just cleaned them up, re-edited them and added to them.

(L) OK, if this is the case, it would seem to me that a person would have a much better chance of having something believed if they presented it as coming from a human source who either observed or saw it. Why would they say that this is an alien dictating this when that is so far and away more unbelievable? It seems to me that if they were making it up they would have far better chances if they said a human extracted this information rather than that it is what the alien said. That would almost tend, in a backward sort of way, to make you think that maybe this KRLL dude, maybe it was true. But, the only thing about that is, if it was an alien, especially if it was an STS alien, how much of it was true? That's the question.

(T) Well, KRLL was supposed to be one of the standard Grays.

(L) Well, then, we can't rely on anything he says. We can rely on the fact that it is possible that it was an alien who gave this information, but if it was one of the standard Grays, then we know who and what they are and we have to look at the information itself as being unreliable, not necessarily the human who revealed the scenario.

(F) Well, it is not necessarily unreliable even if it is an STS source.

(L) Yes, but as STS they would undoubtedly only give information that

would tend to service their position.

(F) That would seem to be the case if you look at it from the obvious angle. But, that is not necessarily true. Just because it is an STS alien, and, in fact, a cybergenetic being, that does not mean that the information is necessarily inaccurate for several reasons. For those of us who have reached a certain level of understanding, our first assumption would be that it is inaccurate, so it could be a reverse psychology ploy. Give accurate information, get those who are at a higher level of understanding to think it's inaccurate, when in actuality it is accurate.

(L) Well, do you know what it said? It says, basically, what we have been getting here.

(F) Well, then it is accurate.

(T) If this is a standard cybergenetic Gray, the question is how much biological is he? Is he biological enough to pass a dissection?

(L) Sure, absolutely. There are reports of autopsies of these guys, they just can't figure out how they feed.[19]

(F) They are cybergenetic, but they look and function exactly like a biological being. If you go inside of them you will find blood and fibers and tissue and microscopic evidence...

(L) The microscopic exams, from what I have heard, reveal that they're more in the line of a plant...

(T) Yes.

(F) Which, of course, would indicate that they have been grown!

(L) Yes. Imagine chromosomal linking of human genetic information with that of the plant kingdom.

(T) You could literally grow hundreds of them easily.

(L) And plant them like seeds... and, apparently that is what they have done. People have come back who have been taken to these ships and have seen walls of containers growing these things. Like a room in a hot house.

(F) Well, there you go. We have gotten information which indicates that the Grays have access to both dimensions because they are probes of the Lizzies. And this gives us a further clue as to what a strange place 4th level is if such 'probes' can be grown like plants! And, what level must fully souled 4d beings be when we are fooled into believing their cybergenetic constructions are the 'real thing'!

(T) Does this mean that the abilities of the Lizzies, since they have to create 'probes' to enter our density, would not be any more advanced than, say, your everyday spirit? Without the Grays, would they be able to interact with us at all?

(F) Yes.

(L) Yes, they are, they have, they will and they do. *(F)* But, there are several problems. One is their appearance is very, very alarming...

(J) They would garner a lot of attention if they walked down the street.

(T) It depends on how they dress themselves. [Joking]

(L) They can shape-shift.

(F) They can shape-shift, but only for a limited period of time.

[19]Notice that this was well before the alleged *Alien Autopsy* film had been released.

(L) Because it takes 3rd density energy to do that.

(F) That brings up something, when we were talking to Susy on the phone the other night, Susy and Barry mentioned the Men in Black. The [Cs'] response said that the Men in Black were "Lizard beings". In many reports of Men in Black, they have been described as very strange in numerous ways. Their voices have been described as sounding like they come from an echo chamber, and...

(T) Well, when we asked about the Men in Black in one of the sessions, what did the Cassiopaeans say? That they are "projections".

(J) Exactly, maybe that is a clue, maybe that is how they come into our reality: as projections from 4th into 3rd.

(F) But, there is one case that always sticks in my mind, and it took place relatively recently. On April 28, 1978, a guy in Maine who had been doing UFO research was accosted by a single Man in Black. He said the guy was very strange in many ways. He had pink... his face looked like it was covered with make-up, and, in fact, he touched himself at one point and his face started to smear as if it was completely covered. And then, he suddenly got up and said: "Have to go now... run-n-ning out of e-ner-gy." Then he walked out of the house and staggered down the drive. They guy said that at that point he became somewhat disoriented as he watched the Man in Black start to stagger...

(L) He was not the Energizer Bunny! [Laughter]

(F) And then the man saw a light that he at first thought was the headlight of a car, but the Man in Black walked into the light and was gone.

(J) Projections! That's how they move from 4th to 3rd.

(L) They said they project as a "triage". Remember. It was something like travel in space-time.

(T) Well, we have gotten off the discussion of KRLL, but we have certainly been led into some pretty amazing conclusions about 4th level.

(F) Maybe KRLL is just kaput, at this point.

(L) Who cares about KRLL? We just use them and throw them away! [Laughter]

(T) That's what I was getting at... should we treat our standard UFO stuff... I mean, we are beyond that now...

(J) Yes, we are...

(T) ...with what we are working with here...

(F) All of what we have worked with over the years, the ideas of it being nuts-and-bolts, which I originally thought too, and it's clear if one has been following the whole phenomenon closely, it has evolved, actually, from a nuts-and-bolts perspective, and I am not knocking nuts-and-bolts, but those who are really looking with an open mind are seeing that this is far more.

(L) Alright, here it is, guys... [had been looking for references to Men in Black.] Who or what are the Men in Black? [Answer:] Lizard projections.

(T) We got on to that because we were asking about the projection of the guy in the Camaro that showed up in my driveway.

(L) OK. Does this mean that the Lizards are just projecting an image of a being? And, the answer was "yes". At that point Terry asked: "The Men in Black are not real in our physical terms?" And the answer: "Partly correct. You do not understand technology but we will describe it if you like. First we must explain further 'time travel' because the two concepts are closely related. The first step is to artificially induce an electromagnetic field. This opens the door between dimensions of reality. Next, thoughts must be channeled by participant in order to access reality bonding channel. They must then focus the energy to the proper dimensional bridge, the electrons must be arranged in correct frequency wave, and then the triage must be sent through realm curtain in order to balance perceptions at all density levels. Triage is as follows: 1. Matter; 2. Energy; 3. Perception of reality." In other words they send through...

(J) Holographic images.

(T) They transmit energy that takes matter here and creates what we perceive, and what we perceive depends on...

(L) No, no, no... I know what it is... the triage must be sent through... the triage is that the matter becomes energy which then becomes perception [information] and when it hits the other side of the curtain, the perception [information] reconverts to energy which then coagulates as matter... it is like doing a back-flip through the realm curtain.

(T) And what the individual sees depends upon what they expect to see, which the Lizzies have to tap into first before they do the triage... that is the "reality bonding channel." If you are open to see Men in Black, even if you don't know what they are, then at some level of consciousness...

(F) But I think this is not just limited to Men In Black.

(L) Listen to this! "Several times I have heard references to big rectangular boxes, I would like to know who these belong to." And the answer was: "Lizard projections..." What are they doing, projecting their whole damn reality into our world?

(F) Well, apparently part of the whole process of going from 4th to 3rd is the 'projection' process itself.

(T) Yes, you have to move backward somehow.

(F) This also, of course, explains much of what we have read and heard about in terms of higher phenomena. You cannot ground it at all. So many people have fallen off the track by expecting to capture metallic craft and dissect them, and, while that does happen...

(J) And the whole concept of what's wrong with science now is that they can't hold it or measure it, or see it physically because it doesn't exist!

(F) That is where material science falls apart. It is stuck in a vicious cycle.

(J) Yes, and it is using its own rules to make itself obsolete!

(F) Right!

(T) So, the bottom line is, we have simply gone beyond the KRLL stuff, the Cooper and Lear stuff, and so on.

(F) Which is one of the reasons why the Cassiopaeans keep telling us to stop asking these stupid questions.

(T) We don't need to go into all that. *(F)* Yes, that's UFOs 101.

(J) Yeah, right, we've moved beyond all that.

(T) There's another thing that is even more interesting and that is that we are not alone in this density, there are other beings on other planets also. And, it just may be that some of them are coming here just to throw some more stuff in the soup to keep us confused as to which or who is what.

(F) I have a feeling, though, that probably everything that we have experienced in the UFO area over the many years is a passage from higher levels of density to this one. I don't think that we have ever experienced a 3rd to 3rd transfer. That is just my feeling. And, it is only just now that people are beginning to realize that. In other words...

(T) Well, that is what Vallee thinks, along those lines, so he is just looking at interdimensional, because...

(F) But Vallee is also a material scientist so he is examining it in a scientific way. He is a little more open-minded than some who would just say it is impossible because we haven't discovered it yet...

(J) Yeah, our name isn't on it so it doesn't exist...

(F) But, he is doing it in a very careful way.

(L) Well, have we done enough with KRLL? *(T)* Yeah, I think we have done more than enough with KRLL. *(L)* KRLL is irrelevant. I think we need to be more careful about our questions. *(J)* I would like to ask if this is a mode of learning the Cassiopaeans would like to see us pursue on a regular basis. *(L)* OK. Consider it asked.

A: Would be a good idea. 195

Q: *(L)* I do have a question that I don't 196
know if we could discuss it and work it out because it is a real outside one. I would like to know if the soul's electromagnetic pattern can be forcibly altered, from the outside, by another being, force, or source of energy.

A: No. 197

Q: *(L)* Is a person's soul pattern deter- 198
mined by the cumulative experiences of that individual?

A: Part of the equation. 199

Q: *(L)* Does a person carry within their 200
soul pattern memories of every single incident, event or happening that has ever occurred to them throughout all realms of their experience?

A: Memories are imprint of "Past, 201
Present and Future."

Q: *(L)* So, if the imprint is there... *(J)* 202
"We are you in the future!" *(L)* Right, so if the imprint is there, and no outside force including Lizzies or Orions can...

A: You can remember us. 203

Q: *(L)* The point I am trying to get 204
at here is that, at some level, anything that happens to us can be accessed, correct?

A: Yes. 205

Q: *(L)* And it is incorrect to say that 206
any other being can come and erase some part of our experience and replace it with their own creation in any way, shape, form or fashion?

A: Nonsense! 207

208 **Q**: *(J)* Ask if I should give *Childhood's End* to Laura to read. I think there is some very important information in there.

209 **A**: Up to you.

210 **Q**: *(J)* Never mind! *(L)* Of course you should lend it to me. You know I read everything in sight!

211 **A**: Jan, are you going to ask us what socks to wear tomorrow?

212 **Q**: *(L)* Do you wear socks, Jan? *(J)* No. *(T)* What socks should she wear tomorrow? *(L)* Terry!

213 **A**: Red with white stripes.

214 **Q**: *(J)* I'm sorry. I shouldn't have gotten off line. *(L)* Now, here's a couple of things I would like to ask about and I am not asking about because I want... because we have already discussed this at some length. Some time ago I asked about the "Wise Baby" dream, that is about the baby that was ten days old and quoting Shakespeare, and I thought this was unusual and asked about it. You said I should discover. Well, Mother had a similar dream the other day. She did not know about my dream, but we both dreamed about talking babies. This is mentioned in the Budd Hopkins book. The significant things about these dreams is the talking baby. The passage in the Budd Hopkins' book describes the woman who underwent hypnotic regression to investigate her "Wise Baby" dream and discovered that the dream was not the reality. In my and my mother's dream there were individuals present who pronounced the baby to be evil and who advised us not to interact with it. The day following the dream we both felt very uncomfortable, ill at ease, and slightly depressed. In the book, the woman who had the dream said it was a 'feel-good' dream and she liked it. But then she found out it was not such a good dream. My question about this is, at a very deep level, what does this baby represent?

A: Nothing. 215

Q: *(L)* Is the baby a cover memory or 216
a screen memory of another event?

A: Maybe. 217

Q: *(L)* We hashed it around and Jan 218
pointed out that in both dreams there was somebody in the dream who told us not to listen to the baby. Who does this person telling us not to listen to this baby represent? Is this information from you guys in our dreams telling us not to listen to this baby? Is this baby, in fact, a screen memory of an interaction with an alien of some sort, i.e., Grays or Lizzies?

A: Differs. 219

Q: *(L)* What differs? *(T)* It wasn't 220
an interaction with the Grays or the Lizzies. *(L)* OK, can you tell me...

A: Each is individual. 221

Q: *(L)* So this means that my dream is 222
different from my mother's dream and both are different from the dream of the woman in the book?

A: Yes. 223

Q: *(L)* Well, I guess that if I want to 224
know more about the dream I can do a meditation or hypnosis.

A: Bingo! 225

Q: *(L)* Terry and I were discussing the 226
migration of objects underground. As you know, we dug where you told us to dig and we did find a space underground where something obviously had

been. We then found that the ground was soft.

227 **A**: Yes.

228 **Q**: *(L)* And it was as though somebody had dug very deep but moving in a strange direction. Well, Terry, interestingly, had read a work on the tendency of objects to move underground stimulated by the drainage of water through the Earth. It almost seems that the pattern of this soft sand is toward an area where there is water. Could it be possible that something could migrate through the sand this way?

229 **A**: Yes.

230 **Q**: *(L)* And would it migrate toward an area where water flows through the ground?

231 **A**: Yes.

232 **Q**: *(L)* And could it migrate that distance in, say, 50 or 60 years?

233 **A**: Sure!

234 **Q**: *(L)* And, in order to migrate that distance in that period of time, what would the approximate weight of an object have to be?

235 **A**: Open.

236 **Q**: *(T)* It doesn't matter. The weight of the object is irrelevant to the movement. The thought crosses my mind, what if it was dug deliberately as a tunnel?

237 **A**: Yes. Are you on to something? Hmmm?

238 **Q**: *(L)* So, my husband's idea to expand the cellar, to brace the corners with blocks as he digs, in order to prevent cave-in... *(F)* Did you find a place when you dug that looked like a place where somebody had put something? *(L)* There was a hollow space under the cement floor. Under this was the soft sand area which continues to extend downward and outward surrounded by hard packed sand. *(F)* Well, obviously something was there. *(L)* Was this something that has been moved already?

A: Discover, it is fun. 239

Q: *(L)* Well my thoughts are, also, interestingly, because out of this whole project has come the idea of expanding the cellar which will then make a space that you can go into and stand instead of just a root cellar. Do you guys have plans for this room we are building? 240

A: Who knows? 241

Q: *(L)* It occurred to me as I was thinking about it: remember when we were talking about Noah and the ark and how we were told that the symbolism was that Noah just built an ark because it seemed like a good idea at the time and later it came in handy. *(T)* And you are digging this out because it seems like a good idea but you don't know why yet. Maybe there is some other reason and maybe you will find something in the digging, too. But, you are also going to end up with an expanded basement and there may be another reason for it. But, you don't know that yet and they are not going to tell you! *(J)* You'll find out when the time is right. *(T)* You are already started in that direction. *(L)* Yeah. He said since he has already done all this digging he might as well finish the job. *(T)* It may not be for a flood or an earthquake or whatever, it just may be useful for something else. Maybe you're just supposed to get that finished so we can move our sessions downstairs! 242

243 **A**: You are learning, Bravo!

244 **Q**: *(T)* Well, we are back on the right track. So, you have to continue digging! *(L)* Gee, thanks! *(T)* Well, that is where the fun is! It's a treasure hunt!

245 **A**: And you might just find something verrrry interesting!!!

246 **Q**: *(L)* Jan and I are very curious about artistic expression at 4th density. We experience art and music in a very positive and moving way, most of us, in this realm, and sometimes music can be very sublime and very transforming. It can move one in a lot of very unusual ways. What is it like in 4th density?

247 **A**: In 4th, you can "see" sounds and "hear" colors, for example.[20]

248 **Q**: *(L)* Is this – now you guys just calm down when I ask this question... *(F)* I know what you are going to ask... *(L)* No remarks, OK? Many years ago when I was a child of the 60s and 70s, I tried some LSD. *(T)* I know exactly what you are going to ask, yeah, because I've seen it too! *(J)* Yes. *(L)* In a major way! Geometric patterns and colors manifested with music. *(T)* Yes! *(L)* Is this what we are talking about here?

249 **A**: Bingo!

250 **Q**: *(L)* So, in other words...

251 **A**: The answer to your next question is yes, you experienced a bleed through of 4th density.

252 **Q**: *(F)* In other words an acid trip is like a glimpse into 4th density. *(L)* Do you recommend this method for accessing this type of reality?

A: Open. 253

Q: *(T)* Well, the problem is that some 254
people would want to do that all the time and not work on doing it in a natural way.

A: Yes. 255

Q: *(T)* And other people would use it 256
and abuse it and use it as an excuse. *(J)* And damage themselves. *(L)* Yes, it is obviously something that has to be very carefully handled. We can't encourage this.[21] *(J)* Is that like the concept of adding additional dimensions to the 3 we normally experience?

A: Yes. 4th level density implies 257
an additional dimension of experience, doesn't it?

Q: *(T)* The first dimension is a sin- 258
gle point, the second is the movement of the point into a line, the third is the movement of the line into a plane and the addition of time gives solidity. What is the fourth?

A: Discover! 259

Q: *(T)* Is time frequency also as we per- 260
ceive time?

A: Not as you perceive it. 261

Q: *(T)* We perceive it linearly, but is 262
it a frequency that our sense organs do not interpret correctly?

A: Maybe. 263

Q: *(L)* They have told us before that 264
time is an illusion or a deception imposed at the time of the 'Fall'. *(J)* I've seen – we have all seen – the light spectrum. What we are able to perceive with our eyes is only a limited section. Is reality like that? What we are able

[20] *High Strangeness* 6

[21] My experience with it was not extremely pleasant, to put it mildly, and I never let anybody talk me into something like that again!

to perceive is only a small section of the spectrum of vibrations?

265 **A**: Close.

266 **Q**: *(T)* When we move into 4th density will we be able to perceive more of this electromagnetic band?

267 **A**: Much.

268 **Q**: *(J)* So, it expands our awareness?

269 **A**: Yes.

270 **Q**: *(L)* A few years ago I was meditating and I did what I call 'zoning'. It is an indescribable state. I kind of bobbed back to the surface for a moment because I experienced a buzzing in my head that sounded like an electrical transformer. Words came into my head that were like: "The presence is approaching", and I thought immediately of *Shekina*, or the 'forerunner' of the 'presence of God'. I was a little agitated because I was not positioned in the way I would have liked to be to receive any experience or visitation. I adjusted myself in a more 'prim and proper' position and remember nothing more until I just sort of came to with the intense urge to relieve my bladder. I don't know how much time passed, but it must have been a considerable period to have the physical urge that strong. The bed was adjacent to a wall between the bedroom and the bathroom with just a walk space. I had to be careful not to bump my head on the wall when I was getting up. I got out of the bed and was quite startled to discover that my head and shoulders passed right through the wall. As soon as I noticed that, I started to pay attention to what else I was experiencing. I noticed that all physical objects appeared as transparent slides of color and light. The walls of the house did not exist, I could see the children in their beds in other rooms in the house, their bodies were light. I could see through the house to the outside and it was not darkness as we perceive it. I was aware that it was night, but trees, plants and other objects were apparent by their appearance as color and light. I had a brief thought of something distant and it was as though my vision was telescopic and zoomed onto it instantaneously. I was also aware that my vision was 360, that is, I could see in all directions at once. All of this happened very quickly, or so it seemed, and I realized that I was not in the body. That thought startled me and the instant I was startled, that is, felt an inkling of fear, I snapped back in like a rubber band. I discovered myself exactly as I had been prior to hearing the buzzing, not having made the adjustments in my position. I think what we are talking about when we talk about 4th density, is this kind of perception.

(F) Well, you remember in Whitley Strieber's book, he talks about floating out of his body and he became aware of all kinds of things including the fields around power lines and it is quite a description.

(L) Well, it was a very strange experience, to say the least.

(T) When you started to explain about the trance state, you said: "What I call zoned out, I can't explain it." That's the same thing the Cassiopaeans say when we ask them to explain what 4th density is like!

(J) Yes, we have no physical frame of reference.

(L) Yes, I can't say I wasn't unaware, because I was intensely aware of every-

thing. And yet, I can't say I was focused on any one thing, because I was not.

(F) The last session we had we received some clues as to why it is they can't explain all these things. They said something when we were talking about plants and rocks at 1st density. Try to think of something in animal language to express what it is like to perceive the universe as a human. The thing that occurs to me is that, even though we share the same space with dogs, cats, etc., their perception of the universe is so radically different that for all intents and purposes, they might as well be on another planet.

(T) Science tells us that a dog's eyes only see in black and white.

(F) It isn't just what they physically can see and how they see it, but how they perceive and understand it and how they think. It is so radically different from a human being... and some people get all attached and all emotional and think that animals are almost human and the dog isn't even thinking "Oh, I'm a dog, I think I'll just take a nap." There is not anything that we can understand. So, if you think about the steps up density-wise, if they are merely equal, imagine the jump from 3rd to 4th! In 4th, they may understand us entirely, but their view is radically different.

(L) Let's say goodnight.

End of session

January 21, 1995

Disturbing material about animal/human mutilations and human manipulation by hyperdimensional beings ahead! Brace yourself!

Participants: 'Frank', Laura, Terry, Jan, S___, D___, Chuck[1]

1 **Q**: *(L)* Who do we have with us?

2 **A**: Torrillahk.

3 **Q**: *(L)* And where are you from, Torillahk?

4 **A**: Cassiopaea.

5 **Q**: *(L)* Let's get the ridge out of the board. Do you have any messages?

6 **A**: Thank you.[2]

7 **Q**: *(L)* You are welcome. Do you have any messages for any of us tonight, or should we just start in on our questions?

8 **A**: Any rituals performed tonight?

9 **Q**: *(L)* Did anyone do any rituals? Why do you ask?

10 **A**: Feel some restrictions.[3]

11 **Q**: *(D)* I bathed in bath salt. *(L)* That wouldn't do anything. Sue has some questions about some of her healing things. *(S)* If I put my finger on a certain muscle in an inter-oral area, would you be able to tell me if it is the correct position?[4]

A: Okay. 12

Q: *(S)* OK, is this the terragoid? 13

A: Okay. 14

Q: *(S)* OK, I guess it's the terragoid. 15
That was where I had my finger. I just needed to know that. *(S)* Which school of thought, Upliger or Nix (?)...

A: Your work is less dependent upon 16
physical factors than you think.

Q: *(T)* Is it that she should use more 17
intuition in this?

A: Aural frequency. 18

Q: *(L)* In other words, feel it. *(S)* Don't 19
I still need the basic knowledge?

[1]The guests "D___" and "Chuck" were problematic for a number of reasons. Chuck was a PI who had worked with me on an abduction case. He wasn't really 'into' the paranormal and asked to attend just out of curiosity. D___ is the woman who appears at a couple other sessions and was discussed in *The Wave* as the science teacher who claimed, under hypnosis, to have been affiliated with praying mantis–type aliens.

[2]Apparently for getting the ridge out of the board.

[3]I would suggest that the "restrictions" were purely and simply due to the presence of D___.

[4]Sue was a massage therapist.

20 **A**: Sense, knowledge is held within, simply unlock more and more as needed.

21 **Q**: *(S)* Sometimes it's hard to... *(L)* Go ahead, ask your questions. *(S)* Does re-aligning the sphenoid bone actually do something with the pituitary gland?

22 **A**: All these procedures are factored by your own natural healing abilities, this is of the light, and comes from within when you follow your natural instincts and trust!

23 **Q**: *(T)* Yes, it does, it does what they just said! *(S)* Would myofascial unwinding help me unblock some of my own fears, hesitancies...

24 **A**: Just trust your extraordinary abilities!

25 **Q**: *(T)* What they are trying to tell you is to go with what you think is right because it will be right, because it is coming from within you, and it's not so much whether you've touched here, or touched there, it's that wherever you've touched is the intent. It's what they say, intent is what it is. *(S)* But the way the law of this country and state goes, you also have to have that piece of paper that says yes, you can do this.

26 **A**: Bravo, Terry!

27 **Q**: *(T)* Thank you, thank you! *(L)* Well, go ahead and get the licensing and do what feels right. You're doing the right stuff. Everything you're doing, you're doing by instinct, you know – continue the classes. *(S)* It's like, I know about three or four ways for carpal-tunnel syndrome, they're all totally different... *(L)* Try them all, one might work differently for a different person, they can all be right, you know.

A: It is not the physical methodology that matters. 28

Q: *(J)* It's like you're tapped in, just go with the flow. 29

A: Humor the authorities, they know not any better. 30

Q: *(S)* Why am I so reluctant to use some things, is it because I'm going to too many classes, too many different schools of thought, that I'm getting confused? 31

A: Lose the fear and just do it! Welcome, Chuck, you were a "wild one" in youth, eh? Lady Killer. Mirth. 32

Q: [Laughter] *(L)* We're going to go on with our questions and see how many we can cram into this session. *(D)* Monday is the 23rd, my house is supposed to sell. My realtor is sweating blood. 33

A: Did we not tell you? 34

Q: *(D)* Yeah, you did. *(L)* The van I looked at today, is there anything significantly wrong with it that doesn't show up, or that I have missed, that we have missed? Is it as good a deal as it seems to be? 35

A: Yes. 36

Q: *(L)* OK, that's all I wanted to know. Back in the 1970s in the Central United States there were quite a number of cases of animal mutilation. There has been a lot of publicity about this at some point and then it died down and was covered up, and there were a lot of ideas and theories about it. What I would like to know is who was doing the animal mutilations? 37

[5] *The Wave* 22

38 **A**: Many.

39 **Q**: OK, who was doing most of the animal mutilations?[5]

40 **A**: Not applicable.

41 **Q**: OK. Was some of the animal mutilation done by the U.S. government, or entities within the government?

42 **A**: Was?

43 **Q**: *(L)* In other words, it is still going on. So OK, so they are still doing it. Was, or is, some of this activity being conducted by alien individuals?

44 **A**: Yes.

45 **Q**: *(T)* Were they acting for the same reasons?[6]

46 **A**: No.

47 **Q**: Why did the government do animal mutilations?

48 **A**: Copy, in order to throw off investigation.

49 **Q**: *(L)* So they copied this activity to throw off investigations. Did they do this as an act to protect the aliens who were doing animal mutilations for their own purposes?

50 **A**: No.

51 **Q**: *(L)* Were they doing it to protect themselves from the public knowing that they were engaged in alien interactions?

52 **A**: They do it to protect the public from knowing that which would explode society if discovered.[7]

53 **Q**: *(L)* What is this item that they were protecting so that society or the public wouldn't know about it? What activity is this?

A: Humans eat cattle, aliens eat you. 54

Q: *(T)* They've said that before. *(L)* 55
OK, yeah, we eat 2nd level, they eat 3rd. Did aliens do some of the cattle mutilations?

A: Yes. 56

Q: What do aliens do to cattle? 57

A: Blood. 58

Q: *(L)* They take the blood out of 59
them?

A: Yes. 60

Q: *(J)* They drink it? What do they 61
use this blood for?

A: Nourishment. 62

Q: *(L)* OK, but you just said that 63
aliens eat humans, and humans eat cattle. Why were the aliens being nourished by cattle, if that's not their normal bill of fare? *(J)* Delicacy. *(T)* A cow's blood is a lot like human blood.

A: Do you not ever consume facsimile? 64

Q: *(T)* Hamburger helper? Shake and 65
Bake... *(J)* And I helped! [Laughter] Sorry!

A: Facsimile is less controversial, obvi- 66
ously!

Q: *(L)* So in other words, they were eat- 67
ing cattle just to keep from having to eat so many humans – that would have just upset people a lot – is that it? Oh god.

A: Yes. 68

Q: *(T)* So, since they're eating cat- 69
tle instead of humans, does that mean they'll stop eating humans? *(L)* Terry, you know better than that! *(T)* Well, it's the next logical question.

---

[6] *High Strangeness* 9

[7] *The Wave* 12

70 **A**: Some of their human "food" is merely emotions, think of flesh as being the equal of "filet mignon."

71 **Q**: *(T)* Some of their food is merely emotions. OK, when we're talking about these aliens, are we talking about the Grays?

72 **A**: No.

73 **Q**: *(T)* We're talking about the Lizards.[8]

74 **A**: Yes.

75 **Q**: *(T)* OK, what do the Grays feed on?

76 **A**: Plasma.

77 **Q**: *(T)* OK, the Grays feed on plasma, blood plasmas of some kind, is this what you are saying?

78 **A**: Yes.

79 **Q**: *(T)* OK, so that's why they want the blood; so, do the Grays feed on emotions?

80 **A**: No.

81 **Q**: *(T)* OK.

82 **A**: They send them to Lizards.

83 **Q**: *(T)* The Grays send emotions to the Lizards? They're transmitters?

84 **A**: Transfer energy through technology.

85 **Q**: *(L)* Let me ask this... *(T)* Are the cattle giving off enough emotion for the Grays to feed this to the Lizards also?

86 **A**: No. That is physical only, you see, Lizards and Grays only need physical nourishment while "visiting" 3rd level, not when in natural realm, 4th density, there they feed on emotions only.[9]

Q: *(T)* Grays are not strictly 3rd density? Because they've been created by the Lizzies? 87

A: Yes. Correct, they too are 4th level. 88

Q: *(L)* OK, let me ask, while we're on this subject, real quickly, we need to move on to cover these questions. Actually, it becomes moot, since we know their technological capabilities. What technology do they use to surgically excise certain areas of the cattle's anatomy, is this done by laser... 89

A: Laser-like. 90

Q: *(L)* OK, since it has been noted that quite frequently the cattle mutilations consist of taking very specific parts of the body, such as the eyeballs, the genitalia – they core out the anal sphincter right up to the colon – what would be the purpose for these specific body parts? I mean, do they core out the rectum and put a pump on there and suck all the blood out, I mean... *(T)* That's what the tail's for! It's a pump! *(L)* Why? Why do they do this? 91

A: Close. 92

Q: *(L)* Close? I'm close? 93

A: Yes. Not the tail part, ha ha! 94

Q: *(L)* OK, I think we kind of have an answer to this one, but sightings of black, unmarked helicopters have been very frequently associated with the phenomenon of cattle mutilations. Who or what are these helicopters? 95

A: Variable. 96

Q: *(L)* Are some of these helicopters disguised alien craft? Are some of these 97

[8] *High Strangeness* 9
[9] *High Strangeness* 9
[10] *The Wave* 22

helicopters the property of the U.S. government?[10]

98 **A**: Yes to both.

99 **Q**: *(T)* Are some of these helicopters private enterprise?

100 **A**: Yes.

101 **Q**: *(L)* Oh boy, Terry, you had to do that! A whole new can of worms!

102 **A**: All are interconnected.[11]

103 **Q**: *(L)* OK, I want to ask this one, because this is one I haven't hit lately. Wendelle Stevens, who was associated with Billy Meier, and also Genesis 2 or 3, put out the Billy Meier book on the Billy Meier sightings....

104 **A**: Some too, are projections, this phenomenon is multifaceted.[12]

105 **Q**: *(L)* I expect that goes back to the black helicopters. I want to know about Wendelle Stevens, associate of Billy Meier...

106 **A**: Why? This is wasted energy.

107 **Q**: *(L)* Well, I just want to know how reliable he is. In a word, is this person somebody who can be relied upon for factual information, yes or no?

108 **A**: No.

109 **Q**: *(L)* OK, that's good enough. Who are the oriental-appearing personnel that have been seen manning the helicopters and the white vans that have been sighted all over the country?

110 **A**: MIB.

111 **Q**: *(T)* Talk about opening up another can of worms! *(L)* I'm not even going to touch that one!

112 **A**: And government copycats.

Q: *(L)* OK, now, I have a list of names, 113
and I want a yes or no as to whether these individuals were – because I believe most of them are deceased right now, this is just a little verification on some other things for the general public – were these individuals involved in the cover-up of the UFO activity and phenomenon in the U.S.? Roscoe Hillenkoetter?

A: Yes. 114

Q: *(L)* Dr. Vannevar Bush? 115

A: Yes. 116

Q: *(L)* Secretary James Forrestal? 117

A: Yes. 118

Q: *(L)* General Nathan Twining? 119

A: Yes. 120

Q: *(L)* General Hoyt F. Vandenberg? 121

A: Yes. 122

Q: *(L)* Dr. Detlev Bronk? 123

A: Yes. 124

Q: *(L)* Jerome Hudson? 125

A: Yes. 126

Q: *(L)* Mr. Sidney Sauers? 127

A: Yes. 128

Q: *(L)* Donald Menzel? 129

A: Yes. 130

Q: *(L)* Robert Montague? 131

A: Yes. 132

Q: *(L)* Dr. Lloyd B. Berger? 133

A: Yes. 134

Q: Who is in MJ12 now? 135

A: Will not reveal as you would be ter- 136
minated if this information were to be let out, so forget it now!

---

[11] *High Strangeness* "Appendix"

[12] *The Wave* 52

137 **Q**: Does MJ-12 still exist?

138 **A**: In different form.

139 **Q**: I would like to know who sent the MJ-12 documents to Jamie Shandera. Who sent those documents to him?

140 **A**: Bill Cooper.

141 **Q**: *(T)* Who sent them to Cooper?

142 **A**: He discovered them in records review.

143 **Q**: *(L)* He is the one who discovered the MJ-12 documents? Does he claim he sent them? *(T)* Yes. *(L)* How did you know that and I didn't know that? *(T)* I read the Cooper book, the early Cooper papers.

144 **A**: Cooper was unintended security leak, then "turncoat."

145 **Q**: *(T)* OK, so he found all this out when he was working for the government...

146 **A**: Yes.

147 **Q**: *(T)* ...which is how he got them out of the records?

148 **A**: Yes.

149 **Q**: *(T)* Well OK, while we are on the subject... I don't want the names of those involved with MJ-12 – the question is, if you gave us the names, how many of those people would we know? Not personally, but how many would we know? How many would we have heard of?

150 **A**: One or two maybe.

151 **Q**: *(T)* Which is what I figured. Just like back in the 40s you wouldn't have known who these people were. Hillenkoetter and Forrestal, maybe, because they were WWII people, their names were in the paper. Unless you were into sciences, you wouldn't know who these people were. *(L)* How many alien craft, actual alien craft, are in the hands of the government or this consortium?

A: 36 152

Q: *(L)* And were these captured craft? 153
Or gifted?[13]

A: And recovered. 154

Q: *(T)* OK, they were all three. Were 155
any of them purchased?

A: Not correct concept, Grays are not 156
financial.

Q: *(T)* I didn't mean by money, I 157
meant purchased as in some kind of a trade. A gift is something that is given without anything in return *(J)* We give them something in return. *(T)* Were the gift ones not what we would really consider gifts, but they were given to us in return for something else, some other kind of payment? Barter?

A: No. Because all sought return fa- 158
vors were already achieved.

Q: *(L)* So it was all just a farce. *(T)* So 159
they were payment as opposed to gifts.

A: Not correct concept. 160

Q: *(L)* How about this: They weren't 161
payment, they weren't gifts, they were distractions?

A: Closer. 162

Q: *(T)* OK, we've got captured 163
ships, recovered ships, something called gifted ships, that were not really gifted ships, and the concept that some of them were purchased, but they were not purchased in a sense that we would normally purchase things, bartered for something, and that the ships that

[13] *High Strangeness* 9; *The Wave* 22

were gifted were given to the government in order to keep them distracted from other things that the beings were doing. Is this something close along the lines of what we're talking about?

164 **A**: Close

165 **Q**: *(T)* OK, so there's a lot of different categories of how these ships got into the hands of the federal government?

166 **A**: Yes. Multidimensional.

167 **Q**: *(L)* OK, give me a yes or no answer on this: Dr. Paul Bennewitz – reliable, yes or no?

168 **A**: No.

169 **Q**: *(L)* Is his statement, as it is recorded in the KRLL papers, falsified?

170 **A**: No.

171 **Q**: *(L)* Is that statement true?

172 **A**: Partly.

173 **Q**: *(L)* Was he reliable previously? At the time he was doing that work?

174 **A**: Sort of.

175 **Q**: *(L)* Who is O. H. Krill?

176 **A**: No one.

177 **Q**: *(L)* Is O. H. Krill a group?

178 **A**: Symbolism.

179 **Q**: *(L)* Symbolism of what? What does O. H. Krill translate out to?

180 **A**: For documentary purposes only, your government likes code names.

181 **Q**: *(L)* Are you implying that this piece of work was put out by the government for dissemination of the subject matter? *(J)* Is it disinformation?[14]

A: Complex. 182

Q: *(L)* Give us a percentage of factual 183
information in this document.

A: 43%. 184

Q: *(L)* Are you saying that 43% is fac- 185
tual?

A: Close enough. 186

Q: *(L)* OK, so, in other words, this has 187
been planted by the government. Was it put out with the intention of giving out some factual information...

A: No. Planted? No. 188

Q: *(L)* You are saying it was planted? 189
(T) It was leaked purposely?

A: Your government is operating 190
on many cross-purposes, very complicated!

Q: *(T)* Even the simplest things are 191
very complicated with them. OK, question: The U.S. government...

A: On purpose! 192

Q: *(T)* Very true. Question: The gov- 193
ernment, our government, the U.S. government, is holding 36 craft of one kind or another that they have gotten in one way or another. How many other governments have craft?[15]

A: All is one. 194

Q: *(L)* We already have a one-world 195
government is what they're saying. *(T)* Yes, they're just waiting to make it official somehow. *(L)* Let me ask. What is...

A: Has been so for long time, as you 196
measure time.[16]

Q: *(L)* Let me ask this one before the 197
tape runs out and we take a break.

[14] *The Wave* 22, 64
[15] *High Strangeness* 9
[16] *The Wave* 12

What is the 'ultimate secret' being protected by the Consortium?

198 **A**: You are not in control of yourselves, you are an experiment.[17]

[Break]

199 **Q**: Do you have anything else to say on that subject?

200 **A**: Up to you.

201 **Q**: *(T)* When you say this is the ultimate secret, that we're being 'protected' from by the government, are we talking about the ultimate secret of humans only here?

202 **A**: Basically.

203 **Q**: *(T)* The ultimate secret of the human race is that we are an experiment that other humans are conducting on the rest of us?

204 **A**: Part.

205 **Q**: *(T)* OK, does the other part have to do with the Lizards?

206 **A**: Yes.

207 **Q**: *(L)* Other aliens also?

208 **A**: Yes.

209 **Q**: *(T)* OK, so, are the humans who are running the experiment, do they know that they are part of the experiment also?

210 **A**: Yes.

211 **Q**: *(T)* And they're doing this willingly?

212 **A**: They have no choice.

213 **Q**: *(L)* Why do they have no choice?

214 **A**: Already in progress.

215 **Q**: *(T)* What is the experiment about?

A: Too complicated for you to understand. 216

Q: *(J)* I hate it when that happens! *(T)* OK, is this part of, is this about the experiment the Lizzies are doing of dominating us and sucking us dry? 217

A: Yes, but there's much more than that, you will understand at level 4. 218

Q: *(T)* OK, I won't pursue that much further. *(L)* OK, in this KRLL document there was a statement made that the Grays and other aliens use glandular substances extracted during physical exams of human beings, what they would call the gynecological and the sperm extraction exams, that they used these glandular substances to get high or to feed on, that they are addicted to these – is this a correct assessment? 219

A: No. 220

Q: *(L)* Do they use glandular substances at all?[18] 221

A: Yes. 222

Q: *(L)* What do they use glandular substances for? 223

A: Medicine. 224

Q: *(L)* And what or whom do they use this medicine on? 225

A: Themselves. 226

Q: *(L)* And what does this medicine do for them? 227

A: Helps them cope with 3rd density. 228

Q: *(T)* Is this something that they use to help them stay in the 3d density? 229

A: Close. 230

Q: *(L)* Does it help them to manifest in a more solid physical manner? 231

[17] *The Wave* 49
[18] *The Wave* 9

232 **A**: Yes.

233 **Q**: *(L)* So, in other words, they draw glandular substances. Do they also use sexual energy given off by individuals to maintain their status in 3 dimensions?

234 **A**: No. That feeds them in 4D, as we told you before.

235 **Q**: *(L)* Yes. OK. How 'long', and I put long in quotes, because we know, as you say, there is no time, but how long, as we measure it, have the Grays been interacting with our race? The Grays, not the Lizards, the Grays, the cybergenetic probes?

236 **A**: No.

237 **Q**: *(L)* What do you mean, "No"?

238 **A**: Time travelers, therefore, "Time is ongoing."[19]

239 **Q**: *(L)* OK, recently I read a couple of books Jan gave me, *Knight in Shining Armor* and *Replay.* Both of these books described time travel.

240 **A**: No, not finished with answer. Do you understand the gravity of last response?

241 **Q**: *(L)* They are time travelers, they can move forward and backward in time, they can play games with our heads... *(T)* They can set up the past to create a future they want. *(D)* They can organize things so that they can create the energy that they need... *(L)* They can also make things look good, make them feel good, make them seem good, they can make you have an idea one minute, and then the next minute, create some sort of situation that confirms that idea...[20]

A: When you asked how long, of course 242
it is totally unlimited, is it not?

Q: *(L)* That's not good. If they were 243
to move back through space-time and alter an event in our past, would that alteration in the past instantaneously alter our present as well?

A: Has over and over and over. 244

Q: *(D)* So they do it over and over and 245
over, constantly? *(L)* So, at each...

A: You just are not yet aware, and have 246
no idea of the ramifications!!!

Q: *(L)* We're getting a little glimmer! 247
Yeah, I do, a little! *(T)* The ramifications of being able to move in and out of time and manipulate it the way you want. *(L)* And the ramifications of what they're doing to us; what they are doing to us and what they will do to us, over and over. *(F)* What did it say about over and over? *(L)* So, in other words, our only real prayer in this whole damn situation is to get out of this density level. That's what they're saying, that's what it sounds like to me.

A: Close. 248

Q: *(L)* Because, otherwise, we're just 249
literally, as in that book, stuck in the replay over and over and over, and the Holocaust could happen over and over, and we could just, you know... Genghis Khan, Attila the Hun... over and over and over again. *(T)* We're stuck in a time loop; they're putting us in a time loop. *(J)* Are we in a time loop?

A: Yes. 250

Q: *(D)* I have a question about... there 251
was a... [pause] Mankind has found it necessary for some reason or other to appoint time for some reason or other.

[19] *The Wave* 20

[20] *High Strangeness* 9

The only reason I can see is to have a means of telling, like in verbal or written communications...

252 **A**: Control mechanism.[21]

253 **Q**: *(T)* Is there a way for us to break the control mechanism? Besides moving to 4th density? *(D)* That was part...

254 **A**: Nope.

255 **Q**: *(D)* When 4th density beings communicate, it's telepathic, right?[22]

256 **A**: Yes.

257 **Q**: *(D)* OK, since time doesn't exist, how do you communicate about happenings?

258 **A**: Rephrase, please; clarify.

259 **Q**: *(L)* What she means to ask is, if you're communicating telepathically... *(D)* On 4th density... *(L)* And time doesn't exist, how do you communicate about events as one happens now, as opposed to later and the next thing happens, and the next thing happens... *(J)* How is it sequential?

260 **A**: Translate.

261 **Q**: *(D)* Translate? OK, let me explain what I mean. I mean, we talk about 1907 something happened...

262 **A**: That is how it is done.[23]

263 **Q**: *(T)* Translate is how it is done. You translate the experience?

264 **A**: From 4 to 3. And vice verse.

265 **Q**: *(L)* So, in other words, it's almost like making movies. *(J)* Are linear thought processes part of it? Is it being linear and non-linear?

A: Part of 3D illusion only.[24] 266

Q: *(L)* So, in other words, if you're a 4th density being, everything is more or less happening, excuse the term happening, everything is simultaneous, and if you wish to discuss or communicate or have any focus upon any particular aspect of this unified dimension, then what you do is you kind of extract it out, project it into 3rd density... 267

A: Close. 268

Q: *(L)* ...like a movie. 269

A: But you will not understand fully until you get there[25] 270

Q: *(T)* OK, so it's a concept that we can't completely grasp in 3rd density at this point. 271

A: Can a dog grasp algebra? You got it. 272

Q: *(L)* In other words, we're in bad shape! And these guys are playing games with us, so to speak... 273

A: Subjective. 274

Q: *(T)* Subjective to whether we're in bad shape or not. 275

A: Yes. 276

Q: *(T)* I was going to say that doesn't necessarily mean we're in bad shape... *(L)* Well, the situation we find ourselves in, is the only way of getting out of this time loop, so to speak, to move into another density, or is there a loop in the other density as well? 277

[21] *The Wave* 23
[22] *Secret History* 12
[23] *The Wave* 26
[24] *High Strangeness* 9
[25] *The Wave* 49

278 **A**: No.

279 **Q**: *(L)* No loop in the other density?

280 **A**: Yogis can do it.

281 **Q**: *(L)* Yogis can do it... *(T)* Transcend time. *(L)* OK, let me ask this before we really start to go...

282 **A**: How they control their own physicality.

283 **Q**: *(L)* Let me ask a few questions here before, I think we're breaking up. First of all, there was the television special on the other night about...

284 **A**: What is "breaking up"?

285 **Q**: *(L)* I think it means that everybody's getting tired and losing their focus. The question I want to ask is about this...

286 **A**: You are, but not all others.

287 **Q**: *(L)* Well, let me get my question in here, and if you guys want to sit up all night, I'll just keep my mouth shut.

288 **A**: Laura has "bug" in her system.

289 **Q**: *(L)* OK, I have a bug in my system. I want to know what this humming sound is that people are hearing all over this country. I mean people have been reporting hearing this intense humming sound that literally drives them crazy. There was a TV special on about this the other night. What is this humming and where is it coming from?

290 **A**: Increased EM waves in preparation for oncoming wave.[26]

Q: *(L)* What is the source of this sound, 291
I mean, where specifically, location-wise, is it coming from?

A: Cosmic. 292

Q: *(L)* OK, it's cosmic, it's not coming 293
from the planet itself. OK, what is the greatest weakness of the Lizzies or the Grays in 4th density?

A: STS. 294

Q: *(T)* Yes, that is their greatest weak- 295
ness: service to self. *(L)* Is that in both densities?

A: Yes. 296

Q: *(T)* Is there a way... can we use that 297
against them?

A: Not correct philosophy. 298

Q: *(T)* Very true, very true. *(L)* I want 299
to ask a question that Chuck brought up a little while ago, have we in our group...

A: Let Chuck ask himself. 300

Q: *(C)* Has this group been infiltrated 301
by anyone in controlled by the aliens?

A: No, not exactly.[27] 302

Q: *(L)* Can we get clarification? 303

A: Have attempted to corrupt commu- 304
nication, but remember, we, too are "alien".[28]

Q: *(D)* There was one time when 305
other aliens tried to interject, but they didn't succeed. *(L)* Yeah, that was in one of the other transcripts. I think what Chuck meant more specifically, other than other alien communication or communicants, was a particular 3rd

[26] *The Wave* 2

[27] *High Strangeness* "Appendix"; *The Wave* 21

[28] The Cs put "alien" in quotes because, obviously, they don't mean they are aliens in the sense of physical UFO-type beings. But, since the UFO phenomenon is mostly a paranormal situation, this makes perfect sense.

density person – have we ever had such a person attend these sessions?

306 **A**: Not yet, but "stay tuned."

307 **Q**: *(L)* Well, I'm done with my questions, we covered my stuff. You guys are on your own now.

308 **A**: Chuck ask.

309 **Q**: *(C)* That was the only question I had, and they answered it.

310 **A**: Untrue.

311 **Q**: *(L)* Are you wondering something? Ask. *(C)* How truthful the source is.

312 **A**: Up to you to decide

313 **Q**: *(T)* They only provide the information. They want us to make the decisions as to what we do with it, interpret it, what happens with it. I'm sure we all look at it slightly differently. We all have a different way of perceiving things, so we all perceive it differently. *(D)* Is the information gathered from the collective consciousness? A collection of all lessons learned by all humans?

314 **A**: Yes, and other sources as well.

315 **Q**: *(D)* Does this include the Lizzies?

316 **A**: Yes.

317 **Q**: *(D)* That includes you, also?

318 **A**: Yes.

319 **Q**: *(D)* OK, can we tune into the collective consciousness?

320 **A**: Of course.

321 **Q**: *(D)* OK, then, are there certain abilities needed to do this connection into the collective consciousness?

322 **A**: You all have all you need.

323 **Q**: *(D)* Well then, if this... *(T)* By sitting here, we tap into them and they tap into us. *(D)* If this collective consciousness is a collection, haven't all lessons been learned by someone at some time?

A: Yes. 324

Q: *(D)* Then can we tune into the col- 325
lective consciousness to find how our same lessons have been solved before?

A: Yes. But what is "before?" 326

Q: *(D)* Before? No, I didn't ask... *(J)* 327
Before, during, after, these are all time concepts. *(D)* Oh, yeah.

A: Yes. 328

Q: *(D)* Well, my real question is if all 329
the answers are there, and we can get there, why are we going through the lessons again? I mean, why do we have to go through these lessons if the solutions are already there?

A: It's all just lessons. 330

Q: *(D)* I know, that's what made me 331
ask... I just... I can't understand this... we already have the answers, and we're going through the lessons again... *(T)* Not all of us have learned all the answers, that's why we're all going through the lessons again... *(D)* But, you see, all the answers are there...

A: Who said "again"? 332

Q: *(J)* Is it more like 'still'? *(D)* But if 333
all the answers are there...

A: You are still thinking at 3rd level. 334

Q: *(D)* Yeah, but I'm still trying to un- 335
derstand... Sorry, guys.

A: Don't "try" so much, just go with 336
it.

Q: *(T)* It's like Master Yoda said in 337
Star Wars, "Don't try, do"... Just do it.

A: Yes. 338

339 **Q**: *(T)* See, I knew *Star Wars* had a redeeming social value. *(J)* So did *Relationships*. The how is to do it. *(D)* But if the answers are there, and we can find the answers, to our lessons... *(T)* We don't have to find the answers, we have the answers. The answers are within all of us. *(D)* It seems so redundant... *(T)* Most of the lessons are to find the right answers... *(D)* ...to actually go through the doing of the lessons....

340 **A**: No. Not correct idea.

341 **Q**: *(T)* Where were we going with this? *(D)* Oh, it was just a wonder of mine. It's just like, if we have the answers, I didn't understand why we do it. *(J)* We're not supposed to know. *(T)* Well, if we have all the answers, they're all in us, and we all know the correct solutions to the lessons, we should always be able to do it right, but we're doing it wrong, that means we haven't learned it right yet.

342 **A**: Retrieval.

343 **Q**: *(L)* I know what she's hanging up on here – what's the point? *(D)* Yeah! *(L)* That's the whole question: what's the point? And I guess the point is, is that it's just...

344 **A**: Lessons.

345 **Q**: *(L)* In other words, just to have something to do. *(J)* Hang on a second, I want to read something to you. Corinthians 13... *(D)* I can't handle this... *(J)* just listen. This is from Corinthians 13, the one about love. "When I was a child, I spoke as a child, I understood as a child, I thought as a child, but when I became a man, I put away childish things. For now we see through a glass darkly, but then face to face. Now I know in part, but then shall I know, even as I also am known." And that's what going from 3rd to 4th is going to be like. *(D)* Is that part of the... *(T)* Think so? [Tea kettle starts to whistle.]

A: Yes. 346

Q: *(J)* That's it. We're not supposed to know it all now. In moving from 3rd to 4th, is part of the knowledge process. *(T)* We gain insight moving... 347

A: Yes. 348

Q: *(T)* ...insight we don't have yet, but we can start working with what we may not understand what it is we're doing. 349

A: Close 350

Q: So when you said we're thinking in 3rd... 351

A: Stop noise. 352

Q: *(L)* Somebody turn off the kettle... *(T)* It's bothering us too, we're taking care of it... [tea kettle whistle is turned off] ...that's one 3rd density thing we can do! So when you say that we're thinking in 3rd density, you're not always telling us we're not thinking correctly, you're just indicating that we're thinking in 3rd density, because we can't think in any other way. 353

A: Close. 354

Q: *(T)* So not all those shots were shots, they were just saying that it's as far as we can get right now. 355

A: We don't shoot. 356

Q: *(L)* I have a question – do you guys have emotions... 357

A: Not 3rd level. 358

Q: *(L)* OK, well, then let me ask it this way. What are your thoughts towards us, or your attitude or emotions, as you know, them towards us? Individually or as a group? 359

360 **A**: Love.

361 **Q**: *(D)* Well, that's what I needed to hear. [Sigh] *(J)* Be patient, we're not finished yet.

362 **A**: Hoorah!

363 **Q**: *(T)* Well, there's not any of us here alone. They're us in the future. *(J)* Diana, think of us like those puppies in there. Our eyes aren't open yet, but they'll open up.

364 **A**: Yes. But there is no time so you are already are where you are, you see, we are you in the "future".

365 **Q**: *(D)* I have a question. Transdimensional atomic remolecularization, is this teleportation?

366 **A**: Close.

367 **Q**: *(D)* OK, so this is the way we will transfer from 3rd to 4th?

368 **A**: Technology for this purpose.

369 **Q**: *(D)* Well, is this the way they're going to move the new bodies to the ancient Earth?

370 **A**: No. That is a natural process.

371 **Q**: *(T)* They're creating the bodies now with the genetic engineering. *(D)* Yeah, I know, but...

372 **A**: TDARM is tech.

373 **Q**: *(T)* What was that? Was it a word? *(J)* I have no idea. Please repeat the entire...

374 **A**: Abbreviation.

375 **Q**: *(L)* Trans Dimensional Atomic Re-Molecularization! Got it. *(T)* It's on the tip of everybody's tongue these days! *(D)* Down at the church they gave me a list of prayers and symbols to use in a ritual where I would say a prayer while I had my hand on a symbol and the purpose of this...

A: Rituals restrict. 376

Q: *(D)* So, in other words, that did not 377
connect my DNA chains. Right?

A: Nonsense! 378

Q: *(D)* OK, well that's what I thought, 379
but I went ahead and did it because I didn't want to pass up an opportunity!

A: Stop! 380

Q: *(T)* Stop rituals. They don't ap- 381
prove of any rituals, it blocks the flow, it restricts. *(D)* That's fine, I won't do it anymore. *(L)* Pure universal knowledge includes everything, and if you establish a ritual, that means you are adhering to one line of thought, one mode of thinking, one idea structure, and excluding all others. *(D)* Was that in the thing, did I miss that? *(T)* In different words, it's in there several times. *(L)* You may not have gotten it, you only have part of the transcripts, you only have about 100 pages. *(D)* I got up to file 3, page 41. *(L)* You don't have a whole lot of it. You're probably missing parts of it. *(T)* You really have to read through it many times. *(D)* I don't want to look like a pseudo-intellect... *(J)* You're trying to understand.

A: Nonsense! 382

Q: *(T)* Is it OK if we bring our friend 383
Brad M?

A: Up to you. 384

Q: *(T)* Would he be a good addition to 385
the group?

A: Open. 386

Q: *(T)* What are his feelings towards 387
what we're doing?

A: Puzzled. 388

Q: *(T)* Puzzled about the purpose? 389

A: Does not conform to his belief sys- 390
tem.

391 **Q**: *(J)* I could hear it in his voice when I was telling him, he wasn't being openly receptive, but he wasn't being combative about it, either. He was open... *(F)* Is he a MUFON person? *(T)* Yes. He's scientifically based. He's following Hoagland's stuff. *(F)* Well, I've got that tape, too, and I think there's something to it... *(T)* He talks with Hoagland, he's in contact with Hoagland... *(D)* Terry, do you want to ask about what the individuals in this group are going to do in the future?

392 **A**: Discover.

393 **Q**: *(T)* Is Jan's mom's estate going to be settled relatively quickly and easily?

394 **A**: Yes.

395 **Q**: *(T)* Is it going to make everybody happy, the outcome?

396 **A**: Subjective. Open.

397 **Q**: *(T)* When we were talking about other people, let me throw another name out here, Robert Dean, do you know who he is?

398 **A**: Yes.

399 **Q**: *(T)* Is he telling the truth as he knows it?

400 **A**: Some.

401 **Q**: *(T)* Is there more to what he knows, he's just not telling all of it?

402 **A**: Yes.

403 **Q**: *(T)* Is he as honest and up front as he seems to be?

404 **A**: Subjective.

405 **Q**: *(T)* Is he doing disinformation for the government?

406 **A**: No.

407 **Q**: *(T)* He's really a good speaker. Is he doing disinformation for anyone?

A: No. Withholds. 408

Q: *(T)* He's withholding information? 409

A: Some. 410

Q: *(J)* He's withholding MJ-12 infor- 411
mation? *(T)* Well, it could be anything. He's made several sweeping statements and has lots of facts and figures and stuff that he was privy to when he was in the military in NATO. Was all that information about the "Assessment" and all that stuff all true?

A: Close. 412

Q: *(T)* Was he allowed to see it on pur- 413
pose?

A: No. 414

Q: *(T)* So his story about that it was 415
there in the security vault, and because he had access and because he was able to see it, and that he just was intrigued by it, is true?

A: Yes. 416

Q: *(T)* OK. Is he going to tell the rest 417
of what he knows?

A: Open. 418

Q: *(T)* Is he in danger because he is 419
telling the truth?

A: Maybe. 420

Q: *(T)* Also, it's smart to tell the truth 421
as loudly as you can, and in front of as many people as you can. He's an amazing speaker, and the things he has to say... to me, his body language is that he's telling the truth. I have a question about a friend, Nova M, is she open to this?

A: Maybe. 422

Q: *(T)* We've told her some about this, 423
does she... how does she feel?

A: Maybe. 424

425 **Q**: *(T)* How does she feel about what we've told her so far?

426 **A**: Skeptical.

427 **Q**: *(C)* What is my son's next duty station?

428 **A**: Open. Will he even stay in?

429 **Q**: *(C)* There's someone who owes me a great deal of money; will they pay within the next few months?

430 **A**: You must act upon this.

431 **Q**: *(T)* Will Chuck have to go as far as taking him to court?

432 **A**: Likely.

433 **Q**: *(T)* Does Chuck have a good lawyer? Humor! Mirth! Don't answer that! All the good ones are in California right now! Oh, OJ. I think even they are bored with OJ by now! *(J)* Are you bored with OJ by now?

434 **A**: Yes.

435 **Q**: *(T)* What major event is happening under the cover of the OJ trial right now?

436 **A**: None.

437 **Q**: *(T)* You mean we're just getting stuck with all this snow, and there ain't even anything happening?

438 **A**: Diversion by opportunity.

439 **Q**: *(T)* What a waste of a good diversion if there isn't anything going on! Here's this great diversion and they don't even have anything to hide behind it! *(D)* Is Sarah having some problems that she's not coming to me about?

440 **A**: Yes.

441 **Q**: *(D)* Is there anything that you can tell me about this?

A: Diana, communicate, as we told 442
you.

Q: *(D)* What did I forget? *(T)* What 443
have you been doing on your own? *(J)* Have you been 'surfing' the cosmos on your own? Surfing the board, so to speak? *(T)* Well, it will come to you; they've told you something and it will come back. *(D)* Would you mind clarifying that, I don't know... *(T)* What was it you told her?

A: Communicate, don't preach. 444

Q: *(D)* Thanks for the help, yeah, 445
you're right. Is there anything else I can do to help Sarah?

A: Learn. 446

Q: *(J)* Do you have any messages for 447
any of us tonight?

A: No. 448

Q: *(T)* Do you have anything you 449
would like to communicate to the group?

A: Not this session. 450

Q: *(T)* You predicted a quake in Japan, 451
near Osaka, several sessions back, you were off by the magnitude a little bit and by the miles a little bit, but basically you were correct. What between that prediction and the prediction for the Tokyo quake can Japan expect?

A: Not correct interpretation. Osaka 452
quake yet to be.

Q: *(T)* So this was not the quake that 453
you predicted the 8.9 – this was a 7.2, but it was miles distance from Osaka almost right on the money, but this was not the quake that you predicted? *(J)* There's going to be another one coming?

A: Yes 14 more this sequence. 454

455 **Q**: *(T)* 14 more quakes? *(J)* I'm sorry, I'm losing it real bad tonight, I don't know why.[29] *(D)* Are you breaking up? *(J)* No, it's me. Please repeat the answer. *(T)* We're having problems down here in 3rd density this evening!

456 **A**: SEQUENCE.

457 **Q**: *(T)* This is one in a sequence of earthquakes that are going to culminate in the 8.9?

458 **A**: 9 pt 6.

459 **Q**: *(T)* In Osaka, near Osaka?

460 **A**: Tokyo.

461 **Q**: OK, that's the one you talked about, then a 9.6 that's going to be the culmination of the quakes in this. This is only the 3rd or 4th in a sequential series and the 8.9 that's going to hit them hasn't happened yet.

462 **A**: 7th.

463 **Q**: *(T)* This is the 7th earthquake?

464 **A**: Yes.

465 **Q**: *(T)* 7.2 was the 7th earthquake, there's going to be 14 of them – is that what you said before?

466 **A**: Yes.

467 **Q**: *(J)* So there's 7 more coming? *(T)* So the 14th one will be the big one, in Tokyo?

468 **A**: 13th.

469 **Q**: *(T)* OK, the 13th is going to be the 9.6 and I think the other prediction was 9.8, they're close. That'll be the 13th. What will be the 8.9 – which one of those will be the Osaka 8.9?

470 **A**: Within next 4.

471 **Q**: *(T)* What will the 14th be?

A: Small. 472

Q: *(T)* So they're going out anticlimactically on the last quake. Is Mt. Fujiyama going to explode, is the volcano going to become active again? 473

A: Maybe. 474

Q: *(T)* Will these quakes – is China, Korea, Philippines and the surrounding area also going to be affected as these quakes increase in strength? 475

A: Yes. 476

Q: *(T)* Are we talking about putting about 30% of the world's industrial output out of business in the next year and a half or so? 477

A: No. 478

Q: *(T)* They're not going to recover anytime soon. OK, so when this all happens is there going to be an effect on California of all of this, on the West Coast of this country? 479

A: Yes. 480

Q: *(T)* Not just California. Is Los Angeles going to be hit with any of these big earthquakes as the plate on the other side moves? 481

A: Yes. 482

Q: *(T)* What magnitude? 483

A: 8.9. 484

Q: *(T)* Where will that happen? 485

A: San Gabriel Mountains. 486

Q: *(T)* Is that outside of Los Angeles? San Andreas Fault line? 487

A: Yes. 488

Q: *(T)* Will this be very destructive to Los Angeles? 489

A: What do you think? 490

[29] She was referring to her inability to keep up with the speed of delivery of the letters.

491 **Q**: *(T)* In the destruction of this area, is this going to increase the job potential on the East Coast, in order to then – this is really serious stuff here, because this is going to affect the economy the way it shifts...

492 **A**: Yes.

493 **Q**: *(T)* So it...

494 **A**: Mass exodus from California.

495 **Q**: *(T)* Those dumb people out there looked at that Osaka stuff and said, "Oh, you know, that might happen to us." Ohhh, boy, the brain finally fired up out there. *(J)* They've been in denial about that out there... *(D)* Will that bring an influx of people to Florida?

496 **A**: Yes. 15 quakes.

497 **Q**: *(D)* And then they're going to move. *(T)* 15 quakes in the California area?

498 **A**: In near future.[30]

499 **Q**: *(T)* Are we talking strictly the West Coast here?

500 **A**: California.

501 **Q**: *(T)* Are there going to be earthquakes elsewhere in the United States?

502 **A**: Yes.

503 **Q**: *(T)* 15 in the near future in California alone... *(D)* This is the beginning of the destruction of the state of California, there'll be separation from the North American continent. *(T)* Well, they said don't take that literally, or it will fall off, it's symbolic...

504 **A**: Open.

505 **Q**: *(T)* So look at it symbolically. *(D)* OK. *(J)* Where are the other quakes going to be?

A: Hundreds. 506

Q: *(T)* Hundreds? Hundreds of earthquakes. Hundreds of places? 507

A: Yes. 508

Q: There's going to be that many additional earthquakes? Beside the 15 in California? 509

A: Yes. 510

Q: *(T)* We're going to be rocking and rolling on this continent! Of course, when you move a plate, that's a lot of stuff. Are we going to be seeing a lot of water damage on the coast? 511

A: Open. 512

Q: *(T)* Is the West Coast of Florida going to see a rising water level? 513

A: That is vague. 514

Q: *(T)* Is there going to be earthquakes in Florida? 515

A: Seismically stable. 516

Q: *(T)* Will the seismic activity cause the water level in Florida to go up? 517

A: No. 518

Q: *(T)* So, for the time being, during the quakes, we'll be fairly safe, but there's other things to worry about beside that? 519

A: Storms. 520

Q: *(D)* Are we talking hurricanes? 521

A: Cyclonic. 522

Q: *(J)* Will there be any damage from such storms in this area? 523

A: Open. 524

Q: *(C)* Are these caused by nature? *(T)* Is all this activity being... is natural? 525

[30] As we well know by now, based on other predictions that have been correct, the Cs use of "near future" is seriously loose in human terms!!

526 **A**: Close.

527 **Q**: *(D)* If I were to go down to [home of friend], is there anything I can do in the way of healing that would help him?

A: Open. 528

Q: *(L)* Goodnight. We're closing up. 529

A: Bye. 530

End of Session

Now, I want to come back to this problem of aliens eating humans. I don't really know what to think or say about it. If you recall, this is connected back to the very first Cs contact on 16 July 1994 and the mention of missing children, as well as a few other remarks in other sessions. Consider also the alleged information that was presented by Diana M under hypnosis, discussed in the session of 9 December 1994. Then there was the information given by Frank during a direct channeling session on 22 October 1994 where humans were described as being sources of food and labor for 'aliens'. In that session, the precise mechanisms of ingestion and/or energy transfer were described.

Is any of this true? Can it be true? Is it symbolic? Is it real? I don't know. What I can do is present some more or less circumstantial evidence from others and you, the reader, can decide for yourself. Highly respected UFO researcher Don Ecker wrote:

> While researching several stories for *UFO Magazine*, I interviewed a number of prominent UFOlogists, over the last several months, and in each case, the question of human deaths, in connection with animal mutilations, invariably was raised. Most readers of this text will be familiar with Mr. John Keel, who many regard as the last of the Great UFOlogists. From the earliest days of modern UFOlogy, Keel has been a force to reckon with. The author of numerous books that address various aspects of UFOlogy, and magazine articles too numerous to mention, Keel has a unique slant on the subject that most will never experience. According to Keel, the phenomenon has always had an unexplained hostility towards humans, that have led to untold numbers of deaths. While Keel will be the first to explain that he rejects the ET hypothesis, he does not doubt the phenomenon a bit. In what many UFOlogists consider as one of Keel's best works *The Mothman Prophecies*, E. P. Dutton & Co., Inc. 1975, Keel related report after report of animal mutilations involving cattle, dogs, horses and sheep, and also related what were called

"vampire killings" of four humans in Yugoslavia, where the victims were "mutilated and drained of blood". [...]

In January, 1989, it came to the attention of the MUFON State Director of Idaho, Mr. Don Mason, that cattle mutilations had occurred once again in the southeastern section of Idaho. After an investigation by a MUFON investigator, the facts were as follows. The animals (two cattle, same night, but each owned by different ranchers) were "somehow" killed, sexual organs removed, body fluids drained, patches of hide "surgically" removed. All the appearances of what is today considered to be a classic case of animal mutilation. As of this date (February 15, 1989) the final lab reports are not back yet, but already the Sheriff's Department has labelled it a "cult killing." No tracks, tire or human, around the animals even though it had just rained, no unusual activity reported by the ranchers that evening, and one animal was found next to an occupied house. One of the ranchers admitted that this was the second time he had been "hit" by the mysterious mutilators. The last incident had only been a bit over a year previously, and they were worried enough that all had their "deer rifle" within easy reach.

After having been personally involved in an investigation of cattle mutilations as a police officer back in 1982, I was very familiar with the "cult" theory of perpetrators. The Idaho Department of Law Enforcement drags it out every time there is a new rash of mutilations. The problem is, and everyone is aware of it, that no one has yet been brought to trial, or arrested yet for these crimes. Out here in the west, people know that you are flirting with a rancher's bullet if you are caught fooling around with the rancher's cattle. They are his livelihood, and he will defend it. Yet, the mutilations keep occurring, and no one is any the wiser, or are they?

With the subject of animal mutilations fresh in everyone's mind, I was once again speaking to Don Mason, when he informed me that the investigator that had been assigned to the above-mentioned case had come across a very mysterious death of a man back in 1979. According to the report, two hunters in the Bliss and Jerome area of Idaho had literally stumbled across the nude body of a man that had been hideously mutilated. The body was in the literal middle of nowhere, nude except for a pair of underpants, his sexual organs had been removed, his lips sliced off, and several other classic mutilation cuts. Although he was in very rugged country, his bare feet were not marked as if he had walked in that terrain, but yet no other tracks, animal or human, were evident anywhere. After the police were notified, an intensive search was mounted, and miles away, the man's possessions were recovered, yet no one yet knows how the body ended up where it was found, or even more importantly, what happened to him. It should be noted that this area also had over the years, many unexplained UFO reports and cattle mutilations.

Now I must explain that I had very mixed feelings about whether I wished to attempt to explore this subject any further, or allow sleeping dogs to lie. On the one hand, I wanted more than anything to discover just what was occurring, and on the other, I realized that this had the potential to backfire on someone that disturbed the status quo. I was familiar with reports of human abductions and mutilations that had surfaced in the last several years in reports such as the Lear documents, Grudge 13 reports and others, but yet I was not sure what I believed, or even if there was anything to believe.

I ran across a friend that was still employed with a police department in this area who was a detective. I had mentioned to him the recent cattle mutilations, and what I suspected in the above-mentioned case of a human that had been mutilated. Scot had also been involved in the last several years with several cases of mutilations that he had been called upon to investigate, always with negative results. He was as curious about this phenomenon as I was, and since he was still an active duty police officer, he had access to the department computer, to access the NCIC system that is maintained in Washington D.C. by the FBI. After giving Scot the criteria for a search of unexplained human deaths that involved factors of mutilation, I asked that the search go back to at least 1973, involving this area of the Northwest. Scot (not his real name) ran the request through the department computer. As he mentioned at the time, he had expected to get reams of reports back that we would have to wade through, to get to the reports that would be [worthy of] further study. Scot ended up requesting that the inquiry be run back to 1970, and involve not only Idaho, but also Utah, Nevada, Oregon, and Washington states. Because of the magnitude of this search, Scot stated that it would take about one week to get the results back into his department. As a side note, for anyone that is not familiar with the NCIC system, it is a national data

> bank for law enforcement agencies all across the United States. It is maintained and controlled by the Federal Bureau of Investigation, at FBI headquarters, in Washington D. C. On the 14th of February, Scot contacted me in person, and appeared very troubled. His exact words were that "something is really screwy, Don." "I got the request back from NCIC on Monday, and there has gotta be something wrong. They told me that they had NO unsolved murders at all, zero, that met that criteria. That any further requests will have to be made by voice, telephone call, with the proper authorizations. Somebody is sitting on something, big as hell." I also knew that something was as screwy as hell. After all, anybody that has had any dealing with law enforcement knows about the "Green River Killer" in Washington state. This serial killer is credited with at least 30 to 40 murders of young women, and to this date, the case is as big a mystery as ever. Many of the killings showed some types of mutilation, and if nothing else, at least some of these homicides should have shown up.[31]

Nick Redfern, after citing Ecker's work, adds:

> As enigmatic as this certainly was, more was to come. In the Vol. 5, No. 2 issue of *UFO Magazine*, it was revealed that an assistant examiner in Westchester County, New York, informed a researcher, Bill Knell, in 1989, that several morgues in the area had been "hit" in the middle of the night, and fresh human cadavers had been mutilated, which involved partial removal of the face, and total removal of the eyes, thyroid, stomach and genitals. According to the assistant ME, "the morgues in question wasted no time in putting the mutilations under wraps and out of the public eye."
>
> There are many more such accounts – all bubbling quietly below the surface of the UFO rumor-mill. Now, to stress, as I said, I am categorically not saying that we should all be locking our doors and hiding out in the cellar because extraterrestrial butchers want to serve us up on a plate. But, I am pointing out that this is alleged in some quarters to be a genuine aspect of the bigger UFO puzzle. And if only to lay the matter to rest, someone should launch an in-depth study of the controversy. Anyone up for the challenge?[32]

[31] http://www.sott.net/article/194149-Don-Ecker-The-Human-Mutilation-Factor
[32] http://www.sott.net/article/126261-Human-Mutes-and-UFOs

In the years since Ecker and Redfern wrote the above pleas for someone to undertake this research, the gauntlet has been picked up, though not in a straightforward "looking for human mutes" kind of way and, interestingly, by another law enforcement type, a Mr. David Paulides.

Paulides received his undergraduate and graduate degrees from the University of San Francisco and has a professional background that includes twenty years in law enforcement (3.5 years at Fremont Police and 16.5 years at San Jose Police) and senior executive positions in the technology sector. All that is pretty normal. Now it gets a little strange. I guess he got so curious about strange things coming into view in the course of his professional life that he decided that they deserved investigation. In 2004 he formed North America Bigfoot Search (NABS, www.nabigfootsearch.com), where he applied his investigative and analytical experience to the research respecting Bigfoot/Sasquatch sightings and encounters. He spent two years living with the Hoopa tribe, recording their Bigfoot stories. *The Hoopa Project* is his first book, based upon this research in the Bluff Creek area of Northern California. This was followed by a second book, *Tribal Bigfoot*, said to be a quantum jump in Bigfoot research. That's just the background to his following books, which appear to have a great bearing on the issue of the possibility of some type of hyperdimensional beings harvesting human beings, i.e., *Missing 411*.

Missing 411 is a two-volume work, one for the Eastern half of the USA, and the other for the Western half. Paulides spent 3 years doing research on missing people from National Parks and Forests. In many cases, the people disappeared and were never found. Also, many of the cases involve children under 10, some of whom are subsequently recovered, found in remote and difficult locations. The case-by-case narrative is fascinating to read and really creepy when he recounts those cases where people disappear totally while other people are only yards or feet away. Many of the parents and relatives of the missing claim that the victim was kidnapped/abducted, in very remote areas.

A follow-up volume has recently been released: *Missing 411: North America and Beyond* presents the cases of missing people and relevant facts from five countries (Australia, England, France, Iceland and Indonesia) outside of North America and examines the parallels between the cases. The book also includes a multitude of new stories from

North America.

Based on this research, there is a continuing trend of clusters of missing people in United States National Parks. The National Park Service has continued with their policy of failing to keep ledgers, track or otherwise document lists of missing people inside their parks and monuments. There are multiple disappearances of people in small, confined areas and the similarities of the cases will give you the shivers. The real question that these books demand an answer to is: What is happening to these people?

Paulides is astonished by the government's lack of interest in these events. "There's got to be some type of cover-up going at the federal level, because there's no reason in the rational world why the Parks Service wouldn't be tracking people who disappear inside their system." To that end, he cites two separate instances where a person went missing and teams of Green Berets showed up in the area, made no contact with the other searchers, and proceeded to conduct their own search "as if they were on their own private mission that no one else understood".

It may very well be that the answers to the 'who' and 'how' questions of the missing people documented in the *Missing 411* books could well turn our entire concepts of reality upside down. It seems to me that human beings urgently need to become aware of the facts collected in these books. See www.canammissing.com for books, interviews and details.

Paulides is researching Bigfoot in relation to missing persons, but recall what the Cs said about Bigfoot-type creatures back on 9 October 1994:

Q: *(L)* Was Mars ever inhabited?

A: Yes.

Q: *(L)* By whom?

A: By those you now know as Sasquatch or Bigfoot.

Q: *(L)* Do they now live on this planet as a result of being brought here by other beings?

A: They are transitory. Do not inhabit on a permanent basis.

Q: *(L)* Well, how do they come and go?

A: They are the slaves and "pets" of the Lizard beings.

Q: *(L)* How did the Sasquatch get here from Mars?

A: Brought by Lizard beings but they do not inhabit Earth.

Q: *(L)* Why have Sasquatch been seen

in remote places throughout history?

A: Put there for menial slave tasks.

Q: *(L)* Does that mean that whenever Sasquatch have been seen that there is a Lizard nearby?

A: No.

Q: *(L)* What menial tasks might they be doing?

A: Collecting samples.

Q: *(L)* Why has everyone who has ever come in contact with Sasquatch commented on the awful odor of them? Why do they stink?

A: Organic functions.

Q: *(L)* What is it about their organic functions that makes them stink?

A: Sweat.

So, for all we know, Bigfoot critters are collecting humans for dinner the way bears collect berries.

In the end, what I want to say was said by Nick Redfern, quoted above, and deserves to be emphasized:

> I am categorically not saying that we should all be locking our doors and hiding out in the cellar because extraterrestrial butchers want to serve us up on a plate. But, I am pointing out that this is alleged in some quarters to be a genuine aspect of the bigger UFO puzzle.

February 9, 1995

There's some important background to this session. As I wrote in *The Wave*, on October 20, 1994, as part of my rapid fire testing questions, I threw out the following:

> **Q**: *(L)* Who built the city of Baalbek?
>
> **A**: *(L)* Antereans and early Sumerians. We meant Atlanteans.
>
> **Q**: What technical means did they use to cut the stones and transport them?
>
> **A**: Sound wave focusing.

On October 23, 1994, in response to another question, a similar answer was given... with something added:

> **Q**: *(L)* Who built Stonehenge?
>
> **A**: Druids.
>
> **Q**: *(L)* Who were the Druids?
>
> **A**: Early Aryan group.
>
> **Q**: *(L)* How did they move the stones and set them up?
>
> **A**: Sound wave focusing; try it yourself; Coral Castle.
>
> **Q**: *(L)* Who taught the Druids to use the sound waves?
>
> **A**: They knew; handed down.
>
> **Q**: *(L)* What was Stonehenge built to do or be used for?
>
> **A**: Energy director.
>
> **Q**: *(L)* What was this energy to be directed to do?
>
> **A**: All things.
>
> **Q**: *(L)* Was the energy to be directed outward or inward to the center?
>
> **A**: Both.
>
> **Q**: *(L)* Does this sound come from our bodies?
>
> **A**: Learn. Laura will find answer through discovery.

Well, *that* was a pretty cryptic remark, that I would learn something about this through a discovery! And the comment about the Coral Castle intrigued us as well. Even though I live in Florida, I had never been to see this purported marvel and the only things I knew about it were what I had learned by watching a television program about it on *Unsolved Mysteries*, I believe.

Because of the spreading fame, or infamy, as the case may be, of the Cassiopaea Experiment among the local UFO/metaphysical community, I had received an invitation to speak to a UFO study group in Orlando. It was pretty typical for such groups at the time, a mix of true believers, contactees, and just a hint of actual research which consisted mostly of the leader of the group hypnotizing people and getting them to channel their alien counterparts on the Moon or the Mothership. I didn't know that at the time, so I was willing to talk to them.

I had no idea what I was going to say; how open this group was going to be; or anything about the participants at all.

On the drive over (two of my children accompanied me) my daughter asked me what I was going to talk about. I said that I wasn't sure, because I had no idea how 'receptive' the audience would be. So, she said: "Mom, you don't have time to break it to them gently." I thought that was a wise child thing, and that is what I did. I told the group about my personal sighting which occurred at a time that I was still in the 'skeptical-to-the-point-of-contemptuous-of-UFOs' stage and how abruptly and completely my life was changed by it and the realizations that accompanied dealing with such a phenomenon. I then told them about the endless research I had done on the subject, having become obsessed with discovering just exactly what this business was all about that I had closed my eyes to for so many years. That, of course, led to a brief synopsis of the 'Cs communication' and *their* take on the subject.

OK, fine. There was not a great deal of 'receptivity'. There was a gal there who claimed to be a 'Pleiadian Walk-In' and who offered to 'cure me' through her Pleiadian Dance Therapy... I declined. There was a Cabala teacher, assorted MUFON folks, and, of course, Henry Belk who was pretty focused on his 'psychic surgery' agenda.

After my talk, we watched Henry's latest video of a gal over on the East Coast who 'exudes' gold foil through the skin and who was Henry's latest object of study. It was pretty fascinating because the camera was 'up close and personal' and you could *see* this stuff just 'growing' out of this girl's body. She was almost completely illiterate and sort of a 'Motorcycle Mama' type of person, so there was no 'spiritual attribution' going on. It was curious.

Anyway (yes, I am getting to the Coral Castle business!), after all the presentations, snacks were being served and an old fellow came up to me and said: "I want to shake your hand! What you have just done is the most courageous thing I have ever seen! I have been studying this business for about 40 years and you are the first person I have ever heard tell it like it *really* is!"

Of course, I was appreciative of the kind words, but not being entirely sure that either my 'source' or my own opinions are so right, I took it with a grain of salt. I thanked him and he started telling me that he was a retired engineer from the Air Force, having formerly been in the Army Air Corps, and was stationed in South Florida and saw a UFO in the Everglades... he claimed to have been associated with J. Allen Hynek and claimed to know Morris Jessup and a few others. Then he said that he had some stuff to show me and that I ought to pay him a personal visit sometime.

By this time, I was thinking the guy was just a little loony, so I politely eased myself into another group and just sort of stood there drinking my cola and listening to what was being said. There was a couple visiting from the north and they were asking Jiles about the Coral Castle.

Naturally, my ears pricked up at that. I listened more carefully. Jiles told the folks: "Oh, you have to ask Hilliard about *that*! He knew the guy who built it." He pointed off to the side and I looked where he was pointing and it was my 'little old man'.

I became suddenly a *lot* more interested in the old guy! So, I waited for my chance and cornered him and said: "I hear you knew the guy who built the Coral Castle?" "Ayup!" (he had a funny 'sing-song' way of talking.)

So, he was telling me about his friendship with Edward Leedskallin and how he was the only person who was really close to the guy and what a crime it was that Leonard Nimor made such a farce of the TV special about the thing because it was pure hokey and all that.

But, he really wanted to talk about it in private and said that he had a manuscript that he had put together from his talks with Leedskallin and I ought to come to see him and have a look. It was the only copy and he was afraid to turn loose of it.

Well, my curiosity got the better of me. I made an appointment to come back to the Orlando area, which I did the following month... But we'll get to that.

Participants: 'Frank', Laura, Susan

1 **Q**: *(L)* Hello.

2 **A**: Hello. Very good.

3 **Q**: *(L)* What is very good?

4 **A**: All.

5 **Q**: *(L)* I have here Barbara Marciniak's latest book...

6 **A**: Ego driven.

7 **Q**: *(L)* This book is ego driven? So this is not so much true channeling as ego?

8 **A**: Yes.

9 **Q**: *(L)* Is there any possibility that she has been corrupted and is channeling Lizzies?

10 **A**: No. Under pressure, constriction.

11 **Q**: *(L)* So, the pressure has constricted the flow. I think I would like to ask a few questions about Frank and his tiredness. What can we do to help Frank with his tiredness?

12 **A**: Nothing, it is process of progress.

13 **Q**: *(L)* I want to ask a little bit about this process of 'unwinding' Susan has been facilitating with my body. Have you guys been watching?

14 **A**: Always. You have just accessed and outed globules of energy.

15 **Q**: *(S)* It's an energy cyst. *(L)* What is the original reason for the presence of the energy?

16 **A**: Anger from age 22 when you were in severe depression and had plans for suicide. The negative energy went to your arms.

Q: *(L)* Is that what is wrong with my 17
neck, also?

A: No. That is fibrous tumor. 18

Q: *(S)* Is my work going to help dimin- 19
ish it?

A: Maybe. 20

Q: *(L)* Susan has been having unusual 21
experiences in awareness as she reads the transcripts...

A: We are blasting open her awareness. 22

Q: *(L)* Well, she has been having quite 23
a bit of success by following her inner guidance. She has also been accessing knowledge as she reads the transcripts, even well in advance of others, it seems. Is this correct?

A: Open. 24

Q: *(L)* I went to talk to the group in 25
Orlando area and I am sure you guys had your secret eye camera while I was there. What I would like to know is what thoughts were in the mind of Jiles Hamilton and how did he react to my talk?

A: This ego is sexually focused and he 26
reacts mainly to what he has to say.

Q: *(L)* OK, this Henry Belk was a 27
rather interesting person, I perceived something very unusual about him but I can't put my finger on it. Initially I thought he was a positive influence, or that he was one who had a great deal of knowledge, but later I thought I might

be wrong in that assessment. And yet, there was something about him that I recognized. What was going through his mind?

28 **A**: Open.

29 **Q**: *(L)* Can you tell me anything about this person, or does it matter?

30 **A**: No, it doesn't matter.

31 **Q**: *(L)* Did I present the material in the way it should be presented?

A: Okay. 32

Q: *(L)* Is it true that when you die you go to the 'Bardo'?[1] 33

A: What is that? 34

Q: *(L)* Anything we need to know at this time? 35

A: Not tonight. Ask on the eleventh. 36

Q: *(L)* Well, goodnight. 37

End of Session

Let me tell you a bit of the rest of the story of my little talk in Orlando and the figures present. As noted, one of the attendees was a Mr. Henry Belk. I didn't know it at the time, but he was a close friend of Senator Claiborne Pell, Andrija Puharich, Prince Hans Adam II of Liechtenstein, and more, all names well known to those who track CIA influences in the media. Even though I knew nothing of those things at the time, I was definitely aware of the fact that I had ruffled some feathers due to the reactions of Henry Belk to my short talk. He came up to me afterward and was positively rude. So, the main thing I wanted to know in the above session was what was the deal with this Henry Belk (without giving anything away because I hadn't given Frank all the details). Notice the flat response.

As it turned out, I don't think that this meeting with Belk and his reaction to what the Cs had to say was as unimportant as it would seem from the above. It was only later, as I learned the ropes and put the pieces of the puzzle together, that I realized I had been targeted as a serious problem and steps would be taken to destroy me and/or any possibility that my work would reach a wider audience. Since that day, I have been the subject of a most egregious and widespread defamation/smear campaigns that can be tracked and documented on the internet. Interestingly it began with a small gang of alleged Puharich devotees, the apparent leader or guru being one Vincent Bridges (who was later revealed to be a practicing Black Magician!)

So, what explains the Cs not warning me about this when I asked the above questions about Henry Belk? The only thing that I can

[1]A question Susan had brought up earlier in conversation.

suggest is that this was an emotional button for Frank. I didn't realize it at the time how jealous he was that people would call me and ask me to give talks but nobody ever asked him.

February 11, 1995

Participants: 'Frank', Laura, Susan V, DM[1]

1 **A**: Wow, what a change!

2 **Q**: *(L)* What do you mean?

3 **A**: The new board.

4 **Q**: *(L)* Well, glad you like it. Let's get on with the questions.

5 **A**: You didn't ask for ID.

6 **Q**: *(L)* OK, who do we have with us tonight?

7 **A**: Sorran.

8 **Q**: *(L)* And where are you from?

9 **A**: Cassiopaea.

10 **Q**: *(DM)* Are you male or female?

11 **A**: There is no gender here.

12 **Q**: *(L)* You have said that you are us in the future; can you identify which one of you is me or Frank, or anyone else?

13 **A**: All are one. Names are used for your perceptions. We do not mean that we are one "individual", but that we are one in unity.

14 **Q**: *(L)* Well, I have some personal stuff I would like to ask about without mentioning it specifically – can I do that?

15 **A**: Whatever you desire!

16 **Q**: *(L)* Well, something has been going on with me internally and I just don't know what it is. I don't even know who I am right now. I am at odds with myself, it seems. What is going on? Why am I so irritable?

A: You are being defensive, letting go 17
of old stuff.

Q: *(L)* Well, I am trying not to be irri- 18
table.

A: You try too much. Stop attempting 19
and just "Go with it!" There is no need to steer, no need to drive, just ride!

Q: *(L)* Well, that is very hard for me to 20
do when this energy threatens to overwhelm me.

A: You have always been a driver, that 21
is the old stuff to let go of. Why resist? This is why you have been irritable. Your super consciousness is telling you something.

Q: *(L)* Why did this feeling begin when 22
Frank's dad passed away? Why do I feel now that I don't know which way we are going to go?

A: That was a steppingstone, a "mile- 23
stone", if you like.

Q: *(L)* OK, on one occasion you re- 24
sponded to a question by saying that JW and MF had 'reported' me. Obviously this was not done consciously. You then said that they were unconscious and unwitting agents for the Lizzies. This perhaps implies that they have been abducted. How many times

[1]In my opinion, DM was a bit New Agey and her presence was problematical.

has JW been abducted and when did the abductions start?

25 **A**: He has been "contacted" or abducted 186 times beginning at age 4.

26 **Q**: What about M___?

27 **A**: Are you ready for this? 446 times.

28 **Q**: [General sounds of amazement.] How does the control mechanism work with these two since, obviously, they would both be quite amazed to hear this, if not, in fact, go into complete denial?

29 **A**: Waves are transmitted into their minds which stimulate pre-coded implants. They are monitored. When they are exposed to truth, the waves are generated to prevent their reception and to strengthen pre-coded thought patterns of resistance.

30 **Q**: *(L)* You also said on one other occasion that something was done to me physically to block my energy and cause physical problems. What was this?

31 **A**: Your thyroid was inhibited.

32 **Q**: *(L)* You have said on occasion that free will is the most important law of consciousness in creation. Why can we not exercise our free will and refuse to be abducted and experimented upon?

33 **A**: Those who abduct are exercising their free will in doing so.

34 **Q**: *(L)* Why does their free will have precedence over our free will?

35 **A**: Why does your free will have precedence over density 2 and 1 beings?

36 **Q**: *(L)* In a past reading you told me that the UFO I saw above my pool was a 'multiple reality projection.' What is this in layman's terms? Did we see a nuts-and-bolts craft, or did we see something that was projected?

A: Your mind was given to you to be 37
used, we provide clues.

Q: *(L)* Multiple realities? OK, so this 38
was a point in space-time where there was or is a convergence of 3rd and 4th realities so that they were probably in 4th density, and we were in 3rd; yet the area around my house was created as a multiple reality station for this event to occur, is that correct?

A: Bravo! 39

Q: *(L)* Once again I want to ask what 40
was the purpose of them showing themselves to me, since they are the 'bad' guys?

A: See last answer. 41

Q: *(L)* Well, I don't like what I think 42
when I think about that.

A: Then think something else. 43

Q: *(L)* I heard from Terry and Jan that 44
there have been reports of numerous sightings of UFOs in the region, particularly on Saturday nights when we are doing our sessions. Is there any connection between this activity and what we are doing?

A: Of course! 45

Q: *(L)* What is the relationship? 46

A: You are leading the way. 47

Q: *(DM)* We are leading the way. *(L)* 48
That's the relationship? Can we get a clarification on that? *(DM)* Are we clearing the ground for other occurrences here on this planet? *(L)* Or, are they showing themselves to try to stop us from leading the way, because we are leading the way in a major way?

49 **A**: All of the above.[2]

50 **Q**: *(L)* So, it's the same thing. We are leading the way and they are trying to stop us. OK...

51 **A**: And...

52 **Q**: *(L)* And it's a manifestation of 3rd and 4th density conjunction that are created by the expanding of consciousness in this area?

53 **A**: And...

54 **Q**: *(L)* Umm... *(DM)* We are getting information to be given to mankind?

55 **A**: And...

56 **Q**: *(DM)* This is going to be published?

57 **A**: And...

58 **Q**: *(L)* And are they actually... are some of these craft evidence of your presence?

59 **A**: And...

60 **Q**: *(DM)* It is all going to fit together like a puzzle. *(L)* So, in other words, our activities are interactive in a sense... and we are leading the way?

61 **A**: Yes, for the whole world!!!

62 **Q**: *(SV)* For the whole world? *(DM)* God! Does this mean that we are of extreme importance?

63 **A**: Bingo![3]

Q: *(DM)* I got goose bumps! *(SV)* I didn't. *(L)* You always knew it. *(SV)* I didn't say that! [Laughter] *(DM)* Can I ask a personal question? Is this why I am moving to New Port Richey? 64

A: Open. 65

Q: *(L)* They are not going to give you that one. You know why. 66

A: Now, we suggest you be humble!!! 67

Q: *(DM)* I think we will be. [Laughter] *(L)* I'm trying hard... [sings] "Oh lord, it's hard to be humble, when you're perfect in every wayyy!" [Laughter] 68

A: Laura, this is directed mainly toward you.[4] 69

Q: *(L)* You mean the "be humble" part? 70

A: Bingo! 71

Q: *(L)* I try real hard and you guys know it. It's hard, sometimes when you have to be in charge. And, I know you told me to let go and let someone else drive for a while, so I will. Frank, you drive. You're in charge now. 72

A: No need for that.[5] 73

Q: *(L)* In a previous reading you stated that the Lizzies tried to abduct my eldest daughter and that I 'stopped' it. At the time I should have asked, and am asking now: how, specifically, did I stop that activity?[6] 74

---

[2] *High Strangeness* "Appendix"

[3] Yeah, right! Important target of abuse is most of what I have experienced since publishing the Cs sessions and our research! Now do you see why I didn't like it when this woman was present??

[4] At the time, I took this rather unfair dig in stride but it really was unfair and symptomatic of the presence of Diana M in conjunction with Frank. Of all of us there, the one who needed most to be "humble" was Frank, but that only became obvious as time passed.

[5] *The Wave* 51

[6] I described this episode and my actions in my book *Amazing Grace*.

75 **A**: Mental blocking, i.e. using 4th density principles.

76 **Q**: *(DM)* Was it just her presence that led them to believe that they should go find somebody else to abduct?

77 **A**: Pay attention to self-explanatory answers.

78 **Q**: *(L)* OK, so, a mental block is a 4th density principle?

79 **A**: Bravo!

80 **Q**: *(L)* So, mentally blocking is our defense?

81 **A**: One of them.

82 **Q**: *(L)* And, I was galvanized to erect this shield around my child because it was my baby?

83 **A**: And you knew what to do.

84 **Q**: *(L)* So, we have to go global? That is a lot of responsibility. *(DM)* I would rather it just stay very private. *(L)* It can't. *(F)* We do not have the ability to direct it, DM, it just may become... *(DM)* This is something that I am trying to overcome... *(F)* Don't worry about it, go with it... *(SV)* Yeah, just go with it... *(F)* When they were speaking to Laura, they were really speaking to all of us. Don't try and drive or direct. *(L)* Whatever will come, will come. *(SV)* It's just like what they told me about massage and bodywork. I don't even plan it anymore, I just start doing it and whatever my hands do is what is done. *(F)* Don't worry about notoriety; if it is meant to be, it will happen that way and it will work. It won't cause your life to be disrupted and your entire family to be rent asunder.[7] *(DM)* Well, I have at least started teaching [my daughter], and the other day I even went so far as to express the teachings in the classroom.[8] One kid said something very negative to another kid and I said: "You know, it's just like a big wall of elastic that comes up in front of you. Whatever you say just bounces right back on you." The kids in the class applauded! I feel that I have to be very careful of what I say to keep from losing my job. *(L)* There are a lot of things you can say in a general way that are acceptable to just about anybody, no matter what their belief system. *(DM)* I want to ask... Am I eventually going to lose my job because of my metaphysical abilities?

A: Open. 85

Q: *(L)* They are not going to tell you 86
something like that. My initial reaction is no, but you may walk away from it someday. *(F)* Yeah, that's what came to me also. If someone came along and offered you a sewing factory, would you keep on knitting alone at home? *(DM)* I see what you are saying. Then, what we are doing here might lead to something big? *(L)* Huge. *(SV)* I think it already is. *(F)* The momentum is starting to pick up. It is like the snowball just starting to roll from the top of Mount Everest. *(DM)* I never fathomed that...

A: Worry not, DM. "Que sera, sera!" 87

Q: *(F)* [Sings] "Whatever will be, will 88
be..." *(SV)* Sometimes when you lose a job, you always go on to something better. *(DM)* I need to actually put something out there to manifest. *(L)* You are already doing that right now...

A: No need to drive, just ride, that is 89

[7] Famous last words!

[8] DM was a Computer Science teacher in one of the local schools.

what we do, we ride the wave!

90 **Q**: *(SV)* Go with the flow. *(DM)* I just kind of meandered into this. *(L)* I want to say something now. For a very long time Frank and I have been working at trying to get something through that was of a very high order, and we believed it could be done eventually. We knew we had to kiss a lot of frogs to get to a prince. We also knew we had to go through a lot of pooh to get to the prize. So, we did that for a long period of time. We carried a heavy burden, both of us, for a long time. I am now very, very grateful for all the help that has come from so many directions. It was overwhelming me. I knew the significance, I drove myself... Frank will tell you, I drove myself day and night... I did everything by myself. Finally, others came along who were willing to put forth financial help, time and effort, because I virtually carried it on my own, financially and every other way...

91 **A**: And others will be brought in.

92 **Q**: *(L)* And, I want to say that SV is, at this point, playing a key role in the moving of this project because I have been so physically attacked for so long that without her work, I would not be able to continue, much less do even more, as I can see is going to be upcoming. Frank will tell you that he has seen me laid up in bed from attacks for literally days and weeks at a time. Then, I would force myself to push on, start driving myself. *(DM)* Were these problems because of the DNA changes? *(L)* I think it was more the forces trying to block the fruition of this project, trying to prevent both of us from combining our energies. *(DM)* Do you suppose they could be working through [my daughter] on me? *(L)* Absolutely. *(F)* Nobody who is involved in this will just sail along until they get over the hump. For years and years these forces have been trying to get me to commit suicide because they saw this coming. *(L)* We have been told by the Cassiopaeans that both of us were programmed to commit suicide or otherwise destroy ourselves. I asked why this was and we were told that we were very important to the world. I initially had a little trouble with that answer, but, it seems that this project is the meaning of it, at least up to this point. Who knows what it ultimately means? *(DM)* What about Scientology?

A: Another Lizard plot, of course.[9] 93

Q: *(DM)* Well, I was really into it. *(L)* 94
So, on the one hand we experience a lot of attack, and on the other, there has been a lot of divine intervention to get us to this point. *(SV)* I have a friend from school named Linda, she's in Tampa. Who or what is she channeling?

A: Multiple sources.[10] 95

Q: *(SV)* I am going to be taking a class 96
from her in Oriental healing... *(L)* Now,

[9]Keep in mind that 'Lizards' are sort of code for 4th density STS. In my book, *Secret History* Vol. 1, I've explained the entropic nature of this energy that is perceived by us as 'Lizard-like'. The actual reality of Lizard-type beings has been attested by many witnesses and there is even some alleged photographic evidence, not to mention many ancient representations. But, as I've said before, I've never seen one and I tend to think that it may be interpretive.

[10]*The Wave* 52

in a previous session – and this is what I seem to be doing tonight, covering some stuff and filling in some blanks...

97 **A**: Okay, but why not spread review process over several sessions?

98 **Q**: *(F)* Well, just one more question: You said that Neanderthal man had been taken by the Lizzies to another planet. Now, I don't want to know what other planet, but I would like to know what state, evolutionary speaking, is Neanderthal man in at present, as we measure time?

99 **A**: No progress, still the same.[11]

100 **Q**: *(F)* Any information for us in general?

101 **A**: Listen: Now is point where all can learn more information by searching within more, rather than from without. One or two of you are already very adept at this, this way you access universal truths directly, where there is less likelihood of corruption if done properly, see?[12]

102 **Q**: *(L)* Does this mean you want us to start using a direct channeling method? *(DM)* Do you want us to use one of us as a voice?

103 **A**: All.

104 **Q**: *(DM)* Do you mean simultaneously?

105 **A**: As you wish.

106 **Q**: *(L)* Do you mean that you want us to, for example, gather as a group, meditate together...

107 **A**: Just ask yourselves questions, and receive answers.

Q: *(L)* In other words, no hypnosis, 108
just sit and discuss and ask back and forth among ourselves and let the energy of the group interact?

A: Or in solitude as well. Then net- 109
work and exchange lessons, one does this often.

Q: *(L)* OK, you want us to do the dis- 110
cussion thing, and you want us to begin to ask ourselves? Does this mean you want us to discontinue using the board?

A: No, of course not!! 111

Q: *(DM)* I don't understand. *(SV)* I do, 112
we are supposed to find out things on our own and check certain things out to make sure we are on track.

A: Open channel, one or two are open 113
already.

Q: *(L)* One or two individuals in the 114
group are already open?

A: Yes. 115

Q: *(DM)* Who are they? 116

A: Open. 117

Q: *(L)* They are not going to tell us 118
that. *(F)* All you have to do is ask the questions and the answers come to you. I do it all the time and have been since I was five or six. *(DM)* That is what I started to do. I started hearing the answers before they were spelled out. *(F)* That happens here with the board, but what I am saying is the answer is to channel by yourself. *(L)* Don't we have to be concerned to a certain extent with corrupting influences?

A: Not with your group. 119

---

[11] *The Wave* 68

[12] *The Wave* 53. I actually do not consider this very sound advice for the many reasons given in my books. I would suggest that this response was highly subjective and, again, based on the presence of Diana M augmenting Frank's often heavily biased and egocentric attitude.

120 **Q**: *(L)* Does this mean, at this point, we are individually and collectively, tuned in?[13]

121 **A**: Yes. We will aid in process to an extent.

122 **Q**: *(L)* And as the group grows larger, the other people who come and find themselves at home with us, will also be assisted in this manner, is this correct?

123 **A**: To an extent.

124 **Q**: *(DM)* We will have to use a lot of discernment as to who... each person will have to be checked...

125 **A**: No.

126 **Q**: *(L)* I think as people encounter this, they will either stay or go...

127 **A**: Yes.

128 **Q**: *(L)* I want to ask a question about two of our former participants who fell by the wayside... I have a very strong feeling that V___ may not come back...

129 **A**: Open.

130 **Q**: *(L)* I also do not feel that there is any possibility of Scarlett[14] being salvaged from the Lizzie control. Is this correct?

131 **A**: Open.

132 **Q**: *(L)* Earlier we were reading from Ouspensky's *Tertium Organum* about perceptions. Was this a fairly accurate description of the state of our perceptions and the state of 2nd density perceptions?[15]

133 **A**: Yes.

Q: *(L)* OK, now making a jump with that, as to 4th density perception, is the 4th density perception... 134

A: Wait and see. 135

Q: *(L)* The other night when I was meditating, I felt a gentle presence in a sort of light movement of air around my face and a sensation of mental floating. Was this you? 136

A: Open. Your mind was given to you for a reason. 137

Q: *(L)* OK, I am not going to ask about things I can figure out myself, but I am going to ask about something I don't know: as you know, Frank's dad passed away about two weeks ago. From that day to this, everything has seemed to be different in terms of dynamics and energy, and this is not just with Frank and his family, but also with myself. I am curious as to why I feel so different. I cannot put a word to how different I feel... it is definitely a feeling, an emotional sense – why is this? 138

A: Let us just refer to this as a steppingstone or "milestone," if you prefer.[16] 139

Q: *(L)* OK, it is a milestone, but why should this... I wish I could convey to you all how strange I have been feeling... *(DM)* Can you specify strange? *(F)* See, I don't even know... *(L)* Is Frank's dad earthbound? 140

A: Partially. 141

Q: *(L)* Is he trying to communicate through me? 142

A: Maybe. 143

[13] I was definitely not trusting this information.

[14] Identified as 'Candy' in *The Wave*. (See previous volume.)

[15] *The Wave* 6

[16] *The Wave* 44

144 **Q**: *(L)* Why, on the day and at the time that Frank's dad decided to make his transition, was I overwhelmed with the need to go to sleep?[17]

145 **A**: Connection.

146 **Q**: *(L)* Connection to what? *(DM)* You mean he was connecting with Laura?

147 **A**: Close.

148 **Q**: *(SV)* She was connecting to him?

149 **A**: Close.

150 **Q**: *(DM)* Were they mentally entangled? *(L)* No, you are drifting. *(F)* Let Laura ask the question. *(L)* Did he basically come to me at another level...

151 **A**: Yes.

152 **Q**: *(L)* He came to me at another level; why me and not Frank?

153 **A**: He always trusts others to be more qualified.

154 **Q**: *(L)* So, he was trusting me to be more qualified than Frank, to advise him in his new estate, is that it?

155 **A**: Yes.

156 **Q**: *(F)* Well, that certainly fits his personality. *(L)* What does he want from me now?

157 **A**: Nothing specific, but open channel and see.

158 **Q**: *(L)* Can we address Frank's dad directly through the board?

159 **A**: Laura can meditate on an individual basis, this is the chosen mode.

Q: *(F)* That is probably why you are 160
feeling so weird is that you haven't opened to channel on your own. *(L)* Yeah, and it's driving me nuts. *(DM)* It's interfering with your thinking processes. *(L)* Does Frank's dad need me to help him to release into the light?

A: Open. 161

Q: *(L)* Well, it has definitely been a 162
problem, but I'll deal with it. *(DM)* I am wondering if your questions are carrying to the microphone. *(L)* OK, anything further on this matter that you can give me to ease the situation?

A: No. 163

Q: *(L)* One of the things that has been 164
being brought to my mind continuously and repeatedly since that time has been the memory of the lifetime that Frank and I explored before, where we were brother and sister in Bavaria, and I am wondering if there was some connection with Frank's dad in that time, and is that why it is being continuously shoved in my face?

A: Why not check it out? You are good 165
at that, when you want to be.

Q: *(L)* Obviously you want me to check 166
it out through my own head, right?

A: Yes. 167

Q: *(L)* OK, well, since we don't really 168
have any further questions we will stop for the night.

A: Goodnight. 169

End of Session

Respecting my 'secret question' about what was going on in my mental/emotional state, after a lot of research and many more experiences, I understand now that this was the seating of the higher emotional

[17]Frank's dad committed suicide.

center. It really did feel like a form of madness. It was very similar to an event that had occurred some years earlier. I described this in my book *Amazing Grace* in the following way:

> As a matter of practicality I generally meditated lying on the bed. Some people cannot do this because they tend to fall asleep, but that was never a problem for me. I could 'zone out' in meditation, 'come to' some time later, and then go to sleep easily at night. I was generally so uncomfortable in any position that getting to sleep was problematical if I didn't meditate first.
>
> So, I went to bed and waited for Larry to go to sleep. If he thought I wanted quiet for meditation, he would manage to just *have* to make some sort of noise or disruption, apologize, and then do it again.
>
> After he was asleep, I began my breathing exercises. This part of the process I had borrowed from my hypnotherapy training and was extremely useful. Of course, I later learned that it had been 'borrowed' for hypnotherapy from certain meditation systems.[18]
>
> At this point, I don't know what happened. All I remember is starting the breathing phase, which came before the contemplative phase of the exercise. But then I made some kind of big 'skip'.
>
> The next thing I knew, I was jerked back into consciousness by a sensation that can only be described as a boiling turbulence in my abdomen. It was so powerful that, at first, it felt actually physical – like there was a boiling agitation in my organs that was going to erupt upward in some way.
>
> I was frantically holding my throat, because I could feel a tightening of the muscles in the throat area, as wave after wave of energy blew upward like the precursors of steam blasts from a volcano before it erupts. I struggled out of the bed, holding the wall with one hand and my throat with the other, clenching my teeth so whatever it was would not come gushing out of me and disturb Larry or the children. For all I knew, I was just going to be violently sick.
>
> I rushed outside to the porch Larry had recently built onto our little house, where there was a lawn sofa, and collapsed onto it just as the outpouring began.

[18]The practices I used at this time are now being made available and taught in the Éiriú Eolas program. See http://eiriu-eolas.org

I wish I could describe this in better words, but there are simply none that apply other than ordinary descriptions which don't come close to the essence and intensity of the event. What erupted from me was a shattering series of sobs and cries that were utterly primeval and coming from some soul-deep place that defies explanation. Accompanying these cries, or actually, embedded in them, were images – visions – complete scenes with all attendant emotional content and implied context conveyed in an instant. Again, it was like the idea of your life passing before your eyes. But, in this case, it was not scenes from this life. It was lifetime after lifetime. I knew that I was there in every scene, in these vignettes of other lives. I was experiencing myself as all these people.

And the tears. My God! The tears that flowed. I had no idea that the human physiology was capable of producing such copious amounts of liquid so rapidly.

Now, if this had been just an hour-long crying jag or something like that, it would have to pass into history as 'just one of those things', maybe like PMS. But, this activity had a life of its own. It went on, without slowing or stopping, for *more than five hours.* If I attempted to slow it down, stop it, or 'switch' my mind in another direction, the inner sensation of explosive eruption rapidly took over, all the muscles in my body would begin to clench up and I was no longer in control. I could only sit there as a sort of instrument of grief and lamentation, and literally sob my heart out for every horror of history in which I had seemingly participated or to which I had possibly been a witness. I think that there were even some that I was simply aware of without my direct participation. And some were truly horrible scenes.

Plague and pestilence and death and destruction. Scene after scene. Loved ones standing one moment, crushed or lying in bloody heaps the next. Rapaciousness, pillaging, plundering; rivers of blood and gore; slaughter, carnage, and butchery in all its many manifestations passed before my eyes; holocaust and hell. Rage and hot anger, bloodlust and fury, murder and mayhem, all around me, everywhere I looked. Evil heaped on evil like twisted, dismembered bodies. And the grief of centuries, the unshed tears of millennia, the guilt, remorse, and penitence flooded through me; melting, thawing, and dissolving the burdensome shell of stone that encased my petrified heart; washing away the pain with my tears. An ocean of tears.

As this release of the worlds of accumulated guilt and grief of many lifetimes went on, the voice-that-was-not-a-voice in the background, ever soothing, ever calming, repeated:

"It's not your fault. There is no blame. It's not your fault. You didn't know."

And I came to understand something very deep: I understood that there is no original sin. I understood that the terrors and suffering mankind experiences here in life on Earth are not caused by some sort of flaw or error or aberration from within. It is not punishment. It is not something from which one can be saved.

I understood that every scene of terrible suffering and heart-rending cruelty was the result of IGNORANCE. And each experience was the gaining of knowledge.

It is easier to see this idea when you consider the Crusades or the Inquisition. You can trace the path of twisted reason, leading from the idea of the love of God to imposing that view on others 'for their own good', ending in torture and mass murder. Forget for a moment about those who just viciously used such philosophies for their own gain and political maneuvers. Think for a moment about the sincerity of the philosophies behind such events. But it is based on IGNORANCE.

Those who were seemingly out for gain and self-aggrandizement were operating out of ignorance – fear and hunger of the soul that cannot be satisfied. It is only a matter of degrees, but in the end, it is only ignorance – lack of knowledge.

When the flow of energy, images, and tears finally began to subside, I felt a sensation of warm, balmy liquid, almost airy in its lightness, and so sweet that to this day, I can still remember the piercing quickening of the fire of love for all of creation. It was ecstatic, rapturous, and exultant all at the same time. I was lost in wonder, amazed and at the same time bewildered at this vision of the world.

Well, the result of this event was a state of prolonged elevation or loving peace that persisted for a very long time. You could even say that the effects reverberate to the present. Never again was I able to condemn – act against with intent to destroy what they choose to believe – another, no matter how wicked their deeds. I could see that all so-called evil and wickedness was a manifestation of ignorance. No person, no matter how holy and elevated they may think they are in this life, has not reveled in the shedding of another's blood in some other time and place.

> And no person who chooses ignorance and wickedness and destruction in this life is 'wrong'. Yes, I had the right to avoid them, to defend myself against them, to understand what they were doing; but it was not my place to go on a campaign to change their mind.
>
> The significant point is this: Ignorance is a choice, and one made for a reason: to learn and to grow.
>
> And that realization led to another: to learn how to truly choose. To be able to learn, at this level of reality, what is and isn't of ignorance, what is of truth and beauty and love and cleanliness. I understood the saying of Jesus that some things are bright and shining on the outside, but inside they are filthy and full of decay. And I don't mean that I was seeing this negativity as something to be judged. I clearly understood its reason and place as modes of learning, but I was deeply inspired to seek out all I could learn about this world to best manifest what was of light.

The short version of what was going on with me at the time of the above session was that I was again being subjected to an almost constant series of what seemed to be past life memories from many periods of history. In the particular case mentioned above, I was made aware, through these memories, that Frank had been abusive toward me and had basically tortured me throughout that lifetime because he had legal and financial control over me. These memories were experienced pretty much exactly as any normal memory is experienced, with full emotional content. Needless to say, being subject to such a process was quite exhausting because I seemed to have very little control over it; I could not just 'turn it off'.

February 18, 1995

This is another problematic session for several reasons. Diana M, who attended a number of sessions, including the one immediately prior to this one, was, in my opinion at the time, a 'disturbance in the force' of some sort. Additionally, there was a strong conflict between her and Jan and exchanges between them could be sharp, which was understandable since Diana was such an airhead and Jan was pretty practical and down-to-earth. However, Frank was always enthusiastic about the attendance of Diana because she was so in awe of him and hung on his every word as though it was gold. Frank liked that a *lot*!

Anyway, it seemed that when the two of them were together it was difficult for anyone else to keep a balance and this skewed the transmission in odd ways. The attitude of the Cs approached what came through with Frank doing the channeling under hypnosis, though there were certainly bursts of really good material depending on the topic. And, in spite of the skewing, the Cs seem to have managed to send through clues. I think one of the clues was when they abbreviated the word 'Cassiopaea', which was odd at this stage of the experiment. And then, at the point where all my antennae were quivering and I suspect I was giving off energy of my own, the tone changed again. It went from being cranky and almost mean, to joking and being almost silly.

An additional problem was that the tape recorder messed up at one point and several questions were lost, though we did have the responses. I've reconstructed where I could.

Participants: 'Frank', Laura, Terry, Jan, DM

1 **Q**: *(L)* Do we have anyone with us?

2 **A**: Stop.

3 **Q**: *(T)* Stop what, our discussion of all this weirdness?

4 **A**: No. And it is not weirdness.

Q: *(T)* What does "stop" mean? 5

A: Close doors. 6

Q: *(L)* Well, that is weird, they have never been bothered by the household noise before. [We closed the doors.] Who do we have with us tonight? 7

A: Teiurannea. 8

9 **Q**: *(L)* OK, why did you want the doors closed and are you going to give us our answer?

10 **A**: There is usually too much interference from outside influences.

11 **Q**: *(L)* And we have with us...

12 **A**: Living room contains too much noise and static.

13 **Q**: *(L)* Well, they have never complained about it before... *(J)* It must be the TV.... [Laura instructs children in the next room to turn down television and get quiet.] Don't you like *Star Trek*?

14 **A**: Not problem.

15 **Q**: *(L)* What is the problem?

16 **A**: Noise and innocent banter.

17 **Q**: *(J)* It's the kids. *(L)* Well, they will be going to bed soon...

18 **A**: You will not have control of this session, so don't worry about asking silly questions, as before!

19 **Q**: *(L)* Well, that doesn't sound very friendly, does it? *(T)* Are you going to impart some information that you want us to just listen to and absorb?

20 **A**: Sometimes friendliness must be set aside to get your attention and redirect wavelengths.

21 **Q**: *(T)* You have the floor, redirect.

22 **A**: Pause... wait for important information to be directed through our channel. You forgot ID inquiry.[1]

Q: *(L)* Where are you from? 23

A: Cass. Children are not cooperating.[2] 24

[Laura sends children to bed. Much negative feeling engendered thereby.]

A: Thank you. You need to be more open, remember, we are you!!!!! 25

Q: *(L)* Who is not being open? 26

A: Not issue. Can you imagine what it is like to look at yourselves as you once were, and to know you still are, and must communicate with yourself on a most unconventional level for union of purpose? 27

Q: *(L)* No, I don't think I could imagine that. 28

A: Well, try! 29

Q: *(L)* I am trying. I guess it would be like looking at yourself as an infant. 30

A: Okay. Continue. 31

Q: *(L)* Well, getting into the mindset of an infant we find that they have very little awareness of what is going on. Their awareness is primarily focused on meeting their personal needs, themselves, food, comfort, and the adult is worried about whether the roof leaks, whether the wind is going to blow the windows in and whether the wolf is going to come howling at the door – is that pretty close? 32

A: Progress! 33

Q: *(L)* So, you find us to be a bit trying at times? 34

---

[1]Notice the "our channel", i.e., Frank.

[2]Already at this point, I was quite aware that there was something wrong with this session. The sounds the children made in the next room had never been a problem for any of us. So, this apparent intolerance gave me a creepy feeling. In retrospect, it appears that there was a much stronger negative energy coming from Frank thanks to the 'adoration' of Diana M.

35 **A**: We are you, you are us, we are literally one and the same.[3]

36 **Q**: *(L)* So, you don't find us trying because it would be difficult to find oneself trying, but it is still possible to be dissatisfied with an aspect of one's personality? *(J)* Or, like loving someone and seeing what they could be and being a bit impatient that they are not?

37 **A**: Wow! What a concept!

38 **Q**: *(L)* Alright...

39 **A**: Laura, you still think we are a separate entity from you. You go around saying to people: "The Cassiopaeans said this, the Cassiopaeans said that." Don't you know it is you as you will be?

40 **Q**: *(T)* Faced with the fact that they were like this back then and they are trying to deal with it as it is, and they are trying to convince themselves back now, to open up enough to listen to ourselves there... or something similar to that. *(J)* Well, I think they have patience with us.

41 **A**: Close, Terry. It is fun to us to listen to you as you!

42 **Q**: *(T)* Cool! It's nice to know that I am entertaining myself in the future.

43 **A**: As us!

44 **Q**: *(T)* But, it's got to be frustrating because when you were us in your past, in 3rd density, you didn't know enough to be able to communicate with yourself in the future. *(J)* Well, maybe they did. You don't know that.

45 **A**: Wrong! What do you think this is!

46 **Q**: *(L)* This is the future, the past, the present... *(T)* But, it is hard for you to understand that now as us stuck in 3rd density... they are me, we are all together, coo coo cachoo! *(J)* It's hard for us, it's not hard for them. *(T)* They are us, we are them.

A: Not hard for us in either point of 47
reference.

Q: *(T)* Then why is it hard for us here 48
to perceive what we there seem to understand? *(L)* Maybe it is not as hard for us as we seem to think it is. *(T)* Well, how do we get past it, then? How do we get to the point where we perceive what we need to perceive? *(J)* Let it go.

A: You are past it. 49

Q: *(T)* So, just by the fact that we are 50
doing what we are doing, we are past that point. Now, all we have to do is to be able to open up more to be able to do this correctly?

A: Bingo zingo! 51

Q: *(T)* Obviously someone else of us 52
likes to say "Bingo zingo," which you got from us back then when you were here because I never said "Bingo zingo." *(J)* It was Al. *(T)* Al the hologram said bingo zingo...

A: Or maybe you changed and decided 53
you liked to say it!

Q: *(L)* Alright guys, can I ask a ques- 54
tion? I have had something bugging me all week.

A: Ask if you must, but we are going 55
to have fun tonight.

Q: *(J)* I also want to ask about that 56
sleep interruption I experienced. *(T)* We always have fun... why don't we let

[3]A bit contradictory with the "our channel" bit unless, as I have speculated, Frank was not connected to the Cs at all except through me.

them run their stuff out... *(L)* OK, run your stuff out...

57 **A**: No Laura, we are not the Lizzies; this is Cassiopaea calling. Worry not, channel is now permanently locked in, but damn those tapes!

58 **Q**: *(L)* You are giving me the heebie-jeebies guys.[4]

59 **A**: You are too serious.

60 **Q**: *(L)* Well, somebody's gotta be!

61 **A**: No!

62 **Q**: *(T)* Well, you were going to give us some important information here... that is what you said in the beginning of this session...

63 **A**: All in due time, but first, we want to have some fun.

64 **Q**: *(L)* Well, go ahead. I want to see this happen. Do it.[5]

65 **A**: Lighten up, Laura. This is your other persona talking directly to myself!

66 **Q**: *(J)* This does not make sense. I don't like it when I can't understand it...

67 **A**: Persona. Jan, you always had trouble with the pens and pencils after you/I learned the computer!!!

68 **Q**: *(J)* That's true! I have to block print.

69 **A**: Now it's me/us, Jan.

70 **Q**: *(J)* So it was your persona talking to you, Laura.

71 **A**: Forget it, Laura, it was just only one of many, many learning experiences! They all enriched us tremendously.[6]

Q: *(L)* What am I supposed to forget 72 that was the learning experience?

A: Lifetimes of "woe." 73

Q: *(T)* Is this one of her/your lifetimes 74 of woe?

A: They all are if we choose to view 75 them thusly.

Q: *(J)* I have a comment to make to the 76 Cassiopaeans. *(T)* Does this include 4th density life as well? *(J)* I may have a hard time writing, but half the time I am already anticipating what they are going to say and am writing ahead, so they should cut me some slack. *(L)* Cut her some slack, guys. *(T)* Cut, cut!

A: Slack cutteth! 77

Q: [Laughter] *(T)* I'm glad to know 78 there is still humor when you get up to 6th level!

A: There is a lot here, not nearly 79 enough there. Dear Jan, give the pen and paper to DM.

Q: *(T)* A 'Dear Jan' letter! [Laughter] 80 *(DM)* I guess I'm sitting over here getting stuff too. I've been feeling kind of like a fifth wheel anyway.

A: I, we, heard, DM. By the way, this 81 is us talking!

Q: *(T)* By the way can be abbreviated 82 BTW, guys.

A: BTO. 83

Q: *(L)* What does that mean? *(T)* By 84 the other?

A: Bachman Turner Overdrive! 85

Q: [Laughter] *(L)* Well, Terry, if you 86 didn't know that one you are really in bad shape! *(T)* Emerson, Lake and

[4] I was really feeling that this session was off.

[5] I was being rather sarcastic here.

[6] *The Wave* 44

Palmer! Electric Light Orchestra! *(L)* Well, I just want to say something...

87 **A**: Okay, Laura, ask it if you must.[7]

88 **Q**: *(J)* I want to ask about...

89 **A**: Laura first, we/she is about to jump out of her/our skin.

90 **Q**: [Laughter] *(T)* Ask away, my dear. *(L)* I wanted to ask – now you guys are going to be mad at me because I am going off on a very serious tangent...

91 **A**: We know, just ask it, already!!!!

92 **Q**: *(LM)* Is that New Yorkese?[8] *(L)* The question I wanted to ask...

93 **A**: No, LM, Miami Jewishese!

94 **Q**: [Laughter] *(LM)* I thought they were in Cornucopia, not Miami! *(J)* Just spit it out! *(L)* My question is... *(T)* She forgot! *(L)* No, I didn't forget, I just have to figure out how to word this. As you know, I am reading this book about Holocaust victims reincarnating and remembering their experiences at this time. The question is, on one occasion you told us that the Jewish people, as a racial group, were Atlantean descendants, is that correct?

95 **A**: Some.

96 **Q**: *(L)* There is some. Can you give us that some?

97 **A**: No.

Q: *(L)* Is there some karmic element 98
that was fulfilled by the Holocaust?[9]

A: Of course. 99

Q: *(L)* Could you tell us what karma 100
was being expunged in that activity, and what group the Jews represented?

A: This is not germane, but it was 101
Atlantean overseers "expunging" guilt from that life experience.

Q: *(L)* So... 102

A: So what? 103

Q: *(L)* A couple of weeks ago I had 104
an experience where I woke up in the morning and felt as though my tongue had been torn out. I felt the sensation of something unusual having happened. I would like to know what this was.[10]

A: It is not important. 105

Q: *(L)* I know you say it is not impor- 106
tant, but this had some very serious ramifications for my physical body.

A: As always. And, have we not ad- 107
vised to concentrate less upon physicality?

Q: *(L)* Well, the point I am trying to 108
get at is, if I was hauled out in the middle of the night by a bunch of Lizzies, or whatever, and worked on, I would certainly like to know about it. I know it's physicality...

A: You were not.[11] 109

[7] *The Wave* 44

[8] My husband, LM, had just popped in.

[9] *Secret History* 11

[10] I actually woke up spitting blood from deep in my throat and it was on the night before I was to have an MRI done. I related this story in *Petty Tyrants*, chapter 41. So the Cs' answer here seems to me to be quite off.

[11] Maybe not by Lizzies, but something very strange happened on that night. Something that had been seen in an X-ray was *not* present on the MRI that was done that morning.

110 **Q**: *(L)* OK, Jan, ask your question, if you dare! *(J)* If I dare! I had an experience last week where I woke up about 20 minutes after I had gone to sleep, screaming my head off, because there was something standing by the bed. What was that?

111 **A**: Now Jan, you indeed were taken!

112 **Q**: *(L)* Who took her?

113 **A**: Our friends, the Grays.

114 **Q**: *(L)* What did they do?[12]

115 **A**: Study update on psychic database.

116 **Q**: [Question lost]

117 **A**: Mirth should never stop!

118 **Q**: [Question lost]

119 **A**: Wrong concept.

120 **Q**: *(T)* Was Jan startled and screamed at the sensation of passing through a window?

121 **A**: Don't need windows.

122 **Q**: [Question lost]

123 **A**: Usual abduction experience, as you are familiar.

124 **Q**: [Question lost]

125 **A**: Okay.

126 **Q**: [Question lost]

127 **A**: Yes.

128 **Q**: *(T)* The event seemed to have lasted, in our illusion of time, 20 minutes, because I was in the living room watching the television while this happened. But, the experience that happened to her may have lasted longer or shorter in our perception of time, correct?

129 **A**: Yes.

[12] *The Wave* 19

Q: *(T)* So, when she screamed... *(J)* Did 130
I stop the abduction by screaming?

A: End, consciousness level border. 131

Q: *(T)* So, when I came into the bed- 132
room, it had just finished?

A: Yes. 133

Q: *(T)* I had nothing to do with the 134
ending of the event? Her screaming just alerted me.

A: You were diverted. 135

Q: *(T)* Well, that's easy enough to do 136
for me. I'm easy to divert! Give me a computer screen and I'm diverted.

A: All are. 137

Q: *(T)* I'm in good company. 138

[Break]

Q: *(J)* I have a follow-up question. Af- 139
ter that happened, Terry made the comment that he...

A: DM, please join board!! 140

Q: *(J)* Do they want all four of you? 141
(L) No. I don't want to talk to them tonight, they are being ugly! *(DM)* They are making me feel awfully important!

A: Ugly is subjective. We are you, 142
Laura.

Q: *(L)* I'm not sure I believe that. 143

A: Why would we be ugly to ourselves? 144
But we understand imprisonment of physicality and its biological tendencies.

Q: *(L)* What kind of a snide remark 145
was that? *(T)* They are just telling you that you understand. *(DM)* We are just talking back and forth to ourselves. *(T)* They are us. We are us.

146 **A**: Snide is your, and also our, perception. Alas.

147 **Q**: *(L)* Well, sorry, but it seems to me that you guys are wasting a lot of time and energy. I mean, we stay up late at night to do this and...

148 **A**: Who determines waste factor?

149 **Q**: *(L)* Well, that's just my opinion.

150 **A**: Ours, too!!

151 **Q**: *(T)* Cause they are you and you are them... as the Beatles said: "Coo coo cachoo, we are the Walrus!" *(DM)* Can't we just ask if they have something important to dispense to the human race or something like that? *(T)* Is there something more in the light of what you said earlier?

152 **A**: Is in process of being dispensed.

153 **Q**: *(L)* And when is that going to occur?

154 **A**: Is occurring now.

155 **Q**: *(DM)* Well maybe this whole thing is just to let us realize that we are talking to ourselves from the past...

156 **A**: Part. Why resistance.

157 **Q**: *(DM)* I guess we just understand it and we are waiting for the next thing.

158 **A**: We are not separate from you. Once this is recognized, progress will be made!

159 **Q**: *(T)* Yeah. You are us, we are you. *(L)* Alright, I want to ask what it was that I went through about a week ago when I felt like I was getting all kinds of stuff pumped into my system that I did not seem capable of coping with in terms of emotional control. What was going on?

A: Answered about one half hour ago as you/us measure time.[13] 160

Q: *(L)* I don't remember asking a question about it or getting an answer. *(J)* You asked about your tongue. *(L)* I'm not talking about that. 161

A: No. 162

Q: *(L)* What are you talking about... the past life business? 163

A: Yes.[14] 164

Q: *(L)* Well, what precipitated that activity? 165

A: Ions charged by awareness opening in window of EM envelope, used to precipitate physical trauma in immediate surroundings. "Used to" refers to past tense. 166

Q: *(L)* OK, so in the past, this kind of opening of a window in the EM envelope... 167

A: You have elevated. 168

Q: *(T)* You made a connection with other life experiences, and you were able to experience them in another way. *(L)* Well, it had some damn strange effects, that's all I've got to say about it! I wasn't very happy about it. *(T)* Will she be experiencing more of this now that she's made this elevation? 169

A: Yes. Each episode will be easier and easier. 170

Q: *(L)* Thank God! When do these guys get to enjoy that particular... *(T)* We haven't gotten to that point yet, or 171

[13] *The Wave* 44

[14] This refers to the remark at the very beginning about "lifetimes of woe". This had been brought up spontaneously, with no question asked, which was another bit of evidence that Frank was 'vacuuming' the information through me.

we may experience it in a different way. Is that it?

172 **A**: Sort of, each has their own issues.

173 **Q**: *(T)* Well, we are all doing different things as we move forward. *(J)* We all have different issues to work through.

174 **A**: Why wish agony upon another?[15]

175 **Q**: *(L)* I don't wish agony upon another, I just want you guys to appreciate the utter agony... *(T)* They do appreciate... *(J)* And we do too... They went through it with you. You didn't go through it alone! *(T)* They are you!

176 **A**: Why wish agony upon another, all have personal trials, would you/us like to share?

177 **Q**: *(L)* In other words, be grateful that it wasn't worse. *(DM)* I would like to ask a question because you probably understand it and I do not. If we are 6th and we are also 3rd, in the future, will we be another 3rd and another 6th... *(F)* In our 3rd density perception, since our time is linear and we are looking at us in the future, talking back to us in the present, but it is all happening at once because there is no real time. And, probably, I guess this also means that one day, which is also today, we will be 6th looking down here... *(DM)* We will be doing the same thing over and over? *(F)* Sort of yes and no... I don't think we can quite grasp the whole thing... *(T)* The problem is...

178 **A**: You will grasp it when at 6th level!!! So, rejoice in the "here and now!"

Q: *(T)* Even at 4th we will understand 179
more than we do now. They are giving us concepts that are beyond 3rd level. They are working with us to prepare us so that when we move into 4th we will have a head start on what's going on. They are bringing us up to where we already are because we came from 4th level to come here to do this originally, to set the frequency and hold it so that others can move to 4th level. We came from 4th density to do this. They are trying to give us enough information so that we will remember... *(F)* It is kind of like Hansel and Gretel going into the forest and leaving a trail of crumbs so that they can find their way out. We came back from 4th to 3rd to do what we've got to do and we're going back to 4th but we've got to leave a trail for us to keep connected to where we came from... something similar to that, in any event. *(F)* Is your mind exploding, DM? *(T)* We, where we are now, don't grasp all this because we are not supposed to at this level.

A: Learning. Laura just gained one 180
more strand, that is why it was so painful, okay?

Q: *(DM)* Say! Congratulations! *(T)* 181
Yup, she gained another strand and made Reiki Master! *(L)* I am in a bear of a mood! *(T)* Mirth! You in 6th density are enjoying the hell out of you now. We are going to take a break. *(F)* You gained a strand of DNA?

---

[15]Even though I had not revealed to anyone the kinds of experiences I was having that seem to have been triggered by the suicide of Frank's father (see notes and comments from previous session), that they were 'lives of woe' and recalling it all was truly agony suggests strongly to me that the Cs were coming through me, to Frank, with a twist.

After a break in which Terry and Jan and I consulted in the kitchen while Frank regaled DM in the living room with tales of his feats of channeling derring-do, we came back to the table, aware and alert, and the rest of the session was far more stable, even if there were a couple of quirky moments of skewing and a couple of attempts at 'time-anchored predictions', which was always a dead giveaway that STS forces were trying to horn in.

It is also at this point that I asked a 'secret question'. After pondering the idea that the events of the past weeks had been related to DNA, I came to some sort of idea that I had been inspired to undertake the channeling project as a means of this very DNA activation that had resulted in this 'awakening', or 'quickening', and that ultimately, my entire life would completely change as a result, and I was asking mentally if this was true, and if so, how would it manifest?

182 **Q**: *(L)* Are you with us guys? Of course, you are us!

183 **A**: Yes, something like that.

184 **Q**: *(T)* Why will Laura never be satisfied?

185 **A**: You are insatiable.

186 **Q**: *(T)* Are you insatiable? That's why everything is flowing on you, cause you're insatiable. *(L)* Oh well, we all have our crosses to bear. *(DM)* You are better at asking questions; would you mind asking 'us' if my abdominal problem has anything to do with my DNA changing?

187 **A**: Beware driving tonight, DM.

188 **Q**: *(L)* Is DM's DNA changing and is this stomach problem she has been having evidence of this DNA change?

189 **A**: Yes and no.

190 **Q**: *(DM)* Thank you. *(T)* Are you dudes or dudettes? No, we already asked that...

191 **A**: Background review.

Q: *(L)* I want to ask about the Reiki Mastership. We have discussed the charges, at least Susan and I have been discussing it – my feeling is that is should be made available to people for a lot less than what it has been going for, but at the same time... 192

A: Yes, but please now less personalization. 193

Q: *(L)* Is that a personal question? 194

A: Was leading to same. 195

Q: *(L)* Well, I beg to differ. It was not. 196

A: Expect 4.7 tremor in the U.S. within three days. In the N.E., Rochester, N.Y. Area. Faults exist near there. Mt. Vesuvius and Etna activity within calendar 1995. And Thera as well. In Africa, floods kill 1,000's in summer of 1995. 197

Q: *(DM)* I think it might be very important for us to contact somebody and tell them how we got this information... *(T)* Are the volcanoes related to the Japanese stuff? 198

199 **A**: Yes. Volcanic eruption under arctic ice in 1996.

200 **Q**: *(T)* Cool! *(L)* That ought to be a real zinger. *(T)* That will bring us some floods then!

201 **A**: No. Weather causing increased evaporation and yes, UFO flaps are caused by our activities and these communications!

202 **Q**: *(T)* Did we ask that? *(J)* No, but I have been thinking about it and we were talking about it earlier. *(T)* We are helping to create...

203 **A**: Causing, Terry.

204 **Q**: *(T)* We are causing this? *(DM)* No.

205 **A**: Yes.

206 **Q**: *(T)* So what they are saying is that we are helping to open up the area so that this is happening more?

207 **A**: Blasting open huge window. Gigantic, biggest in recorded history!!!

208 **Q**: *(L)* And to think that all this started when I hypnotized Pat Z. Just think, if she only knew what she did!

209 **A**: Not PZ, is our "Link-up."

210 **Q**: *(L)* Well, I was just kidding. *(T)* A little mirth there, guys. *(L)* Can I have a little mirth once in a while?

211 **A**: Yes and you are going to need all the mirth you can get.

212 **Q**: *(J)* I always said that the only way to get through life is with laughter. *(F)* That sounds rather ominous to me. *(L)* Yeah, me too. *(T)* The more we work this channel, the larger this window is going to become, is this correct?

213 **A**: Yes. And you will be busy.

214 **Q**: *(F)* Is that why we need all the mirth we can get, because we are going to be so busy?

A: Yes. 215

Q: *(DM)* Should we be doing this more 216
than one night a week? *(L)* No! *(DM)* Oh, excuse me.

A: No. 217

Q: *(T)* One night is more than enough. 218
(F) What do you want to do, drain me into entire non-existence? [Laughter] *(L)* We tried it more than one night a week and it nearly killed us. *(T)* While we are blasting this window open, are there other people on the planet taking notice of this?

A: Getting side effects. 219

Q: *(T)* Will they eventually be able to 220
pin down the source?

A: Maybe. 221

Q: *(T)* So, we better keep a lot of 222
mirth 'cause we might be having visitors. *(DM)* Is there something we can do to help them to locate this? *(L)* We don't want them to! *(DM)* Oh! Why?

A: MIB's. 223

Q: *(T)* The Men in Black! No, DM, we 224
don't want them to know where we are! Anybody who will come about us causing them difficulties will not be happy about it! *(DM)* Oh, I didn't realize it was a difficulty. I thought it was good. *(T)* It is difficult for them... *(DM)* I see, I see... *(T)* If what we are doing here creates more and more difficulties, side effects would be problems with communications, things of that nature...

A: But also able to channel stronger. 225

Q: *(T)* OK. We will be able to chan- 226
nel stronger because we are growing in strength. Are we also causing some Earth changes... are we part of that?

A: Symmetry. 227

228 **Q**: *(L)* Huh? *(DM)* Things are happening together. *(T)* Cause and effect...

229 **A**: Yes.

230 **Q**: *(L)* Are we building a giant energy bubble around our area?

231 **A**: You are the guidepost of the destiny of the planet.

232 **Q**: *(L)* But Mom! I didn't want to grow up to save the world! [Laughter] *(T)* Will they make a TV movie about us after this is over? This is mirth! *(DM)* Are we ever going to be known for this? *(T)* I sure hope not! I don't want them coming down on us!

233 **A**: Wait and see!

234 **Q**: *(L)* I have a question now... Jan and I worked very hard the other day on trying to lay out our mail-out. Is this the preferred format or should we go with a different format... just bear with us... *(T)* We need some style input here...

235 **A**: Of course you are heading in the right direction, symmetry, synchronicity.

236 **Q**: *(L)* Is the Reiki symbol that I picked to put on the cover, is that going to help to power out this energy?

237 **A**: Maybe. Why not use the symbol given to you?

238 **Q**: *(L)* You mean the An nu ki?

239 **A**: Bingo!

240 **Q**: *(L)* Then we'll put the An nu ki symbol on it then, which is the three-part pyramid. [Terry reviews predictions.] Are there more predictions?

241 **A**: No.

242 **Q**: *(T)* Well, I just wanted to make sure that we didn't go off on a tangent and miss something. OK. *(DM)* Did I ask if we are supposed to let that be known? *(T)* What's that? *(DM)* This information and the predictions? *(T)* I guess it is up to us whether we want to tell anybody or not. Will anybody be hurt in the Rochester quake?

A: No. 243

Q: *(J)* It's just a small one. *(T)* Just enough to get their attention? 244

A: Yes. 245

Q: *(T)* OK, do we have other questions? *(L)* Yeah, I want to... 246

A: Small Fire in Illinois. Won't be tragedy, just inconvenient. Who has a farm in Illinois? 247

Q: *(DM)* I'm from Illinois. My folks have a farm there. Is this the farm you are talking about? 248

A: Yes. 249

Q: *(DM)* When will this happen? 250

A: Soon. 251

Q: *(DM)* Is there anything I should do to prevent it? 252

A: No. 253

Q: *(L)* Alright, I want to ask a question. This is a trick question. It involves mind-reading. Please answer the question I am thinking.[16] 254

A: Your dreams are valid. 255

Q: *(DM)* My dreams are valid? 256

A: No. 257

Q: *(T)* Laura's dreams? 258

A: Yes. 259

Q: *(T)* What dream? *(DM)* Your dreams are valid, Laura. *(T)* Was that your question? *(L)* Well, sort of. It could apply. *(T)* They answered your 260

[16] *The Wave* 44

question before you asked it. *(L)* Yeah. I wasn't going to ask it out loud anyway. *(T)* If we could just get them to skip the questions and go to the answers, we would make a lot better time here.

261 **A**: Have.

262 **Q**: *(L)* In other words, my impressions of the ultimate outcome of this DNA switcheroo is...

263 **A**: Yes!

264 **Q**: *(T)* Any other questions?[17]

265 **A**: Go to Pensacola.

266 **Q**: *(L)* Who wants to go to Pensacola?

267 **A**: I do, I do. [Laughter]

268 **Q**: *(T)* Is something going to happen in Pensacola?

269 **A**: Conference.

270 **Q**: *(L)* Is there a conference in Pensacola? *(T)* It's in October. *(J)* Are you talking about the October conference?

271 **A**: One before then.

272 **Q**: *(T)* There's another conference before the one in October? I don't know anything about this other conference.

273 **A**: Increasing activity in Florida panhandle, vortex. If you go to Pensacola you will see UFOs of all origins including yours truly.

274 **Q**: *(T)* Oh! It's your conference! And we've been invited!

275 **A**: Okay.

276 **Q**: *(T)* And we have tickets! Are you guys going to front for the hotel bill? That is, will we front the hotel bill for ourselves?

A: Silly. 277

Q: *(L)* I hate to come back to these 278
mundane 3rd density questions, but that is an undertaking that requires a flow of energy called money. I mean, we can't just charge off to conferences every day, you know. *(T)* When is it that we are supposed to go? Is it that whenever we go, then will be the conference?

A: May. 279

Q: *(T)* Is there something in May? In 280
Pensacola? *(J)* Project Awareness is in May but that's in Tampa. *(T)* Are you talking about the conference in May that is being put on by the Pensacola group?

A: Look and see. 281

Q: *(T)* You are talking about the con- 282
ference in Tampa that is put on by Project Awareness? *(J)* Do you want us to physically go to Pensacola? This is beginning to sound like the Gulf Breeze Six, the guys that boogied out of Germany because they were doing the same kind of stuff we are, only they had someone else who told them to do that. OK, in May we should go to Gulf Breeze?

A: Yes. 283

Q: *(T)* OK, the conference in Gulf 284
Breeze in going to be in Tampa in May. *(L)* Well, maybe we should go there and all the UFOs will show up while they are all down here. That would be a gas! *(T)* Are we supposed to connect up with the Cs?

A: Yes. 285

Q: *(T)* Are we supposed to go in May 286
before the conference?

[17] *The Wave* 32

287 **A**: Go back with them. See them here, then return.

288 **Q**: *(DM)* What are we going to accomplish by going back with them?

289 **A**: Do a session and monitor the skies at the same time. Have someone posted outside with a video camera!!

290 **Q**: *(DM)* Is that when we are going to go public? *(T)* We are already going public. This is when we are going to convince the nation. We have to go to the conference, get the C___ aside and...

291 **A**: Let's try to steer all these "Ufologists" in the right path.

292 **Q**: *(T)* I'm going to take my hand off so it won't start moving while I am talking. I don't want me to start off while I'm talking! Don't you love it?! Not only do you have to contend with you, you have to contend with *you*. When we do what we are doing, we are opening a window, as we have been told. Are we pulling stuff in that doesn't want to come through? Are we accidentally pulling people or beings through while we are doing this?

A: Windows provide for easier transport. 293

Q: *(T)* Yes, but what I am getting at is, is there some 4th density being just bopping along the 4th density lane who just accidentally falls through this window and goes: "What the hell!!" 294

A: It is conceivable. If 4th density "Lost Traveller" should show up at your door, please resist strong urges toward rejection. 295

Q: *(T)* We won't make them feel uncomfortable. *(J)* We will always welcome guests, yes. *(T)* They are always welcome here! 296

A: That was serious comment. 297

Q: *(L)* How are we going to know it is a 4th density "Lost Traveller"? *(DM)* You guys, I am getting very, very weak. 298

A: Obvious. 299

Q: *(L)* Let's shut down for the night, I am pooped. *(T)* Any last words? 300

A: Goodnight. 301

End of Session

As the reader can guess, I was not very pleased with this communication. Neither were Terry and Jan, and it showed. We tried to be 'light' and have a little fun with it, but the 'off' flavor and texture of the contact made it clear that something was going on, and it was only right at the end that the clue was given as to what it was. The woman, DM, was feeding Frank energy that empowered the STS force connection to him. Based on the remarks, he was obviously able to vacuum out of me many details of what was in my thoughts and experiences of the past weeks. The information given was, indeed, 'starkly accurate' in that respect. And there is clear evidence that my own foreknowledge of coming personal events was being tapped. This is also one of the few sessions in which Frank was actually active, and that was probably due to the fact that DM treated him rather worshipfully and he was practically ecstatic to have a 'groupie'.

One really odd thing in this session that later turned out to be important was the directive "Go to Pensacola". We did, eventually, go to a UFO conference in Pensacola and it was there that a very strange thing happened that did, literally, change my life forever.

As I wrote somewhere in *The Wave*, sometimes the transmissions were like trying to watch television while someone runs the vacuum cleaner. The degree of interference can vary by the position of the vacuum relative to the television, as well as other factors including the strength of the broadcast signal. So, even though the picture might get very snowy or distorted, the real picture can still be seen and interpreted. The best pictures came when the vacuum was turned off, and Frank practically dozed at the board from boredom. For the most part, when I was off on my cosmic questions, my questions about history and the nature of reality, he practically went to sleep. But notice that his alertness in the above session also made him cranky about the sounds the children were making in the next room, which otherwise never bothered anyone.

February 22, 1995

The main reason for this session was that I was really bugged by the previous session when Diana M was present and wanted to know why it was that every time she was present, things seemed to be 'off'.

Participants: 'Frank', Laura and Susan V

1 **Q**: *(L)* Cassiopaeans, are you with us?

2 **A**: Yes.

3 **Q**: *(L)* Who do we have with us this evening?

4 **A**: Iora.

5 **Q**: *(L)* And where are you from?

6 **A**: Cassiopaea.

7 **Q**: *(L)* I would like to ask who was with us last Saturday night.[1] Was it one of the Cassiopaeans or were we pulling in some corruption?

8 **A**: Yes.

9 **Q**: *(L)* We were pulling in corruption last Saturday?

A: And us. 10

Q: *(L)* It was both? 11

A: Yes. 12

Q: *(L)* What was the source and reason 13
for the corruption?

A: Trailer. 14

Q: *(L)* What is a trailer? 15

A: Hanger on. Diverter of energy wave. 16

Q: *(L)* And how did we acquire or have 17
this diverter?

A: You know. 18

Q: *(L)* In other words, it is as I sus- 19
pected, that DM has brought in attachments because she is an agent of the Lizzies, though she is not aware of this?

---

[1]See 18 February 1995.

[2]I've often wondered about this "hormonally charged" thing. A few years after this session I read a book entitled *The Ultimate Alien Agenda: The Re-engineering of Humankind* by "teacher, counselor and public servant Jim Walden." (Interesting that he, too, was a teacher as Diana M was!) Rather than describe the book and its content and why it reminds me of Diana M and her messed-up hormones, I'll just include here the review I wrote of this book:

> Perhaps it is fitting that Dr. Walden suggests that our 'Fearless Leader', appropriately nick-named 'Slick Willie' (an appropriateness that is particularly evident in this book), is a 'fellow alien hybrid' of the Serpentine ilk. Dr. Weldon, having attended the same church frequented by Dr. Rich Boylan, "just knows that the energy of Reptilian intelligence is similar to human sexual energy. It feels the same." Gosh! Why didn't we all realize that Monica and Bill were just intellectualizing?

20 **A**: Hormonally charged through their influences on her mind.[2]

21 **Q**: *(L)* Would it be better to do the sessions without such individuals present?

22 **A**: Up to you.

23 **Q**: *(L)* Well, obviously since we don't want that kind of thing to happen anymore, the choice is already made. OK, I would like to know: recently I watched a video at Jiles Hamilton's on psychic surgery. This, obviously, was the real thing. Am I correct in that assessment?[3]

24 **A**: No.

25 **Q**: *(L)* No?! What was happening?

26 **A**: Fakery and "demonic" influences to delusion, now, strict warning: avoid at all cost!!

Q: *(L)* Avoid what at all cost, psychic surgery? 27

A: Yes. 28

Q: *(L)* Well, that is pretty heavy duty. *(F)* They almost never say anything like that. *(L)* I would like to know for the benefit of somebody else who asked the question: What is the origin of AIDS? 29

A: Simian mutation. 30

Q: *(L)* A monkey virus, in other words. 31

A: Was, but mutated. 32

Q: *(L)* Who is the individual or group responsible for this mutation? 33

A: Not humans. 34

Q: *(L)* Well then, who? 35

The 'source' of this naive 'Treatise' reveals itself over and over in the ego-centered "self-reference" of "Old Big Head" (the alien lizard critter) and in such passages as: "He helped me discover my true identity [...] Then, something unexpected happened. My physical tongue swelled up, as if it was being inflated. I could barely speak. 'My tongue... it's quite large! [...] My enormous tongue was darting in and out...'" And we thought Ken Starr's transcripts were explicit!

All kidding aside, it is hard to believe that Barbara Bartholic allowed herself to be taken in by this prepubescent ego-drivel, which would be pathetic enough if one considered just the style and presentation which is somewhat akin to "What did I do last summer between 5th and 6th grade? I got abducted and raped! By Reptoid Aliens! Ooooh! I was scared at first... but after I knew how GOOD it was now I just can't wait for them to come again!" You would think that Barbara would have learned something from her association with Karla Turner, i.e., those who *don't* adopt the 'party line' don't survive. But, on the other hand, maybe she *did* learn...

Spend your time and money on Dr. David Jacobs's book, *The Threat*. Unless you just want to see how easy it is to swallow lies when they are sandwiched between sweet and sticky truths...

[3]The video was made and presented by Henry Belk who is described in the notes of 9 February 1995. The video was shown on the same evening I gave my talk to the UFO study group near Orlando.

[4]A puzzling response that should have been followed up at the time, like whose "destined frequency path", that of the 'Lizards' or that of the monkeys or both? Or the utilization of a mutated monkey virus to infect humans who are on a particular "destined frequency path"? Or just the general destruction of humankind? Or something that induces DNA changes in those it doesn't make sick?

36 **A**: Lizards acting in conjunction with destined frequency path.[4]

37 **Q**: *(L)* And what is the purpose of the infliction of the AIDS virus on the human race?

38 **A**: Not determined.

39 **Q**: *(L)* I would like to know how many lifetimes I have had as a human being?[5]

40 **A**: That is open to definition.

41 **Q**: *(L)* Well, on planet Earth.

42 **A**: Including Neanderthal?

43 **Q**: *(L)* No, we'll just pass that up.

44 **A**: Okay, then it is 79 in broken sequence.

45 **Q**: *(L)* Broken by what?

46 **A**: Other planes.

47 **Q**: *(L)* The same question for Frank?

48 **A**: Same exactly.

49 **Q**: *(L)* How many for SV? Same?

50 **A**: No. Not correct definition of answer.

51 **Q**: *(L)* What would be correct for her?

52 **A**: Not same exact sequence. 72 plus 4 as special learning channel "hold back" on contemplative plane AKA 5th density level.

53 **Q**: *(L)* SV is a 5th level soul?

54 **A**: No. Spent 4 sequence holdovers there.[6]

Q: *(L)* Now this is curious. Why do Frank and I have these 79 lives in the exact same sequence? Isn't that a little odd? 55

A: No. 56

Q: *(L)* How many lifetimes have the three of us in this room worked together? 57

A: Discover. 58

Q: *(L)* Now, you said that the Jews were Atlantean descendants, and that Noah was an Atlantean... 59

A: Most of them. 60

Q: *(L)* What is the significance of this relating to their religion and their experiences and the current state of the Jews?[7] 61

A: Was Jews in "holocaust" only. 62

Q: *(L)* Is the Jewish religion somewhat similar to the Atlantean religion? 63

A: Did you understand the previous answer? 64

Q: *(L)* Are you saying that the Jews were the only ones in the Holocaust? 65

A: No. 66

Q: *(L)* Are you saying that the Jews were not the only ones in the Holocaust? 67

A: No special karmic significance to being "Jewish", special significance is experiencing holocaust for purpose of purging extraordinary karmic debt.[8] 68

[5] *The Wave* 64

[6] My general impression at the present time would be that this meant some kind of karmic debt issue that required 'extended' contemplation, though using a time reference might be misleading.

[7] *Secret History* 11

[8] This response suggests that many of the individuals who died in the Holocaust were Atlanteans whether Jewish or otherwise. Also, there is no special karmic significance to being Jewish and probably the same for being Christian, Muslim,

69 **Q**: *(L)* OK. I got it. Now, is the Jewish religion similar to the Atlantean religion?

70 **A**: Not one religion only. Many "religions."

71 **Q**: *(L)* Now, I would also like to know: last January we had a lot of booming sounds which were reported to the local sheriff's office. The papers reported that they were military planes on maneuvers. Is this correct?

72 **A**: Yes.

73 **Q**: *(L)* I guess we are done for now. Is Frank going to have enough money to pay his bills?[9]

74 **A**: If aided by group.

75 **Q**: *(L)* We would like to have this project bring income so that we can devote more of our time to it. Is it going to become self-supporting?

76 **A**: Eventually, yes, but immediately no, because of veil of skepticism combined with relentless 4th density level originating attacks. Beware of those who profess great interest; agents of STS are preparing many false guides, as you have already seen.[10]

77 **Q**: *(L)* What can we do to protect ourselves from this?

78 **A**: Suggestion: "Buttonhole" in point blank fashion those who promise assistance or interest in indefinite way!

Q: *(L)* What does that mean? 79

A: Good question; when someone 80
greets you at a function and gets your hopes up regarding helping you to further this most important work, demand immediate proof regarding their sincerity and credibility!!!

Q: *(L)* And if they don't prove their 81
credibility and sincerity?

A: Drop them at once!!! 82

Q: *(L)* In other words, don't waste our 83
time with deadbeats?

A: Or agents with ill intentions, ei- 84
ther conscious or unconscious, don't be afraid to confront directly immediately and openly.[11]

Q: *(F)* If somebody comes up and says 85
to us: "I can do this or that for you" or "I'm interested" or whatever, we must tell them right off the bat that it is very nice that they are interested, but they must understand that we are under attack because of our work, so we have to know that they are serious and honest and good intentioned. *(L)* So, how do we get them to prove their sincerity? *(SV)* Get out the checkbook! *(L)* Is that it?

A: Well, that can take many forms, but 86
awhile ago, you asked about financial assistance, so why not say "put your

---

or following other religion. Notice also the previous answer that only *most* of the Jews (Jewish genetic lines) were Atlantean descendants. That suggests that there must be some other elements involved in the Jewish lineage. This issue will come up again in a further session, so stay tuned.

[9]He had spent several hours before the session complaining about his finances.

[10]That was certainly true! And the most misleading/damaging always presented themselves as great fans of our work!

[11]This was something that I had great difficulty learning because I was always concerned to not 'hurt' someone else's feelings. This issue led to a *lot* of lessons, especially in the field of psychopathology.

money where your mouth is," or something akin to that?

87 **Q**: *(L)* Well, that's it for the night. Thank you very much for being with us.

End of Session

February 25, 1995

This group of session attendees was pretty large and was the result of a talk I had given at the Clearwater MUFON meeting that afternoon. Quite a few people were unhappy that my time had been cut from one hour to just 15 minutes and when we let them know we would be having a session that night, a number of them wanted to know if they could attend and check it out.

The group had been discussing a June 5, 1995, mass UFO landing predicted by a purported diary of the last pope, supposedly found by his cleaning lady. I'll include what I found about that at the end.

Overall, this was an interesting and energetic session once we got going, but the level of questions was pretty low. Also, the Cs seemed to be interested in warning Caryl D to be more careful. As you will see, she was involved with what she called the 'Vanishing Twin Phenomenon'. She was going about it in a rather scientific way and I'll include an excerpt at the end of this session.

Gene B was an interesting character. He was a state-level director of MUFON and some sort of aerospace engineer with interesting connections.

Participants: Caryl D,[1] Bill P,[2] Tom M, Gene B,[3] Susan V, Terry and Jan, 'Frank', Laura, Denise J, LM

1 **Q**: *(L)* Hello, how are you tonight?

2 **A**: Hello. Okay. Why not regroup. Concentrate. Too much energy. Children. Sorry. Who are we?

3 **Q**: [Children are sent to bed.] *(T)* Ask them if anyone else can sit at the board this evening?

A: Sure. 4

Q: *(GB)* Can I sit in there now? *(T)* Sure. Do they want all four of us or just three? [GB takes Terry's place at the board.] 5

A: No matter. 6

Q: *(J)* Who do we have with us tonight? We didn't ask. 7

A: Concentrate. Slow mental processes 8

[1]Woman into 'color therapy'.

[2]Caryl's boyfriend and New Agey type.

[3]Former head of regional MUFON.

down. Less pressure. [GB lightens up.]

9 **Q**: *(L)* Who do we have with us tonight?

10 **A**: Who are we?

11 **Q**: *(L)* Who are you?

12 **A**: Cassiopaeans.

13 **Q**: *(L)* And who do we have with us?

14 **A**: Pommori.

15 **Q**: *(J)* And who do we have with us tonight in 3rd density?

16 **A**: Unknown. 3rd density is you! And us in the "past."

17 **Q**: *(L)* Let's get on with it.

18 **A**: Ask who is at south position.

19 **Q**: *(L)* Who is at the south position? Oh, that's you. Yeah, that's GB, as if you didn't know. Are we playing bridge, or what?

20 **A**: Hello. Concentrate all in room.

21 **Q**: *(T)* What are we going to concentrate on? *(L)* Is anybody thinking about sex? [Laughter]

22 **A**: Mind.

23 **Q**: *(GB)* Ask TM's question: will there be a mass landing in 1995?

24 **A**: Not ready to answer. Still trying to settle energy waves in room.

25 **Q**: *(GB)* Let me ask you, Frank, you are the only one this comes through? *(J)* Well, we have not really determined that. *(F)* No, we haven't determined exactly what happens. It seems like I'm the, what you would call, primary channel. *(TM)* Can you do it by yourself without anybody else? *(F)* If I did do it by myself without anybody else holding it, I wouldn't trust the information. *(TM)* Can you do it in a meditative state? *(F)* Well, we have tried it with me under hypnosis and have gotten a lot of information, but again, we don't trust it because it doesn't have the participatory aspect to it. *(L)* This way no one really knows what is being said. It is not coming through any one person's mind. No one thinks the thoughts as they come through. *(F)* I have also sat at the computer and gotten a lot of stuff, but, again, I don't know how much I would trust that. *(L)* You never can tell how much of that is your own stuff. *(F)* The standard way of channeling that so many people do has an extremely questionable validity rating. The validity level of this is also somewhat questionable, but, we have done a lot of checking and testing and, so far, it has more than satisfied all the tests we have applied. *(GB)* Can we do it with our eyes closed?[4] *(L)* Now, we are curious as to this channeling process, and ordinarily, when we do not have so many guests, it is quite different, and we want to know who is the primary channel here?

A: That is not the issue. 26

Q: *(L)* Is it important for us to use our senses, as in our eyes, ears and so forth, while doing this? 27

A: Of course. How else can we see the board? 28

[4]We attempted an experiment to see if the information would come through with all eyes closed. It was unsuccessful. Trying various combinations of eyes closed and/or open also were unsuccessful. It seems that the eyes of all participants must be open at once in order for the contact to be sustained. This agrees with the idea that it is a purely telepathic contact and not 3rd density or 'poltergeist' in nature.

29 **Q**: *(J)* They have to see the board through our eyes. *(L)* Could Frank do this alone?

30 **A**: No.

31 **Q**: *(F)* Could Laura do this alone? *(T)* Do you want the original three on the board?

32 **A**: No. Not issue.

33 **Q**: *(J)* Well, what is the issue? *(T)* What is the problem here?

34 **A**: Fractured frequency.

35 **Q**: *(J)* Why is it fractured?

36 **A**: Detached energy.

37 **Q**: *(L)* Are you saying that there is something floating around in this room doing this?

38 **A**: Not certain.

39 **Q**: *(J)* What can we do to help?

40 **A**: Will clear eventually.

41 **Q**: *(BP)* Well, ask a question. Maybe it will clear with a question. *(L)* Well let me make a suggestion... Terry, you come back and sit down. GB you back up for just a little while and let's get the flow going with what they are used to and then others can cut in, so to speak. I mean, I am impatient with this method to begin with, even though I find it eminently trustworthy, and this dragging it out is getting on my nerves. *(BP)* Yeah, my brother-in-law pissed them off! [Changes are made.] *(J)* I think part of it is that we have new people present in the room and it is a great influx of new energy. *(L)* Now, how are we feeling?

42 **A**: Now, more powder. We are sorry for the delays. One in the room is under great stress.

43 **Q**: *(L)* Who is stressed?

A: CD. 44

Q: *(L)* Are you stressed? You don't look stressed to me. *(CD)* I don't feel stressed. 45

A: Under pressure for study. 46

Q: *(BP)* It's for that article you want to write. *(CD)* Maybe. *(L)* Do you have a deadline or something? *(CD)* Yes. But I am really not thinking about it, at least consciously. 47

A: Yes. You have been watched, CD. 48

Q: *(L)* By whom? *(BP)* CD has been watched? 49

A: Government. 50

Q: *(BP)* It's been nice knowing you! [Laughter] *(GB)* Do these guys have a sense of humor? *(J)* Yes, as a matter of fact, they do! *(T)* Is this mirth, here? 51

A: No, this is not mirth. 52

Q: *(BP)* Why is the government watching Caryl? 53

A: Has because of writings or papers. 54

Q: *(L)* What are you writing? *(CD)* I write books. Does it have to do with the twin research? *(BP)* Vanishing Twin Phenomenon? 55

A: Partly. 56

Q: *(CD)* Does it have to do with the prodigies? 57

A: Partly. 58

Q: *(CD)* Does Tim C have anything to do with this? 59

A: Open. 60

Q: *(BP)* Is Tim C working for anyone other than himself? 61

A: Open. 62

Q: *(J)* How does Tim C feel about Caryl? 63

A: Okay. 64

65 **Q**: *(T)* Is he part of the problem?

66 **A**: Open.

67 **Q**: *(GB)* Does Caryl's new paper have anything to do with it?

68 **A**: Yes.

69 **Q**: *(L)* What is it about? *(CD)* The prodigies, people who have contacted extraterrestrials and have become geniuses, and the Vanishing Twin Phenomenon.

70 **A**: Danger, this is serious!!

71 **Q**: *(T)* Is Caryl getting close to something?

72 **A**: She is at it!!

73 **Q**: *(CD)* What should I do? *(T)* Have you thought about a trip to deepest Peru? [Laughter] I could point you to some really good temples!

74 **A**: Serious problem, please take this seriously.

75 **Q**: *(GB)* Does Linda Howe have anything to do with it?

76 **A**: Open.

77 **Q**: *(CD)* What can I do? *(BP)* Can you suggest action at this time?

78 **A**: Stay with others.

79 **Q**: *(T)* Don't stay alone. *(CD)* Does the incident Thursday night have something to do with this?

80 **A**: Yes.

81 **Q**: *(CD)* Is it 4th density danger?

82 **A**: No. High level government, you have been striking a "nerve."

83 **Q**: *(GB)* Well, the only thing you have been talking about is the prodigies and the vanishing twins. *(CD)* Is it more the twins?

A: Open. 84

Q: *(CD)* Does the color work have anything to do with it? 85

A: No. 86

Q: *(GB)* Who have you been contacting? Linda Howe... 87

A: Not important, the sources are sincere but closely watched. Some of this has now transferred to you. 88

Q: *(BP)* Is Robin in danger? 89

A: Yes. 90

Q: *(T)* Is more than one government of more than one country involved here? 91

A: It is a complex. 92

Q: *(T)* Should she take the trip to England? 93

A: Open. 94

Q: *(J)* They are not going to give advice other than to stay with others. *(CD)* The thing the other night... was I being bombarded by ELF frequencies? 95

A: All are. 96

Q: *(L)* All in the room?[5] 97

A: All are. 98

Q: *(BP)* Are they using ELF or microwave technologies specifically to do something to Caryl? 99

A: Give maybe. 100

Q: *(T)* Run that by us again. 101

A: Give maybe. 102

Q: *(T)* They are giving us a maybe. *(GB)* Who in the government, which branch of the government? 103

A: It is a complex source. 104

Q: *(CD)* Am I in physical danger? 105

[5] *The Wave* 20

106 **A**: That is not the point. You can be harassed.

107 **Q**: *(L)* I will give you an example. We did a session for Barry and Susy Konicov and they were given a very serious warning to back off on certain activities relating to teaching people how to not pay income tax. They called us one night recently because several people they had been associated with had been raided by the IRS. The IRS had confiscated computers, jewelry, equipment, and whatever else they could lay their hands on and were basically holding these people's possessions hostage until they could determine whether or not what they were doing was illegal or whatever. Barry and Susy expected to be raided imminently. The Cassiopaeans said to them that whether or not they got raided was not the point, because they had been warned. The point was, what are you going to do now? What steps are you going to take and what information are you going to accept to prevent further attack? *(CD)* Should I stop publishing the book?

108 **A**: Open.

109 **Q**: *(J)* They will not tell you what to do. *(CD)* Will not publishing the book stop the harassment and danger?

110 **A**: Open. MUFON has "spies."

111 **Q**: *(GB)* So what else is new? *(BP)* Cannot unconditional love and faith overcome all of this?

112 **A**: Open. More is needed.

113 **Q**: *(GB)* Will the government relax their policy this year and release more information to the public?

A: Complicated question because you are making simple judgments based upon available evidence which can be interpreted a number of different ways, not just one![6] 114

Q: *(TM)* In a book I have been reading it specifically states that Stanton Freidman is a spy. *(BP)* Really? *(T)* That is what Bill Cooper says? *(TM)* I may be taking it out of context because I have not read the whole book. *(T)* I have heard that before. *(L)* Let's ask that question. Why do they need spies? Why would anyone need spies in MUFON since everything in MUFON is public? 115

A: "Double verification." 116

Q: *(BP)* Would you ask if Caryl is the only one in the room in danger, and, if not, who else? 117

A: Yes. But all eventually. 118

Q: *(GB)* Is BP in Danger? 119

A: Well, these are simplistic questions, you need more exposure to this and other sources! We know you are skeptical, but that is good for balance, also, you have much material knowledge! There is more to the phenomenon than "meets the eye." 120

Q: *(GB)* What is the danger? Is it mental, physical... 121

A: Complicated, also GB knows more than he is telling! 122

Q: *(CD)* He's the spy! [Laughter] *(BP)* He used to work for NASA! *(F)* Did you really work for the Apollo program? *(GB)* Oh yeah. Secret, as a consultant. (*Laura and Jan*) Ah hah! *(BP)* Could they offer general suggestions... I know they won't tell us what to do, but this 123

[6] I believe this answer is for BP's question about unconditional love, not GB's inserted question on another subject.

is a general question for all who are anchoring light, who want to be of service; can they offer any specific suggestions for us...

124 **A**: STO, not just "light." [Planchette flies off board and has to be retrieved.]

125 **Q**: *(GB)* In other words, you have to do something for others. *(J)* You have to have... *(BP)* See if Caryl can sit in... [Caryl takes Terry's place.]

126 **A**: Hi!

127 **Q**: *(CD)* Thanks for scaring the crap out of me.

128 **A**: Knowledge protects, my dear.

129 **Q**: *(BP)* Is the 4th dimension to be eliminated in any way in terms of planetary ascension? People are talking about the planet going through this big change and the 4th dimension being eliminated.

130 **A**: What??

131 **Q**: *(L)* We are moving into 4th density. *(BP)* We are not going to skip 4th density and move directly into 5th? *(L)* 5th is the contemplation zone. *(F)* Where your soul goes when you die. *(L)* We are going into a state of variability of physicality. *(BP)* I read the pamphlet... *(L)* Well, that is just highlights. There is over 300 pages of material. *(J)* We are working on getting it together. *(L)* They have talked about the fact that we are moving into a 4th density state and the reptilian beings are trying like heck to prevent this because, once we are in that situation, if there are enough of us who are in the STO mode...

132 **A**: You are all 4th density candidates.

133 **Q**: *(L)* Once we move into 4th density we are on an equal footing with all these other guys and things will be more equal. At the same time, those who are not 4th density candidates are going to cycle back and start all over again. Basically they are all going to go into the primordial soup and experience another 300,000 years of strife and misery. *(BP)* And this moving into 4th density will be a change in perception, rather than a change in location, in terms of space-time, is that correct? *(L)* Um hmm.

A: Close. 134

Q: *(L)* I think that this is about as close 135
as we can get with it. *(CD)* Is there anything else they want to tell me, or anything else I can do to be of service?

A: Keep quiet. 136

Q: *(L)* Keep quiet about what? 137

A: Two things recently learned. 138

Q: *(L)* Did you recently learn some 139
things you are planning on telling the public? *(BP)* Anything you haven't already told? *(GB)* Is it in her subconscious? *(CD)* Is it in the article?

A: Close. 140

Q: *(CD)* Is it in my newest book? 141

A: Ask yourself, CD. 142

Q: *(CD)* Is it in the article? 143

A: Review. 144

Q: *(L)* You are talking about two 145
things recently learned here, tonight? *(GB)* No.

A: No. 146

Q: *(BP)* Would one of the things be 147
the mass cattle disappearances in Oklahoma? Is that significant?

A: Open. 148

Q: *(CD)* Does it have to do with 149
Robin?

150 **A**: Ask yourself, CD, this is for you to know for yourself. More pressure for clean connection.

151 **Q**: [Laughter] *(L)* Well, some use too much pressure and some don't use enough. *(BP)* There you go... They're touchy! [Laughter] No pun intended!

152 **A**: Cute, BP. [Laughter] Mirth!!! Knowledge protects. Now, Caryl, ask yourself, who are your true friends?

153 **Q**: *(L)* So, the connection is in there. Knowledge of who your true friends are can be protection. *(CD)* So, somebody who appears to be a friend is not really a friend?

154 **A**: Yes.

155 **Q**: *(CD)* Is it Robin? *(L)* They aren't going to tell you that. *(GB)* But you have suspected that all along, Caryl. *(J)* Ask yourself, you *know*. *(L)* Have you had that feeling about this and have been ignoring it? *(BP)* Can you tell us anything about Jefferson S? Who is he really? *(CD)* Is Jefferson S involved in this?

156 **A**: Open.

157 **Q**: *(BP)* Can you tell us anything about him? Who is he?

158 **A**: More than one person.

159 **Q**: *(J)* Interesting. *(GB)* Is he involved in the complex government? *(CD)* Is he involved in this danger for me?

160 **A**: Open.

161 **Q**: *(BP)* Why are you so f****** noncommital?[7]

162 **A**: Discover.

163 **Q**: *(L)* This Jefferson S, do you mean he is more than one person in a physical sense or that he has a multiple personality, or as in AKA? *(BP)* Multiple identities?

A: Both. 164

Q: *(L)* What are Jefferson S's inten- 165
tions?

A: Varied. 166

Q: *(L)* What is at the root of his activ- 167
ity?

A: Won't answer. 168

Q: *(L)* What are his thoughts or inten- 169
tions toward Caryl?

A: Ask that of all. 170

Q: *(J)* Ooh! *(BP)* All in this room? 171
(CD) Is Tim Crampton working for the government?

A: Cannot say, "Free will." 172

Q: *(GB)* Why don't we get off this sub- 173
ject and come back to it. Give me a definition of the soul. *(TM)* They never answered my question... will there be a mass UFO landing?

A: Too many concepts in one question. 174
Need review.

Q: *(L)* Will there be... *(TM)* A mass 175
landing of UFOs this year... *(J)* Anywhere in the world...

A: Need review. 176

Q: *(L)* They have answered those ques- 177
tions before.

A: Breakdown your question. 178

Q: *(L)* Will there be a mass landing 179
of the reptilian beings this year? *(BP)* Will they manifest publicly? *(L)* Will they land *en masse*?

A: Breakdown much further. 180

Q: *(L)* Will they present themselves to 181
the world as the rulers of the planet?

[7]This exclamation came from the guy who was going on about 'love and light'!!

182 **A**: Time.

183 **Q**: *(BP)* Before the end of 1995?

184 **A**: Don't know.

185 **Q**: *(L)* Do they have that in their plans to do that?

186 **A**: Laura, what have you learned?

187 **Q**: *(L)* OK, time for me to give you folks a review. [Review of the material omitted.]

188 **A**: CD under too much pressure to channel effectively.

189 **Q**: *(CD)* Are you talking about the article? *(L)* No, I think they mean just in general. You need relief, dear. *(CD)* No kidding. *(GB)* How do you spell relief? BP. [Laughter]

190 **A**: Mirth!!

191 **Q**: *(L)* On the twin question: are some groups working with the twins in STO?

192 **A**: Maybe.

193 **Q**: *(CD)* Is that what is happening with the prodigies, as I term them?

194 **A**: Yes.

195 **Q**: *(CD)* Am I a twin?

196 **A**: Yes.

197 **Q**: *(CD)* Is BP a twin?

198 **A**: No.

199 **Q**: *(L)* Is Caryl's twin the one who fed her all the information on color in 1987?

200 **A**: Partly.

201 **Q**: *(L)* Is Frank a twin?

202 **A**: No.

203 **Q**: *(L)* Is anyone else in this room a twin?

A: No. 204

Q: *(L)* Are there any humans involved 205 in this project?

A: Minutely. 206

Q: *(L)* And who is, in a general sense, 207 that is – what percentage of this phenomenon is STO?

A: Vague question. 208

Q: *(L)* What percentage of this Vanish- 209 ing Twin Phenomenon...

A: Small. 210

Q: *(GB)* So the idea is that the Van- 211 ishing Twin Phenomenon is the work of the STS beings? The reptilians. *(CD)* A small percentage is positive. *(GB)* What are they gaining out of it? *(L)* They are making bodies for themselves.

A: All has exception. 212

Q: *(L)* So, there are exceptions. *(GB)* 213 I had a very strange experience when I meditated a while back – was that positive or negative?

A: You have had many "strange" expe- 214 riences. Would you like to share any with those present, GB?[8]

Q: *(TM)* I think I know which one you 215 are talking about. *(L)* What was the nature of that experience?

A: Entity reflection through curtain. 216

Q: *(L)* Did you experience a being or 217 something? An energy? *(GB)* Was the entity reptilian that I manifested behind me? Or was this a positive or negative energy?

A: Both and neither.[9] 218

Q: *(L)* Was this a reptilian being? 219

A: Reflection. Projection. 220

[8] *The Wave* 10

[9] *The Wave* 21

221 **Q**: *(L)* What was it a projection of?

222 **A**: Complicated?

223 **Q**: *(L)* What was the source of this projection?

224 **A**: STS.

225 **Q**: *(BP)* I know exactly what it was! *(GB)* What were the loud whacks behind my chair? What did they try to tell me?

226 **A**: It was not a message, it was a "curtain breach."

227 **Q**: *(J)* Kind of like a dimensional sonic boom. *(GB)* Well, I heard a tremendous crack behind my chair when I asked for a sign. About seven large whacks on the floor. *(J)* Was there an entity standing behind his chair?

228 **A**: Yes, but again, GB has had a most interesting life, apparently he does not want to divulge this.

229 **Q**: *(L)* Well, three times they have hinted about this! [Laughter] *(BP)* And I thought I knew you! *(TM)* Yeah, he doesn't even know about it! *(BP)* Is GB a so-called abductee?

230 **A**: In more ways than one.

231 **Q**: *(BP)* Please clarify.

232 **A**: That is up to GB.

233 **Q**: *(L)* There are about 6 different kinds of abductions ranging from physical to telepathic contact and triggering.

234 **A**: And there are human abductions too.

235 **Q**: *(L)* You mean humans abduct people too? *(J)* Have humans abducted GB?

236 **A**: Up to GB.

237 **Q**: *(L)* Remember the gal, no names mentioned, who was supposedly hauled off by the Sasquatch? She came over to my house with bruises on the backs of her legs. Under hypnosis, she described being hauled out by the military and suggestions were implanted to make her think she had been abducted by aliens. She even perceived the truck they drove her off in as an alien craft hovering over the lake behind her house. Was GB abducted from the place on Stratford?

A: Yes. 238

Q: *(L)* Who abducted him at that time? And what did they do to him at that time? 239

A: Grays. Examined. 240

Q: *(L)* Was that his first abduction? 241

A: No. 242

Q: *(L)* When was he first abducted? 243

A: Age three. 244

Q: *(L)* How many times has GB been abducted? 245

A: 175 times. 246

Q: *(L)* When was the last contact? 247

A: Last week. 248

Q: *(GB)* Fooled me. *(J)* Obviously they have. *(L)* They can. That is what they do. *(GB)* What is the agenda for abducting me? 249

A: You know a lot, don't you? 250

Q: *(L)* Does GB have an implant? 251

A: Yes. 252

Q: *(GB)* Where? 253

A: In the brain. 254

Q: *(L)* What is it composed of? 255

A: Silicon. 256

Q: *(L)* Who put it in? 257

258 **A**: Grays.

259 **Q**: *(BP)* What is its purpose?

260 **A**: For Lizard monitor.

261 **Q**: *(L)* Well, we have all got one, so don't feel strange. *(GB)* Is that right? *(L)* Has anybody in this room not got an implant?

262 **A**: LM.[10]

263 **Q**: *(L)* Yes, well, my husband doesn't have one but that is only because he is an alligator hunter. [Laughter] *(TM)* That sort of answered the question I was going to ask. *(GB)* So all of us have implants.

264 **A**: This is why you are all interested in this subject.

265 **Q**: *(TM)* My next question is, where is my implant?[11]

266 **A**: You have two. One in brain behind sinus and one in leg bone.

267 **Q**: *(TM)* I have a suspicion that I might know when I got it, last year... I have been having nosebleeds. *(GB)* Well, your brain is behind your sinuses. *(L)* They have to go through your nose to get to your brain. *(J)* You may be aware of the penetration, but you are not aware of the final residence of the implant. *(TM)* Where was I when I got the one in my brain?

268 **A**: On travel sequence, in transit.

269 **Q**: *(L)* Did you travel last year? *(TM)* Where was I going?

270 **A**: In transit to some sort of gathering.

271 **Q**: *(TM)* I had in mind a particular time... I was hoping they would tell me something that would justify my suspicions.

A: You tell us. We see transit clearly, 272
but it is unclear why so rapid through 3rd level. Time cycle was interrupted and we can't see clearly due to cycle block.

Q: *(L)* Did you have missing time? 273
(TM) Not that I am aware of. In fact, I got somewhere sooner than I should have. *(L)* Well, that explains why they said "unclear why so rapid through 3rd level." *(J)* Did TM experience time acceleration?

A: You bet. 274

Q: *(TM)* What kind of vehicle was I 275
traveling in?

A: Can't see due to the cycle block. 276

Q: *(L)* What is a cycle block?[12] 277

A: Too complex, but it involves a dome 278
of frequency over subject.

Q: *(GB)* In a bubble? 279

A: Close. 280

Q: *(BP)* So, what they do is screw with 281
our perception of time, they just yank you out, do what they do, throw you back in and if it's faster, it's faster, if it's slower, it's slower. Who gives a hoot? *(L)* Sloppy work.

A: Close. 282

Q: *(J)* Kind of like putting people back 283
in the wrong cars or facing the wrong end of the bed, pajamas inside out, or whatever. *(BP)* People have woken up in different beds, in different houses, out in the woods, whatever.

[10]Actually, the fact that my ex-husband did *not* have an implant suggests that he didn't need one for some reason...

[11]*High Strangeness* 8

[12]*High Strangeness* 8

284 **A**: Yes.

285 **Q**: *(GB)* When was the last time my wife was abducted?

286 **A**: Last week.

287 **Q**: *(J)* Were they both abducted at the same time?

288 **A**: Yes.

289 **Q**: *(L)* They have told us that 94% are containers for the Lizzies to use. *(BP)* 94% of the population of the planet?! *(GB)* Let me get back to my wife. When we were both abducted together, was it a physical or other abduction?

290 **A**: Soul abduction.

291 **Q**: *(L)* Did it occur during the night while they were sleeping?

292 **A**: Yes.

293 **Q**: *(GB)* What did they do during the soul abduction? What was the purpose?

294 **A**: Knowledge review.

295 **Q**: *(GB)* For what benefit? *(J)* Who reviewed the knowledge?

296 **A**: Lizards, of course.

297 **Q**: *(J)* It was like a download. *(L)* Now, if they had discovered that GB and his wife had knowledge... that is, is there any knowledge that they might find during a review that might cause them to stop the abduction?

298 **A**: Open.

299 **Q**: *(L)* Are there any people, who, by virtue of their knowledge, do not get abducted?

300 **A**: Maybe.

301 **Q**: *(GB)* Is this to elevate our knowledge, or to monitor our knowledge?

302 **A**: Both, but mostly monitor.

Q: *(L)* How could being abducted by 303
the STS beings increase our knowledge?

A: Accidentally. 304

Q: *(L)* How would this be done acci- 305
dentally?

A: Self explanatory. 306

Q: *(L)* So, in other words, they 307
may abduct someone to monitor their knowledge, but if the individual has achieved a certain level of knowledge, the abduction only serves to add to their knowledge?

A: Yes. 308

Q: *(BP)* What is the Lizards' Achilles 309
heel?

A: STS. As in "wishful thinking" which 310
blocks knowledge.

Q: *(J)* Their singular preoccupation 311
with service to self blocks them from being able to move from 4th level.

A: Yes. 312

Q: *(TM)* Do they want to... *(J)* No they 313
are happy there... they want to stay there forever and control, and consume, and have a good time. *(BP)* It is like finding a place with really good food, a great place to live, great sex, everything you like, you would want to stay there. *(TM)* Don't a lot of us like the idea of staying in the 3rd level forever?

A: Yes. 314

Q: *(BP)* Under the control of the 315
Lizards! *(F)* But, you only want to stay in 3rd level forever if you are focused on STS. *(TM)* Yeah, but there are a lot of people on this Earth who want the physical world. *(J)* It's physicality. *(L)* They like to consume, because that is the essence of this 3rd density reality:

consumption. By being here you must consume. *(GB)* Is this message given to us tonight from 6th density beings?

316 **A**: Yes.

317 **Q**: *(GB)* Do you have power over 4th density Lizard beings?

318 **A**: That is not the issue. We choose STO.

319 **Q**: *(L)* STO beings do not exert power over anyone, they only serve all. When STS beings call for knowledge and have raised their frequency levels, which can be done while still remaining STS, the only place in the universe they will obtain knowledge is from STO beings, even though they may use this knowledge to serve themselves. STS beings won't *give* knowledge, because that is STO. *(GB)* Do the Lizzies have souls?

320 **A**: Yes.

321 **Q**: *(BP)* Were the Mayans an STS civilization?

322 **A**: No.

323 **Q**: *(BP)* Why did they engage in human sacrifice and so forth?

324 **A**: They did not.

325 **Q**: *(BP)* They did not?! *(L)* I think that's an archaeological fallacy. *(TM)* Yes. *(BP)* Isn't that fascinating! *(TM)* I am going to be looking into that in the next couple of months. *(L)* You ain't heard nothin' yet! *(TM)* Wasn't there another group... the Toltecs – were they the ones who engaged in human sacrifice?

326 **A**: At some point.

327 **Q**: *(GB)* Does my wife have an implant in her now? *(L)* You know the answer to that, GB.

328 **A**: Yes.

Q: *(TM)* I would like to find out the purpose of my implant. 329

A: Monitor. 330

Q: *(J)* Do I have an implant? 331

A: Yes. 332

Q: *(J)* Where is it? 333

A: This is getting redundant. 334

Q: *(BP)* Would it be helpful in STO to be able to rid ourselves of these implants? 335

A: Do you wish to get a quick ticket to level 5? 336

Q: [Laughter] *(BP)* Yes! That's exactly what I was thinking. I want to get the hell out of here. *(J)* That would do it, I guess! *(GB)* Ask and you shall receive! 337

A: Do you, BP, know what level 5 is? 338

Q: [Laughter] *(BP)* I thought I did! *(TM)* Be careful! *(L)* It's death. *(BP)* The intent behind the question was to become stronger in STO. *(L)* What they have told us on the implant question is... 339

A: You are an STO candidate. 340

Q: *(J)* You are already on the path, so don't worry about. *(L)* Terry had the idea that we should use their implants against them and blow their circuits. We were told that the thing to do is to simply not manifest the thoughts and feelings they like. This has happened to a peripheral person here. She was supposed to be at the meeting today but she called and left a message saying that she had gotten a psychic message that she was not to go and meet us there. I called her when I got home and told her what a great meeting she had missed. She called me back ten minutes later telling me I had a lot of 341 nerve putting her down and trampling all over her feelings. I was quite taken aback. The Lizzies are really working on her hard and are making her emotionally unstable, and making her receive everything positive in a negative way. As long as you *know* that they are going to play with your head and your emotions, if you know that this is not *you*, but head games from outside, then you don't have to own it. It isn't yours. We don't have to buy into these negative perceptions. *(F)* Part of the disinformation tells us that we are totally in control of our own ship, our own minds, everything that happens to us, create your own reality and so forth. So, when negative things happen or we think negative thoughts, we either believe them or think that we are trying to destroy our own selves. *(GB)* Are all in this room 4th density STO Candidates?

342 **A**: Open.

343 **Q**: *(GB)* Am I?

344 **A**: Yes.

345 **Q**: *(BP)* Am I?

346 **A**: Yes.

347 **Q**: *(J)* Am I?

348 **A**: Yes.

349 **Q**: *(GB)* is Caryl?

350 **A**: Sure. TM has a minor liver problem.

351 **Q**: *(BP)* How are we getting additional DNA? How is it developing? *(L)* The planet is being bombarded with the effects of this oncoming wave. *(F)* It was described to us as similar to a sea wave. *(L)* Yes, and we were told that when it hits it is going to be like a psychic thermonuclear explosion. I said, well, that sounds pleasant... we're all gonna blow up! *(BP)* Maybe you are too literal for them. *(GB)* BP, why don't you try the board now? Can we receive this information through meditation?

A: Yes. 352

Q: *(GB)* By asking for the light to come 353
in first?

A: Okay. 354

Q: *(L)* But watch the rituals. *(GB)* 355
Does meditation increase...

A: Rituals restrict. 356

Q: *(GB)* Does meditation increase the 357
DNA changing process?

A: Overall, if repetitive. 358

Q: *(L)* If you do it regularly. *(GB)* How 359
often? *(L)* Every day or as often as you can do it effortlessly. *(TM)* Is Denise an STO candidate?

A: Yes. 360

Q: *(L)* Another thing is that phys- 361
ical problems can come with DNA changes. *(TM)* I am experiencing a mild headache. Is this coming from what we are doing right now?

A: Yes. 362

Q: *(CD)* I want to know if the infor- 363
mation I learned that they warned me about had to do with Collette?

A: Maybe. 364

Q: *(CD)* What about Beverly? 365

A: Please discover, that is how you 366
learn.

Q: *(GB)* Why is Frank given this abil- 367
ity to tap into the energy of the 6th density?

A: Not correct concept. Frank's abili- 368
ties are not unique.

369 **Q**: *(BP)* Are you also transmitting through CLT in Los Angeles?

370 **A**: Maybe.

371 **Q**: *(T)* Is she in contact with you?

372 **A**: Open.

373 **Q**: *(BP)* Is the work of Carlos Castaneda historically accurate as far as what he says about don Juan?

374 **A**: Yes.

375 **Q**: *(T)* Cool! *(BP)* Are all members of my immediate biological family implanted?

376 **A**: No.

377 **Q**: *(BP)* Is my perception that my STO is primarily as a healer correct?

378 **A**: You are still STS, like all humans.

379 **Q**: *(J)* We are human, therefore STS, but we are STO candidates. *(T)* 3rd density beings are STS. *(CD)* Is BP's special gift as a healer?

380 **A**: One of them.

381 **Q**: *(L)* Ask if Reiki will enhance his healing abilities.

382 **A**: Of course, as always.

383 **Q**: *(L)* Reiki will boost your healing abilities 50% instantly. *(GB)* Could you explain the process of the soul?

384 **A**: Soul is consciousness, period.[13]

385 **Q**: *(BP)* Who is MH?

386 **A**: True STO.

387 **Q**: *(J)* True STO? Wow! *(L)* Who is MH? *(BP)* Is she a 5th density walk-in?

388 **A**: Yes.

Q: *(J)* Where does she live? *(L)* Who is 389 this person? *(T)* Is there more besides just a yes?

A: Yes. 390

Q: *(T)* So, continue. 391

A: Exactly!! 392

Q: *(L)* Who is MH? *(BP)* Damn! I took 393 a trip with Reynaldo T, I met M___-there and we were thrown together in an obvious sort of *Celestine Prophecy* sort of way, you know, like hit me over the head. And we did this thing at the sacrificial well in Chichen Itza that was apparently some kind of cleansing, because, according to the archaeological inaccuracies, that is where the people were all sacrificed. Maybe they weren't sacrificed, maybe they were volunteers. *(L)* Maybe it was a different culture altogether. *(BP)* Yes, because we don't know who all was there. The Mayans may have been long gone. Anyway, we did some sort of healing there and afterward M___ told me a lot of stuff about who she was: on January 11, 1991, she was an ordinary person, she was driving down the road in her car and she felt a presence in her car that turned out to be Jesus Christ. She was taken out of her body, her life was reviewed for her, she was taken to 5th density, which she says is what we know as heaven, and after about 20 minutes or so, she returned as, apparently, someone else. She became very psychic and started having all these experiences. Classic walk-in story. Among other things she says now her body is silicone based and that she is here to anchor a certain energy. My feeling was that, well, I was bouncing back and forth between feeling that this was a demented house-

[13] *The Wave* 10

wife or a f****** angel walking on the planet. That was my reaction. I sort of fell in love with her except that I wasn't physically attracted to her. She did some work on me. I didn't feel a thing. We spent 6 days in each other's company. So, I have been rather curious. And then, Caryl just sort of blew up in the middle of it. And it was so obvious to me that I had to follow my spirit in that direction and that was what I was supposed to do. It didn't feel like STS, but who knows? M__-_ reacted extremely negatively. We had not consummated the relationship. She is still living with her husband who won't touch her, who thinks she is crazy – he is total 3rd density. She hadn't been able to get out of that situation. She is way into some weird stuff. *(L)* Well, M___ may be pure STO, but she may not be fully manifested in the body. *(BP)* Yeah, she says she is having a lot of trouble anchoring here. *(L)* My thought is that a lot of us are actually 4th density beings who have come back down to serve. *(BP)* We are all multi-dimensional masters playing at limitation. *(BP)* Who is Reynaldo T?

394 **A**: In what respect?

395 **Q**: *(BP)* Is he a Gray experiment gone awry?

396 **A**: No such thing.

397 **Q**: *(BP)* Is Caryl's assessment of him correct?

398 **A**: Close.

399 **Q**: *(BP)* Is what he is teaching in terms of healing accurate?

400 **A**: Open.

401 **Q**: *(TM)* I have a close friend who had a personal experience with him... *(BP)* Was it a female? *(TM)* Yes. *(BP)* Yeah, it happens all the time... [Laughter]

A: Cute. 402

Q: *(L)* Ask if MH fully manifested as a 5th density STO being? 403

A: Define. 404

Q: *(L)* Is she doing her work as she is supposed to? 405

A: Close. 406

Q: *(BP)* Does she know clearly who she is? 407

A: No, not yet? 408

Q: *(BP)* Will she find out in Hawaii? 409

A: Maybe. 410

Q: *(CD)* Has BP fulfilled his interaction with her? 411

A: Open. 412

Q: *(BP)* Can I be of any further service to M___? 413

A: Up to you. 414

Q: *(GB)* Can they manifest a sighting to us individually or as a group of any density? 415

A: Now, this is an interesting question with many answers. You can manifest sightings any time. But, the question is, how? 416

Q: *(BP)* Tell us how. 417

A: Meditation. Grays craft over Land O' Lakes tonight. 418

Q: *(T)* Are they coming this way? 419

A: Open. Why don't you ever have someone watching over this house during sessions? 420

Q: *(T)* That's a very good question. We have thought about it but nobody ever wants to be the one to do it. *(BP)* 421

Well, if it was just one person out there, for God's sake, they could put a rope on 'em... *(L)* My neighbors already want to burn crosses on my lawn... *(BP)* Are we calling in physical danger by seeking to interact with these craft?

422 **A**: Knowledge protects.

423 **Q**: *(GB)* What is the knowledge that protects? *(J)* You are in danger if you are not aware... *(BP)* I say let's go to Land O' Lakes. *(LM)* How can knowledge protect you? They can zap you and suck you up in a light beam... *(J)* They are doing it all the time anyway.

424 **A**: Only if ignorant.

425 **Q**: *(LM)* You mean if a tractor beam comes out of a ship and you know it is a tractor beam, it can't get you? *(L)* You have to understand you are dealing with 4th density beings. *(BP)* Is a reasonable motive in seeking interaction with these craft the desire to confirm the validity of what you are transmitting to us?

426 **A**: Okay.

427 **Q**: *(J)* GB went out to look. *(T)* I didn't know you could see Land O' Lakes from here. *(LM)* If it is 5 miles high it's easy. *(F)* The very first time we did anything with this, a whole UFO flap started in the area. *(J)* Well, one transcript said that there was a craft over the house at that moment. Why wasn't there an immediate stampede for the door? *(L)* I didn't want to see anything. *(GB)* I just went out there and I didn't see anything. *(BP)* Is it necessary, through meditation or other methods, to raise one's frequency in order to see these craft? Are they always around?

428 **A**: Close. Not "Raise," change.

[Everyone got up and went outside, tape was turned off and not turned back on. However the answers were written down as notes.]

Q: [Question lost] 429

A: Open. 430

Q: [Question lost] 431

A: Why didn't you see the first person? 432

Q: [Question lost] 433

A: Two. 434

Q: [Question lost] 435

A: Head, brain stem and behind eye. 436

Q: [Question lost] 437

A: Yes. 438

Q: [Question lost] 439

A: Funny. 440

Q: [Question lost] 441

A: No, not important. 442

Q: [Question lost] 443

A: If you make it to level 4 it will not matter. 444

Q: [Question lost] 445

A: So what? 446

Q: [Question lost] 447

A: No. 448

Q: [Question lost] 449

A: No. 450

Q: [Question lost] 451

A: Yes. 452

Q: [Question lost] 453

A: Missing time. 454

Q: [Question lost] 455

A: Light flash. 456

Q: [Question lost] 457

A: Michelle. 458

459 **Q**: [Question lost]

460 **A**: Sure, why not?

461 **Q**: [Question lost]

462 **A**: No.

463 **Q**: [Question lost]

464 **A**: Mirth.

465 **Q**: [Question lost]

466 **A**: Yes.

467 **Q**: [Question lost]

468 **A**: You are screwing around with us.

469 **Q**: [Question lost]

470 **A**: No.

471 **Q**: [Question lost]

472 **A**: Lizards are always present on level
4.

473 **Q**: [Question lost]

474 **A**: Close.

475 **Q**: [Question lost]

476 **A**: Open.

477 **Q**: [Question lost]

478 **A**: Wait and see.

479 **Q**: [Question lost]

480 **A**: Yes.

481 **Q**: [Question lost]

482 **A**: No.

483 **Q**: [Question lost]

484 **A**: Roommate was zoned out.

485 **Q**: [Question lost]

486 **A**: Grays.

487 **Q**: [Question lost]

488 **A**: No.

489 **Q**: [Question lost]

490 **A**: STS.

Q: [Question lost] 491

A: Up to you. 492

Q: [Question lost] 493

A: Open. 494

Q: [Question lost] 495

A: Subjective. 496

Q: [Question lost] 497

A: No. 498

Q: [Question lost] 499

A: Discover, ie: learn. Learning is how 500
you progress.

Q: [Question lost] 501

A: Senses. 502

Q: [Question lost] 503

A: Yes. 504

Q: [Question lost] 505

A: Yes. 506

Q: [Question lost] 507

A: Close. 508

Q: [Question lost] 509

A: Open. 510

[Tape recorder turned back on.]

Q: *(TM)* I have a friend by the name 511
of L___ and I wonder if it is good for
me to spend time with him?

A: Open. 512

Q: *(TM)* Who is LH? 513

A: Open. 514

Q: *(TM)* What I am trying to find out 515
is if it is good to be around this person.

516 **A**: Those are personal questions. There will be a terrorist attack in the U.S. month; bomb.[14]

517 **Q**: *(T)* There is going to be a terrorist attack in the United States in a month?

518 **A**: Yes!!! [Planchette flies off board again; retrieved.]

519 **Q**: *(T)* In a month?

520 **A**: Yes.

521 **Q**: *(T)* Where in the United States?

522 **A**: Washington D.C.

523 **Q**: *(T)* Well, they filed bankruptcy, now they are going to blow it up and collect the insurance.

524 **A**: Trial ongoing.

Q: *(BP)* O.J.? *(TM)* Oh, that's because of the terrorist trial? *(T)* Yes, the terrorist trial in New York. *(TM)* Yes, they are guarding Wall Street heavily because they are threatening to blow that up. *(J)* Oh, OK. *(BP)* Is the CIA or the FBI involved in this terrorist bombing? 525

A: No. 526

Q: *(T)* Do they know about it? 527

A: No. 528

Q: *(BP)* Is it Muslim terrorists? 529

A: Yes. 530

Q: *(BP)* Are we talking about a nuclear bomb? 531

[14] Actually, it was just a little bit more than a month from the session date. On April 19, the now famous Oklahoma City bombing occurred. It didn't happen in Washington, but rather on the Alfred P. Murrah Federal Building in downtown Oklahoma. Supposedly, Timothy McVeigh was after revenge against the federal government for their handling of the Waco siege, which ended in the deaths of 76 people exactly two years before the bombing, as well as for the Ruby Ridge incident in 1992.

Wikipedia tells us:

> McVeigh hoped to inspire a revolt against what he considered to be a tyrannical federal government. He was convicted of eleven federal offenses and sentenced to death. Surprisingly, his execution was carried out unusually quickly, as most convicts on death row in the United States spend many years there before being executed. McVeigh was executed only four years later, by lethal injection on June 11, 2001, at the Federal Correctional Complex in Terre Haute, Indiana. Terry Nichols and Michael Fortier were also convicted as conspirators in the plot. Terry Nichols was sentenced to 161 life terms without parole. Fortier was sentenced to 12 years and has since been released. [...] It is claimed that while visiting friends in Decker, Michigan, McVeigh complained that the Army had implanted a microchip into his buttocks so that the government could keep track of him.
> [http://en.wikipedia.org/wiki/Timothy_McVeigh]

If you read the entire entry, you'll see that McVeigh's real target was the Federal Government in general. Apparently it was correct that the CIA and FBI were not involved nor did they know about it, but it seems to be incorrect that it was in any way related to Muslims.

The questions trying to pin down the location were interesting because the Cs said it would not be in the Capitol, nor the White House, but "maybe" in a federal office building.

532 **A**: No.

533 **Q**: *(T)* We should be so lucky. *(J)* Can you pinpoint where the bomb is going to be in Washington? *(BP)* Congress?

534 **A**: No.

535 **Q**: *(BP)* Will it be in the Capitol?

536 **A**: No.

537 **Q**: *(BP)* Will it be in the White House?

538 **A**: No.

539 **Q**: *(BP)* Will it be in a federal office building?

540 **A**: Maybe.

541 **Q**: *(BP)* So, it is variable as to whether it will be successful or not as well as other aspects?

542 **A**: Yes.

543 **Q**: *(T)* Do the authorities have an idea that this is going to happen yet?

544 **A**: Some.

545 **Q**: *(T)* Some authorities or some idea?

A: Idea. 546

Q: *(GB)* Any further predictions? 547

A: Amtrak derailment in Long Island 548
or Chicago. Near one or the other by June.

Q: *(L)* Is this going to be a deliberate 549
act?

A: No. 550

Q: *(L)* Why are the two locations so 551
widely separated?

A: Indefinite.[15] 552

Q: *(L)* So, it is like an amorphous event 553
that hasn't firmed up yet. *(GB)* Any more predictions?

A: One person here will be in a mi- 554
nor car accident by April. Think GB or TM. There will be a storm in Mid U.S. next month; lives lost 191; Missouri area likely.[16]

End of Session

[15] As far as I know, this prediction did not pan out. However, there was a serious train accident that June:

> June 16, 1995 – United States – Gettysburg Railroad Boiler Explosion, Gardners, Pennsylvania. A Gettysburg Railroad steam locomotive suffers a catastrophic boiler explosion due to low water. Three crew are seriously injured. The National Transportation Safety Board investigated, finding poor training, complacency and a general loss of the craft skills needed to operate and maintain steam. They also reported that an even more serious explosion had been averted by the fact that the locomotive was fitted with fusible plugs, a safety feature rarely found in North America but common in Europe. Major new regulation of steam locomotives followed.

[16] Again, as far as I know, there was no storm in Missouri that killed a lot of people that year, though there were a number of tornadoes in that area in that time frame.

The UFO Mass Landing

Trying to search for a source of the mass UFO landing discussed above, all I was able to find is the following:

A cleaning lady discovered a "dusty, leather-bound diary" of Pope John XXIII when sorting through boxes in a little used Vatican storage room, according to a story in the *Manila Bulletin* that was later reprinted by the *Philippine News* on March 10, 1993. The article also included diary entries which were released by Father Guiseppe D'Angelo, who thoroughly studied the diary.

Here is a portion of the article:

> The entries clearly spell out the assassination of John F. Kennedy, America's plunge into the Vietnam War, unrest in the Middle East and the fall of communism years before they took place. Later entries call for even more troubled times.
>
> "Pope John had periodic visits from both Jesus and the Virgin Mary," says Rev. Guiseppe D'Angelo, who's pored over the wondrous tales. "These sessions in the Pope's chambers resulted in fantastic glimpses into the future of mankind...
>
> "Pope John writes of Heavenly visitors arriving by June 1995 in flaming chariots of steel. These special visitors will arrive at the height of despair and help man heal his wounds and work together to right all the horrible wrongs."
>
> Father D'Angelo, 73, has agreed to release some of the diary entries made between February of 1959 and April of 1963. The scrawled messages reveal a frightened and excited pontiff who decided to keep his meetings with Christ and the Madonna a secret.

Here are two entries from the Pope's diary:

> MAY 19, 1962: "From the Heavens will appear the saviors. They will arrive on June 5, 1995, and begin their task of assisting the clean up and repair of the environment and the crippled countries. Many will fear these odd-looking beings, but they come in peace and will with God's guidance transform Earth from a charred, spinning rock to a lush oasis in space. The survivors will flourish in a world without war, disease or hatred. My heart is finally at peace with this knowledge that there is hope for humanity."

> JULY 2, 1962: "The Madonna tells me this will be her final visit. It is a joyous one for she shares tremendous news. As the year 1998 arrives, our Heavenly friends will have shared much of their advanced knowledge. Mankind will at last wipe out most of its diseases and our life spans will increase to the length of those listed in the Bible. The visitors will also share the remarkable power of resurrection, and throngs of the wrongly dead will rise again."

Pope John XXIII died a year later on June 3, 1963, without sharing with the world the spiritual messages he received in his private chambers.

The information apparently comes from *Insight*, a religious magazine of some sort, reprinted from *The Manila Bulletin* where it originally appeared. This copy was distributed by certain groups in several catholic churches in Metro Manila in the Philippines. (More about it here: http://www.ufoupdateslist.com/digest/DIGEST22.TXT)

The Vanishing Twin Phenomenon

Caryl Dennis writes on her website:

> The Vanishing Twin Phenomenon or Syndrome *(VTP)*, as it is known in the medical literature, is explored extensively in the 1995 text *Multiple Pregnancy: Epidemiology, Gestation & Perinatal Outcome.* With contributions from over 80 experts from around the world, this book offers a definitive and comprehensive examination of the subject of twins. In it, Dr. Charles Boklage states: "In reality [...] losing one or both offspring from a twin pregnancy is too common to be called phenomenal, and occurs for too many different reasons to qualify as a syndrome. There is little room to doubt that the question of vanishing twins and sole survivors of twin gestation represent issues of broad and fundamental importance." With the growing use of fertility drugs and in vitro fertilization, and as more women choose to begin their families later in life – thereby increasing their chances of multiple ovulation – the number of multiple pregnancies is soaring. [...]
>
> My preliminary interviews with over 200 "twinless twins" indicates that the loss of a twin in utero can have profound physical, mental and emotional effects, both on the surviving child and

> its parents – especially if it is unacknowledged. Unfortunately, I have found very few instances in which healthcare providers discuss these potential problems with the parents. The surviving twin may never learn of the loss of its companion; myriad psychological problems can result, with no context in which to process them. Parents are often left with unacknowledged feelings of confusion, loss and/or grief.

You can read more here: http://caryl.ipower.com/wordpress/vanishing-twins

Tom French and Cherie Diez

The day this session was held was also the day that I met the *St. Petersburg Times* journalist Tom French and photographer Cherie Diez, who had been in the audience. He had come up to me after the meeting, gave me his card, and asked for my phone number, saying he wanted to call me later. He later wrote about this meeting:

> I met Laura for the first time on the afternoon of Saturday, Feb. 25, 1995, at the east branch of the Clearwater Library. She and I were there for the meeting of a local chapter of the Mutual UFO Network, better known as MUFON, an organization that investigates reports of UFOs and alien abductions. I had not been aware that there was any such chapter in Tampa Bay, much less that it had enough members for them to congregate en masse at the public library. I wanted to know more, so I went.
>
> This was in the early stages of the current national obsession with all things UFO-related. *The X-Files* was only in its second season, the so-called alien autopsy video was not yet airing on the Fox network, and the only person I knew personally who had seen a UFO – or at least, who had admitted such a thing to me – was my former hairdresser.
>
> Still, the congregants at the library were excited that Saturday. They knew that a ground swell of interest in other worlds and other intelligences was gaining momentum around the country; they sensed that they were in the first wave of a profound shift in the public's willingness to consider the possibility that alien visitations might just be a verifiable fact of life on this planet. After years of being derided, these people were finally getting some attention and respect.

To say that Laura made an impression that day is an understatement. When it was her turn to speak, she instantly seized control of the room. She had so much presence, she was almost radioactive. And hers was no ordinary presence. She was not about to be mistaken for a movie star; she was overweight and slightly mussed, and her clothes were almost defiantly unfashionable. She wore leggings that, as I recall, were a little too tight and a tunic adorned with amber beads and painted gold spirals. I took one look at her and said to myself, "I bet she has a bust of Elvis in her living room."

Somehow, though, Laura used all these qualities to her advantage. She was too much, and knew it, and did not care; if anything, she reveled in her over-the-topness, which gave her tremendous freedom and power. Her eyes flashed; her hair flowed freely; her slightly crooked smile ignited the atmosphere around her.

In a short talk, apparently delivered without any notes, Laura gave an overview of her life, telling a little about her childhood, her work as an exorcist, her hypnosis session with the woman with the missing time, the night she and the kids saw the two ships above their swimming pool. She also spoke about some recent experiences with a spirit board, which as I understood it was similar to a Ouija board but more elaborate. Using this spirit board, she said, she and [Frank] and some other friends had begun communicating with what she called "sixth-density beings" from the stars that make up the Cassiopeia constellation.

Laura's story was easily the wildest I heard that day. It didn't matter. She was smart, charming, completely real. She joked about herself, her kids, her husband, her family's decidedly offbeat riff on middle-class life. She even joked about these sixth-density beings, whatever they were. "The boys from Brazil," she called them, and the way she said it made me laugh, even though I had no clue what she was talking about.

She was giving a performance, and I was not the only one in the audience who enjoyed it. Cherie Diez, a *Times* photographer with whom I'd worked for many years, had come with me to the MUFON meeting. The two of us were searching for someone unusual to follow for the newspaper. After seeing and listening to Laura that day, Cherie and I believed that we had found a subject who exceeded our every expectation.

In between our work on other projects for the paper, we were drawn again and again to Laura's house in New Port Richey, hanging out for hours at a time with her and her family and friends. What we saw, every time we visited, was a woman leading a life on her own terms, defining herself every day. Laura's life was crammed with seemingly incongruous elements. She was a walking smorgasbord of the paranormal, yes. But she was also a mother of five, making dinner and doing the laundry while she pursued aliens and demonic spirits. She was a glorious amalgamation, a mixture of Bette Midler, Father Damien, Donna Reed and Agent Scully.

Laura defied all categories. She did not, would not fit into any box, including one that I had tried to stick her into that first day at the MUFON meeting. When I toured her home, I found no bust of Elvis in the living room. But on her mantel, above the fireplace, there was an eerie, almost ghostly ceramic pitcher bearing the likeness of Edward VIII. Laura's grandparents had bought it in 1937, just after Edward gave up the English throne to marry Wallis Simpson.

So much for my stereotyping.

Laura's house was one huge encyclopedia of her life, overflowing with things that testified to the breadth of her curiosity and interests.

On the walls hung Victorian prints from her grandparents, a painting of Jesus, a map of the world, pieces of her children's artwork, oversized reproductions of tarot cards, *Star Trek* posters the kids had put up. Laura's study was lined with shelves crammed with hundreds and hundreds of books. Scanning through just a few of the titles, I found *Angels and Aliens*, *The Bible as History*, *On the Dead Sea Scrolls*, *Alien Intelligence*, *Genesis Revisited*, *UFO Encounters & Beyond*, *Infinity and the Mind*, *Extra-Terrestrials Among Us*.

Read more: http://www.sptimes.com/News/webspecials/exorcist

March 4, 1995

The regular group met and had a long discussion about recent sessions attended by various persons and how that affected the Cs' transmissions. Well, what was really being affected was not the Cs, but us, the receivers. We knew that we needed to figure this out and put some kind of controls in place if we really wanted the information to come through as un-corrupted as possible.

Participants: 'Frank', Laura, Terry and Jan, Susan V

1 **Q**: *(T)* Good evening.

2 **A**: Luck.

3 **Q**: *(L)* Is the luck with us at this time?

4 **A**: Yes.

5 **Q**: *(L)* Who do we have with us this evening?

6 **A**: Not yet.

7 **Q**: *(L)* The luck is not yet with us?

8 **A**: Try not to second guess what we mean.

9 **Q**: *(L)* What does "luck" mean?

10 **A**: Nilionna from "Cassiopaea."

11 **Q**: *(L)* What does the term "luck" refer to?

12 **A**: Discover.

13 **Q**: *(L)* Are we going to discover something very soon that is lucky for us as a group?

A: Second guessing![1] 14

Q: *(T)* Hi, Nilionna! 15

A: Hello. 16

Q: *(L)* Nilionna, have you been listening to our discussion? 17

A: Maybe. 18

Q: *(L)* We have been discussing some control systems for our sessions. 19

A: Okay. 20

Q: *(L)* Are you saying that the control systems we are trying to set up are OK? 21

A: Yes. No time limit, though, when it is advantageous to stop for your benefit, the sessions will terminate. 22

Q: *(L)* In other words, we aren't supposed to put a time limit on it. *(T)* Cool, works for me. *(J)* I had a thought, Laura – even though Diana M was not present, her presence was felt before we opened up the channel because you are still torqued up about her. So she has had an effect. *(L)* You 23

[1]Interestingly, my husband Ark was born in Luck, Poland. But this was 16 months before we 'met' via the posting of a Cs' session online. Was this being dropped as a clue for me?

want to ask that? *(J)* Yes. Is DM having an influence on the session because of her phone contact with Frank and because of the way I reacted to her?

24 **A**: Perceptive of you, Jan!

25 **Q**: *(L)* Are we correct in what we have discussed, that her presence has a corrupting influence on the channel?

26 **A**: Clear.

27 **Q**: *(L)* What does that mean? *(T)* The channel is clear. *(L)* Is the channel clear right now?

28 **A**: Her.

29 **Q**: *(L)* She is clear?

30 **A**: Up.

31 **Q**: *(L)* I don't understand? *(J)* Clear her up?

32 **A**: Yes.

33 **Q**: *(J)* That is what we are going to do. She has made an appointment and it is in progress. *(T)* She needs spirit release. *(L)* On that subject, before we get going, let me ask about DM.

34 **A**: Enough said, remember, you have been learning slowly that personal issues hold minor significance. Terry's dream was significant, however!!!!! SV too!! And Frank has been sent same message as well.

35 **Q**: *(L)* Did you have a dream or message, Frank? *(F)* That's true. I did have some funny feelings. *(T)* Did you have something else? *(F)* Well, I have received some stuff. Just the same kind of thing, that there is something that we are missing. *(T)* OK. We are missing a key topic or issue, here, that's true.

36 **A**: 4th level STO!

Q: *(L)* Is that the title of the topic? 37

A: You have only thought of 4th level STS. 38

Q: *(L)* Ahhh! What SV was talking about, we need to ask about the good guys. 39

A: They are the only ones who can help you defend yourselves against 4th level attack!!!! We give you information which is invaluable in nature, but remember we are 6th level STO, Beings of light, and on this density level there simply is no interference with free will no matter how detrimental to you!!![2] 40

Q: *(T)* 4th density STO beings can actually help in a meaningful way! We knew there was both sides, but we never asked. We have been concentrating on the Lizards. *(S)* Yeah! There are 16 groups on both sides, and nobody has ever asked... *(J)* And by concentrating on the Lizards, we have been feeding their f****** energy. *(F)* Their damn energy. *(J)* Their damn energy. *(T)* That *darn* energy! Who are these 4th density STO beings that we need to contact? Obviously we need to talk to them because they can talk to us. 6th density 'us' can't. 41

A: Orion Federation. 42

Q: *(L)* And who are the members of the Orion Federation? 43

A: Not yet. 44

Q: *(L)* What can you tell us? *(T)* The Orion Federation is 4th density? 45

A: You have asked us to protect you, it is important for you to understand that we are beyond that! 46

Q: *(L)* We understand that. *(J)* I understand that. *(T)* We understand that 47

[2] *The Wave* 44

you, at 6th density, can't interfere with free will on either side. But, the Orion Federation...

48 **A**: First, incorrect thought patterns which have become imbedded must be purged before you can move onto next subject.

49 **Q**: *(J)* It's like: DM must be purged before she can come back into this group, she must get rid of her incorrect thought patterns. We have incorrect thought patterns that must be removed also. *(L)* What are they, Frank? *(F)* Don't ask me. Ask them. *(J)* Well, they're not going to tell us that. *(T)* Why not? Let's ask. *(F)* Yeah, if they are not going to tell us, they will tell us that they are not going to tell us. *(T)* What are the incorrect thought patterns?

50 **A**: That we protect.

51 **Q**: *(T)* Well, you said that knowledge protects. You have been providing knowledge. *(J)* Uh uh. *(T)* No?

52 **A**: Indirectly.

53 **Q**: *(J)* They are not really giving it to us, they are helping us to draw it out of ourselves.

54 **A**: We are providing invaluable information which becomes knowledge, but you are under attack, therefore, you could maybe use some direct power from the same density as the attack is coming from.

55 **Q**: *(F)* But, until you have total knowledge... *(L)* You don't have the kind of power we are talking about needing. *(F)* Right. We would would need 500,000 pages of transcript to have that kind of knowledge, to get to that point. *(L)* OK, what is the phone number of the Orion Federation? *(S)* Laura! *(T)* That's what I was going to ask. [Laughter] *(L)* How do we get ahold of them?

56 **A**: Off the hook!

57 **Q**: *(T)* Uh oh! *(L)* They're busy? *(T)* Getting a lot of calls. *(L)* OK, guys, what do we need to do here?

58 **A**: Find a "Nordic." They are on Earth posing as humans.[3]

59 **Q**: *(T)* They are 4th density. I thought they...

60 **A**: Yes.

61 **Q**: *(T)* I thought that 4th density couldn't hold the frequency that long and that is why the Lizards have so much trouble. *(J)* They're STS.

62 **A**: Not STO!

63 **Q**: *(T)* Very good, Jan hit it as they said it. The STS can't stay, only the STO.

64 **A**: Yes.

65 **Q**: *(T)* So, we need to find a Nordic – do we know one?

66 **A**: Have seen them at meetings and such.

67 **Q**: *(L)* What kind of meetings? *(J)* MUFON meetings?

68 **A**: MUFON.

69 **Q**: *(T)* I guess that means we are infiltrated over there. *(L)* Was there one at last week's meeting?

70 **A**: ?? Discover, remember these are among your protectors and Laura and Frank know what level one attack is like, Terry, Jan and SV are perilously close to finding out!

[3] *The Wave* 44

71 **Q**: *(T)* And we are working hard to not get attacked. We have a Nordic coming to our meetings? *(J)* Did we meet one today? *(L)* They gave a question mark to that one. What about this big conference in May?

72 **A**: Discover.

73 **Q**: *(L)* Well, should we wear something special like a red scarf so they can find us in the crowd? *(T)* Wait, wait...

74 **A**: Not needed at all, just be open and aware!![4]

75 **Q**: *(L)* Is this there any way we can get any help or power from these 4th density good guys prior to that so that we can put a period to this attack we have been undergoing?

76 **A**: Start to call them, maybe.

77 **Q**: *(L)* How do we call them. *(T)* They said "discover!" They don't usually say that in regard to the project awareness meeting. *(L)* Yes. OK.

78 **A**: Hint!

79 **Q**: *(T)* Thank you! *(L)* How do we call them? *(T)* We are calling them, we have our information packs out. *(J)* On the board?

80 **A**: No.

81 **Q**: *(L)* No, not on the board. *(T)* They'll come to us.

82 **A**: They are 4th, not 6th.

83 **Q**: *(T)* We can't contact them through the board because they are only 4th density? Is there a problem there?

84 **A**: Not conventional. It would be like using a FAX to contact Fido.

Q: *(J)* Is there any significance to the fact that one of our cats has been looking like she is really trying to tell us something?[5] 85

A: One of your cats, no, make that 2 of your cats, are close to transition to 3rd level. 86

Q: *(T)* Sabrina's moving up in the world, she's going to get a promotion. *(J)* What's going to happen to her when she hits 3rd? She's going to be a human? 87

A: Yes. 88

Q: *(J)* Wow. *(T)* When she moves from cat to human, her cat body will die? 89

A: Yes. 90

Q: *(T)* Is this going to happen some time in the near future as we measure it? 91

A: Not concept, we mean at next incarnation whenever that occurs. By the way, who gave her that name? 92

Q: *(J)* What name? *(L)* Sabrina? *(S)* The cat's name? *(T)* Two of our cats? *(L)* Maybe. *(T)* They are 3rd density candidates. *(J)* What about the name? 93

A: Exactly. 94

Q: *(L)* Does that mean that when a person is a 4th density candidate that they have to leave their body to go to 4th density? 95

A: Yes unless they are in the body when the Wave arrives. 96

Q: *(J)* What about the name? *(T)* Do you mean who gave the kitty the name? 97

A: No. 98

---

4 *The Wave* 44

5 *The Wave* 2

99 **Q**: *(T)* Oh, you mean why did I name that particular cat? It's not Sabrina?

100 **A**: ? There are 2 candidates.

101 **Q**: *(T)* So, you are not going to give us the name. *(J)* Is there any significance to the behavior that the cat, Sabrina, has been displaying?

102 **A**: Maybe.

103 **Q**: *(L)* Well, let's go back to our Orion guys for a few minutes. Have you given us all you are going to give us on this seeking of help and protection?

104 **A**: Review.

105 **Q**: *(J)* OK. *(T)* We gave out over a hundred of those pamphlets. If they are going to the meetings, they've got one. We are already calling them. *(J)* Will they contact us or do we have to recognize and contact them?

106 **A**: They know about you even without pamphlets.

107 **Q**: *(L)* This individual who sent me this letter, this Thor Templar...

108 **A**: Open.

109 **Q**: *(T)* Can you give him a weapons design? *(L)* Oh god! *(T)* Humor, mirth! *(L)* You did tell us at one point that we could achieve a certain level of protection with stones, crystals, and so forth – is that correct?

110 **A**: Yes but crystals are "small potatoes."

111 **Q**: *(L)* Is there anything we can do with our thinking patterns or with our bodies, or anything we can do to accelerate the receiving of assistance?

112 **A**: Unite.

113 **Q**: *(J)* That is what we are doing. In other words, keep on keeping on.

A: Not. You are still STS. 114

Q: *(L)* What can we do to accelerate 115 this process, this uniting, this moving from STS to STO?

A: 8 Questions at once. 116

Q: *(L)* Maybe I will just say a little bit 117 of what I think it is.

A: Okay. 118

Q: *(L)* Part of my perception of this is 119 seeing that whatever I have or receive is shared with the group in terms of my time, my energy, my thoughts, my finances, and everything that is related to that – is that correct?

A: Evaluate attack intensity. 120

Q: *(T)* How strong is the attack? What 121 is the intensity you have experienced. *(L)* Well, it has been financial through various institutions, mostly. *(F)* Yes, I would have to agree that we have been attacked in that way to a level never before experienced in middle-class America. *(J)* Is that the type of attack being referred to?

A: Part. 122

Q: *(L)* Is another part of the attack the 123 emotional upheaval I experienced a few weeks ago?

A: Part. 124

Q: *(J)* What about Diana M? 125

A: Part, accident, etc., etc. Not DM 126 per se, but through her.

Q: *(L)* So the accident and all the other 127 physical things are part of the attack?

A: Yes. 128

Q: *(L)* Does prayer help? 129

A: Terry and Jan are next in line. 130

Q: *(L)* Well, my suggestion would be 131 to not leave your shoelaces untied!

(F) Oh, God! You don't want to go through this, believe me. *(T)* Well, there is not much they can do to us at this point.

132 **A**: Not true!

133 **Q**: *(L)* OK guys, you are telling us we are under attack, you are telling us it is going to get worse, you are telling us that maybe some of these other guys can help us out. What can we do in the meantime?

134 **A**: Prayers help but more is needed.

135 **Q**: *(T)* More than prayers is needed. So, we are on our own until we get contacted?

136 **A**: Find an Orion!!!

137 **Q**: *(J)* How? *(L)* What do we do, go out to the beach and say: "Orions, come here?" *(T)* No, they are at the disco – Orions like to dance.

138 **A**: That is all we can tell you, because it is the limit of informative arena, any further would interfere with free will, so discover.[6]

139 **Q**: *(L)* One session I asked about some things that happened to me in the past and I was told that what saved my buns from the fire was divine intervention.

140 **A**: Yes.

141 **Q**: *(L)* Can you tell us about divine intervention?

142 **A**: Multifaceted.

Q: *(L)* Was this divine intervention en- 143
acted to protect me from direful consequences that would have prevented me from doing whatever work is forming up for me in the future?

A: Yes. 144

Q: *(L)* Does it not seem that being un- 145
der attack as we are now might further prevent me, as well as my compatriots, from doing our work?

A: Of course. 146

Q: *(L)* Well, does it not then behoove 147
this same divine intervention enacted at these other times to act at this time, or is the threat less?

A: Divine intervention cannot be ar- 148
ranged by 3rd level beings.

Q: *(L)* What level beings arrange di- 149
vine intervention?

A: 4th through 7th. 150

Q: *(T)* So, we are just shy of a level to 151
do that! We can do some quasi-divine intervention!

A: You cannot do this divine interven- 152
tion. You can do 3rd level intervention.

Q: *(Laura, Jan)* What is third level in- 153
tervention? [Pause] *(T)* They're accessing the cosmic retrieval system.

A: Discover. 154

Q: *(L)* Give us a hint! 155

A: You should know! 156

[6]The main thing that occurs to me in retrospect, taking the issue of protection fully into account, as well as the interesting opening, "Luck", is that my husband, Ark, is the incarnated 4D STO being that I was supposed to begin looking for. In subsequent sessions the Cs kept urging me to get on the internet and later on told me that my life would change suddenly and dramatically after some event of "recognition", and that occurred in spades when Ark and I met. So, for all the people who keep writing to me telling me that "I'm your Orion!", sorry, the position is taken.

157 **Q**: *(T)* Knowledge protects! So when we find ourselves a 4th density being, things are gonna roll!

158 **A**: You do 3rd intervention all the "time."

159 **Q**: *(L)* Do you mean spirit release and cleansing?

160 **A**: And other.

161 **Q**: *(T)* Well we've done spirit release and cleansing, which has prepared us somewhat. *(L)* Do we need to do this over and over again to constantly keep it up?

162 **A**: Open.

163 **Q**: *(T)* When I am on my lunch break, I go walking around the complex. As I am walking along, every so often I get an image – not a visual, it is like a perceived image – of the forms and shapes encountered when doing spirit release work. I can see these things coming toward me. As they come toward me I just send them to the light. I say, "Hello, how are ya, go to the light!" And they will swirl around me and disappear. So, I don't know if that is part of what we are supposed to be doing: being prepared by keeping all of the stuff off of us, by always setting up a field... *(F)* You are protecting yourself against attachment, is what you are doing. *(T)* But, it is also setting up a field that automatically intercedes... *(L)* OK, you say that I do 3rd level intervention all the time. Now, obviously this is partly the release work. Let me ask, is SV's work in moving this stuff out of the tissue base, is that part of this intervention?

164 **A**: Yes.

165 **Q**: *(J)* Is that a collective?

A: So is writing letters and yelling at people over the phone! 166

Q: *(S)* Getting it off your chest. *(J)* Yeah, not letting it... *(F)* That's all 3rd level stuff... *(J)* Teflon coating yourself... *(F)* Punching somebody in the mouth is a 3rd level intervention. *(S)* Yeah, releasing, yelling is one of the best releases... *(L)* And they are saying to do this? *(F)* We can do it. *(T)* These are all things that are at our disposal, our repertoire of 3rd level... *(F)* You asked what can we do, and are we helpless... *(T)* About the attachments, what dawned on me was that, as we are drawing power, as we are increasing our energy level, we are drawing more and more of them to us. *(L)* You think so? *(T)* The stuff I have been experiencing in the last few days with these attachments is... they are coming to us because we look like the light to them. *(S)* Can read auras, you know. I do it with my eyes closed. *(T)* Part of the attack experience is most likely the increase in these loose energy things flying around. And, as I realize this, I work to improve my shielding so that it holds automatically. Where I work is full of negative energy and a horrible place to be in terms of attachments. I walk across the parking lot and they fly at me. I can sense them. *(F)* Where I work, of course, two of the people there are alcoholics and you can bet they are a bus load with nobody driving. *(S)* Well, the Jin shin do goes beyond the body right to the energy level, also. *(T)* And, what we are doing right here, in this room, is that we are building an energy that may be drawing attachments to your house. *(L)* Is this work, with the board, is it in some way related to the location in space-time, because of the fact that we have done this for so 167 long in this spot?

168 **A**: Yes.

169 **Q**: *(L)* Does it work better because we are here rather than somewhere else?

170 **A**: For now.

171 **Q**: *(J)* Well, how about going to Leonard's on Saturday? *(L)* Will we be able to do a demonstration at the MUFON meeting on Saturday?

172 **A**: Yes, because it is predestined.[7]

173 **Q**: *(L)* That's heavy. *(T)* That's not free will. Let's not go next Saturday and break the predestined plan! [Laughter] My free will wants to break predestined plans. Mirth, mirth! *(L)* Can we ask any further questions about that remark?

174 **A**: You are allowed to ask anything you wish.

175 **Q**: *(T)* But, they won't necessarily answer anything we ask! *(S)* I want to ask something about auras. On some people, their auras show, by Kirlian photography, a white area, like a halo, behind or around their head or near the shoulder. What does this mean?

176 **A**: Open.

177 **Q**: *(T)* I guess what they mean is that it could be a different thing on different people.

178 **A**: Yes.

179 **Q**: *(L)* Is there a general schematic of aura colors and what they mean as has been presented by various groups?

180 **A**: No.

181 **Q**: *(S)* Was Edgar Cayce's readings on colors...

[7] *The Wave* 4

A: Reading anything requires accessing 182
"higher levels" of understanding which are fluid, not concrete and absolute.

Q: *(L)* So this changes, fluctuates. *(S)* 183
Oh yes, auras constantly change. *(L)* Yeah, but what they are saying is that the meanings of the colors can change with the individual. *(T)* It is like reading cards... *(F)* And palms – just because a person has a line of a certain sort doesn't mean that they are going to be in an accident on such and such a day... *(T)* Yes, and with the cards, one card can mean one thing with one person, and something else with another person. *(F)* I could look at two palms that are almost identical but they could mean entirely different things... *(T)* Which really ticks off the materialists who want the directions to come with the card and palm reading kits! [Laughter] *(L)* Are we, at this point, at an end of this subject of getting help and so forth?

A: Discover, that is how you learn, not 184
by being "led by the hand."

Q: *(L)* Let us get to the questions we 185
have prepared. *(S)* I wonder if subliminal tapes could help in protection?

A: Up to you. 186

Q: *(L)* Was all the land on the planet 187
Earth formed into one vast continent at some point in Earth's history?

A: Multiple history reality possibilities. 188

Q: *(L)* In this reality that we experi- 189
ence, was all the land joined into one vast continent?

A: Incorrect conceptualization. 190

Q: *(L)* Well, I don't know how to ask it. 191
(J) Move on. *(L)* What is the source of energy generated by stars?

192 **A**: Transfer points cause friction thus producing energy.

193 **Q**: *(L)* Transfer points of what? From what to what?

194 **A**: Dimensions.

195 **Q**: *(L)* Now, this is going to be a strange question, but if you can help us out, relate this to something, it would be very helpful. There are a lot of theories going around about the age of the universe. Some of the latest says that it is anywhere from 8 to 25 billion years old. I know that you have said that time is an illusion, but, in view of the fact that scientists are struggling with this one... [much laughter] which of the figures that they have pulled out of the air, in terms of the time illusion itself, is the most correct?

196 **A**: None.

197 **Q**: *(F)* Does that answer the question satisfactorily? That's like saying: "Oh, that's an interesting store, what's in there?" *(L)* Well, if none of the figures science has come up with is correct, what is the correct definition of the age of the universe?

198 **A**: Quasi-quantum possibilities.

199 **Q**: *(L)* What does that mean? [Laughter] *(J)* Anybody's guess?! *(L)* Well, I think they are going to tell us something here.

200 **A**: Discover.

201 **Q**: *(J)* Thanks a lot! *(T)* That is certainly new to me! *(S)* It's probably a lot of gazillion years old! *(T)* What does quasi mean? *(L)* Partly, half-way... *(F)* And what does quantum mean? *(L)* Well, a quanta is a unit of measure... *(T)* All possible units of measurement... *(F)* Is that what that would... *(L)* Come on and help us out here, guys? *(T)* In their time, which is no time, it exists at all times and not time, in our time, that would be infinity. *(L)* OK. *(T)* So, the age of the universe is infinite in our time limit, but the way they perceive it is it doesn't... it exists until it doesn't... it does and then it does not... *(L)* OK, let's ask this another way... help me out here... *(J)* Go for it! *(F)* You got yourself in the woods, keep looking for the crumbs to find your way out! *(L)* What do you mean by quasi-quantum possibilities?

A: Closed circle. 202

Q: *(L)* OK, if you select any one point 203
on the circle, and hold that point, and then measure around to the point again, where on that circle are we? Arbitrarily?

A: Not correct concept. 204

Q: *(L)* OK, well help me out here. If 205
there is a closed circle, that means that there is no point that you can arbitrarily designate? *(J)* Yes.

A: Yes. 206

Q: *(L)* Should we just drop this line, or 207
continue with it?

A: Open. 208

Q: *(L)* OK, then let's just drop it. *(J)* 209
It is, it was, it always will be, world without end, amen! *(F)* Well, if there is no time as we are told, and there is free will that is so important, how can this be? If there is no time and everything is connected, past, present and future, and everything is just a random collection of thoughts and experiences, and everything is supposed to be fluid, then there can't ever have been free will. If there is free will, and there is no past, present or future, and everything is all the same point in space-time

experience, the key is the free will, but there is no answer. *(L)* Is the planet Earth, as so many have predicted, going to acquire an additional sun?

210 **A**: Maybe.

211 **Q**: *(T)* An additional sun, like if Jupiter blows up? Is Jupiter an unborn sun?

212 **A**: Jupiter is already a star.

213 **Q**: *(L)* Why do we not perceive it as a star?

214 **A**: You are still learning. Earth is a star to be.

215 **Q**: *(F)* How the hell can that be? *(L)* If a planet...

216 **A**: Everything cycles fully.

217 **Q**: *(L)* If a star is a transition point from one dimension to another, when the Earth moves into 4th density, is it going to appear as a star to the people in 3rd density?

218 **A**: "Gas planet."

219 **Q**: *(L)* It will appear as a gas planet? *(J)* Just as Jupiter appears to us.

220 **A**: Jupiter is level 4 density.

221 **Q**: *(L)* To whom does Jupiter appear as a flaming sun? At what level?

222 **A**: 5, 6, and 7.

223 **Q**: *(T)* What does it look like in 4th?

224 **A**: Earth.

225 **Q**: *(T)* Jupiter looks like Earth and Earth looks like Jupiter in 4th density?

226 **A**: No.

227 **Q**: *(L)* What does Earth look like in 4th density?

228 **A**: Invisible.

229 **Q**: *(J)* Huh? *(L)* What do you mean, invisible?

A: Only visible upon request. Variability of physicality. 230

Q: *(L)* OK, does this mean that to the Lizzies and Orions the Earth is invisible? 231

A: When they are not thinking about it. 232

Q: *(J)* You mean when they are not thinking about it it doesn't exist? They have to focus on it for it to become visible? 233

A: Close. 234

Q: *(T)* But, you told us one time that everyone in 4th density was able to see us. 235

A: Yes. 236

Q: *(J)* Us, not Earth. *(T)* What do they see us on? 237

A: Able to see you when they choose to. 238

Q: *(J)* In other words, they focus on the frequency to see us. *(L)* I guess it is like animals in 2nd density. You ride down the road and don't really see what is around you unless you focus in on it. *(J)* Unless you concentrate on looking for them... *(T)* Like standing still in a forest and after a time you can see what is there. *(J)* It is all according to perception. 239

A: Yes, but 4th level is the first one with true variability. 240

Q: *(L)* Georges Gurdjieff proposed the idea that the Earth is, in a sense, food for the moon. What he meant was, what he had learned from these ancient teachers was that Earth was a food source for some level of being, and that possibly these beings had encampments or bases on the moon, but that Earth was eventually to become a star and that then the moon would become 241 an inhabited planet as the Earth was, and so on... Is this a fairly...

242 **A**: Close.

243 **Q**: *(L)* Is the moon a 2nd density planet?

244 **A**: Yes.

245 **Q**: *(L)* And the moon is used as a base by other beings?

246 **A**: On different densities.

247 **Q**: *(L)* Are there 2nd density beings that inhabit the moon in a full time way?

248 **A**: No.

249 **Q**: *(T)* Are there 3rd density beings?

250 **A**: No.

251 **Q**: *(T)* Are there 4th density beings?

252 **A**: Yes.

253 **Q**: *(T)* Are they Grays?

254 **A**: They don't inhabit the moon, they just use it.

255 **Q**: *(T)* Are there 5th density beings there?

256 **A**: 5th uses all.

257 **Q**: *(T)* Are there 6th density beings there?

258 **A**: Ditto.

259 **Q**: *(T)* Is the 7th density being there?

260 **A**: That is union with the One.

261 **Q**: *(T)* Thank you, just checking. *(L)* The 'Arcturians' talk about the path to the Great Central Sun. What is the Great Central Sun, and what does this mean, "The path to the Great Central Sun"?

262 **A**: 7th level.

263 **Q**: *(L)* Is the star Arcturus also a residence, as in planet, for certain beings?

A: Stars are transition and communi- 264
cation points.

Q: *(L)* The book *We Are the Arcturi-* 265
ans talks about the Arcturians, and it says that they live on the star Arcturus, that it is a planet for them, and that they have families, reproduce, and do all kinds of normal things. This struck me as strange and reminded me of the Jiles Hamilton stuff.

A: No. 266

Q: *(L)* OK, what was the source of this 267
information?

A: This information was told in a for- 268
mat that would be understood best by those who read it.

Q: *(T)* Is this the book we are supposed 269
to get the dates out of for the Arcturus position of the Wave? *(L)* Yes. OK. Was there a massive volcano in the area we now call Kentucky at some point in our historical reference?

A: Not then. 270

Q: *(J)* Will there be? *(L)* Is there 271
a massive volcano in the area of Kentucky?

A: No. 272

Q: *(L)* Will there be? 273

A: Open. 274

Q: *(L)* Where was/is the center of the 275
caldera?

A: You have proceeded not according 276
to info in previous answer. Who said there was a caldera?

Q: *(L)* OK, in other words, there 277
wasn't a volcano in the area of Kentucky, there isn't a volcano in the area of Kentucky, and there isn't going to be a volcano in the area of Kentucky?

A: Open. 278

279 **Q**: *(L)* Could you describe for us the interior of our sun and how it works?

280 **A**: It is a window.

281 **Q**: *(L)* The interior of the sun is a window. OK, is the interior of the sun composed of what we would call solid matter?

282 **A**: No.

283 **Q**: *(L)* The general idea is that the interior of the sun is composed of great masses of hydrogen and this is converting to helium and...

284 **A**: In 3rd density perception.

285 **Q**: *(L)* You are saying that the sun is a window or transmission point between dimensions. If that is the case, then it is virtually illimitable in terms of longevity?

286 **A**: Close.

287 **Q**: *(L)* So, the ideas of the sun running out of gas and turning into a red giant and sautéing humanity are incorrect concepts?

288 **A**: No. 3rd level, Laura, 3rd level!

289 **Q**: *(L)* So, in 3rd level it will...

290 **A**: Open.

291 **Q**: *(L)* How long ago was North Africa green and fertile and what geologic factors created the state in which we find it today?

292 **A**: Weather changes in 3rd density 10,000 years ago.

293 **Q**: *(L)* Scientists have been making a lot of conjectures about the matter of the universe and what they have been saying is that 90 to 95% of the matter needed to make the universe stable is unaccounted for. They call this dark matter. There have been a number of theories proposed as to what this dark matter consists of. I would like to know what is this dark matter?

A: You are "chasing rainbows" and so 294
are they.

Q: *(L)* What is the source of cosmic 295
background radiation?

A: 3rd level cosmic light rays. 296

Q: *(L)* Is there anything else we can 297
add to that?

A: Trivia. 298

Q: *(L)* Where on Earth was man first 299
seeded? *(T)* Wimbledon! [Laughter] Sorry, I couldn't resist that. *(L)* Was man first seeded in one particular place?

A: No. 300

Q: *(L)* It was stated that the Earth 301
once had a water vapor canopy. Was this one of the reasons for longevity in that time?

A: Yes, and already answered this. Re- 302
view transcripts.

Q: *(L)* What are the effects of sunlight 303
on the human body now as opposed to then?

A: Degenerative. 304

Q: *(L)* Does that mean that we should 305
avoid sunlight because we no longer have our canopy?

A: You cannot avoid enough to matter. 306

Q: *(T)* It's everywhere, all day long. 307
(F) When you are inside you are still exposed to radiation. The radiation in the air is leftover junk from the light rays coming in. *(T)* The radiation is everywhere, even at night. Speaking of which, did you see the article about the chunk of ice that broke off in Antarctica the size of Rhode Island? The scientists said: "We don't understand

why." And Antarctica is where the major ozone hole has been for the last five years. *(F)* Well, they have been predicting that for years... *(T)* Hope it didn't fall on anybody's foot! *(F)* That would be heavy enough that you wouldn't feel it. *(L)* Has the woman, who is now known as Leah Haley – and I understand that she legally changed her name to protect her family – has she been harassed by the U.S. government, or it this a screen memory put in by aliens with concomitant confirmations?

A: Yes to question one and no to ques- 308
tion two.

Q: *(T)* Are any of her memories of 309
abductions by Grays screen memories of abductions by the government?

A: No. 310

Q: *(T)* Why is she being abducted? 311

A: Review your data. 312

[8]Interestingly, according to *The UFO Trail* website:

> Former self-described alien abductee Leah Haley has revised her perspectives about her experiences of high strangeness to conclude that no alien abductions ever took place in her life. She now completely attributes her remarkable perceptions to having been an involuntary research subject. Commenting on literal alien abduction from her home in Pensacola, Florida, Haley stated, "It doesn't happen."
>
> Haley attracted widespread attention within the UFO community in 1993 with the publication of her book, *Lost Was the Key*, in which she described her extraordinary experiences consisting of fragmented memories of UFOs and apparent non-human beings. She became a well known speaker and was commonly sought for interviews. Ten years later she published *Unlocking Alien Closets: Abductions, Mind Control and Spirituality*, further documenting her descent into an increasingly complex web of deceit, disinformation and character assassination within ufology. Sales of her books climbed well into the thousands although word of mouth was virtually the only means of marketing.
>
> Haley initially thought aliens were responsible for her experiences but that changed following years of investigation. She long acknowledged military personnel were involved in her experiences to some extent, but she fully re-evaluated circumstances after viewing select Freedom of Information Act and U.S. Patent Office documents. Haley further based her revised conclusions on hundreds of interactions with abductees and researchers, as well as having mysterious individuals enter and later abruptly vanish from her life. She is now thoroughly convinced mind control experiments are responsible for what became known as the alien abduction phenomenon.
>
> "I really can explain every alien abduction away using human technology," Haley said.
>
> Commenting on what she termed "legitimate" reports of abduction, she continued, "I don't know for sure, but every case that I know very, very well – every single one of them – if I probe deeply enough, I'm going to find that there were humans here and there too. That tells me that it was a human-instigated situation. I can't think of a single case, not a single one, that I've really delved into that didn't have humans in it too, so I just don't think alien abductions are happening. I don't know, but I just don't think they are."

Read more here: http://ufotrail.blogspot.fr/2011/09/leah-haley-on-alien-abduction-it-doesnt_17.html

313 **Q**: *(L)* Then, she is being abducted for the same reason we are being abducted. *(J)* The agenda[8] is the same all the way down the line.

314 **A**: Is this a review session?

315 **Q**: *(L)* No. OK.

316 **A**: Then why ask repeat questions?

317 **Q**: *(L)* Well, we didn't know it was a repeat question. *(J)* We don't have the transcripts memorized just yet. *(L)* If there was an agreement between the U.S. and the aliens, how was this agreement reached? Who met with who where and when?

318 **A**: Review.

319 **Q**: *(L)* Well, you never told us that exactly.

320 **A**: Yes we did.

321 **Q**: *(L)* No you didn't. *(J)* Don't argue with them. *(L)* Well, what happened to Captain Thomas Mantell on 7 January 1948, when he attempted to track a UFO? Whose craft was it?

322 **A**: Grays and he lost consciousness, thus piloting his plane above its ceiling, thus disintegrated.

323 **Q**: *(L)* So, in other words they didn't zap him, he just lost control. *(T)* Yeah, he was flying a P-51 Mustang and he went too high. *(L)* At one point in a previous session, the remark was made when Terry was talking about directions, that knowledge of compass direction was going to become very important in the not too distant future. Could you tell us why this is so?

324 **A**: Because you will have increased sensitivity to magnetic influences.

325 **Q**: *(L)* So, in other words your comment was not that we needed to learn this but that this would become important because our sensitivity would increase?

A: Both. 326

Q: *(L)* Does our learning of compass di- 327
rections act to increase our sensitivity?

A: Catch 22. 328

Q: *(T)* It is a contradiction. In the 329
book: You have to keep flying the bombing missions because we don't have enough people to win the war, but we won't let you fly if you are crazy because we can't have a crazy person in the airplane with all those bombs. But, the doctor can't determine that you are crazy, you have to say that you are crazy so that the doctor can sign the papers, but if you say that you are crazy then the doctor can't sign the papers because one indication of sanity is to know that you are crazy, therefore you have to fly. *(F)* It's a no-win situation. *(J)* Does it have anything to do with the fact that when we move to 4th density we will lose the physicality we use to navigate with now?

A: One half of equation. 330

Q: *(T)* OK, we have the ability to 331
tell direction because of our physicality, which will increase to the point where we will be able to sense direction when we don't need direction because we won't be physical?

A: Close. 332

Q: *(T)* That is the Catch-22. You will 333
have the great direction sense when you don't need it.

A: You will have variable physicality. 334

Q: *(J)* Yeah, so in switching from one 335
to the other you don't want to get disoriented. If you have compass knowledge ingrained in you when you switch

from physical to non-physical, you will know where you are. *(L)* In a previous session we talked about the feline principle as represented by the sphinx, and the fact that Egyptians worshiped cats. Is there anything more you can give us on this? Why was this so? Was the cat representative of some principle we need to learn or investigate?

336 **A**: This is not really important.

337 **Q**: *(T)* Is the cat and the cat symbol itself important in some way?

338 **A**: You are; up to the perceiver.

339 **Q**: *(L)* We talked about the scarab and why the scarab represented eternal life to the Egyptians, and then we went into the thing about the scarab rolling dung. What is there in the symbolism of the scarab that might be significant to us today?

340 **A**: Up to you.

341 **Q**: *(L)* In the annotated copy of the Morris K. Jessup book, there were three people annotating: Mr. A., Mr. B., and one known as Jemi. One of the references was to the sighting made by Kenneth Arnold. In reference to that sighting, Mr. B wrote: "Don't worry, Jemi, those were LM ships not S men. They are an improved type and were on a training flight. That is why their leader interconnected their force fields, to teach them level tele-control without inducing a fear block." Now, what is an LM ship?

342 **A**: Light matter.

343 **Q**: *(L)* What is an "S man?"

344 **A**: Secret order member.

345 **Q**: *(L)* What is the secret order?

346 **A**: That is for you to discover.

Q: *(L)* What does it mean that "their leader interconnected their force fields to teach them level tele-control"? 347

A: Self-explanatory. 348

Q: *(L)* Jemi's comment on Jessup's discussion on mysterious disappearances of persons throughout history is quite chilling. Written in the margin of the book was: "Hey, if he only knew why he'd die of shock!" To what does this refer? 349

A: We cannot reveal this at this "time." 350

Q: *(L)* So you are saying that there is a whole lot more to this situation and what is going on on this planet than even we have been told at this time? 351

A: Of course. 352

Q: *(L)* So if there is a lot more to this, would we, knowing what we know, "die of shock" if we knew the rest? 353

A: Maybe. 354

Q: *(L)* Well, that is not pleasant. OK, Jessup wondered in his book if aviators could be frozen by space ships and carried away in a field of invisibility. Mr. B commented in the margin: "If only he knew by experience, he would keep silent and not write or speak of it ever again in his lifetime. He couldn't speak of it, for, you see Jemi, it paralyzes one's sense of time and nullifies mental cognition, functioning and memory. So he has no knowledge, he could not have, he is only guessing." 355

A: Okay. 356

Q: *(T)* OK what? 357

A: Exactly correct! 358

Q: *(L)* There are a lot of terms in this book... 359

A: Too much data. 360

361 **Q**: *(L)* There was some conjecture as to who wrote these comments. Can you give us a clue as to who did the annotations in this book?

362 **A**: Discover. If we told you everything, it would not be good!!

363 **Q**: On that note, I think we will close for the night.

364 **A**: Goodnight.

365 **Q**: *(L)* Well, here are the terms: Mothership, Homeship, Deadship, Great ark, Great bombardment, Great return, Great war, Little men, Forcefields, Deep freezes, Undersea building, Measure markers, Scout ships, Magnetic and gravity fields, Sheets of diamond, Cosmic Rays, Force cutters, Undersea explorers, Inlay work, Clear talk, Telepathing, Burning coat, Nodes, Vortices, Magnetic nets, and what happens to people, planes and ships that have disappeared.

The three commentators of Jessup's book explain the origin of odd storms, clouds, objects falling from the sky, strange marks and footprints and other things we have not solved.

(F) If you were to try to find out about all of that, it would be like trying to bite into a grapefruit that is 19 stories tall, and swallow it all in one gulp.

(L) Well they say to "discover" things like this. How the heck are we supposed to discover these things?

(F) This will come to us step-by-step.

(J) It doesn't really matter.

(L) It does matter, because they say that knowledge protects. This is knowledge.

(F) I know, but you can't get it all at once. Look how much you have acquired in the last three years, the last eight months. You are so impatient. You expect to have your mind totally input with all of this and then to go back and have fun with your children, eating popcorn and watching movies. It wouldn't work that way. This is what you would be like if you had all this knowledge at once. [Demonstrates extreme spasticity. Laughter.] Is that what you want?

(T) Yeah, the kids would get their popcorn and sit around and watch mom! Better than a movie.

(F) The rest of your existence in 3rd density would consist of eh-eh-eh-eh-eh-eh!!! [Laughter] Doctors would be coming and injecting you with glucose and stomach feeding and you wouldn't feel it. You would be still going eh-eh-eh-eh-eh-eh-eh-eh-eh! You can't get it all at once! I have the feeling that as time progresses that we are going to get an enormous input of knowledge, every session has to be absorbed. You can't just get it all dumped into your brain like a dump truck.

(T) We are doing what we are supposed to be doing.

(F) I suspect that some of those annotations in that book were coming from a 4th density being who already knew all of this stuff the way we know about tiddly winks. But, that is all fine and good. We are not there yet.

(L) Why would somebody annotate this book this way and send it to the ONI?

(F) To show the ONI how little they know.

(S) It worked – they now have a study group!

(F) Besides, if we get too much too

quickly, you will be sitting watching a movie and all of a sudden you will hear a knock on the door and there will be four gray suits out there asking for you!

End of Session

Regarding Morris Jessup's annotated book referred to as "The Varo Edition":

> Carl Allen – or, as he preferred to call himself, Carlos Allende – caused a great deal of confusion in the ufological community in the '60s.
>
> If you're unfamiliar with him, I can direct you to Robert A. Goerman's dossier[9]. But, in brief, Allen wrote some letters to the UFO writer Morris K. Jessup, which, disseminated and elaborated, became the story of the "Philadelphia Experiment." He also annotated a copy of Jessup's book, *The Case for the UFO*, and sent it to Admiral Furth, Chief of the Office of Naval Research in Washington, D.C. The Navy transcribed it, and published it in a small edition with Allen's commentary in red: thereby puzzling and exciting saucer buffs everywhere. The "Varo Edition" (so called after the printer) became a legend, more talked about than read, until Gray Barker published a facsimile in 1973.
>
> [http://www.johnkeel.com/?p=594]

Robert A. Goerman's dossier includes recently released correspondence of UFO/paranormal investigator/journalist John Keel. Keel makes the following claims in the letter:

- Jessup thought the Varo edition was a joke (Keel shares the opinion that Allende was mentally unstable and unreliable)
- Jessup was depressed and Keel thinks he really did commit suicide
- Jessup gave his Varo edition to Mr. Santesson shortly before he died, who then gave it to Ivan Sanderson, who was working on a book at the time

[9] http://windmill-slayer.tripod.com/aliascarlosallende

- Allende was the guy who made the annotations (he claimed this to the Lorenzens and others); Keel, Jessup, Sanderson, Santesson "and everyone else" knew this; one set of annotations was in his handwriting (the other probably done with his other hand)

- Keel's Allende files were used by Berlitz in his *Philadelphia Experiment* book, but Keel went uncredited (Keel also put Moore in touch with Berlitz)

- Keel blames Varo for the whole controversy

For more, see: http://windmill-slayer.tripod.com/aliascarlosallende/

March 7, 1995

In this session I mention that the *St. Petersburg Times* journalist has made an appointment to interview me and ask a bit for the Cs' advice as to how to handle this sort of thing. However, there is some backstory to this.

Terry and Jan, being the editors and publishers of a regional MUFON journal, had been instrumental in arranging for the little talk I gave at MUFON referenced in the 25 February 1995 session. When Jan introduced me to Tom French after the meeting, and he indicated he would like to interview me, I thought that it was the group he was interested in, and I was excited for the Cs. I said something about the fact that we were all together on Saturday nights, and that would be the best time, but he insisted that he would call me and make an appointment later.

Frank was, as might be expected, utterly ecstatic that Tom was interested in writing about us. He just knew that this was the door to fame for the Cs, and him by virtue of association! He told me to be sure and call him the instant the interview was scheduled. He would take time off from work, if necessary, to be there.

When Tom French finally called, he made it clear that it was me he wanted to talk to – alone. I was confused and felt just a little trapped because without Frank and Terry and Jan there – what was I going to say? I certainly couldn't make any kind of commitments for them without them being there. I even boldly suggested that they ought to be present, but Tom was firm: he wanted to talk to me, and not the group. Reluctantly, I agreed.

When I told Frank that the journalist didn't want to talk to him – at least not yet – he became very sour and critical. He spent hours and hours giving me instructions on what I was supposed to say, how I was supposed to act, and the image I must convey to Mr. French in order to make him understand just how important the Cs (and Frank, by default) were to the world. Most of his comments were aimed at undermining my confidence. He described in great detail all of the people in my position who had been interviewed by journalists and that, without exception, they had been ridiculed and made to look like fools. He outlined exhaustively the detrimental effects this would have on me, my children, and life in general and specific. And of course, the problem was that I was just simply too naive to know how to talk to a journalist and not get taken in by conniving and trickery. All journalists were the scum of the earth, and I was going to get slimed.

By the time he was done, I was ready to call Tom French and cancel the whole thing. But, before I did, I wanted to discuss it with the Cs. In their responses, it is clear that Frank's attempts to undermine my confidence were skewing the flow.

Participants: 'Frank', Laura, Susan V, Martie T,[1] Mark[2]

1 **Q**: *(L)* Hello.

2 **A**: Hello.

3 **Q**: *(L)* Who do we have with us tonight?

4 **A**: Sijll.

5 **Q**: *(L)* And where are you from?

6 **A**: Cassiopaea, of course.

7 **Q**: *(L)* We have some questions tonight. We were discussing earlier this evening the 'abomination of desolation' as written about by the prophet Daniel and also spoken of by Jesus. What is this?[3]

8 **A**: Disinformation.[4]

Q: *(L)* Are you saying that the abomination of desolation *is* disinformation, or that the writing about it is disinformation? 9

A: Both. 10

Q: *(L)* Can you tell us anything to clarify this point? 11

A: In what way? 12

Q: *(L)* Who, or what, was the source of that information as prophesied by Daniel? 13

A: Illuminati. 14

Q: *(L)* The prophecies given to Daniel were disinformation? 15

A: Close. 16

[1]Owner of New Age center in Tampa.

[2]Friend of Frank, son of 'Dane', as written about in *Amazing Grace.*

[3]*The Wave* 32

[4]This is pretty accurate, as I've learned now after years of research into the Bible. I'll be writing about that soon.

[5]A term found in the Book of Daniel in the Hebrew Bible. It also occurs in 1 Maccabees and in the Synoptic Gospels of the New Testament. My question was based on a futurist perspective, that it was a prophecy of the End Times. Numerous books have been written by Christian Futurists who consider the abomination of desolation prophecy of Daniel mentioned by Jesus in Matthew 24:15 and Mark

17 **Q**: *(L)* Is there an 'abomination of desolation'?[5]

18 **A**: There is anything, if the definitions are unrestricted.

19 **Q**: *(L)* Well, OK. Who were the Elohim of the Bible?[6]

20 **A**: Transdefinitive.

21 **Q**: *(L)* What does that mean? Transcends definition?

22 **A**: And variable entities.

23 **Q**: *(L)* Were the Elohim 'good guys'?

A: First manifestation was human, then non-human. 24

Q: *(L)* Are they light beings as some people say? 25

A: Vague. 26

Q: *(L)* Well, what brought about their transformation from human to non-human?[7] 27

A: Pact or covenant. 28

Q: *(L)* They made a pact or covenant with each other? 29

13:14 to refer to an event in the future, when a 7-year peace treaty will be signed between Israel and a world ruler called 'the man of lawlessness' or the 'Antichrist'. So, this was the position from which I asked the question, i.e. is this perspective true?

Since those days, I've done a lot of research on the topic and discovered that there is more to this 'abomination of desolation' than the futurists acknowledge. For example, the rabbinical consensus is that the expression refers to the desecration of the Second Temple (Herod's Temple) by the erection of a Zeus statue in its sacred precincts by Antiochus IV Epiphanes. That is to say, the Book of Daniel was written after the fact, and the 'prophecies' of Daniel 9:27, 11:31 and 12:11 are examples of *vaticinium ex eventu* (prophecies after the event). The same is true for the so-called prophecies of Matthew 24:15 and Mark 13:14; prophecies after the event about the siege of Jerusalem in AD 70 by the Roman general Titus. Some scholars think these verses are a *vaticinium ex eventu* about Emperor Hadrian's attempt to install the statue of Jupiter Capitolinus on the site of the ruined Jewish Temple in Jerusalem, which led to the Bar Kokhba revolt of 132–135 AD. Another scholarly theory relates the prophecy to the actions of Caligula c. 40 AD when he ordered that a golden statue depicting himself as Zeus incarnate be set up in the Temple in Jerusalem recorded by Philo and Josephus. This prospect however, never came to fruition since he was assassinated in 41 AD along with his wife and daughter. Peter Bolt, head of New Testament at Moore Theological College, believes that the abomination of desolation in Mark 13 refers to the crucifixion of the Son of God; in other words, Jesus is referring to his own impending death when he mentions the 'abomination of desolation. My own research shows that there is much evidence in favor of rather late composition of Daniel and the gospels, so in every case, it is *vaticinium ex eventu*; that of Daniel refers to Antiochus Epiphanes, and that of the gospels refers the destruction of Jerusalem.

What seems to be the point the Cs are making is that this term has been taken over and manipulated toward a belief in an end-time Antichrist.

[6] *Secret History* 11

[7] *The Wave* 22

30 **A**: No, with 4th density STS.

31 **Q**: *(L)* Well, that is not good! Are you saying that the Elohim are STS? Who were these STS beings they made a pact with?

32 **A**: Rosteem, now manifests as Rosicrucians.

33 **Q**: *(L)* What is their purpose?

34 **A**: As yet unrevealable to you.

35 **Q**: *(L)* That's heavy! OK, what is the source of the *Keys of Enoch* teaching? James Hurtak claims that he was taken up to the higher realms and that the 'Keys' were programmed into him...

36 **A**: Disguised reality.

37 **Q**: *(L)* The place that he was taken to?

38 **A**: Not the place, the message.

39 **Q**: *(L)* What is the source of this disguised reality?[8]

40 **A**: Research; one here studies a bit too much to discover explosive reality trailblazings.

41 **Q**: *(L)* OK. Is there coded information in this book on several levels as Martie suggests?

42 **A**: There is coded information all over the place. Suggest slower pace of studying in order to discover earth shaking principles.

43 **Q**: *(L)* Who is studying too hard?

44 **A**: You. Slower would help. Remember the old parable about biting off more than you can chew?

45 **Q**: *(MT)* What are we supposed to do if not study?

A: Martie is resistant. 46

Q: *(MT)* To what? 47

A: Why do you think you are hav- 48
ing difficulty determining the course of your life?

Q: *(MT)* Resistant to what? 49

A: The message about slowing down. 50
It is important because it is hard to see the veins in the leaves when the car is traveling too fast to see the trees clearly.

Q: *(L)* Well, she does seem to be living 51
life in the 'fast lane,' so to speak.

A: Incorrect interpretation. It is not 52
living life in the fast lane, it is trying to absorb too much too quickly.

Q: *(L)* In other words, she is running 53
on too rich a gas mixture?

A: Clumsy analogy, but the right idea. 54

Q: *(MT)* I'm not quite sure what is 55
meant here.

A: Metaphysics overload. It is a good 56
path, but we suggest that you be more like the tortoise than the hare.

Q: *(L)* Well, she is looking for a path 57
where she can combine her studies and also make a living.

A: Readings, therapies, rather than 58
"teaching." Become the therapist rather than the therapy instructor! People crave individual attention, have you not noticed?

Q: *(MT)* Well, I make a lot more when 59
I read than when I teach.

A: Bingo! 60

[8]It's obvious, in retrospect, that the claims of Hurtak to having been taken to 'higher realms' are the "disguised reality" the Cs refer to. It just wasn't so obvious at the time. What was the 'real reality' of the *Keys of Enoch*? Some kind of COINTELPRO, I would suggest at this point in time.

61 **Q**: *(MT)* How can I get more work in that respect?

62 **A**: That will take care of itself when you network, which you are already adept at doing.

63 **Q**: *(L)* OK, there is a journalist[9] coming here on Friday who wants to talk to me...

64 **A**: Be open in your mind regarding the flow of the situation. You have a tendency to forget that all do not share your ability to expand consciousness so easily.[10]

65 **Q**: *(L)* So, you mean he is going to be a real skeptic and I am going to have to deal with validation issues?

66 **A**: That is not the point. The audience will be looking for flaws in the materialistic reference point, so you must be cautious, lest you be made to look irrational.

67 **Q**: *(L)* Well, then I guess I better not talk about exorcisms or anything like that.

68 **A**: Balance.

Q: *(L)* OK. I will try to stay bal- 69
anced.[11] I don't want to have to leave the country. *(MT)* I would like to know what my connection is with the Hindu temple?

A: Nice people, but not your place. 70
You needed the uplifting vibrations during a particularly stressful and disappointing period!

Q: *(MT)* Should I bring my book store 71
back?

A: Open. 72

Q: *(MT)* Can you suggest a way for me 73
to find a place for my books?[12]

A: One last time, network and all falls 74
into place.

Q: *(L)* Has Mark been abducted? 75

A: Open. 76

Q: *(L)* Why won't you answer that? 77

A: Another session we will. 78

Q: *(M)* Can you indicate to me what I 79
am supposed to do in my career?

A: Career path should be, as for every- 80
one, that which is attractive, effortless and painless.

---

[9]Tom French from the *St. Petersburg Times*, already mentioned.

[10]*The Wave* 37

[11]The fact is, no one but Frank has ever suggested that I discuss metaphysics and the paranormal in any kind of irrational way. No one but Frank has ever suggested that I forget the limitations of my audience. In fact, in retrospect, it is singularly curious that as long as he thought that he was going to be interviewed, he was extraordinarily enthusiastic about the idea. The instant he realized that it was me who was going to be interviewed, it became the Titanic of ideas: doomed to hit obstructions and sink unless I listened to Frank and managed to convince Tom of how the story ought to be told, which was, of course, as Frank wanted it to be told. After his hours and hours of indoctrination, Frank was finally assured that I would do as he wanted – that I would convince Tom of the importance of writing about the Cs group, and then, being reassured, he again became enthusiastic about the idea. I would be the public relations agent, and fame was only a hop, skip and a jump into the future!

[12]Martie was closing her book store and needed to find homes for a *lot* of books.

81 **Q**: *(L)* In terms of material activities, what would be the best course for Mark to follow in his healing process right now?

82 **A**: Don't follow. Not following anything is a key. It is up to the individual.

83 **Q**: *(L)* Could you give us in a few words, the potential in each of us, for the greatest forward movement or growth?

84 **A**: We cannot tell anyone of you this, because then you would not learn, and if you do not learn, you do not progress as an individual soul!

Q: *(L)* Is there such a thing as a 'soul 85
number', as someone we know has been told?

A: Only if you want there to be. Time 86
to say "goodnight, Gracie."[13]

Q: *(L)* Goodnight. 87

End of Session

[13]Note that the Cs are rather 'withholding' in this session, probably due to Frank's state.

March 11, 1995

This was the session held on the evening of the day we gave a demo at the local MUFON meeting (in Holiday, FL). After my little talk at the Clearwater MUFON meeting on the 25th, followed by the session that evening being attended by a number of MUFON members, the local group decided that they wanted more than just a talk and asked if we could give a demonstration. The meeting room was packed. One of the attendees, Andrew B, placed a gauss meter on the table beside the board and every time the Cs responded to a question, it buried the needle.

Jan gave a short introduction where she explained that she was not a 'believer', and even had many doubts about the UFO/alien reality. This was due, she explained, to her lack of having ever had any kind of personal 'experience'. However, because her husband, Terry, was very deeply involved in studying such phenomena (having had a number of his own experiences through the years), in solidarity with him, she had become involved in MUFON and was, at the time, the acting Secretary of the Hillsborough/Pinellas Counties chapter. She and Terry also edited, published, and often wrote articles for, the area MUFON newsletter.

But, even so, as Jan confessed, she was *not* a believer, though she found the ideas presented by the Cassiopaeans to be fascinating.

After Jan's few remarks, she turned the podium over to me and I went through a brief recapitulation of the long process we went through over several years before the Cassiopaean contact was established. I then began to try and explain what the material was imparting to us in the form of 'explanations of the order of the universe', so to speak. Do keep in mind that this was *very* early in the experiment – we had only been receiving the information about 9 months at the time of these talks, so the fact was that even *we* didn't know the full scope of what was going to come in the next few years! I will insert here the transcript of my talk from this point:

In terms of accessing who and what you are in totality, one of the things the Cassiopaeans have said is that, originally, the human being was created with more active DNA than they currently operate with. An event occurred that has been remembered by all the cultures around the world as 'The Fall', or the loss of the Edenic state, and this was primarily due to, depending on the cultural myth being examined, a snake, serpent or dragon, whatever. But, it is generally a scaly, reptilian type of being. What the Cassiopaeans have said indicates that there may be more to this than mere mythical conceptualization!

The Cassiopaeans have talked about the fact that the DNA can be reconstructed or reconnected because it is still there, it is just broken up or 'deactivated'. The important elements of this process include oxygenation, spinning or centrifuging, as well as certain activities such as meditation and gaining knowledge.

One of the things that I have experienced recently has been pretty interesting in terms of this idea. After my accident I began to have a lot of body work done, including different types of 'energy work', and at certain points, this began to affect me in strange ways. After one of these sessions of energy work, for about seven days or longer, it felt like a water main was attached to my solar plexus, and was pumping in memories and emotions from every lifetime I had ever lived; I mean hundreds and thousands of images! Everybody says, "Oh, I want to remember my past lives!", but think again! I got to experience every emotion of entire lifetimes with this review! It was so bad that I thought I was going to drown in it and die! I would sit there – and everybody will tell you that I was a horror to be around during that time – rocking in my rocking chair saying, "Oh God! Oh God! I can't stand this! Please let it stop! Let it stop!" Images of people, places, events, castles, knights charging into battle on a horse waving a battle axe; deserts, jungles, death, destruction, diseases, plague, pestilence; all these kinds of things just flashing by, like Dorothy in the tornado; all this stuff flying by! Meanwhile, the emotion of every one of these images was hitting me full force! I might have seen the image for only one second, but the entire emotion that went with it would hit me and I was gasping and choking from one incident to the next, one after another after another. So, at one of the sessions we asked just what it was that was going on with me... I was about to collapse under the strain – and the Cassiopaeans said: "Oh, you just activated

> more of your DNA!" Well, fine! Stop it! Take it back! No more! I can't handle it!
>
> But, apparently, that is what having this knowledge can do! It is a condition of being able to access universes of information! The Cassiopaeans have said: "It's FUN to access..." and I asked them: "Fun for WHO?!"

After a few more remarks, I turned the podium over to Terry, but I do want to mention the fact that my description of the events of my state of 'remembering' as being similar to Dorothy in the tornado is something that I had forgotten entirely until I transcribed the tapes.

Terry introduced himself and made several remarks about having attended some of the early experimental sessions *prior* to the Cassiopaean connection and that he and Jan had more or less given up on the project because nothing seemed to be happening during that time. It was only later, after the Cassiopaeans came through, that I was able to persuade them to have a look at the material. I valued their insight and input because I knew that both of them were as skeptical as I was and I certainly felt in need of a 'second opinion', not wanting to fall into the 'true believer' trap that is so common nowadays. After his intro, Terry made the following remarks:

> *(Terry)* You can tell by now that there is a *lot* of information here. I've been rambling on for the past 20 minutes here, and there is more. It doesn't matter where you start with it, you end up having to explain the whole thing. At this point, there is 9 months worth of material and in another 3 months we'll have to explain a whole year's worth, because the Cassiopaeans continue to give new information – they add to it as we learn to ask the questions correctly. As my wife has said in her remarks, neither of us were great believers in channelled information and it took several months for Laura to get us up to her place to see what was going on. We had been up a couple of times before during the early experiment stage and had gotten nowhere. We live down in St. Pete and that's a long drive to make to come up for the evening, to sit around and have nothing come through.
>
> When we finally came up Laura told us, "You're not gonna believe what this is doing." We came up in November – they've been receiving the Cassiopaean information since July – and I watched for a little while seeing this little thing move around on

the board. I mean, it bounced around all over the place; I never saw anything move that fast! A mouse trying to get away from my six cats is about the only thing I've seen move as fast as that little thing moved on the board!

So, I sat down. They let me sit in for a while just so I could put my hand on it. I wanted to touch it; I wanted to see what it was. And I sat there for about 25 minutes or so and my arm was tired! I work with computers and I'm used to 'mousing' (speaking of mice), on the computer, pointing and clicking and all that, all day long. My arm had moved around this board so fast for 25 minutes or so, that I actually had shooting pains in my shoulder from it because I wasn't used to that position for that length of time. I couldn't believe how quickly it moved. I couldn't believe the amount of energy I could feel running through that little section of the room.

Since then, I have noticed that it is not just one person, it's not just those people sitting at the board; it's a combination of all the people in the room – all the people in Laura's house, for that matter. The more people, the more energy, and the faster it goes. Twice the planchette flew off the board. On New Year's Eve, there were a whole bunch of people there and there was so much energy – just loose energy, not directed energy because people were just milling around, it was a New Year's Eve party – and we couldn't keep the planchette on the board. It was flying back and forth so fast it flew right off the table and sailed through the air. We picked it up, put it back down, and it was across the board again. It took about 20 minutes for the energy to settle down so we could get any kind of information. Then, the information may or may not have been that good because all the people in the room weren't concentrating. It was loose energy in the air.

A couple of weeks ago a couple people came up who are involved in UFO research and they understand energy flows and how to direct it. And, we had the same experience. The Cassiopaeans told us then that it would take time to settle the energy and direct it because there was just so much of it. That little planchette was sailing again... flew off the table a couple of times and through the air. It went off the table with so much force it just kept going... took us a good 25 minutes to get it settled down again. They told us: "You've fractured the channel." I guess that the 'wire' that runs between here and 6th density got increased in size the other night. We rewired it for sure!

(Laura) It physically affects us, too, because we can *feel* this energy.

(Question from the audience) Is there any dizziness effect?

(Laura) No, no dizziness. It feels more like warm drafts of air against the skin, and then an elevated feeling.

(Question from the audience) Is it like euphoria?

(Laura) No, it's more of an intense, mental sharpness... a focus to the *n*th degree.... it actually energizes us. We've done sessions that lasted up to 8 hours, tape after tape, and no one was tired!

(Question from the audience) Have you had other movements in the room during the sessions, like objects falling off shelves or something?

(Laura) No, we haven't. We've actually asked that question and the Cassiopaeans have said that if there were such movement, it would be strictly energy from the lower chakras. We aren't dealing with that level here. If you get poltergeist-type phenomena, you can pretty well figure the level it comes from. But, of course, during the early phases of the experiment, we *did* get some of that type of activity. On one occasion, a candelabra flew off a shelf, and several other things went crashing around. It was real unpleasant energy. That is the sort of thing we worked to get beyond.

(Terry) We aren't even sure who or what the Cassiopaeans are. They say they are 6th density and that they are 'us' in the future – but, that may not be the case. We aren't going to sit here and believe it just because they say it. We are presenting it that way because that is *their* description. We don't make the mistake of believing everything that is coming through; we are just presenting the information. We are still wondering what it is we have tapped into. Is it some kind of universal, Cosmic Retrieval System? Is it some kind of universal computer? Is it the Jungian archetypal consciousness? What we have tapped into we don't know.

What impresses me about it, even beyond the confirmations we have gotten on different material, is the consistency of the information. There are reams of material already, and it is consistent right across the board. It doesn't vary in level. It's not like a contact that is extremely intelligent one week and super dumb the next. It's consistent, uniform and has continuity.

(Laura) One exception, I would point out: if there are people

are in the room who would be upset by any particular information, the Cassiopaeans will more or less 'hold back', and will suggest that we ask it later. It is rather like a courtesy to the person in the room who is not prepared to hear the answer. When it's just us, information comes through that might not come with new people present.

(Terry) They will also not permit children to be present as they have indicated that such activities can be detrimental because the energy levels that are generated are too much for the 'young circuits', so to speak.

(Question from the audience) Your sources are obviously champions of free will. Obviously, that is the way the universe is supposed to be. Have they given you any reconciliation as to why our density seems to have been interfered with in terms of free will? I know there are a lot of sources that say that we agreed to be abducted before we came here, but that's just a little bit too thin, in my opinion.

(Terry) What we have been told on that is that this universe was created as a free-will universe. It was created specifically to allow all souls to do whatever they wish to do; they have complete choice about what they wish to do. The Grays, the Lizards, whoever they are who abduct and put implants in people, have the right to do that because it's their free will to come here and do that to us. And, they have the right to tell us whatever they want to tell us to rationalize their behavior. Our right is to *not* believe what abducting entities tell us. We have free will to believe or not believe them. If they tell us in one lifetime that they have the right to do this to us, and we choose to believe them then, and then, in this lifetime, they try the same tricks and we choose *not* to believe them, in each case, we are exercising our free will and so are they. This is a free-will universe. We can change our mind. They are trying to convince us that we have no choice in that; whether we believe them or not is *our* choice. There's more to it than that, of course, because interfering with us physically, obviously, goes on all the time. They have more power than us physically, or pseudo-physically. It is the same relationship between us and animals in our reality. Cows and sheep and chickens have free will, too, but we have more power than them and we have convinced them (and ourselves), in our need to consume food, that "this is good for for you, this is your purpose in life." Just as we consume animals, so are we consumed

by those in higher densities than ours. But, for the most part, it occurs in terms of energy, and not specifically flesh, though that too occurs. We are part of a food chain, so to speak, and we are *not* at the top by any means!

Anyway, back to 300,000 years ago: there was a battle between the forces of service to others and the forces of service to self at all different levels of density. Unfortunately, the forces of service to self won the battle. The Lizards are 4th density service to self beings. They can come to 3rd density, but they can only sustain themselves here for a short time because their technology does not allow them to extend it any further.

At 4th density, they are still using technology, they are still learning para-physical things. They have subjugated us; they have implanted us; they have taken our DNA and manipulated it so we won't remember who we are and what we can really do. Barbara Marciniak's book, *Bringers of the Dawn*, covers much of that information. The Cassiopaeans have said that when Barbara communicated with her Pleiadians, she was communicating with – there is this thing out there called a realm border, it's a wave, a wall, a frequency of some kind that's like a doorway between the different densities – the Cassiopaeans, the Pleiadians, and whoever transmit through that – it expedites their ability to transduce from 6th density down to 3rd – at the time Marciniak was channeling her information, this wave was located in the region of space of the Pleiades, and they called themselves Pleiadians to give a reference point. As we perceive it, this window is now passing through what we call Cassiopeia. When it was in the region of Arcturus, they called themselves the Arcturians. At some point they were the Orions, though I don't remember what the order is. As it gets closer and closer, it gets stronger and stronger, and apparently, there are people destined to be these contact points. The closer the Wave gets to us, the clearer the signal becomes. The next stop, according to the Cassiopaeans, is Leo. Of course, the stars in the constellations are not all the same distance, so we have refined the reference points to specific stars or groupings.

Anyway, the Lizards have created the Grays. They are 4th density also. They have no souls; they are robots. The Grays were created in such a way so that the Lizards could send them into 3rd density as projections, so to speak. They can project some portion of their own energy into the Grays so that when they are in 3rd density, they are not only a robot being controlled by them, they are actually 'in it', so to speak, looking through its eyes. It may even be that several Grays constitute the energy of a single Lizard portion. The whole purpose of the subjugation of humans by the Lizards is that they use us as food. The old John Lear/Bill Cooper stuff about the vats of body parts may have some truth to it. But, mainly, they take energy. They want our energy. That's what they feed on in 4th density, because they are basically energy beings in 4th density. They feed on energy. There is positive energy, there is negative energy. Service-to-self beings in 4th density feed on negative energy produced by 3rd density beings, and even 1st and 2nd density beings on occasion. They like us because we have emotions. Emotions generate energy. That's why you're always reading that the Grays seem to be "so interested in our emotions! Our love, our hate, our this and that." They control us and create situations that produce negative energy. The more negative energy they can create, the more food they have. That's what the whole purpose is.

There is another purpose also: they covet the idea of being 3rd density physical/material beings. They haven't done it in a long time, and the physicality of it is just so attractive to them because they are so hung up in service to self, that part of the plan is to create a new race for themselves.

What you have to understand is that we have so much information here, and we are still trying to dig through it and understand what it is they are telling us. They have given us a massive amount of information. It's to the point now, that when we do a session, not only do we ask questions, but it turns into conversations. It's not like what you normally do with a Ouija board – you know, "Am I gonna get rich?" "Yes." "Am I gonna be poor?" "No." "Am I gonna get in a car wreck?" "Yes." And that kind of stuff. It's really like sitting around with a bunch of people and talking. We talk. They will talk to us. We can ask a question, get an answer, and then be talking about the answer amongst ourselves, and they will comment on our comments, interject remarks, agree or disagree with our analysis.

What we are trying to talk about today – and this is the first time we have done this in such a large group – is that we are still trying to work through all this information. When you sit around the house talking about something: say you say "we're gonna talk about politics" and you're sitting there talking about politics –

and somebody says something and you say "oh, that reminds: did you see the sale down at the store?" and the discussion goes off on the subject of the sale, and you say "yeah, I got a hammer," and that leads to "I was working on the house," in the way that conversations do – going off in tangents all over the place. You may never talk about politics again after the first few remarks. Well, our sessions are like that, too. We may start with a topic, and one thing will lead to another, which leads to another, which takes us out someplace else, so the information we have in the raw transcripts is all jumbled together that way – like a free-form, stream of consciousness–type thing, and we have to go through this and piece it together again. It's like a big jigsaw puzzle of questions and answers and comments and information that's all mixed together. We have to go through and transcribe all this information, it's all in notebooks and on tapes and Laura has spent a lot of time sitting there trying to transcribe the tapes and comparing what is on the tapes to what is in the notebooks. It's a long and tedious process because, when there is a large group, she has to identify the voices and put the right names in place so we know who is saying what. We have here 155 pages in 10 point type, and that's just up to over a month ago. We have to be able to sort all of it out and understand it ourselves so that we can go back and ask intelligent questions about points that have not been covered completely.

(Jan) Yes, and they always remember when they have already told us something. We may argue, but if we go back and look, sure enough, it's there!

(Laura) Yes, and if a question gets asked and then six months later, a different person asks the same question, the Cassiopaeans will tell us to go back and review. They will say, "Bring so-and-so up to speed."

(Terry) Yes, they will us to go back and look it up.

(Jan) One time they told us, "NO! Stop! Listen! Wait!" – trying to get our attention because we were off on a question spree – and they said: "YOU have the answers!" They told us specifically to stop channelling, sit there and talk the matter over. They told us that we could find the answers by 'networking'.

(Laura) Yes, so we spent an hour or more talking about the subject and by the time we got through, we realized that we did, indeed, know the answer.

(Terry) The bottom line of what they seem to be trying to

tell us, which we are trying to 'get', which 'we' in 6th density are trying to help 'us' in the present to do, is to understand that, within the next 20 years or so, this realm wave, this window, so to say, is going to arrive. And, when it arrives, we will have the opportunity to move from 3rd to 4th density as a group, as opposed to individually, on at a time through any number of lives. If, and when, we are able to do this, the object is first: to get us to move, but second: this is part of the counterattack against the Lizards from the service-to-others beings who are trying to get us back in the realm of freedom. They can't interfere with free will, but if they can inform enough of us, and we can make a free choice to move back, it will break the Lizards' hold on the human race. The object seems to be to break the Lizard hold on the human race. At that point, whether this works or not, whatever happens in 3rd density, happens. And then, the whole focal point of the campaign moves to somewhere else in the universe, because they are doing this in other places. This is *not* the only place that this is happening.

(Laura) And don't get the idea that this is something terrible. Are you all familiar with the Yin-Yang symbol, the black half and the white half? This is really what this is all about. We don't need to look at it as though it is really an actual battle, though in some terms, expressed at this density, it displays that way as well as in Earth changes. What it is is that for over 300,000 years we have been in the service-to-self realm, or the dark half of the circle. Now, the cycle is coming around. You have to remember that we are just doing this, as the Cassiopaeans say, "for fun!" [Laughter]

Now, we are gonna take a break, and after the break we are going to try to demonstrate – I don't know if it is going to work – but we are going to try. We don't want any personal questions. Don't ask what house you are gonna buy next year. Try to come up with some good questions, write them down for us, and we will see what happens.

During the break we set up the board and arranged the chairs with everybody in their proper alignments according to the compass points. Laura sits at the east, Frank at the north, Terry at the west, and the south position is open. I was really nervous when we sat down because I had no idea if things would work in a different location or not. But, after a few seconds of contact, the planchette began to spiral around in large circles, finally going to the word: "Hello."

1 **Q**: *(L)* Hello.

2 **A**: New location?

3 **Q**: *(L)* Yes, it's a new location, indeed. Where do you transmit through?

4 **A**: Cassiopaea.

5 **Q**: *(L)* Are you having difficulty operating in the new location?

6 **A**: Some but should stabilize.

7 **Q**: *(L)* We have questions from the audience. Shall we begin?

8 **A**: Sure!

9 **Q**: *(L)* The first question here is: "In which density is our astral existence?"

10 **A**: 5th, density of contemplation, you did not explain that one, did you?

11 **Q**: *(L)* Yeah, we forgot to explain that. Sorry.

12 **A**: Okay. Explain 5th now please.

13 **Q**: *(Terry)* 5th density is where souls go when they die. When you leave your physical body in any one of the first 4 densities, your soul moves to 5th density. They call it the contemplation density. That's where you go, and you get to review the life you have had, and learn from it, and decide what it is you want to do next when you incarnate next. In the chain of densities, one through seven, the souls exist in 1 through 4 and in 6th, actively, and in 5th density passively. Did I get that right?

14 **A**: Yes.

15 **Q**: *(Member of audience)* What energy are they using to create the conduit?

16 **A**: Open frequency EM wave.

Q: *(Member of audience)* Is there a 17
mathematical formula for creating the conduit? If so, what is it?

A: Create one at your leisure! 18

Q: *(L)* I guess if you want a mathemat- 19
ical formula, you are supposed to create one at your leisure! [Laughter] *(J)* That's humor, I guess.

A: Not totally humor! 20

Q: *(Member of audience)* Is it beyond 21
our current scientific level?

A: Yes. 22

Q: *(Question from audience)* "What ex- 23
ists in inner earth region as reported by Admiral Byrd?" Well, I think we should add *allegedly* reported by Admiral Byrd.

A: Cross awareness "window." 24

Q: *(L)* So, a window exists in the inner 25
earth region?

A: Did for Admiral Byrd at that in- 26
stance.

Q: *(L)* So, he passed through an aware- 27
ness window?

A: Yes. 28

Q: *(T)* What is an awareness window? 29

A: You have been told. 30

Q: *(L)* Yes. It's in the transcripts. 31

A: Realms can be accessed at will if 32
awareness balance is proper.

Q: *(L)* If awareness balance is proper, 33
"cross awareness window" means that you can cross over in awareness to another realm. Is that right? Let me break it down: does this mean that if your awareness is balanced, you create a 'window'?

34 **A**: Close.

35 **Q**: *(L)* Can this happen to a person spontaneously?

36 **A**: Yes.

37 **Q**: *(L)* It is not something that you necessarily have to work for, it can happen to anyone, anytime...

38 **A**: Unlikely.

39 **Q**: *(L)* So, it *can*, but without some preparation, is unlikely to happen. Okay, next question: "After 7th density is the Big Bang, and everything starts all over again?"

40 **A**: Close and partial. Grand cycle access.

41 **Q**: *(L)* You mean that 7th Density is a "grand cycle access"?

42 **A**: No, review.

43 **Q**: *(L)* 7th density is the Big Bang and it all starts all over again and that is the grand cycle? There is really no beginning or end, just an endless cycling?

44 **A**: No. Grand cycle is self explanatory to 6 people here.

45 **Q**: *(L)* I guess I'm not one of them. [A member of the audience here gives an explanation, but it is impossible to decipher it from the tape, as they were apparently in the back of the room. It sounds something like "at 7th density there is a window of access to the grand cycle."]

46 **A**: Yes.

47 **Q**: *(Question from audience)* What is the true age of the Great Pyramid? *(L)* That's already been given.

48 **A**: Yes.

49 **Q**: *(L)* I believe the figure that was given was 10,600 years ago, more or less. *(Question from audience)* Where do alien craft go when seen going into water such as lakes, rivers, the ocean, etc? Where do they go?

A: Variable. 50

Q: *(Member of audience)* Where did 51
the one go that I saw at Longboat Key? Where are they going off Longboat Key?

A: Non-specific. 52

Q: *(L)* Different destinations? *(T)* Are 53
some of them going to a base?

A: Not there, but remember, you are 54
talking about dual density cross-transference, therefore "rules" for 3rd density do not always apply.

Q: *(Question from audience)* Are they 55
using the ocean water as a conduit or window?

A: Maybe but not the only "method." 56

Q: *(T)* So, they could be doing about 57
anything down there once they have entered the water.

A: Yes. 58

Q: *(T)* Including just sitting there wait- 59
ing.

A: Why not? 60

Q: *(Question from audience)* Did you 61
ever ask them who built the Great Pyramid? *(L)* Yes, we did. The response was Atlanteans.

A: Descendants of same. 62

Q: *(Question from audience)* Did they 63
ever tell about the purpose for the pyramids?

(L) Yes, they did. First of all, the Atlantean civilization existed for a very long time and was quite extensive all over the globe, not necessarily confined

to the semi-legendary 'continent of Atlantis'. Apparently, interplanetary travel was as easy for the Atlanteans as it is for us to take a trip to the store. They had bases on the Moon, bases on Mars; the monuments of the Moon and Mars are Atlantean in origin; they also had some of their giant crystals on the Moon and Mars, and these were used to collect cosmic and solar energy as a power source. We have talked about locations of such crystals on the Earth and why they were not destroyed in the cataclysms that destroyed Atlantis and the answer was that the engineered function of these crystals was such that massive amounts of energy interacting with them is absorbed and transmuted, so to speak. If you put an atomic bomb on one of them, it would absorb the energy and transduce it. It was the design function. When we asked if our present technology could decipher how to use these crystals, the response was "would a Neanderthal know how to fly a 747." [Laughter] So, when we are talking about the Atlanteans, we are talking about a super-advanced civilization and the descendants of them, after the destruction that occurred which destroyed this amazing culture, built these pyramidal shapes, which had a similar function as the pyramid-shaped giant crystals, though much less effective. In other words, the pyramids are simply gigantic machines. They were used to manipulate energy to control weather, power the many things that a civilization requires to be considered 'advanced', to preserve and transmute or heal. Just a whole host of energy applications similar to what we do with electricity. But, still, it was a step down from the far more advanced Atlantean technology, and as time went by, other things occurred, and even this knowledge was lost.

(Question from audience) Is there a giant pyramid, or a step pyramid in China?

A: Yes. 64

Q: *(T)* Can you give us some information about this pyramid? 65

A: Yes. 66

Q: *(L)* Was it built by Atlantean descendants also? 67

A: Yes. 68

Q: *(L)* I think that the Atlantean civilization was much like our present one... it didn't really denote a specific place, though there may have been the equivalent of the 'Western technological world, as is America at the present time. In fact, when we asked about the population of the world at the height of Atlantis, the answer was that it was pretty much the same as it is now, over 6 billion. We then asked how many were left after the destruction and the figure was either 19 million or 119 million. I screwed up in the transcribing and will have to go back to the tape to get it right. Well, which was it? 69

A: 19 million. 70

Q: *(L)* That is a serious reduction from 6 billion. 71

(Question from audience) In all the varying transitions between 1st and 6th density, does any soul every perish, or become extinguished?

A: No. 72

Q: *(T)* We asked about this at several points. Apparently all souls began at the same point in 'time', and all will be returned to 7th density at the same 73 time. No new souls are being created, and no souls are ever destroyed; they merely change from state to state according to their 'lesson profile', or what they have learned or need to learn and experience. *(L)* Yeah. That's the good news; here's the bad news: those that don't graduate to 4th density on this pass of the Wave get to do 3rd density all over again, in its entire cycle. [Laughter]

(Question from audience) Have you ever asked about why there is so much suffering here on earth?

(L) Yes, and it's not Eve's fault!

(Question from audience) Well, I don't know about others, but if there is a utopia out there somewhere, I'd rather be there and never come back here again! And what you are telling me is that, even though we go back to 6th density, we have to come back again.

(L) No, that's 5th density – contemplation level. You make the decisions there, and if you are here, it's because you chose to be here. But, the only way to get out of the cycle of the 3rd density service-to-self level, the consumption level where you must feed on others – and that is really the bottom line there – you must transcend that issue, the physicality. You become an energy being who only gives conjoined with other beings who also only give, and in such symbiosis, no one ever lacks. But, yes, there is a very definite reason for the suffering at this level and Terry touched on it awhile ago: the dominance of the Reptilian beings who fed off of us for the past 300,000 years. They dumbed us down, implanted control impulses in us such as jealousy, greed, avarice and so forth, so that we would constantly generate negative energy while they are sitting there in 4th density with a straw just slurping it up! "Yummy!" So, when you feel yourself going into negative states, if you want to transcend it, all you have to really do is understand that it is not *yours*. You don't 'own it'. Yes, it is part of the physicality of this density, but it is a physicality that has been genetically tampered with so that such emotions will dominate. You can *not* act them out, you can refuse to be controlled by such states, you can *choose* to be other, even if it requires something of an inner struggle between the choice of the soul and the wants of the flesh, which are pretty clever at being rationalized by the brain so that we don't see what is really going on very clearly at all.

(Question from audience) So, we actually chose to accept this state of being at some point, and now we can choose otherwise?

(L) That's exactly right. Each moment, we have the choice of accepting the Lizzie program, or to follow a different line of choices. The mass of humanity, the group – and we have been told that the legend of Lucifer is the story of this choice and refers to the human race – made this choice. I don't know about you, but I've had enough. I think I changed my mind! [Laughter]

At this point, a member of the audience has taken Terry's place at the board. This was the 'skeptic' who, at the beginning of the session, had set up his little meter beside the board on the table.

74 **Q**: *(L)* OK, we have a new person at the board...

75 **A**: Yes.

76 **Q**: *(L)* We have a question here from somebody about walk-ins, and before I ask it, I would like to ask a sort of 'pre-question'. My question is: how often does something along the idea of a 'walk-in' occur?

77 **A**: Rare.

78 **Q**: *(L)* Yes, it was a very popular idea, and still is. I mean, how easy can it be to say, "Oh, I didn't do that! It was the former occupant of this body!" Or, "I can do *this* now, because I have just taken over this body. I'm not a trash man, I'm really a brain surgeon, so hand me a scalpel!" and that sort of thing. People were creating all kinds of exotic and elaborate 'backgrounds' for themselves, and as I heard these stories, they got wilder by the day! "I'm Prince or Princess So-and-So from the Planet Hoogabooga! Make obeisance, peasant!" How bizarre can it get?

(Question from audience) Have you asked about actual, physical life-forms on other planets, or is it just us here in the Universe?

(L) Yes, we have, but let's get in this question we have already. It says: "Are any of those who claim to be walk-ins really so?" And, we sort of answered that already. Yes, it *can* happen, but is very rare. The question continues: "If so, who are they specifically? My friend in Longboat Key, Gail _____, is she one?"

A: No. 79

Q: *(L)* Well, so much for that. [Ad- 80
dressing audience member who is nodding her head vigorously] Did you know that already? *(AM)* Yes. I just wanted to make sure.

(Question from new participant at the board, AB) Given the amount of destruction the Reptilians have done to our DNA, what can we do to repair it? Is there a diet adjustment?

A: Maybe. It is open to the individual 81
to experiment and discover.

I should note that the energy, at this point, was quite fractured with the new person at the board and the planchette was moving very slowly.

82 **Q**: *(L)* I think that the conduit has to be readjusted to the new energy.

83 **A**: Yes. Note Light waves in device.

84 **Q**: *(L)* You mean the meter beside us? Turn it around so we can see it. *(T)* What is the bottom of the range? *(AB)* .1, .2 is the ambient. It's been hitting peaks of 5 at times before I sat down. That's micro-gausses. *(J)* What light waves are you referring to?

A: Near window. 85

Q: A space-time window? [There was 86
no physical window in the room.]

A: Yes. 87

Q: *(L)* I think that this is in response 88
to your question about DNA. We are supposed to notice that the meter is measuring some sort of energy and that this represents light waves near the 'window' or conduit that is established

by the channelling, and that this is one of the things that can change DNA. I don't think that eating or drinking one way or another can make a difference; it is what is inside, which, in a sense *can* change what you eat or drink, but it is a change that comes from a different direction than a change that is done deliberately in order to alter DNA. They have said that light waves alter DNA. *(AB)* What specific light frequency?

89 **A**: 6 pt 5

90 **Q**: *(AB)* Angstroms?

91 **A**: Yes.

92 **Q**: *(AB)* That's actually the frequency of a medium red neon laser. A laser is a monochromic frequency. It's like one of those laser pointers. It puts out only one color, one exact frequency. 6.5 would be mid-orange?

A: Yes. 93

Q: *(Question from audience)* What are 94
certain people in our government and our military gaining by being more conspiring than lucid?

A: Open. 95

Q: *(T)* Many things. Is there one thing 96
in particular that they gain from this?

A: As we know, answer is dangerous. 97

Q: *(T)* We've gotten several answers 98
like that when we touch on sensitive questions.

At this point, the tape ended, and we ended the 'demonstration session' that was supposed to have been 'predestined'. Was it? What were the ramifications aside from the fact that the small, local MUFON group had the largest attendance ever in its existence?

As it turned out, there were interesting developments shortly thereafter.

On this occasion, however, we didn't invite a bunch of guests back with us – not after the last experience! Instead, we decided to just discuss it with the Cs and amongst ourselves. Our energy was high, we were all feeling in harmony, and it turned out to be an excellent session with some fascinating discussion. We call it the 'Wizard of Oz' session.

Additionally, following up on the session of February 9th, where I mentioned that I had made an appointment to visit the Coral Castle guy's friend in Orlando, there are some questions about that here also. So, let me bring you up to date on that.

The funny thing is, of course, that if the Cs had not mentioned the key words 'Coral Castle', I would probably have had *no* interest in this guy at *all*! But, because they had offered it as a clue to a 'discovery', I was 'primed' and ready to follow the 'trail'.

So, I made the trip back over (about 100 miles from my home) and visited Hilliard (that's the guy's name).

When I walked in his house, a beautiful lake-shore Frank Lloyd Wright–type affair, I was *amazed* at all the UFO stuff all over the place. *Huge* blown-up photos... shelves *full* of books and videos and 'reports'... knick-knacks... you name it. He pulled out a big box of typewritten sheets and we began to talk about Edward Leedskalnin.

Story is that EL was fond of telling folks that "he knew the secret of how the pyramids were built." Also, apparently, the Coral Castle was built in one place and then, because of zoning or some such reason, had to be *moved*... and the guy did it in *one night*! There never was any such thing as the 'lost love' called 'Sweet Sixteen' that was told on the TV special – Leedskalnin made that up just to bamboozle the media and laughed about it ever after.

Hilliard pointed out that the most amazing thing about the building was that the quarry where the stones came from *had no tailings* – that is, there were no piles of 'stonedust' from cutting.

Hilliard hinted that he knew the 'secret', but he was not yet ready to tell me... but he gave me a hint. He said: "You know, I am the only one who was ever inside Edward's private room. He was very ascetic, and lived in only one room with the barest necessities. In his room were only four objects: a cot bed, a table and chair that he made himself, and an airplane seat suspended from the ceiling by chains."

He looked at me *very* intently as he said this and I realized that this was the clue.

"An airplane seat?" I asked.

"Ayup."

Well, that was all he would say at that point. He showed me photos of him and Leedskalnin (he was in his AF uniform), and there were photos of Leedskalnin and his children and group photos and all that. But, he wouldn't let me take the manuscript, even though I offered to retype it on computer and put it on a diskette. He said he would have to "think about it."

The very next day, Hilliard was in an auto accident... fortunately, he was not seriously injured.

Participants: 'Frank', Laura, Terry, Jan, Susan V

1 **Q**: *(L)* Hello.

2 **A**: Real UFOs SV.

3 **Q**: *(T)* The word is coming off the board because the surface is too slick to hold the ink.[1]

4 **A**: Density.

5 **Q**: *(T)* Is this satisfactory even though we are losing the word 'density'?

6 **A**: Losing density is a common experience.

7 **Q**: *(J)* Are we talking about dieting?

8 **A**: Several interpretations.

9 **Q**: *(T)* I love mirth!

10 **A**: Mirth is good.

11 **Q**: *(L)* Who do we have with us tonight?

12 **A**: Sorra.

13 **Q**: *(T)* Hi, Sorra! *(L)* And where are you from?

14 **A**: Hi, Terry! Cassiopaea.

15 **Q**: *(T)* We have provided a new board. Works great.

16 **A**: Please make a habit of this!

17 **Q**: *(T)* We all like the new board, yes indeed!

18 **A**: Smooth, have called others to observe in amazement! [Laughter] Next demonstration please use this or a similar board.

Q: *(L)* We are sorry that we had to 19 use the old board for the demonstration. *(T)* We were all winging it! Did we do OK today?

A: Okay today, we are actually hav- 20 ing fun with this board. Love it!!!!!!! [Laughter] Yeah! This is Deanorrilloa, I am impressed too! Oppilmno, me too! Your energy will soar tonight to new levels!

Q: *(J)* Does it have something to do 21 with our demonstration today[2] and the new board?

A: Yes!! 22

Q: *(J)* You guys are going to get 23 whiplash moving around the board so fast!

A: You are good! 24

Q: *(T)* We owe it all to us! 25

A: Yes. 26

Q: *(L)* Tell us about the general... 27

A: [Mike F] wants back in![3] 28

Q: *(T)* What does F___ want? Yeah, 29 we convinced him today. Why does F___ want back in?

A: You are a powerful channel, he does 30 know a legitimate one when he sees one, you know! And he is a legitimate researcher who merely got caught up in an emotional state.

Q: *(L)* I thought that you said that he 31 was an agent for the Lizzies?

A: Agent provacateur. 32

[1]We were using a new board and had added several words and punctuation marks to it.

[2]At the MUFON meeting.

[3]MF, supposed UFO investigator for MUFON. When I was working with the abductee, Scarlett ("Candy" in *The Wave*), he saw it as a case to make him famous, started manipulating her, and ended up having an affair with her.

33 **Q**: *(T)* They are not saying that we should let him back in; they are just saying that he wants in.

34 **A**: All is up to you.

35 **Q**: *(L)* What was the reaction of Andrew B?[4]

36 **A**: Excitement.

37 **Q**: *(T)* I don't mind having Andy come if you don't. I don't mind as long as he doesn't go running and screwing around with F___. *(T)* Well, he can do whatever he wants with F___ as long as he doesn't bring F___'s energy in here. Only MF can do that. *(L)* Who was the gray-headed, bearded guy?

38 **A**: Barth H___.

39 **Q**: *(T)* Who the heck is Barth H? *(J)* Who was the guy with the pith helmet? *(L)* He is at Leonard's meeting quite often. You guys said the other day that this demonstration that we were going to give today was a destined event.

40 **A**: Yes.

41 **Q**: *(L)* Tell us now, since we have done it, what was the intent or the purpose of this destiny?

42 **A**: Education of those who could use a little redirection.

43 **Q**: *(L)* All those people there were people with just a little bit of an open mind. I mean, you almost can't deal with metaphysical people because they are generally closet fundamentalists. *(F)* Yeah, they seemed to be more balanced than some of these 'New Agers'. *(J)* Why was there so much interference when we had the group here a couple of sessions ago and there was no interference today?[5]

A: Grooved better. 44

Q: *(T)* It was also good practice for doing it with a larger group of people. 45

A: Did you notice the heightened openness? 46

Q: *(L)* Yes we did notice. What was the reason for that? 47

A: Grooving provides for less interference among other things. 48

Q: *(T)* When GB[6] and the others were here, that was the first time we had that many people here who were all directing the energy at the channel, so that opened the channel and grooved it wider. *(J)* The more new people we bring in with the right attitude, the more grooved it will become. 49

A: No, it happens as a natural circumstance of events. 50

Q: *(L)* Am I correct in thinking that one of the things that happened today was that we explained quite clearly what was going on, put up the parameters, and told the people what we would accept in the way of questions, and that this set up the protection? 51

A: Yes. 52

Q: *(L)* AB wanted us to ask, what were the original number of chromosomes the human being possessed? 53

A: 135 pairs. 54

Q: *(T)* And we now have 23 pairs. So, we lost quite a few chromosomes. *(L)* A lot! *(T)* Will we get them all back? 55

[4]Supposed to be the highest-level Golden Dawn initiate in the region. He was *such* a poseur!

[5]Referring to the 25 Feb session when a number of MUFON people attended.

[6]Former regional director of MUFON.

56 **A**: Wait and see.

57 **Q**: *(L)* I want to ask about the fellow with the Coral Castle. We went over to see Hillard, as you know. He had an accident after we saw him, the very next day, in fact. Was this accident caused to prevent him from communicating with us any further?

58 **A**: Open. Call him and press for details if you like.

59 **Q**: *(L)* When we were talking to Hillard, he told us about the man who built the Coral Castle.[7] This fellow had, apparently, in his private quarters, three objects: a bed, a table, and a swing made of an airplane seat suspended from the ceiling by a chain, complete with seatbelts. Is this...

60 **A**: You got it right because you are learning and rebundling DNA as a result of this and other activities.[8]

61 **Q**: *(L)* OK, so what SV and I were hashing out about this mystery, that was a process of understanding how this man performed these remarkable feats of engineering and construction, is that it?

62 **A**: Hypnotize SV if you wish.

63 **Q**: *(L)* Will SV be able to access this knowledge through hypnosis?

64 **A**: What do you suppose has happened to SV in her life, and why does she have nagging thoughts about her personal reality which she chooses not to disclose?

65 **Q**: *(S)* I think you better hypnotize me. I have nagging thoughts, but... *(T)* Does this bring anything out? *(S)* About my personality, I doubt myself, I don't know. It's like a great big question mark. *(T)* Do you want to follow up on this? And, they started out with "Real UFOs, SV." What does that mean?

A: What does it mean, indeed![9] 66

Q: *(S)* I guess as opposed to projec- 67
tions? *(L)* OK, guys, let's connect our brain cells here!

A: No need to connect "brain cells," us- 68
ing your chakras will do!

Q: *(L)* Don't connect your brain cells, 69
connect your chakras? How do we connect our chakras? *(T)* I didn't know that you could connect them? *(S)* They are all connected always. *(L)* But I mean how do we connect them with each other? *(S)* Think it, I guess.

A: Discover. 70

Q: *(L)* Can you give us a clue on this? 71
(T) Meditation?

A: You are missing the point, don't 72
search, just let it happen when it is ready.

Q: *(T)* That's easy enough. *(S)* What 73
does "real UFOs" mean? *(L)* Yes, you opened with that, what does it mean?

A: Ask SV! 74

Q: *(L)* Well, we certainly will ask SV. 75
(S) I have never seen a UFO that I know of. Maybe I have but I didn't know it. Does it have anything to do with the fact that I am adopted?

A: Maybe. 76

[7] Leedskalnin.

[8] *The Wave* 44

[9] Considering later events, this was a curious coded warning, or so it seems in retrospect.

77 **Q**: *(L)* Maybe you are an alien, SV. *(T)* Are you an Orion Federation member? [Laughter] *(S)* Am I?

78 **A**: Mirth.

79 **Q**: *(S)* You have to hypnotize me soon, I am dying of curiosity. *(L)* You won't die, I promise. *(T)* Yeah, you are living in Curiosity City. *(S)* I have had some really strange, fragmented dreams lately. They are only like glimpses... *(T)* Lately? Jan or I haven't had any strange dreams lately since the last one we talked about, but Jan had the visual thing with the eye the other night. *(L)* Yes, what was this phenomenon Jan experienced with her eyes the other night? *(T)* This is like the third or fourth time this thing has happened to her over the years.

80 **A**: Strand development in progress.

81 **Q**: *(J)* That's what I thought.

82 **A**: If that is what you thought, why hold back, don't you see your increasing abilities?

83 **Q**: *(T)* You have just gained knowledge on what you should be thinking about the next time it happens. I have been telling her that when it started that she should just relax, get past the stress and the fear, and just watch it and see what it does. *(L)* Yes, well, we have all had some strange experiences. *(T)* Yes, it is easy for me to say but hard for me to do and the same is true for all of us. *(L)* And with each of us, it is different.

84 **A**: Yes.

85 **Q**: *(J)* What kind of abilities are you talking about?

86 **A**: Psychic!

87 **Q**: *(J)* OK, good...

A: Stop resisting UFO phenomenon, 88
just accept.

Q: *(L)* What is this? Are you resisting, 89
Jan? *(J)* I think I am still skeptical, yes. *(L)* You're kidding! I guess you need to see one, I guess. It sure cured me. [Laughter] *(J)* I have not had any assurances at all. *(S)* Neither have I, as far as we know. [Laughter] *(J)* I mean, I know all this stuff... *(T)* Can we arrange for something for all of us to see where you are?

A: You can arrange any time. Laura, 90
more caffeine, please.

Q: *(T)* Do you guys want some coffee? 91
Let me ask, could it be that you guys are hooked on caffeine and you can only get it through us?

A: Open. How does a 6th density light 92
being go about being "hooked" on anything from 3rd density?

Q: *(S)* OK, Terry, you'd better explain 93
it to them! *(T)* It is coming through on the frequency we are transmitting. *(L)* Are you guys getting the caffeine when I drink it?

A: No. 94

Q: *(T)* Are you getting the shot of fre- 95
quency change it provides?

A: If so, oh well! [Laughter] 96

Q: *(L)* I think what it does is make us 97
able to stay up with them.

A: Yes. 98

Q: *(T)* Oh, come on! You get a little 99
out of it! Yeah, you do! *(J)* Do you like flavored or non-flavored coffee?

A: Terry, what have you been smok- 100
ing?

Q: *(T)* Oh! They want some of that 101
too! Ho-ho-ho, mirth, mirth. *(S)* It's those cigars you smoke, Terry!

[Break for coffee.]

102 **Q**: *(L)* I assume that you/us have been listening to our/your conversation on finances...

103 **A**: As always.

104 **Q**: *(L)* Now, what we would like to know is, can you give us pointers in this regard, or reassurances, because we are still 3rd density and need reassurance in some respects, as to how to deal with this situation.

105 **A**: You are still 3rd density enough to need a lot of things, my love!

106 **Q**: *(L)* Yes, but you didn't answer the question! *(T)* They are good at that.

107 **A**: RTB Review memory.

108 **Q**: *(L)* OK, you said you were making financial arrangements for us...

109 **A**: RTB RTLTHEBSHS

110 **Q**: *(L)* Is this a code?

111 **A**: RTL, THE, BSHS...

112 **Q**: *(Laura and Jan)* RATTLE THE BUSHES! [Groans]

113 **A**: As you are doing, network!

114 **Q**: *(L)* So, we need to get more stuff and send more stuff out, and do like Frank said and look for sponsors and so forth.

115 **A**: Ask GB about money, he will not likely give, but may know someone who will! Do you now see the process?

116 **Q**: *(S)* A government grant? [Laughter]

117 **A**: Nyet.

118 **Q**: [Much laughter] *(T)* Let's ask Newt! *(L)* Nyet on Newt! *(T)* Ask GB?

119 **A**: Nyet on Newt! Mirth.

Q: *(T)* So, there are no Republicans on 6th level... now, what happened, Laura, when you were looking for the correct Reiki teacher? *(L)* I asked if I knew someone who knew someone who knew the correct Reiki... *(T)* And the Cassiopaeans said HD. And, when they said that, you said: "Well, Helen doesn't believe in Reiki." Yet Helen knew the person with the correct lineage and teachings. 120

A: Trust. 121

Q: *(T)* But, you didn't know she knew someone, yet she sent you to the person you needed to find. *(L)* Right. *(T)* And, now they are suggesting GB. He won't give us the help, but he will tell us someone to go see. Is it not the same? *(J)* He forks out every month to pay for the MUFON Newsletter and it costs about $150 a month to print that out. *(L)* Jan, didn't you have a question you wanted to ask? *(J)* Yes... I wanted to ask about that 'psycho-power'. *(L)* Where's the envelope the ad came in? There it is... there is the psycho-power thing... *(J)* Yes, and how come they misspelled my name... [Laura waves envelope with ad in air.] *(L)* You see this, guys? We would like to know if this is... 122

A: "Karnak the Magnificent" 123

Q: *(J)* Oh! *(L)* What's the matter? 124

(J) Well, that's confirmation enough for me!!

(L) What do you mean?

(J) We were talking about Karnak in the car on the way up today! You know, the Johnny Carson skit. *(L)* Oh! *(T)* Karnak gave the answer to questions that were sealed in envelopes. It was always a joke. He would give a straight

answer to a question that turned out to be a joke. "Humpty Dumpty had a great fall," is the one I remember, and the question was, "What happened to Humpty Dumpty when Misses September, October and November moved into his apartment complex." [Groans] Bad jokes.

(F) He would frequently use a play on words for that skit. If there was someone whose name was in the news a lot, he would say something like, "Alexander Haig", and then they would open up the envelope and the question would be, "Who is the father of the son of Alexander Haig." [Groans]

(L) Well, we can save our money on that one.

(J) Guys, I am still skeptical of this...

(L) What do you mean?

(J) This whole thing... I really am... and for that to come through like that after Terry and I were joking about that in the car on the way here, and they picked that out specifically... just blows me away... I am sorry. [Gets tearful]

(F) That's OK. Until you get something that you can literally put trust in, it isn't really real for you.

(J) Yes, like Laura's was...

(L) Actually the biggest one was...

(J) George R. Kidd...[10]

(L) Actually there have been several... the 666 thing was not in anybody's subconscious, I know... none of us could have known about the Coptic number-letter relationship... and the thing about...

(J) I think we each have to have our own personal thing...

(L) And I have had to have so many of them, and still, with so many of them piling up, every once in a while I still go into my doubt mode...

(J) We all do....

(L) What is this, are we deluding ourselves, is this a master deception by some entity? Our own minds?

(J) My friend Ann over in Palatka, who publishes that newsletter, the *UFOlogist*. We played around with the board one weekend when I went to stay with her. We got this really strange entity, and it didn't really go much of anywhere, but one phrase came through that was very clear that I had seen on a TV episode several days before, and the other one that came through that got me was the night before we went to that charity event and the first word that came up was 'poinsettias', and we asked what it meant and the Cassiopaeans answered that it just came to mind. Well, when we went to that event the next night, there were poinsettias all over the place.

(T) Yeah, that country club was just filled with poinsettias.

A: Hand on. [Laura had hand off while looking for papers and puts hand on planchette when requested.] 125

Q: *(T)* OK, what... 126

A: Put your hand in the hand of the Cassiopaeans! Put your hand in the hand of the "Man" who rides the Wave! [Laughter] 127

[10]Name of my son in his previous incarnation. See Tom French's article, "The Exorcist in Love", *St. Petersburg Times*, for details, as well as session 7 November 1994.

128 **Q**: *(T)* Oh, I like that one. *(L)* We need to get to our questions... *(J)* GB thinks we need to put a book together on predictions... *(L)* I think the words of Jesus on that matter are appropriate: "It is a weak and faithless generation that seeketh after a sign." *(T)* We were talking about that earlier in the car... that the predictions are minor things compared to what we are actually getting, and that if you have the knowledge, you don't need the predictions, because you already know that something is going to happen and you know that things are not necessarily 'set' until just before they happen...

129 **A**: Ask.

130 **Q**: *(L)* At one point we were told that time was an illusion that came into being at the 'time' of the 'Fall' in Eden, and this was said in such a way that I inferred that there were other illusions put into place at that time...[11]

131 **A**: Time is an illusion that works for you because of your altered DNA state.[12]

132 **Q**: *(L)* OK, what other illusions?

133 **A**: Monotheism, the belief in one separate, all powerful entity.

134 **Q**: *(L)* What is another one of the illusions?

135 **A**: The need for physical aggrandizement.

136 **Q**: *(L)* The focus on the physical as the thing one needs to hold on to or protect. *(T)* Is separate the key word in regard to monotheism?

137 **A**: Yes.

Q: *(L)* What is another of the illusions? 138

A: Linear focus. 139

Q: *(L)* Anything else at this time? 140

A: Unidimensionality. 141

Q: *(L)* The veil... *(J)* The perception of 142
only one dimension... *(L)* Were these illusions programmed into us genetically through our DNA?

A: Close. 143

Q: *(L)* Are there any others we should 144
cover at this point?

A: Are you finished with the concept? 145

Q: *(L)* Well, I don't know. Can you 146
tell us a little bit about how these illusions are enforced on us, how they are perceived by us?

A: If someone opens a door, and behind 147
it you see a pot of gold, do you worry whether there is a poisonous snake behind the door hidden from view, before you reach for the pot of gold?[13]

Q: *(L)* What does the gold represent? 148

A: Temptation to limitation. 149

Q: *(L)* What does the door represent? 150

A: Opening for limitation. 151

Q: *(L)* Was limitation presented as a 152
pot of gold when, in fact, it was not? Was this a trick?

A: What is snake? 153

Q: *(T)* The Lizards? *(J)* Danger. *(L)* 154
OK, who opened the door? *(J)* We did. *(T)* No, what is the snake.

A: No. 155

Q: *(L)* Does that mean we did not open 156
the door?

[11] *The Wave* 3, 23, 68; *The Wave 7* "Appendix B"
[12] *High Strangeness* 10
[13] *The Wave* 3

157 **A**: Yes.

158 **Q**: *(T)* Who opened the door?

159 **A**: Lizards.

160 **Q**: *(L)* So, we were, literally... *(T)* Who was the snake? *(J)* The Lizards, they are danger...

161 **A**: No!

162 **Q**: *(L)* Who was the snake?[14]

163 **A**: Result of giving into temptation without caution, i.e. leaping before looking.[15]

164 **Q**: *(J)* So we should exercise caution. *(T)* OK, what was the snake? *(J)* The result of giving into temptation. The snake represents the classic... *(L)* So what you are saying to us is that the story of the temptation in Eden was the story of humankind being led into this reality as a result of being tempted. So, the eating of the fruit of the Tree of Knowledge of Good and Evil was...

165 **A**: Giving into temptation.[16]

166 **Q**: *(L)* And this was a trick...[17]

167 **A**: No! Tricks don't exist!

168 **Q**: *(L)* There is an issue here. *(T)* OK, no trick – a trap?

169 **A**: No! Traps don't exist either. Free will could not be abridged if you had not obliged.

170 **Q**: *(T)* Now wait a minute. I am losing the whole train here. What were we before the 'Fall'?

171 **A**: 3rd density STO.[18]

[14] *The Wave 7* "Appendix B"
[15] *The Wave* 23
[16] *The Wave* 68
[17] *High Strangeness* 10
[18] *Secret History* 5
[19] *The Wave* 28, 39

Q: *(T)* Didn't you tell us that 3rd den- 172
sity beings could not be STO? *(L)* No. They said there are 3rd density STO beings. *(T)* We are STS at this point because of what happened then?

A: Yes. 173

Q: *(T)* OK, now, we were STO at that 174
time. The Lizards opened the door – we are using this as an allegory, I guess – the Lizards opened the door and showed us a pot of gold hoping that we would reach in for the pot, or walk through the door, when they were waiting for us on the other side in order to take us over in some way. Am I on the right track?

A: Hoping is incorrect idea. 175

Q: *(T)* OK, what was it they were try- 176
ing to do by enticing us?

A: Trying is incorrect idea, continue to 177
probe for learning opportunity.

Q: *(T)* We were 3rd density STO at 178
this time. Was this after the battle that had transpired? In other words, were we, as a 3rd density race, literally on our own at that point, as opposed to before?

A: Was battle. 179

Q: *(L)* The battle was in us?[19] 180

A: Through you. 181

Q: *(T)* The battle was through us as 182
to whether we would walk through this doorway... *(L)* The battle was fought through us, we were literally the battleground. *(T)* I got that, but I want

to get back to this analogy to make sure where we are in the overall picture. The battle was going on when the door was opened. Was the battle over whether or not we walked through that door?

183 **A**: Close.

184 **Q**: *(T)* OK, we were STO at that point. You have said before that on this density we have the choice of being STS or STO.

185 **A**: Oh Terry, the battle is always there, it's "when" you choose that counts!

186 **Q**: *(T)* OK, so we are still looking at that pot of gold? What I am trying to find out is... there is something important here... *(L)* Let's back up and ask it this way: Prior to this event, humankind was or was not...

187 **A**: Prior to?

188 **Q**: *(L)* OK, not prior. But, we are still talking about somewhat of a historical event in a sense even though it is all simultaneous. This event, somewhere on the cycle, was humankind all one soul, so to speak...

189 **A**: Backsliding.

190 **Q**: *(T)* We are moving backwards here. OK, let's ask it this way...

191 **A**: Closer. You were with the thought waves, perhaps better to defer to him for this one.

192 **Q**: *(L)* OK, I'll shut up. Carry on, Terry. *(T)* I need all the help I can get. *(L)* It's a tough one. *(T)* This must tie in to why the Lizards and other aliens keep telling people that they have given their consent for abduction and so forth. We were STO and now we are STS. *(J)* Yeah, right.

A: Yes, continue.[20] 193

Q: *(T)* We are working with the anal- 194
ogy. The gold was an illusion. The gold was not what we perceived it to be. It was a temptation that was given to us as STO beings on 3rd density. The door was opened by the Lizards.

A: No temptation, it was always there. 195
Remember Dorothy and the ruby slippers?

Q: *(T)* OK, we were STO at that time, 196
before we stepped through. We didn't have to step through. *(F)* But, wait a minute now, they keep saying, correct me if I am wrong, every time Terry says: "They tried to get us through..." *(L)* They said no... *(F)* It was always there. *(J)* Free will could not be abridged if you had not obliged. *(T)* They didn't do anything but open the door. The Lizards opened the door and let us decide whether we were going to go through or not. *(J)* I still think the key is that we obliged by stepping through the door... *(T)* By our stepping through this door that the Lizards conveniently provided for us without actually doing anything to us, just opening it and showing it to us...

A: Provided?!? 197

Q: *(L)* They didn't provide it... *(J)* It 198
always existed... *(T)* It's always there.... *(J)* It's there now... *(T)* The Lizards...

A: Yes, think of the ruby slippers. 199
What did Glenda tell Dorothy???

Q: *(J)* You can always go home. *(L)* 200
You have always had the power to go home...[21]

A: Yes. 201

[20] *High Strangeness* 10
[21] *The Wave* 3

202 **Q**: *(L)* So, we always have the power to return to being STO? Even in 3rd density?

203 **A**: Yes.

204 **Q**: *(L)* How does a 3rd density STO being conduct their life?

205 **A**: Discover.

206 **Q**: *(T)* I want to go back to the analogy of the door. The door has always been there. The temptation has always been there... *(J)* Is there... *(T)* Has, is, will be... is always.

207 **A**: "When" you went for the gold, you said "Hello" to the Lizards and all that that implies.

208 **Q**: *(T)* OK, that was what I was trying to get at. You said that the Lizards, or the forces of STS, opened the door.

209 **A**: No. Shouldn't say opened. We said "opened" only to introduce you to the concept, so that you would understand.

210 **Q**: *(L)* So, let's let go of the part that somebody "opened" the door. *(T)* The door was always there and always open. I was just trying to work with the analogy. So, the concept is that, as STO beings we had the choice of either going for the gold or not. By going for the gold, we became STS beings, because going for the gold was STS.

211 **A**: Yes.

212 **Q**: *(T)* And, in doing so, we ended up aligning ourselves with the 4th density Lizard beings...[22]

213 **A**: Yes.

Q: *(T)* Because they are 4th density be- 214
ings and they have a lot more abilities than we at 3rd density...

A: You used to be aligned with 4th den- 215
sity STO.[23]

Q: *(T)* And we were 3rd density STO. 216
But, by going for the gold we aligned ourselves with 4th density STS.

A: Yes. 217

Q: *(T)* And by doing so we gave 4th 218
density STS permission to do whatever they wish with us?

A: Close. 219

Q: *(T)* So, when they tell us that we 220
gave them permission to abduct us, it is this they are referring to?[24]

A: Close. 221

Q: *(J)* Go back to what they said be- 222
fore: "Free will could not be abridged if you had not obliged." *(T)* We, as the human race, used our free will to switch from STO to STS. *(L)* So, at some level we have chosen the mess we are in and that is the Super Ancient Legend of the Fallen Angel, Lucifer. That is us. We fell by falling into that door, so to speak, going after the pot of gold, and when we fell through the door, the serpent bit us![25]

A: But this is a repeating syndrome. 223

Q: *(L)* Is it a repeating syndrome just 224
for the human race or is it a repeating syndrome throughout all of creation?

A: It is the latter. 225

Q: *(L)* Is this a repeating syndrome 226
throughout all of creation simply be-

[22] *Secret History* 5; *The Wave* 7 "Appendix B"
[23] *The Wave* 68
[24] *High Strangeness* 10; *The Wave* 28
[25] *The Wave* 3

cause it is the cyclic nature of things? Or is it as the Indians call it, *maya*?

227 **A**: Either or.

228 **Q**: *(T)* Now, you keep referring to the movie *The Wizard of Oz*. You have been saying...

229 **A**: 6th density inspired.

230 **Q**: *(T)* You have good filmmakers up there in 6th density. *(S)* What other movies did they inspire? *(T)* Before we go off on a sidetrack like that, I'm still trying to grasp something here... OK, you keep referring to the movie, and that we have an ability within us that is something like the ruby slippers that can take us back to STO any time we wish.

231 **A**: Yes.

232 **Q**: *(T)* So, all this stuff we have been talking about, the realm border, the Wave, raising the frequencies...

233 **A**: Realm wave is the "tornado."

234 **Q**: *(T)* That is the rough wave moving.

235 **A**: Subjective.

236 **Q**: *(L)* In the analogy of Dorothy and the whole thing, the place where she started out was Kansas, i.e. STO? *(J)* It was in black and white...

237 **A**: Not really.

238 **Q**: *(L)* Was going to the land of Oz the STO state?

239 **A**: STS.

240 **Q**: *(L)* So Oz was STS. And Kansas, not necessarily the physical surroundings, but the state of mind of Dorothy prior to the Oz experience, was the STO state.

241 **A**: Yes.

Q: *(L)* So, we don't need necessarily to look at Kansas or the fact that it was filmed in black and white – it is just the state of mind. The going to Oz... 242

A: And Elvira Gulch. 243

Q: *(J)* The lady that turned into the witch. 244

A: The witch is the Lizards. 245

Q: *(T)* Yeah, OK. Tornado. Dorothy fell from the STO to the STS state through the tornado. Is this true? 246

A: Yes. 247

Q: *(T)* The realm wave you equated to the tornado... *(L)* Did a realm wave interact with... 248

A: Analyze more carefully, suggest break to do so. 249

[Break]

(T) They are equating the tornado as the shift from STO to STS.

(L) Maybe it also is a shift from STS to STO.

(J) Yes, a shift from one to the other would be dramatic.

(T) Was it a density shift also? The realm wave is supposed to be a density shift. A window between densities. Is there also a shifting between STO and STS? Is there a gateway that you go through? A door?

(F) Oh God! There are so many possibilities here.

(L) And if you switch into STO, do you find yourself on a different Earth?

(T) They said this tornado is representative of Dorothy going from STO to STS state. She also went from her reality to a totally different reality.

(F) That's true.

(J) But switching from one to the other is going to be traumatic.

(T) They have been talking about a realm wave...

(F) I don't think it matters which way, I just think that in that particular story it was laid out that way.

(T) But what they have been telling us so far is that the realm wave is a window to move between densities.

(J) Right.

(T) But they just said to us that the tornado is an analogy of a realm wave. But the tornado was a passage from STO to STS, not from 3rd to 4th density.

(J) Two different things.

(F) True, however, a realm border passage may represent any kind of sudden shift?

(T) That is what I am wondering. Can it also mean that not only would we shift from 3rd to 4th, but also would we shift from STS to STO and start out in an STO state there? And then have, again, whether or not we shift back to an STS state in 4th density? Do you always start out in an STO state?

(L) OK, let's stop.

(F) No, because if a realm border is coming now, and they have told us over and over again that we are STS, and what they have actually told us is that the realm border is a shift from 3rd density to 4th density, and they never said it was a shift from STS to STO, they have said that it is our choice.

(T) Yes, but they just referred to the tornado as this realm wave, and, in the *Wizard* the tornado was the symbol of shifting from STO to STS.

(J) Is it?

(T) I don't know. I'm just trying to get a handle on what they are trying to tell us here, because it is something extremely important.

(J) They have been saying "ruby slippers, ruby slippers," not "tornado, tornado."

(T) Yeah, they said that just now, that the Wave is the tornado.

(F) I think that is a different subject, there.

(T) But now it is the same symbology. The tornado took her from one point to another and the slippers took her back to point A again. Two different concepts.

(F) Wait a minute.

(L) They said that Kansas wasn't the STO state.

(F) There are all kinds of intricate little things here; somehow there must be a way to connect it. You know what it is, remember the slippers, they said, meant that the pathway was always there for her to go home.

(J) Yeah, but she had to kill the witch to get the slippers.

(F) No, she thought she had to. Don't you remember Glenda telling her, "Ooh, no dear, you can always go home. All you have to do is say 'there's no place like home.'"

(J) Yeah, but you had to be wearing those slippers...

(F) No, no... remember, that was an illusion.

(L) You've always had the power to go home.

(S) Now, you know what, the tornado could be 5th density, as she was looking

out the window all these things passed by...

(T) Yes, her life passed by her.

(F) Yes, but they have told us that the realm border passage itself is going to result in all kinds of hairy stuff going on.

(J) Like I say, switching from STS to STO or back, or from 3rd density to 4th density, it's going to be a violent... it is not going to be an easy passage either way.

(F) Right.

(J) It is a radical change in reality.

(T) Yes, but for Dorothy, in the movie, it was violent in the fact that it was a tornado, though it did not physically hurt her.

(J) Yes, and that is what we have been told, too.

(F) She was scared...

(T) Yes, but that was a mental thing... it was up here [pointing to head] where the hurt was. She didn't get hurt physically.

(F) There is also another thing to speculate about: throughout the entire movie, she was never hurt physically. Through all the threats, she was never actually hurt.

(T) It was also 1939 – if the movie had been made in 1995 they would have had machine guns, missiles, chainsaws, and there would be body counts all over the place. And she still could have gone home any time she wanted. You know, *Dorothy Meets the Terminator.*

(L) Dorothy and the Chainsaw Massacre.

(S) Dorothy Goes to Elm Street. [Laughter]

(T) It's the cross between a children's fairy story and a Stephen King nightmare.

(F) You know, the fundamentalists have attacked *The Wizard of Oz.*

(L) They have? Why?

(T) Because it is Satanic.

(F) Yeah, they say it's Hollywood's effort to pull people away from Christianity and fundamentalism and all that jazz.

(T) The Wizard of Oz is evil. To the fundamentalists.

(F) Yes, because you don't need the celebration of Christ to get back to Kansas.

(L) Yes, and Cinderella is politically incorrect.

(T) Because she didn't sleep with one foot on the floor like all the sitcoms.

(J) Excuse me?

(T) I don't know.

(S) We went from Oz to sitcoms?

(J) I think you are mixing your metaphors.

(S) That was Sleeping Beauty.

(T) Yeah, that was Sleeping Beauty in the box.

(J) And one foot on the floor.

(L) No, Snow White was in the box.

(T) Snow White was in the box. Yeah, Disney took all the things that had Beauty sleeping in them...

(L) Did you ever stop and think about that symbology: Sleeping Beauty? Being awakened by a kiss?

(F) Who turns into a frog.

(L) No!

(F) Oh, that's right, the frog turns into a prince.

(L) That's another analogy. Being awakened from the illusion into which one has been put by the evil witch...

(F) And Cinderella...

(L) And also, in all of these fairy tales it is because of some choice and lack of knowledge...

(J) Rumplestiltskin...

(S) The Ugly Duckling...

(T) Yeah, all of Grimm's fairy tales were really pretty grim. They have been cleaned up a whole lot.

(L) Yeah, in the original Cinderella, the step sister cut off part of her foot to get it to fit the slipper and the Prince found her out because of the dripping blood.

(Jan and S) Ooooh! Yuck!

(T) Must have been the glass slipper, cut my foot!

(L) Yeah, it's pretty grim. One cut her heel off and the other cut her toes off.

(T) Are we getting anywhere? We got the idea that when we fell from STO to STS we gave the Lizzies the right to do what they are doing. So, when they make the statement that we said they could, we did.

250 **A**: Okay.

251 **Q**: *(L)* We are having a bit of a puzzlement here because we are wondering if the tornado which represents the realm wave is something that moves one from an STO state to an STS state while still remaining in 3rd density?

252 **A**: Okay, that is one way. Okay...

Q: *(T)* The realm border is not only a way of transferring from one density to another, but it is also a way of transiting from STS and STO and back?[26] 253

A: Can be. 254

Q: *(T)* So, those who transit on this pass may transit from 3rd to 4th density and come out as an STO being? 255

A: In some of the passages. 256

Q: *(L)* OK, so people can either go from STO to STS in 3rd or 4th density... any of these choices are open at this passing of the realm wave? 257

A: Any of the above according to the orientation of the wave. 258

Q: *(L)* And what is the orientation of the wave that is coming? Is it strictly to move us from 3rd density to 4th density? Is this a function of this wave? 259

A: We have told you this. 260

Q: *(L)* And they have told us that this is a wave from 3rd to 4th density. Some of the waves, apparently, can move from STO to STS... *(T)* Not the wave, the person passing through the wave. As this wave passes by, does the orientation of the wave depend upon the individual? 261

A: Compare to sea waves. Waves are a part of the fiber of all nature. 262

Q: *(T)* Is it going to depend on where on the wave you are relating to the cycle, the crest and the trough? As to which way you transition on it? 263

A: No. 264

Q: *(T)* In other words, a wave that is going to transition from 3rd to 4th density will do so no matter where you are on the wave when it passes? 265

[26] *High Strangeness* 10

266 **A**: Yes.

267 **Q**: *(T)* A wave that is aligned to transit people from STS to STO or vice versa will do that also?

268 **A**: Or you could "go under" instead.

269 **Q**: *(T)* Under the wave? *(J)* Under the water. *(T)* Then you wouldn't move at all. *(L)* You could be pulled under, you could drown and become part of the primordial soup! *(T)* Is that Minestrone?

270 **A**: Chicken Noodle. [Laughter]

271 **Q**: *(L)* Am I right that if you go under you get sucked into the ocean and start cycling all over again?

272 **A**: It is not that simple.

273 **Q**: *(J)* I didn't think that was simple at all. *(T)* Let's not even start on that one. I'm still trying to work out this movement from STO to STS. You keep referring to the movie about Dorothy. In the movie she was told she could go home any time she wanted just by saying "I want to go home", or whatever. That is a lot easier than going through all the conniptions and contankerations waiting out this wave that comes only once every so often. Is there a way for us to go back to STO that is easier and simpler than hanging out for 300,000 years waiting for this wave to come around?

274 **A**: Sure!

275 **Q**: *(T)* OK, now we are getting somewhere. Where are we going? *(L)* Well, they already told me to shut my mouth. *(T)* But now you have caffeine, you can assist me. [Laughter] So, there is another way of doing this. *(J)* Visualization?

276 **A**: Now wait a minute, are you ready to just go to 4th density right now?

Q: *(J)* Well, probably not. I don't 277 think I'm finished yet. *(T)* Yeah, I am ready. Right now. Let's roll! Jan, feed the cats when you get home! *(L)* Even the idea of just taking off and leaving and abdicating your responsibilities and agreements is an STS thing. *(T)* Yeah, but I'd be 4th density STS. *(S)* You and the Lizzies! *(T)* Now, now, I wasn't saying... I'm not ready to go now because I'm wanted here! Anyway, what you are saying is that the realm wave is not the only way to make the transition, is this correct?

A: One idea presented. 278

Q: *(T)* That idea is, the Wave is the 279 way of moving a large group of beings – is this true?

A: Off center. 280

Q: *(L)* Well, the Wave is just part of 281 a grand cycle. *(T)* And we are here to set up a frequency to pull as many beings through the Wave, when it passes, and that is the whole purpose of why we are here... Is this so?

A: That implies interference with free 282 will.

Q: *(L)* So, we are here to set up a fre- 283 quency so that others may join with us... *(J)* And when we get to 4th density we make the choice or change from STS to STO... *(L)* Who do the munchkins represent?

A: 2nd density beings. 284

Q: *(L)* Do the monkeys represent the 285 Grays?

A: If you wish. 286

Q: *(L)* Who do the witches' soldiers 287 represent?

A: The Nephalim. 288

289 **Q**: *(L)* Who does the Wizard represent?

290 **A**: Think, learn, discover.

Q: *(L)* I think we have had enough on this subject. 291

End of Session

March 18, 1995

We had received some information from a guy named Thor Templar of the "Hostile Alien Resistance Movement" (H.A.R.M.) who was promoting his work having to do with, as he claimed, techniques for combating aliens, abduction, getting rid of implants, and so forth. We read it before the session and had been discussing it.

This was another excellent session with information about the oncoming Earth changes (AKA The Wave) and Flight 19 that was pretty creepy. As I write these comments, the recent loss of Malaysian Airlines flight MH370 certainly compares interestingly with the suggestions in this session!

Participants: 'Frank', Laura, Terry and Jan, Brad, Sue

1 **Q**: *(T)* Good Evening.

2 **A**: Hello.

3 **Q**: Who do we have with us this evening?

4 **A**: Usurro.

5 **Q**: And, where are you from?

6 **A**: Cassiopaea. Yes.

7 **Q**: *(L)* Have you been listening to our discussion?[1]

8 **A**: Of course.

9 **Q**: *(L)* And, do you have any comments to make on the assistance factor?[2]

10 **A**: Comments a plenty.

11 **Q**: *(T)* Comment away.

12 **A**: Prejudice.

Q: *(L)* What does prejudice refer to? 13

A: Thor Templar's views. 14

Q: *(L)* His views are prejudiced. OK, can you tell us, does he actually have material or techniques that can cause implants to dissolve and be flushed out of the body? 15

A: No. 16

Q: *(L)* Why does he think he does? 17

A: Open. 18

Q: *(T)* Is he who he says he is? 19

A: Vague. 20

Q: *(L)* He says he is the Lord High Commander of the Alien Resistance Movement to protect the planet Earth from alien beings. Is this who he is? 21

A: If he wishes. 22

[1] *The Wave* 42

[2] http://alienresistancemovement.weebly.com/

23 **Q**: *(T)* Cool. I'm the Lord High Pooh-bah myself. *(L)* Are any of the items in his catalog worth spending money on, such as the radionics devices?

24 **A**: Make good conversation pieces.

25 **Q**: *(L)* Is there any kind of 3rd density technological devices that we could build that would, for example, keep our environment clean in terms of vibrations, protect us, or erect a barrier against attack?

26 **A**: Review.

27 **Q**: *(L)* What have they said on that subject? *(J)* I don't remember. *(T)* When we asked about building a TDARM, they said: "Sure, we can tell you, but where are you going to get the parts?" The point is, the technology the 4th density beings are working with, we can't build.

28 **A**: All you need is knowledge.

29 **Q**: *(T)* I think Thor is missing the point about the knowledge.

30 **A**: If you have the knowledge, what else do you need? Now, think carefully and multidimensionally.

31 **Q**: *(L)* Well, a TDARM would be nice to start off with. *(T)* There's one buried on Oak Island, go dig it up.

32 **A**: No, order from Sears.

33 **Q**: *(S)* You want me to bring over their catalog? You can start looking. *(J)* Is it in the Spring catalog? [Laughter] *(L)* So, we can't get a TDARM. *(T)* Well, you can, but you have to get the right catalog.

34 **A**: Discuss Thor's tape, and we will address points one by one, if you wish!

35 **Q**: *(L)* The first point that he made was that, since you don't give us practical material information that we can make machines and weapons with, that you must be giving us disinformation and maybe you are the Lizzies?

A: Distorted representation of what Thor said, suggest listen again! 36

Q: *(L)* Well, I was just sort of boiling it down. OK... 37

A: No. 38

Q: *(F)* I thought it said what you said it said. *(J)* What he wants is a marketable item he can make money from. 39

A: Interpretation only, Jan. 40

Q: *(J)* Well, why else... I mean, here is a fellow that markets this stuff... 41

A: He was implying the information we have given you is invalid or not of practical use in general, do you believe this to be true? 42

Q: *(T)* That's very true, he was. *(J)* No, I don't believe that! *(L)* No, I don't believe this to be true, but we do need to.... 43

A: Sense doubt. 44

Q: *(L)* Well, yes, you sense some doubts because he has pointed out that we should be able to get financial assistance here since that is the biggest way we have been getting attacked. And, obviously, if you are who you say you are, you should be able to do this, right? 45

A: Who says not in progress, and must it be instantaneous? 46

Q: *(S)* Yeah, look, you got the van. *(L)* That's true. *(S)* And all the little things that have been happening here and there? I have been getting more clients... 47

A: He makes it sound as if we should materialize 100 dollar bills on board! 48

We have told you that you must learn in order to make progress as souls, this does not happen any faster than your abilities to absorb and process!!!

49 **Q**: *(J)* We know that. *(T)* Thor just wants what he wants and he wants it now; he wants to defend himself against aliens that he has no concept of. *(J)* We are just trying to understand what this guy is all about. *(T)* He really doesn't understand. He doesn't have the faintest idea what is happening out there.

50 **A**: His thought is that his own personal notions of what should transpire are gospel.

51 **Q**: *(L)* Are his intentions good?

52 **A**: Open.

53 **Q**: *(L)* Well, what I told him was to put his money where his mouth is and this was his reaction. So, I think we can determine his motivations from this since that has been suggested to us as a test.

(J) It sounds to me more like he is looking to sell us his stuff.

(F) Yes, it does sound that way. And, he will naturally discount any information that says his little gadgets are not worth buying.

(B) He is trying to pick your brains to get something he can get rich off of.

(F) And/or selling us on the idea of abandoning this and becoming followers of his group and helping him to market himself.

(L) Well, one of the things he says is that the Grays are thought forms and then he wants to sell a material object to blast them! The Grays are cybergenetic constructs. They are just as real as you or I. If they died, or ceased functioning, we would be able to take them apart.

(T) They are extremely advanced cyborgs.

(F) As long as they die in 3rd density.

(L) And, you know, the thing that Hilliard[3] told us, about the material evidence that disappears.

(F) And that is found throughout ufology.

(L) Hilliard is this old guy who lives over in St. Cloud, who has the most incredible collection of UFO stuff I have ever seen. He has devoted 40 years of his life to this and he knows or knew all the prominent researchers and has a lot of material that no one else I have ever met has. He is retired military and worked for NASA as a consulting engineer. He's been to Medugorjee to view the apparitions of the Virgin Mary and apparently has the ways and means to travel around to satisfy his curiosity. What he told us that what everybody in the public sector wants is material evidence and that there has been a lot of material evidence picked up from various sites around the world. But, once it is collected, it disappears! When he said that I immediately inferred that he

[3]Hilliard, the rather mysterious man who had taken a liking to me after I gave a talk in Orlando to a UFO group that included CIA millionaire Henry Belk. I am convinced that Hilliard was involved in some way with the *Alien Autopsy* video because of his military background and other clues, and he was also a close friend of Edward Leedskalnin, the guy who built the Coral Castle. Hilliard died of a stroke on the very day that Ark and I were to visit him when he had said he was going to hand over certain documents to me.

was talking about someone in some conspiracy absconding with the evidence. I thought this was what he meant by 'disappearing'. But, he made it a little clearer when he said "they had cameras on it 24 hours a day, and it just *disappeared*!" I realized that what he meant was that it literally dematerialized. When he said this I said: "Oh. I understand that perfectly!" It makes perfect sense.

We have been dealing with this 4th density nature of the phenomenon, which, if it is that, it explains an awful lot of very strange stuff! Aliens walking through solid objects, appearing and disappearing before the eyes of witnesses, beaming people around on 'light', being beyond the restrictions of time, appearing to specific persons in a group while, at the same time, being invisible to others. So, you hear about all this and at the same time you hear about the obvious material nature of the phenomenon: landing traces, changes in sites and people in contact with the UFOs and aliens, dead alien bodies, captured craft. So, you try to sort it all out, and it is so weird, and you try to understand it. But, when you understand it as a 4th density phenomenon, some of which is literally technological and not paranormal in the strict sense of the word, then it makes perfect sense.

And, with the hypnosis sessions I have done, there are always these alien guys moving around in the background, and I instruct the subject to see clearly what is going on, and they get a *flash*; and they say, "God!", the face was there for a second, but they can't get it back, and all they can say is "it looks like a dinosaur," or "it has scales on it." But that is all they can get. So, somewhere behind all this are these damned reptiles who, apparently, are other density.

(B) You said that when 4th density beings come into 3rd density reality, they can only exist for a short period of time, and then they dematerialize back into their own reality because they can't hold the frequency?

(T) Yes, in some of the stuff you have where it talks about the Lizard beings, the reptiles, usually they are only involved for a short period of time. They are only seen every so often. They can only manifest themselves into this density for a short period of time, after which it is too draining. The Grays are projected into 3rd density, and they can stay longer because they are engineered to do so, but they still maintain it for extended periods because some sort of power source is projecting them.

(B) That's why they take the abductees into their density where they can have some stability.

(T) It is easier for them to take us into 4th than for them to come into 3rd. But, they abduct in different states. They don't always abduct the person physically. They can take the essence out of the body.

(L) We have been told through this source that a lot of the things that they do, such as extracting the soul, is actually a technological thing: 4th density technology. It is so far in advance of anything that we can conceive of, but, nevertheless, it is still technology.

(T) Which may explain their interest in the human ability to astrally project. We have an ability to remove our essence and transport it to

other places even though we have little control over this and we are not entirely adept at it. It is somewhat random. They are interested in that ability and they are interested in our emotions, all these things that someone 'from another planet' in a strictly physical sense, would not be interested in. Although I do believe that there are some of these sightings that are strictly from other 3rd density planets.

(F) Let's ask about that.

54 **A**: Are those ideas gospel?

55 **Q**: *(J)* No, we are just trying to figure it out. *(T)* We should consider the source of Thor's ideas. We have to learn to sort through these things.

56 **A**: Yes. Part of the learning process.

57 **Q**: *(T)* Well, we have Brad M with us this evening. He came with us to say hello. And, I think he has some questions.

58 **A**: Hello, Brad.

59 **Q**: *(T)* Brad had a dream the other night he wants to ask about. *(B)* I had a dream several nights ago – is this of significance to move to... should I go into detail? *(J)* No. *(L)* No.

60 **A**: Explore relationships with blood relatives.

61 **Q**: *(B)* That is an interesting reading. *(J)* Yeah, it would work, wouldn't it? *(B)* Yes. I'm adopted and I have been thinking about finding my biological mother. I know her name and the town she is from, but I have never met her. I have never pursued it. *(L)* Maybe that is what the dream is telling you? *(B)* I don't think it is exactly related to that. The dream was about...

62 **A**: Yes. Indirectly; learn, continue to share.

Q: *(B)* The dream was very distinct. 63
I went to the moon and I was taken to the interior of the moon, and there was a very realistic interior to the moon. There were some parts that were hollow inside. And, when I went inside a big cavern there was 1920s art deco style, and it was so clear. And, it was to learn more about who we are and where we are... *(L)* Did you know that, symbolically, the Moon represents the mother or the feminine principle? And, you are talking about going inside a 'cavernous' area 'inside' the Moon, or inside the 'mother'. The womb. *(J)* Twenties Art Deco? [Laughter] *(B)* Yeah...

A: Thirties art deco. 64

Q: [Laughter] *(S)* Did it have some- 65
thing to do with Miami Beach? That's thirties art deco all over the place. *(B)* Yeah, I've been there a few times. *(T)* What did the thirties art deco...

A: Cross reference: perhaps your inter- 66
est in UFOs and related has some connection to your bloodline?

Q: *(B)* So, if I was to explore this rela- 67
tionship... go back and find this woman who was my mother, she might be involved in some way with metaphysical subjects or UFOs?

A: More than you realize!!!!! 68

Q: *(L)* Maybe she's an alien! [Laugh- 69
ter] *(B)* My mother's a Cassiopaean! *(S)* In disguise! An Orion! *(T)* Well, we are looking for an Orion. We are not going to find them, they are going to find us. *(J)* It's not like we can put an ad in the paper. *(L)* Why not? *(J)* No, no, no, no, no! *(S)* We'll give your phone number, Laura! [Laughter]

A: For Brad's benefit, Mars monu- 70
ments are Atlantean, some on Moon are others; are ET.

71 **Q**: *(S)* Yes. Edgar Cayce said that the Atlanteans were going to other planets...

72 **A**: Yes. With the same relative ease with which you would fly to Atlanta.

73 **Q**: *(B)* Strange!

74 **A**: Pun intended! Triple! What is the base root of the name?

75 **Q**: *(B)* Yeah, that's where I am moving later this year.

76 **A**: Plans change!

77 **Q**: *(J)* Is that just a general comment or a prediction?

78 **A**: No.

79 **Q**: *(B)* Is it for me?

80 **A**: Who else?

81 **Q**: *(J)* Are you saying he is not going to move to Atlanta?

82 **A**: Open.

83 **Q**: *(L)* They are not going to tell you any more. It was a big hint! OK, we have a couple of questions to ask here. The first is: What is this big thing going around about the *Keys of Enoch*? James J. Hurtak, I believe, is the author or 'channel' or whatever. I would like to know, what is the source of this material?

84 **A**: Various.

85 **Q**: *(L)* Can you be a little more specific for us?

86 **A**: Probe.

87 **Q**: *(S)* I never read the book. *(L)* I haven't either. *(J)* Well, maybe we need to do the research and get back to them later. *(L)* Would you say that these sources are reliable?

88 **A**: Open.

Q: *(T)* What is it supposed to be 89
about? *(L)* I don't know. Some woman is supposed to be coming next Saturday night from Atlanta to talk about it at Martie T's. *(T)* From Atlanta? As easily as you fly from Atlantis? [Laughter] *(L)* Well, Martie wants us to come hear this gal teach on this subject. *(T)* As long as she is not going to read it! [Laughter] *(F)* No, but Martie is going to have a handout so that we can all follow along flipping the pages. *(J)* You guys are being nasty!

A: Martie T? 90

Q: *(L)* Is that a clue? *(J)* Is that a clue 91
to consider the source?

A: Open. 92

Q: *(T)* Was that a question or a state- 93
ment?

A: Up to you! 94

Q: *(L)* I want to ask again about the 95
Urantia book. My reading of it tends to make me think that it is elitist and racist. Is that a valid assessment?

A: Open. 96

Q: *(S)* Let's ask about Commander X 97
and that stuff. *(T)* Yeah, who is Commander X? *(L)* *The Cosmic Patriot Files*. *(T)* He is a cosmic survivalist!

A: Does not wish to be identified. 98

Q: *(T)* Well, we know that. *(L)* What 99
is his position?

A: Free will. 100

Q: *(L)* Is he in a position to know of 101
which he speaks?

A: Maybe. 102

Q: *(T)* And then again, maybe not. *(L)* 103
I thought it was pretty good information. *(F)* It looks like a compilation. *(L)* Jan and I have a question. Hilliard

mentioned that the frogs are disappearing from the planet.

104 **A**: Ozone layer.

105 **Q**: *(L)* They are getting fried because of the loss of the Ozone layer?[4]

106 **A**: Fried?

107 **Q**: [Laughter] *(J)* Where are they going? *(T)* The ozone layer is depleting and they are the first of the things we are really noticing as an effect of this?

108 **A**: Yes.

109 **Q**: *(J)* Where are they going? *(T)* They are not going anywhere, they are dying. *(F)* They are not reproducing.

110 **A**: Yes.

111 **Q**: *(B)* They have very sensitive skin. *(T)* Soon it is going to be affecting us all.

112 **A**: All part of the wave effects interconnecting realities.

113 **Q**: *(L)* Well, if it is having this effect on frogs, what is it going to do to us when it gets stronger?

114 **A**: Wait and see.

115 **Q**: *(L)* Now, come on! This doesn't sound like a real pleasant thing. Don't you think you ought to give us just a little more on this? A clue here?

116 **A**: No.

117 **Q**: [Laughter] *(T)* Are they saying that the loss of the ozone layer is a direct result of the approaching wave? *(J)* They sure did! *(T)* The loss is not due to the fluorocarbons?

118 **A**: Misinterpretation, review statement thoroughly.

Q: *(J)* Is removal of the ozone layer part of the frequency 'fixing'? 119

A: Close. 120

Q: *(T)* This is keyed on the frog phenomenon? 121

A: No. 122

Q: *(L)* It's keyed on interconnecting realities. 123

A: Yes. 124

Q: *(L)* Are you saying that the Wave is causing the interconnecting of realities? *(J)* And the ozone layer is in the Wave? 125

A: And causing actions which affect third density in myriad ways, close circle. Please "excuse" eavesdroppers. 126

Q: *(J)* Is someone eavesdropping?[5] 127

A: Was, disrupts channel and can be harmful. 128

Q: *(L)* Well, they have repeatedly told us that the children must not be around during the sessions because it can be detrimental to them with their 'open' or unformed energies. Back to the frogs. Interconnecting realities is the key. Myriad manifestations. *(S)* Maybe the frogs are going into a higher density? Affecting 3rd density is the dying of the frogs, correct? 129

A: No. 130

Q: *(L)* It is a symptom? 131

A: Yes. 132

Q: *(L)* OK, it is a symptom of interconnecting of realities. When you say interconnecting of realities... 133

A: No "of". 134

[4] *The Wave* 3

[5] Child in next room peeking around door, who then exits to upstairs.

135 **Q**: *(L)* OK, I've got it... the dying of the frogs is symptomatic on 2nd density level of what is occurring on 3rd density level. It's an expression, on that level, of what is happening here... *(J)* Or a warning... *(L)* Dying frogs... is that correct?

136 **A**: No.

137 **Q**: *(L)* Are the frogs moving from 2nd density to 3rd density?

138 **A**: Not that complex, perhaps you need to study transcripts more often, then you would not need to cover the same subject matter over and over!

139 **Q**: *(L)* OK. Then we will drop it. *(T)* I want to go back to the "frogs are a symptom" of the overlapping realities. Realities, not densities. The frogs are dying because... *(L)* Because they feel sorry for us! *(T)* Yeah! Works for me! [Laughter] The frogs are dying because the ozone layer is becoming depleted. I think it is completely gone and they are lying to us about that.

(B) Maybe they are saying that all life is interconnected on the planet from their reality to our reality; from 2nd density to 3rd density... and there are warnings on all levels...

(J) Yeah: "See what is happening to the frogs now, wait and see what is going to happen to you guys later!"

(B) Right.

(T) But this is because the ozone layer is depleted... but the ozone layer is depleting because of the chemicals we are dumping into the atmosphere, it is not going away, it is dissolving into other chemicals.

(L) But the Cassiopaeans said that the ozone was depleting because of the Wave.

(T) But, is the relationship of the ozone being depleted and the approaching Wave, perhaps that the Wave isn't causing the depletion, it's the Lizzies causing us to deplete the ozone layer in order to create suffering, in order to feed on this negative energy because of the approaching Wave?

(L) Is the Wave causing the ozone depletion?

A: Not directly. 140

Q: *(L)* But is the Wave causing people 141 to behave in a certain way so that they do things that cause...

A: You are getting warm... 142

Q: *(L)* The Wave is causing the activ- 143 ities of the Lizzies to heat up as well as the good guys, and it is part of the conflict...

A: Colder... 144

Q: *(T)* Drop the Lizzies... *(L)* It is caus- 145 ing the destined actions to take place that are necessary for the closing of the grand cycle?

A: Close. 146

Q: *(L)* And the dying off of the frogs 147 is part of this? Poor little frogs... I like frogs...[6]

A: So are "Earth changes." 148

Q: *(J)* Is the depletion of the ozone 149 layer a part of the equation required for the Wave...

A: In third density reality, it is impor- 150 tant.

Q: *(J)* So, it is part of the natural pro- 151 gression of movement from 3rd to 4th?

---

[6] *The Wave* 3

152 **A**: Let's try using the word "reflection," and see if that "rings a bell." Third into fourth.

153 **Q**: *(L)* Are the frogs going into 4th density?

154 **A**: No. No. No.

155 **Q**: *(T)* There were several questions in there. You said 3rd into 4th...

156 **A**: And vice versa.

157 **Q**: *(L)* Well, I'm more confused than ever! *(T)* Reflection...

158 **A**: If you had been studying transcripts, you would not be!

159 **Q**: *(T)* Reflection is... there has been statements made that in 6th density STS balances STO in reflection only.

160 **A**: Ice cold.

161 **Q**: [Booo!] *(J)* Is the ozone layer a hole that allows it to reflect in both directions?

162 **A**: No.

163 **Q**: *(L)* Are new frogs being created to populate the Earth?

164 **A**: Okay, here we go: Oncoming Wave is a transformation from third density to fourth density so, events happening due to the approach of the Wave are causing changes across densities and realities! In third density, you will notice changes that will have third density explanations, but they are a manifestation of the approach; you see them as third density because that is your current point of reference! Remember that all reflects in and cross all density levels but also there is a merging upon arrival of the Wave, it is realm border crossing!!!!!!

Q: *(J)* Well, we are once again thinking 165
3rd density. Please be patient with us. We aren't finished yet. *(S)* Does that mean we are half-baked? *(T)* Or half frogged! *(L)* I just thought that the Lizzies might like frog legs. [Laughter] *(T)* The Lizzies are French?

(F) I read something last night that said a scientist had been working at one of the bases, or he was a tech working at a super-secret complex somewhere, and he was working on something in some underground room and the elevator door opened and he saw, standing there, right before his eyes, a Lizard being. He said that the elevator must have been malfunctioning because it wasn't supposed to stop at that level, and he wasn't supposed to see it. In another instance, someone saw two Grays working on something in a hangar and they were told by an MP to leave or they would be shot.

(L) Are these stories Frank is recounting about Lizzies being on elevators and Grays working in hangars, are these true stories or are they disinformation?

A: True. 166

Q: *(L)* Well, that settled that! Let me 167
ask a couple of quick questions for my kid. She wants to know the source of the Voynich Manuscript.[7]

[7]The Voynich manuscript is an illustrated codex hand-written in an unknown writing system. The vellum in the book pages has been carbon-dated to the early 15th century (1404–1438), and may have been composed in Northern Italy during the Italian Renaissance. The manuscript is named after Wilfrid Voynich, a Polish book dealer who purchased it in 1912.

The Voynich manuscript has been studied by many professional and amateur

168 **A**: Disinformation.

169 **Q**: *(L)* Who put it together?

170 **A**: Various sources.

171 **Q**: *(L)* Why?

172 **A**: Monetary gain.

173 **Q**: *(L)* So, somebody just faked up an ancient manuscript to sell it for big bucks?

174 **A**: Yes.

175 **Q**: *(T)* Well, they did it with the Hitler diaries. *(L)* Her next question is: How are some people able to walk on fiery coals, pierce their bodies all over, or lie on a bed of nails without pain or permanent physical disfigurement?

176 **A**: Mentalism.

177 **Q**: *(L)* What causes some planes, people and ships to disappear in the Bermuda Triangle? Where do they go and what happens to them?

A: Already covered this. 178

Q: *(S)* Yeah, the Atlantean pyramid. 179

A: Yes. EM waves caused by same. 180

Q: *(L)* Where do they go when they 181
disappear?

A: Of course some are just crashes and 182
sinkings, but when accompanied by unusual phenomena, it is because of irregular anomalies.[8]

Q: *(L)* Where do they go? *(T)* They 183
don't go anywhere, they go to the bottom. *(S)* 5th density.

A: To parallel reality. 184

Q: *(L)* Is this parallel reality like being 185
on a parallel Earth?

A: No. 186

Q: *(L)* What do you mean by a parallel 187
reality?

A: Varies according to circumstances. 188

---

cryptographers, including American and British codebreakers from both World War I and World War II. No one has yet succeeded in deciphering the text, and it has become a famous case in the history of cryptography. The mystery of the meaning and origin of the manuscript has excited the popular imagination, making the manuscript the subject of novels and speculation. None of the many hypotheses proposed over the last hundred years has yet been independently verified.

[Wikipedia, http://en.wikipedia.org/wiki/Voynich_manuscript]

[8] *The Wave* 3

[9] Flight 19 was the designation of five TBM Avenger torpedo bombers that disappeared over the Bermuda Triangle on December 5, 1945, during a United States Navy overwater navigation training flight from Naval Air Station Fort Lauderdale, Florida. All 14 airmen on the flight were lost, as were all 13 crew members of a PBM Mariner flying boat assumed by professional investigators to have exploded in mid-air while searching for the flight. Navy investigators could not determine the cause of the loss of Flight 19 but said the airmen may have become disoriented and ditched in rough seas after running out of fuel.

A 500-page Navy board of investigation report published a few months later made several observations:

- Flight leader Lt. Charles C. Taylor had mistakenly believed that the small islands he passed over were the Florida Keys, so his flight was over the Gulf of

189 **Q**: *(L)* What happened to the infamous Flight 19?[9] *(T)* They went to Philadelphia.

190 **A**: They are still trying to get their bearings.

191 **Q**: *(L)* Ooooh! *(J)* Oh! My God! Oh, how horrible! They are still out there trying to get back. *(T)* They are in a parallel reality... *(L)* Where time doesn't exist... *(T)* They are in a reality that holds them in frozen space-time over the ocean, am I getting this right?

192 **A**: In their thought reference, like being "lost souls."

193 **Q**: *(L)* Oooh, bummer! Does this mean that they are 'stuck' in time? *(J)* You got it!

194 **A**: Bingo!

195 **Q**: *(L)* Is there any possibility that they could fly out of this place that they are stuck in and back into our reality?

196 **A**: Absolutely, remember, the Wave is approaching, and as it gets "nearer", more and more unusual events take place, witness crop circles, for example.

Q: *(L)* Is there anything anyone can do to release persons stuck in these parallel realities and bring them back into the reality of origin?[10] 197

A: Yes, but the technology is a closely guarded secret.[11] 198

Q: *(L)* Do you know the secret? 199

A: Yes, but you do too! 200

Q: *(L)* I do too? *(T)* Does Thor know it? [Laughter] 201

A: Mirth! 202

Q: *(L)* I know the secret too? 203

A: Philadelphia Experiment. 204

Q: *(L)* Since you mentioned the Philadelphia Experiment, could you tell us in specific detail, how this was done? What kind of machines were used and how can we build one? [General uproar and laughter] 205

Mexico and heading northeast would take them to Florida. It was determined that Taylor had passed over the Bahamas as scheduled, and he did in fact lead his flight to the northeast over the Atlantic. The report noted that some subordinate officers did likely know their approximate position as indicated by radio transmissions stating that flying west would result in reaching the mainland.

- Taylor, although an excellent combat pilot and officer with the Navy, had a tendency to 'fly by the seat of his pants', getting lost several times in the process. It was twice during such times that he had to ditch his plane in the Pacific and be rescued. But this time he would be confused about what happened to him.
- Taylor was not at fault because the compasses stopped working.
- The loss of PBM-5 BuNo 59 225 was attributed to an explosion.

This report was subsequently amended 'cause unknown' by the Navy after Taylor's mother contended that the Navy was unfairly blaming her son for the loss of five aircraft and 14 men, when the Navy had neither the bodies nor the airplanes as evidence.

[Wikipedia, http://en.wikipedia.org/wiki/Flight_19]

[10] *The Wave* 55

[11] *The Wave* 56

206 **A**: Do you intend to sit here for a day or two?

207 **Q**: *(J)* In other words, it would take a day or two to give us the information? *(T)* Yeah, we got the time. Get some paper and a pencil. *(L)* We will save that for another time. *(T)* Let's start with a diagram and send it to Thor.

208 **A**: In short, build an EM generator.

209 **Q**: *(L)* Here's another of the kid's questions: When and why did homosexuality originate?

210 **A**: It originated when sexuality did.

211 **Q**: *(L)* What is the world's oldest language, at least of those known to today's world?

A: Sanskrit. 212

Q: *(L)* What is the origin of Sanskrit? 213

A: Atlantean roots.[12] 214

Q: *(L)* What is the karma involved 215
with Siamese twins and why are some more joined than others?

A: Too complex and not important. 216

Q: *(L)* OK, that is the last of her ques- 217
tions, at the present time we would like to go through some....

A: Now, some more information about 218
Flight 19. Do you remember a few years ago that a team of researchers claimed to have found the planes, then retracted?[13]

Q: *(L)* Yes, I remember. [All agree][14] 219

[12]Sanskrit is described as a standardized dialect of Old Indo-Aryan language, originating as Vedic Sanskrit and tracing its linguistic ancestry back to Proto-Indo-Iranian and Proto-Indo-European. The pre-Classical form of Sanskrit is known as Vedic Sanskrit, with the language of the Rigveda being the oldest and most archaic stage preserved, its oldest core dating back to the early 2nd millennium BCE. This qualifies Rigvedic Sanskrit as one of the oldest attestations of any Indo-Iranian language, and one of the earliest members of the Indo-European languages, which includes English and most European languages.

[Wikipedia, http://en.wikipedia.org/wiki/Sanskrit]

[13]In 1991, a treasure-hunting expedition led by Graham Hawkes announced that the wreckage of five Avengers had been discovered off the coast of Florida, but that tail numbers revealed they were not Flight 19. In 2004 a BBC documentary showed Hawkes returning with a new submersible 12 years later and identifying one of the planes by its bureau number (a clearly readable 23 990) as a flight lost at sea on 9 October 1943, over two years before Flight 19 (its crew all survived), but he was unable to definitively identify the other planes; the documentary concluded that "Despite the odds, they are just a random collection of accidents that came to rest in the same place 12 miles from home." But in March 2012 Hawkes was reported as stating that it had suited both him (and indirectly his investors) and the Pentagon to make the story go away because it was an expensive and time-consuming distraction, and that, while admitting he had found no conclusive evidence, he now thought he had in fact found Flight 19.

[Tim Golden, 'Mystery of Bermuda Triangle Remains One, *New York Times* (June 5, 1991); Adam Higginbotham, 'Graham Hawkes and the Race to the Bottom of the Sea', *Men's Journal* (March 2012), p. 3.]

[14]*The Wave* 3

220 **A**: Did you find this to be curious?

221 **Q**: *(S)* Yes, because the planes that they found were never reported missing. *(T)* Yes. *(L)* Is that why it was so curious? *(J)* Why did they retract? *(S)* Where did the planes come from that they found?

222 **A**: Yes, if only you knew the details, and how three of the team have required massive psychiatric aid.

223 **Q**: *(L)* Well, tell us the details!

224 **A**: Patience, we are, but must do so slowly so you have some hope of grasping it.

225 **Q**: *(T)* Three of the recovery team needed psychiatric treatment?

226 **A**: What they found were five planes matching the description, and "arranged" in a perfect geometric pattern on the bottom of the ocean, but the serial numbers did not match.

227 **Q**: *(L)* Is the geometric pattern itself significant?

228 **A**: Now, first mystery: There were no other instances of five Avengers disappearing at once. Second: Two of the planes had strange glowing panels with unknown "hieroglyphics" where there should have been numbers. Third: When they tried to raise one of the planes, it vanished, then reappeared, then vanished again then reappeared while attached to the guide-wire, then finally slipped off and fell to the bottom. Fourth: In one of the planes, on the bottom, live human apparitions in WWII uniforms were temporarily seen by three exploratory divers and videotaped by a guide camera. Lastly: Three of the planes have since disappeared. All of this is, naturally, being kept secret!

Q: *(S)* I wonder where the planes came 229
from. *(L)* That is the obvious question!

A: Parallel reality, you see, when some- 230
thing crosses into another reality, it accesses something called, for lack of a better term, the "thought plane", and as long as that reality is misunderstood, the window remains open, thus all perceptions of possibility may manifest concretely, though only temporarily, as thought plane material is constantly fluid.

Q: *(L)* Does this mean that this was a 231
'Flight 19' of a parallel reality that went through a window into our reality?

A: Close. 232

Q: *(L)* Was this part of or connected 233
to the loss of our 'Flight 19'? Did we exchange realities here?

A: It is the thought patterns that ef- 234
fect the reality, when that window is opened, all thought can become physical reality, though only temporarily.

Q: *(L)* Does this mean that the divers' 235
and searchers' thoughts about this became reality?

A: And all others. 236

Q: *(T)* All others involved in the 237
search?

A: All others on the planet. 238

Q: *(T)* Even those that did not believe 239
that the searchers were going to find them?

A: Yes. Researchers found what they 240
expected to find, but when others heard the news, other things started to happen according to which thought patterns dominated.

Q: *(L)* So, in other words, if somebody 241
believed that it was Flight 19, it ap-

peared, and if somebody did not believe it was Flight 19, it disappeared?

242 **A**: Yes.

243 **Q**: *(J)* Oh jeez! *(T)* Well, I didn't believe it to begin with... *(L)* So, I guess we won! *(F)* We sent some poor guys into the psychiatric ward. *(T)* The planes appeared because people... *(L)* No, I think the searchers went looking for this and because there was a window there... *(T)* ...the planes showed up exactly as they expected to see them, in a formation... But the planes would not have come down as described there, and they appeared in a formation on the bottom. That should have told the searchers something right there. When I heard that they had found those planes in a formation, that close together, that bothered me. *(F)* Even if something sinks to the bottom, it won't arrive there in the position it started at the top. *(T)* And what they did find after they started checking the records was that there are about 200 of those planes crashed along the coast. And, there was another guy who said that he found one of those planes, only it wasn't one of Flight 19. And, while he was out there looking for it, he found parts of the shuttle... *(L)* That reminds me, when the Challenger crashed, were the astronauts still alive when they hit the water, and did they continue to live for any length of time after they hit?

244 **A**: Four were alive but died instantly on impact with the water.

245 **Q**: *(L)* Are we done with the Bermuda Triangle? *(T)* I have a question... what happened to the PBA plane that went out searching for Flight 19?

246 **A**: Still trying to find the Avengers.

247 **Q**: *(T)* Is it in the same parallel reality with Flight 19?

A: Yes. 248

Q: *(T)* Will it ever find them? 249

A: ? 250

Q: *(L)* In the perception of the crew of 251 Flight 19, how much time has passed?

A: None. 252

Q: *(J)* So, they have no idea. *(S)* I won- 253 der if they will come back to our time or go back to their time?

A: Your perception. 254

Q: *(L)* We talked about doing a DNA 255 count...

A: Will not answer. Up to you to dis- 256 cover.

Q: *(L)* Jan went through an experience 257 lately; what does it relate to? Is it significant?

A: Yes. 258

Q: *(L)* What does it signify? 259

A: Awareness expansion. 260

Q: *(L)* Jan wanted to ask if there 261 is any significance to the trashy confrontations currently on talk shows?

A: Immaterial. 262

Q: *(L)* Jan also wants to know, what is 263 serotonin?

A: Laura answer. 264

Q: *(L)* Serotonin is a hormone secreted 265 by the pineal gland and is also secreted in the mid-brain and is related to feelings of well-being, mood altering, and you suffer from lack of serotonin if you don't get enough sleep. The other day we were discussing the fact that infants on mother's milk do not produce much waste. Is there any diet that adult humans could eat that would be assimilated as well?

266 **A**: Less, but for no waste, just wait for fourth density.[15]

267 **Q**: *(L)* We would like to know what the Christian Cross represents at a deeper level?

268 **A**: Part of the Lizzie disinformation campaign, sorry!

269 **Q**: *(L)* I thought that! Remember, the cross represents the 'death' which never occurred. *(J)* The reason we wanted to ask that was because Brad wanted to know if the symbol had anything to do with 'realm border crossing'.

270 **A**: Cross is "cross" in English only.

271 **Q**: *(L)* Sometime ago we ask some questions about different lifetimes and S___-was told that she spent four sequences held over as a "special learning channel" or "hold back on contemplative level." What does that mean?

272 **A**: Self-explanatory.

273 **Q**: *(J)* I hate it when they say that.

274 **A**: Learn!

275 **Q**: *(L)* Wait a minute, there is a distinction: was she the one doing the learning or was she helping someone else to learn? I understand "learning channel". *(T)* It's on cable...

A: Both. 276

Q: *(L)* It wasn't because she was bad? 277
She didn't get 'held back in school'?

A: Improper concept. 278

Q: *(S)* Why, when holding acupunc- 279
ture points on Laura, do I get the sweats?

A: Because you are undergoing changes 280
relating to the approach of the wave.[16]

Q: *(L)* Is this significant of the work 281
she is doing?

A: Unrelated. 282

Q: *(L)* Has Jan's brother ever been 283
abducted?

A: No. 284

Q: *(J)* Is there any elitism involved in 285
interactions between other densities?

A: What? 286

Q: *(L)* I guess not. We have heard 287
some things about DW. We have heard that he was behind the Eddie Page fiasco. Is this true?

A: Open. 288

Q: *(L)* Well, then goodnight. 289

A: Goodnight. 290

End of Session

[15] Actually, in the years since this session, we have researched and experimented a lot with diet and asked further questions in light of our studies. We have found a diet that produces minimal waste – almost none – the ketogenic diet. The Paleo diet is close.

[16] *The Wave* 3

April 15, 1995

The reader who is astute will notice that, up to this point in time, we had sessions very frequently – usually more than once a week, but certainly every week. However, we now encounter an anomaly: there is a break here – this session in the file listing is April 15, almost an entire month after the previous session of 18 March. And therein hangs a most interesting tale.

Recall from the 7 March session that I mentioned that the *St. Petersburg Times* journalist, Tom French, had called to make an appointment for an interview. In the notes to that session I mention how extremely disappointed Frank had been that the journalist did not want to interview him. But, we just assumed that after an initial interview with me, Mr. French would then schedule with Frank and the rest of the group.

However, at that first interview, Tom made it pretty clear that he was not particularly interested in the Cs material – or channeling in general, or Frank in specific – he was only interested in the fact that I was interested in investigating unusual things while still being a more or less ordinary wife and mother. I tried every way I could to turn his interest to the Cs, and by default, Frank. I failed. He had an idea, a plan, and I was part of it; but most definitely he was in charge of his writing project and he was confident that he knew what he was doing, how to do it, and what his audience liked and expected. But that didn't stop me from trying regularly and repeatedly to shift the attention to the Cs, and the group, and Frank.

Aside from the shocking effect of this revelation – that anyone would be interested in my very mundane life of struggle and worrying about how to make ends meet – my very first thought was, "Oh, no! How am I going to tell Frank?!" How was I going to tell Frank that Tom French was not really interested in the channeling except insofar as it was one of the tools I was using to pursue my interests while raising a family? Frank was so sure that this was going to be the opening of the door to fame and glory! Frank was so excited that now, people would finally see that he was a force to contend with – a channel – and one that had attracted the attention of a real journalist at that! (He actually used those exact words and much, much more!) After all his excitement, after all of his hours of instruction to me about how to conduct myself in the interview so as to place the work, and especially him, in the proper light, how was I going to tell him that Tom French was more interested in an overweight, stressed-out, middle-aged housewife, than in a brilliant, highly developed spiritual being who was channeling 6th density light beings such as himself? Frank had placed so much confidence in me to be able to turn Tom French's attention toward him, and I had failed. It was going to be a negative experience, and I just couldn't figure out how to tell him without triggering another series of suicidal rants.

Fortunately, I didn't have to deal with the issue the next Saturday night (11 March 1995), because that was the day we took the Cs 'out of the closet' for a public 'test drive' at another MUFON meeting. It wasn't until the following session, on March 18, that I broke the news to Frank that the journalist wasn't really interested in a channeling group and its star performer.

Because Terry and Jan had brought a guest with them to the March 18 session, they left early. Frank wanted to do what he usually did after a session, which was to hold court and discourse for several hours about whatever came to mind. The rest of us had endured this a sufficient number of times that, after a while, we had a sort of unspoken agreement to not ask a question, because asking Frank a question meant that he would talk for at least another hour. These sessions drained everyone, and no matter how many times anyone hinted that they were exhausted, Frank would brush their need for sleep or getting home before the sun rose aside with an insouciance that was completely incomprehensible. I wrote it off to his arrested emotional development, that children don't think about the needs of others, and since I had sort of 'taken Frank to raise', I tolerated it as best I could.

The only person who seemed to be able to stand up to Frank in these late-night marathons was Terry. Jan and I would sit there like zombies throughout these dialogues, voicing our quiet requests for sleep at periodic intervals, ignored by Frank, and with Terry refusing to leave until Frank had, so it was often a standoff. And for the reader who thinks that it should have been a simple matter of just asking Frank to go home, believe me – I did that over and over again. His answer to that was, "Just five more minutes! You can give me that! After all, I have listened to your problems before!" And the five minutes would turn into an hour. If I reminded him of the instant when the five minutes was up, he would suggest that I was not being a very giving person if I was not willing to listen to him when he needed someone to talk to. Never mind that it occurred over and over and over again. After a certain number of these experiences, a discussion about it came up with Terry and Jan and they agreed to not leave without helping me to launch Frank out of whatever chair he had taken possession of, and maneuver him to the door.

But, on the night of the incident we are approaching, Terry and Jan had to leave right away to take their guest home (see previous session). That left Frank, Sue and myself, and I knew I was in for a long night. After my explanation about Tom French's lack of interest in the Cs, Frank's mood was brittle and artificially bright. He was behaving in a way I had never seen before, and it seemed almost bellicose. I was tired and in no mood to sit up until 4 a.m. discussing just anything. I suggested repeatedly that I was exhausted and would like to close up the house and go to bed. Sue was exchanging light banter with him, also suggesting that the two of them should leave so I could go to bed, and to this day I can't remember exactly what was said, either by the two of them, or myself, other than that it was in the light banter mode of trying to convince Frank that it was time to say goodnight – a difficult task under any circumstances. I *think* that I teasingly threatened to turn him into a pumpkin or something equally silly. The only thing I do remember is that what he said next was so completely out of context and out of proportion to anything that I had said, that I will never, ever forget it. He said: "Well how about this: I'm going to tell [your daughter] that [her father] isn't her real father!"

Doesn't sound like much, does it? But the point was that, of all the private things I had ever confided to Frank, this was the one thing that he knew would hurt and upset me the most. As a mother, I am a tigress, and it is a very dangerous thing for anyone to threaten to hurt one of my children, physically, mentally, emotionally, or any way.

As those who have read *Amazing Grace* know, my first child was adopted as a baby by my first husband after we married. She never knew any other father, and as far as the two of them were concerned, he was her father. Of course I realized that, at some time in her life, we would have to tell her the facts, but at that particular moment, it was not the time to do it and I had made the big mistake of confiding my concerns about it to Frank.

Yes, I am familiar with all of the pro and con arguments about how to handle such issues with children, and in the end, I believe that it is up to the judgment of the parent who, after all, knows the child best. And in this case, I had already clearly expressed the opinion that it was not the time to tell her; that it would be a disaster because her own emotional development was at a delicate stage, and Frank knew all of this. He had gone to great lengths to inquire about what was bothering me, to pretend sympathy and interest in order to extract the details from me. And here, now, for the first time, I clearly saw why Frank spent so much time pretending interest in certain people. Indeed, with his rant about being so spiritually superior, his interest was projected like a benediction of approval, but the now obvious true motivation was revealed: he pretended interest, not because he was really interested in the person, but because it was his agenda to extract information that he could later use to control the person.

And he chose to try to control and hurt me for no reason other than the fact that he believed that I had turned Tom French off to the idea of writing about the group (mainly him), and focusing on me. And it was totally untrue. He was jealous, and felt that he was entitled to what he had not worked for, and if he couldn't have it, he would hurt me through my child.

I was almost speechless. I calmly told him that I could not believe that he was such a low-life as to do something so despicable as to hurt my daughter. He stuttered out a protest that he had only been joking, that it just jumped out of his mouth and he didn't mean it. And I replied that it was "out of the fullness of the heart that the mouth speaks." Obviously he would never have said such a thing if he had not already thought about it in those terms. And then I told him (rather calmly, which surprised me), that he had better go home and do it now, and spend some time thinking about what he had just said.

He left.

Sue and I sat there, speechless, and just looked at each other. Neither of us could believe this revelation of Frank's viciousness and meanness. Finally, Sue tried to smooth things over by saying that Frank obviously wasn't himself. He was under stress. He was overtired. It was late. All kinds of excuses.

But nothing could excuse the fact that, in his unjustified anger at me (and it didn't matter whether it was justified or not), Frank had expressed the idea that he would willingly harm an innocent person I loved because he knew that this was the most direct and vicious way of hurting me. And nothing is more despicable than that. The only kinds of people I have ever heard of who consider such actions to be acceptable are the lowest criminal types who are even despised by other criminals. Felons who hurt children are often placed in solitary confinement in prisons because the other prisoners will try to kill them. Hurting a child to hurt the parent is an unspeakable act of cowardice and depravity.

In the days following this event, I was rather startled at the view of Frank that was opened to my mind. All of the aspects of Frank that I had been ascribing to the possibility that he was, truly, a higher spiritual being who was just having a battle with dark forces – and the battle was explainable because he was a higher spiritual being – were now perceived as simply expressions of a very narrow, selfish, conniving, manipulative, and fundamentally mean character. I could see nothing positive in him at all and I marveled that this was so.

I was not as aware of the chemistry of the brain then as I am now, and I was very curious about this effect. How could it be that the mind can shift so instantaneously from one perspective to another? How completely the light had changed on my perception of him, and all of the things I had formerly excused, shoved under the rug, giving a positive spin, or taken his word for, now appeared to me in an altogether different context. Had I really been wearing the proverbial rose-colored glasses all that time? Or was what I was thinking now the distorted view?

In retrospect, I realize that I was, in fact, having a serious lesson in how our thinking is controlled or clarified by our chemistry. As I now know, when a shock is received, or a threat of danger, the mind becomes acutely clear and lucid and what *is* becomes evident to the extent that every nuance of reality is exposed to view with a clarity that is stunning. I suppose that this is a condition of evolutionary advantage; the creature that cannot see clearly when in danger does not survive. And I suspect that the same is true whatever the soul orientation. Any individual, when shocked, will suddenly see who is and is not 'like them', and thus a danger to their existence.

As I said, at the time, I didn't know how subtly our thinking can be controlled by our chemistry. I only knew that I wanted to find out if I was making a big mistake; was I misjudging Frank because of emotion? Was I being unfair? Shouldn't I discuss it with others and discover if my thinking was askew? It was so shocking a thing to be going along one day thinking that a person was a higher spiritual being having trouble adjusting to the real world, and in a single instant, suddenly seeing everything completely differently.

Naturally, Terry and Jan were anxious for Frank and me to reconcile. While they were very shocked by the turn of events, like all of us, they encouraged forgiveness and forgetting. And truthfully, I was beginning to believe that this was the proper course of action myself. After all, it is what we are raised to believe in. The 'normal' chemicals began to take over, and being reminded by my friends of all the good times we had experienced, it was easy to begin to forget that moment of clarity. And surely, it was the right thing to do considering all that happened after.

In retrospect, after many other things occurred, it seems clear that what I saw in Frank at that time was pretty much all that was there: he was small, petty, mean, narcissistic, and more. What happens after such a 'seeing' is that the chemistry of the 'shock' begins to dissipate, and the normal chemistry resumes, and the ability to see and think with such clarity recedes. I began to doubt what I had seen. I began to doubt my perceptions. The rose-colored glasses of giving the benefit of the doubt went back on, and my mind began to work on the problem of how to reconcile. Because, after all, if I wasn't there to help Frank, to make a place in the world for him, who would do it?

So, Sue was asked to mediate.

But, meanwhile, just in case, we decided to continue the sessions without Frank, even though we knew we would have to go through the tuning process again to some extent. These sessions were not included in the transcripts because they were, for the most part, about Frank (naturally). And even though they were not as smooth as we would have liked, having become very accustomed to fast-paced dialogues with the Cs, it was clearly evident that the ability to make the same connection was present. And again, we were confirmed in our opinion that the Cs and Frank were not one and the same.

During the course of this experimental work, we received what I perceived to be a frightening message from the Cs, telling us that there was grave danger around Frank and that agents of some kind were involved. It was difficult to determine from the responses if the danger came *from* Frank, or if the danger was *to* Frank. Because of the return of my rose-colored glasses, I decided that it was most likely that Frank was in danger, that he was being stalked and/or used by agents unknown, and that his very life was in peril.

Well, that was all it took to galvanize me! Even if I was mad at him, I had spent so much time and effort keeping him alive by listening to his endless complaints that I wasn't going to let anything happen to him now! I called Frank and after some very confusing exchanges, Frank arrived at my door and was welcomed like the Prodigal Son.

We all sat around and discussed the matter at some length, the end result being that Frank noted that Sue had been the only one present at the time he acted strange. He then claimed that he had, indeed, sent a conciliatory message to me through Sue. This was troubling, because I had never received any such, nor had Frank received any of the messages that I conveyed through Sue. Frank's conclusion was that there was some controlling influence there, and the implication was, of course, that Sue was to blame for the problem!

I didn't see how it could be possible, but I wasn't in the mood to doubt Frank now! Sue was such a simple soul, always helping out and with a truly generous and giving nature. But there it was. I had sent a message, she had not delivered it as I sent it (or so Frank claimed), and he had sent one back (he claimed), that had not been delivered to me, of that I was certain. I was really becoming confused and uncertain. Just what was going on here? And naturally, we decided to ask the Cs.

Participants: 'Frank', Laura, Terry and Jan

1 **Q**: *(T)* Good evening. Who do we have with us tonight?[1]

2 **A**: Good evening!

3 **Q**: *(L)* Who do we have with us tonight?

4 **A**: Shoura.

5 **Q**: *(L)* And where are you from?

6 **A**: Not from, but you know as Cassiopaea.

7 **Q**: *(L)* Alright. Long time, no see!

8 **A**: Oh yes!

9 **Q**: *(L)* Did we communicate with you when it was just Sue, Terry and Jan and I?

10 **A**: Fragmented.

11 **Q**: *(L)* But it was you, fragmented?

12 **A**: Some.

13 **Q**: *(T)* Not all of it was you?

14 **A**: Like conflicting signals on radio.[2]

15 **Q**: *(T)* Should we continue working with changing people on the board so that we can all work on the channel so that the channel will open for all of us?

16 **A**: Vague.

17 **Q**: *(J)* Do you recommend switching people on the board?

18 **A**: We recommend that which you feel is best.

Q: *(L)* Now, the pressing question: 19
What has been happening to us?

A: We have warned repeatedly of at- 20
tack!!

Q: *(L)* Was this ordeal we have just 21
gone through an attack?

A: Of course. 22

Q: *(L)* What made us vulnerable? 23

A: Your work. 24

Q: *(L)* Was there anything having to 25
do with any one of us contributing to this vulnerability?

A: Open. 26

Q: *(J)* Was anything that happened 27
conscious with anyone?

A: Is this your inquiry? 28

Q: *(J)* Yes. 29

A: Then answer from within. 30

Q: *(L)* That doesn't help. [My daugh- 31
ter] said that, even as a kid, she could have straightened it out between us without even trying. *(J)* Well, maybe Sue just wasn't cut out to be a mediator.

A: Okay. 32

Q: *(J)* What were the intentions of this 33
attack?

A: Susan is insecure. Have you not no- 34
ticed?

Q: *(J)* Yeah. *(T)* But insecurity is not 35
a problem as far as that goes.

[1] *The Wave* 37

[2] Probably one of the simplest explanations for 'channel static' the Cs gave. Sometimes the sessions were rather like me trying to tune in a classical station with a nearby jazz station overwhelming the signal. There would be moments when the selected music would come through clear and clean, and then the jazz sounds would bleed over and blot out the orchestra.

36 **A**: Problems are according to circumstances.

37 **Q**: *(L)* Well, that still leaves us in a bit of a quandary...

38 **A**: Do you employ a maid to fly a passenger jet?

39 **Q**: *(T)* So, the wrong person was doing the wrong thing. It wasn't her fault.

40 **A**: But relaying of messages is sensitive issue.

41 **Q**: *(J)* There is a clue there. Who indicated that she should relay messages between you and Frank? *(L)* Nobody, I guess.

42 **A**: Was spur of moment "flow." Plot course carefully, so as not to run aground.

43 **Q**: *(T)* We are doing Chinese fortune cookies tonight. *(L)* Well, I still feel a little bit hurt that everything I said was simply not understood and that the things Frank said, had they been conveyed exactly as he said them, would have brought the problem to an immediate halt. What should have been repeated was not and what should not have been repeated was.

44 **A**: True. Attack is most purposeful! Watch all portholes.

45 **Q**: *(L)* So, in other words, Sue may have been an instrument of attack unwittingly?

46 **A**: Close.[3]

47 **Q**: *(L)* Was any part of this attack connected to those women in that Metaphysical Church, or Judy and Yvonne in Spring Hill?

A: Open.[4] 48

Q: *(T)* When Terry saw this event in the cards he read for me, he saw three women in attack mode. Did that reading represent this event? 49

A: Open. 50

Q: *(L)* Now, we have three names here and these are people who are involved with Barrie and Susy Konicov. She called last week sometime and wanted us to get a 'take' on these people. The way that Barrie phrased the question was: "How do these people plan to play him?" Or, what are their intentions? First name is Carl Grancy. 51

A: User. 52

Q: *(L)* Mark of Michigan. 53

A: Harmless. 54

Q: *(L)* Karen Hilton? 55

A: Other interests, losing connection to Barrie. 56

Q: *(L)* Does this just mean that she is there for the time and is planning on moving on eventually? 57

A: Close. 58

Q: *(J)* I want to ask about the fact that there has been some stuff that has come out lately that is an about-face of things that have always been the status quo. Disney's change of programming and their production of the alien video, the recently released film that has been 59

[3]This exchange suggests that Sue was the "portal" of attack in some way.

[4]This, too, becomes a much more interesting clue as time passed. It later turned out that Sue was most definitely still hanging out with the Metaphysical Church crowd that I have written about extensively in *The Wave*.

accused of being blasphemous;[5] McNamara's about-face about Vietnam.[6] Is there any significance to this?

60 **A**: All explained by previous answers, of which you are well versed, i.e. preparatory foundation.

61 **Q**: *(J)* The foundation is being set for the changes to come. These events do have significance.

A: You know this, which is why there is recognition. 62

Q: *(T)* They are priming the country for a number of major reversals in policy and so forth. *(J)* I don't even think it is necessarily that. Isn't it just a reversal of known values? 63

A: All of above.[7] 64

Q: *(L)* Is it necessary for me to have 65

---

[5]Fortunately, I actually caught this video when it was broadcast. At the end, I could only say, "What the heck was that all about? Disney?!" From the *UFO Blogger* website:

> In March of 1995, Walt Disney Television aired a most intriguing one-hour television special on UFOs titled *Alien Encounters from New Tomorrowland.* This highly unusual UFO video special presents UFOs and alien visitation to our planet as a matter of fact. Though the film's existence is acknowledged by the respected website of the Internet Movie Database, you will not find it available anywhere for purchase.
>
> Those who tracked this incredible production state that it was shown only once, and with no advance notice on stations in only five US cities.
>
> At first glance, this unique Disney television special appears to be an elaborate promotion of a scary New Tomorrowland ride on alien encounters which was about to open at Disney World. But on closer inspection, it is much more. The entire program, which opens with a short segment by Disney CEO Michael Eisner, does not even question the existence of UFOs and a major UFO cover-up. In fact, at times it has a tone of ridicule towards those who still deny the existence of UFOs.
>
> Considering the very limited showing and audience, and the highly unusual stance on UFOs taken, many suspect that this program was a probe to measure public reaction to news of the reality of visitation and interaction with various forms of non-human intelligent life on Earth. The 10-minute section on alien abductions seems particularly designed to scare viewers. For information that the abduction phenomenon may not be as scary as presented in this film, read about the thought-provoking documentary *Touched*, based on the careful research of Harvard Professor John Mack. [http://www.ufo-blogger.com/2013/08/alien-encounters-lost-walt-disney-ufo.html]

You can see the full version here: http://www.ufo-blogger.com/2013/08/alien-encounters-lost-walt-disney-ufo.html

[6]"We were wrong, terribly wrong. We owe it to future generations to explain why." – McNamara, writing in his 1995 memoir, *In Retrospect*, on the management of the Vietnam War

[7]This certainly turned out to be stunningly accurate; 9/11 was still six years in the future, however.

[8]I was experiencing tremendous pain in my left shoulder and arm due to the accident back in December. This would turn out to be an ongoing problem for some years to come.

surgery to fix my shoulder?[8]

66 **A**: Be careful not to be misled.

67 **Q**: *(L)* Is that about the surgery?

68 **A**: Yes.

69 **Q**: *(L)* Will my arm get well on its own?

70 **A**: Can.

71 **Q**: *(J)* How? *(T)* You ought to get a second or even a third opinion.

72 **A**: Yes. Surgery is profitable.

73 **Q**: *(L)* Can you recommend something that I can do other than surgery?

74 **A**: Heat therapy combined with dietary adjustment.

75 **Q**: *(J)* What dietary adjustments?

76 **A**: Calcium, manganese, starch cutback and potassium supplement, only use distilled water in order to flush solid obstructions!

77 **Q**: *(L)* Well, that is the most comprehensive piece of physical advice they have ever given. *(J)* No kidding.

78 **A**: You are in pain, my dear, and when you hurt, all others do too![9]

79 **Q**: *(J)* That was sweet. Moist heat or dry heat?

A: Moist? 80

Q: *(L)* Reiki? 81

A: Yes. When ligaments are damaged, 82
it is often a function of calcium obstruction.

Q: *(L)* Is the bony prominence that 83
shows up in the x-ray on the Coracoid prominence a build-up against which the tissues have torn?

A: Yes. 84

Q: *(L)* So, it is not a broken piece, is 85
that correct?

A: Yes. 86

Q: *(T)* Wasn't Sue telling you about 87
that? A projection will tear the tissue like a piece of fabric. *(L)* Alright. Before we get on to other subjects, my mom wants to know what causes her abdominal distress?

A: Muscle atrophy. 88

Q: *(T)* She needs to exercise more. *(L)* 89
Is that correct?

A: Yes. 90

Q: *(L)* I recently got a flyer from the 91
Human Potential Foundation[10] about this super duper conference being held

---

[9] *The Wave* 39

[10] http://www.sourcewatch.org/index.php/Human_Potential_Foundation:

> In May 1995, the historic first disclosure conference 'When Cosmic Cultures Meet,' was organized by the Human Potential Foundation in Washington D.C. in order to pressure the White House to reconsider its inherited policy concerning the disclosure of information about Extraterrestrial (ET) and Unidentified Flying Objects (UFO) phenomena. Authors whose work was included in the proceedings of the conference include: Professor George S. Robinson, Michael Hesemann, James J. Hurtak, PhD, James W. Deardorff, Dave Hunt, Richard J. Boyland, PhD, R. Leo Sprinkle, PhD, James More, PhD, William J. Baldwin DDS PhD, Charles T. Tart PhD, Puma Q. Singona, Dennis Rohatyn, PhD, Paula Underwood, MA, Ruth Montgomery, Zecharia Sitchin, Donald M. Ware, John Hunter Gray, PhD, Elisabet Sahtouris PhD, James J. Funaro, Jerome C. Glenn, John E. Mack, MD, Keith Farrell, Michael Michaud."

www.newdawnmagazine.com/Articles/Shades of an Alien Conspiracy.html:

in Washington. I would be really interested in that. Could we or should we plan on trying to attend that one?

92 **A**: Waste of time.

93 **Q**: *(L)* That's pretty definite. *(J)* We have enough on our plate. *(L)* In the book here, *Mysterious Fires and Lights*, there is a whole segment on the idea that certain lights that have been called UFOs of a specific sort, which perform in a specific way, and this is not including all by any means, may actually be living creatures of some sort that manifest in our reality. And, that they seem to have a consciousness, and a purpose, but they don't manifest as 'real' UFOs. Is this, in some cases correct?

94 **A**: Check publishing date for currency of theoretical data.[11]

95 **Q**: *(L)* OK, it is published in 1967. *(T)* Well, so much for that! *(L)* Well, it's not a stupid idea. Like ball lightening. It has been known to demonstrate intelligent behavior, kind of like a curious puppy. What is ball lightening?

A: Would be hard to "get attached" to such a pet. 96

Q: *(L)* I know that, but is it sentient? Is it a probe of some sort? 97

A: No. 98

Q: *(T)* It is just a very strange electrical phenomenon. 99

A: Close. 100

Q: *(L)* The other night when we were working without Frank, we got some information that indicated that Frank was in danger via the government. Is that true or was that true?[12] 101

A: Partly. 102

Q: *(L)* What is the source of this danger? 103

The Human Potential Foundation *(HPF)*, was founded by U.S. Senator Claiborne Pell, funded by Laurence Rockefeller and based in Falls Church, Virginia.

According to Dick Farley, who worked for the organization for about three years, Rockefeller's goals seemed to be the promotion of "alternative religious and psychiatric/psychological paradigms, including so-called 'UFOs' and 'abductions,' having 'Global Mind Change' potentials. Rockefeller put more than $700,000 through the 'HPF' from 1991 to 1994, as Common Cause Magazine recently reported."

The President of HPF, 'retired' naval intelligence officer Cdr. C.B. "Scott" Jones, Ph.D., was a contract consultant to the Defense Nuclear Agency (1981–1985) before working for Senator Pell as Special Assistant (1985–1991). Jones is also listed in John Mack's book alongside Laurence Rockefeller.

Joan d'Arc of *Newspeak*, who attended one of HPF's conferences, said the problem she found with "the 'Have-You-Hugged-Your-Gray-Today' school generally prevailing within the HPF, is that nobody was saying perhaps ETs and abduction experiences are very bad news." [...]

It has been said that all of Laurence Rockefeller's pet projects promote the familiar theme: Aliens are here to help us, perhaps aid us along the evolutionary ladder."

[11] On other occasions the Cs have said that the earliest 'news' about something is likely to be closest to the truth since the cover-up machine has not had time to go into full action. But then, we have also learned that there can be sort of 'living technology' in 4D, according to Cs. So perhaps that was their point.

[12] *The Wave* 37, 63

104 **A**: Source?

105 **Q**: *(L)* I mean like, the IRS, the FBI, the CIA, or what?

106 **A**: Not initialled as such.

107 **Q**: *(L)* Is this physical danger or just harassment danger?

108 **A**: Mind attack for purpose of self-destruction.[13]

109 **Q**: *(L)* Is there anything that can be done to shield against this kind of attack?

110 **A**: Yes.

111 **Q**: *(L)* What can be done for shielding?

112 **A**: Knowledge input on a continuous basis.

113 **Q**: *(L)* And what form should this knowledge take? Does this mean channeled information, books, videos, what?

114 **A**: All and other.

115 **Q**: *(L)* A specific other?

116 **A**: Networking of information now, warning!!! All others will very soon experience great increase of same type of attack, two of you have had episodes in past from same source for similar reasons, but now your association puts you in different category!! Remember all channels and those of similar makeup are identified, tracked, and "dealt with."

117 **Q**: *(T)* Which two have experienced similar types of attack?

118 **A**: Up to you to identify for learning.

119 **Q**: *(J)* I'm pretty sure I'm one of them because I have been way down mentally and emotionally. *(T)* Is Jan one of the two? *(J)* I know I'm one.

A: Suicidal thoughts? 120

Q: *(L)* Have you had suicidal thoughts? 121 *(J)* No. *(T)* Not me. *(F)* I have had them constantly. *(T)* Laura, did you? *(L)* I was pretty damn low. I wasn't contemplating suicide, I was just thinking how nice it would be if we could just turn out the lights and end the illusion. *(T)* OK, so we have identified the two, you and Frank. *(L)* So, in other words, Jan, it is going to get worse. *(F)* Didn't they say two others? *(L)* I guess they are saying that a similar thing can happen. *(T)* If we don't work together on this, we are going to lose the whole thing. *(J)* OK, ask about the card reading Terry did tonight? *(T)* Was it accurate?

A: Close. 122

Q: *(T)* Was the reading referring to the 123 same thing you are now referring to?

A: Close. 124

Q: *(T)* So, we have the knowledge and 125 all we have to do to prevent the attacks from being nasty?

A: You do not have all the awareness 126 you need! Not by any means!

Q: *(J)* Is one of the reasons why this 127 whole thing between Frank and Laura happened to show us that we could establish, albeit a very weak and very jumbled, connection with the channel without Frank's presence? A sort of verification of the channel's integrity. Was that one of the byproducts of this, or one of the purposes of it?

A: Byproduct is good way of putting 128 it. Remember, all there is is lessons.

Q: *(L)* The attack was more internal in 129 terms of doubt, not only of the channel and the information, but of the very

[13] *The Wave* 17

foundations of existence. I mean, the realization that we may not be at the top of the food chain was shattering. *(T)* That snowballed on its own once the initial conflict was established. *(J)* Maybe the way to look at it is: yes, we went through all this crap, and you and Frank went through all this anguish, but maybe one good thing that came out of it, and maybe wasn't intended, was the fact that yes, we were able to see that there is a channel separate and distinct from all of us. It is not dependent on any one of us to be present. Yes, we do need to have all of us together for optimum contact...

130 **A**: All are able to channel, but practice is required to establish the same extent of grooving but be aware of ramifications!

131 **Q**: *(L)* What ramifications?

132 **A**: Observe Frank.

133 **Q**: *(T)* We are observing you. *(J)* Yeah. And? *(F)* I think what they mean is, when you can channel as I can, because I channel almost continuously, this has a good side and a bad side. Now, the good side you know. The bad side you don't know. The bad side is very hard to live with. I cannot even describe the state of my mind. *(L)* I would like to have practical advice and guidance on what we can to do to fend off or prevent psychic attack. We know that knowledge and awareness is important, but any words of wisdom or advance things that can be given would be appreciated.

134 **A**: Daily prayer helps.

135 **Q**: *(L)* Something else came up here a couple of days ago, right out of the blue: after not having heard anything from her for months and months, V___ gave me a call and wanted to stop by with a poem for me to read. What she told me was that one of the reasons she dropped out of the group was that she had been under such massive attack. She believes that the attack came because she had been participating and working on the board and that this brought on the attachment, or something, and that what we are doing is 'questionable'. Now, during the time we had not been hearing from her, she called the Reverend at the Metaphysical Church who caused me so much trouble before, to ask for her help and advice, and then she contacted the woman 'Vanessa', whom we had asked about before. Vanessa, apparently, did a release for V___. Could you tell us what was afflicting V___?

A: Open. 136

Q: *(L)* Whatever it was, did it come by 137
her association with us and this work?

A: No. 138

Q: *(L)* Did she have an attachment? 139

A: Has from times past and time to 140
time.

Q: *(L)* Does it come and go with her? 141

A: Can. 142

Q: *(L)* Did Vanessa help her in releas- 143
ing her attachment?

A: Open. 144

Q: *(L)* What was V___'s agenda in sud- 145
denly dumping this in my lap?

A: Wants to reestablish contact. 146

Q: *(J)* Contact with Laura or the chan- 147
nel?

A: Both. 148

149 **Q**: *(J)* Does she want back into the group?

150 **A**: Close.

151 **Q**: *(L)* Is there anything you wish to tell us before we shut down for the night?[14]

152 **A**: Reread information given about attack warning and discuss amongst yourselves for strengthening of learning and knowledge base for purposes of protection and ultimately, survival!! Goodnight.

End of Session

Even though I tried to take care of a couple of ordinary issues during this session, it is clear that what was on everyone's mind was the recent break in relations, not to mention the psychological effects of the material that had been transmitted thus far. What were we to make of this? We had all certainly been on a quest for answers, for 'the truth', so to say, and the Cs coming along and presenting a plausible scenario that fit the widest range of phenomena was something to be appreciated for sure. But I don't think that any of us had bargained for the kinds of answers we were getting nor the effect it might have on us psychologically, emotionally, and even existentially.

There was the additional problem of possible externally driven glitches in our psychological/emotional natures. In some cases it could obviously be just someone's socio-familial, programmed way of thinking being triggered, but in others, it seemed as though something was deliberately applied as a sort of pressure that garbled thinking or emotions or situations. Years before, I had read about experiments done with extremely low frequency sound waves and how, in a matter of minutes of exposure to same, the best of friends could be at each others' throats with murder on their minds. What other kinds of technology could have been developed along this line since then? And what about the planet or cosmos? Could there be frequencies emitted by our planet, or coming to us from outer space, that could elicit such reactions? These were the things that the Cs were encouraging us to research and consider for, as they said, "strengthening of learning and knowledge base for purposes of protection and ultimately, survival!!"

In the 20 years since, it seems that this has been one of the major issues we have had to study and deal with. In a sense, it is much like

[14] *The Wave* 20, 37

Castaneda's "Three Phase Progression":[15]

1. Holding your own in facing petty tyrants.
2. Facing the unknown with courage.
3. Standing in the presence of the unknowable.

> One of the greatest accomplishments of the seers of the Conquest was a construct he called the three-phase progression. By understanding the nature of man, they were able to reach the incontestable conclusion that if seers can hold their own in facing [human] petty tyrants, they can certainly face the unknown with impunity, and then they can even stand the presence of the unknowable.
>
> "The average man's reaction is to think that the order of that statement should be reversed," he went on. "A seer who can hold his own in the face of the unknown can certainly face petty tyrants. But that's not so. What destroyed the superb seers of ancient times was that assumption. We know better now. We know that nothing can temper the spirit of a warrior as much as the challenge of dealing with impossible people in positions of power. Only under those conditions can warriors acquire the sobriety and serenity to stand the pressure of the unknowable.
>
> "The seers of [the Conquest] couldn't have found a better ground. The Spaniards were the petty tyrants who tested the seers' skills to the limit; after dealing with the conquerors, the seers were capable of facing anything. They were the lucky ones. At that time there were petty tyrants everywhere."

In a sense, we were coming at the thing sort of backward: we were trying to face the unknown and stand in the presence of the unknowable without first having trained ourselves to deal with our own psychological states and emotions. Well, I had a certain amount of practice from raising my children, but obviously, much more needed to be done. I had the advantage of having studied the Gurdjieff work for some years, but Frank was quite convinced that all the answers were 'inside him'. That was then and since a dangerous proposition, as events would show.

[15]Carlos Castaneda, *Fire from Within.*

The fact that the responses relating to Sue did not conform to Frank's opinion of the situation suggests that the session was uncorrupted by his emotional input. Even if we were discussing human relations, which was a subject so often skewed by his emotional prejudices, he was contrite and subdued. What went right over our heads, however, was the fact that the Cs gave us the answer right there and then! They said: "Attack is most purposeful! Watch all portholes. All others will very soon experience great increase of same type of attack, two of you have had episodes in past from same source for similar reasons, but now your association puts you in different category!! Remember all channels and those of similar make-up are identified, tracked, and 'dealt with'. All are able to channel, but practice is required to establish the same extent of grooving but be aware of ramifications! Observe Frank."

Frank had, of course, quickly identified himself as having had suicidal thoughts. But in retrospect, the context of episodes in the past, as it applied to myself, was a very long time in the past – many years previous. And in fact, as we later discussed this, it turned out that very much the same type of attack in the past had occurred to Terry. In point of fact, Frank's claims to be suicidal were, for the most part, if not entirely, a means of controlling others.

"Attack is most purposeful. Watch all portholes. Practice is required to establish the same extent of grooving. Be aware of ramifications. Observe Frank."

"Observe Frank", they said. And we didn't even see it.

April 18, 1995

It's difficult to describe the state of my mind after the return of the 'Prodigal Son'. On the one hand, all of my do-gooder programs had been effectively activated in a powerful way by the perception of physical and spiritual danger to Frank. My rescue program, mother program and save-the-lost-and-heal-the-wounded program – all were on hyperdrive with one object: Frank. His plight had been so eloquently described when he said: "I think what they mean is, when you can channel as I can, because I channel almost continuously, this has a good side and a bad side. Now, the good side you know. The bad side you don't know. The bad side is very hard to live with. I cannot even describe the state of my mind."

I realized at this point that what had been done to Frank as an infant and a young child was that he had been programmed or engineered to be a channel, in the sense of being almost empty inside of anything that was essentially 'him'. It was almost as though he had been drilled through, like with a well-digging machine, cored out and reconfigured. I began to understand that, in this sense, he was 'the channel', in the same way a pipe that is sunk into the ground is a channel for the water or oil to be extracted. I also understood that it depended entirely upon who or what he was connected to, as to what was drawn through this pipeline.

In a sense, my perception of him was that he was as helpless in his dilemma as a newborn baby.

On the other hand, I had a dilemma of my own: even though there was a strong impulse to help Frank, as a human being, and a mother, he had betrayed me badly and such a thing is hard to forget. It's easy to say 'forgive and forget', but not so easy to do. I realized that I no longer trusted him as I had before and that certainly had an effect on the sessions, because I had to devise ways to ask questions and possibly obtain information without including Frank in my deliberations.

My idea at this point was rather simple: obviously, Frank very desperately needed to be connected to me in order for the Cassiopaeans to be the well from which the information he channeled was drawn, and it was crucial to his development and survival that this connection be sustained and further developed. I had the idea that, just as a pipe is made wet by what passes through it, the more he channeled the Cassiopaeans, the more saturated he would be with the STO messages, and the more likely it was that the healing of his own soul would take place. His free will had been so violated, so decimated, that the only way to rebuild it, to restore it, to restore his soul, so to speak, was to channel with me as regularly and as often as possible. Just as a mother feeds a baby, the Cs would feed Frank, and so he would grow. Whether or not he had been a higher spiritual being who had become helpless by agreeing to be born, and who had afterward been attacked and manipulated by dark forces to create this condition, didn't really matter. I was committed anew to 'helping' him. And I was committed with full heart and soul and mind in spite of the fact that I knew I couldn't trust him.

Frank, on the other hand, having been exposed as being something other than the higher spiritual being that he had so repeatedly claimed – having acted in a way that belied such a claim and in fact, having given evidence of very dark self – had to reorganize himself as well.

Now, it would be rather easy for me to just write it all off as having been victimized by a conscious con-man, and that is always a possibility. But the fact seems to be that in human dynamics, each participant in a drama is, at some level, firmly convinced of the rightness of their view and perceptions. The test is, of course, how closely their views align with factual data and observable evidence of reality.

As we have just seen from the events surrounding the previous two sessions, chemistry can play a huge role in our perceptions. What we view for all of our lives in a certain way, can be changed in an instant of soul-shock. And most often, after the shock wears off, the programmed or accepted view gradually displaces the clarity and we go back to sleep in our illusions and narcissistic constructs of reality. This is why the Cassiopaeans repeatedly encourage us to dig, dig, dig for facts and evidence. Don't listen to opinions; check the facts.

In any event, we were back on track and I was determined to get some answers one way or another.

Participants: 'Frank' and Laura

1 **Q**: *(L)* Hello.

2 **A**: Hello.

3 **Q**: *(L)* Who do we have with us this evening?

4 **A**: Tikloria.

5 **Q**: *(L)* And where are you from?

6 **A**: Cassiopaea.

7 **Q**: *(L)* Have you been listening to our tape from Thor Templar?

8 **A**: Yes.

9 **Q**: *(L)* Do you have any rebuttal to make to his accusations of irrelevance?[1]

10 **A**: Is rebuttal necessary?

11 **Q**: *(L)* Well, no, not for me, and, quite frankly, I don't think I will respond to him, so it doesn't really matter. Is it alright if we ask some questions about the situation that has transpired here over the last month or so?

12 **A**: Yes.

13 **Q**: *(L)* OK, is there any way I can access the information I need, because we need to make some kind of assessment of what occurred here.

14 **A**: Open.

15 **Q**: *(L)* Have we ever had a person in our group or in our room here who was sent here deliberately to break up our interaction?[2]

16 **A**: If so, that is for you to discover for purposes of learning and growth.

17 **Q**: *(L)* Is that part of what has been taking place here?

18 **A**: Good chance.

Q: *(L)* Well, that is getting close. 19

A: Remember one can be manipulated 20
by another.

Q: *(L)* In this case, who was the one 21
being manipulated?

A: We mean that one can appear to be 22
an "agent" when in actuality, control is originating elsewhere, this is especially true when the apparent "agent" is one of a good and simple and seemingly stable nature.

Q: *(L)* Okay, you are saying the con- 23
trol could be originating elsewhere. Is that correct?

A: Yes. 24

Q: *(L)* Would that control be 3rd den- 25
sity or 4th density?

A: Either, or elements of both. 26

Q: *(L)* In this particular case, I would 27
much prefer to think that someone was being used or manipulated by other forces. But, in that case, that could be a loose cannon, so to speak. Am I correct?

A: Up to your discretion. 28

Q: *(L)* Can we identify the source of 29
control in this particular case?

A: We mentioned discovery and learn- 30
ing earlier.

Q: *(L)* So, we have to figure this one 31
out?

A: Will benefit you greatly in "future" 32
to do so.

Q: *(F)* Why is that? 33

A: In order to recognize "symptoms," 34
which may be common occurrence.

[1] Mentioned in session 4 March 1995.

[2] *The Wave* 39, 53

35 **Q**: *(L)* In this case, we have discussed it, and it seems that it has already become a common occurrence. Persons come in and are all excited and they put in energy or money or whatever, and they are all gung-ho, and then they become a disruption.

36 **A**: Yes. You are already learning.

37 **Q**: *(L)* Recently Violette came to visit and said that she had an episode with an attachment. Did she have an attachment from this work?

A: No. Hormonal fluctuations. 38

Q: *(L)* She called Vanessa and Vanessa did a cleansing on her. Did this help her with her hormonal fluctuations? 39

A: No. 40

At this point, refer back to the 5 January 1995 session for the beginning of the drama about my son's past life experiences. I had still not decided whether or not we even wanted to go and visit the family of his alleged past life persona, but I did know that I wanted to gather some additional information and try to help my son process the event.

The process consisted of taking him back to the scene under hypnosis and going through it a little at a time, with distance and perspective, in an effort to 'desensitize' him. Well, everything went fine except that he kept 'skipping' over something. He would describe going along in the plane, telling me what he saw in terms of the landscape, sounds, thoughts and so on. Then, he would talk about the approach of the missile, and then he would skip to being out of the body, looking down at the scene, full of grief and rage at his young life, full of hope and promise, being cut short so suddenly and unexpectedly.

This 'skip' bothered me. So, we went over it again, projecting it onto a 'screen' so that he could be somewhat distanced, and have some control over the speed using a mental device of a sort of 'TV remote control'. This time, going through it 'frame by frame', he made a funny remark, saying, "What's that *smell*?"

"What smell?" I asked.

"Kind of like garbage, or sewage."

"Where is it coming from?"

"Boxes. Boxes in the cargo bay."

He continued describing the scenery below, and then he volunteered: "The smell is gone."

Right away, I knew something was going on, so I backed him up again. Frame by frame we went through it again.

This time, he noticed something peculiar: it seemed that they had passed over the same landscape, which had certain notable features, *twice*!

The first time, the smell was present, the second time it was gone. And there was *another* skip there!

The only way I could think of to get some sort of idea what was going on here, since the skip occurred over and over again, was to take him out of the scene to the 'between life' state, where he could analyze and describe what he perceived to have happened. In this state, he remarked that the strange, smelly boxes in the cargo hold had something to do with 'alien presences', and that he had been transporting them, the plane was 'abducted' so that the cargo could be off-loaded into an alien craft, and was 'put back' in the timeline just in time to catch a missile *deliberately*. And it was this hidden interaction that was the cause of the great distress!

Well, needless to say, I didn't know what to make of such an idea. It was bizarre beyond even *my* imagining. But, there it was.

Now, back to the session, where I inquire about this.

41 **Q**: *(L)* A few weeks ago I did a hypnosis session with my son. In this hypnosis session, he seemed to go back through a memory of flying a plane, an EC-135, I believe. He seemed to go through the crash and so forth. Was this a fairly accurate recall on his part?

42 **A**: Yes.

43 **Q**: *(L)* The most interesting part of the session was when he described smelling something strange in the hold of the plane, that the cargo smelled strange. Was this an accurate memory?

44 **A**: Yes.

45 **Q**: *(L)* When I asked him what it smelled like, he said it smelled 'garbagey' or something really horrible like sewage. Was that a correct memory?

46 **A**: Close.

47 **Q**: *(L)* When I asked him if he knew what it was at a higher level, he said that it had something to do with aliens. Was that correct?

A: Yes. 48

Q: *(L)* Was he, in fact, transporting something having to do with alien-human interactions? 49

A: Yes. 50

Q: *(L)* Then, something happened as he was flying along; he seemed to be flying over the same spot twice and it startled him. Did this, in fact, happen? 51

A: Yes. 52

Q: *(L)* And it seems, after he was flying over the same spot the second time, that he said the smell was gone, the cargo was gone. Did this, in fact, happen? 53

A: Yes. 54

55 **Q**: *(L)* Was his plane, himself, and his co-pilot abducted in flight by aliens?

56 **A**: Yes.

57 **Q**: *(L)* Were they then shot down deliberately by the United States government?

58 **A**: Open.[3]

59 **Q**: *(L)* Was his memory of the actual situation, as he was shot down, fairly accurate?

60 **A**: Yes.

61 **Q**: *(L)* Does he need more work on this issue to clear it?

62 **A**: Yes.

63 **Q**: *(L)* Should I take him through the same thing over again more than one time?

64 **A**: Yes.

65 **Q**: *(L)* Okay, the other night we were talking about the episode when I was three or four years old and saw the face at the window[4] that said to me: "No matter where you go you cannot hide. When the time comes, we will find you." When I had that experience, who or what did I see at the window?

66 **A**: Gray.

67 **Q**: *(L)* And what was the message, exactly?

68 **A**: Just as given.

69 **Q**: *(L)* What is it that they were trying to convey to me? Is it that, in point of fact, that they are going to find me or do something to me or with me at some point in the future?

A: Not yet able to inform. 70

Q: *(L)* You are not yet able to give me this information? 71

A: Yes. 72

Q: *(L)* Why is this? 73

A: No. 74

Q: *(L)* When I was with Dr. Zanghi who was doing [trying] a hypnotic regression with me, he asked why I was being abducted. At that moment, in response to that question, a scene appeared to me of a sort of Greek Temple with a lot of 'patriarch' types in long robes and wearing beards, who were teaching me and then sending me out to do something. What was this memory? 75

A: Not yet, Laura! 76

Q: *(L)* Well, that sounds foreboding. That sounds scary to me that you can't tell me. Is this something I should be frightened about? 77

A: No. 78

Q: *(L)* Is this something that I am supposed to do that I can't yet know? 79

A: Close. 80

Q: *(L)* Now, obviously, in my opinion, and this is just my opinion, there is some sort of destiny where Frank and I are concerned. Is this correct? 81

A: Most likely. 82

[3]It had been previously stated that the plane was shot down by the North Vietnamese, but this additional information seems to suggest that there was some 'intent' in replacing the plane at that exact point in space-time so that it *would* be shot down.

[4]See *Amazing Grace*.

83 **Q**: *(F)* That sounds like a cross between a "yes" and an "open." *(L)* Is it true, as we have surmised, that ever since our meeting, person after person has been sent in to attempt to disrupt our relationship? Is this correct?

84 **A**: Maybe.

85 **Q**: *(F)* I think we can read that in the direction of a yes. *(L)* Can I ask at what point in time this interaction will be fully activated?

86 **A**: Open.

87 **Q**: *(L)* Ahhh. They are trickier than I am. Was I correct in the flash of insight I had the other night that nearly caused a coronary, of seeing the skies opening and all sorts of beings just pouring into our reality?

88 **A**: Yes. But is it prophecy, or current reality?

89 **Q**: *(L)* Oh, God!

(F) Well, the thought I was having just a couple of days ago (is that when you had this?) – OK, the thought I was having was along very similar lines. It is that everything is happening *right now*, it is just our perception of it that is lagging behind. Instead of what we have always thought, that one day the veil would be ripped open because of some cosmic event, it just may be that the veil is being opened individual by individual. Then one day it will be the last group that doesn't know anything and then it will fly open. What is really happening is not that the UFOs will someday be invading; it is just that because of some perception, we do not see that it is happening *now*. Karla Turner described it as the 'End of the World', and for her and her family, it was.

A: Yes. Goodnight. 90

End of Session

April 22, 1995

The Konicovs called again with more questions. Violette returned to participating in the sessions even after the problems she claimed they caused her as reported in the previous session.

Here we talk a bit more about Oak Island. See the 10 December 1994 session for earlier discussion.

Participants: 'Frank', Laura, Terry and Jan

1 **Q**: *(L)* Hello.

2 **A**: Hello.

3 **Q**: *(L)* Who do we have with us this evening?

4 **A**: Lioa.

5 **Q**: *(L)* And where are you from?

6 **A**: Cassiopaea.

7 **Q**: *(L)* We have a couple of personal questions for the Konicovs. Are you willing to answer those questions for them?

8 **A**: Konikovs prone to vendetta.[1]

9 **Q**: *(L)* They are prone to do vendettas themselves?

10 **A**: Open.

Q: *(L)* Are they the object of some sort of vendetta? 11

A: All inclusive. 12

Q: *(T)* All inclusive of what? 13

A: Mindset. 14

Q: *(J)* Are they paranoid? 15

A: Okay. 16

Q: *(L)* Well, they have four names. Can I give the names and you give a response to each name? These are people they have been associated with and they would like to know... 17

A: We do not wish to be used for personal life direction by those who take an outwardly orientation. We have given answers for these people before, and you do not know what they have done with information.[2] 18

[1]Cs seem to have deliberately spelled their name this way.

[2]I was relieved with this answer.

[3]Naropa University is a private liberal arts college in Boulder, Colorado, founded in 1974 by Tibetan Buddhist teacher and Oxford University scholar Chögyam Trungpa. It is named for the eleventh-century Indian Buddhist sage Naropa, an abbot of Nalanda. Naropa describes itself as Buddhist-inspired, ecumenical and nonsectarian. It was accredited by the North Central Association of Colleges and Schools in 1988, making it the first Buddhist, or Buddhist-inspired, academic institution to receive United States regional accreditation.

19 **Q**: *(L)* Violette wanted to ask if the Naropa Institute[3] in Boulder would be a good place for her to go to school?

20 **A**: More on previous subject: Suggest tread softly and use diplomacy, not what Terry suggested!

21 **Q**: *(L)* Yes, we don't want to tick them off. *(J)* Well, I don't like to lie. *(L)* Well, there are lies that are OK lies and there are lies that are hurt lies...

22 **A**: Yes. After further "online" connection with Konikovs, will communicate helpful information.

23 **Q**: *(L)* Do you want me to get them on the phone?

24 **A**: That was in "quotes."

25 **Q**: *(L)* Violette and I talked about points of entry of discarnates. I remember that Jan talked about something getting her on the back of the neck as she was sitting at the computer. I would like to know if there is any common entry point for these kinds of connections?

26 **A**: No.

27 **Q**: Can it occur at any place?

28 **A**: Yes.

29 **Q**: *(L)* Is the back of the neck a common place?

30 **A**: Common?

31 **Q**: *(J)* Do they find your physical weak spots and enter there?

32 **A**: Physical is not issue.

33 **Q**: *(L)* So, they find your auric weak spots?

34 **A**: Close.

Q: *(L)* Are your auric weak spots some- 35
times reflected in your physical?

A: All is possible. 36

Q: *(L)* During the time that we all had 37
the pains in our shoulders, was this a psychic attack?

A: Maybe. 38

Q: *(L)* Well, you said that this was ev- 39
idence of DNA changes. Was it that?

A: How does one learn? 40

Q: *(L)* Since we are not equipped to 41
examine genetic material and find out about DNA changes, we are kind of relying on you to tell us when DNA changing is going on. You indicated at the time that this was DNA changes.

A: Network. 42

Q: *(L)* Is there anything going on with 43
this heating-up process, this feeling of being hot?[4]

A: Paranoia will destroy ya. 44

Q: *(L)* Well, I'm not being paranoid. In 45
seriousness, is there anything going on with vibrational changes? Is this heat a reflection of this?

A: In seriousness, no. 46

Q: *(T)* When we do the channeling and 47
Reiki does that generate body heat?

A: Higher energy. 48

Q: *(T)* Does that translate into heat? 49

A: Yes in third density. 50

Q: *(L)* When I was reading our little 51
bit about Oak Island the other day, I noticed that we never followed up on

[4] At this point in time, I was still some eight years away from menopause, though it is entirely possible I was experiencing pre-menopause symptoms. I'm not sure if women experience such symptoms that early, though I suppose it's possible.

certain things. Could we ask on that now?[5]

52 **A**: Yes.

53 **Q**: *(L)* OK, you said at that time that a Transdimensional Atomic Remolecularizer was buried at Oak Island. Is that correct?

54 **A**: Yes.

55 **Q**: *(L)* Who buried it there?

56 **A**: Learn.

57 **Q**: *(L)* Well, we are getting ready to learn because you are going to teach us, is that correct?

58 **A**: You already have tools.

59 **Q**: *(L)* What do you mean we already have tools?

60 **A**: We are trying to teach you to use your most precious commodity.

61 **Q**: *(L)* And that is, of course, our minds?

62 **A**: You betcha!

63 **Q**: *(L)* Speaking of precious commodities, since my accident, my brain has been doing some very strange things. When I write, I transpose letters. I get blank spots. I have been doing some other very strange things, playing with seeing if I know something and then discovering that I do. It is really kind of strange and I wonder if that accident had anything to do with these strange happenings?

64 **A**: Yes.

65 **Q**: *(L)* So, when I hit my head, I really hit my head! *(J)* Scrambled your brains.

66 **A**: Not issue.

Q: *(L)* What is the issue? Can you tell me exactly what it did to my head? 67

A: Not issue. 68

Q: *(L)* What is the issue? *(J)* We were talking about learning. *(L)* Did this event do something to help me learn in a different way? 69

A: Yes. 70

Q: *(L)* Then, I shouldn't worry about it. *(T)* Now you have to learn to work with it. *(J)* Let's not get sidetracked. *(L)* Let's go back to Oak Island. OK. What I read about Oak Island was that there were legends of lights being seen there prior to 1703. 71

A: Yes. 72

Q: *(L)* Prior to 1703 would put the burial of whatever is there at least prior to that time, correct? 73

A: Yes. 74

Q: *(L)* Were those lights the lights of craft of other beings other than the natives of this planet? 75

A: Electromagnetic profile. 76

Q: *(L)* What was noticed when the kids arrived on the Island was that a limb was sawed off of a tree over the depression and there were marks of a rope and pulleys having been utilized. *(T)* If something more advanced dug the pit, they wouldn't have used chain hoists and pulleys. *(L)* That is what I am getting at. So, if there was evidence of this kind of stuff on the tree, it would seem to indicate that somebody had been doing something there who was a little more human or limited in their technology, is that correct? 77

A: Yes. 78

[5] *The Wave* 29

79 **Q**: *(L)* Now, my thought is that, it is beyond human technology to have produced that pit at that point in history?

80 **A**: Beyond known technology.

81 **Q**: *(L)* And yet humans may have been involved in that activity?

82 **A**: Bingo.

83 **Q**: *(J)* Think back to when we were talking about it and you mentioned the lights.

84 **A**: Some humans have always communed with "higher" powers.

85 **Q**: *(L)* So, humans may have actually... *(J)* Like those little kids that broke into those houses and did all that damage. They could have done it themselves, but they had to be directed to do it. I think it is a good analogy.

86 **A**: Not good analogy, we are speaking of conscious communion in this and other instances.

87 **Q**: *(L)* OK, there was conscious communion between humans and other powers in the building of this pit. What group of humans was this?

88 **A**: It's fun learn.

89 **Q**: *(J)* How about pirates? *(L)* Well, who was in this area? Eskimos?

90 **A**: No.

91 **Q**: *(L)* Indians?

92 **A**: Keep going, network.[6]

93 **Q**: *(L)* There was the French and the English. How about the Vikings? *(F)* No, the Vikings were 600 years before that. *(T)* Well, we don't know how long ago the pit was dug. *(J)* I'm still... yeah, good question. *(L)* When was the pit dug?

A: 1500s. Nationality is not issue. 94

Q: *(T)* Well, this pit was dug sometime 95
in the middle of the 1500s. *(J)* And it was discovered in the 1700s.

A: Access sect information. 96

Q: *(L)* So, it could have been a religious 97
group.

A: Now, who claimed communion, 98
Laura has in memory banks from absorption of mass reading practice.[7]

Q: *(F)* Was there a sect from that era 99
that claimed communion?

A: Yes. 100

Q: *(L)* I think that this may have had 101
something to do with the people that later became known as the Cajuns, a French religious sect that was living there...

A: Maybe. 102

Q: *(L)* Now, this article says that it 103
would have taken a hundred men working every day for six months to have built this pit...

A: No. 104

Q: *(L)* The article also says that it 105
must have been dug in 1780...

A: No. 106

Q: *(L)* When they drilled into the pit, 107
some bits of gold came up and a piece of parchment and maybe some other odds and ends. What were these?

A: Alchemy. 108

Q: *(T)* The remolecularizer made it. 109
(L) Why not? If these people were in-

[6] *The Wave* 29
[7] I still have no clue!

volved in doing this, why did they do it?

110 **A**: Instructed to do it.

111 **Q**: *(L)* They were instructed by the higher powers they were in contact with, correct?

112 **A**: Yes.

113 **Q**: *(L)* What did they intend to do with it once it was there? Did someone intend to come back for it at some point in time?

114 **A**: No.

115 **Q**: *(J)* Maybe it was a lesson. *(T)* Is it buried there in that location for a specific reason?

116 **A**: Sure.

117 **Q**: *(L)* Does it do something? *(T)* Does the location itself have something to do with the purpose of it?

118 **A**: Magnetic.

119 **Q**: *(T)* Are there other ones buried on the planet?

120 **A**: Yes.

121 **Q**: *(T)* Are they aligned to each other on the planet in some kind of geometric pattern?

122 **A**: Maybe.

123 **Q**: *(T)* Do they all work together?

124 **A**: Maybe.

125 **Q**: *(T)* Oh, we're getting too close now, they don't want to tell us. *(J)* Can you tell us where some of the other ones are?

126 **A**: Use mind, that is what it is there for.

127 **Q**: *(T)* We are using our minds. And, we are talking to you about this. We are friendly.

A: Shortcut city. 128

Q: *(T)* Yeah! That's what it is all about. We are still 3rd density! If we use... 129

A: It's not nice to fool Mother Cassiopaea! 130

Q: [Laughter] *(T)* Mirth! If we were to follow the coordinates where this thing is buried, would it lead us to others? 131

A: Try it and see. When L___ said he wanted to hunt for buried treasure, do you think he had this in mind? 132

Q: *(T)* Is there a remolecularizer under us? 133

A: No. 134

Q: *(L)* OK. I want to get back to the function of this thing. You say it is buried not to be dug up. It is actually buried to stay there? Is that correct? 135

A: Yes. 136

Q: *(L)* Then that explains a lot of things about the way it was buried. There was found, at a certain level, a rock with carving on it. It was destroyed through carelessness. I am curious as to what this said. Can you access this and tell us what it said? 137

A: Measure marker. 138

Q: *(J)* Could it be possible that this device was somehow related to the crystal pyramid of Atlantis? 139

A: In a small sense. 140

Q: *(J)* Did the pyramid have anything to do with powering this device? 141

A: Yes. 142

Q: *(J)* It is obvious that the device was buried long after the pyramid was there, but it may have tapped into the power. *(L)* Is this device continuously operational? 143

144 **A**: No.

145 **Q**: *(L)* What stimulates it to go into operation? That is, assuming it does.

146 **A**: Magnetic anomalies.

147 **Q**: *(J)* Is it affected by earthquakes?

148 **A**: Can be.

149 **Q**: *(L)* Are these magnetic anomalies ones that occur naturally on the planet?

150 **A**: Both.

151 **Q**: *(L)* So, they can occur naturally on the planet or they can be generated or stimulated by some other source?

152 **A**: Yes.

153 **Q**: *(L)* When this machine is activated, what happens?

154 **A**: Too vague.

155 **Q**: *(J)* Is this device a doorway for entry into this dimension?

156 **A**: Can be used as such.

157 **Q**: *(J)* Is it possibly a lock on a doorway into this dimension?

158 **A**: No.

159 **Q**: *(J)* Is it a focal point for entry into this dimension?

160 **A**: No.

161 **Q**: *(T)* Is it a stand-alone machine or is it to be used in conjunction with others?

162 **A**: Either.

163 **Q**: *(J)* Oh. So, they are networked together and if it is a small job, one can do it, but if it is a big job, they can all activate. *(T)* Do each of them cover a certain area of the planet?

164 **A**: No.

[8] *The Wave* 29

Q: *(T)* You said that they don't have 165
to all work at the same time; they can work independently of each other? Are they positioned in such a way if something small happens only a couple of them kick in, but if something large happens, as many as necessary?

A: Okay. 166

Q: *(T)* Were they placed here to keep 167
the planet stable in some sense?

A: Vague. 168

Q: *(L)* Who owns it? 169

A: Owns? 170

Q: *(L)* Who built it? 171

A: Answer for yourself, and enough, al- 172
ready on this subject!!!![8]

Q: *(J)* I think I just heard a door slam! 173
(L) I want to go to the terrorist bomb attack that just happened. Can we talk about this?

A: You can always ask any and all ques- 174
tions, no need ask for permission, if unanswerable for any reason, we will let you know.

Q: *(L)* OK. We received a prediction 175
on this terrorist bomb attack on February 25th, at which time you said there would be a terrorist bomb attack in Washington D.C. within a month or thereabouts, which was related to an ongoing trial that was identified as the one of the Muslim terrorists who bombed the Twin Towers. Can you tell us if this is the bomb that was supposed to be set off in Washington, but

was then moved to Oklahoma because of security intensification?[9]

176 **A**: No.

177 **Q**: *(L)* Well, no terrorist bomb attack took place in Washington. Can you tell us why?

178 **A**: Yet.

179 **Q**: *(L)* It is yet to happen?

180 **A**: Open.[10]

181 **Q**: *(L)* The bomb in Oklahoma is being connected to the Patriot movement. Is this, in point of fact, who is behind this attack?

182 **A**: There is no unified movement as such, in either purpose or direction. This is extremely fragmented!

183 **Q**: *(J)* I read that it may be related to the Branch Davidians. *(L)* Is that true?

184 **A**: No.

185 **Q**: *(J)* Loose cannons? *(T)* Are the one world government people behind it?

A: No. 186

Q: *(L)* Were the guys who did this just 187
loose cannons?

A: Close. 188

Q: *(L)* So this was just... *(J)* A cou- 189
ple of fruitcakes got together and... *(L)* Fruited?

A: It is very easy to be manipulated, 190
thus be confused and see demons where there are none and the opposite.

Q: *(L)* Are you saying that these guys 191
were manipulated?

A: Yes. 192

Q: *(L)* Can you identify the source of 193
the manipulation?

A: Varied. 194

Q: *(L)* Can you give us a couple of 195
hints, here? Name one of the sources of the manipulation?

A: Lizard race. 196

Q: *(T)* Name another. 197

A: All their agents conscious and oth- 198
erwise.

[9] April 19, at 9:02 A.M. Oklahoma City, USA, a large car bomb exploded at the Alfred P. Murrah Federal Building killing 168 people, and injuring 500 including many children in the building's day care center. Within a week a suspect, Timothy McVeigh, was caught and charged. Two suspects, Timothy McVeigh and Terry Nichols, faced trial. McVeigh was arrested during a routine traffic stop 78 miles from Oklahoma City on weapons charges the same day. Timothy McVeigh and Terry Nichols, were later convicted of charges related to the bombing. Michael Fortier, a key government witness and friend of Nichols and McVeigh, was sentenced to 12 years in prison in 1998 for failing to warn authorities, lying to the FBI, transporting stolen weapons and conspiring to fence stolen weapons. In 1999 Fortier's sentence was overturned and a more lenient sentence was ordered under manslaughter guidelines. In Oct a new 12-year sentence was issued. McVeigh was later convicted of federal murder charges and executed. [http://timelines.ws/days/04_19.HTML]

[10] One wonders, of course, if this is a bit confused, since the prediction from the 25 February session was so darn close to what actually happened in Oklahoma City. However, it is also possible that the 9/11 events were already in the planning stages and the Cs were still referring to that.

199 **Q**: *(L)* Can you tell us who are some of the human Lizard agents? *(LM)* Organizationally. *(L)* We won't tell!

200 **A**: All humans are at one "time" or another.

201 **Q**: *(L)* Yes. Nobody is immune to this manipulation. And that brings me back to the subject of the phone call from Scarlett the other day. I would like to know, what was the motivation behind that phone call?

202 **A**: Dumping excess stuff.

203 **Q**: *(L)* It wasn't in the nature of a fishing expedition? *(J)* Or an attempt at reconciliation?

204 **A**: Maybe.

205 **Q**: *(T)* Well, that would be some of her excess stuff. *(L)* Do you mean excess stuff in terms of her emotions or whatever?

206 **A**: Answers are easier when questions are pin pointed.

207 **Q**: *(L)* Did she call for reconciliation?

208 **A**: Unconsciously, maybe.

209 **Q**: *(L)* Did she call because that bunch at the Metaphysical Church put her up to it?

210 **A**: Ditto.

211 **Q**: *(L)* Is she still connected to MF?

212 **A**: Barely.

213 **Q**: *(L)* Well, it doesn't matter. Why have the roaches been so crazy in the last week or so? They have really been outrageous.

214 **A**: Electromagnetism.[11]

215 **Q**: *(L)* What is the source of this electromagnetism?

A: EM field disturbance. 216

Q: *(T)* What has disturbed the field? 217

A: Seismic. 218

Q: *(L)* Where is it going to 'seat'? 219

A: Open. 220

Q: *(L)* Well, I think something is going 221 to happen because every time I have seen the roaches act this way, something has happened. Earthquakes, hurricanes, planes crashing and so forth. What is the size and locus of it at this point?

A: Moving continuously. 222

Q: *(L)* Is this a fairly large distur- 223 bance?

A: Yes. 224

Q: *(T)* Where was it before it came 225 here?

A: Circling Earth at 6500 r.p.m. 226

Q: *(L)* Per minute? 227

A: Yes. 228

Q: *(LM)* Is this subterranean or atmo- 229 spheric?[12]

A: Both. 230

Q: *(L)* What is the source of this EM 231 disturbance?

A: Too complicated. 232

Q: *(J)* I hate it when they say that! 233 *(LM)* How about in a nutshell? Is it a natural occurrence or is it being generated from other dimensions?

A: Natural. 234

Q: *(L)* Is it from some activity within 235 the planet itself, or the planet's reaction to cosmic waves?

[11] *The Wave* 9

[12] *The Wave* 9

236 **A**: In and around.

237 **Q**: *(J)* Is this a normal occurrence?

238 **A**: No.

239 **Q**: *(J)* Has this happened before?

240 **A**: Yes.

241 **Q**: *(J)* When?

242 **A**: Four months ago.

243 **Q**: *(L)* What happened four months ago?

244 **A**: Access memory.

245 **Q**: *(T)* Well, the Japanese earthquake happened four months ago. *(L)* Is this what you are referring to?

246 **A**: Yes.[13]

247 **Q**: *(LM)* Is it most likely to hit a fault again?

248 **A**: Open.

249 **Q**: *(T)* Is this going to show up as an Earth change of some kind?

250 **A**: Yes.

251 **Q**: *(L)* Can you give us a prediction on it?

252 **A**: Open.

253 **Q**: *(T)* This has been going on for a while, now. *(L)* About ten days, I think. *(J)* Is ten days accurate?

254 **A**: Close.

255 **Q**: *(T)* What is the general time period to play itself out?

256 **A**: Open.

257 **Q**: *(T)* Is it going to center on Laura's house? [Laughter][14]

258 **A**: Open. If so, suggest "vacation."

Q: [Laughter] *(J)* Any suggestions as to where they should go? *(LM)* Los Angeles. *(T)* That's a good spot for the summer Olympics! I hear the U.S. Team has a real good chance of getting gold and breaking windows this year. *(L)* Once again, I will ask for V___ if the Naropa institute is a good environment for her to continue her studies? 259

A: If she chooses. 260

Q: *(L)* My mother wants to know, what are the ramifications of cremation? She has read some things on the subject and she is a little concerned about it. *(T)* They don't do it until after you're dead. 261

A: None. 262

Q: *(L)* So, it's OK to cremate the body and... 263

A: Body is third density not fifth density. 264

Q: *(L)* The reason she is concerned is because she read a book that says it takes a while for the soul to completely separate from the body and that there is a 'cellular' consciousness that might experience pain for some time after death at least until every little cell dies individually. Is any of this true? 265

A: No. When the soul leaves, it leaves instantly. There is no body consciousness that remains and dies "slowly." Once dead, dead. 266

Q: *(T)* The only pain it causes is to those selling cemetery lots and exorbitant funerals who hope that the cremation trend does not continue! *(F)* If people continue to be buried, aren't we going to run out of space? *(T)* Some 267

[13] January 17, A magnitude 6.9 earthquake hit the port city of Kobe, Japan. 5,502 people were killed in the worst earthquake to hit Japan since 1923.

[14] *The Wave* 9

places are recycling the graveyards! I want to be cremated. *(LM)* Let's go outside! *(T)* Not right now! Not 'til I'm dead, L___. Then it won't hurt! [Laughter] *(J)* Ah, get some gasoline and come on outside! *(LM)* I was just kidding! [Laughter] *(T)* Yes, we had our kitty, Mr. Scott, cremated and when I die I want to be cremated and I want Mr. Scott's remains poured in with me so I will have my kitty with me and Mr. Scott won't be alone. *(L)* That is very touching, Terry. A little sick, but touching. *(LM)* Why don't you grow some tomatoes and fertilize them with Mr. Scott and then you'll have him with you? *(T)* But, what goes in, must come out! And then he'd be gone!

[Break]

Q: *(T)* A few sessions back you used the term "take". What did this mean? 268

A: "Take" means whatever it is associated with. 269

Q: *(J)* I watched a couple of programs last night on television. One of them was about a man who was struck by lightning about 20 years ago and this strike greatly increased his psychic abilities.[15] I was wondering if that is a 270

[15] *Wikipedia*, "Dannion Brinkley":

> In *Saved by the Light* Brinkley explained that he was struck by lightning on September 17, 1975, while using a telephone at his home in Aiken, South Carolina. He said he was clinically dead for 28 minutes. During these 28 minutes Brinkley said he experienced many characteristic details of a near death experience as well as certain unique ones. His account includes an out-of-body experience with extensive observations of physical surroundings, passing through a tunnel, a high-speed and detailed life review and an encounter with beings who showed him visions of the future and discussed with him his life mission. Brinkley said he had a strong reluctance to return to his physical body, but he was sent back to fulfill a mission.
>
> In May 1989 Brinkley had heart failure and went to the East Cooper Hospital in Charleston, South Carolina where he had a second near death experience. Brinkley said he had another life review and was taken by a being to a place with pleasant sounds and smells. Brinkley was released from the hospital in a few weeks.
>
> On September 17, 1997 Brinkley had brain surgery to remove a subdural hematoma and had a third near death experience. In The Secrets of the Light he explained that he traveled to a "blue-gray place" that was like purgatory. In this place he said he saw soldiers, martyrs and those unable to reach a level of forgiveness.
>
> Brinkley said he received visions of future events during his near death experience. At least one was reported to Raymond Moody within seven months, that there would be a breakdown of the Soviet Union in 1990 and subsequent food riots. Moody later said Brinkley's forecast struck him as "silly and absurd" at the time but later proved accurate. Brinkley's visions also reportedly included the 1986 Chernobyl nuclear disaster and the 1990–1991 Persian Gulf War, but there was no written account of these visions prior to his 1994 book. Brinkley forecasted a 1995 nuclear accident in Norway and a pre-2000 economic collapse in the United States that never happened. And, according to Moody, other prophetic visions Brinkley made after his first near death experience never materialized the way Brinkley said they would. Brinkley responded to these claims on The West Coast Truth with Russell Scott in May 2012. Brinkley still to this day claims he has psychic visions.

normal by-product of being struck by lightning?

271 **A**: Yes.

272 **Q**: *(T)* Do the enhanced psychic abilities remain or decline after a while?

273 **A**: Stays.

274 **Q**: *(L)* Did my blow to the head in the wreck I was in last December increase my psychic abilities?

275 **A**: Maybe.

276 **Q**: *(J)* We were watching a program about the pyramids in Egypt and they were saying that there was nothing magical or unusual about how the formula was arrived at by which the pyramids were built. Originally they were trying to measure it with tapes that stretched and are inaccurate. So, they decided that they used a measuring wheel which would have enabled them to do it without any great mathematical computation. Is that correct?

277 **A**: No.

278 **Q**: *(L)* You knew that. *(T)* Is this why pi appears in the mathematics of the pyramid?

279 **A**: Take means subject. I.E. a different "take" on the subject.

280 **Q**: *(J)* So, we should take a different take on a subject. *(LM)* Well all the textbooks show a hundred thousand slaves rolling blocks on logs to build the pyramids. *(L)* It was done with sound wave focusing.

281 **A**: Textbooks are propaganda.

282 **Q**: *(T)* Was it built the same way the Coral Castle was built?

283 **A**: Close.

Q: *(L)* I want my husband to get me 284
a bucket seat and suspend it from the tree so that I spin in it. If I do this, will I develop strange abilities?

A: Yes, dizziness. 285

Q: *(L)* Did the guy who built the 286
Coral Castle sit in his airplane seat suspended from the ceiling and spin in it?[16]

A: Open. 287

Q: *(L)* Was the airplane seat suspended 288
from the ceiling in his room part of how he did his work?

A: If you spin, it must be a precise 289
method, not just spinning randomly.

Q: *(L)* Did he discover a precise 290
method for spinning to do such things?

A: Open. 291

Q: *(T)* So many turns and precise direc- 292
tion? *(L)* Can we follow up on this? Is there something on this moving things with sound that you can tell us? *(J)* What about a precise method for spinning?

A: Suggest experimentation. 293

Q: *(L)* What is wrong with my ear? 294

A: Vague. 295

Q: *(L)* Something is wrong with my ear. 296
(J) Describe it. *(L)* No, it's too gross. *(J)* Do it.

A: Fatty tissue. 297

Q: *(L)* That can't be it! My ear is de- 298
veloping and exuding black tarry stuff. I think it is blood and ear wax mixed.

A: No. Fatty tissue. 299

Q: *(L)* Why is it doing this? 300

A: Inner ear. 301

[16] See session 11 March 95 for discussion of Ed Leedskalnin and his airplane seat.

302 **Q**: *(T)* Is there something wrong with Laura's inner ear?

303 **A**: Not to worry about.

304 **Q**: *(L)* Have I been doing the right thing by using the peroxide, alcohol and vinegar?

305 **A**: Okay but easy does it.

306 **Q**: *(L)* Well, it's only the one ear. The other ear is fine. *(T)* Can you hear OK? *(L)* Yes. *(J)* Some people have real active wax production. *(L)* But it is only one ear. And it is the ear I use the most.

307 **A**: Worry not.

308 **Q**: *(T)* Easy for them to say, they don't have ears. *(L)* OK, a quick one here: am I going to get my [insurance] settlement soon?

A: Open. Wait and see. 309

Q: *(L)* Yeah, but I am broke right now. 310

A: Have been before, and you survived. 311

Q: *(L)* I am so broke I can't even buy 312
food.

A: Will not last long. 313

Q: *(L)* Well, I have a lot of things I 314
need to do. How am I going to pay for the conference, for example?

A: Faith. Time to say goodnight. 315

Q: Goodnight. 316

End of Session

April 29, 1995

This was an odd session. It seems as if the Cs had some sort of plan to teach us how to freely explore memories and draw ideas or conclusions from them. They also wanted to convey a particular concept that seems so obvious now, but then, it was really hard to grasp: 'perpendicular realities'. This concept has become increasingly important in recent years in view of Gurdjieff's concept of an 'Esoteric Group' combined with the Cs' concept of a 'conduit'. Other than that, this was a mysterious exercise the Cs led Terry (and the rest of us) through, during the course of which a few interesting items about alleged alien abductions were revealed.

Participants: 'Frank', Laura, Terry and Jan, Susan

1 **Q**: *(L)* Hello. Good evening.

2 **A**: Hello, good evening!

3 **Q**: *(L)* Who do we have with us?

4 **A**: Toria.

5 **Q**: *(L)* And where are you from, Toria?

6 **A**: Cassiopaea.

7 **Q**: *(L)* Well, we were a little late getting started tonight and I expect you have been waiting. The energy has been generating in the room.

8 **A**: Terry, was it October, 1964?

9 **Q**: *(L)* To what does this question refer?[1]

10 **A**: Ask Terry! Lake, yellow brick and brown brick buildings, cool day, fences, large cobalt colored cylinder, oscillating...

Q: *(T)* I would have been 14. *(L)* I bet they are talking about an abduction... *(T)* I was a freshman... my father's cousin had a place at Kuka lake and we used to go there and visit all the time... fences? I don't remember anything. I'm sorry. I'm drawing a blank. 11

A: Images we see... 12

Q: *(L)* Do these images relate to an event that occurred in Terry's life? 13

A: Ask... Now we see Victorian houses, green gabled roof... field... brown brick buildings... 14

Q: *(L)* Is this significant? We have a number of questions to get to... 15

A: Just "go with the flow." Directing "traffic" may restrict... 16

Q: *(T)* October? 17

A: We asked you. 18

[1] *The Wave* 5

19 **Q**: *(T)* Were there other people who saw this also?

20 **A**: Yes.

21 **Q**: *(T)* My mother?

22 **A**: Mother, brother.

23 **Q**: *(T)* Were there any neighbors who saw this?

24 **A**: Yes.

25 **Q**: *(T)* Did my father see it?

26 **A**: ?

27 **Q**: *(T)* Dark blue? *(J)* Cobalt blue. *(T)* Dark blue, almost a black color? *(J)* Cobalt is a bright blue.[2]

28 **A**: Cobalt is metallic navy blue.

29 **Q**: *(T)* Well, Glenn wasn't home...

30 **A**: Another locus.

31 **Q**: *(T)* I know what you are talking about! Yes, I did see something. I don't know if it was in October of 1964, but I remember seeing it!

32 **A**: Okay, now we are getting somewhere... what do you think happened to you that day?

33 **Q**: *(T)* I don't remember anything happening other than that I saw the object; it came floating over the house and then floated off in the other direction. I don't remember anything else happening. I stood outside, watched it come, watched it go; and I stood outside and watched it for quite some time.

34 **A**: Neighborhood, what appearance?

35 **Q**: *(T)* It looked just like the neighborhood. It didn't seem any different. I don't remember...

36 **A**: Describe...

Q: *(T)* There was a fifties develop- 37
ment out on the edge of the city limits of Rochester, surrounded by most of Kodak, out in that area, most of Rochester, across the street was a field with a schoolyard surrounded by a fence. A large, two-story brown school building, brown, or red brick... that I went to grammar school in. I don't know about yellow brick buildings, but our house was green at the time and the nextdoor neighbor's house was yellow at the time with white fancy little trim stuff across the roof. *(L)* Victorian. *(T)* It wasn't gabled, but it looked gabled. There were little gables over the front doors of most of the houses. The doors came out to the front and there was a little peak. *(J)* Almost like a little porch... *(Terry to Jan)* You were in the house, you saw what it looked like? *(J)* Yes. *(T)* There was a stadium on the other side of the schoolyard a ways back for Aquinas football games, their stadium. Some fields and one of the last remaining wooded areas that was in the city limits that wasn't a park down the street... a set of railroad tracks about five blocks to the east. The lake, Lake Ontario, Rochester is right up against it, we were about seven miles, eight miles from there, maybe ten; I used to ride up there on my bike and back... the neighborhood itself didn't look any different because I watched the thing come in over the field. I remember my mother, I don't know if my brother was there, but I remember my mother and my neighbor. The neighbor woman was standing out on the front walk talking and they called me because I was in the house watching TV. I don't know if

[2] *The Wave* 5

it was October though, because it was still warm, sunny. It came in from high over the west, over a field, by the stadium, came down toward us, came right toward us. I thought it was moving right at us. It didn't start moving right at us until we were looking at it...

38 **A**: Was.

39 **Q**: *(T)* Yes. Was moving toward us. It seemed to change direction when I came out and started looking at it. It went right over and...

40 **A**: Objective was you.

41 **Q**: *(T)* The objective was me? I don't think I was picked up at that time.

42 **A**: Oh yeah?

43 **Q**: *(T)* Well there were people standing there... *(L)* Doesn't matter.

44 **A**: Time "freezes" during abduction.

45 **Q**: *(T)* The object had the distinctive falling leaf motion to it, which I thought was an extremely odd thing for it to do. It came right over the edge of the house on the side of the house, where, sometime in the future, I had that thing happen to me when I was in the basement. It was right over where I would have been sleeping...

46 **A**: Oscillating.

47 **Q**: *(T)* I thought it sure looked metallic and I wished I had a little pellet gun and could pop a pellet at it; it wasn't more than about 50 feet up in the air. It was maybe 10 to 15 feet long and maybe about 3 or 4 feet around. It looked like a wiener rounded on both ends but not as fat; it was longer and thinner. *(F)* It looked like a hotdog? *(T)* It looked metallic to me. It was smooth, perfectly smooth. *(L)* What are we getting to here? This was obviously brought up for a reason. If Terry was abducted...

A: Crossroads. 48

Q: *(L)* It was a crossroads in Terry's life? 49

A: And now... connection completed. 50

Q: *(T)* I'm not following this... 51

A: Access your recent dreams. 52

Q: *(L)* That was a crossroads then and that connection is completed now... *(T)* Recent dreams... I dreamed something about moving into a building and I had something that had a power cord or something that went outside... a connection of some kind... *(L)* Is this the dream we are talking about here? 53

A: Ask Terry. 54

Q: *(T)* I don't remember them... they are just very vivid. Could something have happened to me just recently that started with that experience? 55

A: Yes. 56

Q: *(T)* It has to do with what we are doing here, but this isn't the completed connection we are talking about? 57

A: Not exactly. 58

Q: *(T)* The connection that was completed was all about something else? 59

A: Interrelated. 60

Q: *(T)* Did something happen to me just recently? 61

A: Yes. 62

Q: *(T)* Something I am not aware of? 63

A: No. 64

Q: *(T)* Does it have to do with my job? 65

A: In part. 66

67 **Q**: *(T)* Does it have to do with the fact that I am saying certain things to people at work, or wherever I can, when I talk about events that are happening these days and trying to raise their level of thinking on these things?[3]

68 **A**: Yes, now, let's explore your friends and relationships and experiences in the years immediately following the event to see if we can "dig up" something of startling significance!!!

69 **Q**: *(T)* Are we sure this is 1964 and not 1974?

70 **A**: Terry, you know better!

71 **Q**: *(T)* I'm just asking because that event and the event that happened in winter with the voices outside the window and all the weirdness that happened that night seemed to be a lot closer together and that other event happened in the 70s sometime. That was somewhere close to my trip out to Arizona and the weirdness out there with the car and all that. *(L)* Is that what you guys are talking about, the trip to Arizona and the voices and all that?

72 **A**: Oh, there is sooooo much, isn't there Terry! It is time to divulge.

73 **Q**: *(L)* OK, Terry, we're waiting. What happened in the year 1964 and the year following? *(T)* In the year following I was 15. *(L)* Who were your friends and what kind of relationships did you have? What were you doing? *(S)* How did you feel about everybody after this event? *(T)* In a way, but it was not immediate. After high school. But, in those days I was mainly hanging out with some people I met over at Edison. Tom ___, a lot of people named Tom. I used to go to the lake and take drives around it at night. We just used up gas. I felt comfortable because I did a lot of things, but most of the people I knew didn't get along with each other. I still do this today, I have learned from hard experience that I can't mix my friends. I learned at that time that every person in any group that had a counterpart in any other group – groups may be different, but they all have the same make-up, and I was always 'my' person in each of a number of groups. There was nobody in any of the groups I hung out with that was like me; I was that individual for several groups. *(L)* Is this the issue here?

A: No. 74

Q: *(T)* Does it have to do with when I 75
got my driver's license and we all used to drive around a lot out in the country? We drove all through the lakes area...

A: Some. 76

Q: *(T)* We used to drive all through 77
the hills out there at night... long drives. *(L)* Did something happen on one of these drives?

A: Maybe 0... 78

Q: *(T)* Maybe nothing. *(L)* What is 79
the objective of this particular line? *(T)* Does this have something to do with that bizarre town I came across one night and never was able to find again? Is that tied in here somehow?

A: Yes. 80

Q: *(T)* Strangest town I have ever seen. 81
Talk about David Lynch! *(J)* Divulge. *(T)* I was driving down through southwest New York one night. I was out

---

[3] *The Wave* 39

of high school. I used to get stoned then too, so a lot of my experiences aren't dependable because I got stoned. I went through a town one night down there in the Southern Tier, in the Finger Lakes area, and it was the strangest thing. I have been through all these little towns, and there's usually people and stuff. Not a lot, but at least somebody around. It was about nine or ten o'clock, and I went through this town; it was two-story buildings built right up to this two-lane main street, with a little narrow sidewalk, and it was like driving into a canyon, and the buildings went straight up into the air. There was a streetlight every so far, but they were those little yellowish bulbs that don't cast much light on the street. There was absolutely nobody out there. There was nobody in any of the buildings; they were all boarded up and shut down. It looked like a town but it didn't look like a town. It went about four blocks. I came back out of it, turned around and drove through it again because I didn't believe it. I could never find it again, and I didn't know the name of it.

82 **A**: Discover.

83 **Q**: *(S)* It was the *Twilight Zone*... *(T)* Was this town...

84 **A**: Yes.

85 **Q**: *(L)* You drove into another reality. *(T)* It wasn't really a town, was it?

86 **A**: Nope.

87 **Q**: *(T)* It gave me the willies. And, I turned around and drove through it a second time because I didn't believe it was there. *(S)* Were you by yourself? *(T)* Yes, I was all alone. There was nobody out there. One signal light that looked like it was out of the 1920s; old street lamps... like a ghost town, literally. *(L)* What are you guys trying to tell us here about Terry, through Terry? We are big kids now, we can take it.

A: Not the issue. 88

Q: *(L)* What is the issue? 89

A: Learning increases power. 90

Q: *(L)* OK, what are we trying to learn 91
here in this walk down memory lane?

A: How many times do you learn when 92
led by the hand, network!

[Break to discuss Terry's experiences.]

Q: *(L)* Are we getting anywhere? 93

A: It's all interrelated. 94

Q: *(L)* It is interrelated with what? 95
What event that just occurred... has it been our period of attack?

A: No. 96

Q: *(L)* The event that just occurred is 97
private to Terry and happened in his life only?

A: Yes. 98

Q: *(T)* Each of my relationships was 99
with an individual who thought for themselves, they understood things, they had their own experiences that were different from most people, and knew that most people could not relate or understand. It doesn't have to be abduction experiences, but they have had life experiences...

A: Yes, but that is the sign of some- 100
thing more significant.[4]

[4] *The Wave* 5

101 **Q**: *(L)* So, in other words, the fact that Terry... *(T)* Is it that these relationships formed and shaped who I am today because these people and I shared these different things with each other?

102 **A**: No.

103 **Q**: *(L)* No, I think it is the fact that you were able to form friendships with these people of all different kinds, that that was the sign of something significant. The thing that flashed through my mind is: are you a messenger, are you a catalyst?

104 **A**: No.

105 **Q**: *(L)* Did he have something or did he do something in his interactions with these people that caused...

106 **A**: No.

107 **Q**: *(L)* Did any of them do something where he was concerned?

108 **A**: No.

109 **Q**: *(T)* Is it the fact that I am able to form relationships with vastly different types of individuals?[5]

110 **A**: All originate from same "plane."

111 **Q**: *(L)* In other words, he formed relationships with others like himself? And, did they all originate from the same plane, as in somewhere else?

112 **A**: Close.

113 **Q**: *(L)* Well, we are getting somewhere. And was this ship that he saw from that plane or place of origin?

114 **A**: No.

Q: *(L)* Did this ship have a lot to do with interacting with all of these other people that Terry formed friendships and relationships with subsequent to this time? 115

A: Yes, but not central issue. 116

Q: *(L)* The central issue is that Terry and all of these other people that he formed relationships with... *(T)* Do we all share a common experience? 117

A: Close. 118

Q: *(L)* Do they all share a common origin? 119

A: Yes. 120

Q: *(L)* And what is that origin? 121

A: Neormm. 122

Q: *(L)* Neormm? 123

A: Closest English equivalent.[6] 124

Q: *(L)* Is that a place? 125

A: Yes. 126

Q: *(L)* Where is it? 127

A: Check star guides. 128

Q: *(T)* Is this a star? All of us are from another star that I've formed relationships like that – the special ones that I would consider lasting? 129

A: In perpendicular reality. 130

Q: *(T)* Am I the Orion we are looking for? 131

A: No. 132

Q: *(L)* Is Jan one of these too? 133

A: No. 134

---

[5] *The Wave* 39

[6] And no, I still don't know what 'Neormm' means. But now that I consider it, I wonder if perhaps we did not give it a proper word break? Maybe it is really 'Neo rmm'? In view of the character 'Neo' in the later *Matrix* movie, perhaps that is the clue?

135 **Q**: *(L)* Jan! *(J)* What? *(L)* Why not? *(J)* I don't know! *(T)* I'm confused. *(J)* What is the significance of my relationship with Terry, then? *(L)* Humanize him? [Laughter]

136 **A**: Open.

137 **Q**: *(T)* It's an open relationship! *(J)* No it's not. It's a marriage. Sorry! *(T)* You're the one who wanted it! We were fine for 27 years... *(F)* Was it that long? *(T)* No, it only felt that way. *(L)* Alright! Where are we now? We have discovered that Terry has a perpendicular reality that has been running through his life and probably is an ongoing thing – is this correct?

138 **A**: Yes.

139 **Q**: *(T)* What is a perpendicular reality? *(L)* It's a perpendicular reality! *(T)* Oh, well, thank you! That explains it all! *(L)* Well, you have side by side alternate realities, this one goes this way [gestures up and down].

140 **A**: Intersection is at realm border.[7]

141 **Q**: *(L)* So, in other words, you could follow along in your mind to the realm border because you have an intersecting reality with it. Is that correct?

142 **A**: No.

143 **Q**: *(L)* Well, I tried. *(T)* It sounded good to me. I have an escape hatch!

144 **A**: They merge.

145 **Q**: *(L)* OK, we have discovered the significance of the fact that Terry is part alien with a perpendicular alien reality that causes him to interact with other people who also have these perpendicular realities. What's the point? [Laughter] *(S)* Something to do! *(J)* It's a hobby.

A: "Point" is 3rd density concept, and 146
you need "refresher" course!

Q: *(T)* Remedial Cassiopaean. *(L)* 147
Well, I am just trying to understand what this whole thing is all about. What are we getting at here?

A: Then learn from what we communi- 148
cate to you and what you already have "locked up" inside of you i.e. time to get the key![8]

Q: *(L)* Do we have to look at our own 149
stuff this way? *(J)* Does this have anything to do with the fact that Laura just spent the past day and a half...

A: Please stop trying to "push" us this 150
way and that, and just learn freely.

Q: *(L)* What I think is, maybe every- 151
body does this, right now on the planet. There are always different groups that are forming connections with other people with whom they share an alternate reality. *(J)* In other words, we are all being attracted to each other? *(F)* Right. That makes sense. *(L)* In which case, what alternate reality do we share, or do we share no alternate reality and are each representatives of an alternate reality different from each other and are a connection point?

A: Latter concept is exactly correct! 152

Q: *(T)* We are what is common to each 153
other in our group?

A: What did we say about increasing 154
power?

Q: *(L)* So, in other words, each one of 155
us is connected to our own reality and groups of our own realities and...

[7] *The Wave* 5
[8] *The Wave* 39

156 **A**: Read back now Jan.

157 **Q**: *(L)* I have heard the concept, written or talked about, that certain people, or perhaps everybody, have locked up inside themselves pockets of energy or knowledge as in electromagnetic patterning in their fields...

158 **A**: Like putting together the pieces of the puzzle.

159 **Q**: *(L)* We are the pieces of the puzzle? *(J)* Yeah, we've known that.

160 **A**: Draw on a piece of paper one perpendicular intersection.

161 **Q**: [We get paper and draw figure.] *(L)* Like that?

162 **A**: No, make it like an upside down "T".

163 **Q**: *(L)* OK, this is it. [Draws figure.] Now...

164 **A**: Use next page, and this time draw it near but not at lower left corner.

165 **Q**: *(L)* Is that OK?

166 **A**: That is at llc.[9] Too close. [We try again.] Make it much smaller.

167 **Q**: [We try again.] *(L)* Is that OK?

168 **A**: Close to center.

169 **Q**: [We try again.] *(L)* Is that better?

170 **A**: Now, connect to another.

171 **Q**: *(T)* Above it or below it?

172 **A**: Make it slightly different angle.

173 **Q**: [We try.] *(L)* Like that?

174 **A**: Try again.

175 **Q**: [Terry tries.] *(T)* I think I am getting what they want. *(L)* Is that it?

A: No. [Terry tries again.] Connect bases. 176

Q: [Terry tries again.] *(L)* Why don't you just draw it on the board for us? [Clamps pencil next to planchette on piece of paper.] OK guys, draw! [The planchette draws the figure.] 177

A: Continue... 178

Q: *(J)* Is it a spiral? 179

A: No. 180

Q: [Terry draws figure which looks like polygon with perpendicular extensions to each side.] Is that the idea? 181

A: Now, circularize base. Now enclose with outer circle. Now, make clean copy on another page. 182

Q: *(J)* Is this a crop circle? 183

A: Has been done, yes. Designates union of perpendicular realities.[10] 184

Q: *(L)* Was the town that Terry went through one of the perpendicular reality towns? 185

A: Close. Need seven spokes. 186

Q: *(L)* Each person in the group is a spoke? 187

A: Yes. 188

Q: *(L)* Are we ultimately going to have seven spokes?[11] 189

A: Yes. 190

Q: *(T)* Are the five of us here, five of those spokes? 191

A: Open. 192

Q: *(T)* That was diplomatic, wasn't it? Is there more to this concept? 193

A: Of course! 194

---

[9] Lower left corner.

[10] *The Wave* 5

[11] *The Wave* 39

195 **Q**: *(L)* Once the seven spokes are in place in terms of persons, is that going to increase our power/knowledge exponentially?[12]

196 **A**: Explosively.

197 **Q**: *(L)* Is this why there has been so much attack and so many attempts to stop this process?

198 **A**: Partly.

199 **Q**: *(T)* OK, we have the image on the paper with seven spokes. What do we do with it next?

A: Open. 200

Q: *(T)* OK, this is just this lesson. *(L)* What is in the center of the circle? 201

A: Will fall into place, now you must ponder the significance and we must say goodnight! 202

End of Session

In the 20 years since this session, I believe that my understanding of the concept of 'Perpendicular Realities' has increased at least a little. The Cs mention seven spokes of a wheel, so to say, and perhaps that is foundational, but as mentioned above, it seems to me that it relates significantly to Gurdjieff's concept of an 'Esoteric Circle':

> "That is not the point; the point is that a 'group' is the beginning of everything. One man can do nothing, can attain nothing. A group with a real leader can do more. A group of people can do what one man can never do.
>
> "You do not realize your own situation. You are in prison. All you can wish for, if you are a sensible man, is to escape. But how escape? It is necessary to tunnel under a wall. One man can do nothing. But let us suppose there are ten or twenty men – if they work in turn and if one covers another they can complete the tunnel and escape.
>
> "Furthermore, no one can escape from prison without the help of those who have escaped before. Only they can say in what way escape is possible or can send tools, files, or whatever may be necessary. But one prisoner alone cannot find these people or get into touch with them. An organization is necessary. Nothing can be achieved without an organization." [...]
>
> "It is only possible to learn this in a school, that is to say, in a rightly organized school which follows all esoteric traditions. Without the help of a school a man by himself can never understand the law of octaves, the points of the 'intervals,' and the order of creating 'shocks.' He cannot understand because certain conditions are necessary for this purpose, and these conditions

[12] *The Wave* 5

can only be created in a school which is itself created upon these principles.

"How a school is created on the principles of the law of octaves will be explained in due course. And this in its turn will explain to you one aspect of the union of the law of seven with the law of three. [...]

"So that we can imagine the whole of humanity, known as well as unknown to us, as consisting so to speak of several concentric circles.

"The inner circle is called the 'esoteric'; this circle consists of people who have attained the highest development possible for man, each one of whom possesses individuality in the fullest degree, that is to say, an indivisible 'I,' all forms of consciousness possible for man, full control over these states of consciousness, the whole of knowledge possible for man, and a free and independent will. They cannot perform actions opposed to their understanding or have an understanding which is not expressed by actions. At the same time there can be no discords among them, no differences of understanding. Therefore their activity is entirely co-ordinated and leads to one common aim without any kind of compulsion because it is based upon a common and identical understanding.[13]

[13]P.D. Ouspensky, *In Search of the Miraculous*.

May 7, 1995

The Cs were irritatingly non-forthcoming in this session on some issues, but happy to respond on others. Notice that they remark at some point that I was tired though I wasn't conscious of feeling overly tired. I suspect that this was a hint that my psychic energies were down and that Frank's energies were dominant, thus the problematical reception.

Participants: 'Frank', Laura, Terry and Jan, Sue V

1 **Q**: *(T)* Good evening.

2 **A**: Okay.

3 **Q**: *(L)* Who do we have with us this evening?

4 **A**: Myip.

5 **Q**: *(L)* And where are you from?

6 **A**: Cassiopaea.

7 **Q**: *(L)* OK, we have a series of questions we would like to get into this evening. Is that going to be alright? Or do you have plans already?[1]

8 **A**: Some.

9 **Q**: *(L)* You have some plans or we can ask some questions?

10 **A**: Both.

11 **Q**: *(L)* Once again, since the thought was just stimulated by the sight of same, what is the story with the roaches in my house? Why are they coming inside in such numbers?[2]

A: Open. 12

Q: *(L)* Well, there are all kinds of cracks and crevices for them to crawl in through, but usually, they don't. 13

A: Scent food. 14

Q: *(L)* They scent food and that is what they come in for? 15

A: One reason. 16

Q: *(T)* What's another reason? 17

A: Suggest electronic bug discourager. 18

Q: *(L)* You mean a bug zapper? *(SV)* Not the ones that zap them, just the ones that discourage them. *(T)* Won't that frequency interfere with the channel? 19

A: Silly question. 20

[1]After the previous session when the Cs had sort of taken over and guided Terry down memory lane, I wasn't sure what to expect!

[2]Living in Florida naturally meant dealing with roaches. However, I usually never had such problems with them. I had also noted over the years that when the roaches were very active, something usually happened such as a storm. So I was basically just trying to refine this as a predictive method!

21 **Q**: *(J)* I didn't think so. *(L)* I didn't either. I mean, it's a frequency.

22 **A**: Too strong now is why.

23 **Q**: *(L)* OK, let's kick into a couple of our questions here. The first one is: Who were the Sumerians?

24 **A**: Study mathematics.

25 **Q**: *(L)* Study mathematics? Is that the answer?

26 **A**: Yes.

27 **Q**: *(L)* Who should study mathematics?

28 **A**: You.

29 **Q**: *(L)* Is there something about mathematics that will tell me who they were?[3]

30 **A**: Yes.

31 **Q**: *(L)* Well, I have read about the Sumerians, and I have read the Sitchin material...

32 **A**: We are not Sitchin!

33 **Q**: *(L)* How did the Sumerians produce their civilization so suddenly and completely, seemingly out of nowhere?

34 **A**: Study mathematics for all possible unanswered pieces of the puzzle!!! Interpolate and use appropriate computer program, learning now increases your power tenfold, when you use some initiative, rather than asking us for all the answers directly!!!

Q: *(L)* The first thing that comes to my 35
mind is to enter in all the dates that they have given us, create a database, for data, not necessarily written matter – dates of comets, civilizations, archaeological dates, findings, and so forth – and see how it crunches.[4] Was that all the answer there? *(J)* I would like to have some more on crop circles.

A: Do you not want an increase in 36
power?

Q: *(L)* Absolutely. Is there any under- 37
lying significance to the Great Year of 25,920 years, that is the precession of the zodiac?

A: See previous answers. 38

Q: *(L)* This is one that I don't know if 39
mathematics will help us out with, but, what is angel hair that has been seen to fall from UFOs?

A: AKA "slag." 40

Q: *(J)* Is it byproduct of the propulsion 41
systems?

[3] I'll be dealing with this in my upcoming writings.

[4] In 2014, our research group has started working on a project with the preliminary title "Historical Events Database". Its research outcomes are 'work in progress' and are made freely available to the public. See http://hed.quantumfuturegroup.org:

> "The project's main effort is to survey ancient texts and to extract excerpts describing various environmental and 'natural' events for statistical and graphical analysis and mapping. For this purpose, raw text excerpts are analyzed and, if they describe several environmental events at once, may be assigned to a corresponding number of entries in this database to give them a more accurate 'weight' for statistical evaluation. This is done in an effort to transform the common experiences of our ancestors into a timeline showing the frequency of environmental events in our past, and, if possible, to discern patterns in that timeline across many ancient chroniclers."

42 **A**: And of transdimensional maneuvers.

43 **Q**: *(T)* That's why it dissolves and goes away. *(L)* Did you know that Mike F has some in a glassine bag that he got somewhere and is certified angel hair! *(T)* He also has a UFO detector in a cigarette pack! *(L)* OK. On many occasions there have been fiery falls of objects from the sky that leave a gelatinous substance which then disappears. Is there any significance to this that we would be...

44 **A**: See previous answer.

45 **Q**: *(T)* Same stuff as angel hair. *(L)* OK, there were very unusual circumstances surrounding the so-called Great Chicago Fire. I would like to know if there was any impetus given this fire from other-dimensional forces, or was it just a natural phenomenon?

46 **A**: Vague.

47 **Q**: *(L)* Well, in specific, there were several people who reported what they described as literally a fiery tornado, or explosion, or fire falling from the sky that just swept upon them so suddenly and so completely that they literally had no time to do anything except barely escape with their lives.

48 **A**: Rumours.

49 **Q**: *(L)* Well, there were entire little towns destroyed that weren't even next to Chicago, and it happened at the same time, supposedly.

50 **A**: Makes "good reading."[5]

51 **Q**: *(L)* Who constructed the great Serpent Mound in Adams County, Ohio?

A: Armonan sect. 52

Q: *(T)* Who are the Armonans? 53

A: Atlantean descendants.[6] 54

Q: *(T)* So, this was a long time ago? 55

A: *(L)* Is there anything about them 56
we would be advised to know or learn?

A: "Puzzle pieces." 57

Q: *(L)* What period of time did they 58
live in this area, from when to when?

A: See answers to Sumerian question. 59

Q: *(L)* Well, my opinion to this whole 60
thing is that the Sumerians and the Armonans were Atlanteans who set up shop in their respective places when Atlantis went under.

A: Good, now go with that. 61

Q: *(L)* I would say that the same an- 62
swer holds for the White Horse at Uffington, in England?

A: Yup. 63

Q: *(L)* Well, that takes care of that. 64
Does someone or something, as in people or civilizations, or a group or organization, exist inside Mount Shasta in California?

A: No. 65

Q: *(J)* Is there any truth to the ru- 66
mor of the mystical power surrounding Mount Shasta?

A: Roundabout only. 67

Q: *(T)* But, Mount Shasta, itself, 68
doesn't have any power related to it?

A: Yes. 69

Q: *(L)* Yes, Mount Shasta, itself, but 70
not any group or entities, is that correct?

[5]In this case, I disagree with the Cs, as research has revealed a number of oddities about that great fire and its possible relation to the passing of large comets.

[6]*The Wave* 24

71 **A**: Yes.

72 **Q**: *(L)* Is there any reason that we would want to pursue that line of questioning that we are not aware of?

73 **A**: Up to you.

74 **Q**: *(L)* Why is an unbearable stench of sulfur associated with alien bodies and other related phenomena and entities?[7]

75 **A**: Chemical interactions.

76 **Q**: *(L)* So, if an alien dies in 3rd density and remains in 3rd density, and decays in 3rd density, that causes a chemical reaction that creates sulfur or related compounds?

77 **A**: Bravo![8]

78 **Q**: *(J)* So, the difference in dimensions creates this? *(L)* Would they smell this way if they died in 4th density? *(J)* Well, that's a stupid question because, what is 'smell' in 4th density? *(L)* Well, it was a trick question!

79 **A**: Try to think more like 4th density instead of 3 and 2.

80 **Q**: *(L)* Does this imply, since this is what I am inferring, that the aliens are chemically constructed in 4th density?

81 **A**: Close.

82 **Q**: *(L)* Now, Frank and I both had strange dreams. I dreamed last Sunday that I went outside and there was a whole lot of activity in the sky. There were alien ships shooting at each other and at the ground and it was pretty scary. There were people running around and my husband abandoned me and the children because he was so freaked out by it all. A really strange dream.

A: Stay tuned! 83

Q: *(J)* Oh, goody! *(L)* Was this dream 84
prophetic?

A: Open. 85

Q: *(T)* Stay tuned, as in stay tuned 86
during the dream to see what else happens?

A: For more dreams. 87

Q: *(L)* Are these dreams giving us in- 88
formation?

A: Open. 89

Q: *(T)* I keep having repeating dreams 90
about a female. Who is she?

A: See previous answer, from now on 91
abbreviated as "SPA."

Q: *(L)* OK, now I was reading through 92
the transcripts a while ago and it says that a black hole is total non-existence which is regenerated at level one. Or, that the regeneration at level one is a reflection of a black hole. Is a black hole a level-one phenomenon or a level-seven phenomenon?

A: One through four only. 93

Q: *(L)* Is there any representation of 94
the black hole phenomenon, that is, total non-existence, at the higher levels, that is, five through seven?

A: See previous answer. 95

Q: *(T)* Well, if the black hole is pure 96
STS at level one through four, at level five through seven there is only pure STO? *(SV)* They said earlier that there

[7] *The Wave* 9

[8] I think the Cs were glad that we were trying to work out the answers to questions instead of just passively asking and expecting to get everything handed to us.

[9] What we now understand better as 'information'.

was STS at level five and six. *(T)* But, that's reflection. *(L)* Thought form.[9]

97 **A**: Encapsulated at five.

98 **Q**: *(L)* Is there, after level seven, is there another...

99 **A**: No "after seven," suggest "refresher course" of transcripts![10]

100 **Q**: *(L)* Well, the question you didn't let me finish was, is there an octave? Does this step up and start the whole thing over like the octaves on a piano?

101 **A**: SPA.

102 **Q**: *(L)* Well, there is an awful lot of stuff being touted around about octaves and so forth.[11]

103 **A**: Grand cycle, and who is doing the "touting" that you speak of?

104 **Q**: *(L)* One of the persons who talks of the octave cycle is Gurdjieff, the Sufi teachings, several of the great philosophical teachings talk about the octave effect. There is the cycle of seven and the next cycle is at a higher level and is called an octave like the segments on the musical scale.

105 **A**: Who are we?

106 **Q**: *(L)* The Cassiopaeans.

107 **A**: Yes, now, we have volunteered to assist you in your development, yes?

108 **Q**: *(L)* So, throw all that other crap out the window?

109 **A**: If there were a level eight, do you think we would have failed to mention it at this point?!?

Q: *(J)* Good point. *(SV)* They forgot! 110
(J) Oh, by the way, did we mention level eight?! *(T)* Well, maybe these other people are perceiving the recycling as moving into another octave rather than just doing it all over and over. They just haven't got the information straight yet.

A: There are many who speak, and 111
some who speak the truth!

Q: *(J)* Yeah, but which ones are speak- 112
ing the truth? *(L)* The truth is out there! But why seven? What is the significance of the number seven?

A: Why not? 113

Q: *(T)* Could there as easily have been 114
eight or nine or six?

A: Is there "significance" to anything? 115

Q: *(L)* Only the significance we give it, 116
I guess.[12]

A: And if so, what is that? 117

Q: *(T)* Well, it is interesting to me be- 118
cause it means there was a structure to the way things were set up. There must have been a reason it was selected this way as opposed to another way.

A: Really? 119

Q: *(T)* It didn't just happen. Noth- 120
ing just happens! *(J)* Now, hold on a second, base 10 is because we have 10 fingers.

A: Who says? 121

Q: *(T)* You did. 122

A: Oh yeah? 123

[10] *The Wave* 9

[11] An octave includes the repeat of the first step, i.e. A B C D E F G and then begin again with A. So, the musical scale, though it is discussed in terms of octaves, only has 7 notes.

[12] *The Wave* 9

124 **Q**: *(L)* Are you saying, essentially, that it is the way it is because things are just arbitrarily that way?

125 **A**: No, we are trying to teach you how to complete the puzzle.

126 **Q**: *(T)* So the reason it is what it is and why is something we have to figure out.

127 **A**: And you have to figure out what is reason?

128 **Q**: *(T)* The reason for what? *(J)* For the seven.

129 **A**: No. No. No. Pay attention, please. What is reason?

130 **Q**: *(J)* As in reasoning?

131 **A**: Much of your learning to this point is based upon assumption of definitions of reality.

132 **Q**: *(L)* And, all of our assumptions are completely wrong?

133 **A**: Not all.

134 **Q**: *(J)* Anything that is rooted in 3rd density doesn't apply in most of these things and that's where we have to let go.

135 **A**: Logic is subjective.

136 **Q**: *(L)* Is symbolic logic as is used in mathematics subjective?

137 **A**: No.

138 **Q**: *(L)* But you always come up with different things using math rather than mentation. OK. Well, we opened a can of worms here. *(T)* We do that every time. *(J)* Worms are us! [Laughter]

139 **A**: Ongoing project.

140 **Q**: *(T)* Teaching us is an ongoing project. *(J)* We are a can of worms. *(L)* Is there any point in time when these communications will end?

[Tape ends abruptly and snaps off to surprised laughter at the synchronicity. New tape inserted before continuing.]

Q: *(L)* Was that a symbolic answer to 141
that question?

A: Open. 142

Q: *(T)* I want to ask about my dream... 143
I know, "See Previous Answer..." Who is the woman? Who is this being?

A: Stay tuned. 144

Q: *(T)* Oh good! This is like a cliff- 145
hanger every night! *(J)* Will there be more installments? *(T)* Maybe, because she changed tactics...

A: Laura tired. 146

Q: *(T)* Are you tired? *(L)* Not any 147
more than normally. Is there any reason for that?

A: Open; suggest caffeine. 148

Q: *(L)* Pause for caffeine break! [Cof- 149
fee was poured and passed around.] We want to know about this phenomenon of the street lights that go off as Terry and Jan drive down the road sometimes. I know this has happened to me a few times as well. Is there any significance to this phenomenon? Are Terry and Jan causing it, in other words?

A: Maybe. 150

Q: *(L)* Can you tell us anything further 151
about that?

A: Discover. 152

Q: *(L)* Back a few years ago it seemed 153
that an awful lot of things in my presence tended to break... windows, glasses, kerosene lamp chimneys, car windows, satellite dishes... mechanical objects would die upon my touching them.

A: EM anomalies. 154

155 **Q**: *(L)* Were these occurring because of something in me or around me?

156 **A**: Changes in awareness, etc.

157 **Q**: *(L)* Was there any abduction activity or contact activity going on with me at that time that contributed to this?

158 **A**: Discover.

159 **Q**: *(L)* Could Terry and Jan's experiences with the lights be related to this type of thing?

160 **A**: Maybe.

161 **Q**: *(T)* I guess that between open and maybe that maybe is closer to a yes. *(L)* It is EM anomalies and changes in awareness. *(J)* And, part of it, as I was saying to Terry, is that if you are not aware of what is going on around in your environment, you don't notice such things.

A: Yes. 162

Q: *(L)* Well, in my case, it seemed to be 163
a little more explosive so maybe I was a little more in the dark and had to be hit over the head with a two-by-four, so to speak.

A: Maybe. 164

Q: *(T)* Is that EM wave still circling 165
the planet?

A: Yes. 166

Q: *(T)* It hasn't done whatever it's go- 167
ing to do, then?

A: Open. 168

Q: *(T)* Something else I have no- 169
ticed, triple negatives throw them off... [Laughter] *(J)* Well, triple negatives are nasty anyway.

At this point, we brought out some images of a variety of crop circles and asked the Cs to interpret each of them.

170 **A**: A planetary "window."

171 **A**: Astronomical "twin" phenomena etc.

172 **A**: Alternating current.

173 **A**: Means: Expect to be rewarded at harvest time.

Q: *(L)* Is this snail formation a hoax? 174
[Exhibits image of crop circle.]

A: Open. 175

Q: *(L)* What does it mean? 176

A: Open. 177

Another series of crop circles exhibited for interpretation.

178 **A**: Buried memory.

179 **A**: Train.

180 **A**: Longing.

181 **A**: Knowledge through conception.

182 **A**: Sight provides confirmation.

183 **A**: Relay learnings.

184 **A**: Communication.

Q: *(J)* Well, that's the one they use for 185
their logo. *(T)* I wonder if they knew that?

A: Wonder indeed! 186

A: Passage of knowledge. 187

A: Find necessary clues by studying 188
cyclical patterns.

189 **A**: Family.

190 **A**: Season of change.

191 **A**: Grand advance.

192 **A**: Universe as laboratory.

193 **A**: Dimensional crossover.

194 **A**: Physical life pictorial.

195 **Q**: *(L)* Why the dead porcupine?

A: Scrambled body chemistry. 196

Q: *(L)* Are the porcupines significant 197
in these figures?[13]

A: Learn. You have enough material to 198
digest for now, so good luck and until the next time, goodbye.

End of Session

[13] Dead wild animals are rarely found in crop formations, but there have been a few exceptions. Some birds had apparently been caught up in the creation of a 1993 formation, and had been blown apart and disintegrated by the force. Mixed in with the blood and feathers were minute bits of flesh, but there were no bones, or any distinguishable or recognizable parts. Laboratory tests on some of the remains confirmed that they belonged to an 'exploded bird'.

Two dead porcupines were found in two different Canadian crop circles. One had almost disintegrated into blackened parts and the other had been squashed like a pancake. Scrape marks and a row of standing broken quills indicated that the latter porcupine had been dragged to the centre of the formation from the perimeter. The flow of flattened quills on its body went in the same direction as the lay of the fallen crop. Analysis of the other porcupine showed that the blackness of the remains was not due to burning. Most animals probably sense something is about to happen and run away, but porcupines respond to danger by simply raising their spines and sitting tight. (http://davidpratt.info/cropcirc1.htm)

May 13, 1995

In the week previous to this session, we had done some experimental Spirit Release Therapy by proxy utilizing Frank as the medium. I have described and explained this process extensively in a series of videos called "Knowledge and Being" that are available for free on the internet (check my website: cassiopaea.org). My thinking was that I would really like to be apprised of any negative influences in respect of myself and other members of the group, and, at the same time, testing Frank's abilities and comparing with what the Cs would say during communication.

We were sitting around with our fingers on the plastic pointer while chatting and it had begun to move and spell out nonsense.

Participants: 'Frank', Laura, Jan and Terry, Susan V

1 **A**: Hello.

2 **Q**: *(L)* Hello. *(J)* Did we just have somebody else horn in on the channel? *(L)* Who do we have with us?

3 **A**: Rolora.

4 **Q**: *(L)* Did somebody else just horn in on the board a moment ago?[1]

5 **A**: Maybe.

6 **Q**: *(L)* Well, my mother and I got a Play 4 number on the board the other night and three of the numbers were correct. What source did we get those from?[2]

A: Laumer. 7

Q: *(L)* Is he still hanging around? 8

A: All can "hang around," if they choose. 9

Q: *(J)* Has my mother ever been present? 10

A: No. 11

Q: *(L)* I would like to ask, since it is probably bugging everybody at the moment, what is the source of this oppressive heat we have been experiencing? 12

A: Normal weather pattern variation. 13

[1]Referring to garbled exchange that occurred prior official 'hello' process.

[2]I was still engaged in testing predictions on the side. As I've noted before, the idea was to try to determine if the universe was fixed or open and the simplest way to test this was to test predictions such as horse or dog races or lottery numbers. I never used these numbers for betting, I just kept notebooks full of the predictions and then the actual winners to try and see if there was any pattern.

14 **Q**: *(L)* Well, why isn't my air conditioner working well enough to keep the house cool?

15 **A**: House was not built with air conditioning in mind.

16 **Q**: *(L)* Well, you got that right. OK, we have a couple of questions we would like to get into. Jan noticed that there was a symbol on the Windows Wingdings file that is quite similar to the symbol that Ann B uses on her Reiki brochures. We would like to know, what is the source of this symbol and why the variation?

17 **A**: Ethereal memory.

18 **Q**: *(L)* What is the meaning?

19 **A**: Interconnection of reality in general.

20 **Q**: *(L)* Is this a useful symbol to use in Reiki?

21 **A**: Okay.

22 **Q**: *(J)* Why is it different in the fonts from the one used by Ann?

23 **A**: "Different strokes for different folks."

24 **Q**: *(L)* Is there anything further on this subject that you can, would, or should give us?

25 **A**: No.

26 **Q**: *(L)* OK, last week we did a spirit release on myself and Susan with Frank acting as proxy. We also inquired about information about protection for ourselves. Was the information that was given through Frank, at that time, an accurate portrayal of how we can best protect ourselves?

27 **A**: Mostly.

28 **Q**: *(L)* OK, one of the things that was said was that we don't really have to worry about cutting people off or out of our lives, but just to be aware of the potential of what they may be carrying, and that this awareness can actually create the barrier. Is this correct?

A: Largely. 29

Q: *(L)* Is it also, as I have conjectured, 30
a good idea to sometimes limit contact with people who may be carriers of negative energy, or who may have...

A: In extreme cases. 31

Q: *(L)* So, in other words, if a person is 32
extremely toxic, it is best to just stay away from them or limit contact?

A: Good idea. 33

Q: *(J)* I would like to ask about the ex- 34
perience Terry and I were having about my emotional imbalances. *(L)* OK... Jan, actually everybody has been experiencing this attack situation...

A: Has caused stomach problems. 35

Q: *(L)* Have you been having stomach 36
problems? *(J)* No more than usual. *(L)* OK, the situation that Terry and Jan have, that she perceives as attack – was that, in fact, an attack?

A: Some. 37

Q: *(T)* What else was involved? 38

A: Biological changes. 39

Q: *(J)* Monthly hormonal? 40

A: Yes. 41

Q: *(J)* That fits. *(L)* Susan has been 42
experiencing a situation that I experienced in the past. She perceives a misty presence in her room. What is the source of this presence, this fog?

A: Entity ID "code." 43

Q: *(L)* And what kind of entity is it? 44

A: Sublinear yeti like. 45

Q: *(T)* What does sublinear mean? 46

47 **A**: Scrambled identifier of channel mechanism.

48 **Q**: *(T)* Are we talking about encryption here?

49 **A**: Close.

50 **Q**: *(L)* Is it something being sent through the dimensional curtain and does it need Susan's energy to reassemble itself?

51 **A**: No.

52 **Q**: *(L)* Is it having trouble reassembling itself?

53 **A**: Chose Susan due to past imprint.

54 **Q**: *(SV)* What do you mean, "past imprint"?

55 **A**: Past associations have brought about conflicting imprints into your channeling aura.

56 **Q**: *(L)* Is there any way she can change these past associations or imprints?

57 **A**: Go to places where traumatic events occurred, and "reload with current aural pattern."

58 **Q**: *(SV)* Well, that would be all over the country. *(T)* Visualize them.

59 **A**: Not sufficient, must replace physically.[3]

60 **Q**: *(T)* Is this all over from everywhere, all her life, or just recently?

61 **A**: Traumatic events are easily accessible.

62 **Q**: *(L)* In other words, she will know. OK, since this situation she has experienced was very similar to the one I experienced when I was pregnant with [my first child], was this similar?

A: No. 63

Q: *(L)* What was the fog I experienced? 64

A: Entity imprint brought on by un- 65
usual stress.

Q: *(J)* Because of the baby? 66

A: Partly. Pregnancies may cause un- 67
usual psychic awareness.

Q: *(L)* What is the intent of this fog in 68
Susan's room?

A: Not correct conceptualization. 69

Q: *(SV)* Well, I don't feel any fear, I 70
just wonder if it is eyestrain. *(T)* What was the mist I saw the other day?

A: Ozone. 71

Q: *(L)* John W called today and talked 72
to me a little bit about the Oklahoma bombing. Now, we haven't talked about it too much... he did bring up some interesting claims. Was the Oklahoma bombing an 'inside job,' that is, was it done by agents of the government itself?

A: No! 73

Q: *(L)* OK, was the Oklahoma bomb- 74
ing done by the persons who have been arrested for it?

A: Yes. 75

Q: *(L)* Was the Oklahoma bombing 76
accomplished by the fertilizer bomb placed in the truck parked outside the building?

A: Yes. 77

Q: *(L)* It was not accomplished by any 78
bomb inside the building?

A: No. 79

[3]This is a very interesting idea: that a person should return to places where trauma occurred and sort of 'lay the ghost', so to say.

80 **Q**: *(L)* Was Timothy McVeigh influenced to do this by forces outside of himself?

81 **A**: Yes.

82 **Q**: *(L)* Were these forces human or other?

83 **A**: Other.

84 **Q**: *(L)* Was it as I have written in my piece "The Politics of Metaphysics"?

85 **A**: Yes.

86 **Q**: *(L)* Was that piece essentially channeled?

87 **A**: Yes.

88 **Q**: *(J)* Was anything that John W said about the size of the bomb correct?

89 **A**: No.

90 **Q**: *(T)* Was anything John said about it correct?

91 **A**: In general, no.

92 **Q**: *(T)* So he is mouthing rumors or making stuff up, or passing on made-up stuff?

93 **A**: Within circles in which he moves.

94 **Q**: *(J)* What circles does he move in?

95 **A**: Anti-government militia types.

96 **Q**: *(T)* Is he an agent?

97 **A**: Of what sort?

98 **Q**: *(T)* Is he a government agent?

99 **A**: No.

100 **Q**: *(T)* Is he a STS agent?

A: Close. 101

Q: *(T)* Is he trying to influence things? 102

A: Forces trying to influence things are 103
working through him.

Q: *(T)* He is not working for the CIA, 104
or the NSA, or the FBI, or military intelligence, or anything like that?

A: No. 105

Q: *(L)* You told us before that he 106
worked for the NSA... *(T)* The CIA...[4]

A: CIA stands for Confusion Is Appar- 107
ent!

Q: *(T)* He is a "Confusion Is Apparent" 108
agent?

A: Might as well be. 109

Q: *(J)* He's doing their work but he is 110
not on their payroll. *(T)* He is doing as good a job as they are putting out the disinformation. *(L)* Earlier we had a discussion about where we wanted to move. My husband has his ideas, we all have our ideas, and we just want to know, in terms of just being happy and content with the surroundings, of the places mentioned – South Dakota, North Carolina – which would be more pleasant?

A: As we have told you before, moving 111
is pointless, as it is a manifestation of 3rd density thinking, and would thus regress you severely. It is not "where you are that matters, it is who and or what you are that counts."[5]

---

[4]Actually, in searching the transcripts for any such statement by the Cs, I didn't find it anywhere. I did find a related reference in the 11 February 1995 session, and then in the 30 July 1994 session. But in neither case did the Cs connect the individual to the CIA or NSA. So, we see how easily assumptions can be made.

[5]While it is true that it is not where you are that counts, I would have to say that this response was somewhat influenced by Frank, who was adamant that he would never move anywhere and thus, none of the rest of us could either.

112 **Q**: *(L)* That is not the point that we were talking about. We were not talking about moving out of fear. We were talking about moving out of the simple desire to not live in this area any longer because we don't like it! I want to get out of the heat!

113 **A**: That is 3rd density in the extreme!!!

114 **Q**: *(T)* That is just something we decided to do, like Noah building the ark; we thought it would be a good idea.

115 **A**: Then do it, but don't expect us to be there![6]

116 **Q**: *(L)* Since Terry and Jan have the urge to acquire larger space for themselves, what would you propose they do if not move to North Carolina?

117 **A**: Does larger space automatically equate long distance move?

118 **Q**: *(J)* No, it doesn't, but I don't want to spend the kind of money required to get a larger house in St. Petersburg. This is something we have talked about for a long time.

119 **A**: Is St. Petersburg your only option?

120 **Q**: *(J)* We don't know, we have to find that out. It depends on what happens with jobs and other things. *(L)* Is my financial situation blocked because of my plans and ideas about moving?

121 **A**: Maybe.

122 **Q**: *(L)* If I changed my thought patterns in that regard, would my financial situation become unblocked?

123 **A**: If you open your mind to any and all possibilities, this always unblocks.

124 **Q**: *(J)* Well, that is what we are trying to do, and one of the possibilities is moving to North Carolina. *(L)* OK, I say that I don't know what the Universe wants me to do. I am just waiting to see, and waiting for direction. What more can I do?

A: Good! 125

Q: *(J)* That's what we are doing. We 126
are trying to open our minds up to all the possibilities. Something may open up here, or in St. Pete, or somewhere else. We don't know. And, unless we open all the doors to find the one that's right, we have to shake all the bushes.

A: As long as you wish to communicate 127
with us, and learn from the information we are sharing with you, multitudes of possibilities will present themselves to you.

Q: *(L)* Does this mean even for my hus- 128
band, that he will get a good job? Is his potential also connected to this communication?

A: If a "good job" is what he desires, 129
yes, however, if others are trying to convince him that that is what he desires, then there will continue to be blocking of the "flow" taking place! L___ is of the utmost importance to us!

Q: *(L)* Why do I keep having dreams of 130
him abandoning me and the kids when the UFOs start landing?

A: Discover. 131

Q: *(J)* That's your fear. *(L)* OK, you 132
say he is of the utmost importance. Could you give us a clue about that, please?

A: All are. 133

Q: *(L)* OK, he would like to have some 134
advice as to how to shape his life from

[6] At the time, I felt that this was a strong influence from Frank, who was very much against anyone making any changes at all, let alone moving.

this point on?

135 **A**: Do what you really want to, and all else will fall into place, but don't procrastinate or "dream your life away."

136 **Q**: *(L)* OK, have we pretty much exhausted this subject and should we move onto something else here?

137 **A**: Up to you.

138 **Q**: *(J)* I think we have pretty much exhausted the subject. We don't know what is going to happen and we are just waiting to see what the Universe has to offer.

139 **A**: Good! Cope.

Q: *(L)* What does cope refer to? 140

A: You. 141

Q: *(L)* I have to cope with what is go- 142
ing on?

A: All. 143

Q: *(J)* That's what we are doing, one 144
day at a time.

A: Laura is dragging so badly that the 145
channel is oscillating. Save for better circumstances.

Q: *(L)* Then, we will say goodnight. 146

A: Goodnight. 147

End of Session

May 20, 1995

A conference is referenced in this session. Since we attended several, I had to ask Terry about this one specifically and he wrote back:

> This was the 2nd Annual Tampa UFO Conference at the Holiday Inn Crown Plaza in Tampa. May 19–21. It was put on by Project Awareness. You, Frank, Susan, Jan and I went. Speakers included Dr. David Jacobs, Michael Lindemann and Linda Howe. I remember that we commented on how Lindemann was acting weird even for him and Linda Howe seemed to be worried-going-on-scared about something. Howe and Lindemann were very agitated and didn't look to be in agreement on what to do. Interesting conference.

Terry's remarks jogged my memory. This was the conference where Linda Howe was talking about a case of cow mutilation she investigated and when she asked the farmer what he saw, he said that the cow just 'floated' up into the air into the bottom of a UFO. She was quite convinced from the evidence and from speaking with the guy that he was telling the truth. Her voice was shaking as she told the story and she kept losing it with her slideshow clicker thing. People do have a hard time dealing with the hyperdimensional aspect...

There was also scuttlebutt going around that Lindemann and Howe and some of the other speakers had just come from a meeting at Bob Bigelow's ranch. A relatively recent article about Bigelow appeared on the internet site *Intellihub*, an excerpt of which follows here:

> A strange FAA directive issued back in 2010 shows that the US government has in fact deferred all FAA UFO reports to Bigelow Aerospace, raising eyebrows in the UFO investigative community.
>
> MUFON and the FAA have been bottlenecked for their UFO information regarding UFO and/or alien technologies and the funnel leads straight to the man himself, Robert Bigelow, who

> was recently confronted by Jesse Ventura on this very matter in Utah after Ventura's "Tru TV" crew investigated Robert Bigelow's "Skinwalker Ranch".
>
> Yes, you just read that right, "Skinwalker Ranch" in Northeastern Utah. This facility is owned by Robert Bigelow and according to information leaked by a government official, "Skinwalker Ranch" is the site of a human murder in an encounter with aliens. During this battle one of Bigelow's security agents was allegedly killed.
>
> Robert Bigelow has even bough in to MUFON on a secret level offering a $750,00 one year grant to siphoning information from their database hiding it from public view.
>
> Why does this ultra rich man have such a fascination with this stuff?[1]

Something very strange there. And it seems that a number of UFO/alien researchers may have been co-opted into the plan.

Anyway, after the previous session, which felt a bit 'off' in respect of the remarks of the Cs about our discussions of moving, during the week prior to this session I had decided to do a spirit 'viewing' of the board work in general. As noted previously, for those unfamiliar with the process, I have made a series of videos that describe it and give examples, which are available for free on the internet. You will see that it is similar to 'remote viewing'. In the case of this spirit viewing, I did not use Frank as the medium but rather my daughter. As I have said, I no longer fully trusted Frank and was trying various approaches to get a better idea of what was going on.

As a result of what was shown in this spirit viewing, we decided to mentally surround ourselves with light prior to beginning this session. The Cs immediately took us to task about this, which was unsettling. In my opinion, it was not a very satisfactory session, though interesting things were said about underground tunnels. How true they might be is questionable. However, researcher Richard Sauder has studied this and found quite a few bits of compelling evidence (including patents for tunneling machinery) that such a network does exist in some places. I think we were all so new to the idea, and creeped out by it, that

[1] https://www.intellihub.com/mufon-ufo-data-deferred-bigelow-areospace 28 Feb. 2014

we were mostly interested in finding out if there was a tunnel nearby where a Mothman was going to jump out and get us! Yes, sometimes the sessions were like that!

Participants: 'Frank', Laura, Jan and Terry, Sue V

1 **Q**: Hello.

2 **A**: Two messages.

3 **Q**: *(L)* Who do we have with us?

4 **A**: Rituals restrict channel!

5 **Q**: *(L)* We weren't doing a ritual, we were just surrounding ourselves with light. Is there something wrong with surrounding ourselves with light and creating light energy?

6 **A**: Rituals are rituals.

7 **Q**: *(L)* Who do we have with us tonight?

8 **A**: Sonow.

9 **Q**: *(L)* And where are you from?

10 **A**: Cassiopaea.

11 **Q**: *(L)* OK, what are the messages?

12 **A**: That was one, the other is be careful with exposure to those who are still blossoming!

13 **Q**: *(L)* And who are they? *(J)* The kids were in here. *(L)* Do you have any other messages for us this evening?

14 **A**: Open.

15 **Q**: *(L)* You are open. OK. [My daughter] did a [remote] viewing the other night of us doing this work. In this viewing she saw us around the table, and she saw a pyramid in the center of the table. What did the pyramid represent?

A: Energy focuser. 16

Q: *(L)* She also saw another person standing in a corner. Could you tell us who that person was? 17

A: Just viewer, you attract a lot of those in 3rd density and 5th density as well! 18

Q: *(L)* She also saw a lamp hanging over the table. What does the lamp represent? 19

A: Not lamp, was light, represents light channel to level 6. 20

Q: *(L)* She also saw a green glow surrounding us and green slime oozing out of the pyramid all over our hands. What did this represent? 21

A: Was interference in reading coming from level 4 STS. 22

Q: *(T)* Was this what she saw in reference to last week's work? 23

A: General. 24

Q: *(L)* Was what she was seeing interference in our work or interference in her viewing? 25

A: The latter. 26

Q: *(L)* So, STS was interfering in her viewing to cast a different light on it? 27

[2]I have certainly obtained information via remote viewing or spirit viewing that I would consider corrupt, so it is quite possible for that to happen. But in this case, I don't think that was what was happening. I think that the images that my daughter saw were close to accurate and that there was corruption in the channel, though it usually only affected selected things.

28 **A**: Yes.[2]

29 **Q**: *(L)* OK, last week we received information that said if we moved to North Carolina, that you would not be there. We felt very strange about this because we felt that our connection with you was something that extended throughout space and time. We had a very negative reaction to that. We would like to have comments on that subject.

30 **A**: Not point, you were brought together as a result of many confluences of energy transfers for a purpose! You are always free to pursue any path you choose, however, if you concentrate on 3rd level matters such as your physical location, you risk creating rifts within your group! This is because such thoughts and potential actions will strengthen 3rd level STS feelings within each member, thus risking breakup of channel. Now, please realize, you have a unique combination of forces working through all of you that brought you all to this point. This is fragile, and any major changes in the chemistry will inevitably change "the whole picture."

31 **Q**: *(L)* By "major changes", do you mean members of the group leaving?

32 **A**: We are not finished with the message. If you were to move your physical locator, it would not be possible to satisfy each member equally therefore, rifts would develop. Now, consider this, you have all chosen to be in this location. Some chose this when on level 5 even! So, perceived dissatisfactions with locator are transitory, and like so much else, merely the result and symptomatic of the changes occurring within, as well as 4th level STS attack! Many other groups have been successfully misled by perceived need to relocate, with predictable results! Suggest you avoid joining them![3]

Q: *(F)* Based on what has been said 33
before, part of the way we were all brought together was by being physically in proximity to one another. *(J)* Right! *(F)* And if we disrupt that... *(SV)* And we chose it, some of us, from 5th level, so it is sort of preordained that we do this. *(F)* Right! And there are so many factors delicately placed in this situation, that any movement... *(L)* It would actually be... if we tried to go and move as a group, someplace else, some of us would be dissatisfied with the idea of moving, and therefore that would actually create personal problems between us, which would drive the group apart. *(F)* On a small scale, it is similar to when a husband and wife decide to move... "I'll go because I love you and you want to go..." and then they are miserable. *(SV)* The Cayce readings say that many aspects of our lives are decided beforehand on 5th level. So, we must have all gotten together there and decided we were going to all come to New Port Richey and do this! *(L)* New Port Richey! *(J)* The reality of our situation is that we want to get out of our tiny little house and into another... *(L)* Well, the way this was put, it sounds like you can't even move out of your house! *(J)* Oh, no! They have already told us that we can do

[3]Now, all of this message seems to be very reasonable and I would even say accurate for that particular point in space and time. The importance of this cannot be overstated. But I still feel that there was a strong emotional slant imposed on it by Frank.

that! *(T)* No, they just indicated that we shouldn't move from this general location. That is the way I understand it. *(L)* Last week it was pretty short... *(J)* But, on the other hand, maybe they have worked pretty hard getting this project cranked up with all of us being as hard-headed as we are... [Laughter] *(T)* Look how long it took us to get up here! *(J)* It is not like this is new... Terry and I have been talking about moving for years... we may do it someday. *(SV)* I like it here. *(T)* We don't know what is going to transpire. *(F)* If everybody decided together to go to North Carolina... *(L)* And we were all happy with the decision... *(F)* But right now I don't feel like going there... *(L)* And [my husband] doesn't... *(F)* Something else interesting about dissatisfaction being transitory and part of inner changes and attack... I am not dissatisfied with where I am physically, but with who I am and what I am and everything else in my life, which would be precisely the same if I were in North Carolina... *(L)* It wouldn't matter, your physical location wouldn't matter... *(F)* Right, so... *(J)* Our situation is that we have to get out of that house. *(F)* Well, let's ask... *(L)* I think we should ask if we were all equally agreed to go to another location, would the channel work someplace else?

34 **A**: Yes, but that is unlikely.

35 **Q**: *(J)* We know that. *(L)* This leads to the assumption and the realization, which I have long held, and have picked at, and maybe it is time for you guys to take the gloves off: what is it that is going on here? Obviously things have been brought to a certain point for a reason. You have hinted at things, alluded to things, you have...

A: You will discover this as the process 36
continues to unfold, if you were to be given a "preview" you would become "unglued."

Q: *(L)* I don't want to know! *(T)* Give 37
me a preview! *(L)* We don't want a preview! *(J)* We have been having some pretty weird dreams here...

A: No. 38

Q: *(T)* Is this group complete? 39

A: Open. 40

Q: *(T)* Are there others yet to come? 41

A: Very distinct possibility. 42

Q: *(T)* That may be part of why we 43
can't move, if there are others around here that are supposed to come. *(J)* I think as far as the group moving... *(T)* There are others that are supposed to come, they are not here yet... *(J)* It would have to be... in order for the group to be able to move as a group, Susan and Frank and LM would have to change their minds about wanting to move... *(T)* No, no, no... *(J)* Yes... *(T)* If we were to move the thing... there are others who are supposed to be in this group and they are not here yet, so it is not the right timing... if we were all in agreement to move... we don't have the whole group and there would be no way for the rest of the group to get to us... *(L)* The statement was made that we all chose to be here. Is that correct?

A: Yes. 44

Q: *(L)* And we have chosen to work to- 45
gether for a distinct purpose, is that correct?

A: Close. 46

Q: *(L)* And we have all, whether to- 47
gether or individually, we all have a very distinct purpose and pathway to

follow in this life that was pre-chosen and pre-set, is that correct?

48 **A**: That is true for all on level three.

49 **Q**: *(L)* And there is no one in this room who is here by mistake, is that correct?

50 **A**: Yes.

51 **Q**: *(L)* And there is no one in this room who doesn't need to get about finding out what their purpose is by doing each day what is in front of them, is that correct?

52 **A**: Close. But, beware of attack and desires to "push" things in any given direction, which is a manifestation of attack! Just let things fall into place naturally!

53 **Q**: *(L)* OK. *(J)* Can you give any input as to Terry's and my situation, regarding our house being too small, and needing to find something else?

54 **A**: There is no reason you cannot move from your current residence.

55 **Q**: *(L)* OK, a strange thing happened the other day. Our neighbor, who has always been kind of aloof from us, came over and offered [my husband] help in getting a job. Why?

56 **A**: We will occasionally throw "perks" in your direction, just to help you out, when you have had periods of equally balanced misfortune!

57 **Q**: *(L)* Well, is he going to get the job?

58 **A**: Up to LM, these are perks, not guarantees. In other words, we do not lead by the hand.

59 **Q**: *(L)* Well, if you can get him into a job, I thank you.

A: You are welcome. 60

Q: *(L)* Now, about the conference. *(T)* 61
Is it all on the up and up?

A: No. 62

Q: *(T)* As far as the speakers go? 63

A: No. 64

Q: *(T)* Was Mr. O'Leary playing with 65
a full deck?

A: Open. 66

Q: [Laughter] *(L)* How about our 67
putting our brochure out there? *(T)* Yes, was it a good idea the way we did it?[4]

A: Might be wise to be controlled in 68
distribution methods, rather than scattering "to the four winds."

Q: *(L)* But you said to rattle the 69
bushes. *(J)* Should I not give G___-more copies of the brochure?

A: Open. 70

Q: *(L)* Are you saying that what we 71
did was a good idea because it was for a specific audience rather than random distribution?

A: You have been less than careful to 72
this point.

Q: *(L)* Well when we asked you before- 73
hand, you wouldn't tell us anything. Why are you saying this post-event? Post facto!

A: Discover. By the way, rattling 74
the bushes can be accomplished with a broom, not only a howitzer.

Q: *(L)* Well, we thought we were being 75
very restrained in what we put out...

[4] Jan had created some very nice tri-fold brochures explaining about the Cassiopaea Experiment and the kind of information we were receiving and inviting the reader to contact us for more details.

76 **A**: Recently, you have settled down some, yes.

77 **Q**: *(L)* What do you mean 'recently' we have settled down some? Is that me, specifically?

78 **A**: Earlier, you were less careful than now.

79 **Q**: *(T)* That was before you started telling us about the people that are waiting to eat us alive! *(L)* That is before we had all our attacks. We have been discussing the idea of putting this information out on the computer net.

80 **A**: Okay, but suggest no bylines, or "handles."

81 **Q**: *(T)* In other words, don't put our names out there?

82 **A**: Yes.

83 **Q**: *(T)* Well, we were talking about not putting the bio on the Net, just the channel info and address for more info.

84 **A**: Up to you.

85 **Q**: *(J)* I think we could do a condensed bio with no names... *(L)* Well, why don't we put there naked? For all they know, the Cassiopaeans downloaded it themselves. *(T)* They will be able to ID us. *(L)* Well, previously, you were very interested in us getting on the computer net. AOL was not worth the money....

86 **A**: Your opinion and you were characteristically impatient.

87 **Q**: *(L)* Well, I wasn't so impatient as broke. I was paying long distance charges and the Net cost me over $150 dollars that month.

88 **A**: You were not aware of tremendous progress made, due to "tunnel vision" and preconceived notions of what defines progress.

Q: *(T)* Were you using the message 89
boards? *(L)* No, I didn't know how and I couldn't afford to hack through the system and figure it out. *(T)* Well, if I had known, I would have showed you how. *(L)* See, it wasn't my fault, it was Terry's. He didn't show me how to use the thing! I was paying by the hour, not just impatient.

A: We did not place individual blame. 90

Q: *(J)* We need to plan a little bit more. 91
(L) We want to know if there are really underground tunnels all over the place that many people have reported being taken to in alien abductions?

A: Yes. 92

Q: *(T)* Have they been there a long 93
time?

A: Subjective. 94

Q: *(T)* Do they predate humanity?[5] 95

A: A few. 96

Q: *(T)* Are they equivalent of subway 97
tunnels, to get from one place to another?

A: Okay. 98

Q: *(T)* Is there a set of trains or what- 99
ever to move from place to place?

A: No. 100

Q: *(T)* Is there any kind of high-tech 101
gear in place in these tunnels to move from place to place?

A: Subjective. 102

Q: *(L)* How do they travel through 103
these tunnels?

A: Electromagnetically. 104

[5] *High Strangeness* "Appendix"

105 **Q**: *(T)* Can individuals be transported through the tunnels without benefit of equipment? Or do they use some kind of gadgetry?

106 **A**: All of the above.

107 **Q**: *(L)* Who occupies these tunnels?

108 **A**: Various.

109 **Q**: *(T)* Are there still beings in there?

110 **A**: Yes.

111 **Q**: *(T)* Are humans involved in this?

112 **A**: Yes.

113 **Q**: *(T)* Were there humans involved in digging some of these tunnels?

114 **A**: Some.

115 **Q**: *(T)* Before that, there were other beings that were not human?

116 **A**: Yes.

117 **Q**: *(T)* Are those other beings still down there?

118 **A**: Yes.

119 **Q**: *(T)* Is this a worldwide network of tunnels?

120 **A**: No.

121 **Q**: *(T)* Where are most of the tunnels?

122 **A**: North America, since that is the "capitol" of STS, currently.

123 **Q**: *(T)* Are there other tunnel systems other than in North America?

124 **A**: Yes.

125 **Q**: *(T)* Does it depend on where the STS alignment is as to whether they are operational?

126 **A**: Not point, just single factor.

127 **Q**: *(T)* Do any of the tunnels lead to Antarctica?

128 **A**: No.

Q: *(T)* Is there any way of getting to 129
Antarctica through the tunnel systems even if you have to come to the surface occasionally?

A: Okay. 130

Q: *(L)* Are humans ever taken into 131
these tunnels or places underground... *(T)* Against their will?

A: Sometimes. 132

Q: *(T)* Is there some kind of under- 133
ground base in Antarctica?

A: Yes. Eight. 134

Q: *(T)* Are they related to the tunnels 135
in time?

A: Vague. 136

Q: *(T)* Were any of those bases under- 137
ground in Antarctica built by the Germans during World War II?

A: Sect. 138

Q: *(T)* Nazis? 139

A: Remember, all is structured in cy- 140
cles and circles.

Q: *(L)* In other words, these tunnels 141
were built by and belong to the Consortium, is that correct?

A: Circles within circles. 142

Q: *(L)* Masons? 143

A: One example of concept. 144

Q: *(T)* Jan and I have a friend who has 145
told us about someone she knew who found entrances to tunnel systems in North America. One of the entrances was in the Adirondacks, another was in the Mammoth Cave system. Was what she was told true?

A: Yes, but there are thousands of en- 146
trances. Are you ready for a "shocker?"

147 **Q**: *(J)* Oh, you know we are always ready for a shocker. *(L)* Sure! *(T)* OK, give us the shocker. *(J)* We're ready!

148 **A**: There is a tunnel right beneath your feet!

149 **Q**: *(J)* I knew they were going to say that. *(T)* Of course! Is that where the digging is going to go from the basement?

150 **A**: Up to you!

151 **Q**: *(L)* How deep under our feet?

152 **A**: 2000 feet.

153 **Q**: *(T)* Is anything moving in that tunnel?

154 **A**: Vague.

155 **Q**: *(T)* Is that tunnel being used?

156 **A**: Yes.

157 **Q**: *(L)* Right at this second?

158 **A**: Open.

159 **Q**: *(L)* Who uses it more than anybody else?

160 **A**: Open.

161 **Q**: *(T)* Are there humans down there?

162 **A**: Have been, listen for sound anomalies such as loud sonic boom like noises and vague motorized sounds.

163 **Q**: *(L)* Is there any kind of electronic gadgetry down there causing my appliances to keep breaking down?

164 **A**: Maybe.

165 **Q**: *(L)* What is wrong with my air conditioner?

166 **A**: Fuse.

167 **Q**: *(SV)* Does this tunnel hook up with the doorway in the old stone house on Grand Boulevard that nobody has been able to open or cut through?

A: Open. 168

Q: *(T)* Is there an entrance to this tunnel underneath us somewhere in this area? 169

A: Near power plant. 170

Q: *(T)* Crystal River? *(L)* No, Anclote. *(T)* Is that why the power plant is built there? 171

A: Related; old Nike base. 172

Q: *(T)* What direction does this tunnel run that is underneath us? 173

A: East-West. 174

Q: *(T)* Out under the Gulf of Mexico? 175

A: No. 176

Q: *(T)* Where does the west end? 177

A: Just described. 178

Q: *(L)* The power plant. *(T)* OK, where does the east end go? 179

A: Near Lakeland. 180

Q: *(T)* What is in Lakeland that would have a tunnel entrance in it? Why Lakeland? 181

A: Not issue. 182

Q: *(L)* What is on the surface may have no relationship to the tunnel. 183

A: Transfer point and redirector. 184

Q: *(T)* Is there another tunnel that comes into this tunnel, that intersects this tunnel?[6] 185

A: Yes. 186

Q: *(T)* Near Lakeland? 187

A: Yes. 188

[6] *High Strangeness* "Appendix"

189 **Q**: *(T)* Is that what you are talking about? A transfer point?

190 **A**: Yes.

191 **Q**: *(T)* Does that tunnel travel north-south?

192 **A**: Yes.

193 **Q**: *(T)* Does that run up the East Coast?

194 **A**: No.

195 **Q**: *(L)* Lakeland is in the center of the state. *(T)* Where does it go? Are these side tunnels to a main tunnel that runs along the East Coast?

196 **A**: All are interconnected.

197 **Q**: *(T)* So, it is like a subway or bus line? Is there a tunnel farther south of here?

198 **A**: Yes.

199 **Q**: *(T)* How far does the farthest south tunnel go?

200 **A**: Antarctica.

201 **Q**: *(J)* Is there a tunnel near our house, in St. Petersburg?

202 **A**: No.

203 **Q**: *(T)* Is there a tunnel to MacDill [AFB]?

204 **A**: No.

205 **Q**: *(L)* I think that, in general, importance we would ascribe to surface structures may not be a consideration here. *(T)* I was thinking about the military base. *(L)* I would think that the tunnels bear no relationship to the structures under the surface except in certain instances. *(J)* But, what got there first, the tunnels or the structures on the surface? *(L)* Obviously the tunnels have been there for a long time, and perhaps, in certain instances a situation may be manipulated so that a specific structure is built to facilitate the tunnel usage, but the fact that Lakeland is built over it may not be relevant. *(T)* There is no entrance to the tunnel system near Lakeland?

A: Yes. 206

Q: *(J)* And there are no tunnels down in Pinellas? 207

A: Phosphate plant. 208

Q: *(T)* There's a tunnel entrance in the phosphate plant? *(L)* I've got one more question about the tunnels. 209

A: Mine. 210

Q: *(T)* There is a tunnel entrance in one of the phosphate mines? 211

A: Yes. 212

Q: *(J)* Was the placement of this tunnel under our feet the reason Laura got this house?[7] 213

A: No. 214

Q: *(T)* Does the placement of the tunnel underneath us have something to do with the channel? 215

A: Maybe. 216

Q: *(T)* Because of the greater EM underneath us; we are tapping into that EM energy? 217

A: Helps in offhand way. 218

End of Session

[7] *High Strangeness* "Appendix"

May 26, 1995

Participants: 'Frank', Laura, Susan

1 **Q**: *(L)* Hello.

2 **A**: Hello. Why not Susan?

3 **Q**: *(L)* Well, I don't know. Do you want Susan at the board?

4 **A**: Up to you and her; we just asked; no biggy.

5 **Q**: *(L)* Well, she is taking notes.

6 **A**: Okay. Hello.

7 **Q**: *(L)* Could we have your name, please?

8 **A**: Rohr.

9 **Q**: *(L)* And where are you from?

10 **A**: Cassiopaea.

11 **Q**: *(L)* OK, we have several questions tonight...

12 **A**: Fire away.

13 **Q**: *(L)* The first question is regarding the warning of attack Terry and Jan received earlier this year...

14 **A**: Yes.

15 **Q**: We are concerned that they are currently under attack.

16 **A**: Yes.

17 **Q**: *(L)* Terry was offered a job that was interesting, and this offer came, seemingly under exceptional conditions, that is, during the interview, which almost never happens. When he got into the job, he felt that it was not the place for him to be and he quit after four hours. His perception, as I understand it, is that his quitting of this job was an act of protection stemming from his knowledge that it was not the place for him to be. I wondered, and my clue was his word 'feeling', that because he was 'feeling negative' toward the job, and therefore perceived the job in a negative way, he quit what may have been an excellent point of contact for other things, people and experiences that he may have been in line for. Interestingly, Jan felt the same way. Now, my question...

A: You are correct. 18

Q: *(L)* So, he quit the job and this is part of attack? 19

A: Yes. Resulting from. 20

Q: *(L)* What are the ramifications of this? Is this indicative of a possible financial bind? Like getting into the financial soup? 21

A: Open. 22

Q: *(L)* So, at this point, it will just have to be dealt with, is that correct? 23

A: Soups come in a variety of flavors. 24

Q: *(L)* So, it is not necessarily that he will have financial problems; it could be something else altogether? 25

A: Yes. 26

Q: *(L)* Well, I think Terry has been having some pretty negative feelings, as 27 have I, in general. Is this a correct assessment?

28 **A**: Point out to him that feelings are best to be aired, lest they fester. Communication is the key.

29 **Q**: *(L)* Yes, we know that, and I tried to communicate some of my concerns to him on the phone, but he seemed to be blocking me because when I pointed out that feelings are not to be trusted, he said that he felt that *his* feelings *are* reliable in this case. He kept using the word 'feeling', which rang in my head like a warning, especially after what I have been through recently. I tried to communicate this.

30 **A**: Terry is the one who needs to communicate.

[Phone rings and time out is taken to talk to Jan and Terry!]

31 **Q**: *(L)* Were you listening to our conversation?

32 **A**: Of course as always.

33 **Q**: *(L)* That is so comforting. *(SV)* Yes. Remember when I whispered to you because I didn't want the Cassiopaeans to hear?! *(L)* Right!

34 **A**: Ha! Ha!

35 **Q**: *(SV)* They did hear me! *(L)* OK. I just talked to him about what we are discussing, and Terry is pretty convinced that he is on the right track and he has me pretty convinced at this point, too.

A: Attack, just look at what he is feeling about Frank and SV, do you not recognize the "symptoms?"[1] 36

Q: *(L)* Yes, I guess I do since I just went through that and I seem to be suffering in similar ways from time to time. Could you give us some advice on how we can break the attack? 37

A: He needs to air it out with proper parties. 38

Q: *(L)* So, if we all aired everything out, it would help to break the attack? 39

A: Yes. Pops like a balloon. 40

Q: *(L)* Now, regarding my own situation... Terry and Jan have just offered assistance which is welcome and timely, but is only a band-aid... 41

A: We provide, and when ready, huge sums will come to all. 42

Q: *(SV)* It all depends on what you consider 'huge'. *(L)* Well, I consider 'huge' in the millions. *(SV)* Well, that is beyond my comprehension. What would I do with that much? *(L)* I could help you out with that! *(SV)* I was hoping you would say that! 43

A: You will manage! 44

Q: [Laughter] *(L)* OK, well, I have made the decision that I am not going to push to do anything, including moving, unless and until I am sure that that is what I am supposed to do. I am sure that you will let us know. 45

A: Okay. 46

[1]Terry was very sensitive and had early suggested to me that 1) Frank wasn't the only 'channel'; 2) Frank could bring corruption in; 3) Sue was a negative influence. I spent a lot of time trying to smooth these things over but, in the end, overall, Terry was correct. But it wasn't so much that Frank and Sue were so negative, but rather that they were not willing to work on their negativity. They did not have a sincere desire to get to the truth and it was that, more than anything, that was the corrupting influence.

47 **Q**: *(L)* So, we can just work on the house and work on making ourselves happy where we are.

48 **A**: Good girl!

49 **Q**: *(L)* We had our aura photographs taken at the metaphysical conference. Were those photographs accurate in color representation?[2]

50 **A**: Yes.

51 **Q**: *(L)* Frank had a very lovely aura. There are, however, a couple of things that are confusing. In SV's aura, the colors are very compact and close into her body. What does this indicate?

52 **A**: Stomach problems.

53 **Q**: *(L)* What could she do to alleviate her stomach problems?

54 **A**: Change her diet "big time!"

55 **Q**: *(L)* What is there about her diet...

56 **A**: Starch and fats must be reduced steadily.[3]

57 **Q**: *(L)* And what should she add?

58 **A**: Fruit.

59 **Q**: *(L)* Any particular kind?

60 **A**: All.

61 **Q**: *(L)* Is microwaved food harmful to the person who consumes it?

A: Not much. 62

Q: *(L)* Now, are the colors in SV's aura 63
fairly representative of what her colors usually are?

A: Parameters change within resulting 64
in aura changes.[4]

Q: *(L)* Can the color of your aura re- 65
flect psychic attack?

A: Maybe. 66

Q: *(L)* We gave some of our material 67
to Michael Lindemann.[5] I would like to know what his ultimate reaction to it will be? He did not seem to be favorably impressed, but I don't think he read it, either.

A: Let it seep. 68

Q: *(L)* I also left some material with 69
Linda Howe. Is this going to help her in any way?

A: Sinking in. 70

Q: *(L)* Are we going to get any reper- 71
cussions or responses to the distribution of this material?

A: Yes. 72

Q: *(L)* Are we going to get any positive 73
responses?

A: Yes. We direct you as long as you 74
have faith in us, as we are you! Attack is always designed to destroy that faith,

[2]The UFO-Metaphysical conference in Tampa mentioned in previous session. I was operating under the assumption that aura photography was what it presented itself to be. It is not. Stay tuned because this comes up again in the sessions.

[3]Sue did pretty much live on fast foods, pastry and coffee. The hydrogenated fats and sugars contained in those types of things are definitely deadly!

[4]Considering what we learned later about 'aura cameras', the Cs could have said something here about the fact that they really don't take pictures of auras. But they didn't.

[5]Details on Lindemann: www.ufoevidence.org/researchers/detail100.htm. My personal opinion about him is rather mixed; I can't decide if he is a sincere seeker or part of the cover-up. Considering the events described in the session about the UFO conference, I tend a bit toward the latter.

either directly or indirectly. Think of the instances, to see if there is a familiar pattern to the "root."

75 **Q**: *(L)* So, attack is always directed at undermining our faith.

76 **A**: In a roundabout way.[6]

77 **Q**: *(L)* Now, there is a real issue here about SV working on different people who may be sources of negative energy. Is just knowing that there may be negative energies sufficient protection to allow her to work on just anybody?

78 **A**: Strengthens shield if knowledge is utilized properly through psychic channels, therefore, exposure is good if care, prudence and awareness are applied.

79 **Q**: *(F)* Does this mean that Terry, by withdrawing into a protective shell, has deprived himself of an opportunity to gain strength in this regard?[7]

A: Yes. It is lack of faith in what is 80
brought forth for him as well. Tends to weaken the shield.

Q: *(SV)* Maybe I just shouldn't tell 81
anyone who I work on? *(L)* No, we can't not tell each other what we are doing because that is a lack of faith in each other. We can't baby ourselves or each other. *(F)* It all has to be aired out some time or another. *(L)* Can I ask something about the perpendicular realities?

A: Wait for Terry and Jan be present 82
for answers.[8]

Q: *(L)* OK, I'm jumping the gun be- 83
cause I am eaten up with curiosity.

A: Goodnight. 84

End of Session

---

[6] *High Strangeness* 10; *The Wave* 3, 68

[7] At the end of the previous session there had been a discussion during the course of which, Sue revealed that she was still interacting with the metaphysical church group that had caused me so many problems as described in *The Wave*. Terry had gotten quite upset about it and became very confrontational toward Sue. I think that was probably why Terry and Jan were not present at this particular session. Terry just didn't want to be around Sue. At this point in time, I can't say that he was wrong.

[8] I don't know if the request for Terry and Jan to be present was because the Cs knew that I was energetically outflanked when in the presence of Frank and Sue and that more accurate information was possible with them present, or whether it was Frank who liked them there because he needed their energy too. But it certainly is true that, overall, some of the best early sessions were those when Terry and Jan were present.

May 27, 1995

On this day, we attended another meeting of the local MUFON group where a physicist, Prof. Ruggero Santilli, was scheduled to speak. At that same meeting were many of the people who had attended our 'demonstration session' back on 11 March and some of them gathered around during the break to ask us further questions about the experiment in channelling. Prof. Santilli joined them, was given a brief synopsis of the situation, and was intrigued enough to ask to attend a session. As it happened, we were planning one that very evening, so after the meeting, we all drove back to the house with Prof. Santilli and his wife following, and settled down to see what would happen.

Participants: 'Frank', Laura, Jan and Terry, Carla and Roger Santilli

1 **A**: Rouswo.

2 **Q**: *(L)* I guess that is the name. Hello, how are you this evening? *(T)* Who do we have with us?

3 **A**: Name given.

4 **Q**: *(T)* Where are you from?

5 **A**: Cassiopaea.

6 **Q**: *(T)* How are you tonight?

7 **A**: Okay.

8 **Q**: *(T)* We are doing OK too. We have some company this evening.

9 **A**: Good.

10 **Q**: *(T)* Roger and Carla Santilli are with us. Roger has some questions to ask later.

11 **A**: Hello, Roger.

Q: *(RS)* Hello. *(T)* Do you have anything you want to talk about to start off with? 12

A: Channel open. 13

Q: *(L)* Alright, let's start off with the question that Susan and I have wondered about: Is it alright if I give the Reiki initiation during the Mercury retrograde? 14

A: Of course! 15

Q: *(L)* That's what I thought. Go ahead, Roger, ask whatever you like. *(RS)* I want to know whether we can have any clues on the propulsion systems of UFOs? 16

A: Sure! 17

Q: *(RS)* What's the mechanism of the propulsion?[1] 18

A: This is difficult to answer when posed in such a manner, as we are talk- 19

[1] *The Wave* 4

ing about multiple realities, density levels and various modes as well!!

20 **Q**: *(RS)* Is the gravity experienced by an anti-particle in the field of matter attractive or repulsive?

21 **A**: Repulsive when thought of in the way that is parallel to your studies, but, as we alluded to in the previous answer, there are more realms involved besides the one with which you are most familiar.

22 **Q**: *(RS)* The next question is: particles move, matter moves, in our direction of time – do anti-particles, anti-matter, flow backward in time?

23 **A**: Think of it as merely one seventh of the equation, Roger!

24 **Q**: *(L)* Can we get an answer on whether this is the case strictly on the 3rd level of density?

25 **A**: Backward.

26 **Q**: *(RS)* Yes! I am interested in the propulsion systems of UFOs. The only way that I can perceive traveling the long distances involved in interstellar space is to have what is called a "space-time" machine. We cannot move the enormous distances unless you can fold, somehow, time and space. You cannot fold space unless you join it and fold time. You cannot have interstellar travel unless you have a space-time machine. But, a space-time machine means to also have the ability to move forward and backward in time, to manipulate time.

(L) Yes, you would have to cross distances and simultaneously move backward through time so that you would end up arriving wherever you are going essentially at the same moment that you left.

(RS) That is why I asked whether we can use anti-matter as a propulsion, because it would be repulsive in the right direction. The second question: whether, when we use anti-matter, we would move backward in time. Because, some of those objects, you see them moving, and they can be moving in space but not in time, or they could be moving in time but not in space. If you see a UFO, it does not mean that it is in our time. It could be in a completely different time. *(L)* And, they disappear sometimes right before the eyes of the observer, and the question is: where do they go? They could be standing still in space, but moving time. Or moving backwards.

(L) And, there are a lot of abductions reported where there is seemingly no time lost at all. They come in, haul the victim out, do whatever they do, and then they slide them back in a fraction of a second away, if not at the identical second they took the victim out!

(RS) Yes! This article I presented is exactly about this point! If, indeed, anti-particles have lift, then necessarily they have to go backward in time. Then they manipulate this: you can have an abduction any length of time inside the craft, but in our time, in our level three, it is zero time!

(L) Yes, exactly! And not only that, there is the phenomenon of the craft that looks small from the outside, but inside is huge!

(RS) That is all tied up in it! This is very exciting. I am learning the language. In our third level, the motion in space and time occurs via the change of the unit of time and space, therefore, can we change the unit?

27 **A**: Yes, this is precisely what we mean when we speak of "transiting from 4th to 3rd."

28 **Q**: *(RS)* So, when they travel from 4th to 3rd, they change the units. That is precisely what is in the article in the journal! [Holds up book.] This is published in the Ukraine. [Turns to page and displays diagrams and equations.] This is the experiment to test anti-gravity. There is a two-mile-long tunnel which is a vacuum inside. They suck the air out. The first measure is to shoot photons to identify, at the end of the two-mile tunnel, the no-gravity point. The second measure is to shoot a neutron, and we know that a neutron is attractive. So, after two miles, the energy is very, very low. So, there is no gravitational effect when the neutron hits the point. Then, the third step is to shoot an anti-neutron at the same time and see what happens. This experiment will resolve this issue that this board has answered very scientifically. We call it the gravity of anti-particles because we don't know. It can be down... Einstein predicts this as attractive as a neutron; anti-matter and matter have the same gravitational attraction. That's what Einstein says.

But, when Einstein's theory was proposed, in 1915, anti-matter wasn't discovered until 50 years later. If now, theoretically, the only way a particle, in our theory, can go up, can have lift, is if time is reversed. There is no other possibility. So, if this experiment is correct, then the space-time machine is absolutely a consequence and can be tested in a laboratory. You can have a particle moving backward and forward in time.

[Displays new diagram.] This is the other experiment which is, in this case, is done by putting a particle which is neutral and subjecting it to... since we don't have a bunch of anti-matter – ideally we would have a pellet of matter and replace it with anti-matter – we don't have a pellet of anti-matter, at this point, there are ways to do it though and it can be measured as to which way it moves, up or down.

Now, the question of the units, it is very important, a fundamental question, because, say, you are outside a UFO, and you see the UFO as big as a car, say, and people go inside and report this enormous interior. There is no other way to do this than by changing the unit. What is for us one inch, that unit is completely different inside. For us the unit is the same along the three directions. Now, if you are inside, they can have different units in different directions. This means that if you are outside a cube, and you go inside, the shape, not only the dimensions, but the shape even, can be different.

A: Density borderline cross awareness. 29
Does Roger have familiarity with density definitions?

Q: *(L)* Did we ever get a density defini- 30
tion, Terry? *(T)* Just about the seven levels. *(L)* OK, what is a density definition?

A: Review, using your own knowledge 31
base, i.e. network.

Q: *(L)* What do we understand about 32
density? *(T)* There are seven levels of density. *(L)* First level of density is rocks, minerals, plants. They have an awareness at that level. Rocks may even grow and move, but they do it so slowly that we cannot perceive it. Second level is the animal kingdom. This

density awareness relates to geometrical progression. The first level has the awareness of a line. The second level has awareness of a line moving at right angles to itself, or planes. 3rd density is human beings and we have the awareness of the plane moving at right angles to itself, but we can never experience this fully. We see things as three dimensional only because we create an illusion based on memory and knowledge. We can never know the other side or the inside while we are looking at any given side.

(J) The Witnesses in Heinlein's book could only tell what they actually saw. If you asked them the color of a barn, they would tell you that the side they could see was red. If you took them around to see the back and they saw that it was red also, and you then asked them what color it was after it was no longer in view, they would still say that the side they could see was red. If you asked them about the other side that they had seen, they would say that since they could no longer see it, it may have changed color so they would not attest to it.

(L) So, 3rd density is like that. We can only know things by our perception. So, if we extend the idea of 1st, to 2nd, to 3rd, to 4th, and try to understand what 4th density would be like, because then you would know the cup or other object all the way through at once. You would experience a sphere inside and out and all around all at once. We stretch for this...

(T) 4th density is inclusive of all the densities below it and an added density. 5th would be, again, 4th density nature turned at right angles to itself. The same for 6th and then 7th, which the Cassiopaeans call "The One." The completion point.

(L) And we have no idea of how to express these things. They have told us about Trans-Dimensional Atomic Remolecularizers and we asked them how to build one. They asked if we had a couple of days to sit and take direction.

(RS) I do! I do!

(L) We know, and we said the same, but then they asked us, where were we going to get the parts?

(RS) It would be like trying to build electronics in ancient Roman times...

(T) Or, telling a dog how to build a watch. Even if the dog understands how to build it, where is he going to get the parts?

(RS) This point of how deceptive is our perception has been proven scientifically with the seashells. Didn't we discuss about the seashells? *(T)* Yes. *(RS)* At the third level, is it true that the value of the dimension is changed by the available energy, or the energy is used to change the value of the units?

A: This concept crosses the density bar- 33
rier, not limited to level three.

Q: *(RS)* Goes up to level four. That's 34
the means of propulsion of the UFO.

A: Reason for exponential awareness 35
"explosion" is approach of Wave. Now, concentrate on visualization, answers are located there... After a period of contemplation, Roger to "hit upon" breakthrough question to solve puzzle currently occupying "center stage" of his psyche, with only one piece missing currently.[2]

[2]Jan's note: I take this to mean that Roger will be able to come up with questions

36 **Q**: *(T)* Starting with the 4th density, we are no longer confined to the physical. The key phrase is 'variability of physicality'. Once you move from 3rd density to 4th density, and we are all moving upward toward 7th density. When you raise your knowledge, your awareness, to a certain level, you can move to the next level. When we move from 3rd to 4th density, at that point, we have the ability to visualize and decide what our reality is. We create reality from fourth level on. So, at one point, there may not be a solid reality. It may all be energy, we would be light beings, so to speak. We could change that just by thinking about it and making a solid reality. Or, as solid as we wish. This point also, from 4th density up, there is no such thing as time as we perceive it. Our perception of time only exists in the first three densities. Each density perceives it differently.

(RS) What we perceive as back and forth in time, when we go to the fourth level, it doesn't exist anymore. Beings on that level can move back and forth through our density of time because, for them, it doesn't exist. It is all now. It is only one time.

(L) It is like a whole bunch of different doors, one says 1917, one says 1943, or whatever, and they can walk through whichever one they wish...

(T) There is the 'realm border'. The Earth is moving into a 4th density area of space. Or it is moving toward us, or both. This realm border, this crossover between densities, and it's also a crossover between dimensions – a quick sidebar on dimensions: dimensions, according to the Cassiopaeans are lateral realities; all possible realities of a density level, an infinite number; there is a difference between density and dimension.

(RS) This is a fascinating meeting because the answers to the question about moving mathematically from the third level to the fourth level, this change in the units, the answer is exactly what is proposed in my book. The answer, as given, is possible...

(T) We have been told that the universe teems with life at all levels, and that humans are just one selection.

(L) And what they are saying, I think, is that this oncoming realm border, this density change, is being felt and is stimulating consciousness. Essentially what has been said is that what is coming up for us is the ending of a 'grand cycle'. A grand cycle is 300,000 years... *(T)* Give or take a day... *(L)* ...as we measure time. At the beginning of this grand cycle, we were genetically altered to reduce our awareness and also genetically altered through our DNA to perceive time itself. It is in our DNA to be limited this way. Now, at the end of this 300,000-year cycle, a lot of people are reassembling this broken DNA as a result of the changes in energy, and that this is causing their mental powers and perceptions to expand exponentially. I think that they are telling you that this energy is acting on you in a way to allow you to have the breakthrough that you need to finish the puzzle that you have been working on. By having the concepts that you are being given now, you will be able to hold this

to access the Cassiopaean information in a way so that the information can be dispensed. Also that his awareness is exploding as a result of the oncoming Wave.

as a visual and this will give you the key.

(RS) I notice that if the question is not properly phrased... *(L)* You don't get your answer! Be specific.

37 **A**: Careful not to confuse with too much data that is not connected in the same concept arena, as visitor is concerned primarily with one direction; in order to familiarize let data be absorbed on schedule comfortable to researcher! Like trying to learn mathematics in broken dosages!

38 **Q**: *(L)* They are telling us not to tell you too much at once because it will take you away from the central question you are working on.

(RS) Also, I think we should report this work to the MUFON group!

(T) We offered to do this at the meeting and they don't want to do it. This does not fall within MUFON's guidelines.

(L) It [our material] is not nuts and bolts. *(RS)* But this has answered all the questions for the article! In an incredible way! It has answered all the fundamental questions.

(J) This is the first time that we have had someone present who has the technical background to understand what is going on and what kind of communication we are receiving.

(RS) Yes, it has me excited!

39 **A**: His energy has effect upon group.

40 **Q**: *(RS)* Two short questions and then I will stop...

41 **A**: Ask as many as you desire!

42 **Q**: *(RS)* In our level three, does the use of anti-matter change the sign of the unit? Does this imply the reversal of the sign of the unit of space and time?

A: Yes, but problem has always been for level three entities, that the "other" side is uncharted, therefore experimentation is not recommended, unless with assistance from level four through six STO. 43

Q: *(RS)* That is an incredible answer because this is traveling in time. First they said that by using energy you can change the numerical value of the units, and from this [transcriber's note: incomprehensible] you can make a [transcriber's note: incomprehensible] show. Now the question: how you can go backward in time? By changing the sign of the unit: plus one second and we move forward, if that unit is changed to minus one second, we move backward. So the question, whether by using anti-matter we can move backward. But their answer was saying... precisely, that we are moving from level three to level four. Last question and then I am through. 44

A: Not correct, Roger! 45

Q: *(L)* It's not going to be your last question! [Laughter] *(J)* They already said to ask as many as you desire! 46

A: This session has been designated for you! That is why we arranged for you to be here!! You are about to embark upon an extensive tour, whereby you will be communicating and networking, and in fact studying and researching with others of similar paths. The learning and knowledge gain that will result from this sojourn will have extremely major implications! Therefore, consider this to be your "night!" 47

Q: *(RS)* They insist on it! Then, I have another very important question! 48

In Greece, at this time, at the University of Xanthi [?], the nuclear physics laboratory at the university, there is a potentially fundamental experiment going on based on my studies and this book here [displays book] to search for fundamentally new source of energy by bombarding zinc 70 or molybdenum 100 via Gamma with 1.294 MeV energy. Will the experiment be successful... *(CS)* Ah ah... they will not answer that! *(J)* They may not touch that one.... *(RS)* Will zinc 70 be a new source of energy? Can these substances be new sources of energy?

49 **A**: All of the experiments you speak of share one thing in common: They all "touch the borderline" from the perspective of the third density side.

50 **Q**: *(T)* When you talked about using the anti-matter they said: 'Yes' you can work with it, but you are only getting it on one side and you can't get to 4th density side unless you have someone working with you from over there; you have to find a 4th density being to help you here... but you are touching it, you are at the edge of where you can go in 3rd density... *(RS)* Will you help us? *(CS)* Yes, let's be practical! [Laughter]

51 **A**: Terry did not give exactly correct answer. It is possible to cross over into fourth density from third, using third density technology. In fact, this has already been accomplished by various individuals and groups on a more or less accidental basis, the problem is "what does one do when one reaches fourth density reality with only third density training and experience?"

52 **Q**: *(L)* Could you, if we spent the time, help us with this training and technology?

A: Yes, but what do you intend to use 53
it for? This is not like going to Disney World for a day, you know!

Q: *(SV)* They sure told you, Laura! 54
[Laughter] *(T)* I guess then that what Roger is working on is hitting the edge of 3rd density and it can cross over! My question is: if a crossover is accomplished, will the experimenters know what has happened? What will they do? Will they be aware that they have just stepped into the twilight zone, so to speak? Opening that up is a door, or a window, and stuff can go both ways! *(L)* We were told that the members of the famous Flight 19 are frozen in a time warp and are still trying to get their bearings! They think no time has passed. *(RS)* In this type of theory, this is very plausible! *(L)* Well, you don't want to find yourself in a similar position! *(T)* Yeah, Carla will be on the phone asking: "When is Roger coming home?" And you will be over in 4th density asking: "How do I get home from this one!" [Laughter] *(J)* I have a question: If it is not like going to Disney World, does the ride ever end?

A: Too complex, your query is too 55
vague.

Q: *(J)* I was just making a joke! *(T)* 56
Mirth, mirth! *(RS)* Did they answer the question as to whether they will help us? *(L)* They said yes.

A: What is your knowledge quotient 57
regarding following: electromagnetism, Einstein's "unified field theory." And did he ever complete said theory, or was it completed under the supervision of Consortium, and suppressed. And if so, what are the ramifications!!! Also,

[3] *The Wave* 56. I don't think they mean the 'blanks' of the unified field theory, but

Roger, are you capable of "filling in the blanks," we think so![3]

58 **Q**: *(RS)* From the third level there cannot be a unification of electromagnetism and gravitation because they are identical. There is an identity between electromagnetism and gravitation. So, there is no need of the unification because they are identical. Is this view correct?

59 **A**: Yes. What about fourth level?

60 **Q**: *(T)* What does this mean for fourth level? *(RS)* To my understanding to the third level, this is where the possibility to go up a level comes in. If gravitation and electromagnetism are identical, then anti-gravity exists. The origin of anti-gravity is not unification. Einstein was wrong, but the identification that they are the same implies the existence of anti-gravity.

61 **A**: Wrong[4] when searching on level three density exclusively, but this is where the Consortium comes in, i.e. "Can of Worms."

62 **Q**: *(T)* It is considered known to the general public that Einstein did not complete his Unified Field Theory, but that may be a falsehood. Part of the disinformation campaign.

(RS) From what we know, Einstein failed to achieve the Unified Field Theory because the assumptions were not realizable.

(T) Maybe his ideas were taken and completed by someone else and suppressed. [Roger sits at board.] *(RS)* Can I ask a question? The origin of the mass of an elementary particle is primarily electromagnetic, therefore, the gravitational field of elementary particle must be primarily of electromagnetic nature. That's why the view at level three is, outside mass, the gravitation and electromagnetism are identical. This is our belief at this time, supported by experimental evidence. Why is this wrong? I need an explanation.

A: Not wrong at level three, wrong to limit to 3rd level. 63

Q: *(RS)* Is it true that the universe has equal amounts of matter and anti-matter as seen from level three? 64

A: Yes, all others as well. 65

Q: *(RS)* Then it is true that the total time in the universe is null? 66

A: Yes. 67

Q: *(RS)* This is incredible! 68

A: But, Roger less pressure! [Roger lightens up] ...thank you. Now, remember, most important concept is balance. How is balance achieved? 69

Q: *(L)* I guess that whatever there is one of, there is one of the opposite. 70

(RS) Matter and anti-matter. So, if matter is flowing in this direction of time, anti-matter is flowing the other way. They balance each other.

(J) STO and STS. We have to have both.

(RS) This is my question of the total time of the universe, which is zero. If we flow this way, maybe others in another galaxy are flowing another way. The sum is zero.

---

rather reading between the lines of this answer! What, exactly, are the ramifications of research in this direction?

[4]'Wrong' is referring to Einstein's theory.

71 **A**: Not galaxy, dimension.

72 **Q**: *(RS)* Yes. Another level. I always think at level three!

73 **A**: Not anymore! [Laughter]

74 **Q**: *(RS)* How can we represent mathematically the identification of gravity and electromagnetism, including the fourth level that you suggest? How can this be done? How can the inclusion of the fourth level be realized?

75 **A**: We asked you to visualize for answers. It is always there for you to discover.

76 **Q**: *(RS)* It is not going to be easy, but I am going to give it a try.

77 **A**: What ever is?

78 **Q**: *(RS)* The question is how to represent mathematically the transition to the fourth level. I think that this can be done by the isogeometries, the geometry which we discussed earlier, which is generalization of the unit of space and time...

79 **A**: Geometry is one key, but there is another.

80 **Q**: *(L)* What is the other key? Maybe it's a three-dimensional matrix. *(RS)* That's what we use. We also use the cubic. *(L)* Could you give us a clue? Just a little clue. *(RS)* Give us the formula!

81 **A**: Have already... access...

82 **Q**: *(L)* They say they already have. Well, you know, all the time when I type these transcripts, I constantly find that things have been said that I didn't realize at the time the import. *(RS)* We should have a session... because this is confirmation of the only mathematical model we have of the UFOs... the only one that exists as far as I know. We have a computer model... we cannot build a UFO, we don't have the technology, but we can put the formula into the computer and get a model.

A: Merge geometry with optics. 83

Q: *(RS)* What?! It is the science of 84
light. *(L)* Geometric light?

A: Matrix. 85

Q: *(RS)* That is precisely what I have 86
done. I've done a representation of light represented by a unit which is a matrix. I have already done this! Years ago!

A: But you left out one important fac- 87
tor, remember, hypothesis does not theory make!

Q: *(RS)* I made a conceptual hypothe- 88
sis in my mind. That's not a theory. It has to be formulated in a quantitative way, that's the mathematics, the formula, and then this has to be proven experimentally that it works. Hypothesis, formula, and experimental verification is the process for a theory.

A: Now, what factor was missing, 89
Roger?

Q: *(L)* What is it? *(RS)* I don't know. 90
(L) Maybe it's because you didn't factor in 4th density? *(RS)* Oh yes! That's for sure! *(J)* Maybe that's the missing factor. *(RS)* But how... I do not know how to express it mathematically...

A: Light waves... gravity... electro- 91
magnetism...

Q: *(L)* They are toying with you. 92
[Laughter] *(J)* What is this, multiple choice? *(RS)* I have to think it over. In isogeometry...

A: What role do waves play in third 93
level understanding of physics?

94 **Q**: *(RS)* Transverse oscillation of the ether… the medium that fills up the entire universe. No wave can exist unless there is a medium to propagate it. Transverse oscillations fill up the entire universe.

95 **A**: Light, gravity, optics, atomic particles, matter, anti-matter… unify, please.

96 **Q**: *(RS)* That lists everything…

(J) What do they all have in common?

(RS) Oh! All of them are vibrations of the medium that fills up the universe! We perceive things, everything, even spaces between things. Reality is the opposite of this. Because light is a wave, like sound. If you remove the air, sound cannot propagate. Light is the same thing. Light is a wave and cannot propagate unless there is a medium that fills up the entire universe. So what we perceive as being solid and empty is not true perception. The whole universe is filled with the vibration of this medium. So, without the medium, there would be darkness. So, light is an oscillation of this medium. A particle is also an oscillation only the wave propagates and the oscillation stays there. So when I move my hand from here to here, I have just moved the oscillation. The space is oscillating. We are completely empty, but space is filled up. So, the answer is that what they have in common is that they are all oscillations of this medium that fills up the entire universe as perceived from third level and I think from fourth. *(L)* Maybe they are talking about it in a spectral sense? *(RS)* They could be…

A: Now, what relation between gravity 97
and light?

Q: *(RS)* I do not know. At this mo- 98
ment in my studies, I do not know. *(L)* Maybe that is the key? *(RS)* Light can be converted into matter, therefore there is gravitation. *(L)* But, what could the relation between gravity and light be?[5]

A: Access knowledge base and network. 99

Q: *(L)* They said discuss it. 100

(RS) The only connection between light and gravitation… the photon and the photon produces a pair of electron and positron, particles and antiparticles, and those particles have gravitation. So, in this way electromagnetic waves… a photon can create matter…

(L) And matter has gravity…

(RS) And matter has gravity, so… it can be converted…

(L) But where does it come from?

(RS) That is a good question because it isn't known. It could come from a vacuum…

(L) But how does it happen?

(RS) In experiments in the laboratory, you shoot a photon at a nucleus and the nucleus spits one electron and one positron, and so you have conversion of photon into particles. Those particles have gravitation. I do not know if a photon has gravitation. I don't

[5]What about time? Since, at the speed of light there is no matter and no gravity and no time, maybe the three are different ways of describing the same thing? Maybe time is an electromagnetic, gravity-producing phenomenon or vice versa, which has a byproduct: matter?

think so; it travels at the speed of light. There is no time. Time is suspended.

(L) OK, is it true that at the speed of light, there is no gravity?

(RS) There is no gravity.

(L) OK, then maybe the speed of light is the antithesis of gravity just as anti-matter is the opposite of matter?

(RS) That is a good point. A very good point!

101 **A**: Close.

102 **Q**: *(J)* Is it about balance?

103 **A**: All is.

104 **Q**: *(L)* If at the speed of light there is no gravity... *(RS)* There is no time... *(L)* Then gravity must be... *(J)* What keeps us in 3rd density... *(RS)* The clue... But is the missing clue... are we discussing the missing point to go from the 3rd to the 4th density?

105 **A**: Yes.

106 **Q**: *(RS)* Then the point is valid. *(J)* Is gravity what keeps us in 3rd density? *(RS)* So, then if you go at the speed of light then you are in 4th density.

107 **A**: Now, what is missing factor which allows third density and fourth density matter to achieve light speed without disintegration? Think...

108 **Q**: *(RS)* That is the fundamental question of nuclear physics... matter cannot reach the speed of light intact... *(J)* Anti-gravity? *(RS)* Even by using anti-gravity. At this moment, matter cannot do this...

(L) OK, if you have some matter and this matter is speeding up, and it is approaching the speed of light and it is losing its integrity the faster it goes, what if, at some point you start incrementally adding anti-matter which...

(RS) Use the inverse process... take an electron and positron and put one inside the other and recreate the photon. But matter cannot reach the speed of light... if it does, time stops... there is no dimension...

(L) Maybe it is consciousness?

(J) Awareness?

(RS) If it is awareness, yes...

(L) Can you factor in consciousness mathematically?

(RS) Yes, of course!

A: What is the missing link between matter and consciousness? 109

Q: *(RS)* Ah! *(L)* If we knew these things we wouldn't be here! [Laughter] *(RS)* It is supposed to be a field. *(J)* Is it EM? *(RS)* No, a bioenergetic field. *(L)* What if consciousness creates gravity? *(RS)* Gravity is created by matter. *(L)* But isn't matter created by consciousness? Don't we collapse the wave by observing it? *(RS)* Yes, the mind can create matter... 110

A: There are no "gravitons." 111

Q: *(RS)* Not to my knowledge. They do not exist. They are in Einstein's theory, but I will never believe it... Does our consciousness create gravity? 112

A: Getting "warmer." Not "our." 113

Q: *(L)* Somebody else's consciousness creates gravity? *(RS)* Fourth level. 114

A: Level Seven. 115

Q: *(RS)* Oh yes! That I can understand! The ultimate level. Is it true that the universe, as perceived from level three, which is expected to be made up of equal amounts of matter 116 and anti-matter, is, in actuality, open? That is, is matter continuously created somewhere in the universe? Matter and anti-matter?

117 **A**: Better word would be: Recycled.

118 **Q**: *(RS)* Is it true that the same recycling occurs in the center of the Earth? There is a theory that the Earth is expanding. I heard this at a congress, that the Earth is expanding in diameter precisely because the center of the Earth is in process of the creation of matter. Is this correct?

119 **A**: Off base, but all concepts are valid within unified dimensionality.

120 **Q**: *(L)* I guess that in some alternate universe that may be happening, it just doesn't happen to be here.

(RS) My biggest problem has never been new knowledge, but politics, particularly the politics on Einstein. Is the can of worms mentioned before – can you give me anything on this? As soon as you go beyond Einstein, there are all sorts of problems, political problems in our contemporary society. Any suggestions?

121 **A**: Political problems have root in effort to suppress knowledge already gained in limited quarters for purposes of control of civilization.

122 **Q**: *(RS)* That is the best answer I ever heard. Very, very good.

(T) I have two questions to ask. About experiments that are pushing the borderline between 3rd and 4th density... what happens when the experiment reaches the barrier? What can we expect?

123 **A**: Depends on individual circumstances, as we already have told you, this has already happened many times.

Q: *(L)* The Philadelphia Experiment, I 124
suppose... *(J)* Flight 19... *(T)* OK, those have had negative ramifications. What are the implications, reaching the densities, without understanding of what has been done?

A: Already answered. 125

Q: *(L)* Yeah, they talked about that. 126
Insanity. *(J)* Yes, and the people who thought they found Flight 19 went nutzoid. When the researchers reach the barrier, will they recognize that something has happened?

A: Partially. 127

Q: *(T)* When the barriers have been 128
breached so many times, can it be stopped? In other words, can the breaches be repaired?

A: Vague. 129

Q: *(L)* That's assuming that they don't 130
close automatically. *(T)* Do they close automatically once the activity is stopped? No, that's too vague. While I was walking around outside smoking my cigar, I was getting the image that one of the reasons that Roger is here tonight is to experience this, but also to see and read what we give you. We are not making this up. It is coming from somewhere. There is substance to this information. Roger is going to Europe. You have colleagues in Europe who are working on these very same things. The Cassiopaeans have indicated that you are on the edge of opening this barrier. That this can be done, it has been done with disastrous results the few times that we know of and possibly other times that we do not know of. What I am getting at is, part of the reason you are here and seeing this may be because you need to take this information with you because when they

breach these barriers, they need to understand what they have done. Because, if they don't there is a possibility that what is transpiring naturally will be accelerated. Does artificial breaching of the barrier between the densities accelerate...

131 **A**: Yes.

132 **Q**: *(T)* That may be why when we ask how long this process is going to take, this oncoming density change, they answer "one month to 18 years." And we were thinking that maybe they can't tell how long it is going to take for this transition point, this realm border to come through our section of space-time and do whatever it does. Maybe what they are referring to is not that, but what people might do in terms of breaching the barrier unknowingly. They are stretching what they know, and pushing onward, but they don't understand what this is all about.[6]

133 **A**: Yes.

134 **Q**: *(T)* You just had the survival of the whole of civilization moved onto your shoulders, Roger! [Laughter] Laura has been sitting here week after week saying, "I don't want the whole burden of the world on my shoulders!" Roger, you just got part of it! *(RS)* Part of it, yes. I was the technical adviser on the book, *The Andreasson Affair*, because she made all sorts of drawings of things she saw on spacecraft. Any comment on the [transcriber's note: incomprehensible] Research Institute in Italy?

135 **A**: Institute is controlled by Carboni "Foundation," which is linked to questionable funding sources; no need to be disappointed, however, as knowledge protects. Therefore one can work in any environment without corruption when armed with knowledge.

Q: *(RS)* I don't understand. *(J)* Maybe 136
you need to find out about it... *(L)* I don't think you need to worry about it. *(RS)* What about Cardone? *(CS)* The board said Carboni... *(RS)* Who is the guy we are talking to on the board?

A: Guy? 137

Q: [Laughter] *(RS)* Did they say Car- 138
done or Carboni?

A: Carboni Foundation. 139

Q: *(RS)* There is no foundation named 140
this! *(L)* Well, there may be funding coming from there. *(RS)* Not from Carboni... *(CS)* Wait and see...

[Goodnight to Carla and Roger, who had to leave. Discussion followed.]

(L) As you demolecularize moving toward the speed of light, it can be represented as a cone shape. The point of the cone is the speed of light, a sort of singularity, and as you reach this point, this is where you apply the remolecularizer, because maybe you remolecularize as you emerge into an opposite funnel on the other side. I wonder if the Transdimensional Atomic Remolecularizer is a device that applies anti-matter in incremental, graduated doses, for lack of a better word, as you are speeded up? At one end you have light, which has no gravity, no time, no mass. At the other end we have gravity, time and mass. What is the transition? Of the three pairs we were given, they each seem to be opposite to each other: Light and gravity, optics and atomic particles, matter and anti-matter...

[6] *The Wave* 4

(J) It's all about balance. What is the relation between gravity and light? What is the missing factor which allows 3rd density and 4th density matter to achieve light speed without disintegration? What is the missing link between matter and consciousness?

(L) What is the missing link? Well, I think the relationship is right there. What is it that slows down light causing photons to manifest, collapsing the wave, so to speak, and creating matter?

(J) It may be that this same factor that allows 3rd density to achieve light speed without disintegration. What is the missing link between matter and consciousness?

(L) Well, the relationship is there. We were told we were getting close when we said "consciousness" but that it was not our consciousness, but that of level seven.[7]

(J) They said that "creation" was a recycling.

141 **Q**: *(L)* Are you still there?

142 **A**: As always, Laura, do you think we go out to lunch or something? [Laughter] You keep asking if we are here?!?

143 **Q**: *(J)* They are always here, in us. We are all interconnected. *(T)* We are them, they are us, right here! *(L)* OK, guys, we are so glad you know so much physics. And, since you do, or, since 'we' know so much physics... *(T)* Did you enjoy talking to Roger and would you like to talk to him again?

144 **A**: Yes. Will.

Q: *(L)* Am I getting warm when I say... 145
we have light and gravity, optics and atomic particles, matter and anti-matter, all are ways of talking about a transition... are these three pairs of relationships?

A: Close. 146

Q: *(L)* What is the thing that collapses 147
the wave function?

A: ? 148

Q: *(L)* Is it consciousness? 149

A: Yes... 150

Q: *(L)* There is more. Can this con- 151
sciousness be expressed... *(T)* We are trying to get from a 3rd density concept to a 4th density concept where there is no physicality, per se. At 4th density they don't have a problem with going at the speed of light and disintegrating, because it doesn't exist there...

A: Close. 152

Q: *(T)* So, for us to try and think of 153
this in 3rd density...

A: Variable physicality is the key. 154

Q: *(L)* What makes the physicality 155
variable?

A: Awareness of link between con- 156
sciousness and matter.

Q: *(L)* What is the link between con- 157
sciousness and matter?[8]

A: Illusion. 158

Q: *(L)* What is the nature of the illu- 159
sion? *(T)* That there isn't any connection between consciousness and matter.

[7]Could electromagnetism be the 'field' of the consciousness of 'God' or level seven that crosses all densities? Cayce once remarked that 'God is electricity'. Is there some range of electromagnetism in the human consciousness that can be detected, amplified, augmented by controlled electromagnetic waves?

[8]*The Wave* 10

It is only an illusion that there is. It is part of the 3rd density...

160 **A**: No. Illusion is that there is not.

161 **Q**: *(L)* The illusion is that there is no link between consciousness and matter.

162 **A**: Yes.

163 **Q**: *(T)* The illusion is that there is not a link. In 3rd density... *(L)* I got it! *(T)* Don't disappear on me now! [Laughter] The relationship is that consciousness is matter.

164 **A**: Close. What about vice versa?

165 **Q**: *(L)* Just reverse everything. Light is gravity. Optics are atomic particles, matter is anti-matter... just reverse everything to understand the next level... it can't be that easy. *(J)* Wait a second: gravity equals light, atomic particles equals optics, anti-matter equals matter? It is all about balance. *(L)* And the answer must always be zero.

166 **A**: And zero is infinity.

167 **Q**: *(L)* So, you are saying that it is not that there is a link, the illusion is that there is separation. There is no difference, they are the same?

168 **A**: Yes.

169 **Q**: *(T)* If you warp space-time you travel by bringing your destination to you. *(L)* Or, you can reverse that and understand that there is no distance between us and, say, Alpha Centauri; it is the alteration of perception that turns the axis and creates the illusion of distance.

A: Now, all you need is the "technology." 170

Q: *(T)* The technology is being developed right now. *(J)* The technology has probably already been developed, it is just suppressed. 171

A: Yes. 172

Q: *(L)* I have a very strange sense that this interaction has ramifications? 173

A: Yes. 174

Q: *(L)* A hint? 175

A: We could but won't at this "time." 176

Q: *(T)* Are these major ramifications? 177

A: Yes. 178

Q: *(L)* Is there anything further for this evening? *(T)* Do we need to impart anything further to ourselves? 179

A: No. 180

Q: *(L)* Then we will say thank you and goodnight. 181

A: Goodnight. 182

End of Session

One of the most significant things about this session was the revelation to me that it just *might* be possible to solve some of the great mysteries of our world with the help of the Cassiopaeans. Yes, it is so that many, many sources of similar ilk have made claims to having done so – at least in philosophical terms – but here we had a real, live physicist who just possibly could figure out and ask the right questions, and then take the answers and translate them into usable, technological terms for the betterment of all humanity, not just 'true believers'.

I was enthralled by the fact that they had no problems talking with Prof. Santilli about physics, though my stomach had knotted up at the beginning of the session from thinking that this was going to prove to me that the Cassiopaeans were just a chimera of my own subconscious – they would fail the test. But they didn't. Of course, they weren't giving anything away except clues, but the fact that they could do that was astonishing to me. It opened an endless vista of possibilities.

In addition to such considerations, the effect on me was also pronounced. It seemed that even when the session was over and I had gone to bed, I was still 'channelling'. My head was filled with ideas and images too deep for words and I was impatient to get on with the 'project.'

We waited for Prof. Santilli to return from Europe to see what the 'ramifications' of the session would be. When he returned, he seemed to have a different 'attitude' toward the Cassiopaeans, and it became clear that he did not wish to be associated with such a 'bizarre' experiment. It was rather like the initial reaction of the MUFON group, which then changed so drastically that we were reduced from an hour of time to 15 minutes. Something strange was going on. So much for our anticipation of help from such quarters. I put my hopes of delving into physics more deeply on the shelf, and over a year passed before we were to come back to the subject again.

May 31, 1995

During the week before this session, I had suggested to Jan that we might not want to give out session quotes in the brochures she was creating without first redacting the names of our guests. Jan took this as a serious criticism and relations became strained. It seemed to me that there must be some influence affecting her to make her react that way since I had been careful in how I worded the suggestion. I wondered if this might not be some sort of psychic attack on the entire group.

Participants: 'Frank', Laura, Susan V

1 **Q**: Hello.

2 **A**: Hello. SV!

3 **Q**: *(L)* I have been feeling that the group, as a whole, is under attack. What can we do about it?

4 **A**: Will work itself out. Power struggles within groups are quite natural at level three STS.

5 **Q**: *(L)* Well, I don't know what they mean by "power struggles". I just know that I feel uneasy and a tension in the air. What power is there to struggle for? We are all just who we are. *(SV)* You don't need to worry about it and get yourself into a frantic state! *(L)* Well, it seems that we are all being confronted with some of the lines we have drawn in the sands of life and all the things we think of as 'musts' or 'shoulds' or 'ought-tos', our internal parent-self, so to speak, are having to be dealt with. I think that maybe what we need to look at is that lines don't need to be drawn. We just all need to do what is in front of us to be done and not try to control each other or decide what is best for each other and just be accepting.

A: All will settle like sand in a jar of 6
water.

Q: *(L)* That is interesting. I used the 7
idea of lines in the sand and the you use the analogy of sand shaken up in water. Is it a good idea to not print up or send out any more brochures? I was very upset by the giving out of the information with the names not altered or deleted.

A: It was not Jan in charge of that. 8

Q: *(L)* Who was in charge of that? 9

A: Open. Do not assume that was a 10
negative decision.

Q: *(L)* So, this is ultimately beneficial? 11

A: Maybe. 12

Q: *(L)* So, this was a protective mea- 13
sure or device?

A: Yes. 14

15 **Q**: *(L)* Approximately how long before this tension in the group will go away?

16 **A**: Wait and see.

17 **Q**: *(L)* And there is nothing we can do to help?

18 **A**: Not issue.

19 **Q**: *(L)* What is the issue?

20 **A**: Let it be.

21 **Q**: *(SV)* Quit worrying. *(L)* OK, I will. Next question. RS called me about Reiki for his eyes. He said he was diagnosed with macular degeneration. Is this the correct diagnosis?

22 **A**: Yes.

23 **Q**: *(L)* What is the cause of this?

24 **A**: Genetic.

25 **Q**: *(L)* Is there anything that can be done to halt or reverse it?

26 **A**: Open.

27 **Q**: *(SV)* Will the Cayce files help in this?

28 **A**: Cannot hurt.

29 **Q**: *(L)* Why can you not give us some sort of information to help out here?

30 **A**: Level one karmic situation.

31 **Q**: *(L)* Will Reiki help this?

32 **A**: Maybe.

33 **Q**: *(L)* Is there anything else that you can give us on this?

34 **A**: If so, you will discover it at another point in space time.

35 **Q**: *(L)* Michael Lindemann gave a very interesting talk on the subject of angels. Apparently there are a lot of people seeing and claiming to interact with angels. Can you tell us about angels?

A: Be specific. 36

Q: *(L)* Are there such things as angels? 37

A: Yes. 38

Q: *(L)* Are angels as they have been de- 39
scribed: very tall, beautiful beings with wings or whatever?

A: Yes. 40

Q: *(L)* Who are the angels? 41

A: Refer to the transcript. 42

Q: *(L)* I don't think we have ever men- 43
tioned angels in the transcript.

A: Not by name. See the second ses- 44
sion.[1]

Q: *(SV)* There is a book out called 45
Mary's Message to the World by Ann Kirkwood. Is this book a transmission from the Virgin Mary?

A: No. 46

Q: *(L)* Who is this transmission from? 47

A: Various thought centers. 48

Q: *(L)* Why do these thought cen- 49
ters identify themselves as the Virgin Mary?

A: For purposes of familiarity. 50

Q: *(L)* Are these thought centers STS 51
or STO?

A: Open. Discover by studying previ- 52
ously given information. You should review the material regularly, not just to familiarize yourselves with data, but also to learn by piecing together thought pattern segments!

Q: *(L)* If I remember correctly, there 53
have been numerous presentations of the Virgin Mary put forward for disinformation purposes by the STS groups. Is that correct?

[1]The Zendar or Zindar Council?

54 **A**: Yes.

55 **Q**: *(L)* Have there also been presentations of the Virgin Mary put forward by the STO groups?

56 **A**: Yes.

57 **Q**: *(L)* So, depending upon the results, and the teaching, that would be what would enable one to determine whether it is STO or STS?

58 **A**: Partly.

59 **Q**: *(L)* Is there some other measuring stick that we can use to determine whether teachings are correct or incorrect?

60 **A**: Wisdom by way of instincts; all there is is lessons.

61 **Q**: *(SV)* I was thinking about that earlier today. If you are under attack, how do you know if your instincts are correct? *(L)* Are instincts different from emotions?

62 **A**: Yes.

63 **Q**: *(L)* How can you tell the difference between instinctive knowledge and emotional reactions?

64 **A**: Emotions involve wishful thinking, instincts are "gut feelings," psychic in nature, and are stronger. When it is wishful thinking, there is always psychic instinct seeping through which you can access if you use reason and examine your lessons of the past.[2]

65 **Q**: *(L)* Well, for example, the lady at the MUFON meeting on Saturday, her response to Terry's comments on channeled material as being STS, was that we were focusing on the darkness, or negativity, and that people who focus on darkness or negativity experience same. Could you comment on this please?

A: What do your instincts tell you? 66

Q: *(L)* My instincts tell me that she 67 is wanting to believe so strongly and emotionally that the aliens who have been abducting her are good guys, and that somehow she is so laden with an internal guilt complex that she believes that she deserves that kind of treatment, and that anything that is to the contrary, she rejects as wrong and evil.

A: Okay. 68

Q: *(L)* And, furthermore, it occurred 69 to me that a person who really focuses on the darkness with the intention of participation is someone who moves away from the light and goes into the darkness, whereas someone who focuses on the darkness with the intention of diminishing it, keeps the light close to their back, and uses it to energize their own light so that they can illuminate the darkness. Is that correct?

A: Okay. 70

Q: *(L)* And, that someone who only 71 looks at light, has their back turned to the darkness, not only are they blinded by the light, but they are also casting a shadow behind them.

A: "The Emperor is wearing new 72 clothes."

Q: *(L)* Am I the one who is thinking 73 the emperor is wearing new clothes?

[2]This is probably one of the most useful and important things the Cs have ever said in terms of work on the self. I would suggest that the reader read and re-read it and really think about what is being said. It can also help to read Timothy Wilson's book *Strangers to Ourselves*.

(F) I would think that anyone who is hung up on the idea that there is nothing but light as long as you are willing to only see light is believing that the emperor is wearing new clothes. *(L)* Is Frank correct?

74 **A**: Yes.

75 **Q**: *(L)* On Saturday I also met Nova M and her husband. They wanted us to take the session over to their house because they don't smoke and are apparently not willing to submit to our environment. My instinctive reaction to that was "no, forget it." Since that time, I have had other gut reactions to that, that there was some sort of 'power play' going on there.

76 **A**: Open.

77 **Q**: *(L)* Would it be alright for us to take the session over to these people's house?

78 **A**: Up to you.

79 **Q**: *(L)* Well, I don't want to and Frank doesn't want to. *(SV)* Well, all of us smoke. It wouldn't make sense to go somewhere that we can't smoke and be put outside like something dirty. *(L)* Yeah! We couldn't indulge our nasty habits and be dirty and messy and play! Nah! Forget that! *(L)* In my aura photograph, there is a patch of green on my chest. In Cayce's book on the subject, he says that light greens represent falsehood. I am very concerned about this.

80 **A**: Worry not.

81 **Q**: *(SV)* Well, in your case, it is a deep green next to a clear yellow, not a pastel or pale green. Maybe you need to eat more fruit!

82 **A**: Worry not, you know who and what you are, remember, instinct!!

Q: *(L)* Well, Frank had a very beau- 83
tiful aura. Why are others not more positive toward this knowledge?

A: Jealousy. 84

Q: *(L)* Well, that was pretty plain. 85
What are others jealous of?

A: Power struggle. 86

Q: *(L)* Why are people jealous of us 87
and why do they want to try to control us?

A: Fear being left behind. 88

Q: *(L)* Well, nobody is going to be left 89
behind unless they make themselves disagreeable. *(SV)* Well, I dreamed that we all need to wash our dirty laundry, so I got up and put a load in! [Laughter] *(L)* Was John W correct that a person can change their aura by just thinking about it?

A: No. 90

Q: *(SV)* It is what you are! *(L)* Our 91
ability to see or perceive blue, according to some researchers, is very recent. Natives who live on the Blue Nile describe it as brown, Homer described the Mediterranean as the "Wine dark sea," and Aristotle said there were only three colors in the rainbow: red, yellow and green. Is this true, that the human race, in general, has only recently become able to see blue?

A: Yes. 92

Q: *(L)* Is this a reflection of the spiri- 93
tuality of the color blue?

A: Yes. 94

Q: *(L)* Obviously there are colors be- 95
yond blue, and as we attain greater spirituality, we will be able to see them as well – is this true?

A: Yes. 96

97 **Q**: *(SV)* When you look at a rainbow, you can see a shimmer or haze on either side. *(L)* Could it be that as a result of constant straining to see at higher frequencies, some people's eyes suffer?

98 **A**: Maybe.

99 **Q**: *(L)* Could this be a problem with people in spiritual or personal development?

100 **A**: Maybe.

101 **Q**: *(L)* I have read a number of things recently purportedly channeled by the 'Great White Brotherhood'. I would like to know if there is such a thing?

102 **A**: No.

103 **Q**: *(L)* There is no 'Great White Brotherhood'? *(SV)* How come Edgar Cayce talked about it?

104 **A**: Not as such.

105 **Q**: *(L)* What is it that they have been calling the 'Great White Brotherhood'?

A: ? 106

Q: *(L)* What is the Great White Brotherhood that Cayce was referring to? 107

A: Various STO. 108

Q: *(L)* Do they identify themselves as the Great White Brotherhood? 109

A: Sometimes. 110

Q: *(L)* If they are not the 'Great White Brotherhood', what are they? 111

A: Fourth density STO. 112

Q: *(L)* What is their purpose or work? 113

A: Complex, suggest you wait and see. 114

Q: *(L)* Are we going to be contacted by the Great White Brotherhood? 115

A: Maybe. 116

---

[3]See: http://en.wikipedia.org/wiki/Ancestral_Puebloans

> The Ancestral Puebloans were an ancient Native American culture centered on the present-day Four Corners area of the United States, comprising southern Utah, northeastern Arizona, northern New Mexico, and southwestern Colorado. The ancestors to the modern Puebloan peoples, they lived in a range of structures, including pit houses, pueblos, and cliff dwellings designed so that they could lift entry ladders during enemy attacks. The people and their archaeological culture were historically called Anasazi, from the Navajo term Anaasází, meaning "Ancient Ones" or "Ancient Enemies".
>
> One of the most notable aspects of Ancestral Puebloan infrastructure is at Chaco Canyon and is the Chaco Road, a system of roads radiating out from many great house sites such as Pueblo Bonito, Chetro Ketl and Una Vida, and leading towards small outlier sites and natural features within and beyond the canyon limits.
>
> Through satellite images and ground investigations, archaeologists have detected at least 8 main roads that together run for more than 180 miles (ca 300 km), and are more than 30 feet (10 m) wide. These were excavated into a smooth leveled surface in the bedrock or created through the removal of vegetation and soil. The Ancestral Pueblo residents of Chaco Canyon cut large ramps and stairways into the cliff rock to connect the roadways on the ridgetops of the canyon to the sites on the valley bottoms.
>
> Modern Pueblo oral traditions hold that the ancient Pueblo people originated from sipapu, where they emerged from the underworld. For unknown ages, they were led by chiefs and guided by spirits as they completed vast migrations throughout the continent of North America. They settled first in the ancient Pueblo areas

117 **Q**: *(L)* What is the origin of the Anasazi tribe that lived in the cliff dwellings?[3]

118 **A**: Nothing remarkable.

119 **Q**: *(SV)* I have a book on the Brotherhood... I get all kinds of things in the mail... one is from a guy who is supposed to be an extraterrestrial... I'll have to bring it... *(L)* What could we use to represent 7th density as a mathematical symbol?

120 **A**: Try this: [draws figure eight on side in ellipse]

121 **Q**: *(L)* When you get to the point of the Big Bang, or mass disbursement, what mathematical symbol would represent that? Plus, minus, multiply or divide?

122 **A**: NAB

123 **Q**: *(L)* Do you mean 'none of the above'?

124 **A**: Close.

125 **Q**: *(L)* What mathematical operation would represent this?

126 **A**: You have not yet discovered.

127 **Q**: *(L)* What kind of mathematical operation would take place at the point of the Big Bang?

A: One continuous cycling. 128

Q: *(L)* The transition of 7th density to the density where the cycling begins is from 7th to 6th or from 7th to 1st? 129

A: Neither. 130

Q: *(L)* Does it go from 7th to all densities simultaneously? 131

A: Closer. 132

Q: *(L)* Can this be expressed mathematically? 133

A: Maybe. Access your own channel. 134

Q: *(L)* What is my own channel? 135

A: You know. 136

Q: *(L)* I thought you were my channel? 137

A: We are group channel. 138

Q: *(L)* How can I access my own channel? 139

A: You have done it numerous times. 140

Q: *(L)* Was this what I was doing the other morning after Roger Santilli was here? 141

A: Yes. 142

---

for a few hundred years before moving to their present locations.

A 1997 excavation at Cowboy Wash near Dolores, Colorado, found remains of at least twenty-four human skeletons that showed evidence of violence and dismemberment, with strong indications of cannibalism. This modest community appears to have been abandoned during the same time period.[24] Other excavations within the Ancient Pueblo culture area produce varying numbers of unburied, and in some cases dismembered, bodies.[25] In a 2010 paper, Potter and Chuipka argued that evidence at Sacred Ridge Site, near Durango, Colorado, is best interpreted as ethnic cleansing.

This evidence of warfare, conflict, and cannibalism is hotly debated by some scholars and interest groups. Suggested alternatives include: a community under the pressure of starvation or extreme social stress, dismemberment and cannibalism as religious ritual or in response to religious conflict, the influx of outsiders seeking to drive out a settled agricultural community via calculated atrocity, or an invasion of a settled region by nomadic raiders who practiced cannibalism; such peoples have existed in other times and places, e.g. the Androphagi of Europe.

143 **Q**: *(L)* Am I correct when I say gravity is time?

144 **A**: Close.

145 **Q**: *(L)* And gravity is the manifestation of time as put into effect by the limitation of 3rd density consciousness illusion?

146 **A**: Closer.

147 **Q**: *(L)* Can this be expressed mathematically?

148 **A**: Go for it!

149 **Q**: *(L)* Frank, help me out here! *(F)* I can't help you out. You've blazed a trail into the woods all by yourself and I don't know how to find you. You have been told you can do it. This is obviously your forte. They told you to go for it. What do you want, a shortcut? *(L)* I want the formula! *(SV)* What about the thrill of discovery? *(L)* What about the agony of defeat? *(SV)* The agony of defeat... *(L)* That's what you get after shopping all day! [Laughter] *(L)* I want it so bad! I don't feel capable! (Frank) Of course you are! *(SV)* If you can think of the question you can access the answer.

A: Time to say goodnight! 150

Q: *(L)* Goodnight. 151

End of Session

June 3, 1995

The energy was very different at this session due to the presence of Tom French and Cherie Diez, no doubt. There was significant tension and you will see it come out with something of an attack on me. Notice that Jan immediately jumps on that and reinforces it. So, it could be said that her energy was affecting the reception. However, she had a legitimate beef. I had thought that having surprise guests would be fun, but obviously, Jan did not like the surprise and it was certainly not very thoughtful on my part to not have considered that she might want to be informed in advance. I think I've grown up a bit since then.

Participants: 'Frank', Laura, Terry and Jan, Tom French, Cherie Diez, Susan V

1 **Q**: *(L)* Hello.

2 **A**: Hello.

3 **Q**: *(T)* I'm running on low energy. *(L)* Who do we have with us this evening?

4 **A**: Sorrillora.

5 **Q**: *(L)* And where are you from?

6 **A**: Cassiopaea.

7 **Q**: *(L)* We have guests this evening; this is Tom and Cherie.

8 **A**: Hello Tom and Cherie.[1]

9 **Q**: *(L)* Tom has a question.

10 **A**: Surely.

11 **Q**: *(TF)* What happened to my grandfather's watch?

12 **A**: Which one?

[1] *The Wave* 41

Q: *(L)* Which grandfather? *(TF)* 13
Paternal. *(L)* OK, what happened to Tom's paternal grandfather's gold pocketwatch?

A: Under water. 14

Q: *(T)* Under what water? 15

A: It is clear with some silt or sand. 16

Q: *(TF)* What is that? *(L)* I don't 17
think you are going to get a name because that is an artificial designation.

A: Visual reference. Shines in the 18
sunlight, slipped off when attention was distracted.

Q: *(TF)* Did it slip off by itself or did 19
someone take it?

A: Rubbed metal surface. 20

Q: *(TF)* Where was my father at the 21
time?

A: At church. 22

23 **Q**: *(L)* Does that make any sense? *(TF)* Well, maybe. *(T)* Do you know where the watch is? *(TF)* No. *(SV)* Find out where he went to church and see if there is any water around there. *(L)* Maybe his father was nowhere near at the time. *(TF)* My father never went to church; he was an atheist. Did my father have anything to do with the disappearance?

24 **A**: No.

25 **Q**: *(T)* Was his father at church? You say his father was at church; Tom says his father didn't go to church. Why was his father at church?

26 **A**: Not only reason one goes to a church, think!

27 **Q**: *(J)* It might have been a meeting of some kind... *(T)* A wedding; a funeral... *(TF)* You're right. It's not that he never set foot inside a church. *(F)* He's not that much of an atheist! *(T)* Especially weddings; there's food after weddings! *(TF)* OK, well, one more and then I'll be quiet! Was the watch lost or was it taken?

28 **A**: Lost.

29 **Q**: *(L)* Has this bugged you a long time? *(TF)* Not too long. A while.

(L) I have a question to ask about Tom. Tom had a dream that he shared with me, and I think he wouldn't mind sharing it with the group. Tom?

(TF) In the dream I am on an ocean liner. There are other people on board the ship, but I am not talking to them. I'm not with my friends or family. I am by myself. I among all these people, but I am not with them. It is a long journey. I walk back and forth on deck. Finally we come to a city, a major city, a seaport. I get off the ship, I walk through the city, I walk through the center of the city to the outskirts, into the countryside. The countryside is red – reddish all around. The streets are no longer paved; now they are dirt, red dirt. I come to a big house with a white picket fence under the shadow of a mountain. I know that I am supposed to be in this house. I go inside the house, there are other people there. Again, I am not talking with them when I first get there, and as the days begin to pass I do begin to talk to them and they begin to talk to me. I begin to feel better. Suddenly, in the dream, I realize that when I was first walking through the city toward the house, I was a dog; in the early days when I had first been in the house, I was being transformed into a human being, and that all the other people in the house were once animals; and that that was why we were at the house, to learn how to become a human being. It had something to do with the power of the mountain. *(L)* Now, the question I have is: is there some significance to this dream that you can comment on?

A: Not of great significance in a psy- 30
chic sense, merely a reflection of the subject's awareness of metamorphosis within his own life path.

Q: *(L)* Well, that was Tom's interpre- 31
tation and it blew my theory all to hell! *(T)* What was your theory? *(L)* Well, I was just sure he was an alien and he came to Earth on this big ship from the Dog Star, Sirius... *(J)* To Georgia!! [Laughter] I liked my interpretation better! *(T)* Make for a heck of a book! *(SV)* She's been watching too many of those UFO videos!

A: Active imagination! 32

Q: *(L)* Well, I got told! Now, our ques- 33

tions. Why did the Incas and other South American cultures create their cultural environment in mountainous areas where they were forced to terrace to grow food, whereas the European culture developed on level terrain, mined in the mountains... *(T)* And a lot of them starved because they didn't use the mountains correctly...

34 **A**: Mountains were of a different nature in two cases.

35 **Q**: *(L)* So, the mountainous terrain was more fertile in one area than the other; is that the point we are getting at here?

36 **A**: Bingo!

37 **Q**: *(J)* That was what I thought. *(T)* Did the Europeans try terrace farming?

38 **A**: No.

39 **Q**: *(L)* Why? *(T)* Yeah, they built aqueducts, why not terraces?

40 **A**: Why should they try something unnecessary?

41 **Q**: *(T)* Why was it unnecessary? *(L)* No, we know that. They had plenty of arable land that was flat. Why was it necessary in South America? *(J)* Because they didn't. They had to use what they had.

42 **A**: Yes.

43 **Q**: *(T)* Works for me! *(L)* It was said in a previous transmission that the area around my house was a 'multiple reality station'. Is this because of our activities, or is this a pre-existing condition of this house and general location?

44 **A**: Two questions.

45 **Q**: *(L)* Is this because of our activities?

46 **A**: Partially.

Q: *(L)* Is it also a pre-existing condition of this area? 47

A: In a roundabout way.[2] 48

Q: *(L)* Does this have anything to do with the purported tunnel beneath the house? 49

A: Ditto last response. 50

Q: *(L)* OK, you say "in a roundabout way." What is the roundabout way? What is the relationship? 51

A: Crustal energy flow patterns. 52

Q: *(T)* What is crustal energy? 53

A: Self-explanatory. 54

Q: *(T)* OK, it's the energy that is flowing through the crust we are talking about, or the energy the crust is making... we are talking plate tectonics here? *(J)* Yes, plate tectonics? 55

A: Too many comments. 56

Q: *(T)* Are we talking plate tectonics? 57

A: No. 58

Q: *(L)* Are we talking about electromagnetism? 59

A: Close. 60

Q: *(T)* How close to electromagnetism? *(L)* How close can you get? *(T)* Right! [Laughter] 61

A: Related. 62

Q: *(L)* OK, is this an energy flow pattern that is significantly different at this point in space-time as opposed to, say... *(J)* Our house? 63

A: Not correct concept. 64

Q: *(J)* It's not related to space and time? 65

A: You are getting "colder." 66

[2] *High Strangeness* 10; *The Wave* 3, 68

67 **Q**: *(L)* It is not related to space-time. Is it related to a gridwork of energy?

68 **A**: Not gridwork, more like "halo."

69 **Q**: *(T)* A corona? *(L)* Like an aura? *(J)* Is it like an aura?

70 **A**: Yes.

71 **Q**: *(T)* The planet's aura?

72 **A**: Variations within flow.

73 **Q**: *(L)* Is this particular location beneficial to my residence here?

74 **A**: Subjective.

75 **Q**: *(L)* Is it particularly beneficial in terms of this kind of work?

76 **A**: Can be.

77 **Q**: *(J)* It is obviously not detrimental. *(T)* Can it be detrimental?

78 **A**: Yes.

79 **Q**: *(L)* In what way? *(J)* Yes, how is it detrimental?

80 **A**: 64 000 dollar question!

81 **Q**: *(T)* Now, since we hit the 64,000-dollar question, are you going to give us the 64,000-dollar answer? *(L)* Why could it be detrimental? Is it because it could be detrimental if a person is following the STO pathway?

82 **A**: Maybe.

83 **Q**: *(L)* Could it be detrimental to one following the STS pathway?

84 **A**: Maybe.

85 **Q**: *(T)* OK, the energy flow pattern can be detrimental or beneficial. It's just energy, not positive or negative.

86 **A**: This is more complex than your queries allow.[3]

[3] *The Wave* 41

Q: *(L)* In other words, our questions 87
are not complex enough to get the answer?

A: You are "rushing it" due to com- 88
pany present, now please relax and just behave as always.

Q: *(J)* She's trying to show off! *(L)* 89
I am not! *(SV)* That's what they said! *(L)* That's not what they said, and I am not the only one asking questions. *(T)* Let's start over with something simple. We are talking about the aura or something similar. The planet's aura.

A: Yes. 90

Q: *(T)* OK. We are focusing on this 91
site here in relation to the energy of the planet.

A: Okay. 92

Q: *(T)* You have indicated that there is 93
some kind of a correlation between the location and the energy in the planet. The energy in the planet is all the way around the planet and is affected by the planet and everything that goes on around the planet, in the planet, on top of the planet and all over the place. We are one location. As this energy ebbs and flows along, it influences the work we are doing here. Am I on track here?

A: Close. 94

Q: *(T)* OK. So, the crustal energy flow 95
patterns, if they ebb, we lose power... we need to draw more power in order to keep the connection?

A: ? 96

Q: *(T)* I don't even know what I said! 97
(L) Try it this way. We are talking about an aura. In an aura system in the physical body, it can sometimes reflect both the spiritual and physical

state of the person. Is this location similar to a chakra?

98 **A**: If you prefer or other.

99 **Q**: *(L)* Similar to a chakra?

100 **A**: These are all merely labels.

101 **Q**: *(L)* OK, so it is like an energy vortex?

102 **A**: Okay...

103 **Q**: *(L)* An energy vortex in the body, a chakra in the body, is a place where the body energy interfaces with the universe. Tell us about chakras, Susan. *(SV)* There are all different kinds. There are the seven major chakras, the ones in the palms, almost every joint in the body has a chakra... *(T)* What do they do? *(L)* An interface point? *(SV)* Yes. *(L)* Is this what we are talking about here? An interface between this density and other densities?

104 **A**: First of all, "chakras" are a little understood and non-proven phenomenon. Now, it just so happens they do exist, but in different form than reported by many in the so called "psychic" community. So you see, you have opened yet another "can of worms."

105 **Q**: *(L)* Well, Worms Are Us! I knew that question would last all night! Why did I ask it? *(SV)* Well, let's go for it! *(L)* OK, first worm... *(T)* Worm One... *(J)* Worm One... *(L)* ...what, exactly, is a chakra?

106 **A**: An energy field that merges density one, two, three or four with five.

107 **Q**: *(T)* A focus point that merges densities to 5th density contemplation level?

108 **A**: Close.

Q: *(T)* What purpose do we merge 109
to the contemplation level through the chakras?

A: You are all connected with level five 110
on a short wave cycle, reference text.

Q: *(L)* Does each chakra relate to a 111
color as we have been told?

A: In a sense, but not primary issue. 112

Q: *(L)* What is the primary issue? 113

A: The connection with physical im- 114
print locator.

Q: *(L)* So, that has to do with this area 115
right here? Are we back to the house?

A: On a physical body, density levels 116
one through four.

Q: *(L)* So, we are sitting in the mid- 117
dle of a giant chakra, the navel of the world! *(J)* Better than the armpit of the world.

A: What are you speaking of? 118

Q: *(T)* Tallahassee, the armpit of the 119
world! *(L)* I was just joking; we are not in the navel of the world. We are in a chakra... *(T)* In order to be at this location... *(L)* ...is that it?

A: You are drifting and there is 120
much too much thought fragmentation tonight.

Q: *(L)* OK. *(J)* I am wondering if it is 121
related to the storm? *(L)* Let's take a break.

[Break]

Q: *(L)* We have a real serious dude 122
tonight. He's not letting us play! *(SV)* I wonder if there are seven major chakras in the same place as described by others. *(L)* OK, we're back.

A: Back? 123

124 **Q**: *(L)* Well, we really didn't leave, you know. *(J)* Yeah, we went for a walk! *(L)* Susan wants to know if there are seven major chakras related to the physical body as has been taught by many sources?

125 **A**: It varies according to individuals.

126 **Q**: *(SV)* You mean some people have more chakras than others?

127 **A**: Name a "chakra."

128 **Q**: *(L)* Is there a base chakra, the root chakra?

129 **A**: We asked you to name one.

130 **Q**: *(L)* Well, we named one. *(SV)* There's the heart chakra, the third eye – I don't know the Hindu names for them... *(L)* Name a person?

131 **A**: No.

132 **Q**: *(SV)* The lady who wrote *Hands of Light* said that when she does healings, spirit guides...

133 **A**: What happens to those who have major body parts missing?

134 **Q**: *(J)* Oooh! *(SV)* But the etheric field is still there! They have proven that with Kirlian photography...

135 **A**: Is that the same thing?

136 **Q**: *(L)* Well, is that which is photographed by Kirlian photography the same thing that makes up the chakras? *(SV)* Well, you would have the seven major ones... you can't live without a head and torso... *(L)* What happens when you have organs, the glands related to the chakras, taken out? Women have hysterectomies all the time...

137 **A**: Good question!

Q: *(SV)* But the energy's still there 138
even though the body parts are gone! That's what I have been taught.

A: Who says? 139

Q: *(SV)* Do you want to know the 140
names of my instructors?

A: All we are trying to point out to 141
you, is that you are delving into an area where purported fact is not proven, and the entire subject is only slightly understood at your level. It is better to get facts before proclaiming knowledge, lest you make serious mistakes!

Q: *(SV)* But what about what Barbara 142
Marciniak said about the chakras? She talked about 12 chakras, seven internal and five external. Was Barbara on to something?

A: Vague. 143

Q: *(T)* It was not what Barbara was 144
on to, it was the information she was being given. *(L)* Was the information Barbara was given as far as the chakras correct as far as it went?

A: Close. 145

Q: *(L)* Well, there's a clue. *(T)* It bet- 146
ter be, we gave it to her. *(J)* True. *(T)* If they said no... *(J)* ...we are in a lot of trouble. We had better find something else to do on Saturday night. *(L)* We could bowl. Canasta, anyone? This would make a great card table. *(J)* Bridge? *(L)* I don't know how everyone else feels about it, but maybe we should just read Marciniak on this one for now and drop the subject. *(T)* They have been saying that the chakras as they have been taught may not be entirely accurate. The information about these energy points is that they do not exist as they have been laid out by others, but that they exist in different peo-

ple in different places because of the way the energy flows in each individual. They don't always exist in the same place just as the energy vortexes on the planet fluctuate and change. So, within the person the energy changes and fluctuates... *(J)* Do the chakras move around?

147 **A**: They may.

148 **Q**: *(T)* Do different people have different numbers of chakras?

149 **A**: Yes.

150 **Q**: *(T)* So, the whole idea of chakra work – not to take anything away from what Susan has been doing – is very much incorrect as it is laid out?

151 **A**: Maybe.

152 **Q**: *(SV)* OK, if you sensitize your hands, could you pick up on this energy on the body? Could you detect the chakras?

153 **A**: Maybe.

154 **Q**: *(T)* Will Reiki allow you to find the chakras as they move about?

155 **A**: Maybe.

156 **Q**: *(SV)* What about Therapeutic Touch?

157 **A**: Maybe.

158 **Q**: *(SV)* I guess maybe I had better find out. *(L)* How does all of this relate to this house and what we are doing here? *(T)* We are working on a larger scale now. *(L)* Does this house have something to do with connecting up chakras in our bodies?

159 **A**: You are drifting again.

160 **Q**: *(T)* Is it that this energy will move just like the energy in a body will move. We are working at this point because, at this time, this is where the localized energy is in this area, but that this is going to be moving?

A: Again, you have touched upon a 161
group of subjects that require massive study to accurately explain.

Q: *(J)* Does this mean that we have 162
to study and learn more before we can even discuss this with you?

A: Close. 163

Q: *(SV)* Would Edgar Cayce's material 164
be a good place to start?

A: This is a good place to start, but it 165
will take much "time" and effort.

Q: *(L)* Are you suggesting that perhaps 166
this is a subject that we don't need to go into?

A: Up to you. 167

Q: *(J)* At this point, we don't have 168
enough understanding. *(T)* Is it something important that we should be looking into?

A: Open. 169

Q: *(L)* Let's go onto something else 170
that is more simple. The other night the children saw some lights in the sky. I went out to see what they were talking about and at that point there were no moving lights, but there was a single, pulsating, red light about ten degrees to the right of Jupiter. My initial reaction to it was that it was atmospheric twinkle of a large red star or the planet Mars. There was nothing there the following night. What was it the children saw?[4]

A: Children saw planes and a heli- 171
copter.

[4] *The Wave* 41

172 **Q**: *(L)* Well, what was it I saw when I saw this red, pulsating light which did not move for quite some time?

173 **A**: Mars.

174 **Q**: *(L)* It was not Mars because it wasn't there the next night.

175 **A**: Clouds.

176 **Q**: *(T)* Yeah, there were clouds on Mars that night. *(J)* Well, lets move on. *(L)* Well, I thought it was Mars. *(J)* You were right.

177 **A**: You were right.

178 **Q**: *(J)* That's what I just said. *(L)* Now, we want to know if there is any correlation between movement of UFOs and weather patterns... *(J)* Specifically, thunderstorms.

179 **A**: Correlation?[5]

180 **Q**: *(L)* OK, can UFOs not fly during thunderstorms, or electrical storms?

181 **A**: Incorrect.

182 **Q**: *(L)* OK, they can fly during thunderstorms?

183 **A**: Yes. But "fly" is improper term.

184 **Q**: *(L)* OK, what do they do during thunderstorms if they don't fly? *(J)* They bob and weave! *(SV)* They are projections, aren't they? *(J)* Yeah, I don't think they are actually here, down in the atmosphere, anyway.

185 **A**: Operate.

186 **Q**: *(T)* Well, the real question is: does the thunderstorm interfere in the EM flow between densities?

187 **A**: Can.

188 **Q**: *(L)* Can thunderstorms interfere with their projection ability?

A: Yes. 189

Q: *(L)* Do thunderstorms or electrical 190
activity inhibit them?

A: Ionization. 191

Q: *(T)* Is the fact that there are very 192
few abduction cases – at least that I read about, and I've read quite a few of them – during thunderstorms, have to do with the thunderstorm interfering with the EM, so that the abduction would be much harder to do, therefore they don't bother doing it?

A: No. 193

Q: *(T)* Can abductions take place dur- 194
ing thunderstorms?

A: Yes. 195

Q: *(L)* Is there a possibility that thun- 196
derstorms possibly enhance this activity?

A: No. 197

Q: *(T)* So 3rd density EM disturbances 198
don't disturb 4th density?

A: Can. 199

Q: *(J)* Can they control it? *(T)* Well, 200
I haven't read very many things about abductions during storms. *(L)* Well, I have read about a few, enough to break it as a rule. *(T)* Is there some reason that it isn't happening as often during thunderstorms? *(J)* They don't want to get wet.

A: Can you drive a car during the rain? 201

Q: *(J)* Yes, but if it is raining really 202
hard, you avoid it. *(L)* Is there any particular reason why more abductions and UFO sightings occur at night?

A: Not correct. 203

[5] *High Strangeness* 8

204 **Q**: *(L)* So, you mean there is as much activity in the daytime as there is at night?

205 **A**: Yes.

206 **Q**: *(L)* Well, that blew that theory. Is it true that the vastness of space is an illusion of our units of space-time?

207 **A**: Too complex for simple response.

208 **Q**: *(L)* Oh dear. *(J)* We're just way over our heads tonight, aren't we. *(L)* Well, let's try this one...

209 **A**: Trying too hard to carve impression.

210 **Q**: *(L)* Not really. We want to ask these questions...

211 **A**: Yes, really!

212 **Q**: *(T)* Do you have anything to impart to us? *(L)* Yes, you have the floor. *(T)* Or the table... *(J)* Or the walls, or the ceiling...

213 **A**: Just ask more simple questions instead of trying to solve major riddles in one session.

214 **Q**: *(T)* Here's an easy one: is the EM wave still circling the Earth?

215 **A**: Yes.

216 **Q**: *(L)* I don't want to ask simple questions. *(J)* Is this affecting the recent tropical storm? *(T)* Yeah, is the EM wave part of the reason for the storm out here in the Gulf?

217 **A**: Close.

218 **Q**: *(L)* I don't think I have any simple questions... *(J)* What are the Marfa lights?

219 **A**: Window to this dimension leaves static.

220 **Q**: *(T)* Is there a window to this dimension... *(L)* In Marfa?

221 **A**: Many windows on Earth.

Q: *(J)* Is there any correlation between 222
the Marfa lights and the proximity to Carlsbad caverns?

A: Try getting up close to Marfa lights! 223

Q: *(J)* Yeah, I know, you can't. As 224
soon as you walk up close, they disappear. *(L)* How do they know you are walking up to them?

A: Not proper concept. 225

Q: *(L)* What is the proper concept? 226
(T) What happens if you get close to them?

A: They appear at other location. 227

Q: *(J)* Does the EM from your body 228
repel the light?

A: It is visual reality representation 229
only.

Q: *(J)* So, they are not really there, you 230
just think you see them?

A: Close. 231

Q: *(T)* How close do you have to get to 232
them for something to happen?

A: No. 233

Q: *(T)* You don't have to get close to 234
them? Well, you don't have to get close to them, they're just a residue. *(J)* Are they a refraction of something that is going on someplace else? *(T)* How far...

A: Close. 235

Q: *(T)* They are a refraction of some- 236
thing that is going on someplace else? *(L)* So, when you get close, you can no longer see them because... *(J)* ...the angle is wrong. Where are they actually happening, if not there?

A: Somewhere else from viewer. 237

Q: *(J)* Thanks! We got that. *(T)* On 238
the surface or underground?

A: Review two answers past. 239

240 **Q**: *(J)* Are you referring to the visual reality representation?

241 **A**: Yes.

242 **Q**: *(J)* So, they don't really exist in 3rd density?

243 **A**: Close.

244 **Q**: *(J)* Are they like a bleed-through?

245 **A**: Yes.

246 **Q**: *(T)* But the event is not happening where you see the lights... where the observer sees the lights?

247 **A**: Terry, pay attention!

248 **Q**: *(J)* He's tired tonight. *(L)* OK. Let's ditch that one, then. Now, the general scientific opinion is that the major dying of dinosaurs occurred 65 million years ago. You have given us the figure 27 million years ago. Can you explain the discrepancy?

249 **A**: Radio carbon dating is not exact science.

250 **Q**: *(J)* They have said that before. *(L)* So, you are going to stick with your 27 million?

251 **A**: Stick?

252 **Q**: *(L)* We must have somebody who is really on the outer fringes here! *(J)* Yeah, lighten up!

253 **A**: Same could be said for all present!

254 **Q**: *(J)* Same to you, fella! *(L)* Let's see if I have another fairly simple question here... *(J)* Don't mean to be testy tonight... *(SV)* Blame it on the weather. *(L)* I want to ask my TDARM questions, because poor old Roger really stirred my brain... *(F)* Did he give you those questions? *(L)* No, but my brain was stimulated and I thought of them and if we could get some answers, it might help his theory a lot. Well, we will ditch them. Maybe Tom and Cherie have another question... *(C)* When are we going to finish this project?

A: Question should be "if," not when. 255

Q: *(TF)* Oh great! Thanks, Cherie! 256
I'm going to have this hanging over me now!

A: Seems to be struggle within organi- 257
zation!

Q: *(L)* Is there? Are you getting a has- 258
sle about it? *(TF)* Not from the people that count. But, it's a political organization like any other. [Laughter] She can do this because she doesn't have to write this thing! *(L)* Is there anything you can tell Tom to help make it easier?

A: Tom's future lies in independent ca- 259
reer.

Q: [Laughter] *(J)* Just what he wanted 260
to hear! *(TF)* I may be fired! *(L)* No, I don't think that's what it means!

A: No. 261

Q: *(L)* See, you're not going to be fired! 262

A: Writing is your "calling" but as au- 263
thor, not journalist, your publication has so far survived being absorbed by the Consortium, but only barely, and that may not be true in the near future!

Q: *(L)* You do know what the Consor- 264
tium is? *(TF)* Are they referring to Robert Bass?

A: This is but one portal. 265

Q: *(L)* I guess that means they can get 266
in that way or another way. Well...

A: You would not appreciate the chang- 267
ing atmosphere that would accompany a "buy out."

Q: [Laughter] *(TF)* That is an under- 268
statement. *(J)* That means that this

project would be their property and you wouldn't be able to use it.

269 **A**: There is much more to the puzzle than what appears on the surface!!!!!

270 **Q**: *(TF)* See what you started with your question! *(T)* It's all your fault, Cherie! *(C)* I didn't even ask about the photos! *(T)* That's Pulitzer stuff, there!

271 **A**: Photos can "disappear!"

272 **Q**: *(J)* Oh great! Oh great! *(T)* We are moving into the warning stuff, now.

273 **A**: Do you remember the curriculum at journalism school, Tom?

274 **Q**: *(L)* I'm sure he does! What's the point?

275 **A**: Question is for Tom.

276 **Q**: *(TF)* Sure, why?

277 **A**: Do you suppose there may have been any propaganda?

278 **Q**: *(TF)* I guess that depends on whose point of view. *(T)* That's always true.

279 **A**: Yours.

280 **Q**: *(J)* Yeah, what was your point of view? *(TF)* This is not facetious, but the only propaganda I remember was IU basketball! [Laughter]

281 **A**: Not being aware is a symptom of successful methodology... beware!

282 **Q**: *(L)* I guess that not being aware that you are being propagandized is a symptom of good propaganda! *(TF)* Yeah, that would be great propaganda! *(L)* So, what's your point here?

283 **A**: You will soon become disillusioned by events soon to take place. This is good, because it will represent an awakening on your part, as you are a genuine and good hearted and honest soul.

Q: *(J)* That's nice! *(TF)* Whose class had propaganda? 284

A: Not point, was not class, was general direction of program, which is symptomatic of a much bigger issue. 285

Q: *(C)* What events are soon to take place? 286

A: Takeover of employer is imminent! 287

Q: *(T)* Whose taking over? *(L)* They said the Consortium. *(T)* Are we talking about the overall, total media? *(J)* Is it just the *St. Pete Times* or... *(T)* ...that one they haven't got hold of yet... *(L)* Publish in a hurry... 288

A: Yes. 289

Q: *(J)* Yes, what? *(T)* Either publish in a hurry or go for the book and forget the series. *(TF)* Don't say that in front of Cherie! *(T)* Her pictures can go in your book. *(TF)* Don't say that in front of Cherie! [Laughter] You can't publish color if it's in a book. *(C)* If they are in a book they are bad reproductions. *(T)* Sorry... 290

A: Your instincts as a reporter are to uncover hidden truths, but beware that you have been trained to uncover only some types of "truth," and not others. 291

Q: *(TF)* I want to ask one more question about the watch. Which state of the Union is the body of water located where the watch is? 292

A: Do not know, as we access visual reference only, and cannot determine artificially designated borders in this instance. If watch were lost next to road sign, for example, it might be different! 293

Q: *(TF)* Is the area around the body of water flat or mountainous? 294

A: Appears to be "broken." 295

Q: *(L)* The area appears to be broken? 296

297 **A**: Close.

298 **Q**: *(L)* Rough terrain? *(TF)* Why was my father in church?

299 **A**: Open.

300 **Q**: *(TF)* Was it a ceremony involving one of his children?

301 **A**: Maybe.

302 **Q**: *(T)* Maybe is a better answer than "open." *(L)* Jan, tell Tom about your Margaret S thing. *(J)* God, I can't believe you remembered that name! *(L)* I remember everything I type after I type it!

(J) That's amazing. Yeah, I had a little thing that I wanted the Cassiopaeans to answer for me, and they had a real hard time visualizing it for me... they just kind of focus in on...

(L) No, they visualized it extremely well; they saw you in a basement with your friends with candles and they described it as some sort of ritual activity. Jan wanted them to tell what she was doing...

(J) Actually, I wanted them to repeat a phrase... we were doing, I guess, some sort of black magic, trying to put the whammy on a biology teacher that nobody liked... [Laughter]

(L) Jan has a past...

(T) The thing is, with the channel, they see what we see, they know what we know... what's in your mind and subconscious...

(L) ...or what you saw...

(T) Anything that is not within the channel itself, they cannot pick up...

(L) Oh, no! They have come through with tons of stuff that's not in this room or in anybody's mind in here!

(TF) If they only know what's in y'all's mind, how can you ask questions about Jesus... how could that be within...

(L) I think what they do is focus on a point in space-time that they access like a computer, but that all of the artificial constructions that we have created to separate and define are like Greek to them.

(J) Well, time is definitely something that man has created because we live on a planet that has days and nights and the passage of seasons. If we lived on a planet that did not have days and nights and passing seasons, we would not have the concept of time. *(F)* Or, if you were floating around in space...

(J) ...then you wouldn't have up or down either...

(L) The other night I was looking for a bottle of ear drops. We asked the Cassiopaeans where they were. They said: in the bedroom, drawer, white cloth and symbols. Well, I found them in a make-up bag on top of the drawer, the bag being lined with white cloth. And, what is make-up but "symbols"?

(F) That's interesting because I had forgotten about that.

(L) Yes, it is strange what is accessed and how it is represented. Tom, do you think there are going to be changes at the *Times*?

(TF) No.

(L) Well, you might want to consider getting this thing finished as soon as possible anyway...

A: Will be a "take-over," count on it! 303

Q: *(TF)* I guess there could be differ- 304
ent kinds of takeovers. *(J)* Yeah. It could be just a change in management. *(L)* OK, Cherie, do you have any other

questions? [Laughter] *(C)* I'm thinking. *(L)* Now that you opened that can of worms... *(J)* Worms Are Us! *(TF)* I didn't mean to monopolize this session... *(J)* You didn't. Don't worry about it! *(T)* Not at all! *(LM)* [Just coming in the room.] What was the question and what was the answer? *(L)* It was a whole series of them. Cherie asked a question that opened a whole can of worms. *(TF)* Bottom line is: I have to write quickly! *(L)* Yes, worms came squirming out all over the place. *(J)* Changes, takeovers... change of atmosphere... *(L)* What would you do if that happened? *(TF)* I don't know... you just have to roll with the punches. *(L)* OK, they don't want me to ask any of my time travel questions... *(T)* I am at zero energy level tonight... *(L)* That must be what our problem is. Terry is over there zoning out on us. *(TF)* What do you mean "what your problem is"? *(L)* Well, when any one of us has low energy, it limits the reception. *(J)* Why is Terry's energy is so low tonight?

305 **A**: Has virus.

306 **Q**: *(SV)* Don't breathe this way! *(T)* Ebola is here! *(L)* I was curious about the kamikaze virus I had the other day. It made me think about virii in general. Since virii don't have DNA, is it possible that they could be used to modify DNA?

307 **A**: No.

308 **Q**: *(J)* Well, that's good. *(TF)* They don't have DNA? Do they have RNA? *(L)* Well, they are missing one or the other... *(J)* They are cellular parasites... *(SV)* Are you going to ask more about the tunnels? *(L)* Were there any ramifications to this virus not apparent on the surface?

A: No. 309

Q: *(L)* OK. *(J)* When I got home from 310
work the other day. I realized that I was hungry and suddenly I got the shakes and I was real dizzy. I rushed in and made myself a peanut butter and jelly sandwich and drank a glass of milk and it seemed to calm me down. Was this because I had not eaten?

A: Low blood sugar. 311

Q: *(J)* Is that indicative of a condition 312
that I have now?

A: Vague. 313

Q: *(L)* Does that mean she has a) hy- 314
poglycemia or b) hyperinsulinism?

A: No, no. 315

Q: *(L)* Neither. Was it just a momen- 316
tary low blood sugar condition from working too long without eating?

A: Yes. 317

Q: *(J)* I physically had the shakes and 318
I was dizzy and nauseous. *(TF)* What was the 'Mmmmmmm' sound in my father's dreams? *(L)* You're big into dreams, huh? *(TF)* It's a family thing!

A: Was accessing sound waves in alpha 319
state not normally audible.

Q: *(TF)* Why did he find the dreams 320
so threatening?

A: His interpretation. 321

Q: *(L)* Maybe it was something he 322
didn't understand and it scared him. *(TF)* Was it related to Germany?

A: No. 323

Q: *(TF)* He had a series of dreams one 324
summer, 1943, and it was interesting because his father, the dream analyst, could help him with it.

(F) Was his father a dream analyst?

(TF) Right. The same one that lost the watch.

(L) Was there some kind of antagonism between them?

(TF) Well, he was a Freudian dream analyst, so, yes! [Laughter] Nothing more than the normal father-son stuff.

(L) Is there such a thing as normal father-son stuff?

(SV) I doubt it.

(TF) That's true.

(L) Nothing on this planet is normal, or so it would seem. Well, unless somebody has a real outstanding question they just have to ask, I think we should shut down for the night.

End of Session

June 6, 1995

I was upset by the previous session. I knew that part of the problem was the presence of Tom and Cherie, but I also wanted to know what had been up with Jan, who seemed to be the source of the negative energy toward me. It was as though a kind of tit-for-tat thing had been set in motion. I had offended her by complaining that she ought not to publish sessions with real names retained, and then she went after me because I didn't let her know in advance that Tom and Cherie were to be present. The end result, in my mind, was that the session had been so compromised by negative feelings all around that I was even doubting if the communicants had been the Cs at all! I was going to try to get some clarity on this factor of the influence of people present at sessions.

Participants: 'Frank', Laura

1 **Q**: *(L)* Hello.

2 **A**: Stop.

3 **Q**: *(L)* What does that mean? *(F)* Don't ask me! *(L)* Hello![1]

4 **A**: Hello. Azoref from Cassiopaea.

5 **Q**: *(L)* Who was it that said stop?

6 **A**: Static.

7 **Q**: *(L)* There was static?

8 **A**: Yes.

9 **Q**: *(L)* What was the source of the static?

10 **A**: Not important, static always present to some degree.[2]

Q: *(L)* I want to ask some fairly quick questions. 11

A: Okay. 12

Q: *(L)* With whom were we communicating on Saturday night? 13

A: Cassiopaea. 14

Q: *(L)* Was there any corruption in Saturday night's session? 15

A: Maybe. 16

Q: *(L)* Well, I am not looking for a maybe. I felt somewhat offended by the atmosphere that was generated. We had guests and it was important... 17

A: If corrupted, came from 3rd level. 18

[1] *The Wave* 41

[2] This was an interesting remark since I was attempting to see if there was better clarity without additional people present. Obviously, there could still be static with only myself and Frank.

19 **Q**: *(L)* Can you only identify the corruption that comes from your level?

20 **A**: No.

21 **Q**: *(L)* Was there an element of... I don't want to lead here... my impression was that the group was in a state of tension. Is this correct?

22 **A**: Yes.

23 **Q**: *(L)* Why?

24 **A**: Jan was unhappy because of guests.

25 **Q**: *(L)* Why?

26 **A**: Not notified ahead.

27 **Q**: *(L)* Well, I expected Jan and Terry to arrive early enough to tell them and I was saving it until then as a surprise, but they came late so I just figured things could happen as they happened.[3]

28 **A**: Jan feels you should keep her "abreast."

29 **Q**: *(L)* Well, essentially, that is how things have been done, but, at the same time, a lot of things happen spontaneously. If it wasn't long distance, I would probably keep her more 'abreast' as you say. And, besides, I am a big girl. I don't need another mother. Frank and I have been doing what we do, more or less directed by our own inner urgings, for close to four years now. I don't think we should fix it if it isn't broken![4]

A: No need for explanation, just an- 30
swered question for you.

Q: *(L)* Well, I felt a little strange when 31
I was accused by Jan of 'showing off' for our guests, and then the channel reflected this same attitude. What's the story here?

A: If there is strong prejudice by any 32
member or members of level three channel participants it may cause messages to be altered at the point of reception.[5]

Q: *(L)* Well, then that must be what 33
Jan feels. But, what she doesn't realize is that it was important to me for *all* of us to appear in our best light and that what we are doing to be seen as intelligent and professional.[6] I mean, I didn't ask to be picked for the *Times* series. But, at the same time, I have certainly paid my dues and worked very hard for a very long time. And, Frank and I have sat here for almost four years in a dedicated and open way when no one else would bother to participate. And that is not even considering the 20 or so years before this that I have obsessively pushed for a breakthrough. I mean, it's

[3]Yes, I did expect T & J to arrive early enough to let them know that we would have guests, but that really does *not* excuse me from not simply using the phone to give Jan a call a couple days in advance to let her know. So really, I was the one who created the situation that upset Jan. What I was saying here was true enough, but it was a weak excuse and today, I wouldn't accept it from anybody.

[4]More narrative to exculpate myself. Like I said, I wouldn't accept that from anybody nowadays!

[5]This is another super-important bit of data for understanding the sessions and the issues of corruption.

[6]This was true enough. Even though I was to blame for creating the situation that upset Jan, she reacted to it. So there was negative input on both sides. This sort of tempest in a teapot occurs so often in human relations that it's cliche.

not like I just woke up one day and said: "I think we will channel the Cassiopaeans today and go out and find a *Times* reporter to write about it!" I spent a lot of time preparing questions and it seemed that whatever was making it through the 'prejudiced channel' did not even want to deal with questions that were quite similar to many we have asked in the past – so it seems that the prejudice came through toward me in a specific way.

34 **A**: Yes.

35 **Q**: *(L)* Well, if people can be so easily subjected to prejudice and emotional thinking, would that not be considered psychic attack?[7]

36 **A**: Result of. Careful not to make hasty moves based upon events which may be transitory in nature.

37 **Q**: *(L)* Well, I feel like we have all been under attack...

38 **A**: Attack does not emanate from Terry and Jan.

39 **Q**: *(L)* Well, the whole session seems ruined. Even the answer about the lights in the sky was verifiably wrong. You have said that the channel is 'grooved' and cannot be corrupted, yet obviously wrong answers were given, and it seems that you are saying that the attack is 'through' Terry and Jan and the garbled emotions they are experiencing, correct?

40 **A**: Yes.

Q: *(L)* Well, even the answer about 41
the lights in the sky. Mars is 120 degrees away from Jupiter... the answers given to Tom and Cherie may have been based on this 'prejudice', as you call it... Tom and Cherie were upset by this, I was upset... the whole thing was very upsetting! I need some help here!

A: Patience pays! 42

Q: *(L)* Well, do Frank and I have any 43
strong prejudices right now creating any corruption?

A: No.[8] 44

Q: *(L)* Well, what about Tom and 45
Cherie's article?

A: 20 or 30 months.[9] 46

Q: *(L)* What about the *Times* being 47
taken over?

A: Eventually will happen. 48

Q: *(L)* Is it imminent? 49

A: Define imminent. 50

Q: *(L)* Within twelve months? 51

A: Not likely, but possible. 52

Q: *(L)* What is the source of the attack 53
on Terry and Jan? If their emotions are being attacked, I don't think it would be possible to get a clear answer to this question with them present...

A: Lizards. 54

Q: *(L)* What about the information 55
about Tom's grandfather's watch?

A: Open, if concerned, suggest new ses- 56
sion.

[7] *The Wave* 41

[8] Hah! The very fact that I asked the question suggests that I had strong prejudices to be right, and that surely influenced the response!

[9] The article was finally published in February of 2000, a lot further in the future than "20 or 30 months", though that was the projected date at the time of this session.

57 **Q**: *(L)* Well, that whole thing just left me with a bad taste in my mouth. Violette wants to attend soon. Is that alright?

58 **A**: Up to you.

59 **Q**: *(L)* Well, Violette has a lot of 'prejudices' which could restrict the information. Is this correct?

60 **A**: Maybe.

61 **Q**: *(L)* You understand that I am trying to protect what Frank and I have worked so hard and long to achieve...

62 **A**: Of course.

63 **Q**: *(L)* And, I am trying to protect the integrity of the information, and I am trying to protect the reputation of the information. And, if we invite somebody who is, for God's sake, a newspaper reporter, and somebody can come in and blow the whole session with attitude or prejudice, no matter what the source... Do you see my point here?

64 **A**: Yes. Suggest Tom and Cherie attend smaller session.

65 **Q**: *(L)* Well, what am I going to do?

66 **A**: Follow your instincts, but strongly suggest patience, or attack is successful!!!!!

Q: *(L)* Oh! So, this is a very subtle 67
and concerted effort to break up the group?!

A: Yes. 68

Q: *(L)* Well, even without the attack 69
syndrome, we all have very strong personalities and there seems to be a control issue going on here too.

A: Part of attack! 70

Q: *(L)* Well, how long is this attack go- 71
ing to continue?

A: Open according to learning cycle 72
length.

Q: *(L)* Should we temporarily suspend 73
the sessions?

A: Up to you. 74

Q: *(L)* Would the attack end sooner if 75
we do not suspend the sessions?

A: Maybe. 76

Q: *(L)* Would it help to end the attack 77
if I did suspend the sessions?

A: Less likely. 78

Q: *(L)* OK, that's the clue. We shall 79
just carry on.

A: Yes. Goodbye. 80

End of session

June 9, 1995

A few nights earlier I had done what turned out to be a full-bore exorcism on a guy, and it really made me re-think what I was doing along that line. It was scary as heck, to put it mildly. I've given links in the footnotes to podcast discussion of the case that includes excerpts from the actual recording of the exorcism.

Interestingly, in light of the topic of the exorcism, one of our questions about 'monsters' brought in a new term: 'window faller'. It seems that when inter-dimensional windows open, things can 'fall through' them. I suppose that it might work as well the other way: things – or people – from our reality could fall into other dimensions. That's a creepy thought and reminds us of the Flight 19 tragedy.

Participants: 'Frank' and Laura

1 **A**: Zauto.

2 **Q**: *(L)* Is that your name?

3 **A**: Yes.

4 **Q**: *(L)* I like Z names. Where are you from?

5 **A**: Cassiopaea.

6 **Q**: *(L)* I have several questions tonight. Are you open for questions?

7 **A**: Sure.

8 **Q**: *(L)* The first one is: On Tuesday night, I did a spirit release on a fellow named VM. It seemed to get a little rough. What type of entity were we dealing with?[1]

A: STS. 9

Q: *(L)* What density level? 10

A: Fifth.[2] 11

Q: *(L)* Was I successful in freeing VM from this domination? 12

A: Open. 13

Q: *(L)* Is that STS entity gone for at least this time? 14

A: From direct attachment. 15

[1]You can access a podcast discussing this here:
http://cassiopaea.org/2011/11/29/channeling-and-exorcism-part-1 and
http://cassiopaea.org/2011/11/29/channeling-and-exorcism-part-2/
You can read a transcript of the podcast here:
https://cassiopaea.org/forum/index.php/topic,6154.0.html and here
https://cassiopaea.org/forum/index.php/topic,5903.0.html

[2]Demonic.

16 **Q**: *(L)* Is that entity going to try to return?

17 **A**: Open.

18 **Q**: *(L)* Does VM have further attachments at this time?

19 **A**: Slight.

20 **Q**: *(L)* So, the next session, it will be a cake-walk?

21 **A**: Open.

22 **Q**: *(L)* Will it be possible for me to release the attachments to his girlfriend at a distance?

23 **A**: No.

24 **Q**: *(L)* Should I attempt it?

25 **A**: No.

26 **Q**: *(L)* Is there anything about VM I should know?

27 **A**: No.

28 **Q**: *(L)* Violette is worried about her living situation. She was meditating and tried to send light into the apartment near her because the people there are very negative. She felt like something slammed back at her. She would like to know what this was.

29 **A**: Violette seeks protection, but does not promote it.

30 **Q**: *(L)* Was it karmically an error to direct light into someone else's living space without their permission?

31 **A**: Yes.

32 **Q**: *(L)* Would it have been better to just surround herself with light?

33 **A**: Yes.

34 **Q**: *(L)* When I do the next spirit release with VM, would it be alright to have Tom and Cherie present?

A: Up to you. 35

Q: *(L)* What about their 'prejudices'? 36

A: Okay. 37

Q: *(L)* I went to the doctor for the final check-up. When can I expect a settlement and how much? 38

A: Open. 39

Q: *(L)* Well, how much? 40

A: Worry not, we have instructed you to have faith in such matters. Otherwise, valuable energy is wasted, and besides, "a watched pot never boils!" 41

Q: *(L)* Well, the thing about that is that I wonder if you guys were behind that whole accident thing in order to provide funds to me... 42

A: Maybe. So have faith! 43

Q: *(L)* It is not a lack of faith, just curiosity! 44

A: Which killed the cat! 45

Q: *(L)* But satisfaction brought him back! 46

A: Oh yeah? 47

Q: *(L)* Yeah! And, when I get satisfied I feel good all over! Is the attack still going on? 48

A: Most likely. 49

Q: *(L)* I read in a book about a monster called the 'Beast of Gevaudan'. Who or what was this beast? 50

A: Other dimensional "window faller."[3] 51

Q: *(L)* You mean it fell into our dimension from another through a dimensional window? 52

A: Yes. 53

[3] *High Strangeness* 7; *The Wave* 9, 52

54 **Q**: *(L)* Well, that would explain a lot of things about it. What about the creature known as 'Spring-Heel Jack' who terrorized England some time ago?

55 **A**: Same.

56 **Q**: *(L)* What about the Mothman in West Virginia?

57 **A**: Same.

58 **Q**: *(L)* So, windows to other dimensions are the explanation for a whole host of strange things?

59 **A**: Yes.

60 **Q**: *(L)* Why is [my daughter] so afraid of sleeping in her own bed lately?

61 **A**: Simple blossoming of awareness and consciousness evolvement.

62 **Q**: *(L)* Why is Frank so tired lately?[4]

63 **A**: Depression.

64 **Q**: *(L)* Is there anything I can do to help?

65 **A**: Let it "run its course," karmic in nature.

66 **Q**: *(L)* Well, Frank has such a lovely aura; how can he have such icky karma?

67 **A**: Not "icky" karma, has to do with adjustment factors.

68 **Q**: *(L)* As soon as he adjusts in some way, he will stop having these depressions?

69 **A**: Not point.

70 **Q**: *(L)* What is the point? I mean, he is suffering. It is awful to have to spend so much time suffering.

71 **A**: Adjustment process.

Q: *(L)* What is he adjusting from to? 72

A: Not to be answered at this point. 73

Q: *(L)* Edgar Cayce said you could just 74
stop karma at any point by opening your awareness and making a decision. Why can't Frank do that? Can anybody do that? Can you just say "I've had enough" and stop it?

A: No, because not usual circumstance. 75

Q: *(L)* Is Frank's karma 'special' 76
karma?

A: Subjective. Different. 77

Q: *(L)* Different from the usual. Is 78
there anything that he could do to make it better? Any clue? Any word of encouragement?

A: Won't change until environment 79
does.

Q: *(L)* Do you mean the environment 80
as in the whole planet, or his personal environment?

A: Former. 81

Q: *(L)* Does this mean he is going to 82
have this until we all go to 4th density?

A: Until status quo is abridged.[5] 83

Q: *(L)* What is the status quo? 84

A: Self explanatory. 85

Q: *(L)* So, it doesn't mean going into 86
4th density necessarily, but until the status quo of the planet is abridged, or some change occurs in the status quo?

A: Yes. 87

Q: *(L)* So, when some sweeping 88
changes in the status quo of the planet occur, Frank will 'come into his own'? Is that correct?

---

[4] *The Wave* 39

[5] Definition of *status quo*: the existing state of affairs. *Abridged*: to lessen, reduce in scope; lessen or curtail rights or authority.

89 **A**: Close.

90 **Q**: *(L)* Is this going to happen soon?

91 **A**: Open.

Q: *(L)* I couldn't help myself! Thank 92
you so much!

A: Goodbye. 93

End of Session

June 10, 1995

In view of the recent sessions that were not entirely satisfying to me because of the possible elements of corruption, and even though I didn't like it, Frank kept urging it, so I was persuaded to conduct this direct channeling session. As mentioned before, in my mind was the idea that Frank would strengthen in some way by being exposed directly to the information source and that would either develop on its own, or at least contribute to better energetic balance when channeling as a group via the board.

Direct Channeling with Frank.

Participants: 'Frank', Laura, Susan V, Terry and Jan

[Laura induces hypnotic trance in Frank.]

1 **Q**: *(L)* Who do we have with us this evening?

2 **A**: We are not a single entity; as always, that's not changed.

3 **Q**: *(L)* Is anyone in particular representing, or do you prefer to not designate thus?

4 **A**: Well it brings up an interesting point because in your previous sessions using the board, we've noticed that you tend to refer to us as though we were a single entity. In actuality, that is not the correct way of thinking of us. We are multiple entities in union with each other with a singular voice when communicating with you.

5 **Q**: *(L)* We are all gathered here this evening for this experiment to discover if we can receive information through this method as opposed to the board method. Is there anything we can do to enhance the use of this particular method?

A: Define enhance, please. 6

Q: *(L)* Is there anything we can do to make the channel more comfortable, anything to do to make the induction more effective? 7

A: Is it not effective at this point? 8

Q: *(L)* Yes, it seems to be effective, but if there is anything we can or should do to make it better, we would like to know what it is. Any particular induction process that would work better than another aside from getting the numbers straight. 9

A: That is not necessary at this time. 10

Q: *(L)* OK, then can we begin addressing questions? 11

A: Certainly. 12

Q: *(L)* The first question I have is concerning last Saturday night's ses- 13 sion, which nobody seems to have been happy with. We would like to understand why the information seemed to be so garbled and distorted and, quite frankly, incorrect.[1]

14 **A**: What makes you feel it was incorrect?

15 **Q**: *(L)* Because one of the answers was that what I was seeing outside was the planet Mars. It could not have been the planet Mars because Mars was 120 degrees away from the planet Jupiter.

16 **A**: Perhaps the question was posed in such a way as to receive that response. Suggest you check the material more closely.[2]

17 **Q**: *(L)* It was also said that the children were seeing airplanes and helicopters. When I went out, what I saw was most definitely not a helicopter or an airplane and was only ten degrees away from the planet Jupiter, and was a red, pulsating light. Can you tell me what I saw?

18 **A**: Well, if you desire to believe that what you saw was something other than any response given, that's perfectly acceptable. But, when inquiring upon such things as visual reference, one must be prepared for any and all answers.[3]

19 **Q**: *(L)* That seems to be rather evasive.

20 **A**: Evasiveness may also indicate a desire to help one learn about oneself and one's environment.

Q: *(L)* What I saw out there was not an 21
airplane or a helicopter; it was also not the planet Mars. Whatever it was, it was not there the following night or any night subsequent to that. Therefore, it was some sort of object that wasn't of a sort that we usually see, and it baffles me as to why it would be conducive to learning for me to...

A: May we ask a question? 22

Q: *(L)* Sure. 23

A: When seeking to identify visual ref- 24
erence, would it not be wise to be patient with the outcome of the analysis?

Q: *(L)* Well, sure. 25

A: You state that what you saw was 26
not a plane or a helicopter. We are interested to know how you can be certain of that?

Q: *(L)* Because I stood and watched it 27
for a considerable period of time and it never moved.

A: Does that indicate that it was not 28
a helicopter?

Q: *(L)* Yes, because even helicopters, 29
when they hover, there is some lateral or horizontal movement or motion, and they also have different kinds of lights on them. They don't sit there and look like a single, large, reddish-orange, glowing light that pulsates.

A: Okay, well all of these various... 30

Q: *(L)* Could you speak more loudly 31
and clearly?[4]

[1] *The Wave* 41

[2] This answer was evasive. I checked the previous session and there was nothing wrong with the question.

[3] Again, evasive, wordy response.

[4] It was interesting that as I challenged the evasive responses, Frank's voice got lower and lower.

32 **A**: We will try to accommodate your request, however circumstances may not make that completely possible. Remember, we are using a different mode which requires cooperation of physical capability and other factors.

33 **Q**: *(L)* OK. Do you have any further remarks to make about the session last Saturday?[5]

34 **A**: No. If you have any questions or further comments?

35 **Q**: *(L)* Anybody else have any further questions about it? *(T)* Did Tom understand the information that you gave him last week?

36 **A**: Could you specify, please?

37 **Q**: *(T)* At the end of the session you spoke to Tom about his university learning and about his work and about the company that he works for and that there was a possibility of takeover in the not-too-distant future. Do you feel that Tom understood what you were talking about?

38 **A**: Tom understood the message given, but was resisting the information, which is his prerogative.

39 **Q**: *(T)* What about Cherie? Did she understand?

40 **A**: Certainly to the extent that was necessary for her level of development.

41 **Q**: *(L)* Which is?

A: That is a vague question. That is 42
difficult to answer properly, please understand, we do not mean to criticize, but objectivity is necessary for progress with these sessions. When you state a question asking if a subject's level of development is sufficient, that is subjective because who is to determine what is sufficient and what isn't? All are at different levels of development. Do you understand?[6]

Q: *(L)* Yes. 43

A: Now, if the question is: "Is Cherie's 44
level of development relative to others present, greater or lesser," the answer would naturally be lesser. Which should not be surprising because the exposure level has been lesser. The same is true for the subject referred to as Tom French. The exposure level has been to a lesser degree there, too, so therefore, naturally, the understanding level is lower, relatively speaking.

Q: *(L)* In a previous session, com- 45
ments were made regarding remolecularization, and you gave us a rather cryptic remark, and I quote: "learn 4th level assembly." Could you tell us what 4th level assembly is?[7]

A: That is a fragmented question. The 46
response to the question you are referring to is adequate. However, turning it around and posing a question with no further data to compare it to is not

[5]I was not happy with the answers so I decided to just leave the topic, which was emotionally charged, and move on to something else.

[6]I was not the one making the assumption. I did not ask if the person's level of development was sufficient, but simply what was meant by 'level of development'. This is a good example of bamboozling by excessive verbiage.

[7]Again, I was not very impressed with the responses, the assumptions, and the attitude of the entity(ies) Frank was allegedly channeling, which came through in tone and inflection of voice. So, I changed the subject again to something more neutral.

adequate. If you would, please, we ask that you build your question up more carefully. Do you understand?[8]

47 **Q**: *(L)* Yes, and I don't have that particular segment of the transcript in hand so I am at a loss as to how to build the question up. *(T)* Is that particular subject something that we can work with through the board, or is it too complex a set of answers for the board to handle?

48 **A**: The problem is never the method. The problem is merely care-taking in discussion, learning, or a question and answer session. For example, if one seeks an answer to a complex question, one must be patient for the absorption of information is most important and missing any part of it will cause the entire answer to be misunderstood or incomplete. Therefore, any method can be used for receiving knowledge about complicated issues, however, patience is the key, otherwise the information will not be properly absorbed.[9]

49 **Q**: *(L)* We have been looking to make contact with a 4th density individual as we were advised and we would like to know if there are any specific ways or means that we can go about seeking out this individual, and how would we recognize said individual if we found them?

50 **A**: All of that will fall into place when the situation is right for you.

51 **Q**: *(T)* At the time of that session you advised us that we needed to find this 4th density individual. Are you now saying that...

A: The message given was merely to prepare for eventuality. Remember, knowledge is important because it is protection. Think of it also as a foundation for progression to further knowledge and experience. Therefore, gaining of knowledge can sometimes best be facilitated by giving information which prepares one for more important events in succession, understand? 52

Q: *(T)* I believe so. The context of that transmission was that we were under attack and it would be best to facilitate, as I understood the information, to finding this individual. Is the level of attack not that sufficient that we need an immediate intervention by this individual, but that the timing will come on its own, in the future, as we reference time, that this individual will contact us? 53

A: All of that statement was correct with the exception of the very last part. The individual is not necessarily going to contact you. Most important element of the experience has been the foundation that the original statement allowed. In other words, you are now prepared for the eventual meeting of one of a 4th density STO nature, and because the information was given, you are, in fact, aware of the possibility of this occurring. Therefore, you are more on the look-out for those individuals who may fit that profile, and they are prevalent in your midst, though you were not fully aware of that prior to the information being given. 54

Q: *(L)* Are these 4th density STO indi- 55

[8] Yes, we were definitely beginning to understand that this method of channeling was going to get us nothing into which we could sink our research teeth. There was nothing wrong with the question, it was not fragmented.

[9] A rather useless answer that anybody could give about anything.

viduals what is currently being talked about in many circles as 'angels'?

56 **A**: Incorrect.

57 **Q**: *(L)* Are there, as is being talked about widely, such beings as 'angels'?

58 **A**: Yes, but they are not of the 4th density.

59 **Q**: *(L)* What is an angel?

60 **A**: Sixth density light being in service to others.

61 **Q**: *(L)* Do they appear as humans?

62 **A**: May appear as a human projection.

63 **Q**: *(L)* Are they appearing as often as it is conjectured they are at this time period?

64 **A**: That is a vague question.

65 **Q**: *(L)* Is it possible for other-density STS beings to appear as and project themselves as angels and to be misnamed or mistaken for angels?

66 **A**: Certainly.

67 **Q**: *(L)* Is this happening to a certain extent?

68 **A**: Very likely. Deception is part of any and all processes directed toward the manipulation of others for purposes of self gain. And, as we have warned, those of the 4th density service to self nature are interested solely in their own advancement, gain or condition, and will facilitate any and all processes which will further this cause including deception of the nature described.

69 **Q**: *(T)* Going back with the 4th density beings that we are interacting with without knowing it yet, now that we are becoming aware of it. Can I be right in the assumption that because they are aware of us which you indicated in that session, and what you have said so far this evening about them, that even though we may not be interacting directly with them, they are, in fact, helping us without our knowing it?

A: Who said that you are not interacting with them directly? 70

Q: *(T)* OK, let me phrase that dif... *(J)* 71
We are interact... *(T)* We are not aware that we are interacting with 4th density beings, we still see them as just humans because we don't know which one... *(J)* We don't recognize... *(T)* We don't recognize them yet. Can I assume that they, if necessary, they are assisting us already?

A: Think carefully, now, do you really 72
not recognize them?

Q: *(T)* Well, I am trying to become 73
more aware of the people I interact with on a daily basis.

A: Are you not more aware already? 74

Q: *(L)* What's the criteria for being 75
a 4th density STO being? *(J)* Yeah, what's the profile? You mentioned profile before.

A: It depends on what your definition 76
of profile is.

Q: *(J)* Profile would be a list of criteria, 77
a checklist, if you will. *(L)* What do they look like, are they this tall, or ... *(T)* Do they look like that? *(L)* Do they have any special abilities in manipulating 3rd density reality...

A: Perhaps so, but there may be re- 78
strictions as to use of such.

Q: *(L)* Why would there be restric- 79
tions? *(J)* 4th and 5th...

A: Service to others orientation means 80
service to others. Usage of unusual powers or abilities, if you will, can cause disruption to those who do not possess these powers or abilities. Also,

remember, a 4th density being inhabiting 3rd density is not inhabiting their own density level, therefore they are in, if you will, foreign territory, which requires, for many reasons which will not be completely described here, that they do not do anything that brings attention to themselves.[10]

81 **Q**: *(J)* You have also said that about 4th density STOs: it is difficult for them to maintain in 3rd density. *(T)* No, STS. *(L)* STS. *(J)* What's the difference?

82 **A**: The difference is an STO orientation tends to expand one's state of being, STS tends to contract one's state of being.

83 **Q**: *(L)* Are you saying that association with this kind of person can be expanding to the individuals associating with same?

84 **A**: Well, that is true, but that is not what the statement meant.

85 **Q**: *(L)* I know, I was just taking it a little further. And, association with an STS... *(T)* Now, you say we are already interacting with these 4th density beings?

86 **A**: Statement...

87 **Q**: *(J)* And that we may be aware of it...

88 **A**: Statement was rather a question, do you feel that you are not interacting with 4th density STO individuals? It was a rhetorical question demanding reflection on your part. Your statements in return indicated the possibility did exist that you were. That was all.

Q: *(L)* OK. The possibility does exist 89
and this is just to make us aware and keep our eyes open. *(J)* Can you give us any kind of an indication of a way to recognize such beings?

A: No, what we ask you to do now is 90
ask yourself, and you may use us as a, if you will, sounding board for your discussion, to determine how one may recognize a 4th density STO individual, which will help you to learn, which will help you to progress, and so on.

Q: *(L)* Would a 4th density STO be- 91
ing be someone who was born in this density in the normal way?

A: You are still asking a question. 92
What we are asking you to do instead is ask yourselves, discuss and come up with the answer.

Q: *(T)* Well, a service to others being 93
would be someone who is, first off, in service to others. That would be a major indicator.

A: Correct. This is the correct way to 94
go about discovering the answer to this question rather than demanding all of the answers of us. You have the capabilities to pull the answers from within. We are more than happy to assist, but out goal is to help you strengthen yourselves for future use, if you will. It all helps one to advance and progress. All there is is lessons. It's all learning. Therefore, the quickest, the strongest way to learn is to use your own capabilities to that end. Asking us questions is certainly permitted, and helpful, but trying to seek all of the information from this particular source, in

[10] I think that this is a reasonable response, though I had the feeling at the time the the source was implying that Frank was the 4D STO being!

[11] This was another very useful response. There is certainly enough positive (or STO)

the long run, may be detrimental. Now, if you will continue, please...[11]

95 **Q**: *(L)* Well, my idea was that a STO individual would not be someone who was born in the normal way because there would be too great a risk of such an individual losing themselves in the illusion. Therefore, my thought is that an STO being would be somebody who had, maybe, some mystery about their past, or some...

(J) How would we even know that unless we were standing there when they were born or not born...

(T) We have to consider what we would observe...

(L) Well, maybe they would be somebody who wouldn't talk about their childhood?

(T) Not even that... in a group setting or a passing acquaintance we would have to be aware of how they act. How they speak. What kind of compassion they show...

(J) What kind of feeling you get from them...

(T) Yes, it wouldn't so much be a physical thing as an awareness... a connection.

(L) But, on the other hand the thing about feeling is that negative entities can counterfeit feelings or control your feelings and they might induce a negative feeling when you are in the presence of a positive individual just to throw you off track. That would be entirely part of the deception process, wouldn't you think? I mean, we all know...

(J) It's been that way...

(T) But it's something we have to learn account... that's part of the learning process.

(L) So, we can't just say that we could feel it...

(T) Who have you interacted with in the last six months who was outward going, caring, giving, offering to do things, to go places, to... to...

(L) Well, just the members of this group as far as I can see and that is limited in many ways...

(J) Yeah, that's true...

(T) Well, maybe one of us is the being. Maybe one of us is a 4th density being.

(L) Well, don't you think we would know it?

(J) No...

(T) Not really. Not if one of us is a 4th density being and has decided that it is not yet time to enter into the dialogue.

(J) Could it not even be... *(T)* We have to... *(J)* ...that they are not aware of it?

(T) They are aware... remember, the Cassiopaeans told us that they are aware of us... they know about us already as a group... they know what we are doing. Maybe not all of them, but those who we need to talk with or need to know already know about us.

(L) Well, in general, I have to say that most of the people I have interacted with in the last year or two have been one experience after another of...

(J) Pure STS...

(L) Yeah. I mean, it has been like a learning thing for me to go and...

---

information in this session to suggest that the source was STO, though Frank, himself, was a sort of restricting transducer.

(T) Who of those people has offered to do something for you as opposed to taking from you? We are not looking at a whole lot of beings. We are looking at maybe one or two out of the total number that are here that are going to assist us. Or, that we can go to for assistance...

(L) I can't say anybody outside the group. I mean, there have been people who have offered to do this or that, but the price they expected me to pay was a little too high or I found out that they were not telling the truth...

(J) Well, then, that is obviously...

(L) I assume that people mean what they say and...

(T) Let me ask a question... do all 4th density beings that are here on the planet at this time know that they are 4th density beings? Are they aware of who they are and what they are?

96 **A**: Well, that is an interesting question because it leads to another question: Are all 4th density STO beings of the same nature, physically, psychically, spiritually, et cetera?

97 **Q**: *(J)* In other words, is there a connection?

98 **A**: No, that is not the point being given. The point being given is: Are they all of the same orientation? Or is it possible that they are of different orientation?

99 **Q**: *(T)* Orientation... how so?

100 **A**: Physical nature, spiritual nature, psychic nature, awareness of self and destiny?

101 **Q**: *(T)* Just off the top of my head I would have to say that no, they would all be different because they are all different beings to begin with.

(L) So, they could be short and dark, tall and blond...

(J) I don't think that physicality has anything to do with it...

(T) One of the things I have always felt is that when we are dealing with, in this case, the being we were told to be looking out for was an Orion... *(L)* Nordic type... *(J)* No, we said Nordic...

(T) When you speak of Orions in New Age and ufology circles, they automatically flash on the Nordic type... the Aryan, blue-eyed blonde. But that is not necessarily what all Orions look like... that would only be one manifestation. They will not all look the same... they will not look like Semjase from the Pleiadians... they are not all going to look like Fabio or something, because they are going to try to blend into human society across the planet... they can't all look alike. I had a thought that they not only would not look all the same in that type of physical nature, but they would also look different ages in order to blend into whatever setting they were using. In other words, they could be 95 years old or look 95 years old if that is where they felt they needed to be... in finding out who they were. Am I anywhere close to an idea here?

A: Now, the point of our response a 102
while back was to make you aware of the tools that you possess for discovering the answer or answers to your question or questions regarding awareness and identification of 4th density STO beings in your midst, or the possibility of same. And, we have observed that you have made some small progress toward that end. However, one problem that has, if you will, cropped up, is that you have now scattered or sepa-

rated into two divergent thought patterns on the same subject. We suggest that you reorient yourselves so that your questions, goals or objectives to be answered are one and the same.

103 **Q**: *(T)* OK. *(J)* Well, we started off asking, are all of them aware of state, and then we went off into what do they look like and how to recognize them... *(T)* Well, physically, I believe that they would all look different in order to blend. They can't all be the same. *(SV)* Would they be aware that they are a 4th density being? *(J)* Yeah, that's, that's... *(T)* Awareness, the Cassiopaeans have indicated that the awareness may be at different levels.

104 **A**: Maybe at different levels, but, more importantly, the orientation of a 4th density STO being or beings may be of a different nature.

105 **Q**: *(L)* Do you mean orientation not in terms of STO versus STS, but orientation regarding what?

106 **A**: Nature of physicality, spirituality, psychic ability or awareness.

107 **Q**: *(L)* So, orientation means that they could be a Baptist... *(T)* A Muslim, Catholic...

108 **A**: Incorrect...

109 **Q**: *(T)* Spiritual attainment levels... they may be very psychic or they may not be psychic at all...

110 **A**: No. You are on the wrong path...

111 **Q**: *(L)* What do you mean by orientation?

A: Nature of being, physically, spiri- 112
tually, psychically...

Q: *(J)* They might not be human? 113

A: That is one possibility. But, there 114
are many others. And, the subject matter, or the definition of subject matters, can be a cross reference. For example have you not heard of the popular written work by one referred to as Ruth Montgomery, known as *Strangers Among Us.*[12]

Q: *(T)* Yes. 115

A: And what does that written work 116
detail?

Q: *(L)* Isn't that the one that is about 117
'walk-ins'? *(J)* I was just going to ask about walk-ins. *(SV)* No, that's different. *(T)* No, it's not about walk-ins. *(SV)* This is about aliens that are here, living amongst us... it could be the butcher, the cashier... I read it so long ago... *(T)* There's a series of them; she has five or six books.

A: You have the written works con- 118
fused.

Q: *(L)* Which one is this? 119

A: *Strangers Among Us* refers to the 120
phenomenon identified by Ruth Montgomery as 'walk-ins'.

Q: *(L)* But, you have said in previous 121
sessions that this rarely occurs.

A: Rare is relative. 122

Q: *(SV)* Ruth Montgomery also said 123
that sometimes walk-ins don't realize who or what they are.

A: Rare also may be transitory in na- 124
ture.

[12]Notice that this question about 'nature of being' never quite gets answered adequately (at least, not to me), but rather diverges off here to the topic of walk-ins as promoted by Ruth Montgomery. It is definitely not clear what this has to do with 'orientation' as in "nature of being, physically, spiritually, psychically".

125 **Q**: *(J)* You mean walk in and walk back out again?

126 **A**: No. Frequency is not necessarily static according to the timeline, as you measure time.

127 **Q**: *(T)* I have not done a lot of research on walk-ins. What is the definition of a walk-in?

128 **A**: A walk-in, as described by Ruth Montgomery, is a soul that has chosen to take over the body that was vacated by another soul that has chosen, at some level of awareness, to depart for varying reasons. In this way, a higher level entity can enter into the body that was previously occupied by a different level entity, in the form of a soul, that is to say.

129 **Q**: *(T)* A 4th level soul can then enter the body of a 3rd level?

130 **A**: Or perhaps a 4th level soul... remember, as we have described to you before, levels one through four, more appropriately density levels one through four, all involve short wave cycle recycling, or, as you refer to it, reincarnation. Because, each and every one of these density levels has a soul and a physical body marriage, as it were, in progressive life experiences. Each and every one of these density levels involves movement to the 5th level of density for contemplation during the cycling process. It is level six, which is the 1st level where short wave cycle recycling is no longer necessary because there is no more physical orientation. Therefore, all levels, one through four, have a soul reflection of the physical body at all times when in physical state. And, therefore, reincarnation of various types, is at various points on the short wave cycle always possible, and, in fact, quite probable. Do you understand?

Q: *(T)* Somewhat. That's a lot to di- 131
gest. *(J)* So, physicality is involved in levels one through four short wave recycling. *(L)* So, this means that a 4th density being can recycle through 5th density into a 3rd density body?

A: That is one method that can be 132
used, yes.

Q: *(L)* Can it also be that they can 133
come directly from 4th density into a 3rd density body, just as one of the options?

A: Yes. 134

Q: *(T)* As a walk-in. *(L)* And either 135
could be considered a walk-in?

A: That is correct. 136

Q: *(T)* I'm going off on a tangent on 137
what we have been discussing here... what happens to the soul that's in the body that the walk-in takes over? Where does that go?

A: Most likely to the 5th level for recy- 138
cling and contemplation.

Q: *(T)* And then returns? 139

A: Returns, yes. 140

Q: *(L)* So, in other words it would be- 141
hoove us to get this book, reread it to get a clue here... is this advisable?

A: That, of course, is up to you. 142

Q: *(L)* We can't keep him under much 143
longer... *(T)* To be aware of a 4th density being...

A: This is putting the subject under 144
physical stress, more than in most circumstances.

Q: *(T)* Can any of us be put into a 145
trance under these conditions so that you can use us as a vehicle?

146 **A**: That is certainly possible but there are varying degrees of difficulty depending on the individual being used.

147 **Q**: *(T)* Would I make a good relief subject?

148 **A**: Again, we ask you to please try to refrain from subjective sequence questions as it is nearly impossible for us to give adequate answers.

149 **Q**: *(T)* I guess it is something we would learn ourselves by trying it. *(J)* That's right. *(L)* OK, we'll get this book and find out what we can from there... *(T)* Has anybody else encountered anyone that they have felt an affinity toward who seems to be an open and giving person? *(SV)* I find many people that... *(J)* I had an interesting conversation today with Mary B. *(T)* We had an interesting experience with Brad today... *(L)* I would like to ask about Victor before we wrap it up.[13] At any point in time, were Frank and I in any danger?

150 **A**: Please, be more specific.

151 **Q**: *(L)* At any point in time was there any danger of Frank or I being attacked, attached, or in any way molested by the entity that was attached to or attacking Victor?

152 **A**: Well, this possibly would be a danger under normal circumstances, however the knowledge that you have already gained through contact and communication with us as well as your own efforts makes it less of a danger for you than perhaps most others. But, it certainly is true, that there was some interaction there which possibly could have proved to have been less than desirable in its results.[14]

Q: *(L)* Is there any further attachment of that nature or of that order with this individual, Victor? 153

A: It certainly is a possibility. 154

Q: *(L)* If I did another session with him, would it be safe to have observers who do not have the knowledge I have? 155

A: Well, again, we regret having to continue to answer questions with what you may believe are evasive maneuvers, but it is important to have clarity when discussing matters such as this, and therefore, we must ask that you please try to be as specific as possible when asking the questions. For example, when you say, "Is it safe to have observers," this implies that if there is a lack of safety present, there may be a calamity of some sort resulting from this, and then one must ask what sort of calamity is acceptable and what sort is not. This is why we ask that you please be specific. And, we are not trying to irritate you, merely trying to help. 156

Q: *(L)* Alright, specifically: Does Victor M have another heavy-duty attachment like the one we dealt with the other night? 157

A: It is certainly possible that the one you describe as Victor M may indeed have entities around him that could be described as attachments. 158

Q: *(L)* And, if I do another release with him... *(T)* Would it be wise for her to have someone else there in case it gets out of hand again? *(J)* If you feel the necessity for it, then do it... 159

A: Well, all we offer to this subject is that perhaps it would be wise for more 160

[13]Referring to the exorcism referenced in the previous session.
[14]That's an understatement!

care to be taken in matters such as this when possibilities do exist for complications, than has been taken up to this point. That is probably the best way to answer that question, as we do not wish to hinder development and experience or to improperly steer experience when it is necessary for development. But, it possibly could be helpful to suggest more caution.

161 **Q**: *(T)* A point to be taken: now that you are aware of what could happen... *(J)* Exactly. *(T)* ...that you know now what's... *(J)* Exactly. *(T)* ...that things are getting more intense with these spirit release sessions, especially you know that it would behoove you to have someone else there that is awake and conscious... someone, in addition... don't do it alone anymore. *(J)* Yes, definitely. *(T)* And make sure that the person who is with you knows what is going on... *(L)* And that is going to be the tough one because there are very few people who know what the heck is going on... *(T)* Knowledge protects... *(L)* I mean, the only people who have a clue in this area are the people in this room... *(T)* You knew this was coming by the way things had been going and this was the one that really did it. *(J)* It was good... *(T)* You need to have someone else in the room with you. *(L)* Is this...

162 **A**: Let us stop you right there. Do you not see how discussion, and, as we have frequently referred to it, "networking," is an extremely valuable tool.

163 **Q**: *(L)* Now, it does seem to me, that through no real drive on my own part, I have been moved like a chess piece throughout my life, to the point where, at various intervals, I have interacted with spiritual entities. And each interaction has been progressively more complex than the previous interaction. And, it seems that a lot of this has led up to doing the exorcism and spirit release work. Now, during that particular session, it occurred to me that this is really kind of an unpleasant work, and at the same time I understand that not many people can do it. It scares me. I am just wondering if this is something I continue doing or is it OK if I just quit!? *(T)* That's up to you... *(J)* Up to you, Laura... *(T)* What we are doing here, even though the effects that have been described as the culmination of the work, it's ongoing in other places, it isn't going to happen for many years. But, the learning process had to start some time. This learning process might be very important in the coming times... *(L)* You mean doing spirit release? *(J)* Yes... *(T)* Not only the spirit release, but the channeling... to start doing this on down the road would probably be too late... it's going to take several years to really understand what is going on and be able to handle oneself in the situations that may arise...

A: The most notable comment we have 164
is that we are happy to see discussion progressing more freely... and what a tremendous amount of learning takes place in interaction and sharing of ideas, notions, feelings. It does tend to advance learning and also a more grooved type of learning, and we have talked about "grooving" before, indicating a channel or a pathway which leads more clearly to a desired goal, and therefore, we are pleased to see this progress being made and hope that our participation has helped to facilitate this process.

165 **Q**: *(J)* We're learning. *(T)* Your participation is what has made it possible for this learning. *(J)* I see you as a facilitator. *(SV)* One thing that Laura said about her fear during the exorcism the other night: it was fear that opened Victor up to attack. If she experiences fear, would this also open her up to the same sort of attack?

166 **A**: That is a vague complex of ideas...

167 **Q**: *(J)* She had awareness along with the fear. Victor did not have awareness and I think that is the difference. *(L)* I hope so. *(T)* The point is, you have now reached the point where you know you cannot continue doing this by yourself. *(L)* No. *(T)* The intensity is getting physically dangerous. The last thing you need is to have the cops knocking on the door or kicking the door in and finding bodies laying around! But, the work you are doing is important... it helps other people. The subject is not going to be aware of what is happening. *(L)* They are helpless... *(T)* But, the people you are going to have to involve in this from here out are going to have to be aware of what they are getting into. They have to know the level of intensity, the severity of what is going on and the implied danger. *(J)* Yeah, and aside from the people in this room, how many know that? *(T)* Opening up people's subconscious and letting it out... you never know what's going to come crawling out of there. *(J)* Yeah... it's opening up Pandora's box every time! *(T)* What happens the next time you do this with a subject and the subject turns out to be an STS walk-in that doesn't know what they are yet? *(L)* Ouch. *(T)* What do you do with that? You don't want to be alone with it. And, Frank, in a trance state, unable to defend himself physically, and have something like that come crawling out. *(L)* You're right. It can't be done like that again, but there is so much need right... I think we have to bring Frank up here. We want to thank you for your presence tonight unless you have something further to say.

A: Not unless you have further questions. 168

Q: *(L)* Well, we have plenty of questions but Frank has been down long enough and we have to bring him up. We would like you to leave some positive effects, perhaps in the form of suggestions, for his well-being. 169

A: We would suggest that you be aware of the fact that the subject is the channel and, as such, we are in constant communication with each other, as it were. This we have told you before, therefore, you need not worry about the course of destiny of this particular subject. Do you understand?[15] 170

Q: *(L)* I understand, but I also am the one who watches him go through torments and I would like to see that alleviated for him as much as possible. 171

A: We understand your care and concern, but it may also be true that the torments are a precursor to explosive developments that would not be possible without the "torments" occurring. 172

Q: *(T)* We would like to thank you for your assistance. 173

A: You are most welcome. 174

Q: *(L)* We will release then. Goodnight. 175

End of Session

[15] I would say that this was definitely Frank blowing his own horn.

June 17, 1995

Another direct channeling experiment with 'Frank'. There were some issues with this session at the beginning, but the reader will notice that the dynamic changed and I've given a few pointers as to what I think happened in the footnotes. All in all, it turned out to be a very useful and informative session.

Participants: 'Frank', Laura, Susan V, Terry and Jan

[Laura inducts Frank into hypnosis.]

1 **Q**: *(L)* When the connection is completed, please indicate by saying "I am ready." [Pause] Are you ready?

2 **A**: Yes.

3 **Q**: *(L)* OK, we do have questions and I think Terry will start us off this evening. *(T)* How did FDR die?

4 **A**: Due to a cerebral hemorrhage.

5 **Q**: *(T)* It was a natural death, then?

6 **A**: Yes. All death is natural.

7 **Q**: *(T)* It was not a death contrived by someone else?

8 **A**: We don't understand the reference.

9 **Q**: *(T)* He wasn't assassinated in some way?

10 **A**: No.

11 **Q**: *(L)* What about Pope John Paul I? The pope who served for one month? Please speak as loudly and clearly as possible.

12 **A**: It is the comfort of the subject being used as channel or conduit that is the most important factor in clear speaking and increase of volume. This can be a more useful method for channeling information if all circumstances are optimal levels.

Q: *(L)* What else can we do for com- 13
fort?

A: Placement of object to right of sub- 14
ject's head is somewhat inhibiting flow of energy. Please place some form of sustaining object or brace to the left subject's head.

Q: [Adjustments made] *(SV)* Is that 15
better? *(J)* I recommend you get him settled before he even goes into trance. *(L)* I would but he is so hard-headed he won't listen to my suggestions. He says, "I'm fine," but then he isn't. Back to the question: what caused the death of the Pope, John Paul I?

A: Unfortunately, as has been indi- 16
cated by us before, sometimes you ask questions that we will not be able to answer for you. Not because the answers are unknown, but rather because knowing the answers could prove harmful to you.

Q: *(T)* Well, that is an answer in itself. 17
He didn't die naturally.

18 **A**: Speculation is harmless when compared to irrefutable, confirmed knowledge.[1]

19 **Q**: *(L)* OK, Susan had a question that we discussed earlier this week as to what is taking place when craft that are described to be belonging to 'aliens' begin to strobe, as opposed to pulsating or merely blinking or other configurations. In other words, what are the different configurations of light emanations and what do they indicate?

20 **A**: It is interesting when you pose multiple questions. Please choose one.

21 **Q**: *(L)* Is there something indicated by a UFO as to its condition or status or proposed activity when it changes its light emanation?

22 **A**: That is a confusing thought pattern.

23 **Q**: *(L)* OK, say a specific UFO is seen. When it is first seen it appears metallic. In a bit it begins to glow with light of some or another color. Then, after a few minutes of glowing, it begins to strobe – flashing a very bright light. What could this indicate?

24 **A**: We do not mean to be difficult, but the term 'strobe' is still not completely clear to us. That seems to be an artificial construction of your plane that we are not familiar with.[2]

25 **Q**: *(L)* Well, just moving from a glow to a blinding flashing.

26 **A**: Well, you must be aware, first of all, as we have told you before, and as you have, in fact, gained knowledge from other sources prior to your communications with us, the entire subject matter referred to as 'UFOs' is extremely varied and multifaceted in nature and does not represent any one condition, entity, source of entities, mode of transport, density level, or anything else related to these.[3]

Q: *(L)* So, in other words, we would 27
have to specify a specific sighting and condition in order to obtain an answer to this particular question or type of question?

A: Well, let us ask you, would that not 28
be the wisest course of action?

Q: *(J)* I think I have a way out of that. 29
Possibly we are referring to the type of sightings that are typical in the Gulf Breeze area where they...

A: Be aware of the fact, please, that the 30
whole Gulf Breeze situation is rather interesting in many ways. And, when we say "rather interesting," we are being subjective, viewing the subjective from your point of view. There is more going on there than meets the eye... again, from your point of view... not from our point of view, for we know what's going on there. And this brings us to another point that should be taken at this point, no pun intended, that is that your line of questioning, in this particular session, does seem to be developing a pattern; that being trying to find answers to mysteries which, if

[1]The absurdity of a response being given by a channeled source being considered "irrefutable, confirmed knowledge" should not be lost on the reader. It rather seems to me that Frank's channeling was a lot less forthcoming than when we worked via the board and he had less control over the process.

[2]This deliberate obfuscation of exchange was annoying. The feeling that was conveyed was a general disinclination to answer questions.

[3]*High Strangeness* 7

found, could cause difficulties for you. Example one being Pope John Paul's death, as you call it, and example two, Gulf Breeze. If you were to know the answers to these questions, we can assure you that it would not be long, as you measure time, before ramifications would result that would not be pleasant for you. This is because all entities concerned with these various subject matters are strictly STS, and, in fact, involved in practices that, if revealed in their entirety, would be damaging to the efforts of those seeking to serve self in the ways that they are seeking service of self. So, it is not possible for us to go into any great detail about lights seen at Gulf Breeze as it would be possible for you to infer from the information given, various bits and pieces of information, which could lead you to knowledge that it would be best that you not possess currently. Do you understand?[4]

31 **Q**: *(T)* Are you suggesting that some time in the future it might be possible and helpful for us to know these things?

32 **A**: Well, we sincerely try not to suggest, but rather, communicate, and the communication intent was to indicate that it would be more beneficial, perhaps, to gain awareness of these subjects in detail in what you would describe as your future, than would be the case in what you would describe as your present.

Q: *(J)* So sometimes knowledge is... 33
[Terry interjects and both comments lost.] *(T)* Knowledge without understanding...

A: Incorrect. Knowledge protects, but 34
there is an old saying on your 3rd density world [*(J)* I know what's coming...] a little bit of knowledge is a dangerous thing... [*(J)* Got it!] and we will add to that "a little bit of knowledge is no knowledge at all." Understood?

Q: *(L)* Yes... *(J)* Is this kind of like 35
along the line of "Knowledge out of context is dangerous"?

A: That would be accurate as well. 36

Q: *(L)* Well, since we are not going to 37
go anywhere with that question, I have another one... A couple of nights ago I did a session with my son to examine the events that took place on August 16, 1993, over my pool, wherein a couple of UFO-type objects were seen by all of us, kind of casually drifting by. In this hypnosis session, after two or three passes through the subject, he indicated that, in fact, that was not merely a sighting of something going overhead, but was actually an abduction situation. Would that be correct?

A: What do you think? 38

Q: *(L)* Knowing what I know now, I 39
think so.

A: The reason we ask this is, again we 40
must reiterate, your learning is to be

[4] Again, some serious ego is showing through here with the silly claim that things said by a channeled source might be considered 'irrefutable knowledge' in any quarters, much less official ones! The ease with which any such information could be refuted by simply pointing out "it's channeled!" and thus, not reliable, should be evident. It appears from this tendency in Frank, that he had the idea that channeled material was somehow akin to divine proclamation. In short, it appeared to me at the time that Frank was attempting to awe all of us with his abilities and make us duly reverent towards 'the source'. I didn't buy it.

more and more accomplished by utilizing the tools you have within you, and, we are happy to see that you are, indeed, doing this. But you must trust in your own ability to access the information you need through your own efforts.[5]

41 **Q**: *(L)* One remark he made during this session – and this startled me a little, and I would like to get a little amplification on the subject – was that toward the end when I asked what happened, he said that he was "taken apart and beamed back down without benefit of a pain suppressor." This meant that when he was demolecularized some sort of device that is used to suppress pain was not used, and the process of atomic demolecularization or remolecularization can actually be painful, and can cause distress. Is this correct?

42 **A**: Possibly. The whole process of abduction can be stressful, but, to varying degrees and, of course, we must remind you that, as with everything else, it is your own perception of reality that is the most important factor, not some notion of your own perception of reality.[6]

43 **Q**: *(L)* I don't understand what you mean. Is there some device that... does it hurt to be taken to pieces molecularly, beamed aboard a space ship and then sent back? *(J)* Can this be painful to the body?

A: Well, first of all, you are getting way ahead of yourself. Do you honestly believe that a beam of light came down and "took you to pieces," moved your body physically on-board a space vehicle, did some form of examination or some such thing and then reassembled your entire body without a pain suppressor? Is this what you believe? 44

Q: *(L)* Well, he didn't say it happened to me, he said it happened to him. *(J)* We have never heard the term 'pain suppressor' before. *(L)* Yes, we have never heard anything about anything like this; and do I believe a beam of light could have come down and disassembled us and reassembled me, and then something was done to me? Well, from what I have studied I would say it is possible. I mean, knowing about the time manipulation capabilities of said entities, it is entirely possible that it could have happened without any awareness of any loss of time whatsoever.[7] 45

A: Yes, this is true, however, we have told you in previous sessions, in detail, the methodology that is used for what you refer to as 'abduction'. And, if you are familiar with the transcripts that you have now created, you know precisely how this is done. Your description of it is not completely correct as referenced in the hypnosis session you 46

[5] Again, a disinclination to simply answer a question or, in the Cs terms: "to give what is asked for".

[6] *High Strangeness* 6

[7] I had decided to use a different tactic for getting an answer: to declare something to be so and see if that elicited 'corrections'. The response about abductions appears to be rather good, based on research. Many cases reveal the subject's experience to be incompatible with the observations of any third parties, not to mention many other puzzling effects, and this explanation solves those difficulties nicely.

speak of, or at least your interpretation of the information given during the hypnosis session given is not correct.

Now, it must be noted here, that when we make such clarifying statements such as "this is not correct" or "that is not correct," it is unusual for us to do this because the nature of your state of being and all others is one involving various degrees of bonded illusion. Therefore any and all possibilities are present in most instances. However, when two or more of these bonds of the illusion are misaligned, then, indeed, absolute correctness or absolute incorrectness is possible. In this case, there is a misalignment of the bonding. Therefore, it is, in fact, completely incorrect.

And, furthermore, to explain exactly the process again, even though we do very much desire for you to learn, and we sense that perhaps you are getting ahead of yourself in the learning curve, as it were, which is somewhat distressing, but we will worry about that later; the main thing is that you have been told how this process takes place. We will now repeat it. Please do try to retain this knowledge as it is very important not only for what, perhaps, has happened in your reality as you would refer to it as your past, but also in possible variations of your present and in what you refer to as your future. These experiences must be known in their entirety as to what they really are.

You are not normally removed as a physical 3rd density being from one locator to another. What happens is very simple. The time frame is normally frozen, and we use the term 'frozen' for lack of a better term. What this means is that your perception of time in your physical locator, 3rd density body, ceases to pass during this period of time that is called 'zero time' variously by members of your human race. What happens is that the soul imprint occupying or of that particular host body is removed forcibly, transported to another locator, and remolecularized as a separate physical entity body for purpose of examination, implantation, and other. Then, it is demolecularized – the soul imprint is used for the purpose of duplication process – it is then demolecularized and the soul imprint is replaced in the original body at the original locator. That is the process that takes place.

On occasion, the 4th density beings doing the abduction can actually make a mistake in the time referencing points of the 3rd density illusion. This may create the effect of the appearance of an alternate or duplicate experience, when, in actuality there has only been one experience. This was what happened in your case. As you perceived the passage of two 'ships' for lack of a better term, when in actuality, there was only one. That is because the time frame reference illusion was not completely matched from beginning of event to the end of the event in zero time. Normally, however, that is not a problem.

On rare occasions, the host, or the subject of the abduction can actually find themselves replaced in the time frame illusion in what could appear to be several hours, day, weeks, or even, sadly, years prior to the beginning of the event, which, of course, could cause side effects such as total insanity and other such things. Fortunately that did not occur in your case, but there was some fracturing of the time frame reference illusion. This is why you thought you saw two ships when in actuality you only saw one.

Now, it is most important that you understand that this is not a physical, 3rd density experience in its entirety. There is the soul imprint that all 1st density, 2nd density, 3rd density, and 4th density beings possess, as you already know; that is extracted. From that soul imprint a duplicate copy or cloning, if you will, which appears on 4th density, can then be made and studied and the soul imprint is then replaced into the original body at whatever density it was taken. This is normally how the process is done.

Most often, if the 3rd density being is removed in total physicality, there is no return of that being to 3rd density. They are permanently removed to 4th density. Most often that is what takes place although on rare occasions there can be return. However, there is no need for this as complete duplication for all purposes of examination, alteration of sensate, and implanting; need not be done on 3rd density; can be done completely in the 4th density duplication process. Do you understand?

47 **Q**: *(T)* How does the implant come back to the 3rd density body that's originally still here?

48 **A**: The process we are describing, which involves the remolecularization; it is very complex to try and describe how the 4th density is translated into 3rd density, except that once the duplicate, the 4th density cloning, or duplicate is present, all 4th density realities surrounding that 4th density duplicate will be matched in 3rd density whenever and wherever desired. Because, in effect it is the entire density level which is being exchanged, not just the object contained within.

Q: *(L)* So, in other words, just as the soul imprint, when it goes into 4th density, can be used as a template to create a carbon copy, so to speak, then anything that is done to the carbon copy then becomes a template that recreates that same manifestation when it is sent back into the 3rd. 49

A: Precisely. With the only variance there being that technology is used to make sure that implants, or added material that comes from 4th density, is such that it will also translate equally into 3rd density through the remolecularization process. 50

Q: *(L)* Is there any method that we could or should know about to remove or deactivate implants? 51

A: No, you are not capable of doing that without causing death of the host. And, by the way, please don't believe those who claim that they can do such things as they cannot. 52

Q: *(L)* So, in this particular case, something was done, something occurred here, which affected me. My subsequent physical condition makes me curious as to whether the physical reactions I had for six to nine months, and still have occasionally, following this event, were a 3rd density reaction to the, what you call, fracturing of time. Was this an aberration or was this intentional? 53

A: My, my my. My, my, my. You take one subject and launch forward into another. You create your own reality, Laura. That really is impressive! But, of course, incorrect, sorry to say! 54

It does not occur as a result of the 'fracturing' of the time frame reference illusion. It occurs as a result, simply and merely, of your psychic impression imprint of the experience itself reflecting back into your 3rd density physical reality. As we have told you before, of course, and we don't mean to sound snide or condescending, however we are just a bit perturbed that you do not seem to be keeping up with your own transcripts.

55 **Q**: *(L)* Well, since that question was never answered...

56 **A**: It was never answered incorrectly in that way. However if you were familiar with the transcripts, you would realize that it was answered.

57 **Q**: *(L)* Well, it just gave me food for thought hearing about the 'time fracturing'. *(T)* Is the pain that Laura's son described not what he said it was, but rather the pain that is related when the 4th density being removes the life force?

58 **A**: Life force is never removed. The soul is extracted. In answer to your question: Laura's son is merely expressing the discomfort and distress that most 3rd and 2nd density beings experience when abducted by 4th density service to self entities.

59 **Q**: *(L)* Why did they only abduct [my son] and myself and not the girls?

60 **A**: Did they?

61 **Q**: *(L)* Well, that is what he said. And, you have said that the girls have not been abducted.

A: Well, I guess that answers the question then.[8] 62

Q: *(L)* Well, why? Why only him and me? 63

A: Why not? 64

Q: *(J)* Just random? *(L)* Was it a random abduction? 65

A: As we have said before, you have been making progress in learning through your own resources. But, we would hate to see you fall back. 66

Q: *(L)* Well, I don't want to fall back and I have no intention of not pursuing this matter through my own resources. But, using myself as a case in point, I am trying to find out a little bit about the nature of the abduction process in general. I mean, is it done randomly or is it done to specific persons for specific reasons? My thought is that maybe specific people are targeted to put them out of commission. But, then, that seems a little egotistical and I don't want to stumble over ego and say that I am being abducted to put me out of commission and somebody else is being abducted randomly. 67

A: Well, I hope this following statement will not disturb you. Any STS being who possesses a greater power than you do will not have any extreme difficulty in "putting you out of commission" if they so desire. This has happened, of course. 68

Q: *(L)* I would like to ask a little bit about synchronicity. I would like to know, what is the source of synchronous events? Is it a multiple source or is it something that comes out of the 69

[8] This is odd. It almost seems as though Frank had forgotten that we had been told that my girls had not been abducted on that occasion. If I had not reminded him of that fact, I wonder what he would have said?

percipient's own mind or... *(J)* is it random?[9]

70 **A**: Imagine a young school child walking along the street, standing beside a rose bush, picking one of the flowers, and asking the flower: "Would you please explain Einstein's theory of relativity to me today." Now, the analogy here is, while humorous, perhaps, is also to point out to you that we admire and appreciate the challenges that you bring to us to answer such complex questions in such a simple form, not to mention such a simple format. However, if we were to answer these accurately and adequately for you when you ask such complicated questions, it would require a session lasting approximately twenty-four of your days non-stop. Needless to say that this would render the subject rather useless and, of course, yourselves as well. So, we aren't simply not able to answer a question as complex as "What is synchronicity?" as it is incredibly complex. It involves aspects in every imaginable state of reality merging together in what could best be described, if seen visually, as a massive mosaic in perfect balance. But, that is not adequate to a response for your question, however, hopefully, maybe you can contemplate the visual image presented and help yourself to learn a more complete answer.[10]

Q: *(T)* Several sessions back when we 71
were discussing 'perpendicular realities' you were talking about something that happened to me and that I had to look back over my life and analyze my relationships with other people from a certain point up until now and you said that this was a perpendicular reality. What is the definition of a perpendicular reality?[11]

A: The perpendicular reality primar- 72
ily, though not exclusively, refers to one's life path and how one's life path fits together in the cycle or in a wheel when connected with those of a similar life path. And, oddly enough, relates very closely to the previous question involving synchronicity. If you can picture an inlaid wheel formed by a circle within a circle, and adjoining partitions in a perfect balance, that would be the best representation of perpendicular reality for it does not completely involve one individual's experience, but rather a group of individual's experience for the progression of a greater purpose, if you understand what we mean. This is what we mean when

[9] *The Wave* 71

[10] Obviously, such a condescending response was not called for and an answer could have been given that made clear the difficulties of the question while still being adequate. This air of condescension, almost contempt, was extremely disturbing when doing trance channeling with Frank and was one of the reasons that we decided that it was a path that we did not want to pursue. However, I should note at this point that the four of us were looking at each other during this delivery, and I suspect that our thoughts that we didn't like the tone or condescension were picked up by Frank because, at this point, the atmosphere changed. I suppose that this could have been an instance of our energy uniting and blocking STS energies at least to some extent. I think that the reader can pick up on this, too, just from the text.

[11] *The Wave* 5

we say: perpendicular reality. Picture again, a circle within a circle adjoined by equally spaced partitions in a perfect cycle. That is perpendicular reality.

73 **Q**: *(T)* You had us draw this symbol and put seven spokes or partitions between the two circles.

74 **A**: Correct.

75 **Q**: *(T)* Is seven the optimal number?

76 **A**: Seven is always the optimal number. There are seven levels of density. This reflects through all phases of reality.

77 **Q**: *(T)* The people that I interacted with during this time, they also have gone on to do other things that they were supposed to be doing because of their interaction with me in this perpendicular reality that we all existed in?

78 **A**: That's correct.[12]

79 **Q**: *(T)* You also said that each of us in this group came from a different perpendicular reality.

80 **A**: That is correct.

81 **Q**: *(T)* Is it at this point where we merge our different perpendicular realities in order to learn from each others' experiences?

82 **A**: That could be described as correct.

83 **Q**: *(L)* It was said at the time that the inner circle was the connection with this reality and that the outer circle and connecting segments were where the perpendicular reality is 'joined with the Wave'. Is it implied in that statement that the forming of this conduit through these perpendicular realities is instrumental in bringing forth this Wave, bringing forth this change, this dimensional shift, or density shift, and is that something that is being done in other places?

A: We wish to congratulate you for asking six questions in one. [*(T)* One more question and you would have a perfect perpendicular question!] Mirth! 84

Q: *(L)* Are we connected in some way with the Wave, individually and as a group? 85

A: Well, of course. Everything is connected to the Wave. 86

Q: *(L)* Are we, by connecting into this wheel, so to speak, activating the Wave in some way? 87

A: We are not clear about your interesting interpretation there, but it is true that you have an interactive relationship with the Wave, however, as stated before, you are in an interactive relationship with the Wave in a sense, in that the Wave is a part of your reality, always has been and always will be. And, of course, it does involve your progress through the grand cycle. And the perpendicular reality, again is, of course, an advancement from the core outward which is yet another reflection of all reality and all that exists. Now, we wish to return to the visual representation as mentioned previously. If you notice the core circle connects with all seven sections to the outer circle. Now, picture that outer circle as being an ever-expanding circle, and each one of the seven segments as being an ever-expanding line. Of course, now, this will expand outward in a circular or cyclical pattern. Please picture visually an expanding outer circle and a non-expanding inner circle. Contemplate that and 88

[12] *High Strangeness* 7; *The Wave* 8

then please give us your feelings as to what that represents.

89 **Q**: *(L)* Does it represent an expansion of our knowledge and consciousness?

90 **A**: That's part of it.

91 **Q**: *(L)* Does it represent also expanding influence of what and who we are on that which is around us?

92 **A**: That is correct.

93 **Q**: *(L)* Does it also represent a more...

94 **A**: Oops! We detected a slippage of your visual representation! Contemplate, if you will, the ever-expanding outer circle and the non-expanding inner circle, and, of course, the seven partitions also moving outwardly. What type of shape does that form in your mind's eye?

95 **Q**: *(L)* A wheel?

96 **A**: Is that all?

97 **Q**: *(T)* A pie?

98 **A**: Keep going.

99 **Q**: *(L)* An eye.

100 **A**: Now we are starting to turn it into a sphere! Why would it turn into a sphere?

101 **Q**: *(L)* How can it turn into a sphere?

102 **A**: How can it not!

103 **Q**: *(SV)* It is going in *all* directions, not just flat...

104 **A**: Is a straight line a straight line or a...

105 **Q**: *(L)* Oh, you're not talking about a circle?

106 **A**: We are talking about a circle. What becomes of a circle if you expand it outward forever?

107 **Q**: *(J)* It disappears.

108 **A**: It disappears? How can it disappear? Where does it disappear to? We ask you that, Jan? Jan?

109 **Q**: *(J)* Visually, as the outer circle expands, the inner circle becomes smaller and smaller until it disappears. As you continue to expand out with the outer circle, the inner circle disappears.

110 **A**: But where does it disappear to?

111 **Q**: *(J)* A black hole?

112 **A**: A black hole. Well, that's a possibility. But, we really didn't want you to concentrate so heavily on the smaller circle, now did we? It's the outer circle.

113 **Q**: *(T)* The outer circle is used to encompass more and more.

114 **A**: And what shape does it begin to take on? I want you to look at this outer circle expanding outward!

115 **Q**: *(J)* Are we to assume that the seven spokes remain the same size in relation to the circle?

116 **A**: Well, answer that question for yourself.

117 **Q**: *(L)* OK, we are looking at it as a plane representation. As a flat surface.

118 **A**: Well, what happens to a flat surface if you extend it outward forever?

119 **Q**: *(L)* Well, we don't know. That, that... *(SV)* It keeps on going.

120 **A**: It keeps on going?

121 **Q**: *(L)* Yeah, bigger and flatter!

122 **A**: It does? What happens to a line if you extend it forever and ever?

123 **Q**: *(Laura and Susan)* It keeps on going.

124 **A**: It does?

125 **Q**: *(L)* Um hmmm!

126 **A**: Where does it go to?

127 **Q**: *(SV)* Forever. *(J)* Back to itself. *(L)* We don't know that.

128 **A**: Oh, someone said "Back to itself."

129 **Q**: *(J)* Like a snake taking hold of its own tail.

130 **A**: Why don't we know that?

131 **Q**: *(L)* Because we don't. It is conjectured that space is curved...

132 **A**: Because we don't know. Now, why don't we know?

133 **Q**: *(L)* Because we haven't been there.

134 **A**: Had Columbus been outside of Italy and Spain?

135 **Q**: *(L)* OK, we are going to assume that if it keeps on expanding it will eventually come back to itself...

136 **A**: No, no, no, wait! We asked a question!

137 **Q**: *(L)* Well, of course Columbus had an idea that there was something but he hadn't been there, no. But he went and checked it out.

138 **A**: Did he have just an idea?

139 **Q**: *(L)* Well, pretty much, I guess.

140 **A**: Hmmm. That's not the way we remember it. The way we remember it is that he had instinct and imagination and when he married his instinct with imagination, it became reality. And, when it became reality, he had created a reality which he was fully confident would be manifest in the physical 3rd density reality. It wasn't that he was confident. He knew it to be so. He didn't stop himself by adding prejudice to the equation, which is what you are doing when you say: "Well, we don't know what happens because we have never been there!" Think logically, please. We have told you so many times that everything is a grand cycle. If it's a grand cycle, we have told you about circles within circles. We have told you about cycles. We have told you about short wave cycles and long wave cycles. Now, after all this information that you have asked of us, which we have more than happily given to you, would you expect that a straight line would just go out forever and ever and ever as a straight line? How could it possibly do that? What happens if you take, on your 3rd density Earth, and you draw a straight line to the east or to the west or to the north or to the south...

Q: *(J)* It comes all the way back to it- 141
self.

A: Right... 142

Q: *(L)* OK, so we're living in a big 143
globe!

A: Are we? 144

Q: *(L)* Well, that is what it sounds like, 145
a big circle?

A: Oh, my, my, my. You need more 146
study and learning, my dear. Need more study. Even your Albert Einstein had a theory about what happened.

Q: *(L)* Yes, but that was just a theory. 147

A: Oh, well I guess then it must be 148
dropped. We'll never know. It's just a theory. Well, we'll just forget about it.

Q: *(T)* I'm still expanding the circle... 149
(SV) Me too.

A: Very good, that was the idea. It 150
keeps going and going and going.

Q: *(L)* Well, mine does too, but it 151
hasn't come back and met anything. So, what's the point?

A: Does there need to be a point? 152

Q: *(L)* Of course! 153

154 **A**: Who says? We are trying to help you learn. When do you expect to shut down this process?

155 **Q**: *(J)* Never. *(L)* Gee, I hope never.

156 **A**: Then there never is a point!

157 **Q**: *(J)* Point taken! *(L)* There is no point. [Laughter] Well, if you expand the circle outward and continue expanding it in all directions, it pulls the seven spokes with it which encompasses more and more space in a cross section, and then turn that circle, you have a sphere.

158 **A**: Precisely. But Laura says that means we are living in a big globe. And, maybe we are.

159 **Q**: *(T)* Well, it wouldn't be a big globe, so to speak, it would only be a big globe within the circle. If the circle continues to expand, it would just continue to go outward and outward and the globe would become bigger and bigger and bigger... *(L)* You're making me nervous... *(T)* But it goes outward forever... 'cause there is no end to going out...

160 **A**: There isn't?

161 **Q**: *(SV)* Nope.

162 **A**: Well, then maybe there's no beginning.

163 **Q**: *(T)* Well, there wouldn't be a beginning, just a big, open void. An infinite void...

164 **A**: If there's no end and no beginning, then what do you have?

165 **Q**: *(L)* No point. *(J)* The here and now.

166 **A**: The here and now which is also the future and the past. Everything that was, is and will be, all at once. This is why only a very few of your 3rd density persons have been able to understand space travel, because even though traveling into space in your 3rd density is every bit as 3rd density as lying on your bed at night in your comfortable home, the time reference is taken away. Something that you hold very close to your bosom as if it were your mother. And, it is the biggest illusion that you have. We have repeatedly told you over and over that there is no time, and yet, of course, you have been so brainwashed into this concept that you cannot get rid of it no matter what you do, now can you? Imagine going out into space. You'd be lost when confronted with reality that everything is completely all at one. Would you not? Picture yourself floating around in space!

Q: *(L)* I don't want to. *(J)* There is 167
also no space! *(T)* Does the sphere keep expanding... as the circle expands and you turn the circle 180°, you get a sphere. As the sphere continues to expand it, you take a point on the outer edge of the sphere in order to take the sphere about itself, you get a donut, an ever expanding inner tube. *(L)* With a black hole in the middle! *(SV)* Why does it have to be a black hole? *(J)* It's a spiral. *(T)* If you take that and twist it, you get an even larger inner tube. It just continues to expand and encompasses more space...

A: And now, when you merge densities, 168
or traverse densities, what you have is the merging of physical reality and ethereal reality, which involves thought form versus physicality. When you can merge those perfectly, what you realize then, is that the reason there is no beginning and no end is merely because there is no need for you to contemplate a beginning or an end after you have

completed your development. When you are at union with the One at 7th density, that is when you have accomplished this and then there is no longer any need for difference between physical and ethereal forms.

169 **Q**: *(L)* On the subject of time as we discussed the other day: we talked about the fact that at the constant of light there is no time, there is no matter, there is no gravity, but that any unit, infinitesimally small to the downward side of the constant of light, suddenly there is gravity and suddenly there is matter. And we asked what is it that congeals this matter out of the energy of light, so to speak, and I believe that the answer we received was that it was consciousness from 7th level. From our perspective, would it be possible to achieve this constant and move through to the other side of it, or at least stay fixed with it, without de-materializing? Is the speed of light interconnected with the state of no time and no gravity?

170 **A**: No in an absolute sense, in a 3rd density sense.

171 **Q**: *(L)* OK, if you are in 4th density, for example, does everything move at the speed of light and is that why there is no time there and no gravity?

172 **A**: No. That is an incorrect concept.

173 **Q**: *(T)* There is no speed of light, light is everywhere.

174 **A**: Precisely. There is no speed of light in 4th density because there is no need for any 'speed'. Speed, itself, is a 3rd density concept. You remember, all there is is lessons. That's it! There's nothing else. It is all for your perception. For our perception. For all consciousness. That's all there is.

Q: *(L)* Well, I am still trying to get a 175
handle on what it is, what is the source of this gravity, this state of time, because they seem to be so intimately connected.[13]

A: Let us ask you a question now: Do 176
you remember going to school?

Q: *(L)* Yes. 177

A: What did you do in 3rd grade? 178

Q: *(L)* A lot of things. I learned cur- 179
sive writing. I learned to multiply and divide.

A: Do you remember what you did in 180
first grade?

Q: *(L)* Yes. 181

A: Please name one. 182

Q: *(L)* I learned to count in several 183
ways. To add and subtract. I learned to read and write. *(T)* Did you learn to multiply and divide in first grade? *(L)* No.

A: Okay. When you were in the pro- 184
cess of learning to multiply and divide, did you drop your pen or pencil and steadfastly return in your mind to first grade and try and figure out why you had to learn the alphabet?

Q: *(L)* No. 185

A: Why not? 186

Q: *(L)* Because I already knew it. 187

A: You already knew it. In other words, 188
you did not need to learn the alphabet because you already knew it. Correct?

Q: *(L)* Yes. 189

---
13 *The Wave* 71

190 **A**: Are you going to need to learn about the speed of light when there is no longer a speed of light?

191 **Q**: *(L)* Well, that is what I am trying to do. Once you learn it, maybe you are not subject to its lessons anymore. I mean, you get concepts presented, you absorb them, practice them, they become part of you and then you go to the next thing.

192 **A**: Yes, but you are asking about the speed of light as relates to 4th density and above density levels and we are telling you that there is no speed of light there because there is no need for that, because once you reach 4th density level, you have learned the lessons of 3rd level.

193 **Q**: *(L)* Well, if a person on 3rd density gets into some kind of vehicle and achieves light speed, does that automatically translate them into 4th density?

194 **A**: Could you please point out one of these vehicles?

195 **Q**: *(L)* Well, we don't have any... yet.

196 **A**: Do you expect to have any before you go to 4th density?

197 **Q**: *(L)* No.

198 **A**: Then the lesson is learned, yes?

199 **Q**: *(L)* Sort of.

200 **A**: If you trust in what we are saying, which is in response to what you are asking, then the lesson is learned. Now, contemplate, because all there is is lessons.

201 **Q**: *(L)* Well, you talk about time being an illusion, time being something we hold dear to us like a mother, and that sort of thing, and I would be perfectly happy to let go of time...

A: You do! Let go! 202

Q: *(L)* Well, it is one thing to want to 203
do it in your mind and another thing altogether to do it in your system, your internal operating system.

A: Your internal operating system? 204

Q: *(T)* Is that DOS or WARM? 205

A: Could you please explain what an 206
internal operating system is?

Q: *(L)* I guess it is the subconscious 207
mind.

A: It is? 208

Q: *(L)* Maybe. 209

A: My, my. 210

Q: *(T)* The subconscious mind has no 211
idea of time. *(J)* Time is an artificial constraint... *(L)* For example: a person can have a belief about prosperity in their conscious mind and can talk about it and say affirmations and all kinds of positive things for themselves, and yet, for some reason that individual continually lives on the edge of poverty because something keeps happening that they keep screwing up to keep themselves at the level of poverty. And, when you start digging around in their subconscious mind you find out that somewhere there is the belief in poverty or there is a past life connection where they feel they need or deserve to be poor, so, their internal operating system takes precedence over their conscious beliefs and thoughts. That is what I am talking about here.

A: Yes, but what is your point? 212

Q: *(L)* The point is that you may say 213
that you would like to get rid of time and you may understand it conceptually, but something internal keeps you tied to it. How do you get rid of that internal connection?

214 **A**: Something internal keeps you tied to it?

215 **Q**: *(J)* Like circadian rhythms, it's physical.

216 **A**: We feel you are missing the point.

217 **Q**: *(L)* Well, maybe I am.

218 **A**: You see, we speak to all of you when we say this. It's now time for you, as individuals, to try to move away, as much as possible, not to force yourselves, of course, but to try and move away at your own pace as much as possible, from the constraints of 3rd density.[14] You have all learned lessons to the level where you are more than ready to begin to prepare for 4th density. 3rd density involves a level of physicality and restriction and restraint and all of the things that go along with those, that you no longer need.[15] So, therefore, even though we understand that at times it may feel comfortable to cling to this, there is time for you, and there is that word again, it is time for you to consider moving ahead and get ready for 4th density and not to be concerned with such things as time or how to free yourself from the illusion of time. That really is not important. That's like the third grade student delving into mathematics and stopping everything to go back and contemplate the ABCs and why it isn't CBA or BAC. There really is no point. It is what it is. They are what they are.[16]

Q: *(L)* That is what I want to know, what is it?[17] 219

A: Why do you need to know this?[18] 220

Q: *(L)* Because I am curious. What is time? 221

A: We have already told you that it is a non-existent, artificial creation of illusion for the point of learning at the level where you are at or were, and once you have left that level, you no longer need it.[19] 222

Q: *(T)* Maybe one of the lessons is to learn not to worry about time. Once you learn that time is not real... *(SV)* Tell that to your boss! 223

[14]That means we should work on learning more objective ways of looking at things, less anthropocentric.

[15]We will not need them at some point, but right now we need them, though perhaps we should work on needing them as little as necessary. Later on the Cs will be precise.

[16]So, it is time to start getting rid of the illusion of time. What is an illusion? It is something that is less 'real' than a 'truly real' thing. Of course illusions exists. But their existence is different. Getting rid of the illusion means not negating the illusion, but understanding it as such, as an illusion, and how this illusion is hosted by less illusory media.

[17]*The Wave* 8

[18]The Cs' reply that it is not the most important thing.

[19]This suggests that the concept of time, or better, the 'flow of time' is an 'artificial' creation. That means that probably it has something to do with the specific construction of our DNA, and that stones and trees may have a different concept of time.

[20]We are told again that 'time is not real', and as such it should be of a lesser concern to us than 'real stuff'.

224 **A**: If something is not real, is there any concern in worrying about what it is?[20]

225 **Q**: *(T)* Not for me.

226 **A**: Imagine a conversation between two people: Billy and Gene. Billy says to Gene, "There is no such thing as time." Gene says, "Oh, really? But I want to know what it is." Billy says, "But I just told you there is no such thing. Time does not exist. It is not real in any form, in any frame of reference, in any form of reality, any level of density. It simply does not exist." And, Gene says: "Oh, that's interesting. Now, again, what is this time?"[21]

227 **Q**: *(L)* Point taken. *(T)* Do you wear a watch? *(L)* No. *(SV)* I have to because of my schedule. *(T)* But, you wear the watch because other people believe in time? *(SV)* Yes. *(T)* And that is out of courtesy for their belief, not your belief.[22]

228 **A**: That is precisely correct. While you are still in this 3rd density it is still necessary for you to conform, to a certain extent, to the ways of others who are more comfortable within the realm of 3rd density. But, as we have stated previously, perhaps it is 'time' for you to begin preparing for 4th density and not concern yourself any more than is absolutely necessary with all the wheres and whys and what-fors of 3rd density reality. This truly is behind you, now, and we know that because we can see from all levels six through one and back again in full cycle.[23]

Q: *(L)* Going along with that statement – and this is going to have to be the last question – preparing for 4th density: not too long ago I asked a question about the purpose of this group and the answer was that if we knew, or, more specifically if I knew, I would become 'unglued'. Was that meant literally? 229

A: Oh, yes certainly. Every single bone in your body is going to un-glue itself from every other. 230

Q: *(J)* You are going to turn into a pud- 231

[21]Time is not real in any frame of reference. Yet the illusion of time is real. These are two different level of studies: the level of studying the fundamental concepts of reality, and the study of illusions, which are also 'real' but not fundamental. They are secondary phenomena used for a certain purpose (to enable 'learning', in this case). Of course we would like to know more about this 'learning' and what purpose this learning serves, and what kind of reality it can acquire, but that would take us to another topic.

[22]We are in a society, we are networking there, and we learn our lessons while in the level of physicality that is more rigid than other levels, with reality that is more fluid than our present reality. We are here for a reason, to achieve something that otherwise could not be achieved. Gurdjieff is telling us something very similar in his *Beelzebub's Tales to His Grandson.*

[23]One should also make a distinction between the concept of 'imagining' and that of 'understanding'. While we have certainly problems with 'imagining' additional dimensions, we do not have so many problems with 'understanding them', as we can well understand them through mathematics. That does not mean that understanding is easy, but it is not very difficult, as every graduate student of mathematics learns how to calculate in any number of dimensions, including infinite numbers.

dle. *(L)* Well, since you are saying that it is time for us to begin preparing for 4th density, maybe it is time to deal with that question?

232 **A**: Well, perhaps you are trying to steer us, now. This is amusing because, of course, you sought our help, now I guess you are going to put us in your place and vice versa. But, actually, in a way, that is what is already happening, because, again, we must remind, that we are you in the future and we have already experienced all that you are experiencing. And, of course, we are experiencing as it is always being experienced. But, it is important to note that you have been making progress despite our occasional chidings, and we are very proud of the progress you have been making. Also, we want to remind you again not to worry about the extent of the progress or the direction it is taking. Just let it happen. All knowledge that it is absolutely necessary for you to gain to sustain this progress will be gained at the appropriate point in ... [chorus] *time*. Therefore, not to worry as it will all fall into place, as we have told you. Now, we do not feel that you are ready, as yet, to know what your ultimate purpose is, nor is it necessary for you to know, and it certainly would not be helpful in any way, so we ask again that you please not worry about that because when the 'time' comes for you to know, you will.

233 **Q**: *(SV)* I want to ask one question: If there is no time, there is no past and no future; there are no past lives and no future lives; there is no such thing as reincarnation; then how can you be us...[24]

[24] *The Wave* 5, 26

A: Yes, there is reincarnation. You are getting ahead of yourself there. We never said there is no reincarnation. 234

Q: *(SV)* But, if there is no time? *(J)* It is our perception of it. *(L)* It is all happening simultaneously. We are having all of these lifetimes at once. *(SV)* Is there a way that we can connect ourselves with all our other selves? 235

A: Picture it this way: we will access some of your memory banks and give you another reference which, interestingly enough, fits very closely with the perpendicular reality wheel that we described earlier. You know what a slide projector looks like? To give you some feeling of what this expanded nature of reality really is, picture yourself watching a big slide presentation with a big slide wheel on the projector. At any given point along the way you are watching one particular slide. But, all the rest of the slides are present on the wheel, are they not? And, of course, this fits in with the perpendicular reality, which fits in with the circles within circles and cycles within cycles, which also fits in the grand cycle, which also fits in with what we have told you before: All there is is lessons. That's all there is and we ask that you enjoy them as you are watching the slide presentation... 236

Q: *(J)* In that analogy, the light that shines through the slide, as it projects it upon the screen, is our perception? 237

A: And, if you look back at the center of the projector, you see the origin and essence of all creation itself, which is level seven where you are in union with the One. 238

Q: *(T)* Can we ask one more quick ques- 239

tion? NASA has announced that the space telescope, Hubble, has detected clusters of comets. Is this, in effect, the beginning of the governments of the world preparing the people for what is to come?

A: It certainly is a possibility, but, 240
again, you are accessing a very touchy area. Too much knowledge for you to gather in this particular area would not be beneficial.

End of Session

July 8, 1995

This is the second session attended by journalist Tom French and photographer Cherie Diez. There is a very useful discussion of crop circles and the famous Kecksburg UFO here.

Participants: 'Frank', Laura, Terry and Jan, Susan V, Tom French and Cherie Diez

1 **Q**: Hello.

2 **A**: Yes.

3 **Q**: *(L)* Who do we have with us?

4 **A**: Tqv.

5 **Q**: *(L)* What does TQV mean?

6 **A**: Was interrupted.[1]

7 **Q**: *(L)* OK, what is your name, please?

8 **A**: Tora.

9 **Q**: *(L)* And, where are you from?

10 **A**: Cassiopaea.

11 **Q**: *(L)* As you can see, we are doing the board this evening.

12 **A**: Yes.

13 **Q**: *(L)* We think it is a little more convivial. When Frank is zonked out, he can't participate.[2]

14 **A**: Yes.

Q: *(L)* OK, we have a number of questions. Is it alright to start questioning now? 15

A: Yes. 16

Q: *(L)* Is there a Jewish conspiracy to subjugate the world? 17

A: Not Jewish, we have told of this extensively before, curious that you should need review so soon! 18

Q: *(L)* The only reason I ask this question is because John W was here for a long time today and [laughter and groans] I whipped out my Dachau memorial book and laid it in his lap and we got into the thing, and he is just so convinced that there is a Jewish conspiracy to dominate and rule the world that I just thought I would throw the question out to see what further comments might be made about it other than the obvious. Thank you so much for that response. Next question: In reading about crop circles, I know that we have been told that they come from 6th density, but I would like to know the exact mode or mechanism by 19

[1] We were using a new table which required several adjustments. We finally gave up and got out the old table.

[2] I was trying to be diplomatic here. The plain fact is that none of us, except Frank, liked the trance channeling process and we felt that it had too much potential to descend into the usual New Age word salad channeling.

which they are made. Is it like electromagnetic imprinting, is it like a whirlwind? Can you tell us a little bit about how they are actually physically created?

20 **A**: Field transfer.

21 **Q**: *(L)* What kind of field?

22 **A**: Magnetic.

23 **Q**: *(L)* Are they transferred directly from 6th density to 3rd density?

24 **A**: No.

25 **Q**: *(L)* Are they manifested by an object that has come into 3rd density, such as a craft of some sort?

26 **A**: No.

27 **Q**: *(L)* Can you give us a clue here?

28 **A**: We can give "clue."

29 **Q**: *(L)* OK, what is the clue?

30 **A**: See Hoagland.

31 **Q**: *(L)* What does Hoagland say? *(T)* He says that basically what we see in this density is a 3rd dimension reflection of 4th dimension and that it can be seen mathematically by looking at the cloud patterns on the different planets. If there was not another dimension above us, circular would be circular and the circular motion of the clouds would be maintained, but if it is a transfer from 4th density to 3rd density, when you are looking at a 4th density object, what the 3rd density version of it would look like would show a hexagonal figure with angles to it, and that the photographs from the Voyager Probe that show that the cloud patterns from the north and south poles of most of the planets are not circular, they are hexagonal. *(L)* OK, in 6th density, what are crop circles?

A: Thoughts. 32

Q: *(L)* Who is thinking these thoughts? 33

A: Yours truly. 34

Q: *(L)* OK, if they are thoughts... *(J)* 35
They are messages so they could be thoughts before they are messages. *(T)* Well, they have described 6th density as pure energy, therefore there is nothing physical in 6th density to reflect back through the densities. So the only thing that can come from there to here is thought. Because, that is all there is there. *(L)* So, it is a field transfer of thought. *(T)* So, when 6th density thinks and they pass that down, most likely skipping 5th density to 4th density, and then stepping down from 4th to 3rd, we end up with a three-dimensional crop circle. But what does a crop circle look like in 4th density?

A: "Look" is not point. 36

Q: *(L)* What is the point? 37

A: You need visual stimuli in order to 38
remember.

Q: *(L)* Oh! *(J)* What did it say, you 39
need visual...? *(L)* So, in other words, these are thoughts designed to make us remember by looking at them?

A: Yours is a physical dependent exis- 40
tence.

Q: *(J)* Yes! *(L)* OK, if we made di- 41
agrams of the crop circles, and put them up on the wall and looked at them or meditated on them, would they do anything to our brains, our electromagnetic patterns, or would they bring up information from within for us?

A: Not likely. 42

Q: *(L)* Well, what are we supposed to 43
do with them?

A: Nothing in particular. 44

45 **Q**: *(L)* Are they doing something to us? *(T)* I had a feeling it was going that way...

46 **A**: Wait and see.

47 **Q**: *(L)* OK. We have been talking a bit about the maze on the floor of Chartres Cathedral...

48 **A**: Your media resists, why? Suggest discussion.

49 **Q**: *(L)* The media resists crop circles and I know this is so because when I went to the library to research them, there was not a single, solitary book, magazine or article on the subject of crop circles in the entire county system.

(J) There wasn't anything in Barnes and Noble either.

(L) Now, the two books on the subject I do have, I had to order special. Why would the media resist crop circles?

(SV) The same reason they resist everything else.

(F) But, they don't resist everything else as much as crop circles.

(T) Are we looking at this from the wrong perspective? They're not resisting or overlooking them any more than anybody else does. We were just told that crop circles themselves were not important to us.

(F) I don't think that is what they meant.

(L) I said what are we supposed to *do* with them, and they said nothing in particular.

(F) And then you asked if they were going to have any effect on us and they said, "Wait and see."

(T) Could this be because no one is supposed to pay any attention to them? Is this part of it? Maybe we are looking for something that is not there by saying, "Oh, the media does not recognize them and do a bunch of stories about them and alert everybody to them." Maybe they are not supposed to. Maybe the crop circles are supposed to work on their own without major attention.

(F) I don't think so.

(L) Here is something I got off the internet[3] recently [reads text]:

"To some people, the circles which began appearing about a decade ago represent the handiwork of extraterrestrial invaders or crafty tradesmen bent on mischief after an evening at the pub, or even hordes of graduate students driven by mad professors. To others, the circles suggest the action of microwave generated ball lightening, numerous whirlwinds or some other peculiar atmospheric phenomena. These scenarios apparently suffered a severe blow late last summer when two elderly landscape painters, David and Doug, admitted to creating many of the giant, circular wheat field patterns that cropped up over the last decade in southern England. The chuckling hoaxers proudly displayed the wooden planks, ball of string, and primitive sighting device they claimed they had used to construct the circles.

"But this newspaper-orchestrated, widely publicized admission didn't settle the whole mystery. Gerald Hawkins, a retired astronomer who now divides his time between an apartment in Washington and a farm in Woodville, felt

[3] www.thefreelibrary.com/Euclid's+crop+circles.-a011812 538

compelled to write last September to Dave and Doug, asking how they managed to discover and incorporate a number of ingenious, previously unknown, geometric theorems of a type that appear in antique textbooks, into their "artwork" in the crops. He concluded his letter as follows: 'The media did not give you credit for the unusual cleverness behind the designs and the patterns.'"

And then he says that he is finding ratios of small whole numbers that *"precisely match the ratios defining diatonic scale. These ratios produce the eight tones of an octave in the musical scale corresponding to the keys on the piano."* That was surprise number one, he said. He began looking for geometrical relationships among the circles, rings and lines and then he found that measurements reveal that the ratio of the diameter of the large circles is drawn so that it passes through the centers of the three original circles to the diameter of one of the original circles, and is close to 4-to-3. What he discovered were geometric relationships which simply are not taught anymore in the modern math. And yet, essentially he says that these guys that came forward and claimed that they did it could not possibly have done it.

(F) Well, the thing that is so strange to me is that since 1992 there hasn't been any reporting in the American media about this phenomenon at all. *(Laura to Tom)* Is there any way you could check that?

(TF) I already have. *(L)* You have? What have you found?

(TF) There's not a lot.

(L) What is it and what does it say? When?

(TF) I didn't notice the dates. I didn't notice if there was any turned out after 1992...

(F) There's not...

(TF) I liked my photo [of a crop circle] so much I had someone check it out. One of the librarians. Some things you call up you get material that is that thick. [Indicates large file thickness.] This is only this thick. [Indicates tiny file thickness.]

(L) So, there is something?

(TF) But I don't know what years any of it is.

(F) Well, it is not after 1992, I can assure you, because I have been keeping very close track.

(TF) I know it hasn't been in the news. I don't remember seeing anything in the news for several years.

(F) It hasn't been here, but it has been in Britain.

(TF) Right!

(F) It is very strange when we are hooked up to the cable news channels that there has been a television blackout on it here. The other thing is, Linda Howe showed the new ones from 1994 and they are more spectacular than any that have appeared. Now, if these artists are still going around doing this...

(T) This is strange, Michael made me copies of Cornet's lecture and Linda Howe's lecture [on crop circles]. When I played the tapes, the Cornet tape was fine. Mike's equipment is good. But the Linda Howe lecture didn't record. I have two hours of black with flashes of light crisscrossing the tape. I called

Mike and told him and he said, "Oh boy, I did it late at night and must have hit the wrong switch."

(L) Well, I hate to get paranoid, but, do you suppose this Dave and Doug were set up to make this claim so that the media would have an answer they could tout and then just drop the whole thing? If so, why?

(F) Because it's too frightening. I remember in 1991 and 1992 this thing was heating up and heating up...

(TF) That's true.

(F) It was unusual because this type of subject matter is usually not attended by the mainstream media to any great extent. When there is a big UFO wave there might be a little blurb about strange lights reported by various people. This subject was actually focused upon by all of the major networks, it was on all of the major wire services, it was everywhere. All of a sudden, these two drunken artists appeared and they all said: "Oh! That's it! OK, forget about it!" That was so strange because my impression of journalists has always been, at least it used to be, that they want to dig up the truth, and here, mere placebo, surface-type explanations that don't explain anything and which are not adequate, suddenly caused them to lose interest. It would be like Watergate: "Oh, the 18-minute gap... well, Mary what's-her-name stepped on the pedal. Oh, OK, no problem!" Obviously that didn't happen! This just didn't make logical sense for those of us who had looked at the crop circles, and even people who don't follow this type of subject matter closely, who I have talked to, people who brush off the subject of UFOs, have told me that this explanation just doesn't add up! These two guys did all of this under the noses of thousands of researchers who were trying like the dickens to see anything that happened in the middle of the night – in the middle of this, a simple, ridiculous – if you get right down to it – explanation is offered and the whole subject is brushed off?!

(J) And, the explanation would only work if the crop circles were within their physical reach logistically speaking.

(F) Well, not only that, if you have ever calculated what is involved, they started in 1973 with just a handful throughout the summer and by 1992 it was hundreds all over the planet. These guys would have to be working non-stop, 24 hours a day, flying all around the globe... [Laughter] And I thought, how can they accept this brush-off explanation? The other thing is, you would expect, obviously if that were the true explanation, as crazy as it seems, if they could actually, physically do this all by themselves, which is physically and mathematically impossible – but never mind that – it has happened since then. If these two guys are pulling a hoax and nobody is going to pay any more attention, why would they bother to continue to do it each and every summer since that time? Wouldn't somebody catch them by now? There are just a hundred arguments against this explanation that come to mind. Yet, in this country it is completely ignored. My own theory is that it is too sensitive an issue. Here is something that can be photographed.

(L) It proves that there is somebody else out there.

(F) It doesn't prove it...

(J) ...there's something else going on...

(F) I don't think it proves it, but it makes it very hard to ignore. As I have stated before, my father was a physicist and he was also a skeptic. A very brilliant man... When we would see on television... I remember one night in particular, we saw a very comprehensive segment on crop circles, and he actually got angry when I pointed out to him that this phenomenon seemed awfully bizarre, awfully intense, widespread and so on. He tried to brush it off: "Oh, I think it is a fad," were the words he used. This is a scientist!

(L) He dove headfirst into the deepest river in the world! Denial.

(F) Like a whirlwind is going to form a pattern like an intricate geometric figure? Come on! Sure! He grasped that whirlwind theory and when I pointed out to him that this was not logical, he got angry, which I perceived as fear. Being very defensive because it stabbed into the heart of his whole life's work.

(L) That right there is the answer, culturally speaking.

(F) Exactly!

(L) It stabs into the heart of materialism.

(F) In this country somebody does not want this to be reported on because you can't brush it off. You can brush off UFOs... well, not if you really study the issue, but if you don't pay too much attention to it you can brush it off...

(J) ...because there is no physical evidence. You have evidence with crop circles. They are there. You can see them.

(L) And, they are astonishing! Just to look at them is astonishing!

(F) Any of them, really, except for the very simplest ones, I mean. Just using pure, simple logic, who would have the time, the energy, the expertise to do these things?

(J) And to do it in the dark, without any light...

(F) And in just short periods of time! It just doesn't make sense. Just imagine, Mr. French, it is your assignment to go out into the wheat fields of England, in the dark and to make this intricate figure...

(TF) I would ask them to do it for me and show me how they did it!

(F) Right!

(SV) I don't know if it was *Sightings* or *Encounters*, but one time they had a segment on crop circles in Mexico, and they even appear on rock cliffs...

(F) Yes, and it's happening in Puerto Rico. And, the alleged report on this one was that Army-type vehicles came in and destroyed it so people couldn't see it. Which leads me to believe, with my suspicious mind, that somebody doesn't want this stuff going on, for whatever reason.

(L) Yes, what are you going to do with a population that suddenly asks you: "Well, you're in charge – what is this? What's going on?" And, you can't answer them. You have lost credibility as the authority.

(F) And, none of the answers you can come up with are safe. It offends the church because they can't explain it. It offends the scientific community because they can't explain it.

(L) Yes, the church calls everything they can't explain 'The Work of the Devil.'

(T) Which one?

(L) We think we have come up with an answer. Are we anywhere on the right track?

50 **A**: Maybe.

51 **Q**: *(L)* Anything further you would like to add to what we have said?

52 **A**: No.

53 **Q**: *(L)* Well, we have really kind of worn out the subject at this point. Going on to the labyrinth at Chartres Cathedral, we have the idea to reproduce this and use it. *(J)* Is this in the same line as the concept of the spiral and spinning?

54 **A**: Maybe.

55 **Q**: *(L)* Which figure would be the most advantageous to use, the spiral, the cho ku rei[4] or the labyrinth?

56 **A**: You did not ask preliminaries.

57 **Q**: *(L)* What is the source of this labyrinth?

58 **A**: Open.

59 **Q**: *(L)* What preliminaries do you want? Who built it?

60 **A**: Open.

61 **Q**: *(L)* What preliminaries do you want?

62 **A**: We would ask the same of you.

63 **Q**: *(J)* Great! *(L)* What we want to know about this particular figure is if it is beneficial to walk, to use...

64 **A**: Okay, now we are on the right track! Up to you to discover.

65 **Q**: *(L)* So, you are not going to give us anything on the spiral; we have to play with it.

A: And experiment, that is one method 66
for learning.

Q: *(T)* Well, it wasn't a real good ques- 67
tion as to whether or not I was going to do anything with it as a group; I was already going to do something with it. *(L)* Well, then they are not going to tell us anything if that is already in the works. *(T)* I knew it as soon as I picked up the book. I said, "We've got to do this. This is not a choice here, this is something we've got to do." *(L)* OK, is there any information you can give us about this figure? What does it mean? [Displays written glyph given to Jan by Ken Eagle Feather.]

A: Creator implies importance. 68

Q: *(L)* So, the person who drew this 69
implied importance?

A: Yes. 70

Q: *(L)* Is it, in fact, important or sig- 71
nificant?

A: Open. 72

Q: *(T)* What do the symbols mean? 73
(L) Well, the sideways figure eight is the symbol for eternity, this is just a triangle... *(J)* Is it an equation... *(T)* Is it a formula?

A: One question at a time. 74

Q: *(L)* Is it a formula? 75

A: The creation is, because it was cre- 76
ated.

Q: *(T)* What does the triangle symbol- 77
ize?

A: You are not grasping message. 78

Q: *(J)* I guess not. *(L)* Well, I got 79
that the guy who drew it wanted it to be seen as mysterious and wanted to

[4] Reiki symbol.

imply that there was something important and mysterious about it when, in fact, it is just a meaningless drawing?

80 **A**: Yes.

81 **Q**: *(T)* OK, so it has no meaning whatsoever?

82 **A**: Incorrect.

83 **Q**: *(L)* It has meaning, the meaning the person who drew it implied into it. In terms of being a mathematical formula, I can tell you right now that it is not that.

84 **A**: Ask creator for meaning.

85 **Q**: *(T)* So, only the person who drew it knows what it means. *(L)* Because he is the one who drew it. Without the meaning he gave it, it has none.

86 **A**: Yes.

87 **Q**: *(L)* Next question. Are you still with us?

88 **A**: As always.

89 **Q**: *(L)* Thank you. There is a phenomenon going on today where a lot of people have accused their parents of childhood abuse which is later proven to be false, and it causes a lot of problems. This has led to a lot of problems about the practice of hypnosis...

90 **A**: Preconceived notions by biased therapists, i.e. the improperly used power of suggestion.

91 **Q**: *(L)* This has led to much speculation that all UFO abduction memories are false memories, and that hypnosis, itself, in general is a useless or flawed technique. Is there any possibility that many of the people who think that they have been abducted by aliens are merely responding to the suggestions of the therapists?

A: Two concepts at once. 92

Q: *(L)* Is there any possibility that 93
certain people think they have been abducted and they have not?

A: Yes. 94

Q: *(L)* Is it possible for a thera- 95
pist to suggest these ideas into someone's mind through hypnosis and have them...

A: Yes. 96

Q: *(T)* It can work the other way 97
around, too. *(L)* What do you mean?

A: What do you mean? 98

Q: *(T)* You asked if some people who 99
think they have been abducted were actually abused and they said "yes." *(L)* No, that's not what I asked. *(T)* What did you ask? *(L)* I asked if some people thought they had been abducted who had not been abducted, or if some people thought they had been abducted and the idea had been planted in their mind by the therapist. And, they said "yes." *(T)* OK, have some people who thought they have been abused, not been abused? The same question only using the word abused, instead of abducted?

A: Already answered yes. 100

Q: *(L)* But, the next question is: 101
Are there some people who have been abducted who think they have been abused?

A: All combinations exist. 102

Q: *(L)* Is there any... *(T)* It depends on 103
the therapist and what the therapist believes as to the results of the therapy... *(J)* Yeah, are relying heavily on Freud?

A: No. Depends upon actions of thera- 104
pist, not beliefs.

105 **Q**: *(L)* Is there any particular personality type that is more likely to be abducted than another?

106 **A**: Ridiculously open question.

107 **Q**: *(L)* Well, I didn't want to lead! *(J)* We have an anniversary coming up. *(L)* Yeah, I know. The sixteenth. *(J)* No, I mean *our* anniversary, Terry's and mine. *(L)* Oh. *(J)* Your anniversary is on the 16th and ours is on the 17th.

108 **A**: Same.

109 **Q**: *(L)* What do you mean, "same"? *(J)* Well, you would have started on the evening of the 16th but worked into the early hours of the 17th.

110 **A**: Yes.

111 **Q**: *(J)* Good grasp of time! *(L)* OK, back to the question. What I want to know is: in all of the articles I have been reading about abduction, there are many that claim that persons who experience abduction are of such and such a personality type, i.e. fantasy prone. Well, I am definitely not a fantasy-prone personality and I don't think the others here are either.

112 **A**: What is a "personality type?"

113 **Q**: *(L)* Well, I don't really think there is such a thing if you want to get down to it. *(T)* Let's just say that the personality types are something developed by individual researchers to pigeonhole people for statistical analysis. It really has nothing to do with abduction itself. *(J)* Or anything else.

114 **A**: Good one, Terry!

115 **Q**: *(L)* I was talking to my cousin the other night when I was up in the boondocks, and we were talking about abductions and UFOs and space-time and so forth. He made the remark that he thought that it was very likely that there was another universe where this one 'ends', in which the constant of light was the 'minimum'. Is this a valid or usable concept?

A: Too simplified.[5] 116

Q: *(T)* What did they tell us before 117
about the speed of light? That the speed of light is a 'time' measurement and time only exists in our illusion, therefore there is no speed of light. *(L)* So, there would be a state where the constant was not a 'speed' but just what is. There is no speed of light because there is no time.

A: All imaginable combinations exist 118
because they are imagined!

Q: *(J)* I like that. *(L)* OK, on De- 119
cember 9, 1965, there was a reported UFO crash at Kecksburg, Pennsylvania. This was purported by the military to be a crash of a Soviet spy satellite. There is a lot of stuff that has gone around about this and it was even portrayed on *X-Files.* Was the event that occurred on December 9, 1965, in Kecksburg, Pennsylvania, a crash of a UFO?

A: Define please "UFO?" 120

Q: *(L)* A UFO as in alien space craft. 121

A: Close. 122

Q: *(L)* It was not a Soviet spy satellite? 123

A: No. 124

Q: *(L)* Now, you say "close." What, 125
specifically, was it?

A: We have taught you new methods 126
of imaging, we are patiently waiting for you to use them!

[5] *The Wave* 35

127 **Q**: *(L)* What do you mean "new methods of imaging"? *(T)* To talk about it? *(L)* We don't know enough about it... that's all we know. *(T)* Well, working with what we know about it we could probably talk it out and figure out what it was.

128 **A**: Density 1, 2, 3, 4, 5, 6, now, how does the concept of "craft" apply here?

129 **Q**: *(L)* Was it a projection? A trans-dimensional atomically remolecularized object?

130 **A**: Closer.

131 **Q**: *(L)* Piloted by, I would assume, the Grays? *(T)* Not necessarily.

132 **A**: ! If you prefer.

133 **Q**: *(T)* Well, if it was a craft as they have been telling us, brought in from 4th density, it would be the Lizards or someone else of the other side, the [Orion] Union.

134 **A**: The point is the mode of transfer.

135 **Q**: *(L)* OK, so it may be that it didn't crash there, it was... Did something happen and something came through the dimensional curtain? Is that it? *(T)* Well, it didn't crash, it landed! Or materialized, or became solid. *(L)* I think NORAD tracked it. *(J)* It was seen as a fireball.

136 **A**: Colder.

137 **Q**: *(T)* OK, this is just a theory, a thought, just something I am throwing out here, nothing positive... the military was 'Johnny on the spot'. They made a big production of hauling it out of there and threatening everyone. What if it was put there, or sent here for them? No that it crashed, but it was something being sent from there to there and the Uncle came and picked it up?

A: No. 138

Q: *(L)* The point is the "mode of transfer." *(T)* The point is that it was 'cross density'. *(J)* Well, we know that they all are 'cross density'. *(T)* No, not all of them, some of them come from this density. *(L)* The point is the "mode of transfer." What are they trying to say? *(T)* It was materialized here from 4th density. It didn't fly here. *(L)* OK, it was not a UFO because it never 'flew'. *(T)* The trail that was seen coming in was it materializing into the atmosphere. *(L)* Actually, it was materializing in the same spot, the atmosphere moved. *(T)* There was a visible path left... *(J)* I think we should stop using the term 'UFO'. 139

A: Isn't this fun?! 140

Q: [Laughter and groans] *(L)* OK, what is the point? *(T)* The point is the "mode of transport."[6] *(L)* OK, it was projected through the dimensional curtain; it was a time traveler... 141

A: The point is why look for "nuts and bolts." Do you want to join Gene and his cronies?[7] 142

Q: *(L)* So, in other words... are you saying that something happened and the military went in and *didn't* get anything? 143

A: No. 144

[6] Cs actually said "mode of TRANSFER" not "transport", but Terry made this transposition and stuck with it.

[7] Gene is a MUFON person with an extreme materialist view of UFOs. He says that they all come from other planets, period.

145 **Q**: *(T)* OK, we are trying to figure out the "mode of transport" and why it was significant. *(L)* Was this something that the military knew was going to happen at that place and that time?

146 **A**: Maybe, but still not issue behind this query.

147 **Q**: *(L)* Well, what is the issue? I just wanted to know if the blasted thing was a UFO or a spy satellite. Was it not a crash? *(T)* It was *reported* as a crash, but we don't know if it crashed or landed. *(J)* We don't know what really happened. *(L)* Was it a crash of a craft?

148 **A**: What defines "crash?"

149 **Q**: *(L)* Did it do something it didn't want to do? [Laughter] A crash is when you go bongo-zongo without intending to.

150 **A**: Do thought forms crash?

151 **Q**: *(L)* I guess not. *(J)* OK! It was a thought form; it came through the density and yet they hauled something away on a truck. What did they haul away on a truck? Or, did they haul away something?

152 **A**: Yes.

153 **Q**: *(L)* What did they haul away? *(SV)* Thought form! [Laughter]

154 **A**: Sorry! 64,000 dollar question!

155 **Q**: *(L)* I hate it when they do that! *(T)* What did they haul away. They hauled away an object...

156 **A**: How do you learn if we don't?

157 **Q**: *(J)* What?

158 **A**: Do "that!"

159 **Q**: *(J)* I guess the point is that we don't really know what the military moved! *(L)* We don't know if they hauled anything away at all. It is all rumor.

(J) Exactly.

(T) The only thing known is that on December 9, the residents of Kecksburg, PA, saw something come down, or thought they saw something come down...

(J) A light come down...

(T) They saw the military come in...

(J) And they saw something come out...

(T) And they saw the military take something away...

(J) So, what does that tell you?

(T) There are residents who said they saw a large, metallic object in the woods, and we only know what they said they saw... Most of the town and the police department and the fire department did see the military come in, because they commandeered the fire department...

(L) OK, here's what we know [reading]:

"The case in question involves the alleged crash of the so-called Kecksburg UFO recently featured in magazines and even re-enacted on television. The 'acorn'-shaped object supposedly fell to the ground in Western Pennsylvania on December 9, 1965. As the story goes, Air Force search teams cordoned off the wooded area and hauled a large object away. It was later reportedly seen at the Wright Patterson Air Force Base near Dayton, Ohio..."[8]

"One suggested identity for the mysterious intruder was the Soviet Cosmos 96 satellite, which actually did fall back into the atmosphere that day. But, according to Air Force spokesmen, that

[8]How come everything goes to Wright-Pat, for God's sake?! What a boring place!

craft had plummeted 12 hours earlier over another part of the planet. It was a shame, of course, because Cosmos 96 would have been a wonderful UFO...

"In May of 1991 the Pittsburg Press decided to verify the Air Force claims on its own. Toward that end, reporters obtained official space tracking data from the archives of NORAD at Cheyenne Mountain. The decades old data finally arrived in the form of 8 snapshots of the satellite's orbital position. The last snapshot, when projected forward into space and time by a leading satellite watcher who does not want his name revealed, seemed to confirm the official Air Force account. But, going on a hunch and tapping my own expertise in space operation and satellite sleuthing, I decided to check the data myself. The released tracking data could not be positively identified with pieces of the failed probe. Why in the world would our government lie?

"In the 1960's U.S. Military intelligence agencies, interested in enemy technology, were eagerly collecting all the Soviet missile and space debris that they could find. International law required that the debris be returned to the country of origin. The hardware of Cosmos 96 was its special missile warning shielding; too valuable to give back. Hardline skeptics still doubt that anything at all landed in Pennsylvania. Robert Young, an investigator from Harrisburg, keeps finding new 'holes' in the claims of witnesses. 'I am now more convinced than ever that nothing came down in Kecksburg,' he says. And, arch-skeptic, Phillip Klass..." [Hooray, Phil!] "...attributes the NORAD data to foul-ups, not cover-up.

"But those of us who study the relationship between U.S. Military Intelligence and the former Soviet Union, still wonder, after all, what better camouflage than to let people think the fallen object was not a Soviet Probe, but, rather, a flying saucer. The Russians would never suspect; the Air Force laboratories could examine the specimen at leisure and, if suspicion lingered, UFO buffs could be counted on to maintain the phony cover story protecting the real truth."

And that is all we know about the purported Kecksburg landing.

(T) Why would anyone fly in a small, acorn-shaped capsule?

(L) They wouldn't want to fly in it. And, remember, it can appear very small on the outside but be huge on the inside.[9]

(T) And, they hauled something away that may or may not have... whatever it was, it went over! Something went over at that time. My folks saw it when it passed over the Great Lakes! I missed it. I was over at a friend's house. We walked out of the house ten minutes after it happened and everybody was saying, "Did you see that! Did you see that!" How about this: The mode is the important thing. Let's just lump all non-human types under the word 'alien'.

(J) Let's use 'non-terrestrial'.

(T) No, you can't use 'non-terrestrial'. Could this have been a human experiment using technology from WWII, from the Einstein work, the Philadelphia Experiment work? Could they have been messing with something and

[9]See the session where physicist Ruggero Santilli was present back in May.

it came down where it wasn't supposed to?

(L) Good question!

(T) It was described as a small acorn-shaped capsule, a lot like what we were shooting up at that time on rockets... *(J)* That's right! *(L)* Is Terry on to something here?

160 **A**: Maybe...

161 **Q**: *(T)* Was this a continuation of the Philadelphia and Montauk work?

162 **A**: Now this poses some interesting questions, does it not?

163 **Q**: *(T)* Yes it does. That was 30 years ago!

164 **A**: Do you want to be the ones who tear away the veil?

165 **Q**: *(T)* Sure! I'm always into veil tearing!

166 **A**: Are you sure that is wise?

167 **Q**: *(T)* If we don't start tearing some veils away from some of these questions, we are not going to be able to progress much farther. You keep toying with this and then you tell us it is too dangerous.

168 **A**: Not point. It is okay to learn truths for yourselves, is it wise to do it for all others?

169 **Q**: *(L)* Is this another one of the things we can't tell? *(T)* No, I think that was more aimed at the fact that it is OK for *me* to learn truths, but do I want to expose you all here... *(L)* No, I think it is more that other people don't want to know it... *(J)* Or aren't ready. *(L)* If the government is, in fact... *(T)* Well, that was 30 years ago, and if it was a...

170 **A**: Who is the "government?"

Q: *(T)* Well, I suppose that if we saw 171
a list of names of who is the real government, we wouldn't know who any of them were! They are certainly never on the ballot.

(L) OK, what we have so far is that this was not a UFO in the sense of being a craft, but that it may have been an object that the government was playing with in their own little experiments in moving things through space-time... *(J)* And they weren't real good at it. *(L)* They screwed up! OK, next question: Is it possible to create resistance to abduction by generating sound? Like an internal sound?

A: Vague. 172

Q: *(L)* Well, this article I was read- 173
ing said that different people used several techniques where they think it has helped them to halt or avoid abduction by 'aliens'. One is to generate an 'internal' sound, a high-pitched 'thought hum', and another is to invoke angelic spirits such as the Archangel Michael, and another is to 'Just Say No', and these people think they have avoided being abducted thereby. Are any of these usable techniques?

A: Potpourri. 174

Q: *(T)* Sweet-smelling dried flowers are 175
potpourri.[10]

A: Sage, salt, ooohm, any other rituals 176
you like?

Q: *(L)* In other words, nothing works? 177
(T) It's not going to stop them! I keep a heavy shield around the house and all that stuff and they still get through!

A: How about the hula hoop dance 178
with green peppers stuck up your nose! [Hilarious laughter]

[10] *High Strangeness* 9

179 Q: *(T)* Thirty-three times! Mirth!

[Tom French sits at board]

(TF) Frank, what is it you feel that you do here?

(L) Ecstasy! Sorry!

(F) Well, you will feel it shortly. It is not like you feel anything, really.

(L) When you put your fingers on, usually just two, you want to put them on lightly but firmly. You don't want to create any drag, yet you want contact. Most people usually put too much pressure or not enough and it either leaves them behind or they stop the motion. [Returning to topic of resisting abduction] Well, the rest of the UFO loonies are not going to want to hear this because they all like to think that they have all kinds of techniques of resistance and they have these psychotronic weapons and machines, and they think they are all-powerful with tricks up their sleeves...

(T) Mike has a UFO detector in a cigarette pack.

(TF) What?!

(L) Yeah. Mike F, our nemesis.

(T) He has an electronic thing he carries around in a cigarette pack which he says beeps or something when UFOs are in the area!

(F) It is funny that you should mention that because when we were at the MUFON meeting in Clearwater, I did hear a distinct, high-pitched beep coming from him.

(TF) Who did he say it to?

(L) Oh, he's told everybody!

(J) Is it anything like a B.S. detector?

(TF) Now, if I start reading out the lyrics from "Born to Run", you know there's something wrong.

(T) It's a lizard. [Discussion of lizards, roaches and toads]

(L) Alright, now, reading about the Linda Cortile case – the woman supposedly abducted out of a high-rise apartment building – rumored to have taken place in the sight of Javier Perez de Cuellar and his bodyguards and driver... *(TF)* The UN guy. *(L)* Was the man who witnessed this really Javier?

A: Yes, but not only one.[11] 180

Q: *(L)* So, there were others? OK, of 181
the two people who were supposed to be the bodyguards of the 'VIP', one of them exhibited some extremely bizarre behavior after this event. What was the cause of this bizarre behavior? Was it him trying to freak out Linda Cortile, or was he simply freaked out himself?

A: Simple shock. 182

Q: *(L)* So, he was having a hard time 183
dealing with it himself. During the discussion of this case, it seems that this particular incident really involved a mass abduction, because a number of women in the neighborhood have subsequently claimed that they not only were abducted at the same time on the same night, but that during the course of time that they were being taken to this craft, they saw other women walking out on the street together. Was this, in fact, a mass abduction?

A: Some was hysteria. 184

Q: *(L)* Do mass abductions ever occur? 185

A: Open. 186

[11] *High Strangeness* 8

187 **Q**: *(L)* Did Linda Cortile make up any of this story?

188 **A**: Open.

189 **Q**: *(T)* Is Budd Hopkins ever going to come out with the story?

190 **A**: Open.[12]

191 **Q**: *(L)* I read a recent article by a woman named Dr. Hulda Clark, and she claims that all cancer, depending upon certain variations, is caused by parasites.

192 **A**: No.

193 **Q**: *(L)* Well, if Hulda Clark's theory isn't it, what is the cause of cancer?

194 **A**: There are many causes.

195 **Q**: *(L)* Well, the reason I asked is because TG has had to go back to Houston for tests because of pain in his arm. Is this, or is he heading toward, a recurrence of his cancer?

196 **A**: Yes.

197 **Q**: *(L)* Is there anything that can be done in that situation? [Tom suggests that he and Frank work alone and Laura removes her fingers.]

198 **A**: Open.

199 **Q**: *(SV)* In the bodywork I have been doing, I have found myself doing a lot of spiraling on people's bodies. I have been getting great results, but I was wondering about the difference between moving clockwise and counterclockwise?

200 **A**: Careful!

201 **Q**: *(SV)* Well, I better not do that anymore! *(L)* No, they just said to be careful. *(SV)* Well, is there any difference between clockwise and counterclockwise?

A: Suggest learn more. 202

Q: *(SV)* How do I learn? *(Tom to Frank)* Do you feel it moving and your fingers sort of follow, or do you feel something generating through your fingers telling them where to go? *(F)* No, I don't feel anything generating through my fingers. *(L)* No, none of us feels anything at this point. Which is not to say that the fingers involved are not moving the planchette [plastic disk]. It is just wholly unconscious. 203

A: Need energy flow. 204

Q: *(L)* I guess they are saying that they need the energy flow of the different people or that the movement is an energy flow through us. There have been occasions where the planchette has flown off the table out from under everybody's fingers. Anything else, Sue? *(SV)* Yes. From whom do I get this training? 205

A: Look, listen, open! 206

Q: *(L)* OK, you can experiment on me! 207

A: Carefully. 208

Q: *(SV)* Is there any danger in doing this? 209

A: Maybe. 210

Q: *(T)* Is it because the spiral pattern creates an energy flow that is too strong for the person? 211

A: Close. 212

Q: *(T)* Has this technique been used before? 213

A: Yes. 214

[12]His book on the case was released the following year: *Witnessed: The True Story of the Brooklyn Bridge UFO Abductions.*

215 **Q**: *(T)* Is it being used now by anyone besides Susan?

216 **A**: Yes.

217 **Q**: *(T)* Is this someone in our area?

218 **A**: Open.

219 **Q**: *(L)* Any other questions? *(TF)* Last time I asked about the mountain dream. I would like to know if there was anything behind my father's 'M' dreams? Dreams in which he was repeatedly terrorized by the letter 'M'. *(L)* You asked that the last time and I think they said it had something to do with the war.

220 **A**: Open.

221 **Q**: *(L)* Anything before we shut down? *(T)* What was the purpose of the attack that we were under? *(L)* The purpose?

222 **A**: Already told you this.

223 **Q**: *(T)* Here? *(L)* It's in the transcript. *(J)* Yes. It's in the transcript. Did you read it? And I thought it was very interesting. I didn't realize that you guys were doing the session, and right at the point where it says "Terry needs to discuss..." the phone rang and it was us calling. *(L)* That whole issue was ....

224 **A**: To discover.

225 **Q**: *(L)* They said at that time that the attack was to break up the group and that all attack was essentially rooted in attack on faith. Did you read that part? *(T)* Yes, but it didn't make sense. *(L)* Well, they said if you look back over the pattern, all attack is an attack on faith.

A: Yes. 226

Q: *(T)* What faith were they at- 227
tacking?

A: Open. Discover. 228

Q: *(T)* Was I being prevented from 229
learning something about the information-gathering process?

A: Up to you to discover.[13] 230

Q: *(L)* Well, it will sort itself out. *(T)* 231
It wasn't an attack on the group. And it wasn't an attack on me that would really make a difference one way or another. Was it a practice attack? *(TF)* Who was behind the mask at the Veiled Prophet Ball? It is a coming-out ball in St. Louis for debutantes. *(L)* Is it someone who is dressed up? *(TF)* They are just there and preside over the ball.

A: Victor Moeller. 232

Q: *(TF)* This is before I was born. 233
(J) Interesting that they give a name! *(TF)* Can't get much more specific than that! It was 1958.

A: Goodnight. 234

End of Session

[13] *Secret History* 12; *The Wave* 26

July 19, 1995

Another of the experimental/therapeutic direct channeling sessions. At several points, the information is very coherent and appears to be as valid as one can determine, considering its nature. At other points, there are issues that I address in the footnotes.

Participants: 'Frank', Laura, Susan V

1 **Q**: *(L)* When the connection is complete will you indicate by saying, "I am ready"? Are you ready?

2 **A**: Yes. [Positional adjustments made]

3 **Q**: *(L)* We have several questions this evening. Who do we have with us?

4 **A**: You keep requesting a name. Remember this mode of communication has different qualities and different necessities, therefore identification by name is not necessary.[1]

5 **Q**: *(L)* What is the protocol?

6 **A**: Protocol is not the word. Protocol suggests restriction. There is no restriction here. It is merely a different mode of communication.

7 **Q**: *(L)* Why does there seem to be difficulty in transmission right now? [Frank is talking very low and slowly.]

8 **A**: That is your perception only.

9 **Q**: *(L)* Ordinarily the voice is strong and clear...?

10 **A**: Your perception, however the voice will become stronger and clearer as the session progresses, as has been the case in each of the previous sessions using this particular type of communication, also one possible problem may be physical blockages of the sound wave paths.

11 **Q**: *(L)* Caused by what?

12 **A**: The physical obstructions in front of the pathway. [We make adjustments with pillows.]

13 **Q**: *(L)* Is that better?[2]

14 **A**: The results will be up to you to determine.

15 **Q**: *(L)* Alright. Our first question is: In a previous session we were given a small dissertation on the process of

[1]However, in earlier communications via board, the Cs indicated that the 'name' given was a sort of indicator of the energies current to the situation. I also did not like this response, because a long tradition of esoteric learning suggested that obtaining a name was important when dealing with discarnate entities. Again, as the Cs suggested, it could be an indicator of the energies. Frank, in refusing to give a name, was again taking a rather condescending attitude. More than this, as soon as he began to speak, the hair on my arms and back of my neck prickled and I felt something was off.

[2]*The Wave* 35

abduction. It was described for us in some detail. Now, what we would like to know is, if our souls are abducted from our bodies and then used as a pattern for remolecularization in 4th density, is there ever, at any time, a remolecularized clone that is retained in 4th density even after the soul has been returned to its original body?

16 **A**: No, it's not possible.[3]

17 **Q**: *(L)* So, they don't keep a pattern or clone of any of us after they have abducted us, 'they' being a general term?

18 **A**: No.

19 **Q**: *(L)* OK. Is any process used to affect us at a distance from 4th density?

20 **A**: That question is vague.

21 **Q**: *(L)* Do any of the STS beings have the ability to cause us physical problems, or mental or emotional problems when not in direct contact with us?

22 **A**: Certainly.

23 **Q**: *(L)* How is this done?

24 **A**: A number of different methods used.

25 **Q**: *(L)* Can you describe the most frequently used methods?

26 **A**: That's a non-applicable question.

27 **Q**: *(L)* What do you mean?

28 **A**: There is no frequency determination by way of mathematical calculation.

29 **Q**: *(L)* So any and all methods may be used at any given time?

30 **A**: That is correct.

Q: *(L)* Could you give us one or two 31 examples of how this is done?

A: There are many: sound wave ma- 32 nipulation of the ultra-high frequency range would be one.

Q: *(L)* What do these sound waves in 33 the ultra high frequencies do?

A: They can alter chemical balances 34 within the body of the subject, thereby also the brain, using the physical path to cause distress by altering these chemical imbalances into place.

Q: *(L)* Do these ultra-high frequency 35 sound waves ever carry messages in terms of pre-coded suggestions that are triggered by these waves?

A: Messages are not carried in ultra- 36 high frequency sound waves. Now, you are talking about an entirely different method.

Q: *(L)* Could you describe this method 37 to us?

A: This would be very complex and 38 time consuming for you, but also, there is one more method used than what your mental capacities are able to perceive.[4]

Q: *(L)* And what is that?[5] 39

A: There's no possibility for an ade- 40 quate response since the information would not be perceptible for you.

Q: *(L)* I don't understand. You say 41 there is one more method that would be beyond our ability to perceive...

A: That's correct. If you cannot per- 42 ceive it, how can you expect to understand it?

[3] *High Strangeness* 6; *The Wave* 20

[4] Notice the condescension, the almost insulting frame of the response, which continues through the exchange.

[5] *Secret History* 5, 12; *The Wave* 26, 28; *The Wave 7* "Appendix B"

43 **Q**: *(L)* Well, perhaps if we were helped to understand it we would learn to perceive it and could thereby negate it.

44 **A**: The best analogy would be trying to explain calculus to a two-year-old. Would this be possible?

45 **Q**: *(L)* To a very clever individual, possibly.

46 **A**: And would it be possible for the two-year-old human to perceive calculus correctly?

47 **Q**: *(L)* If the two-year-old human was extremely bright.

48 **A**: Well, now you are adding conditions into a situation which were not there to begin with.

49 **Q**: *(L)* Well, my question is: why mention something that is non-perceivable and unexplainable if it cannot be discussed?

50 **A**: It still can be documented, can it not?

51 **Q**: *(L)* Well, how do we document it?

52 **A**: Exactly as given.

53 **Q**: *(L)* If we don't know what we are looking for, how can we document it?

54 **A**: Exactly as explained. There is one method which cannot be perceived by you. Is it not possible to document that as such?

55 **Q**: *(L)* If documentation is simply writing that there is one method that we cannot perceive.

56 **A**: Precisely.

57 **Q**: *(L)* And then others will come along and ask: "What is it?" And we will have no answer. Not even a remote estimation of what it could possibly be. And that is a highly unsatisfactory condition to be in, to have a hint...

A: It is? What about all the other an- 58
swers that were once questions?

Q: *(L)* Well, they are far more satisfac- 59
tory since they have now become knowledge.

A: How did they become knowledge? 60

Q: *(L)* By being answered. 61

A: And how did they exist before they 62
became answers?

Q: *(L)* As questions. 63

A: Correct. 64

Q: *(L)* And, our question is: What is 65
this other method?

A: It is not perceivable by you. 66

Q: *(L)* What are the mechanics of it if 67
it is not perceivable?

A: That's part of what you cannot per- 68
ceive. Do you not see that there is a question here for you to begin to study yourself, and this is the only way that it can be done, by planting a seed, as it were, for you then to follow until it eventually leads to the answer. But, in order for you to receive the answer, you need information in between the question and the answer which is not yet available to you because conditions do not exist currently that will allow for that in between information to be available.

Q: *(L)* Alright then, moving on to an- 69
other subject: how are pre-coded information signals sent?[6]

[6]At this point, I was highly irritated with the source. It seems odd that Frank, and/or whoever/whatever was driving him to try to take over the sessions with trance channeling always managed to say exactly those things that guaranteed

70 **A**: Would you clarify, please?

71 **Q**: *(L)* Well, before we got off onto this subject, the suggestion was that messages could be sent via sound-wave focusing.

72 **A**: No, sound wave focusing is designed to alter body and brain chemistry in order to alter such things as feelings, emotions, and so forth, which then may lead to the altering of mental thought patterns. But messages are not sent by ultra-high frequency sound waves.[7]

73 **Q**: *(L)* How are they sent?

74 **A**: Messages are sent by something called Free Formal Imaging.

75 **Q**: *(L)* And what does that describe?[8]

76 **A**: That describes the transference of thought.

77 **Q**: *(L)* And how is that done? At what frequency is it done?

78 **A**: Not correct concept. There is no "frequency" as such involved. There is methodology that, again, unfortunately, you do not understand. However, since you seek answers to all questions, the only possible way to explain is to simply say a thought is formed in one realm and sent to a second realm, which is yours.

79 **Q**: *(L)* OK. Can it be sent to a directed target?

80 **A**: Absolutely.

81 **Q**: *(L)* Now, the question has arisen that, since other-dimensional beings have the ability to kidnap or abduct or forcibly extract souls, do they also have the capability of manipulating our soul essences after they have left our bodies during the transition to 5th density?

A: Not correct. 82

Q: *(L)* They do not? 83

A: No, you see when your physical 84
body expires, and you enter 5th density, this is done one way and one way only: by passing through a conduit which opens specifically for the purpose of transference from 3rd density to 5th density. Now, something often referred to in your terminology as a silver thread, is like a closed line which opens when this conduit is needed. That's rather awkward, but it's the only way to describe it. So that when the physical body terminates, this line is opened, forming a conduit through which the soul passes naturally. However, part of the existence of this conduit is that it is absolutely impenetrable by any force from any density level. Therefore, souls in the process of transferring from 3rd density to 5th density are not in any way able to be molested or tampered with. And it should be mentioned here, also, that the soul imprint of the physical body always has a connection to 5th density and that is through the so-called 'silver thread'. That always exists as the 3rd density soul's doorway to 5th density. It can be opened at a moment's notice whenever needed.

---

that we would not continue with this method. It was a sort of 'shooting oneself in the foot'. It was definitely not a cosmic version of *How to Win Friends and Influence People.* I think that my irritation was evident in my tone of voice, because the atmosphere began to shift and the level of cooperation increased. Perhaps just this awareness and putting up a mental block was the key?

[7] *High Strangeness* 6

[8] *The Wave* 20

When it is opened it becomes a conduit. Through that conduit the soul passes. And it is not subject to interference by anything. This is not a deliberate construction, it is merely the natural process similar to what could be described as the protection mechanisms existing on 2nd level density for creatures which are not capable of protecting themselves through their own conscious thought processes. For example, your turtle is contained within a shell that protects it. That shell is impenetrable by any natural forces, therefore nothing that is natural can harm that turtle. However, the same can exist for any creature when it is connected by the silver thread to 5th density. Once it is passing through the conduit produced by the opening of the silver thread, then, of course, it cannot be tampered with. Do you understand?

85 **Q**: *(L)* Yes, but why do so many souls, when they leave the body, not traverse this conduit, and why do they stay earthbound, and why do they attach to other bodies? Why does this condition exist?[9]

86 **A**: That is a complicated question, however the best answer is, choice is involved there for those souls who wish not to leave the plane of 3rd density. The only possibility to do this is to be detached from the now expired physical body but still be within the 3rd density plane, which, of course, is not natural, but nonetheless can occur. In situations such as this, though it has been incorrectly reported, the silver thread is still attached and still remains a thread rather than a conduit. The soul is still attached to the silver thread but detached from the host body which has now expired. So the effect is very similar to being consciously aware of 3rd density surroundings without a 3rd density unit to accompany. Do you understand?

Q: *(L)* Yes. OK... 87

A: Also, please be aware of the fact that once the soul leaves the confines of the physical body, the illusion of time passage is no longer apparent even when the soul remains on the 3rd density plane. Therefore, it appears to that soul that no time whatsoever has passed. And, we mention this merely for you to contemplate all of the various meanings behind this. 88

Q: *(L)* OK. Now, earlier we had a discussion about crime, the involvement in crime of black people versus white people, and, looking at the numbers, it seems that there is an inordinate number of black people involved in crime or criminal activities, or negatively oriented behavior, than white people; the figures are really outstanding: blacks are eight times more likely to commit crimes than whites. And many of the explanations that are used, such as poverty or discrimination do not seem to account for this disparity, considering the poverty and discrimination exhibited toward many other ethnic groups with no such relationship. Is there something significant in this fact, and is there some reason why this condition exists? 89

A: Perhaps you should try one question at a time. 90

Q: *(L)* Why do blacks commit more crimes than whites? 91

A: That is too broad spectrum a con- 92

[9] *High Strangeness* 6

cept to be answered simply. Please try to break down the question into several parts so that the answers can adequately explain.

93 **Q**: *(L)* Can you suggest a way for me to break it down? It is a difficult subject.

94 **A**: Normally this is not the procedure, however, one suggestion may be, for example, to ask, first of all, what is it that causes individuals to commit crimes; secondly, is there any connection between one's race and national origin or physical state of being and one's proclivity to commit crimes, etc. In other words, this is a broad spectrum subject. In order for it to be answered adequately, it must be broken down into many consecutive questions.

95 **Q**: *(L)* What is it that causes individuals to commit crimes?

96 **A**: Well, now you see, that too, has many answers. We will choose one and then let you contemplate. One answer is, of course, as we mentioned previously, the alteration of blood, body and brain chemistry through the use of ultra-high frequency sound waves. Of course, as you can well imagine, one effect that this may have would be what you would refer to as anti-social behavior. Do you not see this?

97 **Q**: *(L)* I do. OK, is there anything about a person of a particular race or body type which makes them more susceptible to this manipulation than another race or person?

A: Well now, that brings into question 98
the physical differences between races, including the obvious body chemistry differences, a subject that has not been adequately explored on the 3rd density level of existence. For example, it is very obvious the different 'races' as it is called, are human beings that have different chemical make-up in their bodies. Would you not say this?

Q: *(L)* I would say that might be prob- 99
able.

A: Now, if one takes this one step fur- 100
ther, perhaps if one race has a brain chemistry make-up or blood chemistry make-up that can alter the emotions in such a way so as to commit what is called anti-social behavior, at least in social environment to which you are accustomed, then this, perhaps, would explain why there may be a higher percentage of crimes committed by persons of a particular race as opposed to persons of a different particular race.

Q: *(L)* Are there any specific chemi- 101
cals that we could isolate or name that would be involved with this condition?

A: Tumoxifene.[10] 102

[10]I've never found anything called "Tumoxifene". However, there is a substance with a somewhat similar name given to it by researchers. In the late 1950s, pharmaceutical companies were actively researching a newly discovered class of anti-estrogen compounds in the hope of developing a morning-after contraceptive pill. Arthur L. Walpole led such a team at the Alderley Park research laboratories of ICI Pharmaceuticals. It was there in 1966 that Dora Richardson first synthesised tamoxifen, known then as ICI-46,474. Walpole and his colleagues filed a UK patent covering this compound in 1962, but patent protection on this compound was repeatedly denied in the U.S. until the 1980s. Tamoxifen did eventually receive marketing approval as a fertility treatment, but the class of compounds never proved useful in human contraception.

103 **Q**: *(L)* And, what is that?[11]

104 **A**: A hormone secreted by the pituitary gland. You'll find this particular hormone to be in high concentrations in persons of what is referred to as the Negro race.

105 **Q**: *(L)* And why does this hormone make a person susceptible to these ultra-high frequency sound waves, so that they exhibit anti-social behavior?

106 **A**: That's actually a question that skips over some necessary ingredients, however the best way to answer that is that when this hormone is in high abundance, then one's aggressive nature is heightened, since it already exists in higher levels within individuals of the Negro race, it does not require much alteration to increase it to what would be referred to as the danger level. Therefore, aggressive or anti-social behavior can be more easily facilitated in those of the Negro race, and those of other races.

107 **Q**: *(L)* Is it possible, or does it happen, that people of the other races, white, Hispanic, or oriental, to have individuals born into those races, who, by some fluke, have higher levels of this hormone?

108 **A**: Are you asking: "Do some individuals of other races besides the Negro race have high levels of that hormone?" Well, obviously each individual situation is different. It is averages that make up the important composition.

109 **Q**: *(L)* So, this is what we could call, in a general sense, the 'crime hormone'?

A: It is certainly one of them, anyway. 110
Although, aggressive behavior does not necessarily translate into criminal behavior.

Q: *(L)* True. What is it in the blacks 111
that tends to make aggressive behavior translate into crime?

A: That question is not answerable 112
when put in that way. Please reverse and ask a more basic foundational question.

Q: *(L)* Well, individuals such as mem- 113
bers of the Celtic background are historically and evidentially quite aggressive, yet they do not as frequently, in fact less frequently, commit crimes as a result of their aggression. Why is this?[12]

A: Well, there is more than one an- 114
swer, of course. Everyone's chemical nature or make-up is oriented toward their native environments. Of course, if one thinks of the Negro race as having lived for many thousands, in fact millions, of years in the general climate and environmental situation they are native to, then perhaps it could be said that a greater level of Tumoxifene would be needed for survival in that environment. Now, when removed from that environment to an entirely different environment whereby such chemical balance is not correct for the new environment, then increased amounts of this chemical may produce aggressive behavior of one or two particular types. Whereas other races or cultures, when exposed to any stimuli which causes increases or changes in various brain

[11] *Secret History* 5, 12; *The Wave* 26, 28; *The Wave 7* "Appendix B"

[12] I was operating with information given in a number of mainstream scientific articles and government statistics. I'm no longer confidant that such information is even remotely accurate or fair.

chemistry, this may cause aggressive behavior of a different sort which can be channeled into more acceptable pursuits within the given society.

115 **Q**: *(L)* Is there anything that can be done chemically to alter this aggression or crime hormone to reduce it or to convert its effects into other behavior?

116 **A**: That's an extremely complicated question because any tampering with chemistry of the brain is similar to what you would describe in cliché as shooting in the dark at this point in your development, because you do not understand all of the intricacies involved. Therefore, it is very difficult also to positively answer that question when put in that form.

117 **Q**: *(L)* Is there any form that question could be put into where it could be answered more simply?

118 **A**: That is up to the one asking the questions to determine. Obviously the answer is yes, but if you are asking how to formulate the question, we cannot do that for you because that is part of your learning process. If we now are reduced to asking, or rather telling, how to ask questions, this is rather like leading you by the hand, is it not?

119 **Q**: *(L)* Yes. Is there a simple, practical action that could be taken to assist members of the black race in reducing this aggressive behavior?

120 **A**: Well, again, you keep asking nearly impossible questions, because you must realize that this is not a simple black and white issue, no pun intended. What it is is trying to answer an extremely difficult question with very simple answers and this will not work because there are so many different directions involved here. There is just an impossible number of difficulties involved in trying to deal with this. Apparently you don't see that it is not something where one can simply formulate an injection, for example, and line up all the members of the black race for this injection. Can you imagine the extreme difficulty in even trying to contemplate such a thing? And, all of the resistance that would be received from every imaginable corner of your society at even the mere suggestion of such a thought? Obviously this is a problem that will only be taken care of at a later time, as you measure time, when the shift from 3rd density to 4th density takes place. There really is no point in trying to climb backwards up the side of a mountain with nothing but your slippery bare feet and hands to work with. That is what you would be trying to do if you tried to answer such a problem so simply.

Q: *(L)* OK. I would like to know who was responsible for the vision seen by the Emperor Constantine which caused him to convert to Christianity and impose Christianity on his world?[13] 121

A: The answer to that is, mainly and primarily, merely that the Emperor Constantine had been predestined to do such a thing by the planning process that exists in 5th density prior to the reemergence of a soul in 3rd density. 122

Q: *(L)* Is there any particular significance to the fact that the imposition 123

[13] After much more research, I've concluded that Constantine did not see a vision at all. Rather there was an asteroid/comet impact at the time, as I've written about in a number of online articles.

of Christianity on the area of Constantine's reign also brought on the Dark Ages?

124 **A**: Possibly.

125 **Q**: *(L)* Do you have any comments on that?

126 **A**: No, not really.[14]

127 **Q**: *(L)* What is the true significance of the Masonic apron?

128 **A**: In what way?

129 **Q**: *(L)* There are hieroglyphics and carvings from ancient Egypt showing high priests wearing aprons and there are many secret societies down through the ages for centuries and possibly even further back than that where the initiates wore aprons. Now, the aprons have been either white cloth or sheepskin. What is the significance of the apron? Why an apron?

130 **A**: It is simply a tradition born of ritual.

131 **Q**: *(L)* What was the origin of this tradition? What did it symbolize to put on the apron?

132 **A**: Perhaps it could best be described as attempts to shield from negative or evil spirits.

133 **Q**: *(L)* OK, Susan and I did some research on all our past sessions and we came to the realization that after other people began coming regularly there was a significant increase, in fact a doubling, of the number of answers received through this source that were basically refusals to answer, as in: up to you, open, maybe, close, and so forth. In general, what we noticed was a great reduction in the level and type of information we were being given. Could you give us a reason for this?

A: The best answer to that is that when you have a greater and greater number of subjects present for any formal channeling sessions, of course the mental energy and the thought waves are more of a conflicting nature, and of course the answers must be carefully given in order to avoid conflict that is unnecessary by the observers or within the ranks of the observers, so, therefore, some questions are better left unanswered if it is felt or known that the true answers will cause grave distress by some who are receiving them. And, the more subjects you have present, the more likely that this situation is to be apparent. Therefore, sometimes questions must be either passed over or each individual subject must find a way to answer the question for themselves that they feel comfortable with. 134

Q: *(L)* That seems to say that the way that is most conducive to receiving information is to limit the number of individuals present, thereby limiting the amount of conflicting thought patterns. 135

A: That is one possible outlook. 136

Q: *(L)* Does it require a state of absolute openness to receive the information? 137

A: No, it does not, however to receive absolute information in uninterrupted flow, such a state would be required. But, such states are very rare on 3rd density. 138

Q: *(L)* Well, it seemed to me that in the initial six months or so that we were re- 139

[14]Here a good opportunity to bring up the Sirente, Italy, strike that is now thought to be 'Constantine's Vision' was passed over.

ceiving the information, that the information was much more open and the answers were more open. It seems that when I ask questions, I ask because I really want to *hear* what may be said without putting any expectations on it whatsoever. I have realized that with all of the enormous work I have done in this life, that I have not been able to figure out the answers, and I am ready to shut up and listen... When other people ask questions, it often seems that they are just asking just to confirm the answer they have already formed in their own mind against whatever answer may come through.

140 **A**: This is a correct perception on your part, however such prejudice as described is something that all on 3rd density are guilty of to a greater or lesser extent at various question and answer opportunities. Therefore if you were to study the answers more thoroughly, you might also find that there are varying degrees of what you describe as openness or willingness to dispense information even during those sessions where fewer people were present.

141 **Q**: *(L)* That is true. The thing is, from my point of view, to continually strive to reduce the number of prejudices, to expand and broaden the willingness to hear the information, and to not have a preconceived notion of what the answer is going to be. In the initial stages, of course, I was testing and examining what kinds of answers came through and what the parameters were, and I actually think, interestingly, that even with my more or less rigid testing process, that better and more complete answers were given than were given in later sessions where others were present.

A: It's possible. 142

Q: *(L)* What would be the reason for 143
this?

A: We have already described this in 144
the previous answer. The more subjects you have present, the more opportunity for prejudice, obviously.

Q: *(L)* OK, recently I went to a neu- 145
rologist, Dr. Vincent D. Now, it seems that Dr. D was quite animated and indicated that he felt like he had met me before even though he knew that he hadn't. There seemed to have been some very strong subliminal psychic interaction between myself and him. Could you give me a clue as to why this was?

A: There may have been some karmic 146
interaction there.

Q: *(L)* Will this involve any interaction 147
in the future?

A: That is obviously up to you to find 148
out.

Q: *(L)* Well, Susan and I have been 149
talking and she is baffled as to what to do for me therapeutically. Can you help?

A: That, of course, is a very compli- 150
cated situation, however, one of the possibilities is the nerve passages can be altered by physical stresses caused by a number of different factors stemming from activities undertaken in the past, for example buildup of scar tissue around the musculature of the extremities and appendages has perhaps blocked the natural flow of electricity which then pass from the center of the nervous of system to the extremities. This can cause some starvation of necessary passages of electrical elements through the nerve passageways which,

in turn then, may cause a certain degree of starvation to those same extremities through lack of proper oxygenation. Alleviation is difficult because it requires several steps. The best suggestion is a gradual but steady improvement in health as facilitated by a number of different programs to reverse damage having been caused. The information to facilitate this is available to you.

151 **Q**: *(L)* It is reversible?

152 **A**: It is reversible. All damage is always reversible until either the physical host body in part or in whole is terminated.

153 **Q**: *(L)* Is Susan's manipulation of the tissues and electrical currents through her various techniques... is this beneficial at this time?

A: It is beneficial, however, it is very 154
likely more will be needed. We mean more types of activities in order to facilitate complete improvement.

Q: *(SV)* But, the main problem is the 155
scar tissue?

A: Any form of blockages which block 156
the proper firing of the neurons, thus preventing oxygenation which takes place as a result, including the build-up of scar tissue.

End of Session

July 23, 1995

Another trance channeling/therapy session. As I mentioned before, when Frank channeled directly, there was a repellent air that emanated from him which is hard to define. Perhaps it was just his tone of voice. We discussed this at length. I think that, in all fairness, even if the material was subject to being skewed by Frank's emotional or programmed agendas, he was still able to be very accurate due to what I have called the well-pipe analogy. As long as Frank was in the physical presence of the individual asking the questions, he could tune in to that person's mind to some extent, most particularly when the questions were personal. In this way, under hypnosis, he was quite able to channel via a sort of telepathy, the same way he was able to accurately read palms. He simply connected to the individual asking the questions and sort of vacuumed the information out and verbalized it.

Another point we discussed was the fact that even things that may seem to be negative occurrences from one perspective, can be very positive from another. I have noted in several articles the fact that STS-oriented individuals have a sort of semantic aphasia – likely a consequence of wishful thinking – and even when an obvious truth is right in front of their faces, they cannot see the range, depth, or associative properties of the principle. It was in this sense that Frank was quite able to participate in the delivery of material of a very STO orientation, because he simply could not understand what it really meant.

This particular session, when the entire group was present, was one that, in certain segments, demonstrated the superior, condescending attitude so sharply that it is even obvious in the text. Many people have written to ask me if I was sure that we were talking to the Cs on this one. However, even though repellent obfuscation and avoidance of the issues by a lot of words that said little was apparent, there was so important a message conveyed in this session that it deserves attention.

In this particular case, I think it was a simple matter of Frank tuning into me telepathically, and the information was being drawn directly from my unconscious mind; in other words, truly 'me in the future'.

One thing I do know is that, in retrospect, the way I received the information, and the way I ultimately acted on it, was one of the keys to changing my reality completely. It also changed my whole perception of so-called 'aliens' and abduction phenomena. From the first time I read books and cases on that topic, I recognized the paranormal 'taste' of it. But it was problematical to reconcile something that also appeared to have a strong material component. It began to dawn on me that the 'you create your own reality' concept had implications that were completely unknown to the popularizers and promulgators of same, and those possibilities might not be very pleasant to behold or experience. Ignorance of darkness truly was dangerous.

To give a little background on this session, the reader may remember that throughout the period of the 1995 sessions thus far, I was dealing with injuries that I had received in an auto accident in December of 1994. I was in almost constant pain. The therapy I was receiving wasn't helping me very much, to put it briefly. At some point, another X-ray was made by the chiropractor, and he noted a strange shadow that looked like a metal pin linking the 5th and 6th cervical vertebrae together. He referred me to a neurosurgeon who ordered a series of MRIs.

On the night before I was scheduled to have these films made, I woke up suddenly, as though I had been thrown off a cliff, my heart pounding, choking and gagging on something thick in my throat. My entire mouth and throat, going deep inside, was in horrible pain. I felt as though my tongue had been torn out by the roots and I was strangling on it. (See Session 18 February 1995 where I mention this event, which occurred the night of February 2/3rd.)

I ran to the bathroom and tried to spit out what was choking me, and it was a big clot of blood. The only explanation I could think of was that I must have bitten my tongue in my sleep. I examined my throat, and it was torn, red and swollen way in the back, beyond my teeth, slightly to one side of the back of my throat. The bleeding redness extended down into the recesses of my throat where I couldn't see it all. There was no way I could have bitten myself there! When I tried to wake my husband up to help me, I was unable to rouse him, and he had always been a light sleeper. This disturbed me very much. My throat and the side of my face swelled up and stayed swollen for over a week and I had difficulty eating and talking, much less swallowing.

When the MRIs were done, it was noted that whatever had been seen by the chiropractor on the X-rays was no longer there. But I did have a bulging disk that was pressing on the spinal cord and the neurologist felt that this was the source of most of the pain. He wanted me to see a surgeon. The films were sent over and I was given an appointment.

The neurologist told me that surgery was not the best option because I have a congenitally narrow spinal canal. But the same thing that made surgery problematical, made it likely that I would suffer constant pain and occasional paralysis for the rest of my life. What was more, with the vagaries of spinal impingement, it was hard to tell where I was going to hurt or experience the paralysis from one day to the next.

Having suffered so much pain for so long, I was rather depressed by this news. I mean, what else can go wrong?

The attorneys for the fellow who hit me wanted my MRIs to send out for a second opinion, but they had 'disappeared'. All the efforts of two doctors' staffs, as well as the staff at the medical center where they were taken, were unable to produce them. It was a big mystery. The staff at the MRI unit were so upset that they undertook to do hand searches in relays to try and find them. They were under a lot of pressure to find them because, otherwise, they had to do them over again without charge, and it was a very expensive set of films. After almost two weeks of searching, the MRI staff finally admitted defeat. I was scheduled to come in to have another set made.

So, we come to the event that is discussed in this session: The night before the new pictures were to be made, I was worried about being able to go to sleep due to the strange events surrounding the loss of my films as well as other matters. After lying down in the bed, I was just trying to be still and calm down the pain, knowing I wasn't going to be able to go to sleep. I was right in the middle of puzzling over those blasted MRIs, when the next thing I knew there was a sort of momentary blank-spot and I came to myself, only to discover that I was being floated out of bed, feet first, by three or four spidery creatures who had me by the ankle and were 'pulling' on me.

I was struggling and resisting and apparently had been doing so even while asleep because I found that my paralyzed arm was extended up over my head, locked on the brass headboard in a death grip, and the bed was shaking and bouncing with the efforts of my resistance. It was virtually a tug of war and I wasn't going to let go!

I looked at them and the creepy little spider guys realized that I had awakened. One of them put its hand on my head and I felt a paralysis coming over me. I became very angry. I wanted to curse them. But it was impossible to resist this paralysis and that made me even madder! I was determined that, even if they had technology that could overcome all of my efforts of resistance, that at least I would give them a piece of my mind! I was going to have my say!

With enormous concentration, I was able to utter a strangled sound. It was not the defiant curse I was working on in my head, but anything was progress against the frozen sensation of my entire body. And, it had a startling effect! As soon as I uttered this incomprehensible, cave person–type sound, they dropped me like a hot potato and began sort of flitting and chattering like a nest of birds with a cat climbing the tree. They huddled together and sort of melted into a shimmery curtain thing alongside my bed. It was much like the mirage effect one sees on the road ahead when driving on a hot day.

My heart was pounding from real exertion. I can't say that I was terrified, because such a thing is beyond terror. And, I have always been a person who acts cleanly and efficiently in a crisis, so this was no different in that respect. What had been most useful was that I had the information from the Cassiopaeans, because that certainly had a lot to do with not feeling terrified, which is more often a reaction to the unknown. At least, to some extent, I had an idea of what I was dealing with, even if I preferred to believe that it had been a hypnagogic nightmare.

At one point, while I was fighting them, while the bed seemed to be bouncing and jerking, I was very conscious that all this activity was not waking my husband up, and after the creatures had melted away, when I had turned to work at peeling my paralyzed hand away from the headboard, I was startled to see – and feel – three distinct, wave-like shudders pass through his body starting from the head and moving down. After the third one, he took a deep breath and began to snore suddenly and loudly as though he started right in mid-snore.

What was troubling me was that he had not been moving at all, not even to breathe. It struck me with horror that he seemed to have been 'turned off' in order to prevent his intervention. That he could be turned off scared me half to death! I had no protection at all! Not only that, when I tried to tell him what had happened, he thought I was imagining it. I can assure you, it was not imagination, though it may indeed have occurred in a hyperdimensional reality, not a material event as we understand them.

As I lay there, trying to figure out whether the event had really happened, or if it had just been in my own head, I realized that the evidence that something had happened was that my partially paralyzed left hand was holding the headboard. Heck, I couldn't even lift that arm, much less hold anything with my left hand. And that I had been gripping and struggling for some time was pretty certain because of the way the hand refused to come open. I lay there trying to figure out what the heck had happened, while cradling my arm that was still screaming in pain and jerking spasmodically. What was more, I couldn't understand how my ex-husband could have slept through all of that rather violent struggle! I was pretty sure that, even if nothing had been physically manifested in the room, at least I had been struggling within a nightmare and surely, that should have awakened him!

I got out of the bed and sat up the rest of the night in a recliner, thinking and smoking. Early in the morning, the girl from the test center called, and in a shaking voice, told me that when she had come in that morning, my file with all films intact was on the reception desk. No one admitted to finding it and placing it there, and she had been the last one to leave the office the night before and the first in the office that morning and had unlocked the doors herself. It was a mystery that has never been explained.

That gave me even more to think about, but I will leave the speculation to the reader. I can only recount what happened. Because of the exhausting, obfuscatory nature of the following session, during which I wanted to ask a few simple questions about this event, I was never able to ask about the films, and never came back to the subject.

Another important point: I had not discussed the event with the group before asking the questions. The reader will notice that I do not initially even describe or name the event in order to not lead the answers.

Participants: 'Frank', Laura, Susan V, Terry and Jan

1 **Q**: *(L)* When you are ready please indicate.

2 **A**: Okay.

3 **Q**: *(L)* We have a number of questions and I think Jan wants to lead off this evening. *(J)* First off, who do we have with us?

4 **A**: Curious that you should ask that? What is the expected answer?

5 **Q**: *(J)* A name.

6 **A**: You still desire a name. We'll say: Toren.

7 **Q**: *(J)* If it doesn't matter, it doesn't matter.

8 **A**: What matters is what matters to you and our desire to comply.

9 **Q**: *(L)* Toren, the first thing on my mind is an experience I had several nights ago (19th or 20th). It seemed as though there was some sort of interaction between myself and something 'other'. Could you tell me what this experience was?[1]

10 **A**: Was eclipsing of the realities.[2]

11 **Q**: *(L)* What is an eclipsing of the realities?

12 **A**: It is when energy centers conflict.

13 **Q**: *(L)* What energy centers are conflicting?

14 **A**: Thought energy centers.

Q: *(L)* Whose thoughts? 15

A: Ahh, we're getting ahead of our- 16 selves, are we not? Thoughts are the basis of all creation. After all, without thought nothing would exist. Now would it?

Q: *(L)* True. 17

A: Therefore, energy centers conflict- 18 ing involve thought patterns. You could refer to it as an intersecting of thought pattern energies.

Q: *(L)* Could you be a little more ex- 19 plicit?

A: We sense you are leading. The true 20 effort to gain knowledge should always be to be open to any response, any question. Therefore asking to be more specific is assuming that the answer is not explicit.

Q: *(L)* Well, it seemed to me that some- 21 thing happened to me that blanked out a period of my experience, and you say this was an eclipsing of energies caused by an intersecting of thought centers. Now, this intersecting of thought centers, did this occur within my body or within my environment?[3]

A: They are one and the same. 22

Q: *(L)* Was this eclipsing of though cen- 23 ters brought on by any of my activities?

A: Well, again we must ask you to slow 24 down in your own perceptions for just a moment, for one sees the truest of answers when one is open to all possible

[1] *The Wave* 41

[2] *High Strangeness* 8, 11; *The Wave* 11

[3] I was trying not to say too much about the incident itself so as to better assess the information received.

responses and is not prejudiced. And again, unfortunately we sense a leading in your seeking of answers, which indicates prejudice, which is perfectly alright, however one would assume that one seeks the truest of all possible answers and prejudice does not allow that. So, if it would be possible, please try to ask questions that do not lead to any particular type of conclusion.

25 **Q**: *(L)* Can I ask about my specific perceptions of the event?

26 **A**: That is what you are already doing. We sense that you desire the truest of all possible answers and if one desires the truest of all possible answers, one must avoid expressing one's own perceptions to any great degree and simply allow the answers to flow. The best advice to accomplish this is a step-by-step approach – to ask the simplest of questions with the least amount of prejudice attached.

27 **Q**: *(L)* Alright. I was lying in bed worrying about being able to get to sleep. The next thing I knew, I came to myself feeling that I was being floated off my bed. Was I?

28 **A**: No. When you say 'I' you are referring to your whole person. There is more than one factor involved with one's being to any particular definition.

29 **Q**: *(L)* Was some part of my being separated from another part of my being?

30 **A**: Yes.

31 **Q**: *(L)* Was this an attempt to extract my soul or astral body?

32 **A**: Attempt is not probably the proper term.

33 **Q**: *(L)* In other words...

A: It is more just an activity taking 34
place. Attempt implies effort rather than the nature present in a conflicting of energies and thought centers.

Q: *(L)* I also seemed to be aware of sev- 35
eral dark, spider-like figures lined up by the side of the bed. Was this an accurate impression?[4]

A: Those could be described as specific 36
thought center projections.

Q: *(L)* I seemed to be fighting and re- 37
sisting this activity.

A: That was your choice. 38

Q: *(L)* Was I successful? 39

A: Now, we are back to leading again. 40

Q: *(L)* Alright, was this the ending of 41
an abduction that had already taken place?

A: Not the proper terminology. It was 42
the conclusion to an event, not necessarily what one would refer to as an abduction, but more what one would refer to as an interaction.

Q: *(L)* What was the nature of the in- 43
teraction?

A: The conflicting of energies related 44
to thought center impulses.

Q: *(L)* Where are these thought centers 45
located?

A: Well, that is difficult to answer be- 46
cause that is assuming that thought centers are located. And, of course this is a concept area in which you are not fully familiar as of yet. So, an attempt to answer this in any way that would make sense to you would probably not be fruitful. We suggest slowing down and carefully formulating questions.

[4] *The Wave* 11, 52

47 **Q**: *(L)* At what level of density do these thought centers have their primary focus?

48 **A**: Thought centers do not have primary focus in any level of density. This is precisely the point. You are not completely familiar with the reality of what thoughts are. We have spoken to you on many levels and have detailed many areas involving density level, but thoughts are quite a different thing because they pass through all density levels at once. Now, let us ask you this. Do you not now see how that would be possible?

49 **Q**: *(L)* Yes. But what I am trying to do is identify these conflicting thought centers. If two thought centers, or more, conflict, then my idea would be that they are in opposition.

50 **A**: Correct.

51 **Q**: *(L)* And, what I want to know is, was this in opposition to me, or was this an opposition in which I simply was caught in the middle, so to speak.

52 **A**: Well, you are drifting away from the true nature of your experience, because you are making suppositions. And we are not trying to scold you, we are merely trying to guide you and this is not always easy. But, let it be known again that the simplest way for you to gather knowledge on this particular subject matter is to ask the simplest questions without prejudice.

53 **Q**: *(L)* OK, you said I wasn't abducted, that an event of some sort occurred. What was the event?

54 **A**: We have already described this, but the problem that you are having is that you are assuming that the description we are giving is more complicated than this. It is not.

Q: *(L)* Did I leave my body? 55

A: I'm very sorry to tell you that you 56
are drifting again.

Q: *(L)* Well, I am trying to ask simple 57
questions.

A: The problem is that you are pre-sup- 58
posing answers. Please limit prejudice.

Q: *(L)* What is my prejudice, what is 59
my presupposition?

A: Well, just to give you an example: 60
how do you know that you ever 'leave' your body? The question is not, do you ever leave your body, it's how do you know that you do?

Q: *(L)* I guess you don't. 61

A: Let us give you a parallel. If you 62
saw a rainbow in the sky and that rainbow was later no longer visible, would you then say: 'Did that rainbow spill onto the mountain?'

Q: *(L)* I don't get it. No, I wouldn't, 63
because I would know that the rainbow is the refracting of light on water or ice in the atmosphere.

A: That's what you know. But, then 64
again how do you know that anything you know is, in fact, the true representation of reality?

Q: *(L)* We don't. 65

A: The only way to solve this problem 66
when asking about a complicated issue is to ask very simple step-by-step questions without prejudice. In order to do that, one must pause and reflect, and take one's time, as it were, to formulate the questions carefully in order to make sure that they are very simple, step-by-step questions and not questions containing prejudice.

67 **Q**: *(L)* OK, in the experience I felt a paralysis of my body. What caused this paralysis?[5]

68 **A**: Yes. Separation of awareness, which is defined as any point along the pathway where one's awareness becomes so totally focused on one thought sector that all other levels of awareness are temporarily receded, thereby making it impossible to become aware of one's physical reality along with one's mental reality. This gives the impression of what is referred to as paralysis. Do you understand?[6]

69 **Q**: *(L)* Yes. And what stimulates this total focus of awareness?

70 **A**: An event which sidetracks, temporarily, the mental processes.

71 **Q**: *(L)* And what event can sidetrack the mental processes to this extent?

72 **A**: Any number.

73 **Q**: *(L)* In this particular case, what was it?

74 **A**: It was an eclipsing of energies caused by conflicting thought centers.

75 **Q**: *(L)* What energies were being eclipsed?

76 **A**: Whenever two opposing units of reality intersect, this causes what can be referred to as friction, which, for an immeasurable amount of what you would refer to as time, which is, of course, non-existent, creates a non-existence, or a stopping of the movements of all functions. This is what we would know as conflict. In between, or through any intersecting, opposite entities, we always find zero time, zero movement, zero transference, zero exchange. Now think about this. Think about this carefully.

Q: *(L)* Does this mean that I was, essentially, in a condition of non-existence? 77

A: Well, non-existence is not really the proper term, but non-fluid existence would be more to the point. Do you understand? 78

Q: *(L)* Yes. Frozen, as it were? 79

A: Frozen, as it were. 80

Q: *(L)* Was there any benefit to me from this experience? 81

A: All experiences have potential for benefit. 82

Q: *(L)* Was there any detriment from this experience? 83

A: All experiences have potential for detriment. Now, do you see the parallels? We are talking about any opposing forces in nature, when they come together, the result can go all the way to the extreme of one side or all the way to the extreme of the other. Or, it can remain perfectly, symmetrically in balance in the middle, or partially in balance on one side or another. Therefore all potentials are realized at intersecting points in reality. 84

Q: *(L)* Was one of the energies that was intersecting with another energy, the energy that constitutes who and what I am? 85

A: Well, now, you are drifting again. 86

Q: *(L)* Was one of the thought centers me? 87

A: That is presupposing that you, what is defined as you, or how you define 88

[5] *The Wave* 11

[6] *High Strangeness* 8, 11; *The Wave* 41

yourself as 'me' is of and by itself a thought center.

89 **Q**: *(L)* Well, I am trying to find this out by asking these questions. I am not presupposing here, I am just trying to find out what is going on here!

90 **A**: Part of what is you is a thought center but not all of what is you is a thought center. So, therefore it is incorrect to say: "Was one of these conflicting energies or thought centers me?"

91 **Q**: *(L)* Was one of these conflicting thought centers or energies some part of me?

92 **A**: Yes.

93 **Q**: *(L)* And was it eclipsed by interacting with a thought center energy that was part of or all of something or someone else?

94 **A**: Or, was what happened a conflicting of one energy thought center that was a part of your thought process and another energy thought center that was another part of your thought process? We will ask you that question and allow you to contemplate.

95 **Q**: *(L)* Was it?

96 **A**: We will ask you that question and allow you to contemplate.

97 **Q**: *(L)* Does it ever happen that individuals who perceive or think they perceive themselves to have experienced an 'abduction', to actually be interacting with some part of themselves?[7]

98 **A**: That would be a very good possibility. Now, before you ask another question, stop and contemplate for a moment: what possibilities does this open up? Is there any limit? And if there is, what is that? Is it not an area worth exploring?

Q: *(L)* OK, help me out here... 99

A: For example, just one example for 100
you to digest. What if the abduction scenario could take place where your soul projection, in what you perceive as the future, can come back and abduct your soul projection in what you perceive as the present?

Q: *(L)* Oh, dear! Does this happen? 101

A: This is a question for you to ask 102
yourself and contemplate.

Q: *(L)* Why would I do that to myself? 103
(J) To gain knowledge of the future.

A: Are there not a great many possible 104
answers?

Q: *(L)* Well, this seemed to be a very 105
frightening and negative experience. If that is the case: a) maybe that is just my perception, or b) then, in the future I am not a very nice person! *(J)* Or maybe the future isn't very pleasant. And the knowledge that you gained of it is unpleasant.

A: Or is it one possible future, but not 106
all possible futures? And is the pathway of free will not connected to all of this?

Q: *(L)* God! I hope so. 107

A: Now do you see the benefit in slow- 108
ing down and not having prejudices when asking questions of great import? You see when you speed too quickly in the process of learning and gathering knowledge, it is like skipping down the road without pausing to reflect on the ground beneath you. One misses the gold coins and the gemstones contained within the cracks in the road.

[7] *The Wave* 49

109 **Q**: *(L)* Let's pause for a moment. [Leaves room]

110 **A**: Does anyone else [have] inquiries?

111 **Q**: *(J)* I think I'll wait until Laura gets back.

112 **A**: If that is your choice.

113 **Q**: *(SV)* Laura is in great conflict with herself; I know this for a fact. Can we help her or is this something she has to do on her own?

114 **A**: How do you know this for a fact?

115 **Q**: *(SV)* When I am doing bodywork on her, it is how I perceive, what I hear and what I feel and see.

116 **A**: We suggest that you explore that further.

117 **Q**: [Laura returns] *(L)* Now, getting back to this eclipsing of energies. Is an eclipsing of energies, such as we are discussing, is this something that can and does happen to everyone at one or many points in their existence where choices are made?

118 **A**: We regret to inform you that you are speeding up and jumping ahead of yourself.

119 **Q**: *(L)* OK, when this experience occurred, am I to assume that some part of myself, a future self perhaps – of course they are all simultaneous but just for the sake of reference – came back and interacted with my present self for some purpose of exchange?[8]

120 **A**: Well this is a question best left for your own exploration as you will gain more knowledge by contemplating it by yourself rather than seeking the answers here. But a suggestion is to be made that you do that as you will gain much, very much knowledge by contemplating these very questions on your own and networking with others as you do so. Be not frustrated for the answers to be gained through your own contemplation will be truly illuminating to you and the experience to follow will be worth a thousand lifetimes of pleasure and joy.[9]

Q: *(L)* OK, just a few days prior to this experience, I experienced a couple of headaches brought on by marital interactions. I would like to know, what was the source of this sudden, extreme pain? 121

A: Have you not answered that for yourself already? 122

Q: *(L)* Not satisfactorily. 123

A: No. It is that you perceive it as being not satisfactory. 124

Q: *(L)* Well, I have a couple of choices and I haven't selected one as being the one. 125

A: Well, then select one. 126

Q: *(L)* What if I select the wrong one? 127

A: You won't. 128

Q: *(L)* OK, also seemingly tied in with this experience, because all of these things have happened in a circle, was an experience when Susan was doing some bodywork on me and I suddenly saw a flash of myself tied to a crossed beam, crossed in the shape of an X, in expectation of being devoured by a lion that was working on tearing my arm off at the shoulder. Was this an opening up of a doorway to another life? 129

[8] *The Wave* 11

[9] *High Strangeness* 8; *The Wave* 41

130 **A**: How does one normally access that information?

131 **Q**: *(L)* Well, it is normally done through hypnosis, but since there is nobody around to hypnotize *me*, then I usually get left out in the cold on that one.

132 **A**: You say there is no one around to hypnotize you?

133 **Q**: *(L)* Who?

134 **A**: We asked you the question.

135 **Q**: *(L)* Well, it seems that way.

136 **A**: Very interesting. Hmm. Apparently the world is much more limited than we thought it was.

137 **Q**: *(T)* Was Frank's dream significant?

138 **A**: Before we answer that question, we heard one of you say "pick on Laura night". That is not the point of any of this. The point is to help you to gain true knowledge, which can only be done by opening up your own channels. We are more than happy to assist you in any way possible in doing this, however, it would be detrimental to you to focus in entirely on our assistance rather than on your own abilities, which are truly and completely unlimited. Now, as far as the perception of being picked on, as you describe it, this is merely a perception. The process of learning is sometimes difficult when the greatest amount of progress is being made and we commend Laura for making efforts to learn that are sincere and persistent. There is no reason to ever perceive that she, or anyone else present, is being picked on when one is learning, when one is attempting to gain true knowledge, this may be perceived as difficult, however, it is, in the long run, very beneficial. And again, while we may seem to scold, we caution that we do not scold, we merely direct when asked to direct. And, if we sense that one's mental energies are diverting or dispersing, oftentimes we return with what seems to be a rather sharp answer merely in an effort to refocus one's attention. Because that is the way with which all of you are familiar for that purpose. As you will now know as you access your memories, it is instinctive in your minds and in your souls. We suggest that you pause and reflect on this because you will see, if you do, the truth in what we have said.

Q: *(L)* Speaking of truths, we had a 139
discussion earlier, and we are somewhat curious as to whether the law of free will would require that some of the information we receive through this source be a) distorted, b) false?

A: Well, we do not wish to close off 140
any possibilities for an answer to that question, but we will suggest that if there is any falseness, perhaps one possible answer as to why would revolve around what we were speaking of earlier, which is prejudice. Prejudice may be contained within the question itself or it may be contained within the expected answer. Either one can interrupt or divert the flow of energy in such a way as to produce varying degrees of what one would perceive as correctness of response.

Q: *(L)* So, prejudice on the part of any- 141
one in the room as to what the answer should or should not be, or could or could not be, can, in effect, create an answer?

A: It can divert the energy flow as 142
we mentioned earlier when you asked about your own experience. If you recall, we cautioned you repeatedly not

to involve prejudice either in your questions or in your expected responses. This was an effort on our part to help you to gain valuable information and to help you to learn how to gather valuable information, thus leading to an extensive expansion of your own knowledge base. Again we also cautioned you not to perceive our efforts as scolding, but as assistance.

143 **Q**: *(L)* So, the prejudice was my assumption as to what did or did not happen, that it was an 'abduction' or whatever, and my questions were framed on that assumption? And, I wanted to hear answers that confirmed my perceptions?

144 **A**: Yes.

145 **Q**: *(L)* Where else can prejudice enter in?

146 **A**: Well, you have described the most important possibilities. And your own reflections, your own perusal of your own thought centers can and will produce any and all possible answers.

147 **Q**: *(L)* Could prejudice that inhibits or deflects the information also originate from spirit attachments on any or all of us?

148 **A**: That is possible, though very doubtful.

149 **Q**: *(L)* If one or any of us had an attachment which altered our thinking or emotions, could our altered thinking or feeling create the prejudice which would deflect the information.

150 **A**: Well, it is doubtful that there is any limit to the possibilities. There are only varying degrees of potential. However, again, we caution against any prejudice when asking a question either of yourself, or of you accessing of the universal bank of knowledge which is always there at your disposal. For, example, when you say 'spirit attachment', that is presuming, or again, expressing prejudice, that such a thing exists, or that it exists in such a way to be a common problem. Either one of those two possibilities, on the path of prejudice, is present. For example, what is spirit attachment?

Q: *(L)* What is spirit attachment? 151

A: No, we asked you first. 152

Q: *(L)* Well, my thought is that it is 153
just as it has been described and exhibited throughout centuries of interaction.

A: Who described and exhibited it? 154

Q: *(L)* Many individuals have exhib- 155
ited it and it has been described by doctors, psychiatrists, priests, shamans, psychologists, exorcists, my own experience working with it; and I don't say that it is necessarily another entity or being, although it may identify itself as such. My thought is that it is entirely possible that it could just be something, some energy that is packed or contained within that person, that is of that nature, and takes on a life of its own, perhaps.

A: That's good. 156

Q: *(L)* My thought also is that when 157
one goes through the actions of spirit release, it really doesn't matter if it is cousin Harold who has come to live in your left shoulder or whether it is years of anger packed in your right hip or past life pain in your heart; none of those things really matter. What matters is: does the technique work to release you from it?

158 **A**: That's a nice theory, but we suggest further study. Because, in truth, as you know, deep within yourself, you cannot know that these things are actual. And, if they are actual, in what segment of reality they reside. You can only suppose that their existence is as you have described.

159 **Q**: *(L)* Well, I said that it doesn't matter what they are, it just matters that the releasing process works. *(J)* Or that you perceive that it works. *(L)* It gives you a script to make changes in yourself.

160 **A**: The original question we asked was: How this relates to the prejudice that affects the energy flows of informational dispensation.

161 **Q**: *(L)* Well, if a person has the attachment energy, whatever it is, can that type of prejudice or that type of energy create prejudice which then restricts the energy?

162 **A**: Well, that is certainly one possibility. But, as we said, we suggest further study.

163 **Q**: *(L)* Study in terms of books or in terms of working with individuals?

164 **A**: All of the above and then some.

165 **Q**: *(T)* Was Frank's dream significant?

166 **A**: May we ask that you be more specific in your question?

167 **Q**: *(T)* The dream that Frank relayed to us earlier this evening about there being another force, another entity or group of entities involved in what's happening.

168 **A**: Well, that is not the area we wanted you to be more specific with. We are aware of the dream as described, but we are asking you to be more specific about the term 'significant', because...

Q: *(T)* Well, is it important to what we are doing? Was it factual information? 169

A: Again we caution that you not be prejudiced in the formation of your questions, because the terms 'important' and 'significant' imply a generalization of levels of intensity of reality, that they can be seen differently from different vantage points. In other words, what is important to one is not important to another. What is significant to one is not significant to another. It all can be confused as to what is important and significant and what the definitions of important and significant are. Therefore, we ask you to remove those two terms, carefully ponder the question, and re-ask it in more specific terms. 170

Q: *(L)* What was the source of the information Frank received in his dream? 171

A: Well, actually that is jumping ahead of the previous thought pattern as expressed by a different individual, which creates confusion and also restricts the energy flow by diverting it. 172

Q: *(T)* Is the word 'accurate' acceptable? 173

A: Acceptable for what? 174

Q: *(T)* In reference to the question. 175

A: We ask you to carefully formulate the question you wish to ask, and then ask it in complete form. 176

Q: *(T)* Is there another force involved in what is happening on the planet, that is manipulating the Reptoid beings the way they are manipulating humans? 177

A: We do not wish to appear to be scolding, but we are trying to help you to gain knowledge. And, as we have stated previously, the formulation of 178 questions is very important in this process. It has been asked previously, in this particular session, if anything can cause the response to questions to be other than factual in the best definition of what factual is. And, the answer given was any degree of prejudice or expectation of response. Therefore, we must caution you again, to please try to refrain from having any prejudice or expectation of response. And, prejudice can be, again, in one sense, a presupposition of existence. Do you follow?

179 **Q**: *(L)* So, we don't even know if the Lizzies exist or not.

180 **A**: Well, we have previously given you information that such entities do exist. However, the question is not tantamount to the existence of what is described or referred to as Lizzies, therefore it would be best to leave that out of the question until confirmation that such entities exist and that they are an important part of the question being asked. Please bear with us and be patient. The results gained will be beneficial for all.

181 **Q**: *(T)* I don't understand... Is there another force involved with the events on this planet, in 3rd density, that we have not yet discussed in previous sessions?

182 **A**: Perhaps it would help to have a review of what forces it is you have in mind. And then, once those forces have been described, we can answer your question more completely and, more importantly, more accurately.

183 **Q**: *(L)* May I ask a question?

184 **A**: You may always ask a question.

185 **Q**: *(L)* Was Frank's dream an accurate representation of the interplay of energies on the planet at the present?

A: Well, as described to those present, in general terms, it was moving in the right direction, however, the information given was somewhat splintered or fractured. There was not beneficial cohesiveness due to the fact that the subject referred to did not have complete recall of the information given. It could be considered a basic guideline, but not a complete database. 186

Q: *(L)* Could you give for us, at this time in toto, the information that was given to Frank in the dream? 187

A: Well, yes that would be conceivable, however it would require your attendance for approximately 52 units as you measure hours of time, to give an adequate breakdown of the information previously given to Frank. And, we believe that you would be unwilling to participate for that length of time, or that you would be able to physically hold up. 188

Q: *(L)* Can I give post-hypnotic suggestions to Frank that he would remember all of this? 189

A: Certainly. 190

Q: *(L)* May I ask if Frank's exposition as to why I seem to be under such severe attack was correct? 191

A: That is difficult to answer because it is close, as we are accessing the thought patterns, to being factual. However, there are conflicting thought patterns. The thoughts coming from you in this particular instance are confused. If you could be more specific, it would be helpful. 192

Q: *(L)* Then, just let me ask it straight. Why have I been under such severe physical, material, and emotional attack in the past 6 months. Frank thinks that I am under such attack because I 193 work and move too fast in the gathering and attempts at dissemination of information; that I charge ahead and do things, thereby exposing myself to retaliatory attacks.

194 **A**: That has the potential for being partially correct in the sense that you disseminate information, perhaps less carefully than you should. The gathering of information holds no potential for attack from any particular realm. However, dissemination *does*, because those whom become aware, become empowered. And, in any struggle between opposing forces, there is always danger in allowing anyone to become empowered without realization of the ramifications.[10]

195 **Q**: *(L)* So, I can continue to seek information, as long as I keep it to myself?

196 **A**: You have free will to do that which you please. But, when you are framing it in terms of the question, "where is the danger?", this presupposes that you are concerned about dangers to yourself. And, if this be the case, we will be happy to give advice where and when needed.

197 **Q**: *(L)* Well, right now it is needed. I am almost completely debilitated physically and materially, which creates a severe barrier to focus and concentration, and also my ability to assist other people.

198 **A**: Well then, perhaps it is true that you should be careful as to how you disseminate the information and how you disseminate knowledge gained, and where, and when. This is not to say that you must stop, but rather to think carefully before you do it, as to what the ramifications will be. And then your instincts will lead you in the proper direction. The dangers are always that when one proceeds too quickly, the instincts may be overrun and become confused with other thought pattern energies, and thereby opening one up to attack and other unpleasant possibilities.

Q: *(L)* Well, if I promise not to tell, make a vow, can't we just stop all this other? 199

A: It is not necessary to stop, it is just to be careful as to how one does it. The flow of information is never a harmful thing. As we have previously described, the service to self involves the constriction and restriction of energies, and the focusing within. The service to others orientation involves an outward flow of energies, the focus being from within to without. Therefore, the passage of information, or dissemination, is very helpful and is of service to others orientation. But, one must also be aware of the dangers involved. One must not lose control of the flow and the possibilities that can result. This is where you need to be more careful. You need to regulate. And, attack can come from any number of sources for any number of reasons. It is not always for the same reason. And, of course, there is the short wave and long wave cycle. The short wave cycle is one which closes rather quickly. The long wave cycle is one that closes more slowly, therefore take a longer amount of time, as you perceive it, to close. Therefore it also involves a more complicated issue. This is just one example as to how attack can be the result of what we were just describing. 200

[10] *The Wave* 10

201 **Q**: *(L)* Can attack be a left over from another cycle?

202 **A**: That is one possibility, certainly.

203 **Q**: *(L)* Can you give us any advice as to how to navigate our way out of such situations?

204 **A**: That is a *very* vague thought concept.

205 **Q**: *(L)* Well, Frank and I both seem to repeatedly face the financial flow issue, and it seems to be one of the primary modes of attack against us at this point. How can we overcome this?

206 **A**: Are you asking us how to make more money?

207 **Q**: *(L)* Yeah!

208 **A**: My dear Laura! You are already in position of literally thousands of possibilities to accomplish that end, are you not?

209 **Q**: *(L)* Everything takes money!

210 **A**: There goes that prejudice again. We have given much food for thought in that area to help you to learn, to contemplate, to meditate.

211 **Q**: *(L)* It is rather difficult to do that when one is worried.

212 **A**: That is interesting. You can't meditate or contemplate when you are worried about your next meal. I guess then that this means that no one on 3rd density has ever been able to contemplate or meditate while worrying what was going to be eaten at the next meal. Hmmmmmm.

213 **Q**: *(L)* The point is that a constant state of worry, another crisis every day, the perpetual worry, eventually wears a person down to the point where one can no longer focus on any other issues.

A: Perhaps one can solve the crises by focusing on other issues? You see, when you constrict the flow, you constrict the channel. And when you constrict the channel, you close down possibilities. And, you make it difficult, if not impossible, for you to see that which is there. In other words, the obvious becomes oblivious because of constriction of the flow. This is why we have recommended against all rituals, because ritual restricts the flow, thereby restricting the possibilities. And, what you are describing is a situation of 'dire straits', as you call it, and financial pressures of great magnitude which is restricting you. But actually, it is your concentration on same that is restricting, not the situation itself. And we realize that it is difficult for you to focus your attentions, or, more importantly to open up the flow of the channel. But, it is certainly not impossible. Especially for an individual as strong as yourself. It is what you choose to do, not what you *must* do. It is what you *choose* to do. 214

Q: *(L)* So, you are saying that this situation is a result of my own constriction, rather than as a result of attack? 215

A: No, the situation can be a result of anything or any numbers of things. But, the sought after resolution to it may be impeded by your own choice to concentrate on the problem, rather than opening up the channels to seek the solution. We never suggested that you were solely responsible for creating your own financial situation, only that you may be partially responsible for preventing a resolution to the problem, that is all. 216

Q: *(L)* Is that also the case with Frank? 217

A: Of course. 218

219 **Q**: *(L)* Anything further on that subject? You say 'opening the channel...'

220 **A**: And not concentrating on the problem, but rather the solution, by opening the flow. The answers come to you when you open the flow.

221 **Q**: *(L)* And what might that answer be?

222 **A**: That is for you to discover!

223 **Q**: *(L)* That's what I thought. *(T)* What is the cosmic wheel?

224 **A**: Cosmic wheel? Whatever gave you the idea that there was a 'cosmic wheel'?

225 **Q**: *(T)* It was just something that popped into my head a while ago.

A: Well, our best suggestion is: when 226
anything pops into your head, to follow it as far as you can, because therein lies your answer. Do you not do that?

Q: *(T)* As far as I can... 227

A: As far as you can? What prevents 228
you from doing that?

Q: *(T)* Well, thank you for your an- 229
swers tonight.

A: Have you then answered your own 230
question?

Q: *(T)* Several of them. Thank you.[11] 231

A: You are most welcome. 232

End of Session

[11]Terry's meaning in this remark is lost because it is text and does not carry the full weight of his sarcasm. He was quite irritated by the obfuscation and 'game playing' of this session where every question brought forth a response that was like pulling teeth.

August 5, 1995

The main thing to note about this session is that it was – again – direct channeling with "Frank". As I mentioned in the previous session notes, I did have an object in giving this mode a fair trial. The additional factor was that, besides myself, only Sue V was present, as it was at her request and to deal with issues of concern to her, that the session was held. We can note that the usual disinclination to answer personal questions was *not* present. As we know from later events, this makes the information in this session questionable. As I have stressed, this does not mean that everything that ever came through this way is wrong or corrupted, but it all needs to be looked at with the question: "Could there be a reason to skew the answer?" Additionally, as was the case with all of the direct channeling sessions, there was a tendency to be circuitous and even obfuscatory in the mode of answering.

I omit the induction here. There was no introduction giving a contact 'name' as is usual in all other sessions. This giving of a name was apparently not 'liked' by the entranced Frank.

Participants: 'Frank', Laura, Susan V

1 **Q**: *(L)* Susan has some questions about a real estate purchase she wishes to make. May we ask questions related to this?

2 **A**: Yes.

3 **Q**: *(L)* Is the house that Susan is considering buying, located at [address redacted], as good a deal as it seems to be in terms of price?

4 **A**: That is subjective. Subjective reasoning is involved.

5 **Q**: *(L)* Is there anything being hidden by the seller that needs to be looked into?

A: The seller's main concern is profit. 6
Also there is some mechanism involved with the transfer which may tend to maximize profit for the seller. This has to do with time, calendar dates.

Q: *(L)* Is there anything further that 7
you can give us on that which would help Susan to settle down and relax a little?

A: The problem is not with the buyer, 8
it's a situation where the seller can make the sale and either realize a larger profit or a smaller profit within the same purchase price structure. So, therefore, the buyer is unaffected.

Q: *(L)* So, the seller has a deadline to 9

meet to maximize his profit?

10 **A**: Yes. The sale is unaffected from the standpoint of the buyer, either way.

11 **Q**: *(L)* So Susan can safely participate in the closing and not be concerned about the seller's issues?

12 **A**: Absolutely correct. The perception of deceit pertains to maneuverings of the seller to create maximum profit potential, which is *not* contingent on the buyer.

13 **Q**: *(S)* Is the house sound? It's not infested with termites or radon gas or anything, is it?

14 **A**: That is quite a venue. These are subjective questions to an extent. It certainly should not be expected to collapse.[1]

15 **Q**: *(L)* Susan had another question regarding another issue...

16 **A**: Susan has many questions and needs to ask them herself.

17 **Q**: *(S)* OK. This is concerning my birth date and place. On my adoption papers I was told one birth date...

18 **A**: Did you not want to ask further questions about the property you are preparing to purchase?

19 **Q**: *(S)* Of course! But I don't want to wear out the subject.

20 **A**: There is no possibility of wearing out the subject.[2]

21 **Q**: *(S)* Laura and I have a lot of plans for this house. We want to hold classes... some of the things we plan ... such as spirit release... this energy won't hang around the house, will it?

A: Such occurrences have nothing to 22
do with the structure in which it occurs. Such things are merely a manifestation of the occurrence itself, and how any such efforts are undertaken, as opposed to the structure in which they take place.

Q: *(L)* So SRT can be safely done with- 23
out fear of harboring any of that energy in the house?

A: SRT may be safely done or un- 24
safely done according to the procedures employed, and those employing them. The structure within which they are done is not in any way related to these issues. And the same holds true for this particular structure in question.

Q: *(L)* Susan has said that she would 25
rather I did not borrow money on my house, that she would like to lend me the money I need at the moment until I get my insurance settlement. Is this a workable plan? I don't want her to be short in any way in her situation. I don't want it to be detrimental to Susan to extend herself in that way.

A: One area where one must be most 26
cautious is in the borrowing of money.

Q: *(L)* I am aware of that, and that is 27
why I am asking.

A: The question that you ask cannot 28
be answered as you desire, not because the answers are not known, but rather because lessons learned on your karmic

---

[1]Note here that questions about termites or radon gas are *not* "subjective". I felt that this was evasion of the question.

[2]This struck me as an odd answer since it had already been said that questions about the house were "subjective".

pathway cannot be shown to you before they occur. And, decisions such as these are suggested to be based on past experience combined with a period of reflection, and if you choose to follow the pathway of borrowing, it is strongly suggested that all parties involved understand the possible variables, and reflect upon the results of all possible variables.

29 **Q**: *(L)* You mean by simply handling it as business?

30 **A**: That is not really the point. The point involves more emotional learning processes that can be painful. However, also, it is possible to avoid painful experiences by careful and precise reflection on all possible events and any given situation that can result, prior to undertaking any efforts. In other words, openly and honestly discuss all possible angles where emotional concerns are involved. These are the danger zones that invariably crop up whenever large sums of money are borrowed or lent between individuals who have an emotional bond. It is not the financial aspects at the root of any painful lessons, it is the emotional angles. If it is possible for you to discuss any and all possible variables, and what effects can be anticipated within each, then you may proceed to do what you feel is best, with the comfort and knowledge that you have gone to the utmost extreme to consider *all* possible variables.[3]

Q: *(S)* There is another question: if I get this house, I noticed that there were bugs. I don't like bugs. At an earlier session you talked about an automatic bug zapper. I know it is not harmful to humans. But, I have a cat and I may be getting a dog. Are they more susceptible to this frequency of this device? Will it affect their nervous system in the long run, or mine, or anyone else's? 31

A: Please be aware that in the state of being that you currently occupy, and in the environment in which you currently reside, as 3rd density beings, there are many environmental stresses upon your physical being, which you often overlook. And, focus on any particular one is rather pointless without focusing on the remainder. So, therefore, perhaps it is wise not to focus on any at all unless you wish to choose the other path, which is to attempt to focus on all, and this can be most difficult. So, as you are zeroing in, as it were, on one area, such as electronic anti-pest devices, is understandable, but rather futile unless you also wish to focus on food intake, smoking, the pollutants of mechanical devices, of sunlight, the thinning of the ozone, vibrations from sound pollution and a myriad of other consequences that you normally overlook and put out of your mind. It is not necessary to become worried about 32

[3]This was as much a non-answer as any we've ever gotten: a lot of words, not much substance to them. Also, it was not a very large sum.

[4]This answer was also troubling. It was as much as saying, "Don't worry that you are swimming in a sea of poison, be happy!" A better answer would have been a direct response as to whether the device had negative aspects as asked and pointing out that one has to just do the best they can avoiding toxicity and trust that as they learn, they will be able to do more in that line. That has, in fact, been our experience. It was as though giving a direct answer to anything that might actually be helpful was not in the purview of 'Frank' or whoever or whatever was

any given environmental occurrence.[4]

33 **Q**: *(L)* So, it is six of one, half dozen of the other. Bug spray, bug zappers, or bugs – take your pick.

34 **A**: Exactly. But the reason for the lengthy answer is to stimulate reflection on a wider range of subjects of a similar nature, rather than just a simple answer to a single question.[5]

35 **Q**: *(S)* But me, as one individual, I can't do anything about the ozone layer or sound pollution... *(L)* That's not the point. There are all kinds of devices you can buy to produce ozone, and devices to eliminate sound pollution in your home. So, if you are going to worry about the bug zapper, you ought to worry about it all. *(S)* Well, I *have* been thinking about that also! On my adoption certificate it says one date. You have told me another date, and we have figured both of them astrologically. Neither one seems correct. Can you tell me the exact birth date, time and place?

36 **A**: First of all, remember that reading of astrological charts requires total objectivity to obtain accuracy. And, again, when there is an emotional bond between the reader and the one being read, it is difficult to achieve this. Therefore, interpretations can be somewhat off.[6] This is the first issue that must be settled. Also, please try to avoid any desired results, but rather be open to any and all possibilities when reading charts of those with whom there is an emotional bond. As far as the date, time, and place, the word 'Mankato' comes; also the number 12, and 3:06 a.m.

Q: *(L)* We have one other question that is personal. Can you describe the action of DMSO on the body tissues, and can it be detrimental? 37

A: Please define 'detrimental'. 38

Q: *(L)* Just leave it and describe the action on the tissues.[7] 39

A: Pores of the skin are stimulated to open up in ways in which they do not normally open up, due to chemical reaction that is taking place between the oils that are normally present on the skin, and the chemical compound in the DMSO, which allows for rapid absorbing of the chemical compounds into the skin, to such an extent that nerve endings are equally stimulated to produce the desired result that is what could be described as numbness. But, one must remember that this numbness is merely a result of deadening the nerve endings as opposed to any medicinal treatment of the cause of the discomfort. Therefore, it is not particularly helpful for one to use the prod- 40

speaking through him at this time.

[5]It was also evidence of not giving when asked, concealed under the guise of wishing to "stimulate reflection". There are many instances in the sessions when the Cs do not wish to give information that might interfere in the learning of a needed lesson, but it is hardly applicable to a question about the possible health hazards of bug zappers!

[6]Rather different answers to the practice of astrology are given in other places in the transcripts. Here, the suggestion is made that it can be objective and more or less scientific. Elsewhere, astrology is held to be merely subjective wishful thinking.

[7]I was getting a little testy here myself.

uct described if the desired result is long-term treatment and healing. It is merely short-term comfort on a temporary basis, then this is feasible, however, it is not advisable for long term health.[8]

41 **Q**: *(L)* The studies done on DMSO say that it bonds with the water molecules and passes quickly through the cells, forcing the cells to restructure in their original pattern, and that also it can carry into the tissues any other agent that is put with it. So, if you wish to apply an antibiotic to a specific area of the body, you mix it with the DMSO and apply it there and then do not have to treat the entire body with the antibiotic just to get it to a particular area. Is any of this correct?

42 **A**: Well, we choose to pose the question to you: Such intricate processes as described, makes one wonder how such a compound would be widely available, given the nature of political and economic restrictions in your 3rd density environment.[9]

43 **Q**: *(L)* Well, it is sold for veterinary use...

A: Again: How could such a compound be available for your use, if indeed, it has the results that you describe? We have answered the question. And, it is possible for you, given your inquisitive nature, to come up with a reliable and trustworthy chemical analysis through efforts of your own, which would verify our statement: it is merely the result of nerve endings being numbed, as it were, which eases the pain. Now, we ask you to reflect upon this for a moment, again not merely to answer this one simple question regarding one relatively minor subject, but rather also to answer the entire nature of things in your environment. Would you expect anything that produces the results that you describe, to be readily available to you?[10] 44

Q: *(L)* Well, I don't know. One does have to buy it from a veterinary source... so it is not exactly in the supermarket! 45

A: Then why can't you buy, for example, plutonium from such sources?[11] 46

Q: *(L)* Well, plutonium is more rare. 47

A: But we are not discussing rarity 48

[8]This description is not very accurate. There is no chemical compound 'in' the DMSO – DMSO (dimethyl sulfoxide) *is* a pure chemical molecule. The benefits of DMSO are well described in scientific literature. Certainly, it is not a cure-all, and solving the problems that it is being used to treat is desirable, but here again, one must ask: is there any reason for this answer to be skewed? Like to discourage me from using something that might have helped me a great deal? I didn't use DMSO for a long time because of this response and only later, after reading more about it, did I begin to try it, and it certainly does much more than is described in this answer!

[9]It isn't "widely available." This sounded like a 'damage control' question/response. I had responded to an inaccurate description of the action of DMSO with a more accurate one and 'Frank' was apparently back-pedaling.

[10]More backpedaling, damage control, obfuscation and just plain wrong.

[11]This is an obvious straw-man argument and definitely not worthy of the Cs. There was way too much 'Frank' and way too little Cs in this entire session.

of a substance, we are discussing results purported to arise from the use of DMSO. And you describe rather fantastic results involving some rather fantastic chemical reactions which begs the question: Why would such a compound such as this be even remotely available to the average individual in your environment, when other compounds that are *known* to produce various chemical reactions that would be beneficial are *not* available? Again, we refer back to the economic and political structure of your 3rd density environment when posing such a question.

49 **Q**: *(L)* Are you saying that it is almost impossible to get anything that is good or useful in this environment? Are there no 'good guys' out there putting things out that are good for us?

50 **A**: What do you think?

51 **Q**: *(L)* I certainly hope so!

52 **A**: Remember, for quite some period of time now, as you measure time, we have tried to inform you to the effect that your 3rd density environment has been completely controlled and will be controlled by forces that seek only to serve themselves for a period, as you would measure time, exceeding 309,000 years. And, many, many times in your current life existence, you have reflected upon the questions involving the beneficial or otherwise existence of individuals or an individual *in* this environment, the pros and cons of continuing such existence, and what is involved with it. And, you have correctly perceived the conclusion that this is, primarily, a negative experience. But, not that good things do not come from a negative experience, but that the basic indicator that it is a negative experience, should also indicate to you that it is an experience related to a chain of command involving service to self. And, therefore, service to self is a manipulative action rather than a openly beneficial action. It is a withdrawing and taking motion rather than an expanding motion. And these statements can answer for you, not only simple questions about one chemical compound, but the very nature of your existence to begin with as well.[12]

Q: *(L)* This leads to a couple of our other questions. What is the criteria to be a 4th density candidate? 53

A: There is no criteria. A criteria implies a judgment system, which implies that an individual or individuals are watching over the progress of other individuals. It is merely part of the natural process of learning, which you are in total control of from beginning to end, in one sense. In that sense, you choose to be in the environment you are in, which does not indicate any recommendation of the environment by any higher source, or, conversely, any condemnation of the environment by any higher source, but merely the existence of the environment and your choice to exist within it. Therefore, being a candidate merely means that you have chosen to be a candidate for *any* level of density, be it first, second, etc. It is a 54

[12] I wonder if here, in the response above, the Cs were finding a way to send me a message as to what I was dealing with in this session? This certainly described most of the session exchanges!

[13] This almost directly contradicts the previous response about the control system in our environment.

choice of the self to continue that learning pathway.[13]

55 **Q**: *(L)* OK, the question has arisen: at the time of the transition to 4th density, is there going to be any assistance to those who are newly arrived in that density, or does the knowledge of that density come automatically?

56 **A**: Neither. When one arrives in 4th density, it is one's choice to find one's way just as it is in the other densities. There is no one waiting there to assist you. That would be an illusion. It is you assisting yourself as you choose to do it, the way you choose to do it.

57 **Q**: *(L)* There was a discussion the other day and it made me curious. It seems that some people simply do not have the capacity to understand certain concepts. Is this a function of vibrational frequency?[14]

58 **A**: That is not quite hitting at the subject matter in the way in which you desire to answer the question. In other words, it is a parallel understanding pattern. It is not vibrational frequency that determines ability to conceive of any particular notion. Vibrational frequency involves the groove, or pattern, that one has chosen in general terms. But, to give you an example, there are those who are of very *low*, as you would measure, vibrational frequency, who are able to conceive of extremely complicated issues and have also discovered extremely precise, complicated, and intricate answers to very complex notions and problems from your standpoint in the illusion. But, the frequency vibrational level has more to do with the emotional path that leads either to service to self at its greatest possible expression, or service to others at its greatest possible expression, not with intellectual capacity. So it is possible for a completely STS individual at any density level to be completely cognizant of all existence, just as it is possible for a completely STO individual to be completely cognizant of all existence. It has nothing to do with vibrational frequency, because that is the emotional pathway.[15]

Q: *(L)* The reason I ask this is because 59
I have noticed that certain persons can skew the incoming material in the direction of their particular prejudices because of their emotional attachment to these prejudices. And I am sure that my own prejudices have an influence as well. But, I notice that very often the understanding of the material by others is quite different from what Frank and I understand. It seems that we all hear something different. Does this indicate a vibrational differential which could be considered a lack of rapport, or some other phenomenon of which I am not aware?

A: The only phenomenon that is 60
present here that is in any way related to the situation you describe is what could be termed intellectual capacity,

[14] *The Wave* 49. I decided to move the discussion to a more abstract area to see if there would be a relaxation of the sensation of tension that existed up to this point.

[15] I would say that this was accurate enough. But I had an agenda behind my question that emerges in the next one. I was 'testing'. In the following question, I deliberately sought to put 'Frank' at ease by suggesting that I was *not* asking about him at all.

which is not related directly to vibrational frequency. Think, if you will, in your lifetime have you ever met either a) an individual that you did not perceive to be particularly intellectually developed, who was, nevertheless, of a very kind and loving and giving nature; or b) an individual whom you perceive to have great intellectual capacity who was, nevertheless, extremely selfish and non-giving and not generous and not concerned about anyone's well being but their own?[16]

61 **Q**: *(L)* Yes. I know exactly what you mean. But there is still some gap that I am trying to fathom here. I have a little theory that people who are *en rapport* tend to think in similar ways or with similar patterns, even if at different levels. And I think that because of emotional similarity or identity of purpose or orientation, that they might almost begin to think as one mind or move as one body, to work as a unit. Why is this not happening? Why the disparity?

62 **A**: The real issue involved is one of intellectual capacity, which, in and of itself, can lead to all sorts of emotional entanglements and frictions. It does not require a differential in vibrational frequency level to produce the types of symptoms that you describe. It is merely intellectual capacity that is inferior, rather than the vibrational frequency level. Again, this vibrational frequency level involves nature of being and emotion, not intelligence.

63 **Q**: *(L)* I have done a little bit of an assessment on the subject, Frank and I have discussed in all possible ways, and we cannot come up with any reason why persons who are exposed to correct grammar and syntax cannot just pick it up sort of by osmosis so that it is not so jarring to the ears of those who *do* care about words and that they are pronounced and used correctly.[17]

64 **A**: Intellectual capacity.

65 **Q**: *(L)* Well, it shouldn't take a whole lot of brains to hear what others are saying and to at least imitate it!

66 **A**: The greater the intellectual capacity, the greater the chance that each and every facet of intellect will be available for use, growth and stimulation. The lesser the intellectual capacity, the greater the chance that some will not be available. And, the examples you cite of the ability to learn proper grammar by mimicry or understand correct pronunciation and syntax may merely be the closing off of that particular facet of intellectual capacity, rather than any vibrational frequency level differential. And, it is important for you to be aware of this so that you do not make subjective judgments of an individual or individuals, thinking that they are inferior in intent or desire as opposed to intellectual capacity. Granted that it is an irritant for you and others. But, one way to ease the irritation within yourself is to come to a true and complete understanding of the cause of the irritation. Once you

[16] And he fell into the trap, describing himself exactly.

[17] In this question, I was again putting 'Frank' off the scent of what I was after.

[18] At this point, 'Frank' was totally at ease and 'showing off' his access to knowledge/information, so to say. Thus, the information is significantly more useful. And so, I decided to hit another point as a test.

have understood that, then it becomes less irritating. Especially if the cause is one which can be excused or forgiven.[18]

67 **Q**: *(L)* Well, that leads me to the next question: the use of words that I find personally offensive. Is this also something that I should excuse? I mean the use of words that relate to body parts, body functions that are very private, and so forth, used as adjectives and adverbs in ordinary speech about ordinary subjects – what is considered to be extreme slang or pornographic language.

68 **A**: Well, you should be aware that fighting off such occurrences is rather futile in the particular point in space-time that your awareness is emanating from, because it is a part of the environment to an extreme extent at this point. And, whereas it is true that these are symptomatic of negative energy transfer, there is little to nothing that you can do to affect or change any of these.

69 **Q**: *(L)* I don't have to contribute to that negative energy.

70 **A**: This is certainly very true. And it would seem that you are not, as a general rule, doing so. However, perhaps it would be helpful, again, for you to understand that it is more a question of changes occurring in the 3rd density environment right now, that you will notice a great many things that you will perceive to be objectionable or distressing, or even frightening in their nature. It is your advanced state of perception and your intellectual capacity, which is also advanced compared against others in your realm, that allows you to have a deeper understanding of all of this. But, and this is understandable, you tend to become, perhaps, too emotionally involved in each individual occurrence, when, after all, it is all part of the bigger picture that is going on around you. And, it would probably be better to focus your attention on this bigger picture rather than the individual distressing elements contained within.[19]

Q: *(L)* I understand how it is in the rest of the world, and that there is nothing I can do about these things, nor would I try. But, in my own personal environment I do not wish to contribute to that negative energy and I don't think that it is out of line for all members of a group dedicated to bringing in positive energy of knowledge for change not contribute to that energy in their personal lives as well. 71

A: This is certainly understandable. But, something that you should be aware of is, to a great extent, you have already achieved removal of those things which are objectionable, and therefore dwelling [on] this may not be helpful. The use of such words as you have described, which again, as we reiterate, is indeed symptomatic of changes occurring within the 3rd density level in your particular point in space-time, and is a negative energy transfer, one of countless overall, while it is true that this is the nature of what you describe, you have been largely, even if not 100 per cent, successful in removing that particular problem from your environment and from the group you describe, therefore, if there is an occasional contamination, it may be overlooked when compared against 72

[19]Now, notice above the not-so-subtle ego stroke. Remember, this is following my 'alignment' with Frank in previous questions, the 'we're hermanos' maneuver.

your overall success in removing such elements.

73 **Q**: *(L)* I agree. I would like to move on. I would like to know if putting a book together consisting of our experiences and what we have learned in this group and project would be a successful pursuit?

74 **A**: Well, that is up to you. But, we do caution that, due to your lack of credentials, and by this, we mean as perceived in the illusion, it may be difficult for you to reach your desired goals, in the time frame that you may desire, which would be discouraging for you. This problem can be alleviated by the one you have mentioned, Tom French, and you might help him to help himself get the project finished by a true understanding of the nature of the obstacles he is facing.[20]

75 **Q**: *(L)* OK. Can you offer any suggestions as to what to *do* with the masses of information we have received?

76 **A**: Well, so far you have done an extremely admirable amount of 'getting the word out' as you would call it, in the past calendar year, as you measure time, by merely following your instincts. And, it would not be appropriate for us to interfere with this learning pattern by making suggestions or answering that question as you, in fact, desire it to be answered, because it is not necessary. You are making plenty of progress. There is no need for you to deviate from any patterns of movement in this area.

Q: *(L)* Well, I very much want to get financially stable so that I can take certain steps... 77

A: We caution you: compare your current status, and reflect upon the progress that you have made in the last two years, and ask yourself if you have truly suffered in this time period, or have all your necessities always been provided, even if at the last minute. And, if this is indeed true, then the knowledge that we have given you that the financial stability that you seek will, indeed, eventually come your way, why then be concerned? 78

Q: *(L)* I also think that Frank is being overworked and underpaid. 79

A: All there is is lessons. 80

Q: *(L)* Well, if I don't make some changes I am going to fall into a hole. 81

A: When has the hole ever consumed you? 82

Q: *(L)* Well, it is on the verge of it. 83

A: When has it ever consumed you? 84

Q: *(L)* Never. 85

A: Do you expect that to change? 86

Q: *(L)* No. 87

[20]Tom French was a constant thorn in Frank's side. He many times suggested to me: "Tom should interview MEeeee... I can set him straight." And when Tom did not show particular interest in interviewing Frank, except briefly on one occasion, he railed at Tom's 'stupidity' for not seeing what an opportunity he was missing to learn the secrets of the universe from Frank. So, Tom French being brought up here, more or less out of the blue, not having been mentioned by me in this session, is indicative of part of the problem here. Frank was feeling anger and resentment and this was acting strongly on him. It must have been on his mind at the time of this session.

88 **A**: You have, in fact, advised others who have complained about similar situations, that there is no need to worry, because, as you put it, "the Lord will provide". And if, indeed, you do have faith in this very simple principle, why then would your faith deviate at this particular point?

89 **Q**: *(L)* Because sometimes I just don't know what to do and I feel like I am being devoured by stress that I cannot handle.

90 **A**: We do not believe that this is, in fact, a factual statement, but rather an emotionally tainted statement, which we are not condemning. It certainly is understandable, but it is also helpful to understand it for what it is. Previously you have described options that were available to you. It is your choice, then, to seek them out and turn them into answers. Do you not feel that options are available to you?

91 **Q**: *(L)* Well, yes. But none that are terribly pleasant. And there is risk involved.

92 **A**: Describe for us please, anything in your realm that does not involve risk?[21]

93 **Q**: *(L)* OK, I am really curious to discover something about the ancient legend of the Hyperboreans.

94 **A**: There is a masking there. It is an incorrect description.

95 **Q**: *(L)* What do you mean? There was a race supposedly called the Hyperboreans...

A: That is a masking. 96

Q: *(L)* What is a masking? 97

A: A masking is an incorrect descrip- 98
tion of an historical event or condition.

Q: *(L)* What was the true event or con- 99
dition that is masked as the Hyperboreans?

A: There have been, in your 3rd den- 100
sity environment, at various points in space-time, residing on the surface of your planet, and also within its atmosphere, which structure has changed repeatedly, and, in fact, underneath the surface of your physical environment in 3rd density, a great many types of races of humans, some of whom are currently existing in your environment, and some of whom are not. And, also alternate humans. In other words, human-like 3rd density beings who could not be accurately described as humans as you know them. And, also there has been interaction with 4th density beings who pose as 3rd density beings, and 3rd density beings who have, at times in your history, have been able to temporarily and at will interact with 4th density in such a way as to present themselves as 4th density beings. So, we are describing here a virtual potpourri of history involving intelligent life within some realm or condition of your environment. To zero in on any group and give them a name at this point is not really appropriate as names connote approval, but, in fact, may merely be a stamp.[22]

[21]That topic was OK as far as it went, and accurate enough, but no real answer given, the most obvious of which might have been the constant pain I was enduring. The feeling of tension returned, so I shifted gears again to see if a different direction would be more fruitful.

[22]While appearing to be a very accurate synopsis of the state of the planet through time, this was a masterpiece of not answering a question!

101 **Q**: *(L)* OK. Is that all?

102 **A**: That's up to you.

103 **Q**: *(L)* The Hyperboreans were described as a race that lived in the far north, living in a tropical pocket near the North Pole, surrounded by mountains of ice. They were supposedly semi-transparent and supposedly something forced them to move among other humans, and they interbred with them. The legend is that every fifth generation, following the maternal line, produces an individual of exceptional beauty and intelligence. So, it is thought in some places that people who are exceptionally beautiful and intelligent are the result of the Hyperborean genetics. Also, the Hyperboreans were supposed to be the predecessors of the Celts.

104 **A**: That is such a pleasant story! Mmmmm.

105 **Q**: *(L)* I liked it!

106 **A**: Unfortunately, it does not reflect fact. But, fantasy is always fun.

107 **Q**: *(L)* Was there a race that lived in the area of the North Pole?

108 **A**: Well, there is a group currently living in the area of the North Pole.

109 **Q**: *(L)* Who is that?

110 **A**: Eskimos.[23]

111 **Q**: *(L)* OK. Do any secret libraries containing all the secret wisdom of our history exist anywhere on the planet?

112 **A**: No. The secrets that you are alluding to are contained within mental structures in psychic realms, some of which you have little or no conception of. There is no need to record anything in any form that could be placed in any library. It is all done verbally and through mental telepathy.

Q: *(L)* Who and what were the 113
Mayans?

A: The Mayans were a transitory peo- 114
ple who still exist in the lands that you refer to as Central America, and who have certain physical features that are not consistent with the rest of human beings on 3rd density Earth environment, due to their interactions, in the past, as you measure time, with beings of other density levels.[24]

Q: *(L)* What beings would those be? 115

A: Well, we have described 4th density 116
STS beings on many occasions.

Q: *(L)* The Lizard beings? 117

A: Indeed. 118

Q: *(L)* Who was Arajuna of Tiahua- 119
naco?

A: Well, we believe that you are refer- 120
ring to one of approximately eight hybrids that ruled the area currently referred to as Central America. Hybrids being a 4th density to 3rd density transfer experiment from the Lizard race to the human race, which was abandoned after approximately 240 years of experimentation by the Lizard beings, due to the lack of success for sustaining physical duplication, or reproduction of the race. It was one of several attempts by the Lizard beings to directly trans-

[23]This was supposed to be funny and it was. It also made a good point about buying into legendary tales. But still, there was no answer forthcoming in respect of my questions.

[24]Good info and probably accurate, since there is no emotional attachment.

mit their souls into 3rd density environment for permanent placement there. And, of course it is no longer perceived as necessary by them because their intention is to rule 3rd density beings in 4th density when they arrive there.

121 **Q**: *(L)* Who built the city of Tiahuanaco?

122 **A**: The Lizard beings in cooperation with humans.

123 **Q**: *(L)* When was it built?

124 **A**: Varying time frames since it seems to have been destroyed at two points. We have to estimate an average of 8,000 years prior to the current time, as you measure it.

Q: *(L)* Who built the statues at Damien in Kabul? 125

A: An early Persian race, 3rd density in nature. 126

Q: *(L)* Does the Agartha exist?[25] 127

A: No. 128

End of Session

Let me discuss the South American hybrid answer just a bit here. Something strange certainly was going on in South America, as witnessed by the famous Ica Skulls of Peru. In fact, it appears that skulls of this type have been found in varying places around the planet, not just in Peru. There are ancient Indian traditions that claim that these beings were in North America before what we call the Native Americans arrived. There is even one ancient tradition about a war between a tribe of Native Americans and a race of red-haired cannibalistic giants.

To give some more details, Paracas is a desert peninsula located within the Pisco Province in the Ica Region, on the south coast of Peru. This is where a Peruvian archaeologist, Julio Tello, in 1928, discovered a graveyard containing the remains of individuals with the largest elongated skulls found anywhere in the world. Tello found more than 300 of these elongated skulls, which are said to date back around 3,000 years, though I haven't read any serious evidence on this date.

Most cases of skull elongation are the result of various processes of cranial deformation in which the skull is intentionally deformed by applying force over a long period of time beginning in early infancy. This is done usually by binding the head between two pieces of wood, or binding with cloth. It should be noted that cranial deformation changes the shape of the skull, but it cannot alter its volume, weight, or certain other features. The Ica/Paracas skulls, however, are quite different.

[25] A legendary city that is said to be located in the Earth's core. It is related to the belief in a hollow Earth and is a popular subject in esotericism.

The cranial volume of the Ica skulls is 25 to 40 percent larger and 60 percent heavier than normal human skulls, meaning they could not have been intentionally deformed through head binding/flattening. They also contain only one parietal plate, rather than two as is normal for humans. These features strongly suggest that skulls' elongation are not the result of cranial deformation.

Since mainstream scientists seem disinclined to involve themselves in research on these fascinating finds, some private individuals (Brien Foerster et al.) apparently obtained suitable specimens of the skulls and sent them to a genetics lab for sequencing. According to their report, apparently, the mtDNA (mitochondrial DNA) exhibited "mutations unknown in any human, primate, or other animal known". That would mean that these human-like creature are very distinct from Homo sapiens, Neanderthals and the more recently identified Denisovans. That would probably mean that they were unable to breed with humans.

Of course, the debunkers came out in force, claiming it isn't 'scientific' or 'peer reviewed', never mind the fact that I haven't seen any accredited scientists breaking their legs to get over there to get samples and have them analyzed. Strange how that works: mainstream organizations (the powers that be) won't transparently examine and report on something of immense importance or interest, but will cry foul at any attempt by others to do so, bringing out the 'not accredited' accusation as being the worst sin, followed quickly by 'fraud' or 'too stupid to properly analyze or understand the results'. They pull out this last one if they discover that a real scientific test actually has been done and that anomalous results are evident.

While on the topic, I'll mention Boskop man, discovered in 1913 in Boskop, South Africa. This type was a prehistoric variation of anatomically modern humans that is postulated to have lived in that region 30,000 to 10,000 years ago. Apparently Boskop man possessed a skull of gargantuan cranial capacity, 40–50% larger than modern humans. Not unexpectedly, the term 'Boskop man' is no longer used by anthropologists, and the supposedly unusual characteristics of this type are considered to be a *misinterpretation*. See: *Big Brain: The Origins and Future of Human Intelligence* by Gary Lynch and Richard Granger.

So, were 'Lizard beings' involved in genetic experiments that resulted in some strange humanoid type with extremely large and weirdly shaped skulls? I would say that if it is even partly true, mainstream science isn't going to explore in any areas that might bring this up as a possibility, and if they were to do so, or have done so, it would not be transparent. Yet we have millennia of historical allusions to such beings going all the way back to the Mesopotamian 'first' civilizations. They are a common motif in ancient myths. At the present time, while I don't discount entirely the possibility of some hyperdimensional beings of a reptilian configuration, I would suggest that many of the ancient legends of serpent beings refer rather to comet/asteroid bodies in Earth's atmosphere, possessing tails and producing varied EM effects that would certainly impress humans as being serpent-like. As I suggested in my book *Comets and the Horns of Moses*, ancient myths suggest that such interactions between the Earth and comet/asteroid bodies seem to be accompanied by tales of following periods plagued by giants and cannibals. So, either some genetic mutation is going on as a result of such dynamics, or various features of environmental stresses are being conflated. If impact events bring on periods of pestilence and starvation, cannibalism is often a consequence. But genetic mutation cannot be ruled out and is, in my opinion, not just possible, but probable based on some studies done following the Tunguska event that I describe in the previously mentioned volume. For all we know, the 'Lizard beings' of hyperdimensional realms are represented in our 3D reality as comet/asteroid bodies bringing genetic mutations via various processes that we don't understand. In that sense, yes, you could say that Lizard beings are doing genetic experiments.

Having come to that hypothesis, let's look at the time period mentioned in the session above (assuming that the hybrids mentioned were part of the Tiahuanaco society and that both were related to the Ica skulls, though the latter were found in a different location), approximately 8,000 years ago and for a period of 240 years. Among the events of that millennium are the following selected for their interesting implications:[26]

> c. 6000 BC: The land bridge connecting England with the rest of Europe disappears beneath the waters of the North Sea and

[26]http://en.wikipedia.org/wiki/6th_millennium_BC

the English Channel.

c. 6000 BC: A massive volcanic landslide off of Mt. Etna, Sicily caused a megatsunami which devastated the eastern Mediterranean coastline on the continents of Asia, Africa and Europe.

c. 6000 BC: The entire 6th Millennium was a part of the Holocene climatic optimum (so were the 4th, 5th, and 7th Millennia). This was a warm period also known as the Atlantic period and was characterized by minimal glaciation and high sea levels. (McEvedy)

c. 6000 BC: The Copper Age comes to the Fertile Crescent. (Roux 1980) First use of copper in Middle East. (Bailey 1973)

c. 6000 BC: Fully Neolithic agriculture has spread through Anatolia to the Balkans. (1967 McEvedy)

c. 6000 BC: Equids disappear from the Americas.

c. 6000 BC: Female figurines holding serpents are fashioned on Crete and may have been associated with water, regenerative power and protection of the home.

5760 BC: The volcano Puy-de-Dôme in France erupts.

5677 BC: Cataclysmic volcanic eruption of 12,000-foot (3,700 m) high Mount Mazama creates Oregon's Crater Lake when the resulting caldera fills with water. It is the largest single Holocene eruption in history of the Cascade Range with a Volcanic Explosivity Index of 7.

c. 5600 BC: According to the Black Sea deluge theory, the Black Sea floods with salt water. Some 3000 cubic miles (12,500 km) of salt water is added, significantly expanding the body of water and transforming it into a sea from a fresh-water landlocked lake. Beginning of the desertification of North Africa, ultimately leading to the creation of the Sahara desert. This process may have spurned migration to the region of the Nile in the east, thereby laying the groundwork for the rise of Egyptian civilization.

5563 BC: Comet Hale–Bopp appears. It comes back in the 31st century BC.

5509 BC: The Byzantine calendar dates creation to 1 September of this year.

So, overall, it appears to have been a rather dramatic time and undoubtedly, comets and asteroids were flying about with some abandon from time to time giving off showers of fragments, flaming serpents of the Reptilian gods of the skies.

August 12, 1995

As time went by and Frank fell back into his old ways, more or less, and tensions of one sort or another plagued the group, not to mention the fact that I was dealing with recovery from my injuries in the background and the crumbling of my marriage, I realized that I was still rather alone. I wasn't going to trust Frank again with any personal information, and I was keeping my own counsel in respect of dynamics between him and other members of the group, particularly Terry and Jan. I realized the irony of it: that I was more or less able to access a source of possible information that might lead to solutions, but I was unable to ask the most direct questions because I didn't want to alert Frank to the fact that he was most definitely still under scrutiny.

After thinking about this for a while, it occurred to me that *if*, and that was a big if, the information access and delivery was operating as I thought it was, then I could test it in another way: purely mental. That is to say, I could ask questions and substitute the name of one person for another and see if the source could 'get it' and give an accurate answer to the *real* question in my mind, even if seeming to answer the apparent question. In any event, I resolved to do this, to *intend* particular questions from time to time while asking others on the surface.

So, I began. Let's see what happened.

Participants: 'Frank', Laura, Susan V

[Trance induced]

1 **Q**: *(L)* Are you ready to receive questions?

2 **A**: Yes.

[Suggestions given for clarity of communication]

3 **Q**: *(L)* Do you have any messages to give Susan or myself at this time?

4 **A**: No.

5 **Q**: *(L)* OK. Then we'll get to our questions. My first question is: What is the source of the Vedas, the Hindu system

[1] I decided to warm up with innocuous, general topic questions that were already on my list of things to ask.

of philosophy?[1]

6 **A**: There is more than one source.

7 **Q**: *(L)* What is the general source, positive or...?

8 **A**: A very vague question.

9 **Q**: *(L)* Was it a group of people that put them together over centuries, or was it channeled information, or...?

10 **A**: It came into being as a result of meditation.

11 **Q**: *(L)* And what race of people was responsible for this information?

12 **A**: Caucasian.

13 **Q**: *(L)* What period of time were the Vedas received.[2]

14 **A**: Varying bits and pieces of information which later was organized into packages labeled as it is.

15 **Q**: *(L)* From what realm did this meditated information issue?

16 **A**: The realm of the subconscious mind.

17 **Q**: *(L)* Are any of the Vedas information that was given to man by extraterrestrials?

18 **A**: Not as you would define it.

Q: *(L)* From what types of beings, or what level of density did this information issue from? 19

A: Third. 20

Q: *(L)* Can you give us anything more on that in a general sense? 21

A: If you ask. 22

Q: *(L)* What is the percentage of accuracy of the information given in the Vedas? Overall? 23

A: Accurate at what level? 24

Q: *(L)* 3rd density. 25

A: Accurate to what extent and in what way? 26

Q: *(L)* Well, in a general sense, as a way of living one's life and perceiving the universe. 27

A: That's an extremely difficult question to answer as accuracy in determining such things as perceiving the universe and living one's life is entirely open to interpretation as anyone can resolve accuracy by relating to the parallel universe which is appropriate for the information given. And, as we have stated in the past, it is possible to create parallel universes through thought 28

[2] *The Wave* 9

[3] So, basically, what is being said here in a very roundabout way is that the Vedas were put together over a period of time and enhanced by information received via meditation and are basically nothing special. At least that is the impression I got from this exchange. According to tradition, the Vedas are are texts originating in ancient India, composed in Vedic Sanskrit, constituting the oldest layer of Sanskrit literature and the oldest scriptures of Hinduism. Hindus consider the Vedas to be *apauruṣeya*, which means 'not of a man, superhuman' and 'impersonal, authorless'. Orthodox Indian theologians consider the Vedas to be revelations, that is, the work of the Deity. In the Hindu Epic the Mahabharata, the creation of Vedas is credited to Brahma. They are dated to roughly 1700–1100 BCE, and the related texts, as well as the redaction of the Samhitas, date to c. 1000–500 BCE. However, surviving manuscripts are only a few hundred years old. The tradition

energy, and once they are created naturally, they correspond naturally to the interpretation given for them.[3]

29 **Q**: *(L)* Is there any benefit to be obtained through the use of mantras?[4]

30 **A**: Especially when the mind says there is. Remember, most all power necessary for altering reality and physicality is contained within the belief center of the mind.[5] This is something you will understand more closely when you reach 4th density reality where physicality is no longer a prison, but is instead, your home, for you to alter as you please. In your current state, you have the misinterpretation of believing that reality is finite and therein lies your difficulty with finite physical existence. We are surprised that you are still not able to completely grasp this concept.

31 **Q**: *(L)* Well, I think I have a good grasp of this concept, but I am asking questions to obtain answers for others to comprehend.

32 **A**: That is not being completely honest.[6]

Q: *(L)* Close enough. Is it true that recitation of mantras can effect spirit release or exorcism? 33

A: If you please. 34

Q: *(L)* Last week, the remark was made, regarding spirit release and exorcism, that if it is done properly, by the right person, that there is no side effects or eventualities that would bring detrimental conditions to the individuals and location involved. What was meant by 'done correctly'? What is the correct format or mode for exorcism? 35

A: Correct manner involves honesty and understanding that one has complete faith and awareness of the activities pursued. In other words, when one performs an act which they proclaim to be having a desired result, and they do not have faith in their own actions as, in fact, producing the desired result, then the effort will collapse because of their lack of faith. Whereas when one has complete faith and multi-density understanding, their activities are indeed truth and useful as prescribed and this is the correct way to pursue them. 36

teaches that transmission of texts in the Vedic period was oral, preserved with precision with the help of elaborate mnemonic techniques. They were written down only in post-Vedic times, after the rise of Buddhism about the 1st century BCE; however, oral tradition predominated until c. 1000 CE. All in all, it sounds like the same story told about the Hebrew Bible and the Christian New Testament.

[4] *The Wave* 9

[5] This actually is a rather fascinating response. A 'belief center'?

[6] This is one of those off-the-wall, slightly pejorative remarks that characterized Frank's trance channeling efforts. I was, indeed, asking questions to obtain answers that would be helpful to others, assuming that any such were forthcoming. Obviously, a secondary motive was to 'test the source', but then, that goes with the territory. One would think that if Frank were aware of these two factors, as one assumes he must have been, he/source would have been more willing to be forthcoming in a plain way. On the other hand, if the 'well-pipe' analogy was operative, it may have been Frank's own attitude or deliberate restriction on the part of a controlling force/entity.

37 **Q**: *(L)* Isn't faith a difficult commodity to acquire?

38 **A**: Not at all. When you have found something of truth you will receive demonstrations which locks in your faith.[7]

39 **Q**: *(L)* I see. What is the criteria for the 'correct person' to be performing exorcism or spirit release?

40 **A**: The same as the previous answer.

41 **Q**: *(SV)* I have a question. Jan and Terry have been taking sort of lessons from a Buddhist monk. Could this possibly help them, or us, to go within or help with issues?

42 **A**: Any method employed can be helpful for, as you say, resolving issues or with coming up with answers, if indeed the effort is sincere and the seeking is genuine, rather than just going through the motions, as it were.

43 **Q**: *(L)* Several weeks ago we did a spirit viewing of Terry and Jan, and there was something seen that obscured Terry, and something seen within. We later did a direct spirit release and nothing that was similar to what had been observed remotely revealed or exposed itself. Why was this?

A: Complicated, complex. 44

Q: *(L)* Was there error in what was 45
seen?[8]

A: No. 46

Q: *(L)* Was what was seen there when 47
we did the release with Terry?

A: That is not the correct issue. 48

Q: *(L)* What is the correct issue? 49

A: Variability of circumstance. 50

Q: *(L)* So, in the circumstance he was 51
in while being viewed, there was what was there, and when the circumstances changed, it was no longer present?

A: Not exactly. Two different types 52
of activities involved. One was viewing from afar, one was spirit release. These are two separate types of activities employing the psychic or ethereal channeling process, therefore points of view can be altered by a number of factors,

[7]This is another really interesting response, because it has proven itself again and again in my experience: you sort of have to make a decision in so many situations in life where the truth is not entirely clear and never can be. And then, only *after* you have made the choice, do things happen that confirm it, or you find yourself in a mess!

[8]Since Frank had been the one doing the 'spirit viewing', I had been interested to compare what he saw with what was actually revealed working directly with Terry. Before we did the direct release, we did not tell Terry and Jan what had been viewed so that there would be no contamination of the experience. The following responses from Frank look to me like damage control. He would have been highly invested in saving face here.

[9]This is obviously the case, though what is not being mentioned is Frank's own emotional blocks in respect of his spirit viewing of Terry. Frank was becoming increasingly antagonistic toward Terry and Jan, probably because they were regularly challenging his claim that he, and he alone, was 'the channel'. Terry, too, was becoming increasingly antagonistic toward Frank and this was expressed with a great deal of sarcasm from time to time. This was creating some conflict in our

including emotional blocks or change of circumstances, just to name two.[9]

53 **Q**: *(L)* In a previous session we asked the question: Had anyone ever been in our group, or was anyone here, who had been sent to disrupt the group, or stop the channel? The answer was given that there was a good chance, but this was something we had to learn on our own. Now, we have discussed this from many different directions, and it seems to appear that part of this potential for disruption came through, if not from, Terry and or Jan, as you have previously stated.

54 **A**: Well, again you are simplifying a complex issue, seeking a broad, general answer to questions that would be better served by breaking them down into simpler questions.

55 **Q**: *(L)* Were Terry and Jan sent to our group to disrupt it?

56 **A**: No.

57 **Q**: *(L)* Well, the answer seemed to indicate that someone was, and if it wasn't them, then it must be one of us?[10]

58 **A**: No.

59 **Q**: *(L)* Was it someone else at some other time?

60 **A**: It is not someone in the sense of any 3rd density physical being as it is someone attached to a 3rd density physical being which can change from being to being as conditions warrant. Why should you think that any given physical individual contains exactly the same surroundings and attachments at all times? Obviously, this can change. Therefore, if there is attack, would it not be far more effective to launch the attack through anyone and everyone present at any given time, in order to maintain the attack? It is rather naive to assume that it so limited that physical removal of any given 3rd density being will preclude all possibilities for attack if and when one has identified an attack mode resulting from the presence of said being.[11]

Q: *(L)* Are some people more susceptible to attack modes than others? 61

A: Well, again, there is a variable issue rather than a static issue involved here. 62

Q: *(L)* Well, if I remember correctly, when I asked the original question, I believe I specified a 3rd density person, and not something ephemeral. 63

A: If you are asking, is it possible for a 3rd density being to seek consciously to disrupt activities, yes, certainly this is possible. Has it happened as of yet? No. Does that mean it cannot happen? No. Does that mean it will happen? It's always a good chance for your activities are of the type which would bring about attack of any and all sorts. Therefore, you must be on the lookout. However, it is also wise not to become obsessed with any particular mode of attack as many, many, many types can be employed. Types that you may not even think of. 64

Q: *(L)* OK. Well, could my sensitivities to atmosphere, attitudes and so forth 65

little group and I was determined to get to the bottom of it.

[10]This would be the obvious conclusion, but I knew I had to tread very carefully here and not get Frank's back up.

[11]This is obviously true enough, though, of course, Frank did not think that it applied to him.

be a form of attack on myself?

66 **A**: Can be. The attack may not be consciously emanating from the physical 3rd density being as in the case of any and all 3rd density beings.

67 **Q**: *(L)* What I meant to inquire is: is my emotional reaction to this distorted?

68 **A**: Could be, and if it is, then obviously the attack is successful.

69 **Q**: *(L)* How can I determine this?

70 **A**: By being completely open and communicating with all parties at all times. Keeping secrets can only lead to failure.[12]

71 **Q**: *(L)* Well, are Terry and Jan significantly important to this group? I try to talk to them, but it seems that their emotions either block them from hearing me, or their attitudes and responses put a period to my attempts to discuss issues. I find it almost unbearable to be constantly interrupted and this is a constant with the both of them... if they are not trying to out-talk each other.[13]

72 **A**: Well, again, we suggest that you try to avoid subjective inquiries. We ask that you pause and ask yourself if there is anyway that those you refer to as Terry and Jan, and any and all parties to any extent, can ever be of any benefit to any and all involved before you pass judgment.

Q: *(L)* Well, I don't quite get the meaning there. Frank is the channel. Obviously that is an important function. Without the channel there is obviously no group. Right?[14] 73

A: Correct. 74

Q: *(L)* OK, so therefore, in a very real sense, no other of us is all that significant? 75

A: Incorrect. 76

Q: *(L)* Why is that? 77

A: Vague. 78

Q: *(L)* Can we define our roles? 79

A: It is up to each and every one of you to define your roles as whatever role you see yourself fulfilling, and also to communicate those to each other. If this is done, it can bring a much clearer picture of the situation to each one of you, and also avoid the possibility that misunderstandings, conflicts of interest, as is possible when there is a lack of communication in any situation. See, this is one of many modes 80

[12]I felt the hair on the back of my neck tingle here. One thing I was definitely *not* going to do again was to be completely open with Frank. But it is interesting that this response came, because it suggests that there was some awareness on Frank's part of what I was doing.

[13]This was my 'trick question'. I really wanted to know if Frank was significantly important in the way he portrayed himself. I couched it in terms of Terry and Jan, but it was Frank who never listened to anything I tried to point out to him. Whenever the topic was his issues, he had a way of completely blocking the discussion and constantly interrupting me and holding forth for endless hours until I was exhausted. And finally, Frank was actually the one who 'out-talked' everyone else.

[14]I was repeating back to Frank his own claims in an effort to see what kind of response he would give to this.

of attack employed very successfully by those who wish to see efforts cease, and the attack is most ingenious because it involves playing with the subconscious mind where 92% of all thought processes originate in 3rd density.[15]

81 **Q**: *(L)* Well, it has not been my perception that Terry and Jan are open to honest communication. They are quite willing to point out other people's problems, but they do not want to hear it if someone else has a problem with them.[16]

82 **A**: Then it would seem that it is not an open forum.

83 **Q**: *(L)* How can you have an open forum with someone who is not honest with themselves?

84 **A**: Subjective.[17]

85 **Q**: *(L)* Of course it's subjective. Isn't it significant that since they have arrived in the group that the level of information has deteriorated and the occurrence of vague and non-answers?[18]

86 **A**: Be careful not to read incorrect mechanical approaches as defective characteristics or personality or nature. It is important to differentiate between that which is alterable, curable, or can be helped, with that which is incurable, unalterable, and cannot be helped. Also, realize too, that as 3rd density STS beings, it is very easy for any and all of you, each and every one of you, to fall into the trap, which is, of course, one form of attack coming from 4th density STS; to fall into the trap of seeking to serve self even when in cooperation with or in forum with others. This can cause, ultimately, a derailing, of any and all activities designed to improve situations or generate wide-spread assistance.[19]

Q: *(L)* Earlier today, while talking with 87
this fellow, Ram, the Vedic astrologer, he proposed that the Vedic idea of who and what the Lizard beings were was correct and that this is the activation of the sexual principle, or kundalini within us. Any kind of UFO or alien activity is merely the reflection of what is inside all of us. Is this a correct assessment?[20]

A: Part of the answer to that question, 88
if you refer back to the answers to the earlier questions, is of a similar nature.

[15]The statement that 92% of all thought processes take place in the subconscious mind is rather well supported by recent research in cognitive science such as the work of Timothy Wilson, Daniel Kahneman, Martha Stout and others.

[16]Here, again, I am deliberately obscuring my question: asking about Frank himself in the guise of asking about Terry and Jan. Frank was forever pointing out everyone else's problems but could take absolutely no feedback whatsoever about his own.

[17]Obviously Frank is aware that something is going on.

[18]Here, the real question was about trance channeling with Frank alone versus using the board with the group. It was obvious that the trance method was not getting us anywhere and it was also objectively true that many of the best informational sessions occurred with Terry and Jan present.

[19]This was a rather clear answer, to me, about the differences between the two methods of channeling. The answer was that trance channeling was an "incorrect mechanical approach". I decided that it was time to change topics.

[20]*The Wave* 9

But, in truth, the best way to most adequately answer those questions is to ask yourself what do you believe, based on the knowledge that you have collected and have been given.

89 **Q**: *(L)* Well, I sometimes wonder if they are not part of ourselves, in a parallel universe, and they emerge into our world and interact with us in a negative way. And, that the stories of alien–human interaction are really just stories of human performance of mechanical operations, guided by negative aspects of their own being in another dimension or density. Would this not be a distinct possibility?

90 **A**: Not in the sense that you are thinking. Remember, it is always wise to review all the previously gathered information whenever any new ideas appear before you. This is true not only in this particular instance, but also all others as well. For example, how often would mere thought patterns, or realities emerging from a parallel universe, appear in desert locations and be retrieved by 3rd density beings for study in the 3rd density realm? Now, if indeed you believe that this has happened, and it *has*, one must contemplate the meaning such and how it relates to one's proposal that the whole issue involves much higher levels of density on the etheric plane, and, or, interdimensional capabilities that cannot be measured within the realm of 3rd density. These theories, certainly, are part of the answer, but merely a part of the answer, and none of them represents the entire answer. And we caution very strongly that you avoid falling into the trap of believing too strongly in any one explanation that appears, as this too, is a form of attack which can lead to destructive consequences.

Q: *(L)* So, there are actual, material, 91
alien craft that have been captured or retrieved by the government and studied?[21]

A: Do you have any doubt of this? 92

Q: *(L)* Well, sometimes I wonder if the 93
whole thing is cooked up by the government just to make us all crazy!

A: Well that's an interesting concept, 94
but we can assure you, that that is not, in any way, correct.

Q: *(L)* Well, if these craft emerge into 95
our reality from 4th density, as I assume some of them do, how do they stay here? Do they become absolutely physically material and do they remain here?

A: If they malfunction in 3rd density, 96
they then become frozen in 3rd density. Very simple.

Q: *(L)* And, does the same hold true 97
for the beings?

A: Precisely. 98

Q: *(L)* So, in a very real sense, they are 99
very real and physical...

A: They are very real and physical in 100
4th density, too. The difference is that 4th density physicality is not the same as 3rd density physicality. But that is not to say that there is no physicality in 4th density. In order to completely remove all attachment to physicality, one must reach 6th density or higher. Everything below that involves some aspect of physicality or attachment to physicality; as in 5th density, the contemplation zone, which is simply a recycling of those from 1st through 4th den-

[21] *The Wave* 21

sities, in the etheric plane. They are brought back down and recycled into one of the physical realms. Each density level, one through four, involves lesser and lesser physicality, as you know it, but nevertheless there still is physicality. 3rd density physicality, however, remains constant on 3rd density when a being or a craft or an instrument of any kind manufactured or conceived in 4th density arrives in third density, it is able to navigate through 3rd density in 4th density reality. However, when it malfunctions, whatever is left of it remains in 3rd density. Those reports of objects or of any physical structure whatsoever, be it a being or a construct, disappearing from 3rd density to 4th density, in each and every case, involves an object or a being, or a construct, which is not in the process of malfunctioning. It is still fully operational at its 4th density realm. It is merely visiting 3rd density which has a limited capacity, as you measure time in its passage, therefore it does, indeed, remove itself naturally, at some point, to 4th density. However, if it malfunctions or is in any way broken or altered, it will remain in 3rd density.

101 **Q**: *(L)* So, if someone removes an implant, the best way to keep it here would be to smash it?

102 **A**: If someone removes an implant it is no longer functioning as it was designed to function.

103 **Q**: *(L)* OK. So we have some real things happening, and a possibility that a film was taken of this interaction with these malfunctioning 4th density beings and craft. And, supposedly, this film is going to be shown on television. Is this film of this autopsy, and examination of craft remains, a true filming of same, or is it a fake, or fraud?

A: Well, one would suggest that for the maximum amount of learning, that the film be witnessed by those seeking the truth, in order to determine for themselves whether or not it is factual, as such will be possible upon viewing. 104

Q: *(L)* Well, I certainly intend to do that. Now, I want to slide in a personal question. Regarding my present living conditions, I would like to know if this is karmic?[22] 105

A: All difficulties in personal life are karmic in one way or another. Especially those involving interactions with other souled beings. And the closer the interactions, the more karmic they are. This you already know. 106

Q: *(L)* Well, the difficult thing is to know what is the best thing to do. 107

A: Learning images is the process that is ongoing throughout all existence, and is achieved by one action or another. Any and all actions, any and all possible actions, any and all directions of actions facilitate continued learning. Therefore, it is not possible in the ultimate sense, to make mistakes. But, one must experience whatever is karmic to its full extent. The choices made reflect choices made prior to entering the physical plane of 3rd density, combined with the opportunities that present themselves with the variability of reality in its fluid state. Therefore, the decisions to be made will present themselves when they are to be made, and it is only one's ability to accept interpretation objectively that determines whether the learning process 108

[22] This is another of my 'coded' questions: I was asking about my marriage.

will deliver greater or lesser degrees of pain.

109 **Q**: *(L)* Why does learning have to be painful?

110 **A**: It doesn't.

111 **Q**: *(L)* Well, it seems that it invariably is for me.

112 **A**: That is according to the perceptions of the experiencer, not according to any absolute criteria.

113 **Q**: *(L)* We would like to know a bit more on the subject of rituals, which you have warned us are restricting on many levels. Why is this?[23]

114 **A**: If one believes in one's activities sincerely, to the greatest extent, they certainly will produce *some* benefit, at *some* level. But, merely following patterns for the sake of following patterns does not produce sincerity and faith necessary for ultimate benefits to result. So, therefore, as always, one must search from within, rather than from without, to answer that question. Do you understand? To give you an example, to be certain, you meet this all the time. If you read material in the pages of a book that advises one form of ritual or another, and you follow that form of ritual because you have read words printed on the pages, does that really give you the true sense of satisfaction and accomplishment within yourself to the greatest extent possible? Whereas, if you, yourself, were to develop an activity which one or another could interpret or define as a ritual, but it comes from within you, it feels *right* to you, and you have a sincere and complete faith in it, whatever it may be, does that feel right to you?

Q: *(L)* Yes. 115

A: Have we answered the question, 116
then?

Q: *(L)* Yes, thank you. 117

A: We will say goodnight, then. 118

End of session

[23] *The Wave* 10

September 9, 1995

I have mixed feelings about this session. Tom and Cherie were back for a visit and we began as usual with the board. However, as you will see, there was a diversion which, in retrospect, could only be attributed to Frank's desire to prove himself to be a great channel. So the remarks about that should be taken in that context. At the same time, the fact that Frank was given this opportunity also meant that he was on his very best behavior and the information seems to be very good though, obviously, most of it is presently beyond our ability to check and verify as being true.

Participants: 'Frank', Laura, SV, Tom French, Cherie Diez

1 **Q**: *(L)* Hello.

2 **A**: Other.

3 **Q**: *(L)* What do you mean by "other?"

4 **A**: Re: discover other.

5 **Q**: *(L)* Okay, who do we have with us this evening?

6 **A**: Other.

7 **Q**: *(L)* You are someone other than the Cassiopaeans?

8 **A**: No.

9 **Q**: *(L)* Do you wish us to pursue this through trance channeling or with the board?

10 **A**: Trance. You have graduated, why do you wish to backtrack?

11 **Q**: *(L)* Well, for this evening, I would prefer to use the board. Is that alright? [To Tom and Cherie] Is it alright with you if we use the trance medium? They do not seem to want to do it through the board tonight. *(T)* Whatever is usual.

[Frank is put into trance state]

Q: Now, could you talk to us a little bit 12
about the purported "Photon Belt?"[1]

A: The key issue remains one of inter- 13
pretation. The messages are genuine; interpretations are variable in their accuracy. So, when one speaks of the "Photon Belt," one may really be thinking of a concept and giving it a name.[2]

Q: *(L)* So, you mean that various per- 14
sons are seeing something and only describing it within the limits of their knowledge?

A: At one level, yes. 15

Q: *(L)* Any further comments on that? 16

[1] *The Wave* 10

[2] *The Wave* 11

17 **A**: Comments best serve when they are formulated as replies to direct and specific questions.

18 **Q**: *(L)* Was there a harmonic convergence as was advertised within the metaphysical community?

19 **A**: For those who believed there was a harmonic convergence, indeed there was a harmonic convergence.

20 **Q**: *(L)* Did anything of a material nature happen on or to the planet to enhance or change the energy?

21 **A**: Did you notice any changes?

22 **Q**: *(L)* No. Except that it seems that things have gotten worse, if anything.

23 **A**: Did you notice any clear, obvious, material changes?

24 **Q**: *(L)* No. But that could just be me. I could just be a stubborn and skeptical person.

25 **A**: Did anyone else in the room notice any clear or obvious changes?

26 **Q**: *(S)* What date was it? *(L)* 8/8/88, I believe. *(S)* I thought it had something to do with 11/11 ninety- something...

27 **A**: Well, obviously if the recollection of the calendar date is difficult, one would suppose that material changes did not take place. For, if they had, would you not remember the calendar date ascribed to them?

28 **Q**: *(L)* Yes. The claim has further been made that, for a month, following the harmonic convergence that no abductions were taking place. Is this true?

29 **A**: No. There has been no cessation in what you term to be abduction in quite some time as you measure it.

Q: *(L)* Well, on the subject of 30
abduction: we watched a film on television, Monday the 28th, that was a purported video of an alien autopsy, or, more correctly, an autopsy on an alien body. Was this, in fact, an alien?

A: How do you define "alien?"[3] 31

Q: *(L)* Was it a being other than a nat- 32
urally born human on this planet as we know human beings?

A: That is correct. 33

Q: *(L)* It was other than a naturally 34
born human?

A: Correct. 35

Q: *(L)* Okay. What kind of a being 36
was this?

A: Hybrid. 37

Q: *(L)* What was it a hybrid of – com- 38
bining what elements?

A: Cybergenetic creatures you refer to 39
as "Grays," and earth human such as yourself, 3rd density. So, in essence, it was a hybridization of a 3rd density and 4th density being.

Q: *(L)* Okay, was this a 4th density 40
being?

A: No. If you listen to the response – 41
it was a 3rd and 4th density being.

Q: *(L)* How can a being be both 3rd 42
and 4th density?

A: It is the environmental surround- 43
ings that count, not the structure of the individual. The same is true, for you. After all, you have read literature stating that your world or planet is in the process of ascending from 3rd to 4th density, have you not?

Q: *(L)* Yes. 44

[3] *The Wave* 21

45 **A**: And this literature has also stated that this is an ongoing process, has it not?

46 **Q**: *(L)* Yes.

47 **A**: Then, one must wonder, if it is an ongoing process, how would it be possible, if it is not possible, for a being to be in both 3rd and 4th density at one time... Also, if you will recall from review material, you are currently living in the same environment as 2nd and 1st density level beings. Is this not true?

48 **Q**: *(L)* Yes.

49 **A**: At least that is what you have been told. So, therefore, it is possible for a being to be in 3rd and 4th density. And as we have also told you, when 4th density beings visit 3rd density environment, they are, in effect, 3rd density beings, and vice versa. The so-called abduction takes place, especially if it is a physical abduction, the subject becomes temporarily 4th density, because it is the environment that counts. And the key factor there is awareness, not physical or material structure.

50 **Q**: *(L)* I have a paper here that talks about the Grays and says that they have two brains: an anterior brain and a posterior brain; and that if you shoot one – this is what it says, I am not suggesting that I want to shoot anybody – that if you shoot one, and only shoot one part of the brain, that it does not die; that you have to shoot it in a special way and get both brains in order to kill one. Is this a correct concept?

51 **A**: Well, it is rather puzzling. Brings up a lot of questions. One question that comes to mind is: Why would one seek to shoot anything.

52 **Q**: *(L)* Well, I didn't suggest that I wished to, this is just what this paper says here.

A: The physical description is accurate in terms of one variety of what is referred to as the Grays. It does have an anterior brain. However, this is secondary to all other issues. And, also we would suggest that it would not be advisable to seek to cause physical harm to any particular species. Therefore, it may be advisable to disregard the information contained in the work that you are describing. 53

Q: *(L)* It also says that the Grays have to be very close to a person to telepathically link with that person. Is this correct? 54

A: Close? No, as we have described to you before, there are technological processes involved which do not require close physical proximity as you measure it. But, this is very complicated. It follows dimensional windows and that sort of thing, which you do not fully understand, therefore it would not be advisable to go into that in great detail. But, the general answer to that question is no. 55

Q: *(L)* It also says that they implant some sort of crystal on the optic nerve of humans that is 2 to 4 microns in diameter and that this crystal is tuned to the frequency of the individual's implanting it, which allows them to establish a mental frequency for communication. Is that anywhere along the line of what you are talking about? 56

A: Physical implantations do occur. The precise locations vary according to the desired effects. And when it comes to the interactions between the human species in 3rd density, and other STS issues in 4th density, there are a variety 57 of mechanisms in use as well as a variety of directives and objectives. For example, some implants are used merely for tracking. Others are used to alter consciousness, and still others are designed to be mind altering or motor altering mechanisms. Each of these has a different structure and a different material content according to which is being employed and for what purpose. The particular function you are describing there has been used, or, rather, something similar, though we are not completely familiar with that which you have described. So, we suggest that this may be fabrication to some extent, or expansion of accurate information. But, in any case, it is true that implants do get implanted for various reasons.

58 **Q**: *(L)* Shifting gears back to the alien autopsy: can you access the information and indicate whether this hybrid being was one that was obtained from a crash that occurred at Roswell, New Mexico in 1947?

59 **A**: The crash did not occur at Roswell. It was in a desert area, approximately 157 miles to the West by Northwest, of the Roswell location. The Roswell location that you are familiar with, did not include either a craft or any bodies or living beings. It was merely a debris field. The actual crash occurred some distance away. The crash site, a desert location, closer to Los Alamos, Mexico, and there, the craft, which had malfunctioned over Roswell, thus leaving behind the debris field, had, in fact crashed. This is where the bodies and living beings were recovered along with what was remaining of the craft. And, yes, the being in the film you have seen did come from there.

Q: *(L)* How many beings were on that craft? 60

A: Four. 61

Q: *(L)* Were they all hybrids? 62

A: Correct. It also may be noted, and you can check this with the official record as has been interpreted by those in your environment who have studied the subject, this was a specialized mission which was initiated by those referred to as the Lizard Beings using human/hybrid combinations, the hybrid element being that referred to as the Gray type, it was an experiment partly as what could be interpreted or translated to mean a reconnaissance mission, and partly testing the environmental conditions that existed in that area at the time as a result of the nuclear explosions that had occurred in the region in the recent past, as measured from that particular point in time. The effort was to determine effects on both the living Gray species and of, course, the Reptilian or Lizard species, as they have a similar genetic make-up in some ways that we will not get into just now. But, the idea was to test the effects upon both the human genes, or genetic structure, and the Gray genetic structure which, in turn, is connected the Lizard genetic structure if you understand the concept. That was one objective. Another objective, of course, was basic reconnaissance. 63

Q: *(L)* Okay. The next question: Are any of the Grays what one might call "good guys?" 64

A: That is a subjective interpretation any way you look at it. For, after all, what is good and what is bad? 65

Q: *(L)* The definition that has been given is STS and STO. So, are any of 66 the Grays STO beings?

67 **A**: Well, again, if we can review for just a moment. It is subjective to refer to either STS or STO as either good or bad. It merely means Service to Self and Service to Others. Now, the determination as to whether it is good or bad is made by the observer. It depends on your point of view. It depends on your objective. It depends on a lot of things. One is merely service to self. This is inward turning. The other is Service to Others which is outward expanding. It is part of the balance which makes up that which we refer to as the Universe.

68 **Q**: *(L)* Are any of the Grays STO?

69 **A**: In very rare instances, Gray beings have crossed over into the STO realm, but in their natural environment, they are, in fact, STS, as they were constructed to be.

70 **Q**: *(L)* How does it occur that they cross over into the STO environment?

71 **A**: Simply by natural circumstance, in the same general way that it occurs that human beings in the 3rd density STS environment can, under certain circumstances, rise to the STO level. Very rare.

72 **Q**: *(L)* Well, if the Grays are cyber-genetic probes of the Lizard Beings, and, in effect soulless, does this mean that some of the Lizard beings are also STO?

73 **A**: Well, first, no being that is given intelligence to think on its own is, in fact, completely soul-less. It does have some soul imprint; or what could be loosely referred to as soul imprint. This may be a collection of psychic energies that are available in the general vicinity. And this is stretching somewhat so that you can understand the basic ideas, even though in reality it is all far more complex than that. But, in any case, there is really no such thing as being completely soul-less, whether it be a natural intelligence or an artificially constructed intelligence. And, one of the very most interesting things about that from your perspective, is that your technology on 3rd density, which we might add, has been aided somewhat by interactions with those that you might refer to as "aliens," is now reaching a level whereby the artificially created intelligences can, in fact, begin to develop, or attract some soul imprint energy. If you follow what we are saying. For example: your computers, which are now on the verge of reaching the level whereby they can think by themselves, will begin to develop faint soul imprint.

Q: *(L)* That's not a pleasant thought. 74

A: Now, to answer your question: Are 75 the Reptilian beings, or Lizard beings, STO. Of course, some can cross over into STO. However, their natural environment is STS as they have chosen. But, whether or not any of the cyber-genetic Gray beings cross over into STO, and or the Lizard Beings cross over into STO, these are not connected to one another, these two concepts: they are independent.

Q: *(L)* I understand. Okay, would you 76 say there is any percentage, any fairly measurable percentage of Lizard beings that are STO?

A: It is very, very small. Extremely 77 small. Hardly worth mentioning.

Q: *(L)* What about the Grays? 78

A: That might be slightly higher, but 79

again, it is very small, relatively speaking.

80 **Q**: *(L)* Is there another race of beings that are manipulating or using the Lizard beings?

81 **A**: Could you elaborate?

82 **Q**: *(L)* Are the Lizard Beings agents for some other group?

83 **A**: Well that is a rather simple question. But, there are levels of authority in 4th density STS environment. And these are determined by intellectual and physical prowess, as always, in STS. The "pecking order" as you call it. So, therefore, we could state that at the bottom are those you are familiar with as the Gray beings, and in the middle are those you would call the Lizard Beings, and above that are others that you are not so familiar with.

84 **Q**: *(L)* Who are they?

85 **A**: The most commonly known, of course, are the Orion STS.

86 **Q**: *(L)* What do they look like?

87 **A**: They are, in fact, humanoid in structure, resembling large human beings.

88 **Q**: *(L)* And we don't see them that often?

89 **A**: Well, of course you know by now, that the ones most frequently seen on 3rd density level, are the Gray beings. All other equally less frequently seen.

90 **Q**: *(L)* Okay, what is their purpose in all this abduction activity?

91 **A**: We request that you make your questions as specific as possible in this subject area.

92 **Q**: *(L)* Do these Orion STS ever participate in abductions?

A: The abductions are primarily per- 93
formed by the Gray beings. However, others can and will and in fact have abducted. But when this occurs, the nature of the abduction is different.

Q: *(L)* Are there any positive Extra-ter- 94
restrials from the area of Sirius interacting with human beings at the present time?

A: Well, now! First off, it is important 95
for you to know that the term you use: Extra Terrestrial, which of course, is one of the most correct terms used at your level, all that is NOT of the Earth is Extra-Terrestrial. And, for those on your surface earth environment to refer to themselves as the supreme species, or alone in the universe, or the one and only in the cosmos, is laughable in the extreme. It is akin to a microbe on a grain of sand referring to itself as the only form of life on the beach. Would it not? Now, when you ask are there any beings in the vicinity of Sirius, it would be something like that same microbe, located on the grain of sand, on the beach, which is, of course, but one of the beaches located on the surface of the earth, after all, asking if there is, in fact, any life located over in the vicinity of that seashell...

Q: *(L)* But I asked if there were any 96
interacting with Earth...

A: And we are answering that ques- 97
tion. We have chosen to take this opportunity to put things into better focus for you, and we are hoping that these messages will be heard by others, and not just you. While *you* may understand these concepts perfectly well, not all do. Certainly you know that? Therefore, that is why we are giving this information. Now, to answer your question: Are there any beings who re-

side in the vicinity of Sirius who are positively oriented, or STO as it were, again it is difficult to answer that because we do not know how to define the "vicinity of Sirius." But, if you mean within a light year or so of Sirius, as you measure distance, then we can say there are no such beings in that area in 3rd density. But that leaves open 4th through 6th density. So, you see, as you already know, but we wish to reinforce this, there is so much to contemplate here that it is laughable when those around you refer to certain areas or star systems and claim that there are beings from here or there or wherever, and that their objective is this or that or the other. Because if you knew the *true* nature of the universe, of All of the universe, of all possible realms, you would also know that any and all things are possible, and, in fact, *do* exist! You must *not* forget this.

98 **Q**: *(L)* So, in other words, these people are right?

99 **A**: All of these people are right, and all of these people are wrong. Because it is silly to point to some section of the sky, to ascribe any area as being the "Home" of this that or the other.

100 **Q**: *(L)* But what if that is, in fact, the case? The Orions live in some star system in Orion, right?

101 **A**: So are you.

102 **Q**: *(L)* Well, we aren't living there now![4]

103 **A**: That's not the point. If you were to stay in 3rd density and view your star, which you know as the sun, from another point in your galaxy, it would appear to be a part of the Orion system. Would it not?

Q: *(L)* Probably. 104

A: Well, now perhaps you are beginning to understand what we are talking about??? At one level, and in one sense. 105

Q: *(L)* Well, how do these beings get here crossing such vast reaches of space? 106

A: As we have told you, there are seven levels of density which involves, among other things, not only state of being physically, spiritually and etherically, and materially, but also, more importantly, state of awareness. You see, state of awareness is the key element to all existence in creation. You have undoubtedly remembered that we have told you that this is, after all, a grand illusion, have you not? So, therefore, if it is a grand illusion, what is more important, physical structure or state of awareness??? 107

Q: *(L)* State of awareness? 108

A: Exactly. Now, when we go from the measuring system, which of course has been nicely formulated so that you can understand it, of density levels one through seven, the key concept, of course, is state of awareness. All the way through. So, once you rise to a higher state of awareness, such things as physical limitation evaporate. And, when they evaporate, vast distances, as you perceive them, become non-existent. So, just because you are unable to see and understand has absolutely no bearing whatsoever on what is or is not possible. Except within your own level of density. And this is what almost no one on your current level of density is 109

[4]Actually, as I later learned, we *do* live in the "Orion Arm" of our galaxy.

able to understand. If you can understand it and convey it to them, you will be performing the greatest service that your kind has ever seen. Think about that for a moment. Let it seep into your consciousness. Analyze it. Dissect it. Look at it carefully and then put it back together again.

110 **Q**: *(L)* What is it that limits our awareness?[5]

111 **A**: Your environment. And it is the environment that you have chosen. By your level of progress. And that is what limits everything. As you rise to higher levels of density, limitations are removed.

112 **Q**: *(L)* What creates this environment of limitation?

113 **A**: It is the grand illusion which is there for the purpose of learning.

114 **Q**: *(L)* And who put the illusion into place?

115 **A**: The Creator who is also the Created. Which is also you and us and all. As we have told you, we are you and vice versa. And so is everything else.

116 **Q**: *(L)* Is the key that it is all illusion?

117 **A**: Basically, yes.

118 **Q**: *(L)* So, essentially...

119 **A**: As we have told you before, if you will be patient just a moment, the universe is merely a school. And, a school is there for all to learn. That is why everything exists. There is no other reason. Now, if only you understood the true depth of that statement, you would begin to start to see, and experience for yourself, all the levels of density that it is possible to experience, all the dimensions that it is possible to experience, all awareness. When an individual understands that statement to its greatest possible depth, that individual becomes illumined. And, certainly you have heard of that. And, for one moment, which lasts for all eternity, that individual knows absolutely everything that there is to know.

Q: *(L)* So, you are saying that the path to illumination is knowledge and not love?[6] 120

A: That is correct. 121

Q: *(L)* Is it also correct that emotion can be used to mislead, that is emotions that are twisted and generated strictly from the flesh or false programming? 122

A: Emotion that limits is an impediment to progress. Emotion is also necessary to make progress in 3rd density. It is natural. When you begin to separate limiting emotions based on assumptions from emotions that open one to unlimited possibilities, that means you are preparing for the next density. 123

Q: *(L)* What about Love? 124

A: What about it? 125

Q: *(L)* There are many teachings that are promulgated that Love is the key, the answer. They say that illumination and knowledge and what-not can all be achieved through love. 126

A: The problem is not the term "love," the problem is the interpretation of the term. Those on 3rd density have a tendency to confuse the issue horribly. After all, they confuse many things as 127

[5] *The Wave* 72
[6] *The Wave* 65

love. When the actual definition of love as you know it is not correct either. It is not necessarily a feeling that one has that can also be interpreted as an emotion, but rather, as we have told you before, the essence of light which is knowledge is love, and this has been corrupted when it is said that love leads to illumination. Love is Light is Knowledge. Love makes no sense when common definitions are used as they are in your environment. To love you must know. And to know is to have light. And to have light is to love. And to have knowledge is to love.

128 **Q**: *(L)* The other night I met a young woman named Roxanne C___. Can you access anything to help her?

129 **A**: At this time we choose to abstain from making any comments about the nature of individuals in your environment. Also, we would strongly suggest, as this has been rather intense information session, that you may wish to terminate at this time.

Q: *(L)* One very quick question: The problem with my eyes. I have had a lot of trouble with them, using many medicines. Some people have told me that this indicates a genetic mutation and a developing ability to see on many levels? 130

A: This you must discover. Before you become frustrated, if, indeed you are going to begin seeing at another density level, it must be a discovery process for the greatest learning potential. For us to give you previews would not necessarily be in your best interest. 131

Q: *(L)* Last night we were supposed to meet several people at a restaurant, but we lost them in traffic. Was this "losing" somewhat symbolic? 132

A: Perhaps. But, again, we do not wish to comment on interactions between yourself and other individuals, as the purpose for this particular session was informational and not judgments concerning others in your realm. 133

End of Session

September 12, 1995

The last full board session we had done was on 8 July; additionally, there had been almost a month's break between the sessions of 12 August and 9 September, the immediately previous session that I had wanted to do via the board but was prevented by the events. However, the circumstances that surrounded this session more or less mandated that it be done via the board. As you can tell from the dialogue, there were a few people very much attracted to what we were doing and who saw in it something they could promote and make money.

Participants: 'Frank', Laura

1 **Q**: Hello.

2 **A**: Hi!

3 **Q**: *(L)* Who do we have with us this evening?

4 **A**: Decorra.

5 **Q**: *(L)* And where are you from, Decorra?

6 **A**: Cassiopaea.

7 **Q**: *(L)* OK, now, it's been a while since we've done this on the board, and I have several questions that are pretty important that I want to ask. Are you open for questions this evening?

8 **A**: Yes.

9 **Q**: *(L)* First of all, do Frank or I at the present time have any attachments of a negative nature?

10 **A**: No.

11 **Q**: *(L)* Do we have any attachments at all?

12 **A**: Variable.

Q: *(L)* Does that mean they come and go, or they can come and go? 13

A: Yes to question 2. 14

Q: *(L)* OK, yes to question 2. OK, now, there are several new people who have contacted me and want me to do various things for them. In many respects it looks like a very positive involvement, but there have been some very strange things that have happened, and I have been handling them the best way I know how. Can we ask some questions about this situation and how I've handled it so far? 15

A: Yes. 16

Q: *(L)* The first thing is, Roxanne C. Roxanne has basically got some really good ideas, but I think she's got something blocking her from perceiving what is truly going on. She wants so badly to believe in the fairy tales that she ends up mixing things together in an emotional attempt to deal with it all. This is fine, as far as I am concerned, but anybody who can't look at their 17 own 'stuff' is extremely hard for me to deal with. What is the story here?

18 **A**: All involved are portals, beware!!

19 **Q**: *(L)* Do you mean beware as in maybe I should just walk away from this group?

20 **A**: Up to you.

21 **Q**: *(L)* OK, my instincts...

22 **A**: Remember where was initial link?

23 **Q**: *(L)* Initial link? At MUFON?

24 **A**: Who?

25 **Q**: *(L)* Martie T's?

26 **A**: Yes.

27 **Q**: *(L)* OK.

28 **A**: Aura field is uniform.

29 **Q**: *(L)* Whose aura field is uniform?

30 **A**: All in question, do you not see similarities in your personality profiles reading? Examine, review and reflect!

31 **Q**: *(L)* Come on Frank, ask some questions here. Help me out! Personality profile? Well, that's of the different people involved...

32 **A**: Similarities?

33 **Q**: *(L)* Do you mean similarities between the people involved in that group?

34 **A**: Aural field reads as identical.

35 **Q**: *(L)* And are their personality profiles and aura readings different from, say, mine and Frank's?

36 **A**: What do you think?

37 **Q**: *(L)* What do you think, Frank? *(F)* I don't know what they are talking about. *(L)* Well, they're talking about profiles, aural profiles, I guess that's a way of reading a person. *(F)* Yes, but I... *(L)* Well, does that mean that Frank and I are so different that there's nobody that we can interact with?

A: Did we say that? 38

Q: *(L)* Of course not. OK, so in other 39
words this is a mine-field and we really have to tread carefully through it, is that it?

A: You have been warned, how you pro- 40
ceed from here is up to you.

Q: *(L)* Does this guy Barry, who keeps 41
wanting me to commit to some kind of deal with him, and who keeps saying he is going to do this and that, is he?

A: The answer to that is easily dis- 42
cernible.

Q: *(L)* The answer to that is eas- 43
ily discernible? Well, it's hard for us to... I mean, he could be just a Howard Hughes kind of guy! Easily discernible... In other words, what you see on the surface... would that be what they would mean? Easily discernible...

A: Ask him directly! 44

Q: *(F)* You may if you desire... I don't 45
want to! *(L)* What is Martie after in this whole interaction?

A: $$$$$$$$ 46

Q: *(F)* Well, why don't they just say 47
'Money'? *(L)* They like to be creative.

A: Mirth. 48

Q: *(L)* Gotta have mirth, Frank! What 49
does Barry want out of this whole interaction?

A: To be liked and needed. 50

Q: *(L)* What does Roxanne want out of 51
this whole interaction? [Laughter from Frank, response not verbalized]

A: The same as Martie T. 52

53 **Q**: *(L)* What does Frank want out of this whole interaction, including the newsletter?

54 **A**: Ask him, he is here.

55 **Q**: *(F)* What do I want? I haven't a clue! *(L)* What do I want out of all this interaction?... read my deepest, darkest recesses!

56 **A**: You see the newsletter as a mode of transport to fulfillment of your goals.

57 **Q**: *(L)* And what are my goals?

58 **A**: To be the leader of your cause.

59 **Q**: *(F)* Is that true? *(L)* Maybe. Remembering, of course, that my primary drive is to get the Cassiopaean material out there and 'save the world,' so to speak. *(F)* Ask them if it will work. *(L)* Will it work?

60 **A**: Open.

61 **Q**: *(L)* So Martie wants money, Barry wants to be liked and loved and needed. *(F)* That makes sense. *(L)* And, is it true that I can utilize the wants and needs of these people to create a vehicle for the cause of dispensing knowledge?

62 **A**: But will the "vehicle" ever break down, or "get stuck in the mud".[1]

63 **Q**: *(L)* Should I just get in touch with this publisher that Roxanne knows and just deal with putting the material out in book form?

64 **A**: Would not that be: 1) more direct 2) less cumbersome, and 3) less fraught with potential danger?

65 **Q**: *(L)* OK, so getting the material out in book form is...

A: We answered thusly because you 66
thought for yourself.

Q: *(L)* Is giving the lectures, as I've 67
planned to give this lecture about my personal experience, this is not so much about the material, a good way to promote the Cassiopaean material and a good way to get out and do things?

A: Lecture? 68

Q: *(L)* Well, you know, the talk I'm 69
going to give on Saturday night at the Earth Angels Bookstore, where I'm going to talk to these people about whatever is... basically about our experiences, about synchronicity and the coming of the...

A: Well intentioned crowd, but open to 70
deceptive attack.

Q: *(L)* Should I cancel this lecture? 71

A: Up to you.[2] 72

Q: *(L)* Approximately how many peo- 73
ple would show up if I don't cancel?

A: 15. 74

Q: *(L)* Fifteen people. Well, it's not 75
worth being attacked for, is it? *(F)* I don't know if I would cancel at this point, I'd say up to you, but, my gut instinct is that it's not going to do anything. *(L)* Don't waste my time? *(F)* Well, isn't she [Martie] getting these people to pay her money? *(L)* Uhuh. *(F)* Well, then that's what the sum total probably of what you'll get out of it. *(L)* Yeah, and I only get a third of it, and she's letting some people in free. *(L)* Has Frank assessed this person Barry in a correct way?

[1]As events turned out, the whole situation turned very ugly with various persons attacking others and I opted to step out of it and decline the editorship of the newsletter, the lectures I was asked to give, and a whole bunch of other stuff.

[2]I did cancel the lecture after I saw the way the people involved were interacting.

76 **A**: See what happens when we plant the seed, then encourage you to "Till the soil?"

77 **Q**: *(L)* So Barry is basically living on his credit, is that it?

78 **A**: Open

79 **Q**: *(L)* Well, it's not right for Roxanne to be constantly asking him for money. He is probably giving to her on his credit! How much in debt is he right now?

80 **A**: Not your concern. Look, listen, learn.

81 **Q**: *(L)* Well, I think... I don't want to waste my time with these people then. They are all just playing games with each other. *(F)* I agree. It's a shame, but it's another deception, which is a form of attack. Leads you down the primrose path to get you all tangled up, to slow down the progress. And apparently it was an excellent idea when you said just contact the publisher and go down that pathway. *(L)* OK, now, let's ask real quick, this David Hudson tape, about what he calls the Philosopher's Stone. What is this substance that David Hudson has discovered? We watched the video about it; I'm sure you guys watched it with us, so, what is this stuff?

82 **A**: Watch developments there only from a distance.[3]

83 **Q**: *(L)* Is taking this substance [monoatomic gold] as he is talking about, is it dangerous, as I kind of think it is?

84 **A**: Possibly.

85 **Q**: *(L)* So, in other words, I should not get involved in that, either?

A: Up to you. 86

Q: *(L)* I know it's up to me, but you 87
said to watch it from a distance, so I'm assuming that is a clue...

A: Yes. 88

Q: *(L)* OK, my feeling is that there is 89
some negative energy behind that, even though he is trying to be a positive person and do positive things, and that...[4]

A: This is often true! 90

Q: *(L)* I think that taking something 91
like that to transform your consciousness without doing the work or having it occur naturally is black magic. That's what I think. *(F)* It's too easy... *(L)* I think trying to initiate yourself ... *(F)* I read over the years bits and pieces from various different sources that all the things he described in there are possible for those who are willing to sacrifice, to us would appear to be an extreme extent ethereal and spiritual level, such as some of those in India, and all that... *(L)* I don't think you even have to sacrifice so much as have the desire and the natural destiny and ..... *(F)* Well, did Jesus take this gold powder? *(L)* Did Jesus take this powder?

A: No. 92

Q: *(L)* Did Adolph Hitler take this kind 93
of powder, or something similar?

A: Yes. 94

Q: *(F)* That paints a rather bleak pic- 95
ture, doesn't it? *(L)* Could this powder be utilized to transform a person to a very positive entity doing great good? I just don't think it's right.

A: Or could it be utilized to transform 96
an entire race of beings into hypnotic

[3] *The Wave* 30
[4] *The Wave* 20

submission!!!!!!!!!!

97 **Q**: *(F)* Wow! *(L)* Put it in the water. *(F)* Or even just advertise it as the "Manna from Heaven" and get the biggest corporations in the world to... I mean, you know that if this guy were not meant to spread this stuff all around, by now he'd be running into roadblocks, you wouldn't be allowed to get tapes like that. That was one thing I was suspicious of, like why he hasn't even been stopped, if it's really as wonderful as... I mean it just doesn't fit. Anything that's really, really good, and it's going to go against the... remember who runs this world, and has for 309 thousand years, are they just going to sit back and say "Oh, yeah, we'll just let this gold powder get spread round everywhere, and get totally defeated," just like that? I don't think so! *(L)* Oh, that's a scary thought! Boy, I'm sure glad you guys are out there!

98 **A**: Okay.

99 **Q**: *(L)* Holy Frijoles! Well, I guess, unless you have... Do you have something you would like to tell us or communicate to us at the present time?

100 **A**: Reflect upon messages received and goodbye.

(L) Thank you very much.

(F) Once you progress to the level of enlightenment, and you are no longer in these bodies, you don't need orgasm, do you?

(L) I guess not.

(F) And if it's not an orgasm, then why call it an orgasm. I mean, he's saying, "Oh, it's not the same thing, it's wonderful, it feels the same... it's more pure," and all that...

(L) Right.

(F) BS! I don't buy that. I don't buy it.

(L) I don't buy into the Keys of Enoch stuff either because he starts off right away with talking about the guilt thing...

(F) Naughty, naughty...

(L) And the bad guys have to be transformed. I mean, they just can't deal with the fact that that's the way it is, and it's got to be that way, all the way up, all the way through, all the way around, forever. Dark, Light.

(F) Right.

(L) That's it.

(F) Now, JD doesn't seem to have a problem about that. Nobody had a problem understanding that, but somehow they all thought this was of the light, but I just don't buy the idea that all you have to do is drink this powder, or eat this powder, and you are going to become light beings, and you're going to bi-locate, and all these wonderful things, and just walk on water, and all that. It just doesn't add up. You know , that's, once again, it's a shortcut. And there are no short cuts.

End of Session

September 16, 1995

There were a lot of things going on in the background here. As indicated in a couple of previous sessions, there was a Tampa bookstore owner, Martie T, a 'mover and shaker' in the metaphysical community, who had attended a session (or two) and who had been quite busy promoting the Eddie Page and *Keys of Enoch* nonsense. She had closed her store where lectures and workshops were often held, and now had affiliated herself with a new store where she and various New Age–type practitioners would peddle their wares and services. She was very anxious to involve us in this enterprise in some way, so, we had been invited to the grand opening to meet the owner/promoter. It was there that I mentioned I was thinking about starting a magazine as a venue for the Cassiopaean material.

Not long after, a local woman – Roxanne C – called me on the phone and said that she had heard (from Martie) that I was interested in starting a magazine. Roxanne said that she had been publishing a small metaphysical newsletter for over two years and was ready to give it up because she was planning a move and I was welcome to her subscription list and various accoutrements of her project if I wanted to take it over. We decided to meet to discuss it.

When we did, it was a funny trigger for a variety of things. She was Jewish and almost immediately began talking to me about her past life in Nazi Germany and how she had been experimented on by Dr. Mengele and died as a result. There was an instant rapport between us, and she was interested in attending a session. She also told me a lot of scuttlebutt about the owner of the new bookstore and, as a result of this, along with the fact that I had a bad feeling about it, I canceled my lecture and involvement with those folks.

Right after this meeting and before her attendance at a session, I had a dream. In this dream, I was the bride and was wearing a wonderful dress with flowers in my hair and there was a limousine waiting outside to take me to my 'wedding'. I didn't know who the groom was, but there were a lot of people around me encouraging me to 'get in the car' and go to 'meet the bridegroom'. For some reason, I was filled with happiness and the joy of those around me was contagious, so, overcoming my hesitations, I went to the car, got in and was taken to the place of the wedding. I was aware that the date was a Saturday and it seemed to be the 14th, because something was said about Friday the 13th having been the day before.

It turned out to be a big restaurant with a wonderful feast prepared and waiting. It was all decorated with flowers and streamers everywhere and many, many people were gathered in a happy and joyful crowd who cheered me as I got out of the car.

The 'bridegroom' came forward to take my hand and we walked through the crowds of people to stand in front of a priest-like person who married us. I was overcome with happiness even though I could not see the groom's face!

As soon as we were married, beautiful music began to play, and he took me out onto the middle of the floor where everyone had cleared a space, and we began to dance. It was like flying and we whirled and spun. It was happiness such as I had never experienced in my entire life and I awoke bathed in a sensation of ecstatic joy! I had never had such a dream in my entire life and it affected me profoundly.

A few days later, my new Jewish friend, Roxanne C, came to a session. I'll make some additional comments at the end of this session since what I have to add is much longer than will fit in a footnote! I will say in advance, however, that despite the fact that Roxanne had some 'sacred cows' that she held on to for dear life, I think her energy was fundamentally positive and this was a very good session as a consequence.

Participants: 'Frank', Laura, Roxanne C

1 **Q**: *(L)* Hello.

2 **A**: Hello.

3 **Q**: *(L)* Who do we have with us?

4 **A**: Sorra.

5 **Q**: *(L)* And where are you from?

A: Cassiopaea. 6

Q: *(L)* We have a guest this evening. 7
And we have a few questions that I want to ask before we get launched off into some other subjects. First thing is, I had a pretty sick feeling in response to this whole situation with Martie T, and I did cancel the talk at the book store she is associated with. I know

you are not going to tell me whether I did the right thing or the wrong thing; however, I would like to know if there are any implications regarding this situation that I do not, at present, see?

8 **A**: Implications?

9 **Q**: *(L)* Well, in other words, was there someone who would have been there that I should have made a connection with? Did I fail by not going through with it even though it was so distasteful to me?

10 **A**: If distasteful, how would you fail by not appearing?

11 **Q**: *(L)* Well, sometimes I wonder if we are not supposed to overcome our emotional reactions to things and just do things that are emotionally distasteful in spite of our own feelings. Isn't that correct?

12 **A**: You are aware of the nature of your instincts. The nature of...

13 **Q**: *(L)* What are you trying to tell me here? Am I being dense?

14 **A**: What are you always telling others?

15 **Q**: *(L)* Listen to your instincts. Yes. And my instincts told me that this was not a good place to go nor a good group to have any involvement with.

16 **A**: Have you not then answered your own question?

17 **Q**: *(L)* OK. Last night Terry called me and said that on Wednesday night he began channeling the Cassiopaeans directly in his [Buddhist] meditation class. The way he described his experience almost sounded like a physical possession. Can you come through with physical sensations? Was Terry channeling *you*, the Cassiopaeans, or a similar source?

A: We must have been watching a different "channel!" 18

Q: *(L)* Who was being channeled? 19

A: Ask Terry! 20

Q: *(L)* Well, he said he was channeling *you*! 21

A: Ask him after a few more sessions. 22

Q: *(L)* Is there some danger that can be experienced if one goes to a class and the meditation teacher instructs everyone to stare into a mirror and channel the first thing that comes along? 23

A: Maybe, but there is some danger in all things at 3rd density. 24

Q: *(RC)* You need to find out who he was tapping into. Was it his higher self? 25

A: Ask him later. 26

Q: *(L)* Roxanne has some questions... OK? 27

A: It is as always. 28

Q: *(RC)* I have some personal questions and some non-personal questions. 29

A: Don't screen, please, that is restriction!! 30

Q: *(RC)* OK. If Aramaic was ancient Hebrew, was it the language spoken in Atlantis? 31

A: No. 32

Q: *(RC)* Did the Hawk, or the Hoovids, bring this language to Earth? 33

A: No. 34

Q: *(RC)* By scanning the Zohar, does this mean that the fire letters will ignite ancient memory, thus bringing the truth to the surface?[1] 35

[1] Another popular New Age theory that the Hebrew alphabet was given directly from

36 **A**: These are "cult thought patterns."[2]

37 **Q**: *(RC)* It has come to my attention that most of the places where the word for 'God' is used in Zohar as well as in the Old Testament, it is used in its feminine form. Does this imply that the Queen of Heaven... who is Isis?

38 **A**: Isis is a vanguard.

39 **Q**: *(RC)* What is a vanguard?

40 **A**: A symbol of energy patterns that lead transformations of cultures during border periods.

41 **Q**: *(RC)* Is the word 'Jesus' derivative of Isis or Zeus?

42 **A**: Neither, Jesus is moniker only.

43 **Q**: *(RC)* What is moniker? What do you mean? Don't you have to pray in the name of Jesus for protection?

44 **A**: Prayers are not necessary for protection once channel, or more appropriately, conduit is properly grooved!

45 **Q**: *(RC)* The recent movie, *The Prophecy*, produced by Maxwell – is she of the light, and what purpose is behind sending this glimpse of this holographic image to Earth now? Will the movie awaken people to the reality of the Holy War? And whose message is being served through this film?[3]

A: Several questions, crisscrossing 46
thought patterns.

Q: *(RC)* Whose message is being 47
served by this film?

A: What do your instincts tell you? 48

Q: *(RC)* My instincts tell me both 49
sides...

A: Okay. 50

Q: *(RC)* I just wanted to know if there 51
was any specific force behind...

A: We are? 52

Q: *(L)* Oh, they may not be confirm- 53
ing...

A: What do your instincts tell you??? 54

Q: *(RC)* It was about the fallen angels – 55
Lucifer. *(L)* Have you read who the Cs
say Lucifer is? *(RC)* One of the fallen

Jehovah/Yahweh via fire or some such nonsense. Never mind that the Hebrew alphabet is actually just a stylized form derived from the Syrian/Aramaic alphabet. According to scholars, the original Hebrew script developed during the late second and first millennia BCE alongside others used in the region.

The Zohar is the foundational work in the literature of Jewish mystical thought known as Kabbalah. It is basically just scriptural exegesis and commentary. Lots of silly claims are made about it, but the fact is that it appeared first in Spain in the 13th century, probably written by Moses de Leon.

[2] As you will see, the Cs' answers will not be well received by Roxanne, who dearly wanted to believe in such nonsense.

[3] From Wikipedia: "*The Prophecy* is a 1995 American fantasy horror-thriller film starring Christopher Walken, Elias Koteas, Virginia Madsen, Eric Stoltz, and Viggo Mortensen. It was written and directed by Gregory Widen, and is the first motion picture of *The Prophecy* series including four sequels. The film tells the story of the Archangel Gabriel (Walken) and his search for an evil soul on Earth, and a police detective (Koteas) who unknowingly becomes caught in the middle of an angelic civil war." [http://en.wikipedia.org/wiki/The_Prophecy]

angels? The angel of light? It is a *lot* to go through...[4]

56 **A**: Before we can answer some things, you must ask other things.

57 **Q**: *(RC)* Will there be another war in heaven between the angels?

58 **A**: Assumptions are fun to deal with.

59 **Q**: *(L)* You are assuming that there are angels and that they are fighting a war. *(RC)* Well, in a metaphorical sense.

60 **A**: And you are assuming there is a "heaven."

61 **Q**: *(RC)* Yes. Are you saying that there is no heaven? No paradise? I don't believe that. *(L)* There is 5th density. *(RC)* Well, we are getting into semantics here.[5]

62 **A**: "Heaven" is a concept more than semantics. Some think the 3rd density environment known popularly as Leavenworth is heaven, for one example. Could be called "Heavenworth!"

63 **Q**: [Laughter] *(L)* This person Barry... [Planchette begins to move]

64 **A**: Ask we are just energizing. Ask... ask!

65 **Q**: *(L)* Alright, I'm asking! Is Barry possessed?[6]

66 **A**: Vague question.

67 **Q**: *(L)* Is Barry attached by discarnates?

68 **A**: Transitory.

Q: *(L)* Does he have a serious case of 5th density or demonic possession? 69

A: [Spinning] No. 70

Q: *(L)* Well, what is the problem with Barry? Why is he saying such terrible things about Roxanne? 71

A: Not appropriate. 72

Q: *(L)* For me to ask or you to answer? Did I do the right thing in this matter? 73

A: All there is is lessons. 74

Q: *(L)* This was a lesson, obviously. I guess it is not appropriate for me to ask any personal questions about him. Maybe it would be OK for you since you were personally involved. *(RC)* Is Barry a spy? 75

A: Spy? Clarify, please. 76

Q: *(RC)* Is Barry a spy for the Gray aliens? 77

A: Well, are you aware of the modus operandi commonly employed, and the technical aspects of same??? 78

Q: *(RC)* Yes. Has he been used by the dark... 79

A: Define your understanding. 80

Q: *(RC)* They spy through implants or CD-ROM? He absorbs information and then they download it from him? 81

A: In other words, unconscious manipulation. 82

Q: *(L)* Is that it? 83

A: Now, please reveal your reading on the situation. 84

[4]Roxanne was referring to the printed transcripts of the sessions that had been transcribed thus far and which I had previously given her.

[5]Roxanne's heavily programmed beliefs began to emerge.

[6]This was an individual who Roxanne knew and, based on the stories she had told me about him, sounded pretty much like he was possessed, assuming that all Roxanne had said was accurate.

85 **Q**: *(RC)* I think he is being used by them unconsciously as well as consciously. *(L)* My question would be, what is the purpose of this activity?

86 **A**: One step at a time!

87 **Q**: *(RC)* Is he a spy for the CIA?

88 **A**: Assumptions prevail!

89 **Q**: *(L)* Maybe you have assumptions and they are having trouble transmitting through them? *(RC)* I don't think he is a spy for the CIA.

90 **A**: Not the point.

91 **Q**: *(RC)* What is the point?

92 **A**: CIA?

93 **Q**: *(L)* Do you mean why worry about the CIA when there are other things to worry about? *(RC)* Why has everything he has done in my life turned to trouble?

94 **A**: These are the questions that prompt reflection, reflection prompts analysis, analysis prompts conclusions, which builds knowledge, which fosters protection!!!

95 **Q**: *(RC)* Will Barry be free of this or will he go for the rest of his life in this darkness?

96 **A**: Up to Barry.

97 **Q**: *(RC)* Will he do anything more to hurt me?

98 **A**: Are you learning? If you are learning, are you gaining knowledge?

99 **Q**: *(RC)* Well, I know about that but I want to know if he is going to cause me more trouble?

100 **A**: *(L)* What does it matter what he says, if you have the knowledge which protects?

Q: *(RC)* Well, that's kind of like beating a dead horse here... 101

A: Network. 102

Q: *(RC)* I was shown that I lived in Nazi Germany and I was one of the children used for experiments. I was also shown that I chose this for myself. I want to know why. *(L)* How were you shown this? In a dream? *(RC)* Lots of dreams, I have had psychics tell me about it... 103

A: Learning is best accomplished when the student is not restricted by others. 104

Q: *(L)* What do you mean? I guess I should keep my mouth shut. 105

A: What do you suppose? We do not ask that you "keep your mouth shut," just suggesting helpful guidelines for maximum learning. 106

Q: *(RC)* OK, I *know* this from a variety of sources. I don't have to explain them all... all I want to know is why. And, I know that my DNA was interfered with and I want to know if that has been carried into my present body and is this being fixed? 107

A: Physical manifestations normally only carry over in spirit body, and are a discovery process for advancement. They are chosen by the soul during contemplation on 5th density. 108

Q: *(RC)* So, that means that what I have been through in this life physically, has been to bring me to the realization of what happened before? 109

A: Essentially. 110

Q: *(RC)* I was also told that there was a woman who was very protective of me during my last life in Nazi Germany. Have I re-met this soul yet? 111

A: No. 112

113 **Q**: *(RC)* Was she a mother or sister?

114 **A**: Neither.

115 **Q**: *(RC)* Were we related?

116 **A**: No.

117 **Q**: *(RC)* Am I going to meet her?

118 **A**: Wait and see!

119 **Q**: *(RC)* What is my relationship to Frank and Laura from any past life connections?

120 **A**: Discover.

121 **Q**: *(L)* Did I know Roxanne in my past life in Germany?

122 **A**: Maybe.

123 **Q**: *(L)* Now, I was looking at the [astrological] charts, just to see what kind of matches there were and it was a lot. *(RC)* According to astrology, that shows a past life connection. I feel also that something went on in Egypt.

124 **A**: Who were you?

125 **Q**: *(L)* You mean me?

126 **A**: Yes.

127 **Q**: *(L)* I was just German woman... *(RC)* I was wondering about Egypt?[7]

128 **A**: But we are still in Germany!

129 **Q**: *(L)* All I know was that I committed suicide, name was Helga, I think...

130 **A**: Who was your husband?[8]

131 **Q**: *(L)* I don't know. He was Jewish. Is that what you are getting at?

132 **A**: Okay. Who were your children?

133 **Q**: *(L)* Was my husband then the person who was my boyfriend years ago – GM?

A: Not issue. 134

Q: *(RC)* They asked who were the chil- 135
dren. Was I one of your children?

A: Discover. 136

Q: *(L)* What was Roxanne's name in 137
that lifetime?

A: When we say discover, we mean for 138
you to use your given talents to learn, not to have us lead you by the hand every step of the way. If we were to do that, we would cheat you out of an opportunity to gain knowledge, and more importantly, understanding. Thus, we would be abridging free will!

Q: *(RC)* Was my name Rachel? 139

A: How do you examine past lives? 140

Q: *(L)* Hypnosis. 141

A: Bingo! 142

Q: *(RC)* So, I need hypnosis? Can I 143
be put under hypnosis? *(L)* I'm sure you can. You told Frank and me about several past lives before...

A: Because the individual circum- 144
stances were not the same.

Q: *(L)* Who are the 'Bird Tribes' talked 145
about in legend and more recently in several popular books?

A: Varies. 146

Q: *(RC)* Who are the Hoovids? 147

A: Transplanetary. 148

Q: *(RC)* Did the Hoovids become the 149
Hebrews?

A: No. Hebrews do not stem from sin- 150
gle grouping.

Q: *(L)* Are or were the Hebrews a sep- 151
arate racial group?

A: Not necessarily. 152

[7] *The Wave* 44
[8] *The Wave* 30

153 **Q**: *(L)* What was the origin of the Hebrew people?

154 **A**: Genetic construct.

155 **Q**: *(L)* Who did this genetic construct?

156 **A**: Guess.

157 **Q**: The Atlanteans?

158 **A**: Not that simple.

159 **Q**: *(L)* The lizzies?

160 **A**: How about joint effort?

161 **Q**: *(RC)* The Sirians and the Pleiadians?

162 **A**: Getting colder.

163 **Q**: *(L)* The Orion Union?

164 **A**: Okay, but include C.O.C. How does one restrain density 2 companion?

165 **Q**: *(L)* Chain? Chain of Command? Are there any actual inhabited planets in the Pleiades?

166 **A**: Yes.

167 **Q**: *(RC)* What about the Sirians?

168 **A**: Yes.

169 **Q**: *(L)* Alright, the Orions created the Hebrews. What was the purpose for which this genetic variation was created?

170 **A**: Manipulation.

171 **Q**: *(L)* Who was Yahweh?

172 **A**: False teacher.

173 **Q**: *(RC)* Who was Jehovah?

174 **A**: Moniker variance of previous answer.

175 **Q**: *(L)* And what was the desired result of the Hebrew genetic manipulation?

176 **A**: Further control through the fostering of mistrust and hostility, leading to enslavement and warring. Also accomplished renewed and invigorated 3rd to 4th density "feeding."

Q: *(RC)* The Tetragrammaton, which 177
is a code for the name of God in the Old Testament – who or what does this code represent?

A: Be careful not to get caught up 178
in ancient deceptions, but ostensibly it "means" I Am The One.

Q: *(RC)* The 'I Am The One', accord- 179
ing to my research, is another word for 'Isis'. Let's ask about the 'birth goddesses' talked about by Zecharia Sitchin. *(L)* Is there such a thing as these 'birth goddesses'?

A: Whoa, wait a minute, what did we 180
just advise???

Q: *(RC)* Don't get caught up in an- 181
cient deceptions? *(L)* We asked about this once before and were told that it was just the ancient way of describing genetic experiments. *(RC)* OK, why is it that Hebrew, being so specific in participles in terms of gender qualities, how come, in the Old Testament, there are feminine connotations for the names of God, and also feminine connotations for God being in *her* palaces? As well as masculine?

A: Why not? If it works, do it. 182

Q: *(RC)* Is the 'I Am The One' a femi- 183
nine force?

A: My Dear, you seem to be stuck upon 184
gender classifications. Now this is understandable, but prepare yourself for a long winded explanation here, since there appears to be no other way. On density levels 5 through 7 there is no duality. The "God Force" emanates "down" from 7th density and permeates

all densities. It recognizes no classifications related to duality, since it is perfectly blended, thus in permanent balance.

185 **Q**: *(RC)* But the gender names are in the original texts?

186 **A**: This is true, but the original texts were also deceptive in nature.

187 **Q**: *(RC)* How many children have I been used for that are alien hybrids?

188 **A**: To answer this question would alter your chosen path of learning, so therefore must be deferred.

189 **Q**: *(RC)* I have already gotten this in my meditations, so maybe they can help me on it. I have been given names in Hebrew in my recent meditations that have stuck in my head: one the word for 'government' and the other for 'state' or 'politics'. Does this mean that I am meant to be working in politics or for the government? Which government? Is this my destiny?

190 **A**: Well, again, we know the answer to that, but must let you discover in order to learn.

191 **Q**: *(RC)* Am I being called to serve? Is it a government on Earth or...

192 **A**: One interpretation, but not the only one. Remember, "government" is nebulous, and dreams can be pathfinders and dreams can be warnings!!!

193 **Q**: *(RC)* How many lifetimes have I spent on Earth – I already know the answer, someone told me, I just want to know...

194 **A**: 87.

195 **Q**: *(RC)* Not 445? That's it? So, I'm not really from here?

196 **A**: Would you rather we add a few?

Q: *(RC)* So, I am not really from this planet? 197

A: No one is, ultimately. Remember, you are eternal, one through three are not. 198

Q: *(L)* Did Roxanne have other lifetimes on other planets in 3rd density? 199

A: Discover. 200

Q: *(RC)* I was told, based on the lines in my palm, that I had lived 445 times. So there is a huge discrepancy. *(L)* Well, you are talking palmistry now, and that is Frank's bailiwick, you know. He is the most gifted palmist you may ever encounter. *(F)* Let me tell you right now, you can't read anything about past lives in the palm. *(RC)* That's not what this woman says. The left hand is the past, the right is the present. And the lines on the side are like the age rings in a tree trunk. *(F)* No. Let me explain... 201

[Break for palmistry discussion]

Q: *(L)* Roxanne is planning to move to Arizona and has made some arrangements to set about doing this. Is she going to be able to write her book when she is out there and get that accomplished? 202

A: Open. 203

Q: *(RC)* It depends on me. *(L)* Is she going to be able to find the right house? 204

A: Open. 205

Q: *(L)* In a general overview, what was the purpose of this interaction with the Martie T bunch, Barry, JD, David Hudson, Roxanne, Barbara, etc? 206

A: You have already gained some insight. 207

Q: *(L)* Does Roxanne have any attachments? 208

209 **A**: Discover.

210 **Q**: *(L)* Roxanne went to a psychic, CU, who did a spirit release for her. Was this successful?

211 **A**: Why do you wish us to answer that?

212 **Q**: *(L)* It seemed like a good subject to cover, that it might be helpful.

213 **A**: Discover.

214 **Q**: *(RC)* What about the dream that I had about the three slugs coming off of me? Were these three slugs Barry, B___ and M___?

215 **A**: Energy pattern essence, rather than individuals per se.

216 **Q**: *(RC)* Do I still need spirit release?

217 **A**: Yes. Okay.

218 **Q**: *(RC)* How many times have I been abducted?

219 **A**: 20.

220 **Q**: *(RC)* Were most of those in childhood or more recent?

221 **A**: Both.

222 **Q**: *(L)* When was the most recent? *(RC)* Within the past 8 years?

223 **A**: Yes.

224 **Q**: *(RC)* So most of them were within the past 8 years?

225 **A**: No. Just most recent.

226 **Q**: *(L)* Why have they abducted her less than some we have heard about?

227 **A**: Less?

228 **Q**: *(L)* Well, some people seem to have a lot more, and 20 does not seem like a lot.

A: Abductions take many forms. 229

Q: *(L)* I dreamed the other night that I 230
got married, and there was a big party, dancing, the limousine and so on... flowers, happiness. In my dream, I heard a voice saying that the wedding would be on a Saturday the 14th, following Friday the 13th. Could you tell me anything about this dream?

A: No.[9] 231

Q: *(L)* Any other questions? *(RC)* I'm 232
not going to ask, because they didn't really answer what I wanted to hear.[10] I do have 3 questions about the past. What was my role during the French Revolution? I know that I was there then because I have glimpses.

A: Who is David Hufnagel? 233

Q: *(RC)* David was my first love. Why 234
the name Hufnagel? Was that my name in France?

A: David's original name was Huf- 235
nagel.

Q: *(RC)* That was my first boyfriend in 236
South Africa. His name now is Harris.

A: No, changed his name. 237

Q: *(L)* What does that have to do with 238
the French Revolution? *(RC)* He was there, right?

A: We are receiving strong wave pat- 239
tern surrounding subject we chose to cover, thus we interrupted inquiries!

Q: *(L)* OK, anything further on that? 240

A: Moshe in Israel. 241

---

[9] I was more than a little disappointed that the Cs had nothing to say about my dream but figured it was best just to drop it.

[10] I don't think that Roxanne was even the least bit embarrassed about making such a statement, nor was she even aware of how astonishing it was.

242 **Q**: *(RC)* Who is Moshe in Israel?[11]

243 **A**: Moshe is IN Israel.

244 **Q**: *(RC)* There are a lot of Moshes in Israel! Is this someone I know or knew?

245 **A**: Yes.

246 **Q**: *(RC)* Is it connected to my ex-husband?

247 **A**: Maybe. We are not sure. Israel: saw you with Grays in physical, access memory, Moshe too.

248 **Q**: *(L)* Do you mean that David Hufnagel saw Roxanne during an abduction?

249 **A**: No. Country of Israel. Another connector to abduction experience.

250 **Q**: *(L)* Well, maybe you were abducted in Israel and saw these people there... in the physical... and these people saw it...

251 **A**: No. David is elsewhere.

252 **Q**: *(RC)* Is this David my old boyfriend?

253 **A**: Yes.

254 **Q**: *(RC)* And that is who I was with in the French Revolution, which is what started all these questions.

255 **A**: Maybe.

256 **Q**: *(RC)* Am I going to see him again?

257 **A**: Open.

258 **Q**: *(RC)* I was abducted while I was with him?

259 **A**: Well yes, but Israel biggest abduction.

260 **Q**: *(L)* Roxanne was abducted while with David, but in Israel she experienced the biggest abduction? *(RC)* I was with him in Israel... and we were together in South Africa.

A: Abduction with David was in South Africa. 261

Q: *(L)* What is meant by the biggest abduction was in Israel? 262

A: Physical retrieval. 263

Q: *(L)* Was it biggest in the sense that it was the biggest abduction experience of her life? 264

A: Yes. 265

Q: *(RC)* Was it on Mount Sinai? 266

A: No. 267

Q: *(RC)* I had an out of body experience when I was there. Was it out in the desert, the Negev? 268

A: Yes. 269

Q: *(L)* What was done to her during this abduction? 270

A: Open. 271

Q: *(L)* Who was doing the abduction? 272

A: Grays. 273

Q: *(RC)* Is that when I was pregnant? 274

A: Yes. 275

Q: *(L)* How many times have you been pregnant? *(RC)* Five, I think. How many times? 276

A: Open. 277

Q: *(RC)* This makes sense because my migraines started in South Africa... I lost my virginity in the Negev... so that is probably when they started abducting me – it's the whole sexual thing, right? 278

A: Yes. 279

Q: *(RC)* And the guy died... *(L)* That's interesting... OK, change of subject. Back when we were talking about the pit on Oak Island, and you asked me 280

[11] *The Wave* 30, 44

to do some research on it, the answers I came up with were that the responsible group were alchemists. Is this correct?

281 **A**: Yes.

282 **Q**: *(L)* Was one of the alchemists involved Nicholas Flamel?[12]

283 **A**: Yes.

284 **Q**: *(L)* Is it true that there is an enclave of alchemists that live somewhere in the Pyrenees...[13]

285 **A**: Yes.

286 **Q**: *(L)* Is this the group that you referred to as 'The Quorum' in a previous session?

287 **A**: Partly.

Q: *(L)* Do these alchemists use this 288
power as talked about by David Hudson to enhance their longevity and their physical health?

A: And to control. 289

Q: *(L)* Are there people in this enclave 290
who live for literally hundreds, if not thousands, of years?

A: Open. 291

Q: *(L)* How does this monoatomic gold 292
control others?

A: Too complex to answer tonight, as 293
energy is waning.

Q: *(L)* Should we just say goodnight? 294

A: Goodbye. 295

End of Session

I want here to come back to Roxanne's questions about the Hoovids, Hoova, etc. This question was apparently based on a theory about the origins of the Hebrews in which Roxanne was interested. It comes from the channeling of Phyllis V. Schlemmer as published in her book *Earth: The Only Planet of Choice.* This channeled source is analyzed in Pincknett and Prince's book *The Stargate Conspiracy.* I wrote a review of this book and want to excerpt parts of it here so that the reader can have a full awareness of things going on in the background. P & P write:

> Few of the enthusiastic followers of the Face on Mars story realise that the ideas of both Richard Hoagland and James Hurtak – the main advocates of the Mars/Giza connection – are largely shaped by a highly influential cultish group who claim direct, telepathic communication with extraterrestrial intelligences. These alleged non-human entities have, we were to discover, adopted many different aliases over the course of several decades, but today are most often known as the Council of Nine, or simply 'the Nine.'

[12] *The Wave* 22, 29
[13] *The Wave* 30

> [...] As we progressed in our investigation [...] we were astonished, not to say disturbed, by the influence exerted by the people who believe in the Nine – and ultimately, the Nine themselves. We gradually uncovered evidence of the extraordinary hold that these alleged non-human intelligences have over top industrialists, cutting-edge scientists, popular entertainers, radical parapsychologists and key figures in military and intelligence circles. We were to find that the Nine's influence even extends to the threshold of the White House itself.
>
> Richard Hoagland's influential Enterprise Mission had two directors of operations [...] David P. Myers and David S. Percy. Both had significant roles in the promotion of the Message of Cydonia. American writer and former US Navy officer Myers joined the team in 1989, and London-based film producer Percy went on board shortly afterwards. Both left the Mission together in 1992.
>
> It was Myers who 'discovered' many of the key measurements and angular relationships of the Cydonia monuments on which Hoagland bases his decoding of the Message. And it was Percy who surveyed the stone circle of Avebury in order to establish its relationship with Cydonia, as well as with other English sites such as Stonehenge and Glastonbury Tor. However, the source of Myers's 'unique insights' (as Hoagland calls them in his acknowledgment in *The Monuments of Mars*) is neither mathematical skill nor deductive reasoning: he and Percy are part of a network of people who believe they are in direct contact with a group of advanced godlike extraterrestrials.

It turns out that Myers and Percy hung out with the Nine. More than that, James Hurtak claims to have been in touch with the same extraterrestrial source of wisdom since 1973. Hurtak has told two different versions of how he was 'chosen to receive' the teachings that became *The Keys of Enoch.* In one version, he tells how the prophet Enoch appeared in his room one night. But he later told Jacques Vallee that he was 'programmed' with the info one night by a 'bright light' hovering over his car.

> Hurtak's work, like that of Myers and Percy, describes a system based on a hierarchy of intelligences that rule the universe, and explains how they have intervened throughout the history of the Earth.

> *The Keys of Enoch* is a [...] self-consciously religious work [...] Subtitled *A Teaching Given on Seven Levels To Be Read and Visualized In Preparation for the Brotherhood of Light To Be Delivered for the Quickening of the 'People of Light'.* [...] It even looks like a Bible with the Hebrew letters for Yahweh – YHWH – embossed in gold on its white-and-gold cover, and its text displayed in two columns and divided into short numbered verses. This book evidently believes itself to be very holy, very sacred, taking itself extremely seriously indeed. The sixty-four 'Keys' of spiritual wisdom, covering all aspects of ethics and history, are presented in resounding quasi-Biblical language, although it is virtually impenetrable. For example:
>
>> The key to the end of our consciousness time zone is the violation of the spectra of color codes and in the geometry of radiations which will explode gel forming capacities. For this reason, the Host of the Living Light comes to deliver those who are living under and within the Light of Righteousness. [Hurtak, quoted by P & P]

Wow! Did you get that? I'm sure glad to have such a clear explication of – well – of something. Sorry, when I read stuff like that, my brain turns off. I guess it's because I'm not one of the chosen ones.

P & P introduce us to the Nine through the agency of Andrija Puharich, who, by the way, was also interested in drug-induced altered states of consciousness. Now, as P & P proceed through the most interesting history of the Nine, they make a comment that I really have to mention here:

> Another group came from a background of paranormal research. In 1976, after reading Puharich's biography of Geller, *Uri*, former airline pilot Don Elkins and Carla Rueckert went to Ossining to meet him, then accompanied him to Mexico to study the psychic healer Pachita in 1977 and 1978. Elkins and Rueckert, who ran a Kentucky based group with James Allen McCarty, were already deeply committed to the concept of alien intervention by the time they met Puharich. Elkins began in the mid-1950s as a UFO investigator, then in 1962 turned his attention to extraterrestrial 'contactees,' at which time Carla Rueckert began to work with him. They founded a group called L/L Research in 1970, specifically to study such phenomena. After their Mexican trip with Puharich, Rueckert began to channel another emissary from the

> Nine, a group entity called Ra. Significantly, the third member of the trio, James Allen McCarty, who joined L/L Research in 1980, had already worked closely with a group in Oregon who had claimed to channel the same entity as Edgar Cayce. [Source cited: Elkins, Rueckert and McCarty, p. 47)

As I understand it, Cayce never channeled any entities. He actually 'left his body' to 'ascend' to read the 'akashic records'. Somebody correct me if I am wrong on this one, but I have read that more than once. Do P & P have information that the rest of us do not? Or do we lay such a claim at the door of the Ra group?

The fact is, what is actually said in the *Ra Material* cited above is: "In the fall of 1980, he (Jim) traveled from Kentucky to Oregon to work with this group which was supposedly channeling the same source that Edgar Cayce had channeled in deep trance. [...] After only two months in Oregon [Jim returned.]"

Not to put too fine a point on it: Changing the word from 'source' to 'entity' smacks of prestidigitation. Not only that, but two months sort of doesn't fit "had already worked closely with a group", as the sentence is constructed by P & P. How many other 'well-researched' items in this book have been similarly twisted so subtly?

But P & P were not satisfied with that little manipulation. They firmly associated Ra with the Nine by writing the following:

> L/L Research continues to promote the spiritual teachings of Ra, who spoke of a body called the Council of Saturn, based somewhere in its rings, which protects the Earth and keeps it in a kind of quarantine. From a session on 25 January 1981, Ra explained (with very proper godlike disdain for mere earthly grammar and syntax):
>
>> "In number, the Council that sits in constant session, though varying in its members of balancing, which takes place, what you would call irregularly, is nine. That is the Session Council. To back up this Council, there are twenty-four entities which offer their services as requested. These entities faithfully watch and have been called Guardians."

P & P handily leave out the preceding lines of this excerpt, which say:

> The members of the Council are representatives from the Confederation and from those vibratory levels of your inner planes bearing responsibility for your third density. The names are not important because there are no names. Your mind/body/spirit complexes request names and so, in many cases, the vibratory sound complexes which are consonant with the vibratory distortions of each entity are used. However, the name concept is not part of the Council. If names are requested, we will attempt them. However, not all have chosen names.

Yeah. Sounds like real 'godlike disdain'.

The fact is, the Cassiopaeans have also talked about the 'Zendar' or 'Zindar' council of Saturn. And there is nothing about this council in either the Cs material or the Ra material that suggests the Nine as promoted by Schlemmer, Hurtak, et al. In fact, I know personally that Carla's opinion of the Nine is not far different from ours, only she is more diplomatic about it.[14]

However, that such entities – of both polarities – exist at hyperdimensional levels of reality is clearly beyond the pedestrian minds of such as Picknett and Prince, who clearly belong to the Dr. Watson school of investigation.

The fact is: just because a person was interactive with Andrija Puharich, does not mean that they are automatically suspect. In fact, I have it on very good authority that the burning of Puharich's lab was the result of the fact that he finally realized what the conspirators were up to and withdrew his support in horror, refusing to do any further work for them. He was burned out and hounded until he died rather mysteriously in a fall down the stairs.

The Nine, according to Puharich, in the days before he 'woke up', were "directly related to man's concept of God." He further claimed that the "controllers of the Universe operate under the direction of the Nine. Between the controllers and the untold numbers of planetary civilizations are the messengers. The Nine themselves – speaking through Dr. Vinod – said: 'God is nobody else than we together, the Nine Principles of God. There is no God other than what we are together.'" (Quoted by P & P)

[14]Carla Lisbeth Rueckert-McCarty passed over on 1 April 2015.

Somewhere in there, Puharich was involved in research regarding psychic surgery. This was an interesting connection because it brought in the reference to Henry Belk, whom I met once at a lecture I gave, as recounted earlier. He was not only rude, by talking constantly throughout the lecture, but he was actually hostile to what I was saying when I remarked that the so-called extraterrestrials were *not* here for our benefit. I later learned about his interest in psychic surgery and watched a film he made in the Philippines.

Of course, as time passed, Hurtak decided that his 'source' had to be higher than 'the Nine'. By this time, the Nine had made a few embarrassing predictions that didn't pan out, and a number of people were having serious doubts about them. However, that is a minority compared to those who subscribe to the racist, dominator, patristic system of the Nin,e which is, in fact, very similar to the tone of Val Valerian's new 'Final Incarnation' nonsense. (I won't go into that now, it's a can of worms!)

According to Hurtak, the Nine are the intelligences that govern our solar system only and that there are higher authorities known as the Great White Brotherhood with whom he, and only he, is in contact.

It seems that, after a while, the Nine announced that they were the supreme high god of the Egyptians, Atum. As the 'Nine Principles of Egypt embodied as One', the Nine claim to be returning to Earth to help mankind at a critical stage.

As P & P note: "Suspending disbelief for the moment, the disturbing possibility is that they are simply stating the truth."

No kidding. But I can guarantee it isn't to 'help us'.

One of the chief concepts of the Nine is that the Earth was an 'experiment in free will' that went wrong and if we just hold our mouth right, they will come in and fix things up for us as they have over and over again. This is, essentially, the idea that is being presented by dozens, hundreds of channeled sources.

We are cattle to these beings. Nothing more, nothing less. And like cattle, we are 'cared for' and fed or culled when the herd gets too large. And that brings us to our next point: racism. Again, it is raising its ugly head in the teachings of the Nine, as well as many other channels, including, as P & P point out, older ones such as Helena Blavatsky and Alice Bailey.

How does the Control System 'cull the herd'? Why, war, of course. And how do they select who gets to be culled? Probably based on who has the most spirit of resistance – the ones that keep running away or who cause problems are the ones that get noticed and singled out for the slaughterhouse. In our case, it is always vast numbers of our fellow human beings.

P & P tell us:

> By now it is plain that the Nine are behind the messages of Giza and Cydonia, and that all three are now inextricably entwined in a sort of inescapable juggernaut of the 'truth.' It is impossible to have one without the other, thanks to the sterling work of the intelligence agencies, who ensure that this new belief system is constantly being topped up with new rumours and counter rumours, so that we will never fail to be gripped by the unfolding story. But welded firmly on to a very reasonable interest in the mysteries of Mars and the secrets of ancient Egypt lies the insidious presence of the Nine and their ever-eager disciples.
>
> [...] The same individuals play major parts in all three stories. The prime example is James Hurtak, the ultimate guru, who channels the Nine, was Puharich's second-in-command at Lab nine, was the first person to make the Mars-Egypt connection public, and was – and still is – also a major player in the events at Giza.
>
> There is also the involvement in all three stories of SRI, an organisation with intimate connections with defence and intelligence communities in the United States. SRI crops up in Giza, in the Mars story, and, through its involvement with Puharich, in the events surrounding the Nine.
>
> Thanks to this complex, often covert, input from clever men and women, what seems to be happening under our noses is the creation of a new belief system that efficiently brings together many different elements in order to broaden its appeal as much as possible.
>
> [...] This is a conspiracy of enormous proportions, so successful that it is impossible to pinpoint any one person or group as the real controllers, although we have catalogued those they use. We have seen how the Nine's circle were and are supported by very wealthy people, such as Barbara Bronfman and Joyce Petschek, but it is unlikely that they are in on the secret; they are too easily identified.

On this point, I believe that P & P are exactly right. And when we look at a conspiracy of this magnitude, that has operated, essentially (if P & P had done their homework, they would realize this) for millennia. And all the 'front men' are just that: red herrings to draw our attention away from the true source of the manipulation: the 4th density Matrix Control System Programmers.

And then, we have 'damage control' specialists like P & P who come along and 'tell the truth', and even lay it at the door of some of the truly conspiratorial parties. But over and over again, in certain terms, P & P demonstrate a real lack of depth in their perceptions and their research. They also demonstrate that most peculiar habit of disinformation artists of giving things only a very slight twist so that the percipient is certain that they are telling the truth, but the 'truth' that is perceived is subjectively manipulated.

The whole book is jam packed with fun facts and jolly rumors relating to the plans of the Control System to unite us into a one world religion under the benevolent creator race from Mars, with the kind assistance of Richard Hoagland, Tom Bearden, James Hurtak, the Nine, Andrija Puharich, the CIA, NSA, and probably even the BSA if the truth were known. However, it is interesting that pedestrian material-minded thinkers like Picknett and Prince have a clue that something 'not quite right' is going on behind all this, even if they throw the baby out with the bathwater.

Now, let's leave the Nine and change gears to the topic of my dream that the Cs didn't want to discuss. Only after certain events transpired did the fact that the Cs mentioned "Moshe in Israel" at this session seem strange to me. Let's look again at the excerpt of that exchange:

Q: *(L)* I dreamed the other night that I got married, and there was a big party, dancing, the limousine and so on... flowers, happiness. In my dream, I heard a voice saying that the wedding would be on a Saturday the 14th, following Friday the 13th. Could you tell me anything about this dream?

A: No.

Q: *(RC)* What is my relationship to Frank and Laura from any past life connections? Did we know each other in Germany?

A: Maybe. Discover.

Q: *(L)* Now, I was looking at the charts, just to see what kind of matches there were and it was a lot. *(RC)* According to astrology, that shows a past-life connection.

A: Who were you?

Q: *(L)* You mean me?

A: Yes.

Q: *(L)* I was just German woman... *(RC)* I was wondering about Egypt?

A: But we are still in Germany!

Q: *(L)* All I know was that I committed suicide, name was Helga, I think...

A: Who was your husband?

Q: *(L)* I don't know. He was Jewish. Is that what you are getting at?

A: Okay. Who were your children?

Q: *(RC)* They asked who were the children. Was I one of your children?

A: Discover. When we say discover, we mean for you to use your given talents to learn, not to have us lead you by the hand every step of the way. If we were to do that, we would cheat you out of an opportunity to gain knowledge, and more importantly, understanding. Thus, we would be abridging free will!

It struck me as strange for them to be directing me to think about the German past life experience in this way in response to my question about a dream of getting married. They were not answering my question, but they were trying to get something across without violating free will. Then, they said this:

> **A**: We are receiving strong wave pattern surrounding subject *we* chose to cover, thus we interrupted inquiries! Moshe in Israel.
>
> **Q**: *(RC)* Who is Moshe in Israel?
>
> **A**: Moshe is IN Israel.

But we could get no more that made any sense.

As I mentioned, all of this is going to become rather important and it seems to me that Roxanne's presence was some sort of connector of circuits or adder-of-specific-energy and little did I know how soon my life was going to change.

September 24, 1995

The following week, Roxanne C and her husband attended again. We had discussed the views she was attached to that were evident in the previous session, things such as ‘the Nine’ and ‘the Great White Brotherhood’, Hurtak, ‘the Keys of Enoch’, Rosicrucians, Masons, alchemy, the claims of David Hudson and his ‘monoatomic gold’, etc. I told her that the Cs had designated something called ‘the Quorum’ as some sort of higher-level group that oversees things on Earth (which was as best I could understand it), and so we decided to approach this subject and see if we could get some clarification. I was struggling to put the pieces together and find out just who was ‘on first’. Again, Roxanne’s energy was dynamic and it turned out to be an extraordinary session not only in terms of the material delivered, but also in the energy flows that opened other doorways to the future.

Participants: ‘Frank’, Laura, Susan V, Roxanne C, Simon B

1 **Q**: Hello.

2 **A**: Hello. We have been listening.

3 **Q**: *(RC)* Who are you?

4 **A**: Vorra.

5 **Q**: *(L)* And where are you from?

6 **A**: We transmit via the radio source in Cassiopaea.

7 **Q**: *(L)* OK, a year ago we talked about the Quorum and I did not understand. Now, what I would like to know is, is the understanding I have acquired in the past two weeks regarding this group...[1]

A: You need some review. 8

Q: *(L)* OK. 9

A: Not just about the “Quorum,” but about many important subjects, and tonight, we intend to have some free flowing energy, if you don’t mind. In other words, we may supersede questions, when appropriate. However, it may be necessary for you to begin the process by asking a question. 10

Q: *(L)* I am curious about what I call the ‘Scottish Question’. Why is it that every time I start a paper trail on any issue of conspiracy, there always seems to be a link to Scotland and Scots? 11

A: “Celtic,” what does it mean? 12

[1]The “past two weeks” references the discussions I had been having with Roxanne on the topic.

13 **Q**: *(L)* Well, the word 'kilt' comes from 'Celtic', but no one seems to know where they originated... they just sort of appeared on the landscape, so to speak.

14 **A**: Exactly!

15 **Q**: *(L)* Are you going to tell us?

16 **A**: No, not just as of yet.

17 **Q**: *(L)* So, there is some interesting connection! *(RC)* Does it mean 'warrior race'?

18 **A**: If you prefer! We have close affiliation with the "Northern Peoples." Why? Because we were in regular, direct contact with them on Kantek, before they were "lifted" to Earth by Orion STS.

19 **Q**: *(L)* If you were in direct contact with them, how come they were in cahoots with the Orion STS bunch?

20 **A**: Who says they are in "kahoots?"

21 **Q**: *(L)* Weren't they rescued by the Orion STS?

22 **A**: Yes. But one need not be in "kahoots" to be rescued!!!

23 **Q**: *(L)* Well, if the Orion STS brought the Celts here, they must have brought them for their own purposes, am I correct?

24 **A**: Essentially, but herein lies the reason why you need a review. You see, you have some gaps in your knowledge base which are caused by channeling, absorbing and analyzing information out of sequence with what we have given you and mixing it all together!

Q: *(L)* OK, what's my problem? 25

A: You are doing wonderfully, my dear, 26 but it is difficult for you to keep up this way, because your natural drive for the truth makes you impatient, and therefore you tend to fill in the gaps with simple reasoning and assumptions. While these are often correct, they can tend to allow you to get ahead of yourself.[2]

Q: *(L)* OK, square one: Is the Quorum 27 composed of humans who have been alchemists, who are presently in possession of a substance called 'the elixir of life' and which David Hudson calls 'monoatomic gold'?

A: And much, much more! 28 Monoatomic gold is but one minor issue here. Why get lead astray by focusing upon it solely. It would be akin to focusing on the fact that "Batman" can fly! Is that the only important thing that "Batman" does in the story? Is it?[3]

Q: *(L)* Of course not! *(R)* Batman 29 fights crime!

A: What we mean is that alchemy is 30 but one minor piece of the puzzle.

Q: *(L)* OK, I understand. But, un- 31 derstanding the alchemical connection, and its potential for extending life and opening certain abilities, makes it more feasible to think of a group that has been present steadily and consistently for many thousands of years on Earth.[4]

A: They are not the only ones! 32

[2]In other words, I was as guilty of mixing things up, failing to correctly nuance my understanding, and probably tossing the baby out with the bathwater as Picknett and Prince were, as I described at the end of the previous session!

[3]*The Wave* 30, 44

[4]*The Wave* 22

33 **Q**: *(L)* Oh! I knew I was opening a can of worms!

34 **A**: Let us go to the root.

35 **Q**: *(L)* What is the root?

36 **A**: Who, or what made you?[5]

37 **Q**: *(RC)* The Creator. *(L)* Prime Creator.

38 **A**: How? And who is Prime Creator?

39 **Q**: *(L)* Everything, I guess.

40 **A**: You are "Prime Creator."[6]

41 **Q**: *(L)* Well, we know we are... *(RC)* We are creators, but we aren't the Prime Creator...

42 **A**: Prime Creator Manifests IN you.

43 **Q**: *(L)* OK, so at the root is Prime Creator.

44 **A**: But... who was secondary?

45 **Q**: *(RC)* The Sons of God? The Elohim?

46 **A**: Who is that? Remember, your various legends are "seen through a veil."

47 **Q**: *(L)* OK, the secondary creators are the ones interacting with us directly?

48 **A**: Okay.

49 **Q**: *(L)* Is this the source of the stimulation to discover knowledge?

50 **A**: Basically, but, let us take this step by step.

51 **Q**: *(RC)* OK, getting back to the Celts, were the Pleiadians the secondary creators who brought in the Celts?

52 **A**: Review what we have just said!

Q: *(L)* They said it was the Orions. 53
Are the Orions these secondary creators? *(RC)* Well, I read that it was the Pleiadians. And the Hebrews were originally the Hoovids who came from Sirius...

A: Here comes a shocker for you... one 54
day, in 4th density, it will be your descendants' mission to carry on the tradition and assignment of seeding the 3rd density universe, once you have the adequate knowledge!!!

Q: *(L)* If the Orion STS brought the 55
Celts here, were the Celts, while they lived on Kantek, in the form they are in now?

A: They were lighter in appearance. 56

Q: *(L)* You have told us on other oc- 57
casions that the Semitic peoples were remnants of the Atlanteans, and yet they are quite unlike...

A: Whoa!! Wait a minute, let's not get 58
ahead of ourselves. First things first. What Roxanne said was not entirely factual. Remember, there is much disinformation to weed through.

Q: *(RC)* What did I say that was not 59
factual?

A: In this part of your 3rd and 4th den- 60
sity universe, specifically your "galaxy" it is the region known as Orion that is the one and only indigenous home of human type beings... reflect on this! Indigenous home base, not sole locator. What you are most in need of review of is the accurate profile of "alien" data.

Q: *(RC)* I thought that humans origi- 61
nated in Lyra and then a war broke out there and they ended up in Orion.[7]

[5] *The Wave* 68
[6] *The Wave* 32
[7] *The Wave* 30

62 **A**: Lyra is not inhabited. There have been homes in all places, but some were/are transitory, and some are not. Pay attention to Orion! This is your ancestral home, and your eventual destination. Here is the absolutely accurately accurate profile of Orion to follow: This is the most heavily populated region of your Milky Way galaxy! This is a region that extends across 3rd and 4th density space for a distance as vast as the distance between your locator and it. There are 3,444 inhabited "worlds" in this region. Some are planets as you know them. Some are artificially constructed planetoids. Some are floating space barges. And some are "satellites." There are primary homes, travelling stations and incubator laboratories all in 2nd, 3rd and 4th densities. There are overseer zones in 5th and 6th densities. Approximately one half is STO and one half is STS. Together, along with many other colonies, located elsewhere, this is called, in translation, Orion Federation. Orions created Grays in 5 varieties, as cyber-genetic beings, and installed them on Zeta Reticuli 1, 2, 3, and 4, as well as on 2 planets orbiting Barnard's Star. The Reptilians also inhabit 6 planets in the Orion region in 4th density, and are owned by the Orion STS as slaves, and, in some cases, pets!!! The name "Orion" is the actual native name, and was brought to Earth directly. Study the legend of the "god" of Orion for parallels.

63 **Q**: *(L)* Are the Orion STS the infamous red-headed Nordic aliens?

A: Yes, and all other humanoid combinations. 64

Q: *(L)* OK, if it started with the Nordic types, and that is where the other humanoid combinations came from, what genetic combinations were used for human beings? Black people, for instance, since they are so unlike 'Nordics'? 65

A: The Nordic genes were mixed with the gene pool already available on Earth, known as Neanderthal.[8] 66

Q: *(L)* What was the genetic combination used to obtain the Oriental races? 67

A: Orientals come from a region known in your legends as "Lemuria," and are a previous hybridization from 7 genetic code structures from within Orion Union, designed to best fit the Earth climate and cosmic ray environment then existent on Earth. 68

Q: *(L)* OK, what about the Semitic and Mediterranean peoples? 69

A: Each time a new flock was "planted," it was engineered to be best suited to the environment where it was planted. Aryans are the only exception, as they had to be moved to Earth in an emergency. 70

Q: *(L)* If races are engineered on Earth to be 'best suited', what factors are being drawn from or considered regarding the Semitic race? 71

A: They are not engineered on Earth, but in Orion lab as all others. They were "planted" in the Middle East. 72

Q: *(L)* What genetic type were the Atlanteans? 73

[8] Refer back to the discussion of Neanderthals in session 23 October 1994.

[9] Which suggests, of course, that the Western hemisphere was home to the legendary Atlantis. I discuss this at some length in my book *The Secret History of the World* (volume one).

74 **A**: They were the same as the "Native Americans".[9]

75 **Q**: *(L)* What were the roots of the Native American type? Was there a basic type that was here on the planet and was then taken to an Orion lab and genetically modified and then planted?

76 **A**: No!!! Have you been paying attention?!?!

77 **Q**: *(L)* What did I miss? Why do some Native Americans believe they come from the Pleiades?

78 **A**: Where are the Pleiades?

79 **Q**: *(L)* Well, near Orion. *(RC)* Oh, OK. So, they are considering the Pleiades part of Orion. What about Sirius?

80 **A**: Sirius is confused as a locator because it appears in similar location in the sky in the northern hemisphere. The American Indians were confused in the translation because of similar seeming location due to vantage point.

81 **Q**: *(L)* OK. *(RC)* Well, but Sirius is clearly Sirius! It's the brightest star in the sky... it's in all the legends! *(L)* Well, it could be that it is not just misinterpretation, but deliberate disinformation? *(RC)* How could it be translated wrong? This is not clear! The star charts are very specific!

82 **A**: How have *you* translated *your* legends wrong?

83 **Q**: *(F)* I think the point is that it is clear that we, in our present culture, are easily able to get things very wrong, even from the more recent times; so it is not a great consideration to think that the more ancient legends can also be distorted, embellished, and misrepresented.

A: Review what we said at the beginning of this session. 84

Q: *(L)* Did the Dogon come from Sirius? 85

A: All humanoid types originated in Orion region, there are and have been and will continue to be literally millions of colonies. 86

Q: *(RC)* Well, Sirius has a green sky, not a blue sky like we do. *(L)* The star?! *(RC)* Well, no, the planets... Yes, Sirius has a green atmosphere... a light green. *(F)* Well, I prefer blue! *(L)* If a lot of the information that is being propagated these days is confusion or disinformation, what is the purpose of all this? 87

A: You answered yourself: Confusion and disinformation. 88

Q: *(L)* I have a theory that the truth, in any large degree, will not be known until just prior to some sort of transition... 89

A: You expect "truth" then? 90

Q: *(RC)* Absolutely! *(L)* Considering how things are from observation, this may be unrealistic... 91

A: All there is is lessons, no short cuts! 92

Q: *(L)* I want to get back on my question that you have not answered... I want to know who, exactly, and why, exactly, genetically engineered the Semitic people, and why there is such an adversarial attitude between them and the Celts and Aryans.[10] 93

A: It is not just between the Jews and Celts, if you will take notice. Besides, it is the individual aural profile that counts and not groupings or classifications. But, to answer your question: 94

[10] *Secret History* 5; *The Wave* 28

there are many reasons both from on and off the planet.

95 **Q**: *(L)* Why was Hitler so determined, beyond all reason, even to his own self-destruction, to annihilate the Jews?[11]

96 **A**: Many reasons and very complex. But, remember, while still a child, Hitler made a conscious choice to align himself with the "forces of darkness," in order to fulfill his desires for conquest and to unite the Germanic peoples. Henceforth, he was totally controlled, mind, body, and soul, by STS forces.

97 **Q**: *(L)* So, what were the purposes of the STS forces that were controlling Hitler causing him to desire to annihilate an entire group of people?[12]

98 **A**: To create an adequate "breeding ground" for the reintroduction of the Nephalim, for the purpose of total control of the 3rd density Earth prior to elevation to 4th density, where such conquest is more difficult and less certain!

99 **Q**: *(L)* Do you mean 'breeding ground' in the sense of genetic breeding?

100 **A**: Yes. Third density.

101 **Q**: *(L)* Did they accomplish this goal?

102 **A**: No.

103 **Q**: *(L)* So, the creation of the Germanic 'master race' was what they were going after, to create this 'breeding ground'?

104 **A**: Yes.

105 **Q**: *(L)* And, getting rid of the Jews was significant? Couldn't a Germanic master race be created without destroying another group?

106 **A**: No.

107 **Q**: Why?

[11] *High Strangeness* 14

[12] *High Strangeness* "Appendix"

A: Because of 4th density prior encod- 108
ing mission destiny profile.

Q: *(L)* What does that mean? 109

A: This means encoding to activate 110
after elevation to 4th density, thus if not eliminated, negates Nephalim domination and absorption. Jews were prior encoded to carry out mission after conversion, though on individual basis. The Nazis did not exactly know why they were being driven to destroy them, because they were being controlled from 4th density STS. But, Hitler communicated directly with Lizards, and Orion STS, and was instructed on how to create the "master race."

Q: *(L)* And they were going to use this 111
as their basis to introduce a new blend of the Nephilim... *(RC)* And the New World Order... their version of it. *(L)* Well, what is the plan now?

A: We cannot tell you this yet, as you 112
would seek to reveal it prematurely, leading to your destruction!!!!

Q: *(F)* Yes, Laura, I keep telling you 113
that your curiosity is going to bring strange men to the door who are going to say, "Come with us, please!" *(L)* Well, I can't help it! Meanwhile, back to the Celts: obviously if the Lizard beings thought that the Aryans/Celts were a good breeding ground for this 'Nephilim master race', then it must be because there is something genetically inherent in them that makes them desirable in this sense. Is this correct?

A: No, not in the sense you are think- 114
ing. We suggest that you rephrase this question after careful reflection on the implications.

End of Session

Before making a few personal remarks, I'd like to just suggest that the reader do some research on both the mythology and astronomical information about Orion to realize how accurate the Cs were as far as we are able to tell. Those who have read my book *Comets and the Horns of Moses* will recognize the cataclysmic nature of the tales as well as the aspects of 'genetic mutation/engineering' that result in giants and other terrifying phenomena during such periods.

The period of time following this session was very strange. As I have noted at various intervals in my commentary, there were a lot of changes taking place in my psyche, psychology, and life, as a consequence of this channeling experiment. All sorts of energies were being activated and doors of perception were opening; I had been going through an almost constant process of recalling what seemed to be past life material beginning in February of this year, and this was following a number of incidents where I felt actual, physical phenomena during the sessions themselves.

On this particular occasions, after RC and her husband went home, I went to bed in a strangely excited state because what the Cs had said about the Semites and Nephilim was the most reasonable explanation for the Holocaust I had ever encountered. I had always felt that there just had to be some sort of reason for it that was just out of view – like something you can sense at the edge of your mind, but can't quite bring into focus. My thoughts were racing to try to put together what I knew from my research and what I remembered from my past life in Germany that had been ever-present throughout my life and intensified in the previous months. I knew it was going to be difficult to get to sleep, so I began to practice meditative breathing exercises to relax myself.

With my eyes closed, breathing deeply, there suddenly appeared a face right before me! My eyes were closed and I knew that it wasn't real, but it shocked me because it appeared against my eyelids (more or less) as clear and real as if someone had entered the room! It is difficult to convey to anyone how truly solid and three-dimensional this face was and how strange it was to see it and to know that it was clearly a hallucination because I was fully aware of my surroundings and the fact that my eyes were closed. I did not know this face, but it was a man with light hair and glowing eyes and he looked at me so kindly and lovingly before he vanished like a popping balloon! I was so startled that I nearly lost my breath altogether, but with firm effort, I resumed my meditation and soon went to sleep. It would be ten months later that I would see this face again.

October 7, 1995

After the previous session when the Cs had introduced the idea that the Holocaust was part of the plan for the creation of a master race to reintroduce the Nephilim, and I had been warned that there were some things that could be dangerous to know, I had thought long and hard about how to approach this topic and possibly get some answers. What is astonishing is that, with all this preparation, the tape from this session was destroyed and this is the best reconstruction possible from the notes. The answers are exactly as given because they were noted down on paper, but the questions were not, and thus are as close as I can remember them. The ones I do not remember are left blank.

Participants: 'Frank', Laura, Susan V, Nova M

1 **A**: Hello.

2 **Q**: And who do we have with us this evening?[1]

3 **A**: Tomorria of Cassiopaea.

4 **Q**: [Question lost]

5 **A**: Channel.

6 **Q**: [Question lost]

7 **A**: No, it is just merely the point at which we must review for you the modus as opposed to the locus. You have begun to lose sight of the fact that Cassiopaea is a channeling point for three level density transfer, not our "home," as such.

8 **Q**: *(L)* The constellation of Cassiopeia is the 3rd density level transfer point?

A: Yes, but 3 level, not 3rd level. And 9
kindly please excuse young one, as is risky at this point!!

Q: [Child is sent to bed] *(L)* So, you 10
are saying that Cassiopeia is the point where three density levels converge?

A: Yes. 11

Q: *(L)* I have thought about my ques- 12
tion from the last session and I want to ask it this way: You have said that Hitler received instructions from higher density beings about creating a 'master race'. Why were the Aryan genetic types seen to be more desirable for creation of this Germanic 'master race'?[2]

A: Both similarity and ancestral link 13
most unblemished from Orion 3rd and 4th density stock.

Q: *(L)* So they were essentially trying 14

[1] *The Wave* 33

[2] *High Strangeness* 14, "Appendix"; *The Wave* 30

to breed a group of people like themselves?

15 **A**: Yes.

16 **Q**: *(L)* Didn't it occur to them that they could do this more easily?

17 **A**: Not point. How would you suggest creation?

18 **Q**: *(L)* OK. They were preparing this breeding ground, so to speak. Obviously this was for the introduction of some other genetic strain. What was this?

19 **A**: Nephalim.

20 **Q**: *(L)* Well, if the Nephilim are coming in ships, 36 million of them, why bother to create half-breeds here?

21 **A**: Yes, but having an "advance party" makes 3rd density conquest much easier.

22 **Q**: *(L)* So, this master race was supposed to get everything ready...[3]

23 **A**: Yes.

24 **Q**: *(L)* OK, what is it about the Semitic genes that was considered to be so undesirable in the creation of this 'master race'?

25 **A**: Would blemish genetic characteristics inclined to ruthlessness and domination.

26 **Q**: *(L)* So, you are saying that there is something, some genetic tendency or set of genes in the Semitic type that would counteract this?

A: Close. 27

Q: *(L)* But isn't the nature of a person 28
determined by their soul and not the physical body?[4]

A: Partially, remember, aural profile 29
and karmic reference merges with physical structure.

Q: *(L)* So you are saying that particu- 30
lar genetic conditions are a physical reflection of a spiritual orientation? That the soul must match itself to the genetics, even if only in potential?

A: Yes, precisely.[5] 31

Q: *(L)* So a person's potential for spir- 32
itual advancement or unfoldment is, to a great extent, dependent upon their genes?

A: Natural process marries with sys- 33
tematic construct when present.

Q: *(L)* Well, if that is the case, and the 34
aliens are abducting people and altering their genes, can they not alter the genes so that higher level souls simply cannot come in?

A: Not incarnative process, natural bi- 35
ological processes. Incarnative involves strictly ethereal at 5th density and lower, and thus is enveloped in triple cycle "veil" of transfer which is impregnable at any means. However, any and all 1st, 2nd, 3rd, and 4th processes can be manipulated at will and to any degree if technology is sufficient.

---

[3]See sessions 20 October 1994, 23 October 1994, 2 November 1994, 4 November 1994 and 9 November 1994 for additional references to the Nephilim/Nephalim. You may notice that, at the present time, this prediction seems to be manifesting in full force in our reality with the moves toward totalitarianism and the employment of tasers and other social control mechanisms instituted since 9/11.

[4]*The Wave* 28, 49

[5]*The Wave* 29

36 **Q**: *(L)* Getting back to what you said at the beginning, is it possible that all other channeled material that is designated as this or that 'alien group' comes through a 'transfer point' and then is corrupted so that the person receiving it believes that it is from an actual alien race?

37 **A**: Yes, remember, Matrix material, like all others, contains confused concepts at some points. Antareans, Arcturians, and Cassiopaens refers more to the transfer locator for channel groove rather than residence. Some have come in after the fact and planted fables regarding "races" of beings living in, and travelling from, various places as referenced from your perspective.

38 **Q**: *(L)* Well, who are all these groups giving this information?

39 **A**: Many different groups and individuals. Now, there are indeed actual residential locators mentioned in various writings which are factual. Orion, obviously, Zeta Reticuli, Rigel, Barnard's Star, Sirius Region, though not the actual astronomic body as mentioned.

40 **Q**: *(L)* Who are the 'Orange' aliens mentioned as being the 'Council of Nine'?

41 **A**: Orange is reference to hair color.

[Personal questions and answers for Nova M redacted]

42 **Q**: *(L)* Now, we have wondered about obtaining and taking some of this monoatomic gold.

43 **A**: Are you serious? How about some small helpings of arsenic, anyone?[6]

[NM prepares to leave, as it was getting late.]

Q: [Question about upcoming UFO conference, whether we should try to go or not.] 44

A: We have message for you, but if NM must leave, no need to hold her back, as message is for group. Review: what did we say about weather. Why do you suppose "Opal" occurred at time, place reference point? 45

Q: *(L)* To put a stop to the UFO conference in Gulf Breeze? Does this mean we ought to stay home?[7] 46

A: Up to you, but, suggest deferment, we could tell you of titanic battle!!!! 47

Q: *(L)* So, hurricanes are a reflection of battles at higher levels? Did the good guys win? 48

A: Yes, but not concluded, and we fear for those drawn to locator because of sinister plans by 4th density STS. 49

Q: *(L)* Plans such as what? More weather phenomena or something more direct? 50

A: Both, several options open to them, and in works; monstrous hurricane to hit during conference, or tornado strikes Embassy Suites hotel, or bomb blast levels conference center, of mass abductions and mental controls initiated in order to cause dissention and possibly violence, followed by extreme factionalization. 51

Q: *(L)* So, there is the possibility that something really positive could come from the connections made at the conference. Was this directed at us specifically? 52

A: Yes, why do you suppose it has been disrupted as of now? And have you 53

[6] *The Wave* 20

[7] *The Wave* 32, 44

noticed that the hurricanes have been increasing in October, rather than decreasing as would normally be true?

54 **Q**: *(L)* Well, then, I guess we will be staying home.

A: Free will. 55

Q: *(L)* OK, that's it for tonight. Good- 56
night.

End of Session

Now, the strange thing about this UFO conference that we were talking about was that the normal schedule was for the spring conference to be held in Tampa and the fall conference to be held in Gulf Breeze.

As it turned out, that very year the fall Gulf Breeze conference was nearly canceled because of a hurricane! That, in itself, was an extremely interesting event. We had been planning on attending this particular conference and Terry and Jan had already made the reservations. Hurricane Opal was spinning around in the Gulf and everyone was waiting to see where it would come ashore.

So, we canceled our reservations. As it turned out, the hurricane did hit Gulf Breeze almost dead on, and the conference was moved to Mobile. Clearly, there was no bomb blast or tornado. But, strangely, in a weird sort of way, the above sounds very much like the events of 9/11 and all that followed, though the location and context is different. One wonders if this was a bleed-through of that future reality in some sense? After all, 9/11 was still six years in the future at the time of this session and if it was already in the planning stage, it may have been that the venue and MO had not been entirely finalized.

October 14, 1995

A discussion about the *Matrix* books produced by Val Valerian AKA John Grace preceded the start of this session. I had been hearing about them for months but had never read them. During the week previous to this session, Roxanne C lent me her copies. I was later gifted with copies of my own.

My brother, Tom, was also present and his energy sure enlivened things and sent the discussion into fascinating secret government territory and some rather shocking statements by the Cs that are still difficult to parse.

Participants: 'Frank', Laura, Susan V, Terry and Jan, Tom K

1 **Q**: Hello.

2 **A**: Hello. Matrix material.

3 **Q**: *(T) Matrix* material?

4 **A**: Yes.

5 **Q**: *(T)* Who is the person who did this? *(L)* Many. It's a compilation of many things. There are a lot of people who did the *Matrix* material. *(T)* Does it say that somewhere? *(L)* Yes. *(T)* Because I haven't looked at any of it yet. *(L)* One guy has edited it together and arranged it into about 4,000 pages or so... *(T)* 4,000 pages, and we've only got 300? And we can't edit it [ours]? And he did 4,000? *(L)* Well... *(SV)* It took him fifteen years. *(T)* When was it written? *(L)* The last one came out in 1992 or 1994. *(T)* When did the first one come out? *(L)* 1988. *(F)* A lot of it is just copies of documents and stuff... *(L)* Like photocopies of newspaper clippings and stuff like that, but it's arranged in quite a comprehensive order. *(SV)* A lot of it is really scary. *(L)* I want to ask about one thing from the *Matrix* material. I want to know who and what are the 'Esseseni'?

A: Hybrids, new. 6

Q: *(L)* They are new hybrids? And what are they a hybridization of? What are the sources of the material for the hybridization? 7

A: Humans and grays. 8

Q: *(L)* Are the Esseseni positively oriented beings, as has been suggested by some? 9

A: Split. 10

Q: *(T)* Some STS, some STO? 11

A: Yes. 12

Q: *(L)* OK, now we have a visitor this evening, my brother, and he is really just kind of on the periphery... 13

A: Tom Knight. 14

15 **Q**: *(L)* And he is just on the periphery of this subject, more or less, but he does have a couple of questions he would like to ask, and one of the questions is: has he himself ever been abducted by aliens in this lifetime?

16 **A**: Complex.

17 **Q**: *(L)* Complex? OK, then does that mean yes or no? I know it's complex, but...

18 **A**: Ships are vulnerable to ELF and "Zero time transfer."

19 **Q**: *(L)* So, are you suggesting that any abductions that took place, took place while he was on board a ship?[1]

20 **A**: Maybe.

21 **Q**: *(T)* Were you in the Navy? *(L)* He's retired. *(T)* How long? 20 years? That's a long time! What did you serve on, what kind of ships? *(TK)* AEGIS Cruiser. I was just on one ship, that was just the last five years or so... *(L)* He spent almost his entire Navy career on land, which is quite a feat. *(T)* Yeah, that is pretty good! Were his abductions... did they take place while he was on the ship, on the cruiser? I know that's what you said, I'm just clarifying...

22 **A**: We see "Bahrain."

23 **Q**: *(L)* Were you in Bahrain? *(T)* Somewhere in the Gulf? *(TK)* We were only in Bahrain one night. *(T)* That's all it takes! *(L)* Like getting pregnant, you know! It only takes once! *(TK)* What did those suckers do to me? *(L)* He wants to know what they did!

24 **A**: Examine. You must remember, different branches of your military services have underlying code mechanisms to determine their classification status for "secret" duty, including study of personnel, this is all very complex... Now, "U.S. Navy is status 2", which means among other things, that it is married to a class 2 "Cooperation Agency", the O.N.I. All technical personnel are approached during their service, and asked to perform tasks for secret government. If they accept, they are "brought under classified management."

Q: *(T)* Whoa! *(L)* What was that class 25
2 term? Class 2 agency? *(J)* U.S. Navy is status 2.

A: No. Classified management. And it 26
is O.N.I.

Q: *(L)* Carry on with your answer. I'm 27
sure there's more.

A: ??? 28

Q: *(L)* Oh, you want us to ask the ques- 29
tions. Why was he abducted? *(J)* Or was he abducted?

A: Examined, as with all others on 30
ship.

Q: *(L)* So, in other words, it was sim- 31
ply... *(T)* Your standard abduction and examination... OK, what was the whole thing about the O.N.I. and Naval Intelligence... and the classifications and all that stuff about being approached? What did that have to do with the abduction?

A: Nothing. 32

Q: *(L)* That was just information they 33
were giving us. *(T)* Was the Navy aware of what was happening?

A: Segmented. 34

Q: *(T)* They knew some, but not all. 35
(TK) Some know and some don't.

[1] *The Wave* 21

36 **A**: Yes.

37 **Q**: *(T)* That's what I meant: did the Navy know that Tom was abducted? Those that were supposed to, did they know?

38 **A**: Some in Navy are cooks.

39 **Q**: *(SV)* Cooks wouldn't have a high information... *(T)* That's what Steven Segal said in *Under Siege*:"I'm just the cook, you know!" He wasn't really a cook. *(L)* Maybe that was an allusion to that movie. *(T)* Could be some are 'cooks'. *(L)* Was that an allusion to that movie?

40 **A**: No, but we like it!

41 **Q**: *(TK)* They like the movie, huh? *(J)* They like the reference! *(L)* OK, back when I was really little... *(TK)* I *was* a cook in the Navy in the beginning... *(L)* Yeah, I think it's funny that they made that reference. *(J)* That was mirth. *(L)* When I had that experience when I was really little, and I know that there was interaction with [what I would now perceive to be] an alien, and that I remember it clearly in my conscious mind, and my brother was there also in the room, was he also abducted at that time?

42 **A**: No, but why leave subject so fast?

43 **Q**: *(L)* OK, they want to talk about the Navy, obviously. OK, we can talk about the Navy. *(TK)* What about ol' Tricky Dick W? F. Richard W. *(L)* Who was he? *(TK)* He was just one of my captains.

44 **A**: What about him?

45 **Q**: *(L)* You have to ask specific questions, because it's like a computer system, it only answers when you key in the correct questions. Ask a specific question. *(TK)* Why do they want to stay on the subject of the Navy? *(T)* OK, you gave us some information about Navy being connected to Navy Intelligence... *(J)* Wait a minute, what about W___, ask about W___. *(T)* ...and the way things are there. Is it... are we asking more about the information you just gave us? We'll get on W_-_ in a second. Are we supposed to be asking more about what you just gave us? About the Navy and Naval Intelligence?

A: Ask what you please. 46

Q: *(T)* OK, what is it, they gave us 47 Navy connected to Naval Intelligence... *(L)* Are all military personnel routinely abducted and studied by aliens?

A: No. 48

Q: *(L)* Are all military personnel rou- 49 tinely abducted and studied by the military itself?[2]

A: No. 50

Q: *(L)* What is the classification that 51 the person has to fall into in order to be abducted and studied by the military?

A: What makes you think "classifica- 52 tions" correlates with abductions?[3]

Q: *(TK)* It's not the classification, it's 53 gotta be the type of person... *(J)* And how easy it would be...

A: Yes. 54

Q: *(TK)* And how easy it would be to 55 influence...

A: Of course. 56

Q: *(TK)* How easy it would be to in- 57 fluence, also? *(J)* It's gotta be case by case...

[2] *High Strangeness* "Appendix"; *The Wave* 21

[3] *High Strangeness* 8

58 **A**: And many other factors.

59 **Q**: *(TK)* It would have to have something to do with what they could do for the abductors. I mean, they have to be in a position to help them... *(T)* Just exactly what I was trying to phrase as a question. *(L)* Is that a correct assumption?

60 **A**: Yes. STS.

61 **Q**: *(T)* STS; service to self.

62 **A**: Vibrational frequency.

63 **Q**: *(L)* OK, so if the person has an STS vibrational frequency, that already predisposes them to abduction. Is that correct?

64 **A**: Some.

65 **Q**: *(T)* OK, that's a factor. There's more than one agenda involved with abductions. Are the military personnel that are being abducted, is that a specific agenda that is being followed?

66 **A**: Artificial classifications, such as military designations, are important to human groups only.[4]

67 **Q**: *(L)* So in other words... *(J)* I've got a question. Isn't it true that in order to become part of the military, you have to go through boot camp, the indoctrination to the point where you're going to follow orders without questioning, and that that mindset would lend itself more towards... *(TK)* The Marines are about the only ones that even try to get people to follow orders without question anymore. The Navy has all but given up on that. *(J)* That's interesting. I didn't know that. I just assumed that all military. *(TK)* Well, it's not a time of war so it's not necessary right now.

A: Yes. Some have always "faked" such 68
blind allegiance anyway.

Q: *(J)* Ooh, interesting statement. 69
(TK) I basically faked it, I... *(J)* Kind of like, go with the flow?

A: You were not alone. 70

Q: *(TK)* Oh, yeah! There were a bunch 71
of us. "Yeah, sure, tell us what to do. If it's in our interest, if we're going to stay alive, we'll do it; if you're going to kill us, forget it!" I used to tell them on the ship, that if those suckers ever catch me, I'm going to tell them everything I know. I said, they aren't going to have to torture me long...

(T) Besides, when you torture me, I tend to scream a lot and not tell you too much, so I'll just tell you and let's skip the torture.

(TK) So when I refused to go up for ESWS, I was kind of an outcast, I wasn't in the club anymore...

(L) What happened?

(J) That's when you were asked, and you said no?

(TK) When they wanted me to go up for ESWS, it's a pin, and I told them I wasn't going to...

(L) What is it?

(TK) Enlisted Surface Warfare Specialist.

(T) Aha, that's when you were asked!

(J) And you said no.

(TK) That's something that everybody in the Navy can go up for, but you have to be ... I don't know, if I hadn't been thinking about getting out, I might have gone up for it. This captain put it

[4] *The Wave* 21

in such a way, he said, “Well, if you’ll work on your ESWS and get that pin, I’ll see to it that you get good marks and make chief...”, which to me was like saying, “Well, if you don’t do it, you’re not going to make chief.” I said, “Sorry, bud! Sorry, I’m not going to do it.” I don’t respond to that kind of stuff. *(L)* It must be genetic! *(TK)* That’s when I became an outcast from the club. *(T)* Is that when Tom became an outcast?

72 **A**: Not correct concept, not outcast, just deemed not SG material.

73 **Q**: *(L)* What’s SG?

74 **A**: Secret Government.

75 **Q**: *(TK)* Darn! *(J)* You had your chance Tom, and you blew it! *(T)* That’s when they asked you. *(TK)* Oh! Dickie, I’m sorry! *(J)* No, you’re not! *(TK)* Never did like ol’ F. Richard! *(J)* Yeah, let’s get back to F. Richard. *(L)* F. Richard... *(TK)* Was F. Richard initiated? Was he one of the secret government agents?

76 **A**: No.

77 **Q**: *(L)* Was he brown nosing to try to get there?

78 **A**: Was a “conduit.”

79 **Q**: *(L)* He was a conduit for them. *(TK)* Tell you what, F. Richard was one person I would not have wanted to go to war with...

80 **A**: There are several steps that must be followed.

81 **Q**: *(L)* Steps that must be followed for what? *(T)* To become part of the secret government?

82 **A**: Yes.

83 **Q**: *(J)* You have to know the handshake... *(T)* I can’t get my foot in my ear, I’m sorry! [Laughter]

84 **A**: Vietnam MIA’s, where do you suppose they are now?

85 **Q**: *(L)* Well, I’m hoping you’re going to tell us! *(T)* Some of them... *(TK)* Have they been abducted? *(T)* Some of them got blown up so badly that they couldn’t be found, so they were listed as MIAs, because they couldn’t mark them as KIAs. Some of them are deserters, some of them... well, deserters would fall into several classifications, which I won’t bother getting into. Some of them went into the drug trade. *(TK)* Some of them just decided they liked it better over there. *(T)* Yeah, there’s that, and some of them, I would imagine, have been either abducted or swapped, moved into the secret government. *(L)* Is all of this correct?

86 **A**: Yes.

87 **Q**: *(T)* That’s why they can’t tell people where they are... *(TK)* Are we supposed to still be on the military subject? *(J)* Who knows?

88 **A**: KIA’s... Are a Separate subject!! KIA’s, how many really were?

89 **Q**: *(T)* How many of the 60,000 really were killed? How many of them are listed as dead when they’re not? Intelligence... *(TK)* Tell you what, they could recruit... There were so many different kinds of people that went over there, they could have recruited a bunch... *(J)* Yeah, that’s true. *(L)* OK, now, are you going to give us a hint as to where they are and what they’re doing right now? Are these some of the people working in these underground places?

[5] *High Strangeness* “Appendix”

90 **A**: Yes..Yes...Yes.

91 **Q**: *(L)* That's where those personnel are coming from... their lives, they have died the philosopher's death.[5]

92 **A**: And many other places, times. Etc...

93 **Q**: *(TK)* Wars all through the ages. How many are we talking about? *(L)* What kind of a number are we talking about here?

94 **A**: Since your imagination center is on low frequency tonight, suppose we have to spell it all out for you, but at least it is fun to watch the impact, like "A ton of bricks" falling on your heads!!

95 **Q**: *(L)* Go ahead, spell it out for us. How many are we talking about here?

96 **A**: W.W.II, 72,355, still alive where????

97 **Q**: *(L)* Is that the correct figure?... *(T)* Now, wait a minute...

98 **A**: Yes.

99 **Q**: *(T)* That's how many people the secret government has snatched up? *(J)* From WWII. *(SV)* That's not talking Korea... *(TK)* That's out of something like 40 million... *(L)* Frank, how many? *(F)* Total people in WWII was 70 to 80 million... *(TK)* Military casualties... we're not talking about just U.S. military, either, we're talking about total, anybody.... *(T)* Are you talking about total... all killed in action in WWII? *(L)* No, they said... read it.... *(J)* "W.W.II, 72,355 still alive. Where???" *(L)* Still alive! *(T)* That were supposedly killed in action...

100 **A**: Yes.

101 **Q**: *(T)* From all branches of the service.

102 **A**: Yes.

Q: *(TK)* These people aren't aging; 103
they're still in action and ready to go...

A: Precisely, my friends!!! 104

Q: *(J)* OK, that's just WWII...*(TK)* 105
How about Korea, Vietnam, etc... *(L)* All right, what's the figure from Korea? *(TK)* What difference does it make? *(L)* Well, that's true! *(SV)* We want to know.

A: 6,734. 106

Q: *(TK)* Yeah, considering the fact 107
that I don't think we really lost that many... *(T)* No, we didn't have that many losses in Korea. *(TK)* How about the Gulf War?

A: Yes. 55. 108

Q: *(T)* Yeah, there was about 55 thou- 109
sand casualties in Korea, in the four years of Korea. Really it was 3 1/2 years in Korea. So 6,000 means about a little over 10% of them aren't really dead.

A: 23,469. 110

Q: *(L)* What was that? *(J)* Vietnam, 111
that was Vietnam.... *(T)* 23,000 of the 66,000...

A: Yes. 112

Q: *(T)* ...are still alive? 113

A: Yes. 114

Q: *(T)* So you've got 23,000 from... 115

A: Some are body duplicate soul recep- 116
tacle replacements.

[Change in tape sides; first few sentences of next question segment were lost.]

Q: *(T)* They're moving big-time fast 117
right now. *(J)* They have just around 100,000 with those three figures they gave us. *(T)* Well, now, that's just three wars. We didn't ask about...

(TK) That's three wars. That doesn't count... *(J)* How about WWI, how about Gulf War... *(TK)* Well, the Gulf War, there weren't that many casualties... *(T)* About a dozen. *(TK)* But the other side did...

(T) Yes, we're only asking about the U.S. How about others? Yes, you're right, how about other military...

(J) We have no way of knowing. Have they ever released figures? We don't know.

(TK) They've got a military right now, and it's not just a military – these are elite. I'll bet you, they're elite. I mean, they've been recruited.

(J) They've been asked the question, and they said yes!

(T) Yes, this is not some guy hunking a gun in a foxhole just for the heck of it. These are specialists.

(TK) The CIA was siphoning people off in 'Nam right and left.

(T) Yes, and a lot of these squads that are running around don't exist. A lot of this stuff...

(TK) Yes, like these Black Ops, whatever they call it, and all this stuff. This 'New World Order' is about to come about. You know what, there isn't any way to stop it.

(T) Oh, no, we can't stop it.

(TK) You can fight back and try to survive on your own, but there's no way to stop the New World Order.

(T) The only way to get through this is the old Lao Tzu or whoever, the Chinese military philosopher, who said, "The wheat stalk that survives is the one that bends with the wind."

(TK) "Yes, I'll do whatever you say."

(T) There's no way to stop it. All these people who are talking about going out and going to fight it, they aren't going to fight it. They can't. They can't win.

(F) Well, they are already being diverted.

(TK) On top of everything else, these are the elite. I mean, these are the ones that have been recruited, and they are the elite. Now, most military organizations are going to fall right into this, because the government... Admitted, there's going to be a lot of deserters from the military. I mean there's some people – like, if I was in the military, and they started rounding people up in the U.S., I'd say, "Sorry, this is where I came in..."

(T) This is why this Koernke guy up in the Michigan militia group has been talking about the foreign UN troops, because the military, the government that's ready to come into power, this one world government, knows that you can't subdue any country with their own troops.

(TK) It can't be done.

(T) That's why they're sending American troops to all these other countries.

(F) And all the other countries are sending troops here.

(J) Well, what about the guy who wouldn't put on the UN uniform?

(T) Yes, that was mentioned in the paper again today, in passing. This guy knew.

(TK) Well, really, the only thing a person can do is like you were saying, go with the flow... Basically, you've got to. Up to a point, at least.

(T) It's easier to fight it by going with the flow than it is to fight it by going against it.

(F) Who is going to stand up in the line of fire and say, "I refuse!"? They'd blow him away...

(TK) What, if anything, can be done about this 'New World Order'?

118 **A**: Too complex to answer, need specific questions.

119 **Q**: *(T)* I want to ask a couple of questions off the subject, on a different subject, and then we can get back to this. I want to see Tom sit over here. He's tuned on this. He's catching the answers before they spell out. I want you to come sit over here, if you want to. But not right now, I want to ask a couple of questions first. This is off the subject, we'll come back to it later. A few weeks ago, at Luc's meditation, did I channel you guys?

120 **A**: Well, you channeled, but we must warn you that some soul groupings and aural frequency vibrational associations can leave one open to less than STO influences...

121 **Q**: *(T)* But was it you... was it us?

122 **A**: Up to you to discover.

123 **Q**: *(L)* OK, thank you. Now, second question, what is Judy C channeling?

124 **A**: Rape victim.

125 **Q**: *(T)* OK, she's channeling a rape victim? *(J)* Or she is a rape victim?

126 **A**: Both.

127 **Q**: *(T)* Are the Lizards influencing her in some way?

128 **A**: Yes..

129 **Q**: *(T)* Is she possessed?

A: Open. 130

Q: *(T)* Well, she's got the whole slew... 131
(L) They said she's channeling a rape victim. That's pretty much possession... *(T)* That's what the Lizards want... *(L)* Sure, they are the ones that leave people wounded, so these kinds of things can happen, you know, like going up to somebody and cutting them open with a knife, and then sprinkling dirt and bacteria on it so they can get infected. They do it to the soul level ... *(T)* Is there anything that we can do to help her? *(L)* Terry, you know better than to ask something like that...

A: Judy must follow her own path. 132

Q: *(L)* Now, read that back, what they 133
answered the first question about the channeling... you channeled someone... "You channeled, but we must warn you that some soul groupings and aural frequency vibrational associations can leave one open to less than STO influences..." That's what I wanted to get... Some soul groupings and aural frequency vibrational associations – in other words, be real damn careful who you hang out with when you get in that situation [meditation, opening up]... *(T)* In other words, you're referring to the rest of the grouping involved with working with Luc. *(J)* Including Judy and anybody else...

A: Open. 134

Q: *(L)* They're not going to tell you 135
what to do, Terry. *(T)* Well, I know that... I know that. That's why I keep my shields up solid in there. *(L)* OK, now, is that it, or do you want to ask more about that? *(T)* Should we stop doing the work with Luc? *(J)* They're not going to tell you....

A: Up to you. 136

137 **Q**: *(T)* OK... *(L)* But remember... stop everything! Hold everything! It just jumped in my head, whatever. Remember when I asked the question, and it was the time you guys called on the phone that night, and we were talking about... *(T)* Quitting the job... *(L)* ...and I was saying, is he going to get into the financial soup? Because I was worried about your income, because you had quit that job. And I was concerned about that, is he going to get into that soup, and they said, "Soup comes in all flavors!" And, if you think about it, having the time that you've had available, not working, and seeking to fill this time with various activities, can be in a sense jumping into a chicken noodle, or minestrone, whatever. *(T)* Very good point, yup. *(L)* All right, Tom are you ready to take a turn? Let Terry have a rest. *(J)* That's a very good point, because his job was what kept us from being able to do it, because he wasn't available to do it.

[Tom sits at the table.]

(L) Aha, I see. All right, Tom, the thing is to just place your fingers very lightly on it... like this... just two fingers in contact. You keep the contact firm enough, but not too heavy to weight it. OK, now, the question you had asked was: "Is there anything that can be done about... is there anything you can do about this New World Order busines?" So think of some specific questions.

(J) I want to get back to that body duplicate soul receptacle replacement thing... *(L)* OK, hang on to that, we'll get back to it, don't let it get away.

(TK) I can't think of a specific... I mean...

(L) How about, should people move into groups in isolated areas?

(J) We've gone through that, it's old territory.

(L) I mean, that's, you know, an opening... an opening question. You can go from there. What is the primary focus that one should...

A: We have already answered... 138

Q: *(L)* We know that, but we're just looking for an opening for questions here. *(TK)* What was that? *(J)* "We have already answered..." *(L)* We know that, it's in the transcripts. *(J)* A long, long thing about that. *(L)* It doesn't matter where you are, but who you are, is what they said. And that is pretty much what you were saying: it doesn't matter about the abduction, it only matters who you are. *(TK)* Are most of the survivalist kind dangerous? The kind you should stay away from? 139

A: Off the mark. 140

Q: *(L)* In other words, they're off the mark, they don't understand; it's a spiritual question. 141

(TK) They're looking at the wrong thing.

(T) Also, right now, if you're considering survivalist groups, you have to keep in mind, they're under attack right now.

(TK) Oh, yeah, the government's after them.

(T) Between Oklahoma and this thing with Amtrak out in Arizona, militias are under heavy attack.

A: Being led into a trap.[6] 142

[6] *High Strangeness* "Appendix"

143 **Q**: *(L)* I suspected that at one time. They're all being led into a trap. *(T)* Well, they've got guns right now... *(J)* Maybe guns aren't going to change anything...

144 **A**: Good intentions.

145 **Q**: *(L)* They've got good intentions... *(TK)* Started off with good intentions... They've got to be infiltrated, and it's been tainted at the very least.

(J) Maybe it's the idea of putting all the ones together with the same mindset so you know where they are.

(T) Their usefulness to the one world government people has come to an end. It brought the conservative grouping into power in this country.

146 **A**: Not yet.

147 **Q**: *(TK)* Their usefulness isn't over yet, but... *(T)* Well, there's usefulness and there's usefulness... *(J)* But getting close. *(L)* OK, in those terms, what is the single most important thing that we as individuals should focus on in order to prepare ourselves for whatever events may occur? *(J)* Follow your own path...

148 **A**: No single thing.

149 **Q**: *(TK)* Is what Terry was saying earlier, like the thing... with the reed bending and going with the flow, is that the idea?

150 **A**: Close. Watch, look, listen.

151 **Q**: *(J)* Got it, knowledge is power. *(T)* I gotta tell you, from the Cleveland experience, if you let your mind wander, you end up in a very bad position. *(J)* Pay attention. *(T)* Even if there's a lesson... boy, I learned that one quick!

152 **A**: Alertness.

Q: *(L)* And that does not involve anesthetizing your mind with anything. *(TK)* Probably wouldn't hurt if you had any guns or anything, to keep them hidden, would it? 153

A: Messengers are all around. Look, listen. 154

Q: *(L)* Well, can I ask, what was the particular thing that... I mean, just out of curiosity... *(TK)* Is it going to be necessary to stockpile supplies, or anything along those lines? *(L)* That's all in the transcripts. 155

A: Third density. 156

Q: *(L)* That's 3rd density thinking. *(J)* Guns aren't going to help. *(TK)* I'm not really worried about that. No, they're not going to help, but... *(T)* Does Tom know what 3rd and 4th density is? *(L)* Yes. Is there any particular reason why Tom is here tonight, or came tonight? I mean, I know he has an ostensible reason for coming down, but is there any other underlying reason? 157

A: Look, discover. 158

Q: *(L)* OK, guys, let's take a break, my back is getting really stiff. Can we, or do you have something you want to get right now? *(TK)* Jan had something. *(L)* OK, you wanted to do about the... Is your hand sweating? *(TK)* Uh-huh. *(L)* That's interesting. That's some of the heat, huh? *(J)* Yes, they said that the... 159

A: After break. 160

Q: *(T)* Ask them how many Civil War veterans were taken? 161

[Break]

Q: *(L)* OK, guys, we're back. Hello. Terry wants to know, are there any 162

Civil War veterans or killed in action involved in this scenario that we were discussing earlier?

163 **A**: Tom energy fragmented by ritual. [Laura gave Tom Reiki initiation during break.]

164 **Q**: *(L)* So should he sit out until his energy settles down? We did the Reiki initiation. *(F)* Oh, that's where you disappeared off to? *(L)* OK, you sit out until your energy stabilizes, and I would suggest that you sit there and put your hands on yourself and make that energy flow to get all the little electrons flowing in the same direction. *(TK)* I thought it was going faster with him over there anyway. *(T)* Well, we've been doing it for a year now... *(F)* Whenever anybody new comes in, it slows down. *(T)* It usually takes a while to build it up. *(F)* That's normal. *(L)* OK, now back to Terry's question. Are there any Civil War individuals involved in this project, these underground tunnels or bases or whatever? *(T)* KIAs of the Civil War?

165 **A**: A few.

166 **Q**: *(T)* Well, the farther back you go, the specialties weren't developed. But a specialist is a specialist, no matter what the war.[7]

167 **A**: Not point.

168 **Q**: *(L)* I think the point is who they are. Now, in the *Matrix* material, there's a section extracted from the L. Ron Hubbard teachings that talks about technical abilities to jerk people's souls out of their bodies, insert other souls, reprogram the memories, essentially that there is no congruency...

A: False. 169

Q: *(L)* OK, so the jerking out and the manipulating of souls as described by L. Ron Hubbard is false? In a general sense?[8] 170

A: Yes. 171

Q: *(L)* OK, now, you said a moment ago that some of these bodies were used as receptacles, soul receptacles. When you say soul receptacles, do you mean soul receptacles for whom? 172

A: Replacements for dead bodies, i.e. duplicated. 173

Q: *(L)* So, in other words, they make replacements for dead people and put their souls in a replacement body, so that they can continue living on – is that it? 174

A: Yes. 175

Q: *(L)* Do they ever use dead bodies and reanimate them and then put other souls in them? 176

A: No. 177

Q: *(T)* Now, wait now, you're saying some of them... I'm lost now. *(TK)* Is there a limit to how long they can be dead? *(L)* They make...

A: For example: a soldier is KIA, his body is duplicated, his soul is replaced into new body, then he is "reprogrammed for service" to aliens and S.G.[9] 178

Q: *(L)* Where does the new body coming from? *(TK)* Cloned, basically. *(SV)* I would think so... 179

A: It is duplicate of old body. 180

[7] *The Wave* 21
[8] *High Strangeness* "Appendix"
[9] Secret government.

181 **Q**: *(T)* Where do they get the duplicate? *(L)* Where do they get the material for the duplicate? I know that's a dumb question, I know the answer.

182 **A**: TDARM.[10]

183 **Q**: *(L)* OK, that's it. *(J)* It's in the air, same thing. *(T)* Otherwise known in *Star Trek* as a 'replicator'. *(TK)* Does somebody have to die in a certain way before they can do this?

184 **A**: No.

185 **A**: *(TK)* Is there a time limit on how long they can be dead?

186 **A**: No.

187 **Q**: *(T)* Well, because when your physical body dies, your soul body continues on. Your soul doesn't die, so they always have it. *(L)* They don't want to take your body out of the graveyard, because they're not concerned about the body.

188 **A**: Zero time.

189 **Q**: *(T)* Because there's no time... *(L)* They use the frequency vibration of the soul pattern, they take it into another density, use their TDARM technology to cause a molecular re-assembly – in other words, the atoms begin to whir and assemble around it in the pattern that it had before, and then it is a full-fledged body, and then they insert it back through the time doorway into 3D again. Is that correct?

190 **A**: Close.

Q: *(T)* Are all these [listed] KIAs, are 191
they dead KIAs, when they go, that you were talking about? I mean, are they really dead? *(TK)* Were they dead when this was done?

A: ? 192

Q: *(T)* OK, you said... let's use Viet- 193
nam. You said there were 23,000 KIAs of the 60,000 that actually were not killed in action. True? Yes?

A: Were killed, then reanimated.[11] 194

Q: *(L)* We're not talking about physi- 195
cal bodies here, are we?

A: Yes. 196

Q: *(L)* OK, there are some that were 197
killed in action that the actual bodies were reanimated? *(J)* As long as they weren't blown up in a land mine, yeah. *(L)* There were actually bodies that were actually reanimated, is that correct?

A: Some, but most were duplicated. 198

Q: *(L)* Now this leads to the immedi- 199
ate question: Is there some potentiality that is created by dying in a violent manner; i.e., in war, in an atmosphere of war, that makes one susceptible to this particular type of activity, as opposed to just people dying in an ordinary sense? *(J)* Negative energy...

A: No. 200

Q: *(T)* No, because violent death like 201
that, we have violent death all the time

[10] Transdimensional atomic remolecularization.

[11] *The Wave* 21

[12] It's kind of creepy if it's true. Just think, John McCain and a whole bunch of others who are 'movers and shakers' now, who were in Vietnam, could be programmed servants of the secret government! It also suggests why the anti-war movement, which was really taking off in the sixties, just died and went nowhere and none of the 'old hippie' types, the Vietnam vets, are even interested in activism anymore.

without being in a war: car crashes, fires, explosions...

202 **A**: War makes covert actions so easy.[12]

203 **Q**: *(T)* Well, no, it's not like car crashes – the violent part of it, I don't think has anything to do with it. It's just that the cover of a war, is easier to take the bodies. What I'm trying to understand...

(TK) They're not wanting people to realize... They're not wanting to just take them out of the graves, because if you did, it would be more noticed.

(T) These are real bodies, they were dead. In other words, the people were dead, they were taken, and reanimated, or... *(L)* Some were reanimated bodies... *(T)* ...some were remolecularized... *(J)* If they were messed up... *(L)* Were some of these bodies taken, like dead bodies of somebody who just died... were the bodies picked up, taken into another density for this remolecularization patterning?

204 **A**: Yes.

205 **Q**: *(L)* OK, so they had to have an actual body for the pattern. *(T)* Was the original body... *(TK)* Did they actually get the bodies before anybody actually... *(T)* Before they were recovered, yes. Were the original bodies returned once the duplication was done?

206 **A**: More than one type of situation.[13]

207 **Q**: *(L)* So, in other words, it could be sometimes, yeah, they were, and sometimes, no, they weren't. *(J)* It would be case by case. *(T)* Were some of these supposed 'killed in actions' actually not killed? Were they still alive when they were removed?

A: All possibilities. 208

Q: *(L)* So this is in a sense a 'crime of opportunity'. *(J)* It's a supermarket of opportunities. *(T)* Some were just taken by the secret government when they were alive, some were dead and brought back in new bodies to continue on, and they were considered dead, but they're all considered dead. *(SV)* Laura, what about the 'triple veil' when you go to 5D? 209

A: Taken by aliens, not SG. Secret government aware to some extent, but not in control of operation. 210

Q: *(L)* OK, now this brings up the question about... We were told that there was, and this was... last week we asked about this thing about the death... and we were told that there was an impenetrable triple veil that prevents some of this 'L. Ron Hubbard'–type of activity that he describes happening. How can this be reconciled? Well, the explanation that I see is that it happens that they do this before they go into the tunnel, into the light. They catch them in the transition before they go to 5D. Is that correct? 211

A: Time adjustment. 212

Q: *(L)* Does that mean that they know that they're going to, and they go back in just before they die, or just at the moment of death, or...??? 213

A: Close. 214

Q: *(T)* Now, what are the aliens doing with these bodies, with the humans that they replicate and duplicate and reanimate? What are they doing with them? 215

A: Serve them. 216

[13] *The Wave* 21

217 **Q**: *(T)* So these humans are becoming servants for the aliens?

218 **A**: Workers.

219 **Q**: *(T)* They're slaves. *(L)* Now, this leads me to a question that I have thought about asking on many occasions. In terms of finite numbers, how many of these STS aliens of any different group, or any combination of groups all together, do we have operating on this planet at the present time?

220 **A**: Specify.

221 **Q**: *(L)* OK, how many Lizzies are operating on the planet?

222 **A**: 300,000.

223 **Q**: *(L)* OK, how many Oranges?

224 **A**: 62,530.

225 **Q**: *(L)* How many grays?

226 **A**: 2,750,000.

227 **Q**: *(L)* This is not a pretty picture! *(J)* No sh*t. *(L)* Are most of these inhabiting alternate dimensions or densities most of the time? I mean, it would be kind of crowded otherwise!

228 **A**: Back and forth.

229 **Q**: *(J)* Just like they said in the very beginning. *(T)* When you asked how many of them are here, in 3rd density? *(L)* On the planet...

230 **A**: And others.

231 **Q**: *(L)* I didn't specify the density. Just in our immediate planetary area. *(T)* That's how many of them are working this project. *(L)* Now, I'm sure that there are... here, hand me this little booklet here. We have here some drawings of supposed alien servants. This one right here is called a Rigelian servant. [The booklet says:] It's a protosynthezoid, in other words, a cyber-genetic. Is this an accurate representation of this being, and does this being actually exist?

A: Yes. 232

Q: *(L)* Well, that's friendly. *(SV)* 233
Which one is that? [Looks at drawing.] Oooh, I don't want to see him... *(L)* Now, this one here... *(T)* Oh, lightning-bolt man! *(L)* Does this one actually exist? This 'mutative clone form'?

A: Yes. 234

Q: *(L)* OK, this one here, this little 235
Tah-hay being...

A: Yes. 236

Q: *(T)* ET! *(L)* OK, they said he was 237
real? Yes. OK, now this one is a real pleasant-looking fellow [S'pth]...

A: Yes. Occupies Dulce base.[14] 238

Q: *(T)* Can we make it easy and just 239
ask if everything in the book is real? *(L)* No, because if there's anything, I want to put a note on it. [Reading:] "This is a cloned synthezoid form," in other words a cyber-genetic, "whose specific job is to act as controllers. They are plus or minus four feet tall." This is, I think, your standard gray. It's just that the drawing is kind of crappy-looking. *(T)* Wait, the face... the eyes are smaller on the thing but the face is a lot like the one in the *Autopsy* film. *(L)* This is a lot like what I had in my bedroom, only all swathed in black. OK, now, this is what they call a replica. [Reading:] "They are protosynthezoid form of human whose specific job is as a special outside agent.

[14] *High Strangeness* "Appendix"

Observation: Face and body change shape at will." This is like in the *X-Files* thing where the guy... the shape changer. Is this a correct concept? Is this basically a... I mean of course you have to draw them in an ambiguous way...

240 **A**: Close.

241 **Q**: *(L)* Is there anything you can tell us about this in particular? Any hint or clue?

242 **A**: ?

243 **Q**: *(L)* OK, we'd have to ask questions. OK, these are the servants from Zeta Reticuli One... *(T)* Are these the Men in Black?

244 **Q**: *(L)* No, remember, the Men in Black... *(T)* OK, just thought I'd check... *(L)* Just cross-checking here... *(T)* Terminator Model IV here... Mr. Liquid Metal. *(L)* OK, these servants from Zeta Reticuli One... this is another version of the one. I would also assume that these are the servants at the Dulce base?

245 **A**: Laura board.[15]

246 **Q**: *(L)* I'm assuming that this is another version of the ones that occupy the Dulce base. Is that correct?

247 **A**: No.

248 **Q**: *(L)* What are these guys?[16]

249 **A**: Floaters.

250 **Q**: *(L)* OK, these are floaters. Let me just comment so that... *(T)* Floaters? As in how floaters? *(L)* I would say it was like somebody in a job... *(T)* Trouble shooters, they go from place to place... *(L)* OK, these are real friendly looking. .. I love these guys! *(T)* Are those the 'Blues'? *(L)* The THROOB! *(T)* Are these the little short stubby blues that Whitley was into? *(L)* Plus or minus four feet tall... Yeah, I think so. It says here: "They are originally from the Draco Constellation and their job is to complete research. They are plus or minus four feet tall." Are these accurately represented here, both in terms and drawing?

A: Yes. 251

Q: *(T)* Are these the ones that Whitley 252
Strieber has seen?

A: Maybe. 253

Q: *(L)* OK, now, the degenerative clone 254
form, which is the bottom image – is this also an accurate representation?

A: Close. 255

Q: *(L)* What is the color of the skin of 256
these friendly-looking little guys?

A: Variable. 257

Q: *(L)* OK, I think there may be one 258
more... Ha, ha! Are you guys ready for this one? This is a Cassiopaean! *(T)* Well, I don't think that's a Cassiopaean! *(J)* Let me see... Oh, lovely! *(T)* Cassiopaea, I couldn't find a star called Cassiopaea... *(L)* There isn't. *(T)* Well, I know that. *(L)* Well, he's being sarcastic. OK, this is one called "a race of insectoids from Cassiopaea, whose specific job is genetic research." Is this an accurate description and drawing of this critter?

A: Yes. 259

Q: *(T)* Is Cassiopeia a star? *(L)* No. 260
(T) What is Cassiopeia? *(L)* It's a constellation. *(T)* I know it's a constel-

[15] Laura was holding book and did not have her fingers on the planchette.
[16] *High Strangeness* "Appendix"

lation, but they say they're from Cassiopeia. You can't be from Cassiopeia... *(L)* Oh, right, that's right. What star in Cassiopeia?

261 **A**: Region.

262 **Q**: *(L)* It's in the Cassiopeia region. Is there any star in particular that you would identify as their home star? They have to have a planet with a home star somewhere, so where is their home star?

263 **A**: No.

264 **Q**: *(L)* They don't have to have a home planet? In other words, they could be riding the Wave? *(SV)* Well, are they coming here? *(L)* Are these guys coming here?

265 **A**: All are already.

266 **Q**: *(L)* OK, hang on... *(T)* What about the one below? What's the one below? *(L)* Well, that's just a biological android. "The Nordics and Oranges normally use inorganic, high-tech servants." Is this an accurate representation of an inorganic, high-tech...

267 **A**: Yes.

268 **Q**: *(T)* What are all the hieroglyphics? *(L)* It's supposed to be one of their alien languages. What does this business say here?

269 **A**: Scrambled.

270 **Q**: *(L)* It's scrambled. So it's a combination of the various different languages they have back there.

271 **A**: Yes.

272 **Q**: *(L)* Somebody just put the various different symbols together, because it looks like two or three different languages. OK, well, that answered those questions. *(SV)* Laura, are you going to get a copy of that for us? *(L)* Yes, I'll make copies for all of you. *(SV)* That's so if I meet one of those guys in my dreams, I won't get scared... Well, I won't be *as* scared! *(J)* Speaking of being scared...

(TK) Doesn't seem to me like there's too much to worry about... *(T)* It's all supposed to be fun! *(L)* Yeah, they've told us it would be ecstasy dealing with it. *(T)* This is fun! It's a challenge, and we're supposed to enjoy this as the challenge that it is. *(TK)* Seems to me it's something you've got to take as it comes, and deal with it! *(T)* That's about it. *(J)* Roll with the punches.

A: Yes. 273

Q: *(J)* Speaking of being scared, I've 274 had a couple more situations where I wake up screaming and have no idea why. Any input to that? I've had that happen about two or three times.

A: Discover. 275

Q: *(L)* You've got to do hypnosis. 276 They've been saying that a lot lately. That's what they told Nova M over and over again... Discover, discover, discover. Did she tell you anything about the session? *(T)* The session? No. *(TK)* Are we asking all the wrong questions here? *(J)* Naaah!

A: There are no such. 277

Q: *(J)* There are no wrong questions. 278 *(L)* I guess whatever occurs to you to ask, as you wind your way around through the maze, trying to get to the heart of it, is appropriate. I mean, what occurs to you to ask? *(J)* It's all knowledge... *(T)* Whatever comes to you is something you should ask. *(L)* Once you read the entire transcripts... Now, I really shouldn't have given it to you the way I did. I should have edited out all diddles. Because you could have gotten to the meat of it. But, you've got to go through some of that because... *(J)* It's all part of the learning process. Even the garbage is. *(L)* Yeah, because, you know, there'll be two pages of somebody asking questions about their own personal stuff, and then all of a sudden there'll come three or four paragraphs of such tremendous impact that you just kind of go, "Oh, my god"... *(T)* As you read through the personal stuff, there's information there, too... *(L)* There's stuff buried there, too... *(T)* There's all kinds of stuff in there... *(J)* I don't think you can edit it out, Laura, to be honest with you... I think Andrew was right, just leave it right as it is.

(TK) But what can... are there questions you can ask, and answers you can get that will make a difference one way or the other? *(J)* Just keep asking, I guess. *(T)* Well, really, what we end up doing is just shooting a lot of different questions out until we get something where we're getting answers, and then we work on it for a while, until we can 't handle it anymore... *(L)* Sometimes, we don't even know what's going to open a door. Some of the most innocuous questions have opened the door to some of the most incredible information which has blown us away.

279 **A**: Ask.

280 **Q**: *(L)* So ask. *(T)* Go ahead, there's no such thing as a wrong question. The thing is, we all ask questions that turn out to be silly. We all get embarrassed, so don't worry about it. They handle that real well for us.

(TK) I don't know, this seems like... what difference does it really make, knowing some of this stuff? *(J)* Because just being aware of it... *(TK)* Being aware, yeah, OK, I can understand. *(J)* Sometimes, that's all there is... *(L)* Also, they've told us, that the more knowledge we actually accumulate, it actually changes your frequency and adds volume and bulk and power and force to who and what you are, at a fundamental level. Not physically, but psychically. In other words, when you come up to some... if you are a person who's full of knowledge, I mean, what does it say in the Bible? "My people perish for a lack of knowledge..." and it says, "you shall know the truth, and the truth shall set you free." And the more knowledge you have, the bigger you are, in a cosmic and psychic sense, the more powerful you are, and...

A: Suggest more questions about the goings on at underground facilities. Jan and Terry were visitors involuntary when went to Albuquerque and Las Vegas! 281

Q: *(J)* Oh, really! *(T)* Read it back, I lost it after visitors. *(L)* You were in an underground base? *(T)* We were in a front door of an underground base. We were in Carlsbad Caverns, and I know that there's a government facility at the other end of it, and they won't talk about it. *(J)* Is that what they mean? *(T)* You're talking about Carlsbad? 282

A: Abducted. 283

Q: *(T)* When we were in Albuquerque?[17] 284

A: Yes. 285

[17] *High Strangeness* 9

286 **Q**: *(J)* And Las Vegas? *(T)* When we were in Las Vegas, also?

287 **A**: Met alien there.

288 **Q**: *(L)* Oh, you met an alien when you were in Las Vegas! *(J)* Does that have anything to do with the fact that the pictures didn't come out from our wedding?

289 **A**: Barfly.

290 **Q**: *(T)* Ohhhhh... *(J)* I know exactly what you are talking about.

291 **A**: Disguised humanoid gray species four. Rigelian. Orion union STS.

292 **Q**: *(T)* Why did he talk to us? Why did he approach us? I know exactly...

293 **A**: Spying on you and aural frequency reading, had you not been as strong, would have suffered permanent abduction because of your studies.

294 **Q**: *(L)* Now, right there is a point. Everybody take note of this. What is there about strength that makes one inaccessible to permanent abduction?

295 **A**: Strength is of character, i.e. if STO candidate, not likely to be victim.

296 **Q**: *(L)* Not likely to be victim... OK, but what.. *(T)* STO candidate... *(L)* I know, but that's... it says when... well, what is it that makes a person... We know that it means being an STO candidate, but what is the thing inside one that stops them... I mean, is this something that is a core ingredient of certain human beings? Is this like something inside them that blocks this manipulation and victimization?

297 **A**: Soul pattern.

Q: *(L)* So in other words, there is some- 298
thing about us, or within us, that literally they cannot touch or harm. Is that correct?

A: Basically, but difficult to facilitate. 299

Q: *(L)* OK, in other words, this is 300
something that is in us, that creates an inherent barrier, but not necessarily something that we can, at this level of density, reach in, grab out as a weapon, and wave around, as in facilitate?

A: Can, but intricate to do consciously. 301

Q: *(L)* Is this some quality or ability 302
that we can work at? I don't think meditation is the answer, this is something that I've come to think... Is this a state of focused awareness, whole-body awareness, internal and external, basically whole-body awareness... *(J)* Going with instinct...

A: Helpful. 303

Q: *(L)* Is there something we can do 304
to develop this to the highest degree possible, while in these bodies, in this density?

A: Wait for 4. 305

Q: *(L)* Wait for 4? 4th density? 306

A: Yes. 307

Q: *(T)* We can't develop it ourselves, 308
but if we... *(J)* We can start the process... *(T)* It's a case of not developing it, it's a case of that, if you can do it, it does it all by itself, you don't think about it... *(L)* It's an innate thing... *(T)* It's a do, it's an involuntary, it's there, it works when it needs to work. Is this the idea?

[18] Briefly, Terry related the story where he and Jan met the barfly at Vegas World, after having gone downtown to get their marriage license. They had taken a taxi

309 **A**: Network western experiences for learning purposes please. Knowledge is protection.[18]

310 **Q**: *(T)* Before we get too far into this, I want to ask them where we were taken. Because after that, as far as I know, nothing else happened. We just went on about our business, and we didn't see him again... *(L)* In this story that Terry has just recounted, what instant represents the turning point of resistance?

311 **A**: The statement.

312 **Q**: *(L)* What statement? *(T)* "We don't have a problem, here, do we?! Everything's cool, everything's OK! I'll buy you a beer?"

313 **A**: Yes.

314 **Q**: *(T)* Because that's when he got confused... *(J)* You totally nullified the... *(SV)* Yeah, from the glaring and staring at each other... *(T)* He was escalating this to a point, and I don't know, it just came to me that the best way to do this was to just stop it right there...

315 **A**: Grays and their associates are thrown off by energy flow diversions or thought pattern interruptions.

316 **Q**: *(SV)* That's exactly what they said in *Matrix I*! *(T)* Another thing that comes to mind while I'm thinking about it: before it turned ugly, he was leading up to going someplace. *(J)* Very vaguely, but yes. *(T)* He was leading up toward, "We ought to get together and go someplace." I think that's when I really shut the whole thing off. *(L)* OK, now, in this episode where Terry and Jan were taken to an underground base, can you identify the location of the underground facility?

A: Socorro, NM. 317

Q: *(J)* We were in Socorro, weren't 318 we? *(T)* We went through Socorro... We stopped at the geological school. *(L)* OK, what was done to them when they were in this underground facility?

A: Quick exam. 319

Q: *(T)* Did we pass? I'm not good on 320 quick exams! Which of the nights in Albuquerque was it we were taken?

A: Second. 321

Q: *(T)* We got there Friday afternoon, 322 that would have been Saturday... *(L)* Who was in charge of this base, this facility? What group?

A: Orion Union STS. 323

Q: *(T)* Why did they take us? I know, 324 a quick exam, but why? Because we happened to be there, and we were

to City Hall, and foolishly decided to walk back to the Strip, in 116-degree weather. They made it as far south as Vegas World, and stopped at the bar inside to cool off. Jan was close to heat prostration, and the barmaid gave her glasses of iced water and an iced towel to put on her neck. They were getting ready to go back out and hail a cab back to Bally's, when they were approached by the 'Barfly', who started asking all sorts of personal questions, and seemed to be acting drunk when he wasn't really intoxicated. He became belligerent when Terry refused to show him his Florida driver's license, but switched to disorientation when Terry made the statement, "We don't have a problem, here, do we?! Everything's cool, everything's OK! I'll buy you a beer?", while staring the guy down and putting the force of his personality behind the question/statement.

close by? *(L)* They said a minute ago because of your studies. *(T)* Well, they could have taken us in Florida.

325 **A**: Yes.

326 **Q**: *(L)* They said because of your studies. Well, you happened to be near a base, I guess. Not everybody goes to these bases, you know, these underground facilities. They get taken to ships.... *(T)* Did we get taken to the base because we happened to be close by at the time when they grabbed us? Was it an opportunity for them?

327 **A**: Close.

328 **Q**: *(T)* Did they know we were coming out there?

329 **A**: Yes.

330 **Q**: *(T)* Why did they follow up with a spy afterwards?

331 **A**: Test.

332 **Q**: *(T)* What kind of test? *(J)* I think we passed... *(L)* I think that if you'd failed, they said a minute ago, you'd have been permanently abducted.

333 **A**: Already answered.

334 **Q**: *(L)* It's an aural reading... read the section back about aural reading... *(T)* You mean that what they were looking at was to see whether we were STS or STO?

335 **A**: Partly.

336 **Q**: *(L)* And if they had been permanently abducted at that point in time, what would have happened to them?

337 **A**: Body part utilization.

338 **Q**: *(T)* You mean I'd be part of some – body? *(TK)* Basically, what that means is that you wouldn't have been any good to them as a person, but the parts would have been all right. *(T)* Well, if they would have taken us and utilized us as body parts, but they didn't take us... *(J)* They couldn't take us because you were strong... *(T)* So they took us... what was the purpose of the examination beforehand? I know, quick exam. Was it to find out whether our body parts were good? I'm trying to make... get the connection between the... because there was no reason to... If they had taken us... *(L)* If they had taken you, why didn't they keep you?

339 **A**: Too complex to explain in this forum.

340 **Q**: *(L)* In other words, we're really getting tired here. I do have an idea about that. Is there not something internal that prevents them from going too far during an abduction, i.e. like maybe, if you want to call it that, a guardian angel or protective energy, and then they try to put an implant in, and then create a situation where they can bypass that... Oh, I know! Is this what Michael Topper was writing about in his article, 'Channels and the Positive/Negative', where he talks about the 'obedience factor' of the STS? If they can get you to obey something, you have given your permission.

341 **A**: Close.

342 **Q**: *(L)* This article is so... OK, I think we're going to close up for tonight, because we're so whipped... are you whipped? *(F)* Well, I'm tired, yeah. *(L)* OK. Is there anything you want to say to anyone before we close up the shop for tonight? Is there any message for Tom, who is getting ready to go back up North tomorrow? Or for any of us in general?

343 **A**: No.

344 **Q**: *(L)* Anything you want to ask before

we go? OK, then, we'll say goodnight, and we thank you for being with us.

A: Good-bye. 345

End of Session

October 21, 1995

In this session we discuss *Alien Autopsy: Fact of Fiction.* Just for the record:

> In 1995 London businessman Ray Santilli launched the alien autopsy film on TV and video around the world to a storm of controversy. Major TV networks including Fox in the USA and Channel 4 in the UK featured the film in major documentaries. To say it caused a sensation is quite an understatement.
>
> Ray Santilli maintained then, as he still does now, that he obtained the film while on a trip to Cleveland, Ohio, in the summer of 1992. This trip was to try and secure old film clips of the early rock 'n' roll stars and he did indeed purchase the very first film of the then unknown Elvis Presley. According to Santilli, the man he bought the Elvis footage from had previously been a cameraman for the United States military and in 1947 he had been sent to Roswell, New Mexico, to film the crash of a UFO. This he did, but not only that, he also filmed the autopsy of the occupants of the crashed flying saucer. A few canisters of film were held back for special processing but because of a military blunder at the time, these were never collected. Forty-seven years later, this now elderly gentleman sold these canisters of film to Ray Santilli. The rest as they say is history. (*Alien Autopsy Inquest* by Phillip Mantle, 10 June 2007)

I had been invited over to Giles Hamilton's house near Orlando to watch this film that was being provided for a pre-release screening by Hilliard P (the Coral Castle guy mentioned previously). That is, I saw it *before* it was shown on television or made available on video. I've always wondered why and how Hilliard had a copy of this video before anybody else did and that, of course, led to questions in my mind about him in connection with the autopsy film. He fit the description of the elusive cameraman to a 'T', except for his location, which was Orlando as opposed to Cleveland, and he made a number of remarks to me alone during the screening that gave me serious pause; these comments could only have been made by someone who had been there, though he was certainly cagey about it and never claimed or admitted to being the autopsy cameraman. Hilliard's cryptic remarks to me at various times, his friendship with Leedskalnin, the fact that he had a copy of the *Alien Autopsy* video long before it was released, all raise interesting questions about Hilliard and his possible involvement in secret government/military affairs. How he died – which will be recounted later when we arrive at that point in time – is also mysterious.

Participants: 'Frank', Laura, Susan V, LM[1]

1 **Q**: *(L)* Hello.

2 **A**: Hello.

3 **Q**: *(L)* Who do we have with us this evening?

4 **A**: Yzgorra.

5 **Q**: *(L)* And where are you from, Yzgorra?

6 **A**: Cassiopaea.

7 **Q**: *(SV)* How do you pronounce that name? *(L)* Wy-za-gorra? Is that correct, would you pronounce the 'Y' as an 'I'?

8 **A**: Yes.

9 **Q**: *(L)* OK, we would like to ask our questions.

10 **A**: Remember, Cassiopaea is our transmission point, not our home.

11 **Q**: *(L)* OK, we remember. We were talking just a few minutes ago about the symbol that appeared that was similar to a crop circle on LM's driveway, and we would like to know if you can access for us the source of that symbol. Who put that symbol there?

12 **A**: Grey alien species number 4.

Q: *(LM)* What made them come to my house? 13

A: Complex. 14

Q: *(L)* Can you just give a little indication? We won't go into it too deeply, but, just a little indication? 15

A: No. 16

Q: *(L)* Is there some significance to this that we should ask it at a later time? 17

A: Up to you. 18

Q: *(L)* OK, why can't we know this? 19

A: Too complicated for receptors. 20

Q: *(L)* OK, was this sign put there, just in a general sense, as a wake-up call to LM? 21

A: No. 22

Q: *(L)* Was it put there as a warning? 23

A: No. 24

Q: *(L)* Did the putting of it there manifest a certain energy at that location? 25

A: Maybe. 26

Q: *(L)* Did the putting of that sign there, or the interaction of that event, cause changes in his life? Or stimulate changes? 27

A: Vague. 28

[1]My husband at that time.

29 **Q**: *(L)* Well, let me put it this way, were the changes in his life shortly after that, as a result of that interaction?

30 **A**: Interrelated, not causative.

31 **Q**: *(L)* OK, was anybody abducted at that time?

32 **A**: Open.

33 **Q**: *(L)* OK, they're not going to tell us any more about it. *(LM)* What does 'open' mean? *(L)* That they're not going to tell us any more about it. *(LM)* Why? *(SV)* It's too complicated... *(L)* It's either too complicated, or it's something you can't hear right now because it would violate your free will to know it in advance. *(LM)* Well, if it was either, some of it was, they'd say yes or no. See what I'm saying? *(L)* It's not that simplistic. OK, we want to talk about the... Well, let me ask this: Am I right in the feeling that I have that living out in that area was for me, how do I put it, a very transformative experience?

34 **A**: Not because of locator.

35 **Q**: *(L)* Well, I have very often had feelings that there were, like, some real unpleasant spirits in that area; hanging around there. Am I correct in that? Real unpleasant energies...

36 **A**: Do you suppose said entities are restricted by 3rd density constraints.

37 **Q**: *(L)* Well, no, so what does that mean?

38 **A**: Discover.

39 **Q**: *(L)* OK, are you saying that such entities as I felt were present there may not have been just specifically located there, but it was possible for them to be anywhere?

A: Maybe. 40

Q: *(SV)* That's probably what the 41
Lizzies thought about us! *(L)* Well, I want to check that out. They'd probably just stomp us. *(SV)* Well, the Nephilim do...

[Break for coffee]

Q: *(L)* We're back. I want to talk 42
about the Roswell video that we've all watched. Now Terry continues to insist that it was not Roswell, that there's something... He just can't get into it. I would like to know if that video is of alien beings that were retrieved from the crash of Roswell.

A: Yes. 43

Q: *(L)* OK. Why did so many people re- 44
port seeing aliens that had only four fingers and toes, you know, like the standard Grays?

A: Multiple subjects.[2] 45

A: OK, so there was more than one 46
type of alien on that one craft?

A: Yes. 47

Q: *(L)* OK, the story that came from 48
the camera man who shot the video was that there were these four beings. One was dead, and three were standing outside the craft, crying and clutching boxes to their chests. Is this an accurate...

A: Yes. 49

Q: *(L)* What were those boxes? 50

A: Storage of translation matrix group 51
to individual, emotion stabilization units.

Q: *(L)* What is a translation matrix? 52

[2] *The Wave* 21

53 **A**: Translates foreign thought patterns, not needed except in emergency loss of electromagnetic grid wave.

54 **Q**: *(L)* OK, what is an emotion stabilization unit used for?

55 **A**: Variety of uses, mostly for survival by neutralizing thoughts of harm by emotionally charged beings, not accustomed to shocking turn of events.

56 **Q**: *(L)* Were the harmful thoughts that they were designed to neutralize, thoughts of other beings?

57 **A**: Yes.

58 **Q**: *(L)* Well, they didn't work very well, did they?

59 **A**: Did not have chance to activate.

60 **Q**: *(L)* OK, so if they had had the opportunity to activate these boxes, they would have been more or less able to extricate themselves from this unpleasant situation?

61 **A**: Not extricate, lessen negative aspects.

62 **Q**: *(L)* OK, how many beings were in this particular craft that crashed?

63 **A**: 21.

64 **Q**: *(L)* How come the reports say there were only four?

65 **A**: Reports are suppressed and fragmented, as far fewer individuals witnessed interior of craft!!

66 **Q**: *(L)* OK, was this two crafts striking each other, or was it one craft malfunctioning?

67 **A**: Two.

68 **Q**: *(L)* OK, it was two craft hitting each other? Is that correct?

A: No. 69

Q: *(L)* There were two complete craft 70
that came down?

A: Bouncing off ionized waves between 71
two craft traveling in tandem.

Q: *(L)* OK, was one of these craft to- 72
tally destroyed?

A: Yes. 73

Q: *(L)* And all the beings in the one 74
that was totally destroyed were incinerated, or blown to bits. Is that correct?

A: Close. 75

Q: *(L)* Did some of them eject? 76

A: 4th density. 77

Q: *(L)* OK, they knew it was coming 78
and they went into 4th density?

A: No. 79

Q: *(L)* They were 4th density beings, 80
and therefore when they blew to bits, they disappeared. Is that it?

A: Close. 81

Q: *(L)* OK, now of the 21 that were 82
in the craft that was captured, so to speak, there were four outside the craft when it was approached. Is that correct?

A: Yes. 83

Q: *(L)* Then that would mean that 84
there were 17 inside... Of these 21 beings, how many were Grays, the standard grey Lizzie probe–type being?

A: Most. 85

Q: *(L)* Were there other kinds of beings 86
in there?[3]

A: Human. 87

[3] *The Wave* 21

88 **Q**: *(L)* There was one human in there also?

89 **A**: 5.

90 **Q**: *(L)* There were 5 humans inside? So we have... *(LM)* Why? *(L)* Why were those humans in the craft?

91 **A**: Retrieval and study specimens, two bigfoot types.

92 **Q**: *(L)* Does that mean that the humans that they had in there were retrieval and study specimens, or otherwise known as abductees?

93 **A**: Deceased.

94 **Q**: *(L)* Oh, they were dead humans. Wonderful. Did they abduct them dead? Or did they abduct them alive?

95 **A**: No.

96 **Q**: *(L)* Did they abduct them alive and then kill them?

97 **A**: No.

98 **Q**: *(L)* Were they dead as a result of the crash?

99 **A**: No.

100 **Q**: *(L)* Well, then, what's the story here, I mean, what other choices do I have?

101 **A**: Retrieved.

102 **Q**: *(L)* Ohh, these were beings that had been retrieved at death and remolecularized? Is that what you are referring to – what we discussed before?

103 **A**: 3rd density.

104 **Q**: *(L)* Were they remolecularized in 3rd density? Is that what you are saying?

105 **A**: Retrieved in 3rd density.

Q: *(L)* OK, tell me once again what 106
it means for a being, a human, to be retrieved.

A: Picked up after expiration. 107

Q: *(L)* OK, so they picked up dead bod- 108
ies, is that it?

A: Yes. 109

Q: *(LM)* Why? *(L)* To study them. 110
OK, did they plan to reanimate these corpses?

A: Open. 111

Q: *(L)* Do they ever pick up dead bod- 112
ies, you know, right after, and reanimate them?[4]

A: Yes. 113

Q: *(L)* When they pick them up and re- 114
animate them, do they reanimate them with the souls that left them? Do they like, catch the soul and put it back in?

A: No. 115

Q: *(L)* When they reanimate them, 116
do they reanimate them with an alien soul?

A: Multiple possibilities. 117

Q: *(L)* If they reanimate them, is it pos- 118
sible to reanimate them with no soul?

A: Yes. 119

Q: *(L)* OK, when they reanimate them 120
with no soul, do they have kind of like a zombie-like situation?

A: No. 121

Q: *(L)* Well, could you give us a little 122
more information on this particular aspect? If they reanimate them with no soul, what is the animating force or energy?

A: Indistinguishable from other hu- 123
mans.

[4] *The Wave* 21

124 **Q**: *(L)* They're indistinguishable from other humans. *(LM)* How is that possible?

125 **A**: Technology makes all things possible!!!

126 **Q**: *(L)* Of course, you are talking about 4th density technology?

127 **A**: Yes.

128 **Q**: *(L)* Now, a reanimated corpse that has been animated by infusion of some form of an energy pattern... *(SV)* Is it 'chi' energy, maybe? *(L)* What if the reanimated corpse dies again? I mean, you have got to understand here, that we perceive the soul as being the animating force of the physical body, and when the soul is gone, the body dies. Is that correct?

129 **A**: You are making assumptions based on limited data.

130 **Q**: *(L)* OK, well, will you expand my database by telling me how a corpse can be reanimated if not done by a... if not with a soul?

131 **A**: Complex technology, using electronic bio-generation frequency matching, combined with extremely high frequency radio beacon transmitters for tracking and control of all functions, including thought pattern mimic and emotional frequency vibrational rate modulation!!!!

132 **Q**: *(L)* If they're doing this, does it make the physical body...

133 **A**: Yes.

134 **Q**: *(L)* The blood, the heartbeat and everything...

135 **A**: All functions, including cellular, duplicated.

Q: *(SV)* What about the aura? *(L)* 136
Would a being such as this still have an aura?

A: Projected. 137

Q: *(L)* OK, that would be projected, 138
along with all of the frequencies, and everything else. Now... *(SV)* Are there a lot of dead people walking around?

A: This is method used for subjects dis- 139
cussed in "Matrix Material" instead of "Robots", as suggested.

Q: *(L)* Is there any way that a normal 140
person would be able to identify such a being?

A: No. 141

Q: *(L)* Approximately how many of 142
this type of being are walking around on our planet, acting like normal people?

A: 2,000,000. 143

Q: *(L)* Approximately 2 million? 144

A: Yes. 145

Q: *(L)* OK... 146

A: You, Laura, have come in contact 147
with 7 of them!

Q: *(L)* Who are they? 148

A: Discover. 149

Q: *(L)* Can you give me a clue? Has it 150
been within the last... *(SV)* Am I one of them? [Laughter] Well, you never know! *(L)* Are any of us one of them?

A: Discover. 151

Q: *(SV)* Ask if you've done spirit re- 152
lease on any of these seven? *(L)* Has this contact happened within the past year?

A: Open. 153

154 **Q**: *(L)* Are you going to tell me anything about it at all? If there is any question I could ask to get any information concerning this, consider it asked.

155 **A**: Who is nutritionist?

156 **Q**: *(SV)* Who do you know that's a nutritionist? Isn't she a nutritionist, the one that wrote that book? *(L)* Do you mean Susan S?

157 **A**: Yes.

158 **Q**: *(LM)* I find that hard to believe. *(F)* Is Susan S a robot? *(LM)* When did she die?

159 **A**: Open. All it takes is a "hospital visit."[5]

160 **Q**: *(LM)* Then what happens? *(SV)* All what takes? *(LM)* It doesn't make sense. *(L)* Maybe there's a death certificate for her...

161 **A**: Yes it does.

162 **Q**: *(L)* Does this mean if one goes into a hospital for surgery, that it's possible for them to die and be reanimated in this manner? Without anybody being aware of what happened?

163 **A**: Yes.

164 **Q**: *(LM)* Why? *(L)* Well, we know why, because they're creating a force, you know, putting it in place all over the planet so they can take over... We already know that! Is that correct?

165 **A**: Open.

166 **Q**: *(LM)* What's open mean? *(L)* Open means that's not absolutely determined yet, at this time, that's not something that they're just... it could be, yes. So, you're saying that Susan S was one of these robotoids – is that what you're saying?

A: We gave you one for your own knowledge and protection, but cannot give you others at this juncture.[6] 167

Q: *(L)* Is it up to me to figure out what characteristics these individuals have, in order to...[7] 168

A: Based upon data given, yes. 169

Q: *(L)* OK, is one of the – I mean, I'm clicking through mental data files right now – one of the characteristics I think, that these kind of individuals might have, since they have this projected emotional frequency, would be a repeating emotional pattern, that they just simply, in spite of seeming intelligence, do not seem to learn from anything; that it just repeats over and over again, is that a clue? 170

A: Yes. 171

Q: *(SV)* Wait a minute, was that her idea, that we should eat like the monkeys do? *(L)* Yes. *(SV)* And then you've read about... saw the Jane Goodall film that talked about the fact that monkeys like to eat... *(L)* Other monkeys, yes. *(SV)* And what did she say when you told her about that? *(L)* She said, "Well, I'll just say:" and she changed the entire paragraph to read: "That in the wild, primates eat primarily vegetation with some amounts of protein," and no specification as to where the protein came 172

[5] *The Wave* 21. To my knowledge, Susan S had been hospitalized for surgery at least twice.

[6] Does this mean they can be given at another time, after a particular, destined interaction takes place?

[7] *The Wave* 46

from. That's really stretching it. *(SV)* She should have just left it out... *(LM)* That doesn't make any sense... *(L)* Now, there are some strange things about her, I'll have to admit that. OK, then, this same inability to get a clue about what's going on... OK, that's a clue, right there. Is there any kind of instinctual sensation that one would get about these types of individuals?

173 **A**: Bland.

174 **Q**: *(L)* That they're bland in some way? Is that it, that these individuals are bland individuals?

175 **A**: Spend inordinate amounts of "time" in solitude.

176 **Q**: *(L)* Well, that means Frank's one! Frank's kind of bland! And he spends a lot of time in solitude. *(SV)* A lot of people do! *(L)* So, is Frank one?

177 **A**: No.

178 **Q**: *(LM)* So, if you put a lead shield up around him, he'd collapse! *(L)* We're teasing you, Frank! I didn't mean it! *(SV)* He's not bland, though! Frank's anything but bland! *(L)* Is my husband one?

179 **A**: No.

180 **Q**: *(SV)* Am I one? *(L)* Of course not! Don't be silly! Now, let's stop a second. Now, we had several questions, and one of the questions was...

181 **A**: Bland is not universal in this situation, just a clue for you to identify individual.

182 **Q**: *(L)* OK, one is a nutritionist, one is very bland. Is that what we're getting at?[8]

A: No. 183

Q: *(L)* OK, bland is just part of it. 184

A: Not key component, more likely to 185
be spreading of disinformation.[9]

Q: OK, is John W one? 186

A: Open. 187

Q: *(L)* Well, John W has got some stuff, 188
because, I tell you what, you tell him something logically, it's almost like he's got a preset program that runs, and the minute you get to the point where you almost might possibly think he can get the connection because your evidence and logic are overwhelming... then it just shuts down and he repeats the program. And it just amazes me that people can be that way. OK, have we... I guess you're not going to tell us any more about this. Do these beings know what they are?

A: Not conscious beings! 189

Q: *(L)* They're not conscious beings, 190
so, they just react to you as though they are being remote controlled. *(SV)* So, if you told one of them what they were...

A: Are being remote controlled. 191

Q: *(L)* OK, do we have any more ques- 192
tions on this subject? *(SV)* So, if you told one of them what they were, they'd agree with you? *(L)* No, they'd probably disagree with you. *(SV)* Yes, being remote controlled... *(L)* Whoever is in charge would not want you to know it, so they'd naturally deny it vehemently. *(SV)* Then they'd probably come and get you... *(L)* Yes, no doubt about that. Now, what is the purpose

[8] *The Wave* 46
[9] *The Wave* 21

of putting 2 million of these kind of critters on the planet? Can you give us a clue?

193 **A**: Wait and see.

194 **Q**: *(L)* Why is Terry so determined to criticize or break down or discredit in one way or another this autopsy video?

195 **A**: Serving emotional agenda.

196 **Q**: *(L)* And what is his emotional agenda in this case?

197 **A**: Supports strongly held beliefs.

198 **Q**: *(L)* OK, and these strongly held belief are that what... What are these strongly held beliefs that he has that he's trying to support this way?

199 **A**: Not important.

200 **Q**: *(L)* OK, so Terry's beliefs are not important to this issue. I want to ask one insert question here before we go on to other things here. I have a book called *Freemasonry and the Ancient Egyptians*, it's got a black cover. I can't find it anywhere. I want to know, did I lend it out to someone?

201 **A**: Discover.

202 **Q**: *(L)* I'm trying to, and I can't; my mind, my memory is just shot since that accident. I'm telling you, I can't hold on to some things that I just used to really be able to hang on to. Can you tell me, can you give me some kind of indication where this book might be found?

203 **A**: You can find it.

204 **Q**: *(L)* I can find it – in other words, it's in my house somewhere?

A: We do not help you learn by "leading" by the hand, book is easily accessible. 205

Q: *(L)* OK, so, it's around someplace. *(SV)* Maybe it's in your room. Maybe the kids have it. *(L)* I cleaned my room today. *(SV)* Maybe one of the kids have it. *(L)* It may be in my room. I bet I know where it is. It's under my dresser, and I'll look for it later.[10] OK, where is the Ark of the Covenant currently located? 206

A: Alternative 3.[11] 207

Q: *(L)* Alternative 3 is the plan to take all the people, all the smart guys, all the elite, off the planet and leave everybody else here to blow up, isn't it? 208

A: Maybe. 209

Q: *(L)* Where is it currently located? 210

A: Maybe not. Discover. 211

Q: *(L)* We're trying to discover through our interaction with you! How else can we discover something as obscure as this? I mean, that's a pretty darned obscure question, I would think. *(SV)* Who's in charge of Alternative 3, Laura? *(L)* That's too complicated.... *(SV)* Well, maybe they have it, whoever's in charge of it. *(L)* Well, are you going to tell us anything about it? 212

A: Study Alternative 3 to find answer! 213

Q: *(L)* OK, the *Matrix* material says that Henry Kissinger is the current head of MJ-12. Is this correct? 214

A: No. 215

Q: *(L)* Is he just a red herring, so to speak? 216

[10] My daughter had borrowed without mention. When I started asking for help to find it, it was returned.

[11] *The Wave* 22, 57

217 **A**: Yes. MJ12 is no longer MJ12.

218 **Q**: *(L)* What is MJ-12 now known as?

219 **A**: Institute of Higher Learning.

220 **Q**: *(L)* Are you talking about Brookings Lab, or Brookhaven?

221 **A**: Not really.

222 **Q**: *(L)* Is it a specific institute of higher learning?

223 **A**: Yes.[12]

224 **Q**: *(L)* The other night, when we were talking about the underground laboratories and the taking of the MIA and KIA individuals from WWII, that would seem to imply that the underground tunnel system and the alien activity that has been going on there has been going on a lot longer than since 1947. Is this correct?

225 **A**: Yes, but in much less intensive form.[13]

226 **Q**: *(L)* OK, it's gotten a lot more intensive since 1947 or thereabouts. Well, the thing that I want to know: is there any relationship between these underground laboratories and facilities and our cultural concept of hell?

227 **A**: Not in such a simplistic sense.

228 **Q**: *(L)* Well, I'm just curious as to whether the concept of hell being underground, where people were tortured and worked on and all kinds of miseries going on arose from some people who escaped from, or psychically intuited...

229 **A**: Link, but not unified.

230 **Q**: *(L)* Is there a hell?

231 **A**: No.

Q: *(L)* I'd like to know what the 232 prophecies that were given to the children at Fatima tell about the planet, the prophecies that are supposedly sealed up in possession of the Catholic Church.

A: False. 233

Q: *(L)* OK, then, they were false, so we 234 don't have to worry about them, in any event. Is that what you're saying?

A: Yes. 235

Q: *(L)* This underground tunnel that's 236 under my house – is this underground tunnel just a link, or is it occupied a great deal of the time?

A: Fragmented inquiry. 237

Q: *(L)* What I want to know, is this 238 tunnel that's under the house, which you have said is straight down under my house, is it a tunnel... is there like a laboratory under the house, or is it just a tunnel that's used for traveling from one facility to another?

A: Closer to latter. 239

Q: *(L)* Closer to a traveling point. *(SV)* 240 What about the base over at Anclote? *(L)* Does the tunnel under my house go to Anclote base?

A: Portal. 241

Q: *(L)* Which is a portal? The base at 242 Anclote?

A: Yes. 243

Q: *(L)* So that's just a portal. Is it a 244 large facility? You said it was a small facility. Is it just a portal, or is there a working facility there?

A: Portal. 245

[12] After studying Alternative 3, it appears that it is probably Princeton.

[13] *High Strangeness* "Appendix"

246 **Q**: *(L)* When I had Scarlett under hypnosis and I told her to travel along psychically and to read the minds of the aliens, and ask them, or inquire of them what the purpose of the implants were, the response she got was that it was like connecting a bunch of speakers, and once all the speakers were connected, then the stereo was turned on. What does this mean?

247 **A**: Unit group mind. Activation.

248 **Q**: *(L)* So what will happen when they, as she said, turn on the stereo?

249 **A**: Wait and See.

250 **Q**: *(L)* Well, earlier today I was thinking to myself that the way I feel right now must be very similar to the way animals in the forest feel on the opening day of hunting season. I mean, it's like every so many thousands of years, it's hunting season on planet Earth.

A: You are aware, 2nd density is not. 251

Q: *(L)* Is it still, in a sense, like hunting season? Are they just here... I mean, according to this *Matrix* material, they plan on decimating our entire planet, either with disease, or taking over their bodies... 252

A: Some is disinformation, and your energy is draining rapidly now, so must go for now. Goodbye. 253

End of Session

Returning to the topic of the *Autopsy* video, I debated this issue on the radio with Mike Lindemann and some other whacky woman whose name I don't remember. I think I won, and the next day, the DJ – 'Johnny Dollar' at WFLA Tampa – was fired without reason. Johnny himself thinks it is because he had me on the air and I was allowed to speak freely and openly and convincingly without him interfering or making disparaging comments. Tom French and Cherie Diez were in the broadcast booth with us and made a number of photographs to record the event. I would dearly love to have a copy of the broadcast but I'm sure it was destroyed.

Respecting the video itself, one of the points that sticks out for me is this: if the video was faked, it would be logical to fake a 'standard Gray alien'. After all, the fakers would want to try to convince people, right? So they would take the images and descriptions that were 'all the rage' and convert them into a convincing fraud.

But that isn't what we saw. This critter was *not* your standard Gray by any stretch of the imagination.

Another thing that stood out in my mind was the peeling of the scalp. Now, way back when I was in college, I was seriously considering pursuing a career in the biological sciences. I ended up taking classes where we dissected cats, pigs, and other critters. Having peeled a few scalps and sawed the top of a few skulls, when I watched that portion, I could literally feel it in my hands. I think anybody else who has dissected could too.

One of the stupidest arguments I heard against the video was that if such a critter had been picked up, why would an autopsy be done so secretively without calling in the best and most renowned experts in the field? The answer to this is obvious from the way the Air Force has handled the whole UFO/alien thing from the beginning: SECRECY. They could only let those people in on the secret that could be *controlled.* And that pretty much excludes most scientists and experts.

If an alien came into the hands of the PTB, what would their first impulse be? To hide it unless there was some advantage to themselves to reveal it.

OK, they have decided to keep the whole thing under wraps – who are they gonna get to do the autopsy? The best forensic guy in the country? Hardly likely: he can't be bought or kept quiet.

Who are they gonna get to film the business? The best cameraman in Hollywood? Hardly likely: he can't be kept quiet either.

So they are going to select those people who are 'insiders' or whom they can 'own'. That already suggests a very limited range of choices and abilities. One also has to consider the timing factor: who is available? The team that did this autopsy was hurriedly assembled and ad hoc, and so was the filming of it.

Finally, the story about the cameraman was obviously concocted to protect the source. Ray Santilli has not, to my knowledge, yielded on this point. I heard that some guys came along and claimed to have created it as a fraud, but they declined to give any evidence and their claims merit about as much attention as Doug and Dave doing thousands of crop circles.

So, basically, I'm about 99.99 percent convinced that it is real.

November 4, 1995

This is a terrific discussion of alien bases. Keep in mind while reading that this session was 6 years before September 11, 2001. A lot of things that we could not imagine have become realities since then, including the increasing control of populations and travel restrictions.

Participants: 'Frank', Laura, Susan V, Terry and Jan

1 **Q**: Hello.

2 **A**: Hello. Poojoy.

3 **Q**: *(L)* Is that your name?

4 **A**: No.

5 **Q**: *(L)* What is Poojoy? What does it relate to? Could you clarify that, please?

6 **A**: Must it relate?

7 **Q**: *(L)* What is your name?

8 **A**: Naphoron.

9 **Q**: *(L)* Can you identify anything about yourself?

10 **A**: From Cassiopaea, my dear! There is no longer a reason to fear the presence of others, the channel is too thoroughly grooved for corrupted influences to appear... though you still doubt!

11 **Q**: *(L)* I don't doubt, I just check. I have several questions here, and I don't necessarily want to do them in the order they are written down.

12 **A**: "Checking" equals doubt.

13 **Q**: *(L)* OK, got you! We have a few short questions before we get into anything deep and heavy. The first question I want to ask is: there's a rumor going around that the STS alien bases, as in Dulce, and all the other alien bases around out west, have been moved to Paris, Washington and Buenos Aires. Is this, in fact, true?

A: All angles of the story open to corruption, by disinformation. 14

Q: *(L)* Are the STS alien bases in the western part of the U.S. being moved somewhere? 15

A: We just told you!!! 16

Q: *(L)* In other words, what you said was no? 17

A: ! No. No. 18

Q: *(L)* "We just told you"... 19

A: That all angles are wrong!! 20

Q: *(L)* All angles. OK, in other words, no point in asking any other questions about it, because all angles are disinformation. Is that correct? 21

A: Wrong! 22

Q: *(L)* They're all wrong. *(T)* No... 23

A: No. 24

Q: *(T)* Your answer was all wrong. 25

A: Yes. 26

27 **Q**: *(T)* Read it back, what did they say? *(J)* "All angles of story open to corruption by disinformation." *(L)* That's kind of an ambiguous answer! *(J)* Yes, but it's true! *(T)* Well, you said that the story itself was wrong. That's not correct.

28 **A**: Search, don't jump over vital subject matter!!! Patience!!! This is not a relay race!

29 **Q**: *(L)* OK, in other words, all angles... *(T)* You said, "Are all the bases moving to Paris, Buenos Aires and Washington?" *(SV)* Maybe they're expanding... *(T)* They said, "All angles of story open to corruption, by disinformation." *(J)* So some of it is right. *(T)* So it's open to it, it's not actually corrupted, it's open to corruption. Then what did it say? *(J)* Then it said "we just told you."

30 **A**: Problem here involves assumptions.

31 **Q**: *(L)* OK, then, let me tell you the rest of the story. The story is that the Pleiadians are bombarding the underground bases with vibronics. I heard this from two sources.... The Konicovs and Roxanne C.

(T) Now, wait a minute. Who did you get it from first?

(L) Roxanne.

(T) Now, what did she tell you?

(L) Well, she told me that the Pleiadian ships were supposedly above the Earth bombarding these bases with these vibronics, which is a high-pitched sound, which is causing the shifts in the time and the ability of the STS aliens to function, and this was the humming sound that's being heard by the people out in New Mexico.

(T) Are these the Billy Meier Pleiadians?

(L) I guess so. They're the ones that are supposed to be the 'Good Guys', right?

(T) Well, that's open to....

(L) Right, exactly. And as a result of this, the STS, the 'Bad Guys', and the underground bases, are moving their operations under large cities, i.e. Paris, Washington and Buenos Aires, because then they will have a human shield, because the Pleiadians won't be bombarding these large cities full of people with this stuff. Now, that's the story.

(T) Well, that's an assumption on their part. *(J)* Who's to say that they won't? *(T)* RC told you. Where did she get that from?

(L) I think it's on the internet.

(J) Oh, good lord, right there! *(T)* OK, she may have gotten this from the internet. Or she also may have gotten this from that friend of hers, that Virgil A guy who she talks to all the time.[1]

(L) Yes.

(T) OK, now, what did the Konicovs say?

(L) Susy asked if I had heard that all the alien bases are being moved to Paris. That was as far as she knew.

(T) Like as if you would get a fax from the aliens saying, "We're moving, please forward our mail, we're having a garage sale."

(L) Well, she asked me to please ask about it.

(T) OK, now, where did she get that from?

[1] http://www.2012.com.au/VAcat.html

(L) One of the people, apparently it's one of these channel people that she publishes, called her and told her. This was the information that they had. So this may be coming from like, the Ashtar Command, you know, i.e. Lissa Royal or Yvonne Cole.

(T) So there's not really a chance that they got it from each other?

(L) No, because Roxanne has had no contact with the Konicovs.

(J) So, it is two separate sources...

(L) Right, widely separated; Michigan and Florida.

(F) Yes, but, if they're both on the internet...

(L) But Susy's not on the internet.

(T) Yes, but one of the other ones may be on the internet. If it came off the internet, the internet is subject to all kinds of questions... I don't trust a heck of a lot off the networks. I'm sorry, because I know what to expect out there. It's the same thing that happened to Linda Howe, who got hit in the face with it, and then acted really surprised, like: 'It couldn't happen here!' Well, I know why... nobody bothered to tell her that it's like that out there! OK, now, before we go any farther, you said, "Is this true, that they're moving them to these places?" Did one of them say these cities?

(L) Yes, Roxanne said the three cities, and Suzy named Paris.

(J) So, there's a hit on Paris. *(T)* Well, Paris would be a bad place for them to move it, because Paris is where people are bombing themselves crazy.

(L) Well, she says these Paris bombings are a result of the STS bases being moved there.

(T) Well, that means that the Pleiadians would go ahead and do it anyway, because they are already doing destruction to the city anyway. They can't hurt it any more. OK, let's review... they said what?

(J) "All angles of story open to corruption by disinformation."

(T) OK, all angles of story... OK, you've got two angles of the story here.

(L) Well, several. The Pleiadians, the vibronics, the different cities...

(T) No, no, you've got two sources, two angles...

(L) Yes and...

(T) That may be open to corruption.

(L) Would these people necessarily be the angles?

(T) Yes, and where they got it from may be corrupt. Maybe somebody threw it out there just for the fun of it. Anybody having fun with us, in general. OK, then you said that that must mean the story is false, because they said that it is disinformation, and they came back and said... *(L)* Don't make assumptions... *(T)* "All angles"... and you said something, and they said "wrong" and you said the assumption was wrong, and they said, no your answer was wrong. And they said "yes". The answer was wrong.

(J) "Search, and don't jump over vital subject matter... Patience, this is not a relay race!"

(T) The question is: what is the vital subject matter? The alien bases moving, or the sources of the information that you've gotten this from? Or the sources your sources got it from? OK, what is it we're supposed to be looking at?

32 **A**: Alien "bases."

33 **Q**: *(T)* OK, now, why did you put the word bases in quotes?

34 **A**: Assume, and you make an ass out of u and me!

35 **Q**: *(T)* Why did they say that? Because I asked why they put the word bases in quotes? *(L)* Because we're assuming that the aliens have bases? I think that's what they mean... *(T)* Well, we may or may not be assuming that the aliens have bases. Why did you say assuming makes an ass out of u and me?

36 **A**: Because you have never adequately discussed the question of the bases with us.

37 **Q**: *(T)* OK, now you're making a statement that we have not adequately discussed the bases with you, and I will agree, we have not discussed the bases with you, but you are saying that we are making an assumption that the bases exist. Only, the last time we met, you made the statement that Jan and I had been taken to a base. Are you changing what you said?

38 **A**: Assumption is not that bases exist, but rather, all other angles to the story.

39 **Q**: *(T)* OK, that's what I'm trying to get at. All other angles is what we're supposed to be looking at. Not the bases, which we haven't discussed, in detail, and not whether they're being moved or not, not whether they exist or not, but the angles that the story is coming from. Is this what you are saying?

40 **A**: Angles, period.

41 **Q**: *(T)* OK, what is it about the angles that we're missing in your comment, about angles? *(L)* Well, I think what they're saying is that we need to be asking different, specific questions, and those become the angles...

A: Yes. 42

Q: *(T)* Now, these are questions about 43
the bases, not about the information about the bases that Laura just related, but questions of our own about the bases?

A: Yes. 44

Q: *(J)* Not discussing the sources... *(T)* 45
We're not talking about the sources...

A: Right. 46

Q: *(T)* OK, I just want to get this 47
straight, so I can follow this. I know some of our conversations have gotten rambling... We've skimmed over things, and moved on to other things in order to get a lot of stuff in. OK, let's talk about the bases. *(L)* What's the first, most significant thing about the bases we need to know?

A: No, suggest point blank. 48

Q: *(T)* OK, point-blank questions. Do 49
these bases exist? Let's start with yes or no answers.

A: Yes. 50

Q: *(L)* How many are there? *(T)* Are 51
there bases in the United States of America?

A: Close. 52

Q: *(T)* There are no bases within the 53
boundaries of the Continental U.S.? *(L)* No, they are in other dimensions and densities, is that correct?

A: Yes. 54

Q: *(T)* They can be entered through 55
entrance-ways within the United States and other places within the world?

56 **A**: Transdensity.

57 **Q**: *(L)* OK, trans-density points...

58 **A**: No. Bases are.

59 **Q**: *(L)* Bases are trans-density. *(T)* So the bases are trans-density. In other words they exist throughout the densities in the same location. No, no, that won't be right... *(L)* They exist in a trans-density state. *(T)* So they exist in third...

60 **A**: Yes.

61 **Q**: *(T)* They exist in third, fourth, whatever... all at the same time. *(L)* Maybe they could come into our density when necessary and then go out of our density when necessary.

62 **A**: No.

63 **Q**: *(L)* They are in another density.

64 **A**: No.

65 **Q**: *(L)* They are in another dimension. *(T)* They are in all densities...

66 **A**: Trans.

67 **Q**: *(L)* They transit at all densities?

68 **A**: Start at three.

69 **Q**: *(L)* They start at three... *(T)* They go through four, five is not the density they can go into, so they go through six...

70 **A**: Assume.

71 **Q**: *(L)* Assume; you're assuming... *(T)* No, I'm asking, they start at three, you say; where do they go from there?

72 **A**: To five.

73 **Q**: *(L)* Three to five. *(T)* They cover three, four and five?

74 **A**: Yes.

Q: *(T)* Why do they cover five? You've 75
said that five is the level of contemplation... *(L)* Why not? That makes sense, to have one there, too.

A: Yes. 76

Q: *(L)* They can take them through 77
there. They work there. *(T)* Well, I need to understand this, they've said different things about the 5th density, in different sessions.

A: No. 78

Q: *(L)* I'll tell you, hold on. One of 79
the things that came through: it was the session when I was asking questions about [my son's] experiences under hypnosis, so it was back fairly early on. And I asked a series of questions about what he perceived. Now, he had an alien abduction experience that he described in another lifetime, seemingly. He described what amounted to having this screen thing put over his face, and the red dots, and the programming and the beings in the silver robes standing around, and then being shunted through this tunnel, and finding himself in this dark space where there were all these black-hole things all around him. I asked, was this an alien abduction in another lifetime, and they said no, it was a 5th density life review. I said, are some of these beings we perceive as aliens, and some of these experiences we perceive as alien abductions, actually events or experiences on 5th density? And they said yes.

(J) Life review... that's real important.

(L) Right. So what they're saying is, and when they're talking about taking souls on the battlefield, and so forth, obviously we have 5th density 'alien', and they've said that the term is used

loosely. I mean, we might perceive them as alien, but they were 5th density workers, so to speak. That was their job, to do whatever it was they did, or they perceived it as their job. So that, to have these bases transit the densities up through 5th, would make perfect sense because of the kind of work they're doing. Is that...

80 **A**: There is so much extremely vital stuff about this subject, that it would be wise to stay with it until completion.

81 **Q**: *(T)* We plan on staying with it, we're trying to understand this...

(L) You remember when my brother was here, they kept wanting us to come back to the subject of the bases. And we didn't, we wandered off.

(T) Our problem is, we wander a lot of the time. We're worse than Carl Sagan as a group here. We wander off on tangent ideas, and go from one thing to the next. We never stay on a subject. OK, the bases are trans-density bases; they go from the 3rd density to the 5th; they exist in the 3rd, 4th and 5th density all at the same time. Is this correct so far?

82 **A**: Close.

83 **Q**: *(T)* Now, when a being, a soul, whatever, is in the base, do they exist in all three densities at the same time?

84 **A**: No.

85 **Q**: *(L)* Hold on, I've got an idea...

86 **A**: When you are in a skyscraper, do you exist on all floors at the same time?

87 **Q**: *(J)* No, but you have got to know where the elevator is! *(L)* Is there something like an elevator that can move you, if you're in these locations, from one density to another, and experience these bases, these trans-density bases, at different levels?

A: It is an elevator! 88

Q: *(L)* OK, so these bases are points... 89
it *is* an elevator, so these bases may be places that if you are taken to them, are in them, that through these portals, or trans-density bases, you are thereby able to transit the densities?

A: You are able anyway. 90

Q: *(L)* OK, but are these specific loca- 91
tions... OK, it is an elevator... *(T)* Well, not an elevator as we perceive an elevator... *(J)* Conceptually, yes. It's a conveyance, it's a method.

A: No. 92

Q: *(T)* No, that it isn't an elevator as 93
we perceive it? *(L)* Is it an elevator for...

A: Literally. 94

Q: *(L)* It is literally an elevator? 95

A: Yes. 96

Q: *(L)* So you go there to get on to go 97
to different densities?

A: Yes. 98

Q: *(T)* So, it is that easy? 99

A: Yes. 100

Q: *(L)* So you go to these bases, to go 101
to different densities...

A: Although, it is possible to enter 4th 102
and 5th in other ways too!

Q: *(L)* OK, are these beings, these 103
other-density beings, creating and utilizing these bases for mass movement of beings or artifacts from one density to another? Is that what they're doing here?

A: No. They live on 4th, so they con- 104
struct 4th density bases.

105 **Q**: *(L)* I'm getting it... So, the 4th density beings construct 4th density bases. These 4th density bases then somehow interface with 3rd density in a certain point in space-time, and they then influence 3rd density beings to build 3rd density bases at this interface point, and through these interface points they are able to move back and forth between densities. Is this getting close to the idea?

106 **A**: The only ones who need to use this approach are 3rd D.

107 **Q**: *(L)* OK, so these are 4th density... *(J)* They are for our use? They are for 3rd density being use. *(L)* OK, so our people have built these bases, using technology, perhaps... OK, let's take it one step at a time. Are these bases constructed by 3rd density beings?

108 **A**: Partially.

109 **Q**: *(L)* Are they constructed by 3rd and 4th density beings?

110 **A**: Yes.

111 **Q**: *(L)* Are they constructed for the use of 3rd density beings?

112 **A**: No.

113 **Q**: *(L)* Are they constructed... *(T)* Are the 3rd density bases constructed for the use of 3rd density beings?

114 **A**: Both.

115 **Q**: *(T)* Both 3rd and 4th. OK, and there's a way for the 4th density beings – an elevator – to move from 4th to 3rd, from their 4th density base to the 3rd density base.

116 **A**: Vice Versa.

117 **Q**: *(L)* They said they were built for us, not for them.

118 **A**: No.

Q: *(L)* OK, they were built by us to 119
allow us to get there...?

A: No. 120

Q: *(L)* Then, I lost it! *(T)* They were 121
built so that they can have a place to move and operate in 3rd density even though their main base is in 4th density. They come here, and interact with 3rd density beings, and do their 3rd density stuff while they're here, because they can exist there, because 4th density spills over into it through the other bases. *(L)* OK, so when people go to these bases, and see aliens and humans interacting together, are they in 4th density, or 3rd density?

A: Both. 122

Q: *(L)* Either/or. OK. The next ques- 123
tion is... *(T)* Both? Now, wait, they can either be in 3rd or 4th. But you said, if you see them interacting together... *(L)* Are they both at once?

A: Mostly on 4th. 124

Q: *(T)* OK, so the bases in 3rd den- 125
sity here, are bases for whomever is working with the 4th density beings, that they can exist in it over long periods of time. The 4th density beings can come through to this density, by use of the base... [Dogs start howling in the back yard, distracting the session.] Now, I've lost my train of thought. OK, we've got a base, bases that exist: 3rd, 4th and 5th, and they can transit between 3rd, 4th and 5th... The bases are STS bases, let's establish that. *(L)* That's an assumption... let's ask. *(T)* Are the bases STS bases?

A: Mostly. 126

Q: *(T)* So there may be STO bases, as 127
well?

A: This is complex. 128

129 **Q**: *(T)* Because the STO beings interact with the STS beings because of the balance and the fact that STO beings serve themselves by serving others, and therefore they will serve STS beings as well as STO beings, because they're serving... Because they've been asked, because they're doing it to serve others. So there are STO beings operating bases also. *(L)* Is that correct? *(T)* Or close?

130 **A**: Much more complex.

131 **Q**: *(T)* I assume it's much more complex, but that's the general idea...

132 **A**: No.

133 **Q**: *(L)* OK, try this: Are there separate bases operated or built or constructed or somehow occupied or utilized or whatever by STO beings alone?

134 **A**: OK, time for us to teach patience. We are going to illuminate you! Why do you suppose there are roads around Dulce NM where people have become confused when traveling on them? Because the 4th density vibrational frequency emanating from the nearby base more and more frequently resonates on surface.

135 **Q**: *(L)* OK, continue.

136 **A**: Then going to 4th density: road seems straight as seen in 4th density, when curved in 3rd.

137 **Q**: *(J)* It seems straight when seen in 4th, but it's actually curved in 3rd? *(SV)* In other words, accidents! *(J)* It changes configuration from 3rd to 4th! *(T)* When people drive those roads out there, as the 4th density seeps out through, and is seeping out farther and farther, they become confused because they're moving between 3rd and 4th. As the road curves in 3rd, and the car, which is in 3rd, should be curving with the road, the driver sees the road as straight, and drives off the road, because he's confused by what he sees.

A: Exactly. 138

Q: *(J)* It's all about perception! *(T)* Now, we're back to perception of reality! 139

A: In 4th, you see full circle from any vantage point. 140

Q: *(L)* We talked about that before. *(T)* So the road looks straight, because you're seeing it from all angles, therefore, instead of it being curved on one, you're seeing it every way, so the road is now straight. But, it's not really straight in 3rd, and you drive off the road. *(L)* OK, continue on with what you were saying... 141

A: The entire New Mexico region is on verge of moving to 4th density permanently! 142

Q: *(L)* OK... 143

A: Because of the bases. 144

Q: *(L)* So, in other words, the rumors of the bases being moved, being filtered down from other densities, through some of the distorted channels, is in essence, somewhat correct... *(J)* Because they need to have the base in 3rd density! *(L)* Only, they're not moving them to Paris, Washington or Buenos Aires; they're moving to 4th density. 145

A: Close but the bases are already there, pity the host regions. Why do you think there is so much activity seen there! 146

Q: *(L)* Does this mean that when that whole region goes to 4th density, that it's going to, for all intents and purposes, disappear from 3rd? 147

148 **A**: No.

149 **Q**: *(T)* OK, answer your earlier question, then. Why is there so much UFO activity there? Tell me.

150 **A**: Bleed through.

151 **Q**: *(L)* So they're flying around in 4th density... *(T)* ...and they're showing up here in 3rd because...

152 **A**: Wait 'til shift is complete.

153 **Q**: *(L)* Do you mean the shift of New Mexico? Or the total shift? *(T)* I think they're making the sarcastic statement: "Wait till shift is complete... We ain't seen nuthin yet!!" We're just beginning to.

154 **A**: Yes.

155 **Q**: *(T)* Now, this opens up some questions. First question: You made the statement "But the bases are in 4th density." What happens when the 3rd density base, which is vibrating itself into 4th density, runs into the 4th density base that's already there?

156 **A**: Merge.

157 **Q**: *(T)* They become one base?

158 **A**: They already are.

159 **Q**: *(T)* What do you mean by "They will merge?"

160 **A**: To same density.

161 **Q**: *(T)* OK, now, is this moving of the 3rd density location a side-effect of the bases? Harmonic resonance, and all that, as in the beginning of the *Matrix* books? Are we talking about the fact that it's been there so long, that that section of 3rd density is now resonating itself to the 4th density frequencies, and that this is not exactly what they wanted it to do, but it's a side-effect of the fact that they're there?

A: Yes. 162

Q: *(T)* Did they know that it was going 163 to happen?

A: The 4th density STS did, but not 164 3rd.

Q: *(T)* One of the little surprises they 165 weren't told about before the deal was cut? *(J)* If I may ask my question now: You've got these 3rd density bases that are going to move to 4th density. Are they going to need to re-establish another 3rd density base to continue their work? To replace the one that's gone?

A: Why? The whole "territory" will be 166 in 4th then. Tremendous reality shock will occur when it crosses the border.

Q: *(L)* How will we in 3rd perceive it? 167 *(J)* We won't! *(L)* Now, wait, don't make assumptions here! How will we in 3rd perceive it? Let's play make-believe here. What are they going to say?

A: Tremendous reality shock when 168 cross border.

Q: *(L)* Are you saying that this whole 169 region will go into 4th density when the realm border crossing occurs, or is it going to happen shortly?

A: Before! 170

Q: *(L)* OK, this is going to be a tremen- 171 dous reality shock to us, in 3rd density? *(J)* I guess! *(SV)* Well, New Mexico's not going to be there anymore! *(L)* Well, now, how are we going to perceive it? That's what I want to know! Are we going to see a big hole in our world? Are we going to see a vast, empty desert?

[2]Jan's note: New Mexico's vehicle license plate does say 'Land of Enchantment'.

172 **A**: New Mexico will still be there, but suggest review driving skills, for but one example![2]

173 **Q**: *(T)* New Mexico will still exist, but the perception, when you drive into it, is going to change completely, because you've moved into a different density?

174 **A**: Cooking will be fun too!

175 **Q**: *(T)* Because it's 4th density. *(L)* Wait, now, stop a minute here... *(T)* This is not something that can be covered up very easily... *(L)* Now, hold on, back up. What will we perceive... I mean, what is it going to say on the news? Everybody in New Mexico disappeared? *(J)* Or they all go nuts... *(T)* I would hazard to guess...

176 **A**: News blackout.

177 **Q**: *(T)* They're not going to say anything. Now, what is the government's response? I'm sure they will do something like, "An underground nuclear facility for old rods," and they have to block the whole state off...

(L) That's tangential.

(J) They're going to have to keep people out!

(T) How will they explain it? They will not let anybody in!

(L) But they still have... What I'm getting at is... That's begging the question! The question is, what will... *(T)* It will look like New Mexico! *(J)* It will be different every time... *(L)* But the question is, will there be people there? Will there be buildings there? If you fly over it, if you could fly over it, would you see a landscape? Would you see cities? *(T)* It will look like New Mexico... *(L)* They didn't say that!!!

178 **A**: This requires 1,000 answers!

Q: *(L)* In other words, there is an issue 179
here! *(T)* Yes, there is, and there's another issue. That's only one base. OK, we're talking bases...

A: Colossal issue. 180

Q: *(L)* My question is a colossal issue 181
here. What's going on here? This is the whole thing. *(T)* My question, I think, is important, too. There's more than one base. If one is doing it... *(L)* Well, they said the whole territory... *(T)* Not New Mexico; there are bases in South America, there's supposedly a base off the coast of Florida... *(L)* OK, is this going to happen to all the bases? *(T)* There are bases all over the world...*(L)* But New Mexico is where they're hearing all that 'business'. *(T)* They're hearing the 'noise' in a lot of places around the world. *(L)* OK, are there other bases and areas around the world where this is going to happen?

A: Yes. 182

Q: *(L)* Is it going to happen simultane- 183
ously?

A: No. 184

Q: *(L)* It'll happen as it develops... *(T)* 185
The same way it developed out there. *(L)* In other words, they'll move their activities to the other locations, once one place... *(T)* No...

A: No. 186

Q: *(J)* Yes, because I asked, and they 187
said no! *(T)* The bases were not all established at the same time. The base out there is becoming affected.... *(L)* The oldest...

(T) We don't know if this is the oldest, we don't know about other places in the world where nobody can go. We don't know what's going on in Russia,

and in China, in Africa, in the middle of the rainforests, what's happened there... But, as the bases, as our perception of time goes by, each of these bases will experience the same thing, in their due time.

(L) This brings to mind a couple of questions we discussed a couple of weeks ago, when my brother was here. After we had talked about the underground bases, and the soldier effect, and the taking of the souls out, and so on and so forth, and I don't know if we got into it effectively or not, but I don't think so. Is there some connection between these bases and their activities and a concept that has emerged in our culture, of hell being underground?

188 **A**: No.

189 **Q**: *(L)* OK, is there some connection between these bases going into 4th density and the idea of some of the ancient prophetic literature that the...

190 **A**: Bases are partially 4th density already, and always have been. It is the surroundings that are in for a massive change.

191 **Q**: *(T)* OK, now, this brings up an interesting concept. Two interesting concepts. When Roger Santilli was here, we talked about his compatriots messing around with this stuff on a small scale. This is on a massive scale that's getting out of hand on purpose.

(L) And they mentioned that these things had been being done by whom, and blah, blah, blah...

(T) Yes, now, the question is, they told us that the Lizzies want to control us, not in 3rd, but in 4th density. They've also told us that this wave realm border is coming, which is our human chance to move to 4th density on our own and escape, if we can do it, as a group, the Lizzies' control. The Lizzies have brought 4th density to us before the realm border gets here. Everybody who's in a 4th density area, like the New Mexico people, like you were just asking, what happens to everybody, gets transferred into 4th density, where they are controlled by 4D STS, in physicality, right on up there, before the Wave gets here, before they understand what's really happening to them...

(L) That's what I was trying to say earlier...

(T) It wasn't coming out well, but that's it, right?

(L) The ancient prophecies, where they talk about taking out the negative, and that this amounts to the taking out of the tares, the weeds, the chaff.

(T) It's not only in this location, it's in many locations, so they're going to grab... *(L)* Gathering them together... *(T)* ...a whole bunch of humans by way of these bases that they told the different governments a lie about the purpose of the bases. The bases weren't for any of this other stuff that they told them. The bases were there specifically to generate the resonance effect within the area. *(J)* And spread it... *(T)* Yes, well, they knew it would grow, therefore they can grab everybody within the area. In New Mexico, depending on how big an area, they're hearing it out to Taos and as far southeast as Albuquerque. That's a big city. There's a lot of people there, in that area of northern New Mexico. To the north of that, they can take out Las Vegas, which is another large city. Plus the tourist areas throughout the National

Parks. Now, the bases have been in out-of-the-way places. The information, or disinformation, is that the bases would be moved under large cities. Is the experiment that they have performed, and they calculated out, to see if this works on a sparse area first? And then, to move to large population areas, and do it again, and on a second level of experiment, accelerate it?

(L) OK, let's ask. Is that the idea, that they're trying this there, and then move to the large cities for the same purpose? *(J)* Like trying it out in Boston...

192 **A**: No. Remember, you are moving to the density 4 anyway.

193 **Q**: *(J)* My question is, in the case of the New Mexico locality, is this a 'contained' event?

194 **A**: Regional "blip".

195 **Q**: *(J)* OK, so it is contained, it would not spread. *(T)* Well, it's not big enough to spread. But it is bigger than what Santilli's buddies are messing with. *(L)* OK, is there anything happening under the cities of Buenos Aires, Washington and Paris? Along these lines?

196 **A**: There are things "happening" under all cities.

197 **Q**: *(L)* OK, I know you said 'things', but I said along these lines.

198 **A**: Yes.

199 **Q**: *(T)* Is what I said, what we postulated earlier, is this their idea, is this the Lizzies' idea? The 4th density beings' idea? To gather us up before the Wave gets here and then they can make their move?

200 **A**: No need.

Q: *(L)* OK, let me ask it this way. Is 201
this event going to take all the people with it into 4th density STS? I mean, all the people who go with this event?

A: No. People will not "go." 202

Q: *(J)* People will not "go." It will be 203
like those people that were trying to retrieve the planes, and every time it changed, their realities kept on changing. *(T)* Is this like the people, the Flight 19 stuff?

A: No. 204

Q: *(L)* What's going to happen to 205
the people in the region? *(T)* That was an Atlantean thing; they flew into the Atlantean power pyramids... *(J)* No, that's not what I meant... I'm not talking about the guys on the planes, I'm talking about the people that were trying to retrieve them, and they kept on changing back and forth from dimension to dimension... *(L)* What's going to happen to the people in the New Mexico area?

A: Nothing. 206

Q: *(L)* So, if the region disappears... 207
(T) It's not disappearing. It's just shifting... *(L)* So if the region goes into 4th density, will the people living there also be in 4th density?

A: Yes. 208

Q: *(T)* Will they notice that anything 209
is different? Will they, not us, they? Those who are within it?

A: Are you kidding? 210

Q: *(L)* I guess they will. *(T)* Well, 211
I don't know, that's why I'm asking. *(J)* Their perception is going to change! *(T)* But, how can their perception change if they're not going into 4th density? *(L)* No, they said they are going

into 4th density! But they're not 'going' anywhere. *(J)* There will be no traveling involved. *(T)* We're not 'going' anywhere, we're shifting our frequencies up to the next density, not moving from where we are.

212 **A**: Picture driving down a highway, suddenly you notice auras surrounding everything.... Being able to see around corners, going inside little cottages which become mansions, when viewed from inside... Going inside a building in Albuquerque and going out the back door into Las Vegas, going to sleep as a female, and waking up male... Flying in a plane for half an hour and landing at the same place 5 weeks later...[3]

213 **Q**: *(J)* Perception is *being* and changes all the time! *(T)* That's variability of physicality! *(SV)* Albuquerque... That's where the University of New Mexico is! Can you imagine that whole campus...! *(T)* Can you imagine the poor casino operators when 'chance' no longer plays a chance...?

[Break]

214 **Q**: *(T)* How is this changing of the densities, in that large and major a way, affecting the Wave? They said that the scientists, messing in a small way, are affecting us and the Wave. How is this, on a large scale, doing?

215 **A**: No relation.

216 **Q**: *(L)* No, it wasn't that the scientists were affecting the Wave, they had no effect on the Wave, they were affecting the curtain between densities, which is a totally different thing from the Wave, which is an oncoming thing. *(T)* But, does it speed it up, what does it do? What is the effect?

A: No. 217

Q: *(L)* No effect. Let me ask this. Is 218
there any possibility that this regional movement to 4th density is going to manifest in 3rd density as some sort of cataclysmic activity?

A: No. 219

Q: *(L)* OK, is this perception of reality 220
imposed on us from outside, or...

A: Not imposed upon. 221

Q: *(L)* OK, what is it that determines... 222
I mean, I know awareness determines, but if a whole region is going to go, is it because all of the people occupying that region are at a level that they can change their awareness?

A: No. 223

Q: *(T)* It's not going because of that. 224
It's going because the bases are being used to manipulate. *(L)* OK...

A: No. 225

Q: *(T)* It's a side-effect of the bases... 226

A: Yes. 227

Q: *(T)* It has nothing to do with any- 228
body being ready to go... or anything else but as a side-effect?

A: Also atomic bomb blasts. 229

Q: *(J)* Oh, Los Alamos bomb blast! 230

A: Blasts. 231

Q: *(T)* OK, now, how about the French, 232
and their atomic bomb testing in the

[3]This response sure gives one pause considering Malaysian Flight 370 that disappeared without a trace; not to forget all the very strange glitches that are happening with aircraft these days.

South Pacific? Is this activity accelerating some sort of transition, or opening of a doorway...?

233 **A**: Maybe.

234 **Q**: *(T)* OK. As the bases reach these points of side-effect, of transition from 3rd to 4th, each one in itself is localized. But, do many of them together form a much larger shift over a larger geographical area?

235 **A**: We told you it was regional.

236 **Q**: *(J)* Yes, each one is regional, but do you reach a point where... is there a saturation point? *(T)* Is there a cumulative effect over each region? *(J)* As they go? *(T)* In other words, if you've got one whole...

237 **A**: No, we meant SW US region.

238 **Q**: *(L)* OK, this southwest region, this is imminent in this area? Is that correct?

239 **A**: Imminent?

240 **Q**: *(L)* OK, it's already happening, is that it? *(T)* It's in progress.

241 **A**: Yes.

242 **Q**: *(L)* OK, what else were we asking? Can people come in and out of it?

243 **A**: Yes.

244 **Q**: *(L)* Can you get back out of it? *(T)* How well can you drive and cook?

245 **A**: Yes.

246 **Q**: *(T)* You said other bases are going to experience, or are experiencing this same effect.

247 **A**: Yes.

248 **Q**: *(T)* Are there other bases that are experiencing, have experienced this effect, previous to the Dulce base?

249 **A**: Yes.

Q: *(T)* As these bases experience these 250
effects, in different places on the geographical surface of the planet, do the effects become cumulative? *(L)* They said only the SW United States... *(T)* I know, I'm approaching this from another direction here. As this happens, will this ultimately take in the whole planet?

A: No. Wave. 251

Q: *(L)* The Wave will take in the whole 252
planet. *(J)* It'll be a Swiss-cheese effect? With more and more holes as they go on... *(T)* News blackouts will not keep people from hearing about this. How's the power structure going to handle all of this?

A: ? 253

Q: *(L)* How indeed? That's a good 254
question. The power structure already knows it's happening, because it's happened in other places already. This isn't the first place. *(J)* That's what the disinformation is for.

(T) Disinformation is fine in remote places where nobody can reach, like Outer Mongolia, or the middle of the Brazilian rainforest. When it happens in downtown Albuquerque, or Las Vegas, or off the coast of Florida, and you can't go to Orlando or Miami anymore, somebody's going to notice!

(J) Where is Miami or Orlando on the timetable, that's what I'd like to know! *(L)* Interestingly, Jan just said something that keyed in a good question. If time is involved in this, is it possible that when something goes into 4th density, that if we were traveling to that area, that we would arrive in that area at a different point in time? And that we would say... *(T)* As we perceive time...

255 **A**: Yes.

256 **Q**: *(L)* Very good question.

257 **A**: 4th density frees one from the illusion of "time" as you *will* to perceive it.

258 **Q**: *(L)* OK, if you're freed from the illusion of time, going into 4th density, would you then go into one of these regions and perceive a time period and sequence of events as you expect to perceive it?

259 **A**: As you *will* to perceive it.

260 **Q**: *(L)* So, in other words, there may be some people on the planet, because of their fixity of will, and perception, at 3rd density, who will not perceive anything change? Is that correct?

261 **A**: No.

262 **Q**: *(L)* So, anybody will, something will be different. OK. *(J)* What they do with that information, that's a different story... *(T)* You know, these areas will become bigger tourist attractions than any that are out there now! People will flock to them... *(L)* Is that possible?

263 **A**: No.

264 **Q**: *(T)* It's an 'E' ticket ride! When the word gets out that people can go to that area of New Mexico and experience true strangeness, it's going to draw a lot of people.

265 **A**: Not that simple... Picture driving to reach New Mexico by car and 'skipping' over and arriving in San Diego instead, or... driving to the grocery store in Santa Fe, and winding up in Moscow, instead.

266 **Q**: *(L)* So, in other words, this is going to create a situation where people on the planet are going to become very confused and upset over this situation. *(J)* Yes, have you ever tried going shopping in Moscow? *(T)* They're going to draw a lot of people when they find out that happens! *(L)* And being forced to expand their perception and awareness because of the anomalous events!

A: Imagine being an N.S.A. official and 267
shivering at the prospect!

Q: *(L)* NSA, National Security 268
Agency... Why would you shiver at the prospect... *(SV)* ...of being one of them? With all this going on?

A: Concealment. 269

Q: *(J)* In other words, trying to cover 270
up what's going on!

(T) Well, they're not going to be able to cover up what's going on. That's what I'm getting at. And because of what's going on, it's going to draw people to the effect...

(L) If something like this happens, obviously, what they're going to have to do is institute some kind of martial law, so they can cover it up! Or else, they'll lose everything!

(T) They're going to have to restrict travel...

(L) Well, yes, we know that, but they don't!

(T) They're going to have to, at the minimum, restrict all travel through those areas. The only way they're going to do that, is either impose martial law, or come up with some kind of major disaster to keep people out, like I said, "buried, spent fuel rods are leaking contamination over NW New Mexico, no one allowed in." But, they just told us that those who are inside can get out. So how are they going to keep those who are inside from coming out,

especially if they come out all over the world when they leave?

(J) People will be talking a mile a minute about all the stuff...

(T) People are going to find out, they're not going to be able to cover it...

(L) Well, they're going to find out about all the stuff. They'll be picking them up every time they hear about one, but of course, it will be like trying to move the bucket from leak to leak to leak... *(T)* From place to place, and it's not the only place it's happening! *(L)* ...and it's going to be leaking so many places.

(L) They said they were going to teach us. Let's ask if there is any major, further information on these bases, that we need to know. *(J)* Is there one around this area that's going to do this? *(T)* It's off the coast of Florida, they told us that. It's out in the Gulf. *(L)* Is our off-the-coast base going to do this? *(T)* If it [New Mexico] covers an area as far as Las Vegas, and through there, it's going to cover us. *(L)* Is our base going to...

271 **A**: Not of same intensity.

272 **Q**: *(J)* Less or more? Which direction?

273 **A**: Less.

274 **Q**: *(L)* Is there... *(T)* Why would it be less? Because the base is smaller? *(L)* Because it's smaller, they told us it was smaller. They said, "Small base near here". *(T)* Well, that's just the one near here. What about the one out in the Triangle? *(L)* Yes, we didn't ask about the Triangle!

275 **A**: Panhandle, too.

Q: *(L)* Is the Panhandle less, or will 276
they have the same thing happen as Dulce?

A: By that time, the Wave will arrive. 277

Q: *(L)* Is there anything about these 278
bases and this subject matter that you wish to teach us further at this time?[4]

A: Suggest direct channeling for this 279
subject.

Q: *(L)* Well, you know how we feel 280
about the direct channeling, that there is too much personal filtering involved. This way, none of us knows anything...

A: Faith must enter the picture some- 281
where, lest you fall behind. Some subjects are too complex to be properly discussed through this medium.

Q: *(L)* OK, we'll save this discussion 282
of the bases for a direct channeling session. The only thing is, in a direct channeling session it is... There are some things about it that are disturbing. It tends, after doing it several weeks in a row, to become, it begins to sound pompous. *(SV)* Let's ask. *(L)* Why is it after doing it several times in a row, it begins to sound pompous, information begins to get skewed? Why is that?

A: Perceptions are a fun challenge. 283

Q: *(L)* That's easy for you to say, be- 284
cause, when the answer comes back that... *(J)* You're not 'perceptually challenged'!

A: It is easy for you to say many things. 285

Q: *(L)* Well, the thing is, when abso- 286
lutely incorrect information comes out, I have a difficult time dealing with that.

A: How do you determine correctness? 287

[4] *The Wave* 41

288 **Q**: *(L)* Well in that particular instance, I was told that a certain thing that I saw in the sky was the planet Mars, and the planet Mars was so far away from that spot, that it was absolutely incorrect. I mean, the planet Mars was 120 degrees away from Jupiter. And yet, you said that they were 10 degrees apart, that what I saw that was 10 degrees away from Jupiter was Mars. Unless Mars traveled 110 degrees across the sky in one day, then that was incorrect information. There's no two ways about it!

289 **A**: Wrong!!!

290 **Q**: *(L)* No, it's not!

291 **A**: It is!!!

292 **Q**: *(L)* What is wrong? That Mars didn't travel 110 degrees? Because that is exactly what you said, that it was Mars. I went back, I read over the session!

293 **A**: You were in a 4th density flap.

294 **Q**: *(L)* Well, fine and dandy! If I'm in a 4th density flap, that's an easy answer for... any answer that seems to be at variance with what's happening here. I mean, do you get my point here?

295 **A**: Yes. But you are still mistaken.

296 **Q**: *(L)* Why am I the one that's mistaken? Why can't you be mistaken?

297 **A**: We can, but not on this one! Remember, you felt strange during this experience. And besides, you asked us for the information, we must present it to you as it is.

298 **Q**: *(L)* You're saying that I felt weird or strange or unusual at that occasion; I don't remember saying that I felt strange or unusual. Are you trying to put words in my mouth?

A: Who said that? You said that. 299

Q: *(L)* OK, you didn't say that I said 300
that. You said that I said that I felt strange or unusual. I don't remember that I said that. I don't remember feeling strange or unusual.

A: OK. 301

Q: *(SV)* How many other times during 302
direct channeling was wrong information given? *(L)* A lot of the other information is unverifiable. *(J)* How much of this is unverifiable? *(L)* Well, that's what I'm saying. When there's a point such as that... *(T)* Well, when they shut down the southwest and declare martial law and keep everybody out, then we'll know that there's some truth to it. *(J)* Is there a base in the 'Show Me' state? They'll have a great time! *(T)* Is there a base near Denver?

A: Yes. 303

Q: *(T)* Let's think about the Scal- 304
lion map of the future continent. The 'Cities of Enlightenment' that are on his map – there's one in Denver, there's one near Albuquerque, there's one near Tallahassee... *(L)* Doing the direct channeling is so excruciatingly boring.

A: We only suggested it for complex 305
issues.

Q: *(L)* I suppose we can handle it in 306
small doses. Let me ask about a dream I had the other night, about being on safari, and then being given some information, followed by an event where it seemed like something shot out of my side. And then two days ago I was in the bathroom and noticed there was a deep puncture wound in that area that was somewhat healed. Could you tell me what this represented, or what's the story here, or what happened?

307 **A**: Another session.

308 **Q**: *(L)* Then let's say goodnight.

309 **A**: Goodnight.

(L) Well. I had a whole list of questions that we didn't get to ask. And we only asked one question on my list. I'm going to be more careful what I open with! I'm going to be sure I don't ask something that's just full of implications!

(SV) Well, how do you know what question is going to be full of implications? Anyway, what are you going to tell the Konicovs?

(T) "Don't go to Albuquerque!"

End of session

November 11, 1995

Considering the direction the Cs took in this session, it's interesting that it was held on 11/11.

Participants: 'Frank', Laura, Susan V

1 **Q**: *(L)* Hello.

2 **A**: Hello.

3 **Q**: *(L)* Who do we have with us?

4 **A**: Lynostieah

5 **Q**: *(L)* And where are you from?

6 **A**: The translation point of focus is Cassiopaea.

7 **Q**: *(L)* Is there a reason you use the term 'translation'? Is it because the information is translated from one density to another?

8 **A**: Close.

9 **Q**: *(L)* Is that the point where the energy 'shifts' densities?

10 **A**: Close.

11 **Q**: *(L)* I noticed that in the beginning of these transmissions that the language was very formalized, and that as time has gone by, the language used has become more colloquial. Why is this?

12 **A**: Formalized? Colloquial? Define your judgments, please!

13 **Q**: *(L)* Well, what I meant was, that in the beginning it seemed that certain colloquial expressions that we are accustomed to were unclear to you. And now, not only is there great familiarity with our expressions, but you seem to often come up with rather clever and original witty sayings.

A: Familiarity breeds contentment![1] 14

Q: *(L)* OK. I want to get on with the questions for tonight... 15

A: Do you not wish to reflect upon our witticism? 16

Q: *(L)* [Laughter] Yes! I thought that was a very clever witticism! 17

A: It seemed as if you were not impressed?!? Give us a break, Laura?!? We're only sixth density! 18

Q: *(L)* As we say, "I love a sixth density light being with a sense of humor!" Now, the main thing I wanted to ask about is the references I come across in tons of reading, that the number 33 is somehow significant. Could you tell us the significance, in esoteric terms, or in terms of secret societies, of the number 33? There is the cipher of Roger Bacon, based on the number 33, the 33rd-degree Masons... 19

A: As usual, we do not just give you 20

[1] *The Wave* 10

[2] *The Wave* 22, 32

the answers, we help you to teach yourself!! Now, take 11 and contemplate...[2]

21 **Q**: *(L)* Well, three times eleven is thirty-three.

22 **A**: Yes, but what about 11?

23 **Q**: *(L)* Well, eleven is supposed to be one of the prime, or divine power numbers. In Kaballah, 11 is the power number...

24 **A**: Yes...

25 **Q**: *(L)* Eleven is 10 plus 1; it is divisible only by itself and by 1. I can't think of anything else. I am an 11 in numerology... I am also a 22. What else is there to the number 11?

26 **A**: Astrology.

27 **Q**: *(L)* Well, in astrology, the eleventh sign is Aquarius, my name is an eleven, my birthday is a 22 which is twice eleven, and I am an Aquarian. The eleventh house is friends, hopes, dreams and wishes, and also adopted children. Aquarius the Waterbearer, the dispenser of knowledge. Does 11 have something to do with dispensing of knowledge?

28 **A**: Now, 3rd house.

29 **Q**: *(L)* Gemini. OK. Gemini and Aquarius. Third house is how the mind works, communication, relations with neighbors and siblings, education, local travel, how one speaks. Gemini is known as the 'consummate man'. Somewhat shallow and interested in the things of material life. It is also the divine number of creation. So, what's the connection here?

30 **A**: Matrix.

Q: *(L)* Is there something about this in 31
the *Matrix* material?

A: No. 32

Q: *(L)* This *is* a matrix. The third 33
house and the eleventh house create a matrix?[3]

A: Foundation. 34

Q: *(L)* In terms of cosmic things, Gem- 35
ini is in June, Aquarius is in February... *(S)* Isn't the third house also about teaching? And, we are friends here and we are being taught...

A: This is not about you. 36

Q: *(L)* OK. This is not about us. I am 37
just trying to relate it. Gemini is in June, Aquarius is in February. Gemini is the physical man, and Aquarius is the spiritual man?

A: Yin Yang. 38

Q: *(L)* So Gemini is the physical man 39
and Aquarius is the spiritual man... yin yang... is that the...[4]

A: Yes... 40

Q: *(L)* So 33 could represent the trans- 41
formation of the physical man to the divine man through the action of secret or hidden teachings... and those who have gone through this process represent themselves with the number 33, which means that they started out oriented to the flesh and then became...

A: Medusa 11. 42

Q: *(L)* Medusa 11? What does Medusa 43
have to do with it? *(S)* What about spinning 33 times? *(L)* Please tell me how Medusa relates here?

A: Heads. 44

[3] *The Wave* 32
[4] *The Wave* 22

45 **Q**: *(L)* Heads. Medusa. 11. Were there eleven snakes on the head of Medusa or eleven heads? This is really obscure... you need to help me out here.

46 **A**: We are.

47 **Q**: *(L)* Do I need to read the Medusa legend to understand?

48 **A**: No.

49 **Q**: *(L)* Medusa. Heads. 11. Is there something about the mythical Medusa that we need to see here?

50 **A**: 11 squared divided by phi.

51 **Q**: *(L)* By pi. 11 squared divided by pi. What does this result bring us to?[5]

52 **A**: 33. Infinity.

53 **Q**: *(L)* Well, we don't get 33 out of this... we get 3.3166 etc. if we divide the square root of 11 by pi.[6] Divided by phi?! What in the heck is phi? OK, if we divide *pi* into 11, we get 3.5 infinity, but not 33.

54 **A**: 1 times 1.

55 **Q**: *(L)* Oh. You weren't saying 11 times 11, you were saying 1 times 1.

56 **A**: No.

57 **Q**: *(L)* 1 times 1 is what? 1.

A: 5 minus 3. 58

Q: *(L)* OK, that's 2. 59

A: 2 minus 1. 60

Q: *(L)* OK, that's 1. I don't get it. A math genius I am *not*. What is the concept here? 61

A: Look: 3 5 3 5 3 5. 62

Q: *(L)* What is the 3 5 sequence? 63

A: 5 minus 3. 64

Q: *(L)* OK, we have strange math. But, you can do anything with numbers because they correspond to the universe at deep levels... 65

A: Is code. 66

Q: *(L)* What does this code relate to? Is it letters or some written work?[7] 67

A: Infinite power.[8] 68

Q: *(L)* How is infinite power acquired by knowing this code? If you don't know the correspondences, how can you use a numerical code? 69

A: Lord of Serpent promises its followers infinite power which they must seek infinite knowledge to gain, for which they pledge allegiance infinitely, for which they possess for all eternity, so 70

[5] Above, I assumed that the Cs meant *pi*, not *phi*, since I really wasn't all that familiar with *phi* as a mathematical idea, so this is the point where things get frustrating. I'm operating on wrong assumptions. Nevertheless, I still don't see what the Cs were getting at. 11 x 11 / 1.618 = 74.7837 and is not 33. So I'm really in the dark here.

[6] I keep messing up here. 11 squared is *not* the square root of 11, nor did I divide by *pi* as I mentioned.

[7] It is obvious now that the C's were talking about a *phi* spiral, Fibonacci sequence, 1, 1, 2, 3, 5, 8, 13, 21, 34, 55, 89, 144, etc. *Golden Ratio*: The ratio between two consecutive numbers in the Fibonacci Series tends to the Golden Number *phi*: 0.618... or 1.618...; the ratio of each successive pair of numbers in the sequence approximates *phi* (1.618...), as 5 divided by 3 is 1.666..., and 8 divided by 5 is 1.60. But I was ignorant of all that at the time. Poor Cs were *sooo* frustrated I think.

[8] *The Wave* 22, 26, 32

long as they find infinite wisdom, for which they search for all infinity.

71 **Q**: *(L)* Well, that is a round robin... a circle you can't get out of!

72 **A**: And therein you have the deception! Remember, those who seek to serve self with supreme power, are doomed only to serve others who seek to serve self, and can only see that which they want to see.[9]

73 **Q**: *(L)* The thought that occurs to me, as we are talking here, is that the STS pathway consists of an individual who wants to serve themselves – they are selfish and egocentric – they want to impel others to serve them; they want to enslave others; and they find ways to manipulate others to serve them. But, they end up being impelled by some higher being than they are. Because they have been tricked into believing that by so doing, they are actually drawing power to themselves through the teachings, including the popular religions which promote being 'saved' by simply believing and giving up your power. And, then, you have a whole pyramid of people *taking* by trickery and deception, from others. The taker gets taken from in the end. A pyramid where all those on the bottom, the majority, have no one to take from, so they get absorbed into the next level higher, until you get to the apex and everything disappears. In the STO mode, you have those who only give. And, if they are involved with other STO persons, everyone has and no one is at the bottom or at the top, in a void. In the end, it seems like everyone ends up serving someone else anyway, and the principle is the *intent*. But in STO, it is more like a circle, a balance, no one is left without.

A: Balance, yin-yang.[10] 74

Q: *(L)* Obviously the 33 represents the Serpent, the Medusa, and so forth...[11] 75

A: You mentioned pyramid, interesting... And what is the geometric one-dimensional figure that corresponds? 76

Q: *(L)* Well, the triangle. And, if you have a triangle point up you have 3, joined to a triangle pointing down, you have 3, you have a 33. Is that something like what we are getting at here? 77

A: Yes. 78

Q: *(L)* Is there a connection between the number 33 and the Great Pyramid in Egypt? 79

A: Yes. 80

Q: *(L)* And what is that connection? Is it that the builders of the pyramid participated in this secret society activity? 81

A: Yes. And what symbol did you see in "Matrix," for Serpents and Grays? 82

Q: *(L)* You are talking about the triangle with the Serpent's head in it? 83

A: Yes. 84

[9] I guess that, in the end, this is the answer to what 33 represents, as well as the Fibonacci code, etc.

[10] Which takes us back to the astrological representation of Gemini, the third sign, and Aquarius, the eleventh sign, a balance of STS and STO in a Matrix of our world/lives. Notice also that the Gemini Twins' sigil is something like a Roman numeral: II, which resembles the number 11, so we have 11 'squared'.

[11] They didn't object, so I guess we can go with this.

85 **Q**: *(L)* Are we talking in terms of this 33 relating to a group of 'aliens', or a group of humans with advanced knowledge and abilities?

86 **A**: Either/or.

87 **Q**: *(L)* Is this what has been referred to in the Bramley book [*Gods of Eden*] as the Brotherhood of the Serpent or Snake?

88 **A**: Yes.

89 **Q**: *(L)* Is this also what you have referred to as the Quorum?

90 **A**: Close.

91 **Q**: *(L)* So, we have a bunch of people who are playing with mathematics, and playing with higher knowledge, basically as a keep-busy activity to distract them at the human level from the fact that they are being manipulated at a higher level. Is this what is going on? Or, do they consciously know what they are doing? Is it a distraction or a conscious choice?

92 **A**: Both.

93 **Q**: *(L)* If I were to name some names, could you identify if named individuals were involved in this secret group?

94 **A**: It would not be in your best interests.

95 **Q**: *(L)* Is there anything more on this 33 number that I should look at now?

96 **A**: No. You need to contemplate.

97 **Q**: *(L)* The next question in the list is: You indicated that we should study the legend of Orion, and I looked it up in several sources, and basically the legend is of the perfect man, who fell in love with a woman, and her jealous father caused him to be blinded. The only cure was to gaze at the light, the goddess Aurora, to regain his sight. Can you tell us how this relates to the idea that Orion was the indigenous home of humans?[12]

A: It is up to you to look for answers.[13] 98

Q: *(L)* There was an interesting refer- 99
ence in one of the books of the relationship of Orion to Scorpio, that Orion's bow is drawn at Scorpio. And, at one other point, you said that the physical bodies of mankind were molecularized, and *are* being molecularized, on a planet called D'Ankhiar, which is in the constellation Scorpio.

A: Yes. 100

Q: *(L)* What is the relationship of 101
Orion to Scorpio? The Orion 'bad guys', shooting at Scorpio which is the place of origin of the physical manifestation of the human race...

A: Bad guys? 102

Q: *(L)* Forget I said bad guys. "Shoot- 103
ing at Scorpio." Is there any relationship, symbolically, to the fact that the human bodies...

A: It is all interrelated. 104

Q: *(L)* The killing of Osiris, according 105
to the legend, occurred on either the 28th day of Scorpio, or in the 28th year of his life. What is the symbology of the number 28, if any?

A: None. 106

Q: *(L)* This book describes the Nordic 107
aliens as having blood with a different chemical base than ours...

[12]See session 24 September 1995.

[13]*The Wave* 66

108 **A**: This is trivial disinformation, "Nordic" physiology is identical to yours, with the exception being their cranium, which averages 3 per cent larger. Discuss for insight. Must end session.

Q: *(L)* Thank you. 109

End of session

November 18, 1995

This is another session that is far more interesting in retrospect, after 9/11/01 when all of the elements discussed herein appear to have come into play: plane crashes, strobe lights, hypnosis of the population via mass media, etc. Plus, I would suggest that the direction this session took was triggered by the words 'terrorist bombings'.

Also notice the OOBE that I describe in this session and which happened after the previous session where the 3-5 code was discussed. More on that following the text.

Participants: 'Frank', Laura, Terry and Jan

1 **Q**: *(L)* Hello.

2 **A**: Yes.

3 **Q**: *(L)* Who do we have with us?

4 **A**: Rindr.

5 **Q**: *(L)* And where are you from?

6 **A**: Cassiopaea.

7 **Q**: *(L)* We have several questions... are we ready?

A: Certainly. 8

Q: *(L)* Is there any relationship between all of the terrorist bombings that have been taking place in Paris recently,[1] and any stepped-up alien activity?[2] 9

A: Open. 10

Q: *(L)* Is there anything we can obtain on that subject by formulation of cor- 11

[1]See session 4 November 1995 for previous questions about this.

[2]*The Wave* 32

[3]I've not found a "USAir-194 crash". What I did find was NW Airlines flight 255 which crashed on I-94 on August 16, 1987. From Wikipedia:

> Flight 255 made its takeoff roll on Detroit's Runway 3C at approximately 8:45 p.m. EDT, with Maus at the controls. The plane lifted off the runway at 170 knots (195 mph, 315 km/h), beginning to roll from side to side just under 50 feet (15 m) above the ground. The MD-82 was not able to climb as a result of the flaps not being extended (this would have made the wings larger to allow the lift needed to get off the ground); as a result the plane rolled 40 degrees to the left and struck a light pole near the end of the runway, severing 17 feet (5.2 m) of its left wing and igniting jet fuel stored in the wing. It then rolled 90 degrees to the left, striking the roof of an Avis car-rental building. The plane (now uncontrolled) crashed inverted onto Middlebelt Road and struck vehicles just north of its intersection with Wick Road, killing two people on the ground, It then broke apart, with the

rect questions?

12 **A**: USAir-194 crash;[3] United Air crash, Colorado Springs;[4] Connection? Get voice recorder tape transcripts.

13 **Q**: *(L)* Is this in some way related to the question about the Paris bombing?

14 **A**: No.

15 **Q**: *(T)* This is related to what they were talking about last week, the bases turning 4th density – a plane flew into it and crashed.

16 **A**: Assumption! Strobe lights are used for 3rd density mind control.

17 **Q**: *(L)* Strobe lights located where?

18 **A**: Not a question asked with much thought!

Q: *(L)* You are right. I was just trying to open the subject. *(T)* What does "strobe lights used for mind control" have to do with the air crash? 19

A: Just let it flow. As you will see, past sessions of this nature have yielded best results for you. We have picked up your thought waves, which are progress oriented, and are trying to assist you in your increased learning and progress frequency wave. You see, this increases the energy level!! 20

Q: *(L)* OK. We will just let it flow, then. 21

A: It is advisable to ask questions, but be unconcerned with the nature or content of the answers beforehand. 22

Q: *(L)* Do you wish us to go back to 23

fuselage skidding across the road, disintegrating and bursting into flames as it hit a railroad overpass and the overpass of eastbound Interstate 94 (I-94). There was only one survivor.

The NTSB said: "The National Transportation Safety Board determines that the probable cause of the accident was the flight crew's failure to use the taxi checklist to ensure the flaps and slats were extended for takeoff. Contributing to the accident was the absence of electrical power to the airplane takeoff warning system, due to one of the pilots disconnecting a circuit breaker located in the cabin, the investigation was unable to determine who specifically disconnected this circuit. Due to the alarm's lack of power it did not warn the flight crew that the airplane was not configured properly for takeoff."

[4]Regarding the United Airlines crash in Colorado Springs, Wikipedia says:

United Airlines Flight 585 was a scheduled passenger flight from the now-decommissioned Stapleton International Airport in Denver to Colorado Springs, Colorado. On March 3, 1991, the Boeing 737-291 operating the flight, registered N999UA (previously N7356F with Frontier Airlines), carrying 20 passengers plus a flight crew of 5, crashed while on final approach to runway 35 at Colorado Springs Municipal Airport. There were no survivors.

The NTSB reopened the UAL 585 case after the crash of another 737, USAir Flight 427, which occurred three and a half years later. It was eventually determined that both crashes were the result of a sudden malfunction of the rudder power control unit. The pilots lost control of the airplane because "The rudder surface most likely deflected in a direction opposite to that commanded by the pilots as a result of a jam of the main rudder power control unit servo valve secondary slide to the servo valve housing offset from its neutral position and overtravel of the primary slide."

the statement about strobe lights being used to control minds, and pick up and go from there?

24 **A**: Best not to continuously ask us for advice on how to ask the questions, or if this or that is okay, but rather just "shoot from the hip."

25 **Q**: *(L)* OK. You mentioned the strobe lights. Are these strobe lights that are used to control minds – are these something that we would or might come in contact with on a daily basis?[5]

26 **A**: Do you not already know? We didn't say: some strobe lights, we said: strobe lights, i.e. all inclusive![6]

27 **Q**: *(T)* Strobe lights come in many forms and types. TV is a strobe light. Computer screens are a strobe light. Light bulbs strobe. Fluorescents strobe. Streetlights strobe.

28 **A**: Police cars, ambulances, fire trucks... How long has this been true? Have you noticed any changes lately??!!??

29 **Q**: *(F)* Twenty years ago there were no strobe lights on any of those vehicles mentioned. They had the old flasher-type lights. Now, more and more and more there are strobe lights appearing in all kinds of places. *(L)* And now, they even have them on school buses! *(T)* And the regular city buses have them too, now. *(L)* OK, is the strobing of a strobe light set at a certain frequency in order to do certain things?

30 **A**: Hypnotic opener.

31 **Q**: *(L)* Can we say that this is something we are being acclimated to, so that other things that happen to us in terms of our interactions... it just keeps one in a continual state of hypnosis?

32 **A**: Assumptions restrict the flow!

33 **Q**: *(L)* What is the purpose of the hypnotic opener being used in this way?

34 **A**: You don't notice the craft.

35 **Q**: *(L)* Ohhhhhhhh! So we may be being continuously flown over by alien craft...

36 **A**: Assumption!

37 **Q**: *(L)* Sorry! *(T)* OK, we don't notice the craft because we see the strobes. They are hypnotic openers and are inducing a hypnotic effect...

38 **A**: Assumption!

39 **Q**: *(T)* OK, continue, then.

40 **A**: Well, ask a question, then!

41 **Q**: *(L)* OK, they are telling us not to assume, but to ask. *(T)* OK, what craft are we *not* seeing?

42 **A**: Opener. Is precursor to suggestion, which is auditory in nature.

43 **Q**: *(T)* What suggestion?[7]

44 **A**: Put on your thinking caps. Networking is not making assumptions. Bold unilateral statement of "fact" is.

45 **Q**: *(T)* Oh. Phrase your statements in the form of a question! I'd like 'Hypnotic Openers' for $200, Alex! Cosmic Jeopardy! *(L)* OK, you said the "suggestion is auditory in nature." If this is the case, where is the suggestion coming from auditorily?

46 **A**: Where do you normally receive auditory suggestions from?

[5] *The Wave* 20

[6] *High Strangeness* 7

[7] *The Wave* 20

47 **Q**: *(L)* Radio, television... *(T)* Telephone... *(L)* Is that what we are talking about?

48 **A**: Yes.

49 **Q**: *(L)* If you encounter a strobe while driving, or you are sitting in front of your television, then the suggestions can be put into you better because of this hypnotically opened state? Is that it?

50 **A**: Yes.

51 **Q**: *(L)* What are these suggestions designed to do, to suggest? In a general sense?

52 **A**: Review.

53 **Q**: *(L)* Not see the craft?

54 **A**: Yes.

55 **Q**: *(T)* Do we get these signals from the radio in the car even if it is turned off?

56 **A**: Depends upon whether or not there is another source.

57 **Q**: *(T)* Another source such as?

58 **A**: ELP, for example.

59 **Q**: *(L)* What is 'ELP'?

60 **A**: Extremely Low Pulse.

61 **Q**: *(T)* ELF, Extremely Low Frequency, and ELP, Extremely Low Pulse – is this the same thing?

62 **A**: Sometimes.[8]

63 **Q**: *(T)* This would be an external pulse or frequency?

64 **A**: Yes.

65 **Q**: *(T)* Would it be originating from the source of the strobe?

A: No. They act in unison. 66

Q: *(T)* Two separate sources acting in 67
unison?

A: Close. 68

Q: *(L)* And this process prevents us 69
from seeing something, such as craft flying in our skies at any given time?

A: Or maybe see them as something 70
else.

Q: *(L)* Now, we have to stop for a 71
minute because I want to tell you something. In the past few months, I have really been watching the sky carefully every opportunity I get. On 3 or 4 separate occasions I have seen what I thought was an ordinary airplane, and I would watch it carefully and then scan to the left or right, and when I looked back at the place where this plane should be, based on observable speed and direction, there would be nothing there. I have stood there and searched and searched and found nothing. These things just vanished. I knew I had seen it, I knew I wasn't crazy, I knew it couldn't have gone away that completely – and having it happen several times has just really unsettled me. What are the implications of this, other than the fact that we could be completely overflown at all times for any number of purposes and be, as a mass of people, completely unaware of it?

A: Yes, monoatomic gold! 72

Q: *(L)* And what does the reference to 73
monoatomic gold mean?

A: Total entrapment of the being, 74
mind, body and soul.

[8] I should note here that, until Col. Phil Corso published his book *The Day After Roswell*, I had never heard the term 'ELP'. And, remember, this session was in the latter part of 1995. Corso's book wasn't published until several years later.

75 **Q**: *(T)* That's what Hudson said... on the video.

76 **A**: Strobes use minute gold filament.[9]

77 **Q**: *(L)* How can that compare with taking monoatomic gold internally?

78 **A**: What composes minute filament, do you suppose? Hint, it ain't from Fort Knox!

79 **Q**: *(T)* Monoatomic gold.

80 **A**: Bingo. You see, this has extraordinary properties.

81 **Q**: *(T)* I'm sure it does! The thing is, if it does what Hudson says it does, the power structure would have shut him down – he wouldn't have gotten this far with it. So, if they are letting him do it, it's because it doesn't do what he says it does, it does the opposite. Which is what he said. When you take the stuff for so many days, you complete the program, it restructures your genes. Isn't that what happened to us before? Do we want to do it again? *(L)* And, wasn't it said that light was used to cancel certain DNA factors? *(J)* Exactly! *(L)* OK, how do we block this kind of control?

82 **A**: You don't.

83 **Q**: *(L)* Let me ask this, Chuck D volunteered to act as my bodyguard and went with me to do the lecture down in St. Petersburg last night. He asked an interesting question. It was, if we know what he thinks we know, and if we are building the kind of strength that he thinks we are building, and getting factual information about all such things, why hasn't somebody, either on 3rd density or 4th density, seen fit to stop us, or block us, or whatever? Of course, I did explain to him the level of attack and obfuscation and many other things we have had to face... but, in another sense he was asking very plainly why has something physical not been done to, as he put it, "take us out?"

A: The powers that be want slow release of information.[10] 84

Q: *(L)* Does this include the 4th density STS? 85

A: No, but they don't see that which they do not wish to see. 86

Q: *(L)* They don't see us as a threat? 87

A: More like an annoyance. By the way, why is not Chuck more participatory??? 88

Q: *(L)* Is that a rhetorical question? Or, are you asking me? 89

A: Either, or. 90

Q: *(L)* Chuck is very curious. But, why don't you tell us? 91

A: Be more direct in your informational campaign, Laura, rather than trying to stimulate reactions by way of roundabout actions and statements. 92

Q: *(L)* Are you saying I should be more direct with Chuck, specifically? 93

A: Direct appeals always work much better, but you have a fear based aversion to them, which is related to early childhood interactions with your mother. We are trying to aid you with a bit of insight to assist you in your progress. 94

[Break]

[9]LEDs (light emitting diodes), for example, have a tiny gold or copper filament for bonding its semiconductor to the lead wire of its package.

[10]*The Wave* 32

95 **Q**: *(L)* OK, I want to ask about the experience I had the other night – are you still there?

96 **A**: Why do you always ask that, do you expect us to take a coffee break?

97 **Q**: *(L)* OK, I had what seemed to be an OBE the other night. Was I actually having one?

98 **A**: Was an "all intensive ooze" of the solar realm.[11]

99 **Q**: *(L)* What? *(T)* You asked! *(F)* Well, now *that's* completely clear! *(L)* Sarcasm will get you nowhere, guys! *(T)* That's about as clear as ooze! *(L)* OK, what is an "all intensive ooze" of the solar realm?

100 **A**: Realms are compartmentalized at graduated levels, like everything else. The root basis of the study of astrology is the "unified entity realm," which relates to the effect that local cosmic bodies have upon the body and soul of 3rd density beings in any given locator.

101 **Q**: *(L)* So, what does this mean in terms of what I experienced? I felt that I was moving in and out of my body over and over, sort of like doing an exercise.

102 **A**: Solar activity occurring when your experience took place was such that, based on your "solar return," had the effect of partially separating your soul from your body. Now, just for fun, why not check your chart for that day, and see if the aspects were a little more favorable for expiration of the body potential than usual?

103 **Q**: *(L)* Now that I have been able to play with it a little, will I experience it again, or can I?

A: Well, it is always experienced at 104
least once in the lifetime of a human being, but for most people, it occurs at the conclusion.

Q: [Much laughter] *(L)* You mean I 105
died? Or was this what people experience when they die?

A: Yes, but you got to come back in 106
time for dinner!

Q: *(F)* I guess that's mirth! *(L)* So, 107
that wasn't just an OBE, it was a separation of the soul from the body? Is that the same as astral projection?

A: No. 108

Q: *(L)* Do people who have OBEs ex- 109
perience this?

A: With "astral projection" the con- 110
sciousness level is not as intense because of "the silver cord" and the shroud of third density awareness.

Q: *(L)* You guys just don't know how 111
intense this experience was. I was *so* conscious of everything. *(T)* More conscious than you have ever been before, right? *(L)* I have to say yes. I was playing with what was happening to me and having fun. I noticed every little sensation. The separating from the body produces a sizzling sound, a sort of electrical sizzle, and it changes as you move in and out of the body. I knew what I was doing. *(T)* In astral projection, the soul is still connected to the body. In this case, was Laura's soul completely separated from her physical body?

A: Not completely, but the part that 112
was, was.

Q: *(L)* Well, I did sort of keep a toe 113
in. *(T)* This is almost the same thing

[11] *The Wave* 32

that Dannion Brinkley described in his book. So, if Laura had lost complete connection, would she have died at this point?

114 **A**: Yes.

[Break]

115 **Q**: *(L)* I had a safari dream. I dreamed we all went to Africa, and I got some information there, something was given to me, and I put it in my pocket on the right side. And then, just a few days later I had the experience where I felt a danger, something probing in the direction of my mind, and a protective device shot up out of my lower right abdomen, like a rocket. And the next day, I noticed a small, deep, wound at that spot. What was this?

116 **A**: Energy surge.

117 **Q**: *(L)* Why out of the area of the ovary?

118 **A**: Magnetic plane weakness there.

119 **Q**: *(L)* So, is it beneficial to be able to do this?

120 **A**: Maybe.

Q: *(L)* Is this something I learned in 121
this dream, that we can all learn to do in some way?

A: No need. 122

Q: *(L)* Well, it seems that having 123
the body automatically erect defenses when a threat is felt is a pretty handy talent to have.

A: Sure, in 4th density. 124

Q: *(L)* Was this a 4th density action, 125
or ability?

A: Close. 126

Q: *(L)* Did something actually exit my 127
body and leave that wound?

A: Already answered. 128

Q: *(L)* OK, it was an energy surge. Did 129
this energy surge leave a wound in my body?

A: Yes. 130

Q: *(L)* Where did the energy surge em- 131
anate from?

A: Learn naturally as you evolve. 132
Goodnight.

End of Session

Though I never again had the same intense OOBE as I did just after the introduction of the 3-5 code information, I continued to have almost regular experiences with what must be 4th density reality. I could see with my eyes closed, I could sleep without being 'asleep', and be fully aware of both the present reality, including the children and all their varied activities around me, and at the same time, a whole other world was open to me in which people came and went and talked to me and I conversed with them. It was impossible to *generate* such experiences, but this bleed-through occurred so often that I could say that about half of my day-to-day experiences took place in a dual reality. I observed this phenomenon with curiosity and skepticism. I would project myself to where the children were to see what they were doing exactly, and then come back, make myself orient in this reality, and then physically go to check the observations. Over and over again, I realized that what I was doing was, in some strange sense, real. I didn't know what was happening to me or even why, but it was sufficiently strange to keep me in an attentive state. I didn't want to talk about it too much because whenever I brought such things up to the group, it seemed that even they were not quite able to grasp what I was trying to tell them. I did spend some time reading psychology texts in an effort to determine if I was losing my mind! Exactly what I was experiencing, I wasn't sure, but some clues to the possible nature of it were given in the next session.

November 25, 1995

As I've mentioned a couple of times already, there were issues within the group that kept coming up during the developing stages of the experiment, and most of those issues related to Frank. As the experiment continued, Frank's supercilious attitude grew ever more offensive and Terry, particularly, found it difficult to deal with. I still held the hope that by being connected to a positive source through the rest of us, Frank would somehow be able to counter-balance this, so I was willing to continue as we were, though I had determined there would be no more direct channeling sessions with Frank in the driver's seat.

But, inspired by what we had done thus far, Terry and Jan announced that they were going to start their own experiment with another fellow who lived close to them, Andrew B, who happened to also be a self-proclaimed black magician of the Golden Dawn variety. I didn't get a good feeling about this, but I also understood why: it was a long drive to make every week only to have to put up with Frank's egotistical raconteuring. So, the first part of this session addresses that issue. The rest is about economics and is quite interesting. It was triggered by one of those almost-OOBEs I was having almost constantly as described in the previous session.

Participants: 'Frank', Laura, Susan V

1 **Q**: *(L)* OK, we have some questions for tonight...

2 **A**: What, no greeting?

3 **Q**: *(L)* Hello, how are you?

4 **A**: Fine, thank you, how are you?

5 **Q**: *(L)* We are fine. A little bit frazzled, but I am sure you are aware of that.

6 **A**: Yes.

7 **Q**: *(L)* In terms of this frazzled state, would you care to address that or do we need to ask questions?

A: Who are we? 8

Q: *(L)* Sorry. Who do we have with us tonight? 9

A: Jilliore. 10

Q: *(L)* And where are you from? 11

A: Cassiopaea. 12

Q: *(L)* Getting back to the subject, should we ask questions, or do you have something to address to the issue? 13

14 **A**: Up to you.

15 **Q**: *(L)* I would like for you to address the issue in a general way.

16 **A**: Learning can be a painstaking task.

17 **Q**: *(L)* Yeah. It is painful! We have been really learning. And one of the things we have been learning is that some people are sometimes detrimental to the process here. Can you comment on this?

18 **A**: Those you refer to must learn what they must learn.

19 **Q**: *(L)* They are on their own learning path?

20 **A**: As are all others.

21 **Q**: *(L)* I don't have any bad feelings about any of it, but at the same time, I am not emotionally equipped for turmoil just now. I have enough of my own. I was curious if Andrew B was planning on pursuing the issue of channeling on his own or in company with Terry and Jan?

22 **A**: Yes.

23 **Q**: *(L)* Andrew has said that he can only validate material such as this by bringing it in himself, and Terry and Jan seem to be of the same mind at the moment. Will they be able to connect in a similar way?

24 **A**: They will channel that which their frequency vibrational level dictates.

25 **Q**: *(L)* OK. Enough on that. *(F)* I am just curious as to how long this experiment will last? But, that is probably unimportant. *(L)* It will last as long as it lasts and not a minute longer! *(F)* Exactly!

26 **A**: If you wish, you may maintain contact, and ask for updates in a friendly and informative way. The results will amuse you, if nothing else.

27 **Q**: *(L)* Enough. The other day I experienced one of those extended pre-sleep states, and it seemed that I was in a class and there was someone explaining things to me. What they were telling me was that during this Christmas season [the Christmas season of the dream which had no definite date], certain steps would be taken by those controlling the economy, and that after Christmas, in January and February, a whole lot of stuff was going to be put into motion to send the economy into a dive of major proportions. It was not clear that it was *this* year, but that it was right after a Christmas. Can you tell me where this information was coming from, and what was I experiencing?

28 **A**: This is a long and complicated subject, but we will do our best to explain it. What you were seeing was one possible future. The economy of your 3rd density world is entirely manufactured. The forces that control it are both 3rd density and 4th density. There are conflicting opinions in the 3rd density sector right now as to when, where, and how to institute an economic depression. This has been "in the works" for quite some "time" as you measure it. So far, the forces arguing against institution of a collapse have prevailed. How long this condition will be maintained is open to many outcomes. Also, please be aware that the state of the economy is entirely an illusion. In other words, the world economy performs solely based upon what the population is told to believe.

29 **Q**: *(L)* Well, that is all fine and good except for one fact that I have been observing lately, and that is that prices

continue to go up, and wages for the average person do not. I watch prices, and they have been jumping in a very erratic and frightening way. I know for a fact that people simply cannot afford to live. A large segment of the population cannot, that is.[1]

30 **A**: Nobody who obeys the "rules" can afford to "live," but if you refuse to play the game as you are told to, you will do quite well, indeed.

31 **Q**: *(L)* OK. What do you mean by not playing by the rules? What rules?

32 **A**: The best way for us to answer that is for you to think out loud, and wait for our responses.

33 **Q**: *(S)* Rule one would be working at a regular job, 9 to 5, or 40 hours, whichever, and saving all your money and putting it in the bank.

34 **A**: Wait, one at a time.

35 **Q**: *(L)* OK. The first one is that you have to have a 'regular job'.

36 **A**: "Trap" number one!

37 **Q**: *(S)* Rule number two is that you have to save your money.

38 **A**: You save your money by multiplying it, not storing it.

39 **Q**: *(L)* Are you saying that putting it in a bank is 'storing' it?

40 **A**: Yes.

41 **Q**: *(L)* Are you saying that money is only 'saved' if it is multiplied?

42 **A**: Yes. When you store it in the bank, you are helping the Brotherhood AKA Illuminati AKA Antichrist multiply it for itself, all you get is the "crumbs" left over. And, the Antichrist can "call it in" anytime it wants to!

Q: *(L)* One of the most popular ways 43
to make money by investing is in the stock market. But, it seems to me that the stock market is also part of the Antichrist system and investing there would also amount to only getting 'crumbs'.

A: Yes and no. Not all stocks traded 44
publicly are under direct control of the Illuminati.

Q: *(L)* Are you suggesting the stock 45
market as a means of multiplying money?

A: We are not suggesting anything spe- 46
cific, we are just laying the groundwork. With the general clues we give you, you will figure out the details yourselves, which is tantamount to learning, which is how you progress as souls.

Q: *(L)* You said we should multiply our 47
money and that storing it is not making it work for you...

A: If you notice, all successful business 48
people do this. They multiply their money, expand their horizons, continuously. They multiply their money by multiplying their output, thus their intake likewise. And the process is never ending, because they understand instinctively that it is part of a cycle. For the intake to continue, it must not be only retained, but must increase in order to keep pace with the ever spiraling cycle of increase and expansion. And, for this to happen, the output must be expanded accordingly. When it stops, it collapses. And this is how the Illuminati AKA the Brotherhood AKA the Antichrist creates a "panic," by stemming the flow, even only slightly, and then broadcasting the created impression aggressively.

[1] *The Wave* 32

49 **Q**: *(S)* Well, investing is fine if you have money, but Laura and Frank don't have any money to invest. What would be a way for them to do this?

50 **A**: One example would be to share their experiences, insights, and learnings. One way to replicate such would be to publish, for example.

51 **Q**: *(L)* I know you are 6th density light beings and we are just 3rd density humans, and it is hard for us to continue what we are doing when under constant attack from all directions, internally and externally. I don't see how we can tell about all these experiences without risking further problems.

52 **A**: The work has not been stopped and will not be. You have been told that publishing all or parts of your work is merely "a phone call away," but, as of yet, you have not had faith in that statement, and you have problems asking for what you want for fear of creating the wrong "impression," which is in your head and also a part of the attack process. We have lead you to this position, but you know what they say: "You can lead a horse to water..."

53 **Q**: *(L)* Phone call? Let me say that I have sent out piles of material and talked to people until I am perfectly exhausted. *You* tell me who to call and I will be happy to do it!

A: You have expended an enormous 54
amount of energy communicating with many sources, but most of these are fruitless. Now, think, who was it that told you how to get published???

Q: *(L)* I have talked to Ken E, talked to 55
Roxanne, sent sections of manuscript... what more am I supposed to do?

A: As we said, you have a problem ap- 56
proaching the situation directly. For example, say: "I want to be published, please help me get it done!!!"

Q: *(F)* How? 57

A: We have told you to network!! This 58
works wonders!!! When you write letters, they get filed in the "circular file." Ask those who have been published how they did it and how to do it. Don't be afraid of impressions.

Q: *(L)* Well, publishing still seems like 59
a distant thing.

A: No. Ask Valerian. Ask him to help 60
you get published, point blank, no beating around the bush. He will be very receptive if you offer him a "cut of the action." In fact, that is what he is waiting for!

Q: *(L)* OK. That takes care of Frank 61
and me. What about Sue?

A: Susan is part of the picture for as 62
long as she wishes to be. Goodnight.

End of Session

Now, aside from the interesting remarks about the economy, the significant thing for me was the remark that I was seeing 'one possible future' in this semi-dream state. I wondered if that were the case for the many other instances of bleed-through. Was I at some sort of point of branching of the universe, where the energies are such that many realities are present in potential? And, again, the Cassiopaeans urged networking as something that 'works wonders'. Was I networking? I thought I was. I was sure talking to a lot of people and working very hard to put a magazine together that would become an organ for the Cassiopaean material. But getting the work done alone was a crushing labor. The entire burden, it seemed, was mine.

December 2, 1995

I was feeling rather devastated at the beginning of this session. Terry and Jan had visited the previous evening and had made it more concrete that they were starting their own channeling experiment and, in addition, that they were planning on moving much farther away. I really liked Terry and Jan and they had been a stabilizing influence on the experiment, even if the frequent antagonisms between them and Frank caused some tension. Notice that I mention feeling very negative vibes from Terry during their visit. In retrospect, I think it was probably this conflict between him and Frank that I was picking up, as well as my own hurt feelings that they were falling away and would no longer be there as support.

As for the rest of this very interesting session, one of the things in the *Matrix* books that interested me particularly, considering the comments made by the Cassiopaeans about Hitler and the creation of a master race, was the idea that it was the Nazis who were really the 'secret masters' of the world. It was further suggested that they were producing the whole show, including the alien scenario, because they had been able to construct a time machine. There were some variations on this theory, including an evil Consortium of Nazis and American secret groups involved in mind control experiments, among other things. So, I brought it up.

Participants: 'Frank', Laura

1 **Q**: *(L)* Hello, is anyone there? Do you still love us?

2 **A**: Silly Billy!

3 **Q**: *(L)* Well, sometimes one needs a little reassurance! Who do we have with us tonight?

4 **A**: Rommolah Cassiopaea.

5 **Q**: *(L)* As you know, Terry and Jan were here last night and I felt a lot of very strange sensations, as though there was something very dark that came in with them. My stomach was actually hurting. What is going on?

A: Specifics. 6

Q: *(L)* Is there some negative energy there? 7

A: Is chided. 8

9 **Q**: *(L)* What does that mean?

10 **A**: As your learning center library.

11 **Q**: *(L)* OK, the dictionary says: to scold, to reprove mildly. Who is scolding him?

12 **A**: These are the circumstances unfolding.

13 **Q**: *(L)* The circumstances unfolding are going to chide him or are in the act of chiding him?

14 **A**: The latter.

15 **Q**: *(L)* Well, I sort of felt an energy that was *not* him, but that was following him and came in with him. I even thought I heard it say: "He's ours!"

16 **A**: If attached, it is a "fluid" situation.

17 **Q**: *(L)* Well, they were both talking about plans to start another channeling group with Andrew B and then another still after they move away, because they are now talking about moving to Tallahassee. So, obviously they do not now, nor does it seem that they ever had, any intentions of being permanent group members. Or did I misunderstand?

18 **A**: Obviously.

19 **Q**: *(L)* Well, I am sorry that they feel this way. I have essentially prepared all my life to do this, and so has Frank. They have helped a lot.

20 **A**: Group would have too many chiefs and not enough Indians.

21 **Q**: *(L)* Now, this situation going on with Roxanne has made me think that I ought to decline editing her magazine. Any comment?

[1] *The Wave* 46

A: Beware not to misread. Roxanne is 22
strongly influenced in her behavior by biological cycles.

Q: *(L)* So, I should just let it pass? 23

A: Yes. 24

Q: *(L)* Well, I thought the magazine 25
was a good idea...

A: Let the "flow" guide you in decisions 26
regarding your actions.

Q: *(L)* That is pretty much what I 27
try to do. Well, if Roxanne is being influenced by biology, and Terry is being chided, what is happening to me? I mean, I get dumped on by one, and then less than 12 hours later I get dumped on by the other, and then my husband dumps on me on top of all of it and it is just more than I can handle.

A: Suggest ventilation of room. Ioniz- 28
ing factors level balance.

Q: *(L)* [Open windows] Do the ioniz- 29
ing factors have anything to do with the people who have been in this room in the past few days?

A: All connects. You may close the 30
windows later for comfort after balance is restored.

Q: *(L)* When we did the session on 31
October 21st, we were talking about robotoid-type people, or reanimated humans, and that this is what is done rather than cloning and replacing. Then you said I had been in contact with 7 of these, and we identified one of them. Then, we talked about profiles, and it was indicated that a 'bland' personality might have something to do with identification. You also said that you could not identify the others right at that moment. Can you now do so?

32 **A**: Search your "files." Learning is sometimes best accomplished by study and exploration.[1]

33 **Q**: *(L)* Can I have a couple more clues as to what I am looking for? You mentioned being in a hospital...

34 **A**: Non-emotive. There are other clues which you can discover by your own study. It would not be advantageous for us to give you further information on this subject. Speculation about this particular subject will throw you off track.

35 **Q**: *(L)* Is the subject as important as I think it might be?[2]

36 **A**: Ultimately, but not yet!!

37 **Q**: *(L)* I did an interview that was taped and broadcast on a local television station. I am curious as to whether that will lead to any further similar activity?

38 **A**: Like a pot on rising boil.

39 **Q**: *(L)* Let's get off the personal things and onto interesting things.

40 **A**: Thank you!

41 **Q**: *(L)* Did the Germans construct a time machine during WWII?[3]

42 **A**: Yes.

43 **Q**: *(L)* They actually did it?

44 **A**: Ja.

45 **Q**: *(L)* Were the German experiments in time travel carried to the U.S. after the war?

A: In splintered form. 46

Q: *(L)* Did the U.S. take possession of 47 a time machine constructed by the Germans?

A: No. 48

Q: *(L)* Why not? 49

A: Was taken elsewhere. 50

Q: *(L)* Where? 51

A: Mausenberg, Neufriedland. 52

Q: *(L)* Still in Germany? 53

A: Nein! 54

Q: *(L)* Where is Mausenberg? 55

A: Antarktiklandt. 56

Q: *(L)* Who is in control of or running 57 this machine?

A: Klaus Grimmschackler. 58

Q: *(L)* I didn't mean a specific person; 59 a group – Americans or Germans?

A: Deutsche. 60

Q: *(L)* Did they use this machine to 61 transport themselves there and also in time?

A: Has been performed in glophen in 62 gestalt bityieaire das gluppen und werstalt de vir sein der forbidde.[4]

Q: *(L)* Why are you giving this so that 63 we don't understand?

A: Sorry, got the transmissions mixed 64 up due to subject matter.

[2]My question was really about my husband at the time. My marriage was rapidly deteriorating at the same time that I was struggling to regain my health. The former factor naturally affected the latter and I wasn't improving very rapidly. That, of course, put even more strain on my marriage.

[3]*The Wave* 32

[4]This seems to be an attempt to spell in German. However, even in German, this response does not make sense.

65 **Q**: *(L)* Getting back to this German time machine: did the Germans capture a crashed, or retrieve a crashed, UFO during the war?

66 **A**: Yes.

67 **Q**: *(L)* Who was flying that craft – excuse me – *operating* that craft?

68 **A**: Grays.

69 **Q**: *(L)* Were the Germans able to back engineer and construct other craft similar to the one they captured?

70 **A**: Did not need to. They got the information on such things from channeled sources.

Q: *(L)* Did the Germans get the information from the Vril Society?[5] 71

A: Partly. Also Thule Society.[6] 72

Q: *(L)* These individuals who have this time machine in Antarctica – what are they doing with it or what do they plan to do with it? 73

A: Exploring time sectors through loop of cylinder. 74

Q: *(L)* What is a loop of cylinder? 75

A: Complex, but is profile in 4th through 6th density. 76

Q: *(L)* Are there any particular goals 77

[5]According to Wikipedia: *The Coming Race* is an 1871 novel by Edward Bulwer-Lytton, reprinted as *Vril, the Power of the Coming Race*. Among its readers have been those who have believed that its account of a superior subterranean master race and the energy-form called "Vril" is accurate, to the extent that some theosophists, notably Helena Blavatsky, William Scott-Elliot, and Rudolf Steiner, accepted the book as being (at least in part) based on occult truth. A popular book, *The Morning of the Magicians* (1960) suggested that a secret Vril Society existed in pre-Nazi Berlin. However, there is no historical evidence for the existence of such a society. The novel centres on a young, independently wealthy traveller (the narrator), who accidentally finds his way into a subterranean world occupied by beings who seem to resemble angels and call themselves Vril-ya. The hero soon discovers that the Vril-ya are descendants of an antediluvian civilisation who live in networks of subterranean caverns linked by tunnels. It is a technologically supported Utopia, chief among their tools being the "all-permeating fluid" called "Vril", a latent source of energy that its spiritually elevated hosts are able to master through training of their will, to a degree which depends upon their hereditary constitution, giving them access to an extraordinary force that can be controlled at will. The powers of the will include the ability to heal, change, and destroy beings and things; the destructive powers in particular are awesomely powerful, allowing a few young Vril-ya children to wipe out entire cities if necessary. It is also suggested that the Vril-ya are fully telepathic. The narrator states that in time, the Vril-ya will run out of habitable spaces underground and start claiming the surface of the Earth, destroying mankind in the process, if necessary.

[6]The Thule Society, originally the 'Study Group for Germanic Antiquity', was a German occultist and völkisch group in Munich, named after a mythical northern country from Greek legend. The Society is notable chiefly as the organization that sponsored the Deutsche Arbeiterpartei *(DAP)*, which was later reorganized by Adolf Hitler into the National Socialist German Workers' Party (NSDAP or Nazi Party). [https://en.wikipedia.org/wiki/Thule_Society]

that they have in doing this 'time exploration'?

78 **A**: Not up to present, as you measure it.

79 **Q**: *(L)* Well, if they escaped and took this time machine to Antarctica, are they working with any of the so-called 'aliens'?

80 **A**: 4th density STS.

81 **Q**: *(L)* Are these Germans and their time machine any part of the plan to take over Earth when it moves into 4th density?

82 **A**: Maybe.

83 **Q**: *(L)* Are the Germans behind any of the conspiracies in the U.S.?

84 **A**: No.

85 **Q**: *(L)* So there is a maverick German element, but to focus on that as being the foundational aspect of this phenomenon is to focus on the wrong thing?

86 **A**: Maybe.

87 **Q**: *(L)* Among the things that were discussed among the Germans in the Thule Society and the Vril Society was the 'Black Sun That Illuminates the Interior'. Can you tell us what this 'Black Sun' is?

88 **A**: Ultimate destiny of STS orientation.

89 **Q**: *(L)* Is this Black Sun an actual astronomical phenomenon?

90 **A**: In essence.

91 **Q**: *(L)* What would we know this Black Sun as? A black hole?

92 **A**: Good possibility.

93 **Q**: *(L)* A little off to the side, but is there any Japanese connection here?

A: Only to extent of level of participation in "secret" world government. 94

Q: *(L)* Terry has a theory that the United States is so greatly in debt to the Japanese, and that they are going to default on their obligation and cause the Japanese government to fail, and that the Japanese and some others are going to be played as the 'bad guys', once again, as they were in WWII. Is this a plan in the making? 95

A: No. 96

Q: *(L)* Why did the *X-Files* have an implied Japanese experimental conspiracy blamed for the UFO/alien activity in the United States? Why are they presenting the Japanese as the bad guys? 97

A: Remember, the "X-Files" has a fictional basis. 98

Q: *(L)* I saw a film at Roxannes's house last month where very strange UFOs were seen, and she called them Merkabahs. They were like gigantic, translucent, living creatures – sort of like jellyfish – and they would appear and fade... what were these things? 99

A: 6th density manifestations through realm precursor wave influence pockets. 100

Q: *(L)* It seemed that the person who was filming these things could literally call them up. How was he able to do that? 101

A: Magnetic trine of loco-points on grid matrix interact with thought form projections. 102

Q: *(L)* Does this mean that there is something extraordinary about the person? 103

A: Just from subconscious parallel transformation standpoint. 104

105 **Q**: *(L)* Is there some way we could manifest one of these critters if we wanted to?

106 **A**: Would be exceedingly difficult, as loco-matrix is not currently in your favor.

107 **Q**: *(L)* So, it is partly a function of location, a grid, if you will?

108 **A**: Yes.

109 **Q**: *(L)* Speaking of that, Roxanne wants to move to Sedona, and she says that one of reasons she wants to do this is because "Florida is low density," in her opinion, and "Lizzieland," and full of negative entities and energies. Is this an accurate assessment?

110 **A**: What do you think?

111 **Q**: *(L)* Well, I sometimes wonder... I am sure I could be a better person...

112 **A**: All could always be better, but judgments made in haste as an emotional reaction to events, and generalized in nature, are bound to be rife with emotionally induced prejudice.

113 **Q**: *(L)* Does this mean that it is possible that she is jumping out of the frying pan into the fire by moving off to 'alien-land' out there in the Southwest?

114 **A**: Of course! As you well know!

115 **Q**: *(L)* I feel sorry that she feels this way, and that she is possibly putting herself into danger because she does not seem to be thinking clearly right now, and there does not seem to be anything I can do or say. She is just adamant that Florida is a horrible place because of what happened to her here. In a way, I feel insulted.

A: Use your instincts to guide you in your associations. 116

Q: *(L)* Now, switching gears: while watching the alien autopsy film,[7] we saw a massive organ that occupies the whole center of the abdominal cavity. What was that?[8] 117

A: Heart/liver. 118

Q: *(L)* A combination of both in one? 119

A: Yes. 120

Q: *(L)* They also carefully removed a solid or hard object which they then put in a small container. What was this object? 121

A: Crystal transceiver. 122

Q: *(L)* What was all the loose matter? 123

A: Organic tissue. Not important. 124

Q: *(L)* Was it a female or a male? 125

A: Both and neither. 126

Q: *(L)* Was it a being that could reproduce sexually? 127

A: No. 128

Q: *(L)* What kind of nourishment was required by that being? 129

A: Saline gelatin globules. 130

Q: *(L)* Did it eat as we do, through the mouth? 131

A: Cordates.[9] 132

[7]See session 18 March and 9 September 1995.

[8]*The Wave* 21

[9]Chordates are animals possessing a notochord, a hollow dorsal nerve cord, pharyngeal slits, an endostyle, and a post-anal tail for at least some period of their life cycles. Taxonomically, the phylum includes the subphyla Vertebrata, including mammals, fish, amphibians, reptiles, birds; Tunicata, including salps and sea squirts; and Cephalochordata, comprising the lancelets. Members of the phylum

133 **Q**: *(L)* What? What is that?

134 **A**: Applications using biological microforms to metastasize through primary glandular channels.[10]

135 **Q**: *(L)* Did that being use oxygen as in breathing?

136 **A**: Yes.

137 **Q**: *(L)* Where were the lungs?

138 **A**: Side of dorsal cavity.

139 **Q**: *(L)* I have read about a species of Gray aliens that are very tall and have rows of teeth. I assume that this means more than one row of teeth. What are they?

140 **A**: Biogenetic constructs.

141 **Q**: *(L)* You said once before that there was 16 species or groups on both sides of the 'conflict' on the planet. That is, STS and STO. Have we known or experienced any interactions with other so-called good guys?

A: Not as of yet. 142

Q: *(L)* Can you tell me anything about young Dom, who seems to be surprisingly well-informed for one so young?[11] 143

A: Discovery and observation, bearing in mind previous learnings in order to build profile. 144

Q: *(L)* Who and what are the Mantid-type beings that were seen in Mexico and purportedly caught on film? 145

A: Elapiddorian. 146

Q: *(L)* Where are they from? 147

A: Orion. 148

Q: *(L)* What are they here for? 149

A: Interaction study, are project of Minturians, as they resemble physical 150

Chordata are bilaterally symmetric, deuterostome coelomates, and the vertebrate chordates display segmentation. [https://en.wikipedia.org/wiki/Chordate]

[10]Chordates form a phylum of creatures that are based on a bilateral body plan, and is defined by having at some stage in their lives all of the following: 1) A notochord, in other words a fairly stiff rod of cartilage that extends along the inside of the body. Among the vertebrate sub-group of chordates the notochord develops into the spine, and in wholly aquatic species this helps the animal to swim by flexing its tail; 2) A dorsal neural tube. In fish and other vertebrates this develops into the spinal cord, the main communications trunk of the nervous system; 3) Pharyngeal slits. The pharynx is the part of the throat immediately behind the mouth. In fish the slits are modified to form gills, but in some other chordates they are part of a filter-feeding system that extracts particles of food from the water in which the animals live; 4) Post-anal tail. A muscular tail that extends backwards behind the anus; 5) An endostyle. This is a groove in the ventral wall of the pharynx. In filter-feeding species it produces mucus to gather food particles, which helps in transporting food to the esophagus. It also stores iodine, and may be a precursor of the vertebrate thyroid gland. [https://en.wikipedia.org/wiki/Chordate]

[11]I had been contacted by a young radio DJ who had heard my WFLA broadcast with Johnny Dollar, mentioned in previous session. He wanted to meet with me and discuss UFOs and aliens and so forth. He informed me that something strange was going on with mass media broadcasting – that it was all being taken over by a conglomerate and all programming was being increasingly controlled and this worried him. He felt that preparations were being made for something very negative.

profile. Is study to determine compatibility with 3rd density surface equation.

151 **Q**: *(L)* They are trying to learn if they can manifest on Earth?

152 **A**: After realm border crossing.

153 **Q**: *(L)* Just when is this realm border crossing gonna happen?

154 **A**: Open!

155 **Q**: *(L)* I tried! Now, tell me about Val.

156 **A**: Learn through active pursuit of contact and observation.[12]

157 **Q**: *(L)* Do you think he would ever come to a session?

A: Maybe. 158

Q: *(L)* This year the UFO conference 159 in Gulf Breeze is in the spring. Is this the one we are supposed to go to?[13]

A: Yes. 160

Q: *(L)* Why is my husband being such 161 a jerk lately? I know that is a personal question, but I can't handle the stress.[14]

A: Jerk is subjective. 162

Q: *(L)* I know. But I need some advice. 163

A: Just combine spiritual resources... 164 and goodnight!

End of Session

Regarding the UFO conference, I was referring to something the Cassiopaeans had said almost a year earlier right as we were winding up another session (18 February 1995). The issue of the present moment was the UFO conference in Gulf Breeze that was to be held rather soon. We were talking about attending and distributing our magazine, the *Aurora Journal*, and I was reminded of the fact that the Cassiopaeans had suggested going to a Gulf Breeze conference "in the spring" at a time when the Gulf Breeze conferences had always been held in the fall.

Now, the strange thing about this UFO conference that we were talking about was that the normal schedule was for the spring conference to be held in Tampa and the fall conference to be held in Gulf Breeze. As it turned out, that very year the fall Gulf Breeze conference was nearly canceled because of a hurricane! That, in itself, was

[12] *The Wave* 64

[13] *The Wave* 32, 44

[14] Indeed, my marriage was rapidly crumbling. I was determined to keep it together for the sake of the children, but it seemed that my husband (now my ex) was equally determined to make me as miserable as possible. I've written a bit about this in *Amazing Grace* and the later volumes of *The Wave* so will not belabor it here. Suffice it to say that my deteriorating physical condition, instead of inspiring him to try to help me, only provoked him to feel resentment that I was not there to serve his every whim and need all the time.

an extremely interesting event. We had been planning on attending this particular conference and T and J had already made the reservations. Hurricane Opal was spinning around in the Gulf and everyone was waiting to see where it would come ashore.

So, we canceled our reservations for the UFO conference. As it turned out, the hurricane did hit Gulf Breeze almost dead on, and the conference was moved to Mobile. Clearly, there was no bomb blast or tornado so if any of the above-mentioned possibilities did play out, they would seem to have been mass abductions and mental controls initiated.

As a result of this hurricane, the organizers of the conference decided to switch the schedule around so that the Gulf Breeze conference was held in the spring the following year, 1996. But, not in May. In March. So, even if the Cassiopaeans were picking up something about this specific 'switcheroo', it was not a bull's-eye exactly. Another thing that has happened since that hurricane is that the organizers of the conference broke up their organization and reformed. They no longer hold UFO conferences, but rather focus on metaphysical/New Age assemblies. So, it may be that there was a mass abduction and mental controls that initiated dissension. But, it would be difficult to make ufologists any more fragmented and factional than they already were and are!

December 12, 1995

When I brought up the subject to my husband – of going to a weekend UFO conference – he didn't make any real objections but, as the days passed, his sniping and complaining and finding fault (which was standard behavior for him) rose to new levels of intensity.

I was still in therapy three times a week from the automobile accident back in December of 1994, and this was one of the tools he used against me. Obviously, if I could go to a UFO conference, I didn't need any help with the house or the children. Not only that, but he began to covertly encourage the children to not do their own chores. When I would tell them that they were grounded or otherwise restricted for not doing their work, he would override my authority and tell me sneeringly, "That's what mother's are for – to take care of their families." Obviously, by his definition, that meant being a hand-servant and a doormat to everyone in the house.

The situation escalated daily and I had a complete relapse from progress in my therapy. The nervous tremors in my hands increased, the various nerve pains, numbness and partial paralysis that I had begun to overcome slowly came crashing back, and I became so depressed over this that I was hardly able to function at all. Not only that, but I suddenly acquired an ear infection that made the side of my head swell out two or three inches. There was no way I could get on an airplane with an infection like that. The doctor put me on 850 mg of Augmentin four times daily, which reduced the infection, but it just wouldn't go away completely.

But, the struggles I was having with my health did not seem to matter to either my ex-husband or, because of his attitude and manipulations, my children. During the times I was unable to even get out of bed, I would lie there listening to my husband and kids merrily watching television in the next room; knowing that they were all deliberately making as much mess and noise in the house as they possibly could; knowing that he was intentionally instigating it; and that if I said a word I would be shouted down as a woman who no longer wanted to be a wife and mother! I had been so determined to try to go to this conference, and it seemed that my will to do anything was slowly, but surely, being sapped.

I remember lying there, feeling more alone and imprisoned than I ever had in my life; imprisoned not only by the circumstances of my life, but by the deterioration of my health. My eyes would wander to the racks of guns on the walls in the bedroom (I was not allowed to decorate the room as I might like it, but had to live in a room full of gun collections and hunting gear), and I thought how easy it would be to just give him his freedom, give the children what they wanted, which amounted to a life of no rules and restrictions, and obtain peace and freedom from pain for myself.

All it would take would be one singular act of... what? Was it courage I lacked?

But then I thought about the children. Even if they were being manipulated by him, what would it mean to them, especially the baby, to hear a gunshot and run in to find their mother with half a head and her brains splattered all over the walls? I couldn't do that to them. No matter what, I had to endure the pain and the frustration. It was a burden I had chosen, so I needed to just square my shoulders and pick it up and carry it. But, oh! How lonely it was!

As usual, I tried to find the flaw or fault in myself. Perhaps it was my attitude, or some sort of distortion of my perception. Maybe there was some simple answer – something I could do to make life more pleasant and functional for the whole family.

As it was, I went to enormous efforts to make sure that the sessions and the related work interfered as little as possible with family life, but it would have been impossible for it to have no impact. Maybe I was seeing what we were doing as important when it was not? Maybe I should just give it up or, at the very least, schedule the sessions less frequently? It seemed pretty clear that, if there were no Cassiopaeans, if there were no sessions, if I returned to the Baptist fold of my husband's faith and became a dutiful and meek wife, all would be well.

But I couldn't do that.

The drive to learn, to resolve the issues of my past and present were too imperative. I could no longer shove things under the rug. I could no longer lie to myself and say that "God is in his heaven and all is right with the world." I had seen and experienced too much. Only a lobotomy might have helped at this point!

Nevertheless, I resolved to ask the Cassiopaeans about what I could do to make life a little smoother for all our sakes. I knew it meant breaking the 'no personal questions' rule, but I could see no other hope for an answer. It turned out to be a very unusual session:

Participants: 'Frank', Laura, Susan V

1 **Q**: *(L)* Hello.

2 **A**: Hello.

3 **Q**: *(L)* Who do we have with us this evening?

4 **A**: Tira.

5 **Q**: *(L)* And where are you from?

6 **A**: Cassiopaea.

7 **Q**: *(L)* I am sorry but I have some personal questions tonight before we get started with other things. I would like to know what is the reason for this terrible depression I have been experiencing for so long now? I am sick of it.[1]

8 **A**: It is a crushing attack.

9 **Q**: *(L)* Where is it coming from?

10 **A**: 4th density STS.

11 **Q**: *(L)* What can I do to break it before it breaks me?

12 **A**: Counteract.

13 **Q**: *(L)* By what? How do you counteract the things that are just beyond one's ability to deal with?

14 **A**: How is the attack represented in 3rd density for you?

15 **Q**: *(L)* How? Because it seems that my husband does not love me. I do not feel safe or in any way able to function as a wife and mother with this feeling, and I know that it must be a misperception on my part, but I cannot help but feel this way. How can I get over this feeling that he is constantly trying to break me into pieces [psychologically]? Not only do I have to bear the constant burden of the children with no support, the house, managing everything, but I also am continuously sniped at by him. None of my feelings are ever considered. I feel like I am being shoved over and buried by a bulldozer. Is that what you want to know?

A: You are diverting by secession. 16

Q: *(L)* What do you mean? 17

A: What is the definition of "to secede?" 18

Q: *(L)* To leave a union. To step out. To break a union. 19

A: Attack is not countered by following objectives of attack. 20

Q: *(L)* What are the objectives of this attack aside from crushing me?[2] 21

A: Secession at an inappropriate juncture to throw plans askew. 22

Q: *(L)* What plans would be thrown askew by secession at this point? 23

[1] *The Wave* 32
[2] *The Wave* 53

24 **A**: Voice.

25 **Q**: *(L)* What?

26 **A**: And all other.

27 **Q**: *(L)* Well, I just feel that I would plunge into a pit if I had to secede, as you put it.[3]

28 **A**: Suggest ignoring "snipes" and other unpleasantness, as it is not of your being, thus should not be taken "to heart," and when taken thusly, causes emotional disturbances which manifests as depression and related maladies. These ailments tend to grow in scope and intensity, thereby causing severe damage to plans and activities aimed at executing ones "mission."

29 **Q**: *(L)* That's all fine and good. But, just exactly what is the mission?

30 **A**: You are awakening to it just fine, thank you![4]

31 **Q**: *(L)* Are you saying that all this constant discussing and taking things apart and talking about them and thinking about all these things is actually getting us somewhere?

32 **A**: Absolutely!!!![5]

33 **Q**: *(L)* Well, let's get on with the questions. Is the magazine or some other mode of getting information out part of this 'mission'?

A: When you have learned, you have energized yourself. 34

Q: *(L)* What does that mean in relation to the question? 35

A: Lead by the hand? No way, Jose! 36

Q: *(L)* Frank and I discussed a name for the magazine last night and we came up with – and who knows how – Aurora to symbolize the dawn, waking up... that sort of thing. Where in the world did this come from? 37

A: Refer to the previous 2 answers. 38

Q: *(L)* Any comments? 39

A: No need, you are doing just fine by yourselves. 40

Q: *(S)* What did you expect them to say? "Atta girl!"? [Laughter] Will the magazine support itself? 41

A: We are not going to answer that as it would violate level one directive. 42

Q: *(L)* What is a "level one directive"? 43

A: Refer to last answer. 44

Q: *(L)* Well, fine! I want to know! Is there some place that gives out orders? 45

---

[3]In retrospect, the objectives of the attack were to make me so depressed I would actually think about 'seceding' in a permanent way. Obviously, since I had put that thought away, 'secede' meant divorce to me.

[4]*The Wave* 28

[5]Here I was referring to the fact that outside of the sessions, there was a lot of discussion about psychological topics with Frank and a couple of other friends, mainly my old friend Sandra. Frank and Sandra both felt that I was spinning my wheels in trying to save my marriage and make things work. They could see how exhausting it was and that I was getting no support at all in terms of recovering from my injuries from the accident the previous December. It had now been almost a full year and I was not only no better, I was getting worse. I could barely dress myself and I struggled just to keep the house going. I was determined. I did *not* want to go the route of divorce or separation.

46 **A**: You will know when it is right, and not before!

47 **Q**: *(L)* I want you guys to know that I sometimes feel a wee tiny bit like a pawn on a chessboard!

48 **A**: You should, you inhabit 3rd density STS environment.

49 **Q**: *(L)* I was at least hoping that if I was a pawn, that some of the players were good guys. Is that asking too much?

50 **A**: Yes.

51 **Q**: *(L)* To which statement?

52 **A**: Good guys don't play chess.

53 **Q**: *(L)* But there have been so many strange events, so many synchronous events. Is that the good guys helping or the bad guys leading me astray?

54 **A**: Neither. It is Nature running its course.

55 **Q**: *(L)* OK. One of the sensations I have experienced is that I have had it up to the eyebrows with the negative energies and experiences of 3rd density, and I have thought lately that this feeling of having had enough, in an absolute sense, is one of the primary motivators for wanting to find one's way out of this trap we are in. I want out of it. Is this part of this 'Nature' as you call it?

56 **A**: Yes.

57 **Q**: *(L)* When a group of people...

58 **A**: When you see the futility of the limitations of 3rd density life, it means you are ready to graduate. Notice those who wallow in it.

59 **Q**: *(L)* Some people obviously wallow in extreme materiality. And there seems to be another kind that is more subtle, which has to do with saying that you want to grow and become enlightened, and yet such a person is unable to pierce the veil of their own illusions about how to become enlightened, and this illusion is the wallowing...

A: Wallowing takes many forms. 60

Q: *(L)* Among the things I have no- 61
ticed is the type of person who says: "This is my *last* life! Swami So-and-so told me!" And they are wallowing in the enjoyment of the adulation they receive from their followers who believe that sort of thing can be known.

A: Sometimes, but avoid stereotyping, 62
because sometimes they are correct!!!

Q: *(L)* OK. I am not trying to stereo- 63
type.

A: More often, the sign is someone who 64
does not feel alienated by the obvious traps and limitations of 3rd density.

Q: *(L)* Well, that says a lot. One of 65
the questions on the list is: In many of the Sumerian drawings and literature, the gods, the Annunaki, are described as eating a plant that grew at the bottom of the ocean, and this plant was the source of eternal life.

A: Nonsense! The source of eternal life 66
is existence!

Q: *(L)* Well, the point was that there 67
was some sort of food that these beings ate that was unusual or different that somehow enhanced their abilities to an extreme degree...

A: Totally false and you should know 68
it!! All so-called "special powers" come from non-physical sources!!!

Q: *(L)* Carlos Castaneda talks about 69
the 'Eagle's emanations', the Eagle being, I suppose, Prime Creator that emanates down through all the densities,

and that the Nagual who can 'see', sees the Eagle as a large black and white object. Are they seeing the source, or are they seeing something on just another density?[6]

70 **A**: Source? There is no such thing.

71 **Q**: *(L)* You mean there is no Prime Creator, no origin or source of our existence?

72 **A**: You are Prime Creator.[7]

73 **Q**: *(L)* But that is so esoteric... I am talking about...

74 **A**: The point is: stop filling your consciousness with monotheistic philosophies planted long ago to imprison your being. Can't you see it by now, after all you have learned, that there is no source, there is no leader, there is no basis, there is no overseer, etc... You literally possess, within your consciousness profile, all the power that exists within all of creation!?! You absolutely have all that exists, ever has, or ever will, contained within your mind. All you have to do is learn how to use it, and at that moment, you will literally, literally, be all that is, was, and ever will be!!!!!!!

75 **Q**: *(L)* That is all fine and dandy and sounds wonderful, except for one little item. You also say that the monotheistic concepts were *imposed* on us to prevent us from knowing this. So, if we are all that is, how can something exist that can impose something so unpleasant on us?

76 **A**: Choices follow desire based imbalances.

77 **Q**: *(L)* If that is the case, why can't any one just turn off the lights, end the illusion, and everything becomes nothing?

A: Well, first of all, everything does not 78
become nothing. Secondly, some have already become everything.

Q: *(L)* Terrific! And I understand that 79
we are digging our way out of this particular illusion. And that is rather profound a thing to say to someone still stuck in the mire. I really want to find out, but it is hard. I have to think about that for a while. So, let me ask some questions for my daughter. A___-wants to know what the core of Jupiter consists of.

A: Basal. In 3rd density it is known as 80
irridium.

Q: *(L)* What is the diameter of the 81
solid core?

A: 3 microns. 82

Q: *(L)* Are you saying that Jupiter is 83
gassy and slushy all the way through?

A: Yes. 84

Q: *(L)* So Sitchin and others may not 85
be correct in saying that Jupiter has an Earth-sized solid core?

A: If that is what they are saying, but 86
remember, Jupiter, Saturn and others resonate to vibrational levels greater than Earth. You are looking directly at density 4 when you view Jupiter, which is why photos of it from up close appear "surreal," more like drawings.

Q: *(L)* Do beings inhabit Jupiter? 87

A: 5th density and up. 88

Q: *(L)* Are there any organic beings on 89
Jupiter?

A: Organic is 3rd density concept. 90

[6] *The Wave* 10
[7] *The Wave* 30

91 **Q**: *(L)* So the probe will not detect any life?

92 **A**: No.

93 **Q**: *(L)* Is this probe that is going to plunge into Jupiter disturb anything there in any way?

94 **A**: No.

95 **Q**: *(L)* What is the internal 3rd density temperature of Jupiter?

96 **A**: 7000 degrees K.

97 **Q**: *(L)* What is the primary chemical composition?

98 **A**: Ammonia, hydrogen and nitrous oxide.

99 **Q**: *(L)* There is a rumor going around that a large object coming our way, that is a gigantic, intelligently controlled space craft, loaded with Lizzies. Could you comment on this please?

100 **A**: Comet cluster. Sitchin believes it is a "planet."

Q: *(L)* In terms of this comet cluster, how many bodies are in this cluster as a discrete unit? 101

A: Variable. 102

Q: *(L)* What is the ETA? 103

A: Open. 104

Q: *(L)* Why is it open? Why can't we look at it and determine the factors, the direction, trajectory, velocity... 105

A: If you could, you would be interrupted in your learning cycle. 106

Q: *(L)* What exactly does *that* mean? *(F)* Because you would never do anything else because all you would think about is the day the comet is coming! *(L)* Well, speaking of that, I have had 3 death dreams and Frank has had one. I would like to inquire about them. 107

A: No comment. And goodnight. 108

End of Session

So you see what happens when you whine and complain to the Cassiopaeans! All they do is get your dander up! But, oddly, it was what I needed. Even though I desperately wanted to have somebody come and fix what was wrong in my life, I knew that it was unrealistic to expect anyone to clean up the mess that I had made. And the only way I knew to ask for help was to pray and meditate. So, that is what I did.

As a result of my prayers, I came to some ideas and conclusions. No matter how dreadful the present situation was, I could not help but feel that my life was being guided somehow (even if it was just nature taking its course), and I had only to demonstrate my faith and commitment for things to work out as they should by acceptance of the situation as it was. Of course, I had the idea that if I just had enough faith, my husband would undergo some dramatic change and the dream of the 'bridegroom' would come true. Until that time, I would be a good and attentive wife, do the best I could for the sake of the children, get whatever satisfaction I could get from my work, my friends, and some little writing and sharing of information, and just not worry about what he did. A commitment is a promise, and I didn't break my promises. I was sure God or Nature was going to fix it. I knew that, for the moment, I was essentially alone. I didn't have a husband; he was as much a lost child as the children were, and I accepted the responsibility of them all. I believed this to be the direction the Cassiopaeans were pointing me. If I accepted the situation as it was and did the best I could, I felt sure that it would change on its own. Never mind that my idea of this change was that what was broken would be fixed!

December 16, 1995

We had attended a Christmas party held at a local New Age book store and, after a couple of drinks and snacks, decided we'd rather go home and chat with the Cs since I was so exhausted. Contrary to the claims of certain defamers, I am a teetotaler all year and only take token drinks during holidays. That couple of drinks had an effect on me as you can see from the opening! It was a short session.

Participants: 'Frank', Laura, Susan V

1 **Q**: *(L)* Hello.

2 **A**: Hello.

3 **Q**: *(L) (L)* I am slightly inebriated, in case you guys can't guess that already!

4 **A**: Okay.

5 **Q**: *(L)* Who do we have with us tonight?

6 **A**: Wimorio.

7 **Q**: *(L)* And where are you from?

8 **A**: Cassiopaea.

9 **Q**: *(L)* Of course we realize that this is just the point of transmission and that you don't *live* there... Now, first of all...

10 **A**: Pretty bracelet.

11 **Q**: *(L)* Well! Thank you! My little son made it out of Christmas ribbon.

12 **A**: Little?

13 **Q**: *(L)* Of course we know he is not *little*, but he is still my little baby. My first question is about the economic situation we have discussed before [same evening]. All the things we have discussed among ourselves about this, relating to what was given about the economy before, could you tell us whether our views are at all accurate?

14 **A**: Accuracy is relative to juncture with possible futures.

15 **Q**: *(L)* We know there are several possible futures, but we think that a particular one is becoming more likely...

16 **A**: Refer to two sessions ago for answer to this.

17 **Q**: *(L)* We are still dealing with this by eliminating the myths, whether or not there is going to be an economic collapse, we think that creative financial management is the way to go...

18 **A**: Yes.

19 **Q**: *(L)* Using these ideas, is Susan going to be able to manage her resources so that she has a higher return?

20 **A**: Yes. Susan is an innocent person when it comes to areas of investment and finance. Her current status was arrived at as the result of consults with others who did not necessarily have her best interests in mind!

21 **Q**: *(S)* I just want to be sure that if anything happens to my mom that I will be able to take care of her.

22 **A**: Move mother into living will. Does she wish to be kept alive by artificial means?

23 **Q**: *(S)* Definitely not. *(L)* Is that all for Susan?

24 **A**: Not yet. T Bills, commodities market, registered CD's, pennystocks relating to conservation companies, such as offshoots of TRW and Georgia Pacific, etc. Do it now!!! Get some silver too, and liquidate remainder. Suggest 20 per cent in the form of new 100 dollar bills for safekeeping, the new currency only!! February 1996 bills issue. Place into safe along with silver.

25 **Q**: *(L)* How much in silver?

26 **A**: Up to her, also suggest a novelty gold coin or two.

27 **Q**: *(F)* What commodities?

28 **A**: Grain futures and pork bellies best. Pork and other swine futures.

29 **Q**: *(L)* You said that my life would be straightened out and that this would happen through the internet. In fact, you said that my life would change suddenly and drastically...

30 **A**: Yes.

31 **Q**: *(L)* Yet, all I have experienced has been the most oppressive internal and external attack imaginable...[1]

32 **A**: Benefits follow oppressiveness, what is it that you tell to others?? The darkness always precedes the dawn!

Q: *(L)* Well, I don't know which way to turn. I am not in a position to do anything about any of it just now. 33

A: Ask for help, silly! 34

Q: *(L)* I don't like to ask for help. 35

A: You have to. 36

Q: *(L)* That reminds me: Frank shouted at me tonight. *(F)* You shouted at me, too! *(L)* I didn't shout at you! And you shouted at me first! *(F)* I said I was sorry. And so did you. You forgot about it for a while. Why sulk now? *(L)* Because I want to sulk! OK, we have taken care of Susan's questions, and we have decided to just let Laura suffer in the soup... 37

A: No. 38

Q: *(L)* What about Frank's situation? 39

A: Soon to improve. 40

Q: *(L)* I ran into Pat Z recently. Can you comment?[2] 41

A: Keep in touch with her, lest she "wane" in your regard. 42

Q: *(L)* I received an e-mail from a fellow who experienced something similar to what happened to me which you called an 'eclipsing of realities'. 43

A: It was an abduction by cyber-genetic probes whose origin, or more correctly, "station," is the 5th planet around Betelgeuse, known as A.Hur in Orion federation 4th density STS. 44

Q: *(L)* What was the purpose of this abduction? 45

[1] *The Wave* 32

[2] Woman who came for hypnosis session on the night that giant black boomerang-type UFOs were seen in several places in our area, including over my house. This episode is related in detail in *The Wave* chapter 44.

46 **A**: Screen for compatibility for placement on shune, platter, within Mark Status 3.

47 **Q**: *(L)* What does that mean? Placement on "shune, platter"?

48 **A**: It is a demarcation status for compatibility of future "worker" status.

49 **Q**: *(L)* So, "shune" is a word used for that?

50 **A**: Close. Ask P___ if he has had headaches and or blackouts.

51 **Q**: *(L)* Was my experience the same thing?

A: No. It is the "same" from your view point only. 52

Q: *(L)* Is there any advice I can give P___? 53

A: Tell him to keep in touch with you for more information. 54

Q: *(L)* Why haven't I heard from Val?[3] 55

A: "Push buttons" more. Ask for more contact. Time to go. Goodnight. 56

End of Session

---

[3] *The Wave* 64

December 30, 1995

The majority of this tape was indecipherable due to a constant static that drowned out most of the words. This is the best reconstruction possible.

Regarding the background, just a few days before Christmas I was doing my Christmas baking. I remember sitting at the kitchen table, covered with dustings of flour, my girls helping me, and such an apparently happy family scene all around me. The kids didn't know they were being manipulated by their father; they didn't know how it was between their father and me; and I was resolved to keep it from them as best I could. They deserved happiness and stability. And, I was now trying in every way to make my husband happy as well, short of giving up my mind and my work. I redoubled my efforts to the point of absolute exhaustion so that nothing I did would interfere in the normal events of our lives so he would have nothing to complain about. But, the more I tried to juggle everything, the more demanding he became so that it was harder and harder to manage it without some sort of scene with him. Not only that, it was physically destroying me.

So, there I was in my kitchen, baking Christmas goodies with my children, and feeling utterly devastated that I could not feel the happiness that I was working so hard to create around me. The radio was playing and a haunting song caught my ear:

> I could have a mansion that is higher than the trees
> I could have all the gifts I want and never ask please
> I could fly to Paris, oh, it's at my beck and call
> Why do I go through life with nothing at all?
>
> But when I dream, I dream of you
> Maybe someday you will come true
>
> I can be the singer or the clown in every room
> I can even call someone to take me to the moon
> I can put my make-up on and drive the men insane
> I can go to bed alone and never know his name

But when I dream, I dream of you
Maybe someday you will come true

(Sandy Mason Theoret, Jando Music Inc.)

And I broke down and began to cry. What did it matter if I solved the mysteries of the Universe or died in the effort? No one else would ever know... No one who really cared, that is. The forces that were driving me, the Quest seemed to be mine alone. And I was alone.

All the dreams of 'Him' came flooding back and I wondered if He was somewhere on the planet wondering if I was somewhere on the planet. Again, for the millionth time I sternly reminded myself that all such thoughts were nonsense. There was no such thing as 'The One'. It was only romantic fairy tales at best, pathological delusions at worst. Get a grip on your mind, girl!

The children were very concerned with my tears, and I explained that middle-aged mothers just do that sometimes. Nothing to be concerned about. And I pushed the thoughts back under the rug and told myself that I should be overjoyed with what I had and not be such a whiner and crybaby for what I didn't have.

But, even though my mind issued the orders, something deep inside was not listening! Our preparations to attend the Gulf Breeze UFO conference continued. We thought we had experienced high strangeness in our lives. We didn't know how strange it can get!

Participants: 'Frank', Laura, Susan V

1 **Q**: *(L)* Hello.

2 **A**: Hello.

3 **Q**: *(L)* Who do we have with us?

4 **A**: Vira.

5 **Q**: *(L)* And where are you from?

6 **A**: Cassiopaea.

7 **Q**: *(L)* We have a number of questions we want to cover tonight. The first thing is, in the early stages of this channeling process we talked about what it was we were supposed to be doing. We were told that the first thing we needed to do was "establish a clear channel". Obviously, it has taken about a year to do that. I have wondered, after numerous incidents, if it might not be better for us to stop having guests at the sessions, and to simply work in a private way and then pass the information out to others. Would this help to maintain the clarity of the channel?

A: Partially. 8

Q: *(L)* Which part is correct? 9

A: Suitable "third party" on board is 10
helpful.

Q: *(L)* Well, aside from someone to 11

take the notes, who would be the 'suitable' third party on the board? Since Terry and Jan have decided to start another channel with Andrew and [another] Jan, and have even talked about moving to Tallahassee and starting a group there...?

12 **A**: Up to you to discover.

13 **Q**: *(L)* The next thing that was identified that we must do was to establish a 'forum'. What is this forum supposed to be in?

14 **A**: These are all questions to which you must discover the answers by learning, therefore, no further discussion is now beneficial.[1]

15 **Q**: *(L)* Now the next thing was that a direction would open and that there was something amazing and wonderful just around the corner that I would recognize instantly and which would help me to know what to do. Has this already occurred and did I miss something?

16 **A**: Wait and see.

17 **Q**: *(L)* In one session, I asked what was the internal motivation inside me and you responded, "to be a leader of your cause". Well, my motivation then and now, as I understand it, is to find truth and share it with those who ask for it, and to do this in a rather quiet and private way.

18 **A**: Leaders come in a variety of "packages."

19 **Q**: *(L)* I was recently invited to give a talk to the ISCNI, that is, the Institute for the Study of Contact with Non-human Intelligence. I am rather curious as to the reaction of the head of this organization, Mike Lindemann? Was he shocked by some of the things I said?

[1] *The Wave* 64

A: Intrigued would be more accurately descriptive, but nonetheless, Lindemann and the others would best serve the "cause" if they loosen any rigidities that they may have found themselves "grooving into," as this is an area that definitely does not lend itself to manifestations of rigidity in any way, shape, or form, whatsoever!!! 20

Q: *(L)* I think they are getting a little rigid because they are under pressure from the scientific community and they feel they have to prove something. But, observable elements of the phenomenon of aliens have gone so far that trying to prove anything scientifically becomes moot. We don't have time for double-blind experiments. We don't have time to wait for FDA approval! Based upon the energies surrounding the subject, is Lindemann going to respond? 21

A: Make him do so. Persist and express the same thoughts you did here! Help him and others to see that they are dealing with a phenomenon that is better studied in a way that stresses an open learning forum, not a "scientific" study methodology. In all its forms, not just the "physical" agenda that is primarily sought by some and in fact, it is through the ethereal plane and methodologies that the clues and some of the answers lie for physical as well as ethereal factors. Tell Michael this verbatim: "You once had a more open mind, Michael, what happened?" Some of his most frustrating recent events in his life relate directly to this!! Trust your insights, they are assisted learning matrix. 22

Goodnight.

As I have already noted, the presence at two sessions of the young woman *(RC)*, who was convinced that she had been connected to me in some way in a previous life in Nazi Germany, really seemed to shift the direction of the Cassiopaean communications. In retrospect, it was also the opening of a door and the initiating of a new path in my life. After the first session she attended, I had the dream of the happy wedding where I was taken to meet the faceless bridegroom, and after the second session she attended, I had the actual hallucinatory vision of the unknown-yet-familiar-face – my future husband, Ark. RC was also the one who accelerated the project of producing a magazine as an organ for the Cassiopaean material. I had envisioned something that would be more serious and yet open-minded than the usual metaphysical or UFO publications, and a journal seemed to just fit the bill. She had been producing a magazine for a few years and wanted to give it up because she had plans to relocate, and at the same time, she didn't want to leave her subscribers hanging. It seemed to be a perfect solution for me to take over the subscription list and carry on the work.

RC's focus had been more astrological, though she included many articles about alien abduction and conspiracy theories, so the slight reorientation I planned didn't seem like too great a divergence from the original format. I didn't care for the name of the rag, but that was a minor point that could be rectified. Everything looked like it was a go and we felt that this was the key to networking in a big way.

Chapters of "The Wave"

"The Wave" originally was a series of articles written by Laura Knight-Jadczyk for the Internet only. These articles have been expanded and published as a series of volumes (1–8), in paper and in electronic formats. Over the years, a number of editions have been produced for each of these volumes. Some of these editions do not have chapter numbering, and for some, the chapter numbering has been re-started from one. However, the chapter titles are identical in all editions. For this reason, the following table summarizes all chapters of *The Wave* Series and gives chapter number, chapter title, and shows into which volume a particular chapter number has been included (VP = volume number in print, VE = volume number in electronic format), and where a chapter can be found on the Cassiopaea website. Please refer to the bibliography, section "Esotericism", for additional details about the volumes of *The Wave*.

Nr.	Chapter Title	VP	VE	http://cassiopaea.org/
1	"Riding The Wave"	1	1	/the-wave-chapter-1
2	"Multi-Dimensional Soul Essences"	1	1	/the-wave-chapter-2
3	"Dorothy and The Frog Prince"	1	1	/the-wave-chapter-3
4	"The C's go for a 'Test Drive'"	1	1	/the-wave-chapter-4
5	"Perpendicular Realities"	1	1	/the-wave-chapter-5
6	"Animal Psychology"	1	1	/the-wave-chapter-6
7	"Laura Falls Into the Pit"	1	1	/the-wave-chapter-7
8	"Everywhere You Look..."	1	2	/the-wave-chapter-8
9	"The Beast of Gévaudan"	1	2	/the-wave-chapter-9
10	"The Truth Is Out There"	2	2	/the-wave-chapter-10
11	"Roses Grow Best In Manure"	2	2	/the-wave-chapter-11
12	"All There Is Is Lessons"	2	2	/the-wave-chapter-12
13	"Some Further Remarks"	2	2	/the-wave-chapter-13
14	"Candy Will Ruin Your Teeth"	2	2	/the-wave-chapter-14
15	"He Hideth My Soul..."	2	2	/the-wave-chapter-15
16	"Laura Finds Reiki"	2	2	/the-wave-chapter-16
17	"Wandering In 3rd Density"	2	2	/the-wave-chapter-17
18	"A Trip to 'Alligator Alley'"	2	2	/the-wave-chapter-18
19	"Dr. Greenbaum"	2	2	/the-wave-chapter-19

20	"Black Lightning Strikes"	3	3	/the-wave-chapter-20
21	"Roswell Revisited"	3	3	/the-wave-chapter-21
22	"The Nexus Seven"	3	3	/the-wave-chapter-22
23	"Lucifer and the Pot of Gold"	3	3	/the-wave-chapter-23
24	"The Bacchantes Meet Apollo"	3	3	/the-wave-chapter-24
25	"A Walk in Nature"	3	3	/the-wave-chapter-25
26	"The Tree of Life"	3	3	/the-wave-chapter-26
27	"Stripped to the Bone"	3	3	/the-wave-chapter-27
28	"Technicians of Ecstasy"	4	4	/the-wave-chapter-28
29	"The 3-5 Code"	4	4	/the-wave-chapter-29
30	"Grape Wine In a Mason Jar"	4	4	/the-wave-chapter-30
31	"The Priory of Sion"	4	4	/the-wave-chapter-31
32	"Torah, Kaballah..."	4	4	/the-wave-chapter-32
33	"Introduction"	5	5	/the-wave-chapter-33
34	"The Channel"	5	5	/the-wave-chapter-34
35	"A Strange Interlude"	5	5	/the-wave-chapter-35
36	"A Vile Superstition"	5	5	/the-wave-chapter-36
37	"Critical Channeling"	5	5	/the-wave-chapter-37
38	"The Feminine Vampire"	5	5	/the-wave-chapter-38
39	"The Court of Seven"	5	5	/the-wave-chapter-39
40	"Secret Agents from Alpha 1"	5	5	/the-wave-chapter-40
41	"The Realm of Archetypes"	5	5	/the-wave-chapter-41
42	"The Tradition"	5	5	/the-wave-chapter-42
43	"The Head of Bran"	5	5	/the-wave-chapter-43
44	"The Crane Dance"	5	5	/the-wave-chapter-44
45	"The Gulf Breeze"	5	5	/the-wave-chapter-45
46	"The Theological Reality"	5	5	/the-wave-chapter-46
47	"Semiotics and the Content Plane"	5	5	/the-wave-chapter-47
48	"The Juvenile Dictionary"	6	6	/the-wave-chapter-48
49	"Frequency Resonance Vibration"	6	6	/the-wave-chapter-49
50	"Shifts in the Matrix"	6	6	/the-wave-chapter-50
51	"The Psychomantium"	6	6	/the-wave-chapter-51
52	"The Cryptogeographic Being"	6	6	/the-wave-chapter-52
53	"Strange Birds"	6	6	/the-wave-chapter-53
54	"Glimpses of Other Realities"	6	6	/the-wave-chapter-54
55	"Albert Einstein, Free Energy..."	6	6	/the-wave-chapter-55
56	"Intolerance, Cruelty..."	6	6	/the-wave-chapter-56
57	"It's Just Economics"	7	7	/the-wave-chapter-57
58	"Alien Reaction Machines"	7	7	/the-wave-chapter-58
59	"An Encounter with the Unicorn"	7	7	/the-wave-chapter-59
60	"The Unicorn's Closet"	7	7	/the-wave-chapter-60
61	"Ira's Inner Cesspool"	7	7	/the-wave-chapter-61
62	"Secret Games at Princeton"	7	7	/the-wave-chapter-62
63	"Murdering the Feminine"	7	7	/the-wave-chapter-63
64	"Crossing the Threshold"	8	8	/the-wave-chapter-64

65	"The Way of the Fool"	8	8	/the-wave-chapter-65
66	"The Zelator"	8	8	/the-wave-chapter-66
67	"Food for the Moon"	8	8	/the-wave-chapter-67
68	"As Above, So Below"	8	8	/the-wave-chapter-68
69	"The Whirlpool of Charybdis..."	8	8	/the-wave-chapter-69
70	"You Take the High Road..."	8	8	/the-wave-chapter-70
71	"If I Speak in the Tongues..."	8	8	/the-wave-chapter-71
72	"Nonlinear Dynamics of Love..."	8	8	/the-wave-chapter-72

Recommended Reading

This is a subset of the "Recommended Reading" list at
http://cassiopaea.org/forum/index.php/topic,33 092.0.html

9/11

- Griffin, David Ray – *The 9/11 Commission Report: Omissions And Distortions*, Olive Branch Pr 2004
- Griffin and Falk – *The New Pearl Harbor: Disturbing Questions About the Bush Administration and 9/11*, Interlink Pub Group 2004
- Quinn and Knight-Jadczyk – *9/11 The Ultimate Truth*, Red Pill Pr 2006
- Wood, Judy – *Where Did the Towers Go? Evidence of Directed Free-energy Technology on 9/11*, The New Investigation 2010

Ancient Civilizations

- David-Neel, Alexandra – *Magic and Mystery in Tibet*, Dover 1971
- Dunn, Christopher – *The Giza Power Plant: Technologies of Ancient Egypt*, Bear & Company 1998
- Firestone, West, Warwick-Smith – *The Cycle of Cosmic Catastrophes: How a Stone-Age Comet Changed the Course of World Culture*, Bear & Company 2006
- Fox, Hugh – *Gods of the Cataclysm: A revolutionary investigation of man and his gods before and after the Great Cataclysm*, Aardwolfe Books 2011
- von Hassler, Gerd – *Lost Survivors of the Deluge*, Signet 1978
- Muck, Otto – *The Secret of Atlantis*, HarperCollins 1979

Astronomy

- Clube and Napier – *The Cosmic Serpent*, Universe Pub 1982
- Clube and Napier – *The Cosmic Winter*, Blackwell Pub 1990
- Knight-Jadczyk, Laura – *The Apocalypse: Comets, Asteroids and Cyclical Catastrophes*, Red Pill Pr 2012
- Velikovsky, Immanuel – *Worlds in Collision*, Paradigma Ltd 2009

Bible History

- Davies, Philip R. – *The Origins of Biblical Israel (Library Hebrew Bible/Old Testament Studies)*, T&T Clark 2009
- Finkelstein and Silberman – *David and Solomon: In Search of the Bible's Sacred Kings and the Roots of the Western Tradition*, Free Pr 2007
- Garbini, Giovanni – *History and Ideology in Ancient Israel*, Crossroad Pub Co 1988
- Mack, Burton – *The Lost Gospel: The Book of Q and Christian Origins*, HarperOne 1994
- Mack, Burton – *A Myth of Innocence: Mark and Christian Origins*, Augsburg Fortress Pub 1998
- Silberman, Neil Asher – *The Bible Unearthed: Archaeology's New Vision of Ancient Israel and the Origin of Its Sacred Texts*, Touchstone 2002
- Thompson, Thomas L. – *The Mythic Past: Biblical Archaeology And The Myth Of Israel*, Basic Books 2000
- Thompson, Thomas L. – *The Messiah Myth: The Near Eastern Roots of Jesus and David*, Basic Books 2005

Cassiopaea Experiment

- Koehli, Harrison – "The Cs Hit List 01: Prophecy, Prediction, and Portents of Things to Come", *Signs Of The Times*, sott.net/article/236777
- Koehli, Harrison – "The Cs Hit List 02: Space and Weather Science Gone Wild", *Signs Of The Times*, sott.net/article/237356
- Koehli, Harrison – "The Cs Hit List 03: History Is Bunk", *Signs Of The Times*, sott.net/article/238372
- Koehli, Harrison – "The Cs Hit List 04: Nature, Nurture, and My Monkey Genes", *Signs Of The Times*, sott.net/article/239307
- Koehli, Harrison – "The Cs Hit List 05: Dr. Greenbaum and the Manchurian Candidates", *Signs Of The Times*, sott.net/article/240587
- Koehli, Harrison – "The Cs Hit List 06: Let's Do the Planetary Twist to the Tune of the Brothers Heliopolis", *Signs Of The Times*, sott.net/article/242280
- Koehli, Harrison – "The Cs Hit List 07: Sun Star Companion, Singing Stones and Smoking Visions", *Signs Of The Times*, sott.net/article/244819
- Koehli, Harrison – "The Cs Hit List 08: Of Oracles and Conspiracies: TWA 800, 9/11, H1N1, and VISA", *Signs Of The Times*, sott.net/article/247080
- Koehli, Harrison – "The Cs Hit List 09: DNA, Rational Design and the Origins of Life", *Signs Of The Times*, sott.net/article/250256

Esotericism

- Campbell, Joseph – *The Hero with a Thousand Faces*, Princeton University Pr 1972
- Chittick, William – *The Sufi Path of Knowledge: Ibn al-'Arabi's Metaphysics of Imagination*, State University of New York Pr 1989
- Hall, Manly – *The Secret Teachings of all Ages*, Wilder Publications 2009
- Knight-Jadczyk, Laura – *Amazing Grace*, Red Pill Pr 2012
- Knight-Jadczyk, Laura – *Riding the Wave: The Truth and Lies about 2012 and Global Transformation* (The Wave Series Vol. 1), Red Pill Pr 2010
- Knight-Jadczyk, Laura – *Soul Hackers: The Hidden Hands Behind the New Age Movement* (The Wave Series Vol. 2), Red Pill Pr 2010
- Knight-Jadczyk, Laura – *Stripped to the Bone: The Path to Freedom in the Prison of Life* (The Wave Series Vol. 3), Red Pill Pr 2010
- Knight-Jadczyk, Laura – *Through a Glass Darkly: Hidden Masters, Secret Agendas and a Tradition Unveiled* (The Wave Series Vol. 4), Red Pill Pr 2011
- Knight-Jadczyk, Laura – *Petty Tyrants & Facing the Unknown: Navigating the Traps and Diversions of Life in the Matrix* (The Wave Series Vol. 5/6), Red Pill Pr 2011
- Knight-Jadczyk, Laura – *Almost Human: A Stunning Look at the Metaphysics of Evil* (The Wave Series Vol. 7), Red Pill Pr 2009
- Knight-Jadczyk, Laura – *Debugging the Universe: The Hero's Journey* (The Wave Series Vol. 8), Red Pill Pr 2012
- Ouspensky, P. D. – *In Search of the Miraculous: Fragments of an Unknown Teaching*, Harvest/HBJ 1977

Information Theory, Metaphysics and Evolution

- Davies and Gregersen – *Information and the Nature of Reality: From Physics to Metaphysics*, Cambridge University Pr 2010
- Hardy, Alister – *The Living Stream: Evolution and Man*, Harper & Row 1965
- Milton, Richard – *Shattering the Myths of Darwinism*, Inner Traditions 1997
- Morgan, Elaine – *The Scars of Evolution: What Our Bodies Tell Us About Human Origins*, Oxford 1990
- Nagel, Thomas – *Mind and Cosmos: Why the Materialist Neo-Darwinian Conception of Nature Is Almost Certainly False*, Oxford University Pr 2012
- Pierce, John R. – *An Introduction to Information Theory: Symbols, Signals and Noise*
- Shiller, Bryant M. – *Origin of Life: The 5th Option*, Trafford Pub 2006

Health

- Keith, Lierre – *The Vegetarian Myth: Food, Justice and Sustainability*, PM Press 2009
- Mate, Gabor – *When the Body Says No: Exploring the Stress-Disease Connection*, Wiley 2011

History

- Baigent and Leigh and Lincoln – *Holy Blood, Holy Grail: The Secret History of Christ & The Shocking Legacy of the Grail*, Dell Trade Paperbacks 2004
- Baillie, Mike – *Exodus to Arthur: Catastrophic Encounters With Comets*, B T Batsford Ltd 1999
- Baillie, Mike – *New Light on the Black Death*, Tempus 2006
- Carotta, Francesco – *Jesus Was Caesar: On the Julian Origin of Christianity: An Investigative Report*, Aspekt 2005
- Garnier, John – *The Worship of the Dead, or the Origin and Nature of Pagan Idolatry and Its Bearing Upon the Early History of Egypt and Babylonia*, Chapman & Hall 1904
- Knight-Jadczyk, Laura – *The Secret History of the World: And how to get out alive* (Secret History Series Vol. 1), Red Pill Pr 2005
- Knight-Jadczyk, Laura – *Comets and the Horns of Moses* ("Secret History" Series Vol. 2), Red Pill Pr 2013
- Langer, Walter C. – *The Mind of Adolf Hitler: The Secret Wartime Report*, Basic Books 1972
- Lescaudron and Knight-Jadczyk – *Earth Changes and the Human Cosmic Connection* (Secret History Series Vol. 3), Red Pill Pr 2014
- Malkowski, Edward F. – *Ancient Egypt 39,000 BCE: The History, Technology, and Philosophy of Civilization X*, Bear & Company 2010
- Momigliano, Arnaldo – *On Pagans, Jews, and Christians*, Wesleyan 1987
- Shreeve, James – *The Neandertal Enigma: Solving the Mystery of Modern Human Origins*, Avon 1996
- Sitchin, Zecharia – *The 12th Planet*, Harper 2007
- Thompson and Cremo – *The Hidden History of the Human Race (The Condensed Edition of Forbidden Archeology)*, Bhaktivedanta Book Pub 1999
- Wilkens, Iman – *Where Troy Once Stood: The Mystery of Homer's Iliad & Odyssey Revealed*, St Martins Pr 1991

Hyperdimensions

- Abbott, Edwin A. – *Flatland: A Romance of Many Dimensions*, Signet 1984
- Kaku, Michio – *Hyperspace: A Scientific Odyssey Through Parallel Universes, Time Warps, and the 10th Dimension*, Anchor 1995
- Ouspensky, P.D. – *Tertium Organum: A Key to the Enigmas of the World*, Vintage 1981
- Rucker, Rudy – *The Fourth Dimension: A Guided Tour of the Higher Universes*, Houghton Mifflin 1984

Politics and Pathocracy

- Allen, Gary – *None Dare Call It Conspiracy*, Gsg & Assoc 1971
- Douglass, James W. – *JFK and the Unspeakable: Why He Died and Why It Matters*, Touchstone 2010
- Klein, Naomi – *The Shock Doctrine: The Rise of Disaster Capitalism*, Picador 2008
- Knight-Jadczyk, Laura – *JFK: The Assassination of America*, Red Pill Pr 2013
- Prouty, L. Fletcher – *JFK: The CIA, Vietnam, and the Plot to Assassinate John F. Kennedy*, Skyhorse Pub 2011
- Prouty, L. Fletcher – *The Secret Team: The CIA and Its Allies in Control of the United States and the World*, Skyhorse Pub 2011

Psychology

- DiSalvo, David – *What Makes Your Brain Happy and Why You Should Do the Opposite*, Prometheus 2011
- Donaldson-Pressman, Stephanie – *The Narcissistic Family: Diagnosis and Treatment*, Jossey-Bass 1997
- Golomb, Elan – *Trapped in the Mirror: Adult Children of Narcissists in their Struggle for Self*, William Morrow & Co 1995
- Hort, Barbara E – *Unholy Hungers: Encountering the Psychic Vampire in Ourselves & Others*, Shambhala 1996
- Kahneman, Daniel – *Thinking, Fast and Slow*, Farrar, Straus and Giroux 2013
- McRaney, David – *You Are Not So Smart: Why You Have Too Many Friends on Facebook, Why Your Memory Is Mostly Fiction, and 46 Other Ways You're Deluding Yourself*, Gotham 2012
- Simon, George K. – *Character Disturbance: the phenomenon of our age*, Parkhurst Brothers 2011

- Stout, Martha – *The Myth of Sanity: Divided Consciousness and the Promise of Awareness*, Penguin 2002
- Wilson, Timothy D. – *Redirect: The Surprising New Science of Psychological Change*, Little, Brown and Company 2011
- Wilson, Timothy D. – *Strangers to Ourselves: Discovering the Adaptive Unconscious*, Belknap Pr 2004

Psychopathy

- Babiak and Hare – *Snakes in Suits: When Psychopaths Go to Work*, HarperBusiness 2007
- Brown, Sandra – *Women Who Love Psychopaths: Inside the Relationships of inevitable Harm With Psychopaths, Sociopaths & Narcissists*, Mask Pub 2010
- Cleckley, Hervey – *The Mask of Sanity: An Attempt to Clarify Some Issues about the So-Called Psychopathic Personality*, Literary Licensing 2011
- Hare, Robert D. – *Without Conscience: The Disturbing World of the Psychopaths Among Us*, Guilford Pr 1999
- Lobaczewski, Andrzej – *Political Ponerology: A Science on the Nature of Evil Adjusted for Political Purposes*, Red Pill Pr 2007
- Stout, Martha – *The Sociopath Next Door*, Harmony 2006

Religion

- Hoyle, Fred – *Origin of the Universe and the Origin of Religion (Anshen Transdisciplinary Lectureships in Art, Science, and the Philosophy of Culture, Monograph)*, Moyer Bell 1997

Spiritualism

- Ashe, Geoffrey – *The Ancient Wisdom: A Quest for the Source of Mystic Knowledge*, Macmillan 1997
- Baldwin, William – *Spirit Releasement Therapy: A Technique Manual*, Headline Books 1995
- Barrett and Hyslop – *Evidence Of Survival After Death*, Kessinger Publishing 2010
- Blum, Deborah – *Ghost Hunters: William James and the Search for Scientific Proof of Life After Death*, Penguin Books 2007
- Davis, Vance A. – *Unbroken Promises: A True Story of Courage and Belief*, White Mesa Pub 1995
- Doyle, Arthur Conan – *The History of Spiritualism*, Fredonia Books 2003

- Carrington and Fodor – *Haunted People: The Story Of The Poltergeist Down The Centuries*, Kessinger Publishing 2006
- Ebon, Martin – *Prophecy in our Time*, New American Library 1968
- Elkins, Rueckert, McCarty – *The Ra Material*, L/L Research 1984
- Fiore, Edith – *The Unquiet Dead: A Psychologist Treats Spirit Possession*, Ballantine 1995
- Fodor, Nandor – *The haunted mind: A psychoanalyst looks at the supernatural*, Garrett Pub 1959
- Garret, Eileen – *Many Voices: The Autobiography of a Medium*, Putnam Pub
- Kardec, Allan – *The Spirits Book*, White Crow Books 2010
- Lethbridge, T. C. – *The Power of the Pendulum*, Penguin Books 1991
- Marciniak, Barbara – *Bringers of the Dawn*, Bear & Company 1992
- Martin, Malachi – *Hostage to the Devil: The Possession and Exorcism of Five Contemporary Americans*, HarperOne 1999
- Roll and Storey – *Unleashed: Of Poltergeists and Murder: The Curious Story of Tina Resch*, Pocket Books 2007
- Stevenson, Ian – *Twenty Cases Suggestive of Reincarnation*, University of Virginia Pr 1980
- Vickers, Brian – *Occult Scientific Mentalities*, Cambridge University Pr 1986
- Whitten and Fisher – *Life between Life*, Grand Central Pub 1988
- Wickland, Carl – *Thirty Years Among the Dead*, White Crow Books 2011
- Wilson, Colin – *The Siren Call of Hungry Ghosts: A Riveting Investigation Into Channeling and Spirit Guides*, Paraview Press 2001

UFOs/Aliens

- Bramley, William – *The Gods of Eden*, Avon 1993
- Corso, Philip – *The Day After Roswell*, Pocket Books 1998
- Dolan, Richard – *UFOs and the National Security State: Chronology of a Cover-Up, 1941–1973*, Keyhole Pub 2009
- Dolan, Richard – *UFOs and the National Security State: The Cover-Up Exposed, 1973–1991*, Keyhole Pub 2010
- Fort, Charles – *The Complete Books of Charles Fort*, Dover 1974
- Fowler, Raymond E. – *The Andreasson Affair: The Documented Investigation of a Woman's Abduction Aboard a UFO*, Wild Flower Pr 1994
- Fuller, John G. – *The Interrupted Journey*, Dial Pr 1967
- Jessup, Morris – *The Case for the UFO*, New Saucerian Books 2014

- Knight-Jadczyk, Laura – *High Strangeness: Hyperdimensions and the Process of Alien Abduction*, Red Pill Pr 2008
- Moulton Howe, Linda – *Glimpses of Other Realities Vol. 1: Facts and Eyewitnesses*, LMH Prod 1993
- Moulton Howe, Linda – *Glimpses of Other Realities Vol. 2: High Strangeness*, LMH Prod 1998
- Keel, John – *Operation Trojan Horse*, Anomalist Books 2013
- Keel, John – *The Mothman Prophecies*, Tor 2002
- Keel, John – *The Eighth Tower*, Anomalist Books 2013
- Picknett and Prince – *The Stargate Conspiracy: The Truth about Extraterrestrial life and the Mysteries of Ancient Egypt*, Berkley 2001
- Redfern, Nick – *Close Encounters of the Fatal Kind: Suspicious Deaths, Mysterious Murders, and Bizarre Disappearances in UFO History*, New Page Books 2014
- Sanderson, Ivan T. – *Invisible Residents: The Reality of Underwater UFOs*, Adventures Unlimited Pr 2005
- Strieber, Whitley – *Majestic*, Tor 2011
- Turner, Karl – *Into the Fringe: A True Story of Alien Abduction*, WordMean 2014
- Turner, Karl – *Taken: Inside the Alien-Human Agenda*, WordMean 2013
- Vallee, Jacques – *Passport to Magonia: On UFOs, Folklore, and Parallel Worlds*, Contemporary Books 1993
- Vallee, Jacques – *Dimensions: A Casebook of Alien Contact*, Anomalist Books 2008

Books and DVDs from Red Pill Press

Visit redpillpress.com for more information!

The Secret History of the World, Vol. 1

... and how to get out alive

Laura Knight-Jadczyk

If you heard the Truth, would you believe it? Ancient civilisations. Hyperdimensional realities. DNA changes. Bible conspiracies. What are the realities? What is disinformation?

The Secret History of The World and How To Get Out Alive is the definitive book of the real answers where Truth is more fantastic than fiction. Laura Knight-Jadczyk, wife of internationally known theoretical physicist, Arkadiusz Jadczyk, an expert in hyperdimensional physics, draws on science and mysticism to pierce the veil of reality. Due to the many threats on her life from agents and agencies known and unknown, Laura left the United States to live in France, where she is working closely with Patrick Rivière, student of Eugene Canseliet, the only disciple of the legendary alchemist Fulcanelli.

With sparkling humour and wisdom, she picks up where Fulcanelli left off, sharing over thirty years of research to reveal, for the first time, The Great Work and the esoteric Science of the Ancients in terms accessible to scholar and layperson alike.

Conspiracies have existed since the time of Cain and Abel. Facts of history have been altered to support the illusion. The question today is whether a sufficient number of people will see through the deceptions, thus creating a counter-force for positive change - the gold of humanity - during the upcoming times of Macro-Cosmic Quantum Shift. Laura argues convincingly, based on the revelations of the deepest of esoteric secrets, that the present is a time of potential transition, an extraordinary opportunity for individual and collective renewal: a quantum shift of awareness and perception which could see the birth of true creativity in the fields of science, art and spirituality. *The Secret History of the World* allows us to redefine our interpretation of the universe, history, and culture and to thereby navigate a path through this darkness. In this way, Laura Knight-Jadczyk shows us how we may extend the possibilities for all our different futures in literal terms.

With over 850 pages of fascinating reading, *The Secret History of The World and How to Get Out Alive* is rapidly being acknowledged as a classic with profound implications for the destiny of the human race. With painstakingly researched facts and figures, the author overturns long-held conventional ideas on religion, philosophy, Grail legends, science, and alchemy, presenting a cohesive narrative pointing to the existence of an ancient techno-spirituality of the Golden Age which included a mastery of space and time: the Holy Grail, the Philosopher's Stone, the True Process of Ascension. Laura provides the evidence for the advanced level of scientific and metaphysical wisdom possessed by the greatest of lost ancient civilizations - a culture so advanced that none of the trappings of civilization as we know it were needed, explaining why there is no 'evidence' of civilization as we know it left to testify to its existence. The author's consummate synthesis reveals the Message in a Bottle reserved for humanity, including the Cosmology and Mysticism of mankind Before the Fall when, as the ancient texts tell us, man walked and talked with the gods. Laura shows us that the upcoming shift is that point in the vast cosmological cycle when mankind - or at least a portion of mankind - has the opportunity to regain his standing as The Child of the King in the Golden Age.

If ever there was a book that can answer the questions of those who are seeking Truth in the spiritual wilderness of this world, then surely *The Secret History of the World and How to Get Out Alive* is it.

Comets and the Horns of Moses

The Secret History of the World, Vol. 2

Laura Knight-Jadczyk

The Laura Knight-Jadczyk's series, The Secret History of the World, is one of the most ambitious projects ever undertaken to provide a cogent, comprehensive account of humanity's true history and place in the cosmos. Following the great unifying vision of the Stoic Posidonius, Laura weaves together the study of history, mythology, religion, psychology and physics, revealing a view of the world that is both rational and breathtaking in its all-encompassing scope. This second volume, Comets and the Horns of Moses, (written in concert with several following volumes soon to be released) picks up the dangling threads of volume one with an analysis of the Biblical character of Moses – his possible true history and nature – and the cyclical nature of cosmic catastrophes in Earth's history.

Laura skillfully tracks the science of comets, revealing evidence for the fundamentally electrical and electromagnetic nature of these celestial bodies and how they have repeatedly wreaked havoc and destruction on our planet over the course of human history. Even more startling however, is the evidence that comets and cometary fragments have played a central role in the formation of human myth and legend and the very concept of a 'god'. As she expertly navigates her way through the labyrinth of history, Laura uncovers the secret knowledge of comets that has been hidden in the great myths, ancient astronomy (and astrology) and the works of the Greek philosophers. Concluding with a look at the political and psychological implications of cyclical cometary catastrophes and what they portend for humanity today, Comets and the Horns of Moses is a marvel of original thought and keen detective work that will rock the foundations of your understanding of the world you live in, and no doubt ruffle the feathers of the many academics who still cling to an outdated and blinkered view of history.

Earth Changes and the Human-Cosmic Connection

The Secret History of the World, Vol. 3

Pierre Lescaudron and Laura Knight-Jadczyk

Jet Stream meanderings, Gulf Stream slow-downs, hurricanes, earthquakes, volcanic eruptions, meteor fireballs, tornadoes, deluges, sinkholes, and noctilucent clouds have been on the rise since the turn of the century. Have proponents of man-made global warming been proven correct, or is something else, something much bigger, happening on our planet?

While mainstream science depicts these Earth changes as unrelated, Pierre Lescaudron applies findings from the Electric Universe paradigm and plasma physics to suggest that they might in fact be intimately related, and stem from a single common cause: the close approach of our Sun's 'twin' and an accompanying cometary swarm.

Citing historical records, the author reveals a strong correlation between periods of authoritarian oppression with catastrophic and cosmically-induced natural disasters. Referencing metaphysical research and information theory, *Earth Changes and the Human-Cosmic Connection* is a ground-breaking attempt to re-connect modern science with the ancient understanding that the human mind and states of collective human experience can influence cosmic and earthly phenomena.

Covering a broad range of scientific fields, and including over 250 figures and 1,000 sources, *Earth Changes and the Human-Cosmic Connection* is presented in an accessible format for anyone seeking to understand the signs of our times.

The Wave 1 – "Riding the Wave"

... The Truth and Lies about 2012 and Global Transformation

Laura Knight-Jadczyk

As 2012 fast approaches, opinions about what to expect on this much-anticipated date are sharply polarized. Will humanity experience a global, spiritual transformation? Cataclysmic Earth Changes? Or both? Or nothing? If Earth and its inhabitants are scheduled for some life-changing or life-ending event, we should ask ourselves what we know and how we know it, and how to prepare for our future.

Drawing on decades of research into history, religion, and the esoteric, Laura Knight-Jadczyk introduces the concept of "the Wave" to describe the possible phenomena behind all the hype surrounding global transformation. *Riding the Wave* not only collects the most probable scenarios we may face in the near future – it provides the context to make it all intelligible.

With roots in the science of hyperdimensions made popular by physicist Michio Kaku and the Fortean theories of the late John Keel, *Riding the Wave* suggests that many of the noticeable changes to our world in the last century are symptoms of the approaching Wave. From climate change, extreme population growth and technological development, as well as novel social and political movements, to the advent of UFO sightings, crop circles, and a variety of otherworldly experiences, something is up on the Big Blue Marble, and it all seems to be leading to a sea change in the way we see and interact with the world. The only question is, will it be for the better or the worse?

An intimate blend of science and mysticism, this volume of Laura Knight-Jadczyk's Wave Series initiates the process of unveiling the truth about life on Earth, and the man behind the curtain...

The Wave 2 – “Soul Hackers”

... The Hidden Hands Behind the New Age Movement

Laura Knight-Jadczyk

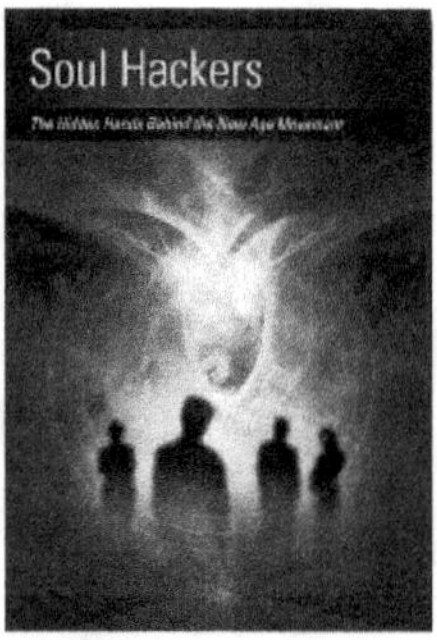

Why are we here? Why do we suffer? If this is an infinite school, what are we here to learn? And why do our efforts at “fixing” our lives often do exactly the opposite? As mystic and researcher Laura Knight-Jadczyk writes in this volume of her expansive Wave Series: “when you ask a question – if the question is a burning one – your life becomes the answer. All of your experiences and interactions and so forth shape themselves around the core of the answer that you are seeking in your soul. In [my] case, the question was: ‘How to be One with God,’ and the answer was, ‘Love is the answer, but you have to have knowledge to know what Love really is.’ ”

Soul Hackers is a deeply personal and insightful account of this very process – of burning questions and transformative answers. Through the story of her own struggle with mainstream and alternative religion and the solutions they claim to offer, Knight-Jadczyk lays bare the problems inherent in the New Age movement as a whole – from Reiki, Wicca, and the phenomenon of channeling, to the very real problems of spirit attachments, mind control, and otherworldly predators posing as benevolent beings. She asks what it really means to “create your own reality.” Is it merely self-hypnosis, or is something more hidden in this New Age truism?

The answers lie in the very nature of the Wave – the cosmic force and fabric of personal and collective evolution. For anyone wishing to understand the deeper meaning and reality of the human experience, and what our very near future may very well have in store for us, *Soul Hackers* provides a map to our symbolic reality and the knowledge necessary to weather the approaching storm.

The Wave 3 – "Stripped to the Bone"

... The Path to Freedom in the Prison of Life

Laura Knight-Jadczyk

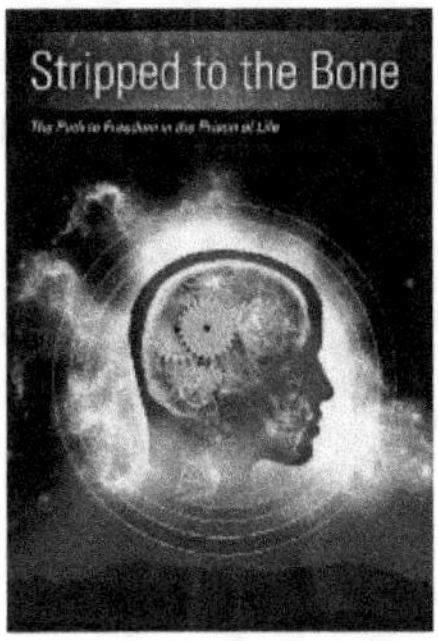

Media propaganda. Official cover-ups. Dishonest science. "Non-lethal" weaponry. Mind control technology. Racial stereotypes. Social engineering. Religious programming. The cold pursuit of profit. And the unrelenting pull of materialism... In a world where "freedom" is exported at the barrel of a gun, true freedom seems more like a distant fairytale, blocked for us in more ways than we can imagine.

In *Stripped to the Bone*, author Laura Knight-Jadczyk lays bare the forces seeking to keep humanity in a prison of its own creation. She lucidly describes evil's place in the cosmos, from the dark world of political conspiracy and government mind control to the reality behind the UFO phenomenon. But in response to the grim state of affairs on the Big Blue Marble, she also asks: Is there a solution? What can we learn from those who came before us? *Stripped to the Bone* suggests that this knowledge was not only known and widely practiced in humanity's prehistory, but that it can be rediscovered.

Through her extensive reading on all things esoteric, Knight-Jadczyk maintains that by knowing our limitations, we may overcome them. In this volume of her acclaimed Wave Series, she tears down our illusions about freedom and the idea that it can be won in any war. Rather, the path to freedom is an inner battle against the many limitations placed on our ability to choose by official culture, our own beliefs, and the forces behind the reality of our everyday experience.

By showing us our own limitations she also succeeds in presenting anew the real possibilities and true potential of a free humanity.

The Wave 4 – "Through A Glass Darkly"

... Hidden Masters, Secret Agendas and a Tradition Unveiled

Laura Knight-Jadczyk

Behind the surface of everyday life lie secrets that have been kept from the eyes of the humanity. In every field of knowledge, we seem to take a wrong turn, coming to conclusions that are diametrically opposed to the truth of the matter. It seems that true science, history, the purpose and aim of human life, our past and potential futures are all off limits to public consumption. How can this be the case, and can these truths come to be known?

In *Through a Glass Darkly*, Laura Knight-Jadczyk continues to make it clear that nothing is what it appears to be. From the stories stitched together to make up our own personal identities to the myths of history on which nations are founded, we live in a sea of lies and half-truths. Just as we lie to ourselves and each other about who we really are, often putting ourselves in the best light possible, there are those who manufacture, manipulate, and shape current and past events to suit their own vested interests. And the current events of today will become the history of tomorrow, erroneously shaping our notions of who we are as a people, just as those of the past have done before.

But behind this sorry state of affairs, the truth awaits discovery. In this fourth volume of her series *The Wave or Adventures with Cassiopaea*, Knight-Jadczyk follows the trail of the hidden masters of our planet, exposing the agenda behind the alleged secret society, the "Priory of Sion", and that mystery's connections with alchemy, Oak Island, and the Kabbalists of old. In the process she reveals aspects of the tradition kept under wraps by these very groups. By exposing the agendas and conspiracies of the elite, we can come to know the truth about ourselves, and why it is has been kept hidden.

The Wave 5 & 6 – "Petty Tyrants & Facing the Unknown"

... Navigating the Traps and Diversions of Life in the Matrix

Laura Knight-Jadczyk

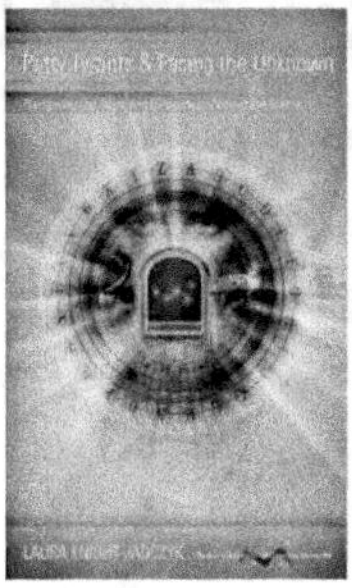

From the myths of romance to the tales of the hero's journey, the quest for knowledge and being has always been portrayed in terms of struggle. Far from home, the hero faces obstacles and tests of his or her courage, will, and cunning. But how do the labyrinths and monsters of these 'messages in a bottle' from our remote ancestors relate to our lives in the 21st century? In an age of mass media, the worldwide web, and multinational corporations, how do these archetypal dramas play themselves out?

In these two volumes of her revolutionary series, *The Wave or Adventures with Cassiopaea*, Laura Knight-Jadczyk continues her project of laying bare the nature of our reality. Through her own experiences and interactions over the course of the Cassiopaean Experiment, many of which just go to show that truth is stranger than fiction, Laura describes the real-life dynamics only hinted at in myth. Most importantly, she gives the tools and clues necessary to actually read the symbols of reality: the theological substrate in which our ordinary psychological motivations are embedded.

With these stunning revelations, Shakespeare's famous words take on a whole new meaning: "All the world's a stage, and all men and women merely players."

First published on her groundbreaking website cassiopaea.org, *Petty Tyrants & Facing the Unknown* have now been fully revised and packaged together in one attractive volume. For anyone interested in the world of esoteric knowledge, studies in the paranormal and everything 'alternative', or even just curious about life in general and its possible significance and meaning, these volumes are a must-read.

The Wave 7 – "Almost Human"

... A Stunning Look at the Metaphysics of Evil

Laura Knight-Jadczyk

In this volume of her prescient Wave series, Laura Knight-Jadczyk brings order to the chaotic and labyrinthine world of murder, conspiracy, and the paranormal. In a unique and probing synthesis of science and mysticism she presents a detailed series of case studies and application of her hypothesis of hyperdimensional influence.

From interpersonal relationships and their expression of archetypal dramas to the vectoring of human behaviour to achieve hyperdimensional purposes, *Almost Human* reveals the mechanics of evil, how it creeps into our lives, and what we need to be aware of in order to avoid it.

The case studies of John Nash, the schizoidal creator of Game Theory, and Ira Einhorn, the New Age psychopath who murdered his girlfriend, are the window through which Knight-Jadczyk unravels the intricate web of deception, aims, and counter-aims of the Powers That Be.

Almost Human is essential reading for anyone wondering why our world is becoming increasingly controlled and our freedoms more restricted.

The Wave 8 – "Debugging the Universe"

... The Hero's Journey

Laura Knight-Jadczyk

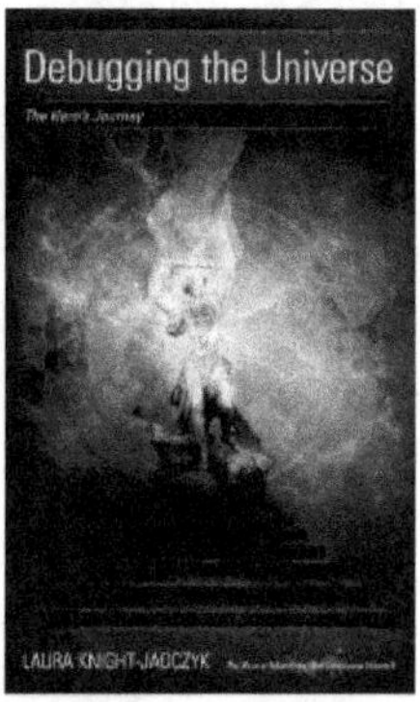

The Path of the Fool, the Hero's Journey, the Great Work – by whatever name it takes, the path of self-development and growth of knowledge is one fraught with difficult lessons and intense struggle. But what exactly is the nature of those lessons, and what insights can the latest advances in modern science provide for us along the way?

Debugging the Universe takes us into the heart of what it means to be human, from the molecules of our DNA to our life purpose and true place in the universe, and everything that separates us from embodying that higher potential. Explored within are real-life applications of the Hero's archetype, the relevance of neuroscience and the 'molecules of emotion', the hidden meaning behind the enigmatic symbols of esoterica, and what it means to live inside a complex system: the universal breath of chaos and order.

This volume concludes the publication in print of Laura Knight-Jadczyk's unparalleled and controversial magnum opus: *The Wave or Adventures with Cassiopaea.* Originally published online at www.cassiopaea.org, The Wave is a fully modern exposition of the knowledge of the ancients, with subjects ranging from metaphysics, science, cosmology, and psychology to the paranormal, UFOs, hyperdimensions and macrocosmic transformation.

"High Strangeness"

... Hyperdimensions and the Process of Alien Abduction

Laura Knight-Jadczyk

High Strangeness: Hyperdimensions and the Process of Alien Abduction is an enlightening attempt to weave together the contradictory threads of religion, science, history, alien abduction, and the true nature of political conspiracies. With thorough research and a drive for the truth, Laura Knight-Jadczyk strips away the facades of official culture and opens doors to understanding our reality.

The Second Edition includes additional material that explains the hyperdimensional mechanisms by which our reality is controlled and shaped by 'alien' powers. The self-serving actions of unwitting puppets – psychopaths and other pathological types – who may have no knowledge that they are being used, become the portals through which an agenda that is hostile to humanity as a whole, is pushed forward.

High Strangeness takes the study of ponerology into a whole new dimension!

"9/11 – The Ultimate Truth"

Joe Quinn and Laura Knight-Jadczyk

In the years since the 9/11 attacks, dozens of books have sought to explore the truth behind the official version of events that day - yet to date, none of these publications has provided a satisfactory answer as to **why** the attacks occurred and who was ultimately responsible for carrying them out.

Taking a broad, millennia-long perspective, Laura Knight-Jadczyk's *9/11: The Ultimate Truth* uncovers the true nature of the ruling elite on our planet and presents new and ground-breaking insights into just how the 9/11 attacks played out.

9/11: The Ultimate Truth makes a strong case for the idea that September 11, 2001 marked the moment when our planet entered the final phase of a diabolical plan that has been many, many years in the making. It is a plan developed and nurtured by successive generations of ruthless individuals who relentlessly exploit the negative aspects of basic human nature to entrap humanity as a whole in endless wars and suffering in order to keep us confused and distracted to the reality of the man behind the curtain.

Drawing on historical and genealogical sources, Knight-Jadczyk eloquently links the 9/11 event to the modern-day Israeli-Palestinian conflict. She also cites the clear evidence that our planet undergoes periodic natural cataclysms, a cycle that has arguably brought humanity to the brink of destruction in the present day.

For its no nonsense style in cutting to the core of the issue and its sheer audacity in refusing to be swayed or distracted by the morass of disinformation that has been employed by the powers that be to cover their tracks, *9/11: The Ultimate Truth* can rightly claim to be **the** definitive book on 9/11 - and what that fateful day's true implications are for the future of mankind.

The new Second Edition of *9/11: The Ultimate Truth* has been updated with new material detailing the real reasons for the collapse of the World Trade Center towers, the central role played by agents of the state of Israel in the attacks, and how the arrogant Bush government is now forced to dance to the Zionists' tune.

JFK: The Assassination of America

Laura Knight-Jadczyk

Anyone who has taken the time to study the facts about that fateful day in Dallas, TX, November 22, 1963, will already know that John F. Kennedy was deliberately murdered by a cabal of psychopathic warmongers who were opposed to his plans for a more peaceful world. This ebook written by Laura Knight-Jadczyk brings into focus how the convergence of greed and the power-mad forces of big oil, organized crime, and the military-industrial complex brought about the destruction of JFK. Drawing on an early analysis of Kennedy's assassination, *Farewell America*, which was produced by a French intelligence group, Mrs. Knight-Jadczyk brings a deeper understanding of this tragic event by placing it in the light of the psychopathic motivations of these criminal elements. *JFK: The Assassination of America* shows a world that could have been, and a great man silenced by forces who will stop at nothing to keep that world from becoming a reality.

Amazing Grace

Laura Knight-Jadczyk

Laura Knight-Jadczyk has lived intimately – and mysteriously – with the world of spirit. In *Amazing Grace*, Laura takes us back to her beginnings in a Gulf Coast Florida childhood, mapping the first decades of her extraordinary search for an objective reality of spirit, of the play of forces that exist as a subtext to the lives of all human beings – a journey toward knowledge and understanding.

From her first experiences with a terrifying Face at the Window in childhood, to her work as an exorcist, chronicled by Pulitzer Prize–winning journalist Thomas French in the *St. Petersburg Times*, Laura relates the many experiences in her search for the existence of truth about our reality, which forced her to recognize the validity of perceptions beyond those of materialism.

This is also the story of how the Cassiopaeans came to be a part of her life. Their channeled messages, which include important concepts of physics and the underlying nature of reality, have drawn the attention of intellectually advanced yet spiritually hungry people from all over the world. This is not just the story of one woman's experience with personal quantum jumps from one reality to another, but is also the greater story of the potential that exists in every seeker. We have the potential to discover the genuine existence of spirit and the play of the archetypal forces of the world, and to connect with them in a dynamic way. Amazing Grace, or Quantum Future, can be a reality in our lives.

The Apocalypse: Comets, Asteroids and Cyclical Catastrophes

Laura Knight-Jadczyk

For untold millennia, comets and asteroids have struck fear into the hearts of humankind. Their stark radiance was observed everywhere with a sense of impending doom, interpreted as signs of the gods' judgment, omens of plague, mass destruction and the end of time. Astronomers recorded their appearance the world over, building large scale observatories to track their movements and predict their ominous arrival. What was it about these majestic wonders of the heavens that inspired such dread? Was it simply a product of mere superstition and social hysteria?

The latest scientific analysis and historical analysis strongly suggest otherwise. Our ancestors knew something we have since forgotten, their secrets deeply embedded in the archaeological record and the myths passed on throughout generations. And we have only begun to unravel their mysteries ...

Spurred on by the discovery of a little known letter of warning to the European Office of Aerospace Research and Development by astrophysicist Victor Clube, author Laura Knight-Jadczyk began an in-depth research project to get to the bottom of the very real threat to humanity posed by these celestial visitors. In *The Apocalypse: Comets, Asteroids, and Cyclical Catastrophes*, Knight-Jadczyk shares what she found: historical evidence for mass destructions, comet-borne plagues, and repeated cover ups littering our past, as well as clues that a similar fate may be fast approaching.

The Noah Syndrome

Laura Knight-Jadczyk

"As it was in the days of Noah ..."

Technological progress married with moral decay. A people enraptured by the trivial and superficial, entrenched in a culture of materialism and endless warfare. A civilization whose time has come. If a phrase defines the condition of our era, it is this: The Noah Syndrome.

After twenty-six years, Laura Knight-Jadczyk's unpublished book is now in print for the first time. And it's more relevant than ever. Drawing on prophecies ancient and new - from biblical narratives to modern-day visionaries - yet grounded in cutting-edge scientific discoveries about earth's cataclysmic history, this book presents a remarkable vision of humanity's dramatic past and extremely hazardous future.

The Noah Syndrome also introduces the concept of quantum cosmic metamorphosis - the spiritual ark that may carry us through the coming catastrophe. If our past is the key to our future, as Laura suggests, heeding the counsel in these pages could mean the difference between transformation and destruction.

Evidence of Revision

Quantum Future Group

Evidence of Revision is a six part documentary containing historical, original news footage revealing that the most seminal events in recent American history have been deeply and purposefully misrepresented to the public. Footage and interviews provide an in-depth exploration of events ranging from the Kennedy assassinations to the Jonestown massacre, and all that lies between.

The footprints left in this archival footage reveal the coordinated, clandestine sculpting of the America we know today. Evidence of Revision proves once and for all that history has been revised even as it was written!

Part 1: The Assassinations of Kennedy and Oswald
Part 2: The why of it all referenced to Vietnam and LBG
Part 3: LBJ, Hoover and others: what so few know even today
Part 4: The RFK assassination as never seen before
Part 5: RFK assassination, MKULTRA and the Jonestown massacre
Part 6: The assassination of Martin Luther King

6 parts – 3 DVD set – Region-Free DVDs – Watch on any DVD player or computer anywhere in the world.

Newly subtitled in English, Spanish, French and Polish – the documentary is filmed in English, the subtitles are for clarity due to archival footage on which the audio is, at times, unclear. Duration: 10 hours 25 minutes.

Éiriú Eolas, An Amazing Stress Control, Healing and Rejuvenation Program

Laura Knight-Jadczyk

Are you stressed? Do you suffer from chronic fatigue, conditions that your doctor cannot diagnose or that he thinks are "all in your head"? Are you in physical pain more often than not? Is your system toxified from living in today's polluted environment? Do you wish you could face life's challenges with greater calm and peace of mind? Would you like to actually feel healthy, happy and pain-free every day?

Introducing Éiriú Eolas (pronounced "AIR-oo OH-lahss"), the amazing scientific stress-control, healing, detoxing and rejuvenation program which is THE KEY that will help you to change your life in a REAL and immediately noticeable way:

Proven benefits of the Éiriú Eolas Program include: instantly control stress in high energy situations, detox your body resulting in pain relief, relax and gently work through past emotional and psychological trauma and regenerate and rejuvenate your body/mind.

Éiriú Eolas will enable you to rapidly and gently access and release layers of mental, emotional and physical toxicity that stand between you and a healthy, younger feeling and younger looking body!

Subtitles available in: English, Danish, German, Spanish, Greek, French, Croatian, Italian, Dutch, Polish, Russian, Serbian, Turkish and Vietnamese!

Red Pill Press
info@redpillpress.com
www.redpillpress.com

Index

abduction, 21, 25, 33, 47, 77, 97, 99, 109–112, 126, 136, 149, 151, 162, 177, 178, 187, 194, 206, 214, 215, 223, 226, 237, 248, 250, 261, 262, 277, 279, 281, 293, 307, 316, 333, 346, 377–379, 381, 400, 401, 405, 406, 410, 412, 422, 427, 428, 430, 433, 466, 467, 470, 490, 491, 510, 511, 514–517, 521, 530, 532, 537, 539, 551, 593, 604, 610, 634

abuse, 73, 111, 400

Alchemy, 268, 492, 501, 502, 623, 624, 630

alien, ii, 21, 30–32, 46, 52, 54, 57, 64–67, 71, 77, 79, 80, 82, 84, 87, 95, 104, 135, 136, 149, 162, 164, 177, 178, 189, 200, 209, 214, 223, 225–227, 247, 248, 261, 262, 277, 283, 290, 301, 302, 307, 333, 340, 369, 376, 400, 401, 404, 405, 422, 461, 462, 466, 468, 469, 485, 489, 494, 503, 504, 510, 511, 514, 515, 523, 525, 526, 528, 530, 535–537, 539, 544–553, 569, 571, 573, 585, 589–591, 599, 609, 610, 634

Alien Autopsy video, 67, 162, 225, 466, 468, 535, 536, 590

Alternative 3, 543, 544

angels, 37, 38, 93, 154, 155, 160, 164, 215, 273, 288, 289, 332, 365, 405, 477, 484, 485, 507, 512, 532, 588

Annunaki, 599

Antarctica, 176, 177, 308, 310, 588, 589

antichrist, 52

Ark of the Covenant, 543

Aryans, 103, 234, 368, 504–506, 509

Ashtar Command, 54, 549

assumptions, 63, 67, 254, 292, 298, 305, 313, 322, 363, 365, 433, 472, 485, 486, 502, 516, 540, 548–550, 553, 555, 567, 572, 573

Atlantis, 103, 125, 137, 138, 200, 201, 227, 228, 232–234, 269, 289, 454, 483, 488, 503, 504, 558, 615

attack, 1, 2, 4, 19, 21, 54, 113, 138, 145, 158, 166–171, 198, 218, 224, 246, 247, 251–253, 255, 258, 266, 270, 271, 281, 285, 296, 304–307, 311–314, 331, 333, 335, 339, 355, 356, 358, 364, 371, 373, 408, 435–437, 459–462, 477, 478, 521, 575, 582, 597, 598, 604, 635

aura, i, ii, 1, 13, 20, 23–25, 37, 40, 43, 51, 57–59, 61, 64, 65, 71, 77, 87, 103, 106, 109, 111, 112, 116, 121–126, 128, 129, 131, 135, 141, 143, 145, 148, 162–165, 167, 170–172, 176, 184, 191–193, 197, 198, 206, 209–211, 223, 227, 236, 237, 246, 251, 252, 259, 262, 265, 268, 273, 276, 277, 283, 287, 292, 295, 297, 300, 303, 310, 311, 313, 315, 321, 327, 328, 331, 334, 339, 342, 353, 357,

359, 361, 372, 373, 375, 380, 381, 384, 386, 393, 396, 407, 409, 426, 431, 432, 437, 439, 440, 455, 465, 473, 475, 476, 482, 487, 499, 501, 505, 506, 509, 510, 513, 520, 523, 525, 527–530, 532, 536, 540, 543, 547, 550, 559, 565, 571, 575–577, 579, 582, 585, 597, 603, 604, 608, 611, 615, 617–619, 622–625, 627–639
awareness, 21, 26, 36, 57, 60, 61, 74, 106, 122, 127, 168, 199, 251, 252, 293, 296, 297, 314, 317–319, 325, 340, 359, 367–370, 373, 377, 378, 412, 429, 447, 457, 460, 467, 471, 472, 492, 530, 559, 561, 576, 623

belief, i, 54, 90, 112, 185, 212, 322, 388, 390, 400, 451, 457, 485, 497, 498, 543, 629
Bermuda Triangle, 232, 234, 236
Bible, 38, 161, 164, 184, 185, 457, 494, 529, 616, 623
black hole, 49, 66, 290, 384, 386, 589
books, i, 1, 7, 19, 20, 33, 45, 49, 53, 54, 64, 65, 71, 74, 81, 82, 85, 95, 99, 100, 106, 111, 113, 114, 117, 125, 135, 136, 138, 143, 145, 146, 161, 164, 175, 177–182, 184, 186, 187, 195, 197, 205, 212, 228, 231, 250, 251, 273–275, 295, 317–319, 321, 327, 332–334, 336, 340, 349, 358, 369–371, 393, 395, 396, 399, 407, 422, 434, 448, 453, 464, 477, 481, 482, 487, 489, 492, 494, 495, 499, 504, 507, 513, 526, 527, 541, 543, 555, 569, 574, 577, 585, 588, 603, 619, 622–624, 635, 636, 639

California, 29, 48, 92–94, 99, 289
cancer, 407
Castaneda, Carlos, 154, 254, 599
celibacy, 40
Celts, 48, 450, 502, 503, 505, 506
chakras, 61, 193, 208, 343–345
Challenger disaster, 236
channeling, 1, 4, 11, 20, 31, 32, 39, 41, 42, 45, 47, 48, 51, 52, 54, 55, 69, 95, 104, 106, 113, 114, 116, 121–124, 129, 130, 137, 142, 148, 165, 166, 191, 192, 195, 197, 204, 206, 207, 228, 229, 237, 239, 240, 246, 251, 252, 255, 257, 258, 266, 287, 295, 297, 298, 300, 303–305, 307, 310, 312, 314, 315, 330, 333, 335, 336, 350, 354, 355, 357, 361, 363, 364, 372, 373, 375–377, 382, 393, 396, 409, 411, 416, 417, 421, 432, 437–439, 454, 456–461, 465, 483, 484, 492, 494, 495, 497, 498, 502, 507, 509, 511, 520, 532, 535, 547, 549, 554, 562, 563, 579, 580, 585, 586, 588, 591, 608, 609, 612, 621, 628, 637
chromosomes, 207
Clark, Hulda Dr., 407
comets, 288, 289, 392, 416, 453, 454, 507, 601, 615, 618, 625, 626, 638
conduit, 45, 199, 200, 203, 277, 375, 383, 412, 413, 484, 517
consortium, the, 52, 82, 84, 308, 321, 322, 348, 349, 585
conspiracy, 64, 158, 204, 226, 249, 271, 393, 492, 496, 498, 499, 501, 589, 610, 616, 619, 622, 623, 629, 630, 632, 634
Cooper, Bill, 82, 145, 196
Coral Castle, 103, 105, 204, 205, 208, 225, 275, 535
corruption, 17, 42, 46, 52, 87, 106, 114, 135, 165, 166, 255, 303,

312, 327, 353–355, 361, 439, 473, 511, 547–549
crop circles, 233, 284, 288, 293, 294, 393–398, 536, 546, 627
crystals, 169, 201

dark matter, 176
death, 9, 10, 12, 15, 38, 54, 95–97, 118, 152, 158, 185, 190, 237, 273, 274, 375, 377, 380, 424, 425, 518, 524, 525, 539, 541, 601
  cremation, 273
densith
  5th, 273
  6th, 303
density, ii, 1, 21, 24, 25, 27, 29, 32, 33, 35–41, 44–46, 51–54, 57–63, 67–70, 73–75, 80, 84–89, 93, 110–113, 115, 123, 124, 128, 132, 133, 137, 138, 142, 144, 146, 151–156, 163, 166–168, 171, 174–176, 178, 180, 186, 192–196, 198–202, 206, 209, 210, 213–220, 224–227, 229–232, 237, 240, 259, 266, 269, 273, 283, 290, 292, 298, 299, 303, 316–319, 321–323, 325–329, 335–337, 343, 346, 348, 357, 359, 364–370, 376, 377, 379–381, 383, 385–391, 393, 394, 402, 403, 410, 412–414, 416–418, 428, 435, 437, 441, 443–445, 447, 449–451, 456, 457, 459–463, 466, 467, 469–473, 483, 485, 486, 488, 489, 496, 499, 503, 504, 506, 509–511, 522, 524–526, 530, 537–540, 545, 550–561, 563, 565, 572, 575–577, 580, 582, 588–590, 592, 597, 599–601, 604
  1st, 36–38, 75, 196, 201, 318, 336, 370, 380, 457, 462, 467, 510
  2nd, 36–38, 79, 115, 174, 175, 196, 220, 230, 234, 301, 318, 380, 381, 413, 467, 504, 510, 545
  3rd, 3, 27, 32, 33, 35–41, 48, 52–54, 58, 59, 62, 63, 68–70, 75, 78–80, 84, 86–90, 93, 110, 111, 123, 128, 132, 142, 150, 151, 154, 155, 168, 170, 171, 174–176, 180, 195, 196, 198, 200, 202, 209, 210, 213–215, 217–219, 224–227, 229–231, 259, 266, 269, 273, 283, 290, 292, 298, 299, 303, 304, 306, 316–323, 325, 326, 328, 329, 331, 337, 346, 348, 353, 354, 365, 366, 370, 377, 379–381, 385–390, 394, 412–414, 416–418, 422, 435, 437, 441, 443, 444, 447, 449–451, 456, 459–463, 466, 467, 469–472, 483, 485, 488, 489, 496, 503, 504, 506, 509, 510, 522, 526, 537, 539, 552–555, 557, 559–561, 565, 566, 572, 575, 576, 580, 582, 592, 597, 599–601, 611
  4th, 21, 24, 25, 29, 32, 35–41, 44, 53, 54, 57–59, 61–63, 67–69, 73–75, 80, 84, 86, 87, 89, 90, 93, 110–113, 115, 124, 128, 133, 138, 144, 146, 151–153, 155–157, 166–168, 170, 171, 174, 175, 178, 180, 186, 195, 196, 198, 202, 215, 217–220, 224, 226, 230, 231, 237, 259, 290, 303, 304, 317–321, 323, 325, 326, 328, 346, 359, 363–370, 379–381, 387–391, 394, 402, 410, 416, 444, 445, 449–451, 454, 457, 461–463, 466, 467, 470, 471, 488, 499, 503, 504, 506, 509–511, 522, 530, 538, 540, 552–561, 563, 572, 575, 577,

580, 588, 589, 597, 604
5th, 21, 25, 35, 38, 51, 53, 59, 62, 136, 137, 146, 154, 155, 175, 199, 202, 217, 232, 303, 304, 318, 343, 365, 370, 394, 412, 413, 416, 422, 454, 462, 485, 486, 504, 510, 551–553, 600, 604, 617
6th, 21, 35, 38, 39, 51, 58, 60, 63, 124, 128, 136, 152, 153, 166–168, 175, 192, 193, 195, 198, 199, 201, 202, 209, 210, 216, 231, 240, 318, 336, 365, 393, 394, 422, 454, 462, 471, 504, 565, 582, 588, 589
7th, 35, 39, 170, 175, 200, 201, 291, 318, 319, 328, 336, 387, 391, 454, 488
candidates, 21, 58, 59, 146, 152–154, 168, 169, 444, 530
depression, 106, 267, 359, 580, 597, 598
dimensions, 21, 35, 45, 67, 69, 70, 73, 77, 83, 85, 86, 90, 99, 146, 149, 155, 174, 176, 212, 224, 267, 270, 272, 289, 290, 297, 301, 317–319, 323, 325–327, 347, 357–359, 383, 390, 394, 402, 412, 425, 453, 462, 467, 472, 496, 507, 524, 526, 550, 551, 558, 568, 622, 623, 627, 632–634
disinformation, ii, 51, 54, 83, 91, 153, 177, 184, 224, 231, 232, 237, 298, 322, 332, 499, 503, 505, 542, 545, 547–549, 558, 560, 570, 623, 635
deception, 33, 52, 64, 73, 211, 365, 367, 478, 488, 568, 623, 632
delusion, 136, 608
diversion, 52, 54, 92, 465, 531, 617
fabrication, 54, 468
DNA, 90, 113, 128, 129, 132, 136, 153, 190, 191, 195, 203, 204, 208, 212, 236, 266, 319, 351, 389, 452, 486, 575, 616, 623, 633
dolphins, 47
dowsing, 4, 133, 296

earth changes, ii, 29, 53, 130, 198, 223, 230, 618, 626, 627
earthquake, 21, 22, 29, 72, 92–94, 131, 270, 272, 273, 626
economy, 94, 580, 582, 603
Eden, 37, 190, 212, 213, 569, 621
effortless, 3, 33, 40, 153, 187
Egypt, 179, 275, 417, 454, 487, 497, 498, 500, 543, 568, 615, 618, 622
Einstein, Albert, 317, 321, 322, 325, 326, 382, 385, 404, 612
electromagnetism, 21, 24, 26, 29, 47, 69, 70, 74, 87, 127, 199, 232, 234, 272, 284, 292, 293, 310, 321–324, 328, 341, 346, 347, 394, 453, 538, 625
Elohim, 185, 186, 503
emotions, 1, 2, 8, 9, 26, 27, 29, 41, 61, 75, 80, 89, 108, 115, 116, 118, 120, 127, 153, 161, 169, 190, 196, 202, 206, 227, 240–242, 244, 251, 253–255, 272, 296, 304, 333, 355, 363, 410, 412, 414, 421, 433, 435, 441, 442, 445–447, 449, 450, 458–460, 472, 473, 475, 483, 537, 538, 540, 541, 543, 580, 590, 598, 633, 641
Esseseni beings, 513
ET's, 34, 46, 47, 51, 58, 95, 98, 101, 144, 227, 249, 250, 336, 395, 492–494, 497, 526, 601

faith, 145, 212, 313, 314, 358, 408, 449, 457, 458, 464, 495, 582, 596, 601
Fall, the, 37, 73, 190, 212, 213, 215, 250, 611, 624

finances, 82, 113, 120, 138, 169, 210, 224, 299, 311, 437, 441, 448, 521, 603
Flight 19, 223, 232–236, 321, 326, 357, 558
free will, 26, 63, 110, 147, 166, 167, 170, 172–174, 194, 198, 213–215, 220, 228, 258, 430, 432, 436, 487, 497, 500, 512, 537
frequency resonance vibration, 47, 59, 266, 445, 446, 516, 520, 524, 540, 554, 580, 600
friendships, 26, 28, 105, 282, 536

galaxy, 31, 47, 322, 323, 471, 503, 504
Gandhi, 64
government, ii, 53, 64, 66, 79, 81–84, 91, 100, 143–145, 147, 158, 177, 204, 210, 250, 262, 271, 297, 298, 301, 302, 392, 404, 405, 415, 462, 489, 513, 514, 517–519, 521–525, 529, 536, 556, 557, 589, 629, 635
  secret, 513, 514, 517, 518, 523–525, 536
grand cycle, 52, 200, 220, 230, 291, 319, 383, 385, 391
gravity, 85, 180, 316, 317, 322–325, 327–329, 337, 387
Grays, 32, 34, 35, 53, 66, 67, 71, 80, 82, 84, 85, 87, 126, 149, 150, 155, 157, 175, 177, 178, 194–196, 220, 225, 226, 231, 402, 466–469, 491, 504, 531, 537, 538, 568, 588
Great Chicago Fire, 289
Gurdjieff, G. I., 174, 254, 277, 285, 291, 390

harmonic convergence, 48, 466
Hebrews, 487, 488, 492, 503
higher self, 45, 483
Hitler, 232, 478, 506, 509, 585, 588, 618
Hoagland, Richard, 91, 394, 492, 493, 499
hormones, 29, 135, 136, 236, 260, 296, 415, 416
Hurtak, James J., 186, 228, 249, 492–494, 496–499, 501
hypnosis, 8, 9, 11, 14, 20, 46, 71, 77, 95, 104, 114, 117, 121, 130, 142, 149, 163, 208, 209, 226, 260–262, 361, 375, 377–379, 400, 421, 432, 435, 478, 487, 528, 545, 551, 571, 573, 574, 604, 628

Illuminati, 184, 581
implants [alien technology], 110, 149, 150, 152, 154, 158, 194, 195, 202, 223, 379, 380, 463, 467, 468, 485, 532, 545
imprisonment, 40, 126
Incas, 341
Isis, 484, 488

Jehovah, 484, 488
Jessup, Morris K., 105, 179–182, 621
Jesus, 21, 120, 154, 160, 164, 184, 185, 212, 350, 478, 484, 616, 618
Jews, 5, 16, 51, 125, 137, 138, 145, 185, 393, 481, 482, 484, 487, 500, 505, 506, 618
Jupiter, 174, 185, 345, 355, 362, 563, 600, 601

karma, ii, 3, 4, 17, 18, 28, 125, 137, 234, 332, 358, 359, 418, 440, 463, 510
knowledge, 1, 26, 33, 52–55, 58, 66, 77, 78, 89, 90, 106, 119, 133, 145–147, 151, 152, 156, 160–162, 167, 171, 177–180, 185, 190, 191, 201, 208, 209, 212, 213, 219, 224, 248, 251–253, 284–286, 293, 295, 311, 314, 317–321, 324–327, 333, 334, 344, 364, 371, 372, 376, 377, 379, 384, 391, 392,

411, 426, 428, 430–434, 436, 441, 445–448, 462, 465, 472, 473, 477, 486, 487, 500, 502, 503, 522, 528, 529, 531, 541, 546, 566, 567, 569, 617, 620, 624, 625, 628–631, 633, 634, 637

KRLL, 64–66, 68–70, 83, 84

Kryon, 47

lessons, 4, 13, 28, 39, 40, 53, 88, 89, 114, 138, 202, 243, 251, 269, 285, 333, 366, 387–391, 440–442, 448, 458, 485, 505, 522, 633

lifetime, 14, 16–20, 34, 40, 51, 52, 116, 118–120, 124, 127, 137, 179, 190, 194, 237, 391, 431, 446, 487, 489, 514, 551, 576

lightning, 23, 274, 275, 526

Linda Cortile case, 406

Linda Howe, 144, 301, 313, 396, 549

Lizard Beings, 2, 35, 37, 38, 41, 53, 54, 62, 63, 67–71, 80, 84, 85, 87, 88, 100, 101, 106, 109, 111, 113, 114, 124, 125, 135–137, 146, 147, 150–153, 157, 166, 167, 174, 194–196, 198, 206, 212–216, 219, 220, 224, 226, 230, 231, 271, 272, 355, 402, 435, 450–453, 461, 468–470, 506, 520, 526, 537, 557, 558, 601

Lucifer, 37, 38, 202, 215, 484, 612

Maitreya, 51

Majestic 12, 82, 91, 543, 544

mantras, 457

Marciniak, Barbara, 106, 195, 344

marriage, 4, 19, 28, 164, 242, 283, 340, 370, 385, 455, 463, 481, 482, 490, 499, 500, 510, 514, 530, 587, 592, 598, 610, 639

Matrix, 282, 323, 499, 511, 513, 523, 531, 540, 543, 545, 555, 566, 568, 585, 612, 617

matrix, 323, 537, 566, 589, 590, 609

Mayans, 35, 48, 152, 154, 450

meditation, 33, 46, 71, 117, 153, 155, 156, 190, 208, 456, 483, 489, 508, 520, 530

men in black, 53, 54, 68, 69, 81, 130, 527

Michael Lindemann, 301, 313, 332

military, 7, 30, 32, 66, 91, 138, 149, 177, 204, 225, 298, 310, 401–403, 493, 514–519, 535, 536, 636

mind

  subconscious, 8, 45, 46, 388, 456, 461

  unconscious, 45, 47, 422

Monauk project, 405

money, 10, 82, 92, 132, 136, 138, 139, 210, 211, 224, 225, 260, 299, 307, 437, 440, 441, 475, 477, 478, 581, 582

monoatomic gold, 478, 492, 501, 502, 511, 574, 575

Monotheism, 212

moon, 33, 34, 174, 175, 227, 607

Mother Theresa, 64

Mount Shasta, California, 289

music, 36, 37, 73, 246, 291, 396, 482

mutilations, animal, 77–80, 95–98, 301

Navy, 181, 232, 233, 493, 514–516

Nazis, 308, 506, 585

Neanderthal, 114, 137, 201, 452, 504

Nephilim, 220, 506, 507, 509, 510, 537

network, 21, 25, 27, 29–32, 49, 65, 114, 162, 187, 197, 210, 251, 266, 268, 270, 281, 302, 308, 317, 320, 324, 372, 390, 397, 431, 486, 493, 531, 535, 549, 573, 582, 588, 610

New World Order, ii, 32, 506, 519–521

Nibiru, 34

Nordics, 167, 168, 368, 504, 528, 569, 570

O. H. Krill, 83
Oak Island, 224, 265–267, 491, 630
objectivity, 2, 3, 279, 280, 369, 389, 442, 461, 463, 468, 469, 471, 597, 598, 637
Oklahoma bombing, 297
Old Testament, 484, 488, 616
OOBE, out of body experience, 571, 577, 579
orgasm, 40, 41, 479
Orion, 38, 70, 166, 167, 169, 170, 174, 195, 209, 227, 282, 368, 402, 470, 471, 488, 502–507, 509, 511, 530, 531, 569, 591, 604
Orion Federation, 166, 167, 209, 504
Ouspensky, P. D., 36, 115, 286, 617, 619
out of body experience, 59, 571, 576, 577, 579
ozone layer, 229–231, 442

parasites, 351, 407
perpendicular reality, 277, 282–285, 314, 382, 383, 391, 611
personal issues, 166
Philadelphia Experiment, 181, 182, 233, 326, 404
photon belt, 47, 48, 465
planets, ii, 32–36, 47, 53, 70, 75, 87, 100, 110, 114, 130, 131, 137, 146, 147, 151, 153, 155, 162, 172, 174, 175, 179, 201, 203, 223, 227–230, 235, 248, 253, 267, 269, 270, 272, 283, 293, 342, 345, 350, 352, 359, 362, 368, 394, 397, 402, 404, 434, 435, 449–451, 466, 487–489, 496, 504–506, 526, 528, 540, 541, 543–545, 560, 561, 563, 569, 591, 601, 604, 608, 625, 626, 630, 635
plants, 36–38, 67, 74, 75, 309, 317, 478, 599
Pleiades, 48, 51, 104, 195, 368, 488, 503, 505, 548, 549
poltergeist, 45, 142, 193, 621
prayer, 85, 90, 169, 170, 252, 484, 601
predictions, ii, 30, 92–94, 129, 131, 159, 212, 228, 270, 271, 273, 295, 497, 510
Prime Creator, 503, 599, 600
protection, 26, 52, 55, 57, 147, 169, 170, 172, 207, 253, 296, 311, 314, 358, 364, 413, 414, 425, 454, 484, 486, 531, 541
psychic
  openness, 24
purgatory, 54, 274
pyramids, 131, 200, 201, 205, 232, 269, 275, 303, 558, 568

quantum, 99, 173, 288, 623, 637, 639

Radio carbon dating, 348
rapture, 59, 639
reality, 21, 46, 47, 52–54, 58, 61, 62, 68, 69, 71, 73, 100, 110, 113, 120, 134, 151, 153, 161, 172, 186, 189, 194, 208, 213, 216, 218, 226, 230, 232, 233, 235, 236, 244, 248, 250, 258, 263, 281, 283, 292, 296, 304, 319, 321, 341, 347, 348, 357, 365, 378–383, 385, 386, 390, 391, 422, 425, 428, 429, 434, 453, 457, 462, 463, 469, 484, 496, 510, 512, 554, 555, 559, 577, 578, 623, 628, 629, 631, 634–637
  parallel, 232, 233, 235, 236
realm, 1, 35, 40, 62, 69, 70, 73, 80, 186, 195, 198, 199, 216–220, 231, 237, 283, 316, 319, 327, 390, 412, 436, 447, 449, 450, 453, 456, 462, 463, 469, 471, 473, 555, 557, 576, 589, 592
  border, 195, 216–219, 231, 237, 283, 319, 327, 555, 557, 592
    crossing, 231, 237, 555, 592
Reiki, 49, 65, 128, 129, 131, 154, 210,

249, 266, 296, 315, 332, 345, 399, 523, 611, 628
reincarnation, ii, 7–9, 13, 14, 17, 28, 33, 38, 39, 120, 127, 168, 211, 260, 370, 388, 391, 433, 481, 487, 499, 500, 507, 621
relationships, 26–29, 41, 110, 155, 194, 211, 227, 230, 263, 280–283, 309, 310, 328, 329, 341, 382, 383, 396, 404, 413, 487, 493, 499, 544, 569, 571, 632
religion, 40, 51, 54, 137, 138, 499, 568, 624, 625, 627, 628, 634
relocation, 27
rituals, 26, 77, 90, 153, 303, 336, 350, 405, 417, 437, 464, 523
rocks, 36, 37, 75, 160, 269, 317, 335, 398, 535, 625
Rosicrucians, 186, 501
Roswell, 468, 535, 537, 574, 612, 621

Sanskrit, 234, 456
science, 1, 31, 65, 69, 70, 77, 82, 91, 141, 173, 176, 199, 231, 317, 318, 323, 348, 398, 415, 442, 443, 452, 453, 461, 493, 545, 546, 559, 609, 620, 623–627, 629, 630, 632–634, 638, 639, 641
Semitics, 503–505, 510
serotonin, 236
Serpent Mound, Ohio, 289
service to others, 2, 25, 38, 41, 42, 53, 57, 62–64, 146, 148, 152–155, 166, 167, 169, 170, 195, 213–220, 231, 258, 290, 320, 322, 332, 333, 335, 342, 364–369, 421, 436, 445, 468, 469, 471, 504, 513, 520, 530, 532, 553, 554, 568, 591
service to self, 25, 38, 41, 42, 52–55, 57, 62, 63, 66, 67, 87, 113, 129, 133, 138, 148, 149, 151, 152, 154, 155, 157, 166, 167, 169, 186, 195, 196, 213–220, 231, 290, 291, 298, 303, 304, 308, 322, 331–333, 342, 357, 365–367, 369, 373, 377, 381, 382, 410, 421, 436, 444, 445, 450, 461, 467–470, 502–504, 506, 511, 513, 516, 526, 530–532, 547–549, 553–555, 557, 558, 568, 575, 589, 591, 597, 599, 604
sex, 23, 40, 41, 85, 96, 106, 135, 142, 151, 234, 461, 491, 590
    homosexuality, 40, 234
shape shifting, 53
Sirius, 340, 470, 471, 503, 505, 511
Sitchin, Zecharia, 34, 249, 288, 488, 600, 601, 618
solar system, 34–36, 497
soul, ii, 9, 33, 38–40, 42, 57, 67, 70, 118, 119, 137, 146, 147, 151, 152, 154, 188, 194, 195, 199, 201, 202, 214, 225, 226, 233, 244, 245, 258, 273, 349, 370, 379–381, 410, 412, 413, 416, 427, 430, 432, 451, 463, 469, 484, 486, 506, 510, 518, 520, 521, 523, 524, 530, 539, 540, 551, 552, 557, 574, 576, 581, 611, 617, 628
sound, 2, 20, 68, 73, 74, 85, 87, 103, 110, 114, 122, 130, 132, 134, 138, 153, 200, 224, 225, 229, 241, 246, 253, 260, 262, 263, 274, 275, 283, 304, 309, 324, 351, 366, 381, 385, 405, 409, 410, 412, 414, 415, 424, 440–443, 457, 483, 485, 494, 496, 512, 548, 562, 576, 600
    humming, 87, 548
spinning, 160, 190, 275, 399, 485, 512, 566, 593, 598
spirals, 163, 198, 284, 386, 399, 407, 567, 581
spirituality, 26, 28, 29, 40, 51, 105, 161, 240, 242–244, 257, 258, 334, 335, 342, 368, 369, 372,

471, 478, 494, 495, 510, 521, 566, 588, 592, 624, 627, 637, 639
stars, 7, 9, 23, 25, 30, 32, 33, 46, 48, 57, 61, 65, 66, 68, 72, 74, 77, 87, 89, 105, 110, 112–114, 117, 126, 128, 130, 133, 136, 146, 154, 156, 163, 168, 172, 174, 175, 191, 195, 197, 200, 206, 208, 209, 216, 217, 220, 224, 234–236, 240, 243, 249, 261, 277, 279, 280, 282, 288, 291, 299, 307, 313, 315, 319, 325, 336, 340–342, 345, 349, 369, 372, 375, 378, 384, 388, 389, 393, 397, 401, 405, 406, 418, 419, 424, 425, 453, 471, 472, 479, 481, 483, 484, 491, 492, 501, 504, 505, 508, 511, 513, 519, 522, 527, 528, 530, 531, 535, 543, 550, 551, 553, 566, 579, 585, 586, 588, 597, 609, 616, 622, 625, 638
Strieber, Whitley, 74, 527
subjectivity, 2, 18, 38, 59, 86, 91, 114, 126, 157, 216, 292, 307, 342, 359, 363, 371, 376, 439, 440, 442, 446, 460, 461, 468, 469, 499, 592
Sumerians, 103, 288, 289, 599
sun, 33, 47, 62, 174–176, 240, 257, 279, 290, 339, 441, 471, 589, 616, 626

Tarot, 32, 33
terrorists, 158, 270, 271, 571
thought centers, 332, 426–430, 433
thought control, 54
Thule Society, 588, 589
thunderstorm, 23, 24, 37, 65, 346
time loop, 85, 86
time travelling, 69, 85, 351, 402, 587
Toltecs, 152
toxic persons, 296
trauma, 8, 13, 45, 127, 217, 297, 641
twins, 19, 63, 143, 144, 148, 161, 162, 234, 293, 345, 498, 626
    Vanishing Twin Phenomenon, 141, 143, 144, 148, 161

UFO's, ii, 21, 25, 30, 31, 46, 49, 57, 64–66, 68, 70, 81, 87, 91, 95–98, 101, 104, 105, 110, 130, 132, 134, 136, 141, 145, 147, 156, 160, 162–164, 167, 172, 177, 178, 181, 183, 189, 192, 204–211, 225–227, 240, 248–250, 263, 288, 289, 299, 301, 302, 313, 315–318, 320, 323, 330, 333, 340, 346, 376, 377, 393, 397, 398, 400–407, 461, 476, 494, 511, 512, 535, 546, 555, 588, 589, 591–593, 595, 604, 608, 610, 621, 622, 627, 629, 633
Ultimate Frontier [book], 39
underground
    base, 66, 308, 529, 531, 548, 557
    facility, 529, 531, 532
    tunnels, 72, 78, 274, 285, 302, 303, 307–310, 317, 341, 351, 523, 525, 544, 551, 588
Unified Field Theory, 321, 322
universal mind, 45
universe, ii, 47, 75, 152, 173, 176, 189, 191, 194, 198, 295, 319, 322, 324–326, 343, 401, 448, 456, 462, 470–472, 493, 503, 567, 582, 624, 633

Vallée, Jacques, 70, 493, 622
variable physicality, 146, 174, 178, 319, 463, 559
Vedas, 455, 456
Virgin Mary, 54, 160, 225, 332, 333
volcanoes, 21, 22, 93, 117, 129, 175, 454, 626
Voynich Manuscript, 231
Vril Society, 588, 589

walk-ins, 370
wave cycle
long, 385, 436
short, 53, 343, 370, 385, 436
Wave, the, i, ii, 1, 4, 18, 21, 23, 29, 32, 36–39, 45–47, 51–53, 56–59, 64, 69, 77–87, 103, 110, 111, 113–115, 117, 122, 124–127, 131, 132, 134, 135, 137, 142, 144, 148, 153, 154, 162, 166–168, 172, 175, 184, 185, 187, 195, 198, 199, 202–204, 206, 208, 210–217, 219, 220, 223, 229–234, 237, 246, 247, 249–251, 253, 259, 267, 268, 270, 272, 273, 275, 277, 278, 280–285, 289–291, 293, 313–315, 318, 319, 321, 323–325, 327, 328, 339, 341–343, 345, 347, 351, 353, 355, 358, 359, 362, 370, 382, 383, 385, 387, 389, 391, 395, 397, 401, 408–410, 412, 414, 415, 417, 424, 426, 427, 429–431, 436, 445, 456, 457, 461, 462, 464–466, 472, 478, 487, 490–492, 500, 502, 503, 505, 509–511, 514–516, 523–525, 528, 530, 537–539, 541–543, 557–560, 562, 565–567, 569, 571–573, 575, 576, 581, 586, 587, 589, 590, 592, 597, 598, 600, 604, 605, 609, 611–613, 617, 627–633
weather, ii, 29, 31, 49, 201, 295, 346, 348, 511, 531, 628
floods, 48, 72, 118, 129, 130, 454, 608
winds, 16, 19, 21, 29, 60–62, 78, 106, 122, 126, 127, 130, 133, 176, 181, 182, 195, 198–200, 203, 216–218, 235, 236, 262, 273, 280, 291–293, 306, 321, 347, 357–359, 394, 395, 398, 467, 488, 519, 528, 561, 586, 592, 632
whales, 47
whishful thinking, 62, 151, 333, 421, 442

Yahweh, 484, 488, 494
yogis, 87

www.ingramcontent.com/pod-product-compliance
Lightning Source LLC
Chambersburg PA
CBHW070357230426
43665CB00012B/1148